THE NEW EUROPE

THE NEW EUROPE

ECONOMY, SOCIETY AND ENVIRONMENT

Edited by
David Pinder

JOHN WILEY & SONS
Chichester • New York • Weinheim • Brisbane • Singapore • Toronto

Copyright © 1998 by John Wiley & Sons Ltd
Baffins Lane, Chichester,
West Sussex, PO19 1UD, England

National 01243 779777
International (+ 44) 1234 779777
e-mail (for orders and customer service enquiries): cs-books@wiley.co.uk
Visit our Home Page on http://www.wiley.co.uk
or http://www.wiley.com

Reprinted September 1999

Other Wiley Editorial Offices

John Wiley & Sons, Inc., 605 Third Avenue,
New York, NY 10158-0012, USA

WILEY-VCH Verlag GmbH, Pappelallee 3,
D-69469 Weinheim, Germany

Jacaranda Wiley Ltd, 33 Park Road, Milton,
Queensland 4064, Australia

John Wiley & Sons (Asia) Pte Ltd, 2 Clementi Loop #02-01,
Jin Xing Distripark, Singapore 129809

John Wiley & Sons (Canada) Ltd, 22 Worcester Road,
Rexdale, Ontario, M9W 1L1, Canada

Library of Congress Cataloging-in-Publication Data

The new Europe : economy, society, and environment / edited by David Pinder.
    p.   cm.
    Includes bibliographical references and index.
    ISBN 0-471-97123-5 (acid-free paper)
        1. European Union countries — Economic conditions.   2. European
Union countries — Social conditions.   3. Environmental policy
— European Union Countries.   I. Pinder, David.
    HC240.N473   1998
    306'.094— dc21   97-31195
                                                                    CIP

British Library Cataloguing in Publication Data

A catalogue record for this book is available from the British Library

ISBN 0-471-97123-5 ✔

Typeset in 10/11.5pt Garamond from the author's disks by MHL Typesetting Ltd, Coventry.
Printed and bound in Great Britain by Bookcraft (Bath) Ltd
This book is printed on acid-free paper responsibly manufactured from sustainable forestry,
in which at least two trees are planted for each one used for paper production.

Contents

Preface

Late in 1989 I had a curious experience. I was embroiled in the final production stages of *Western Europe: challenge and change,* which I had been editing for the Institute of British Geographers and which was being published by Iain Stevenson at Belhaven Press. As each step in the process was completed, the concept of focusing solely on western Europe seemed to become more and more questionable as the socialist era ended in yet another central or eastern European country. Despite this the book went on to be a considerable success, and for some years Iain – who moved with his list from Belhaven to Wiley – pressed me to produce a successor volume. Rather than simply being a new edition, he argued, this should be a much broader book dealing with major issues relevant to both eastern and western Europe.

For several years, with some of the more taxing aspects of the original project still fresh in my mind, I managed to resist his pleas. Then, on 24 January 1995, I was caught off guard. Almost as soon as I arrived at work that morning the phone rang; it was my son announcing the arrival of my first grandchild. Iain Stevenson clearly has a sixth sense for when one's defences are down. Within hours he was on the phone, and in my state of euphoria I stood no chance. The project was agreed, and the outcome is this book.

It will be apparent that, although Iain has now moved on to HMSO, the completion of this project owes much to his persistence. In addition, however, the contributions of many others must be recognised. I am, of course, grateful to the authors for their enthusiastic participation from an early stage. A co-operative spirit has prevailed throughout the exercise, even when I despatched my comments on draft chapters! The contributors must also be thanked for undertaking this project at a time of escalating pressure in the academic world. Faced with increasing and conflicting demands on their time, they have fulfilled commitments which would have been far easier to achieve 10 years ago. Credit is also due to them for dealing with substantial topics within tight word limits. Readers will appreciate that, given such extensive themes, authors could not produce chapters dealing comprehensively with all parts of Europe. Indeed, such an unrealistic task was never in their brief. Rather, they have concentrated on highlighting important trends within their subject areas, exploring the background to those trends, and extending the discussion to consider their implications. By the same token, although some authors have considered both western and eastern Europe together, in many instances it has been more practical to have paired chapters which examine a single theme from the alternative perspectives of West and East.

The aims throughout have been to explore the spatial dimensions of European economic development at a time of far-reaching change; to communicate the complexity of development; and to provide insights not simply into that complexity but also – very importantly – into its wide-ranging social and environmental consequences. In pursuing these goals we hope that we have furthered understanding of the challenges of European life on the eve of the twenty-first century.

David Pinder
July 1997

Acknowledgements

The production of any book requires the assistance of many people behind the scenes, and this is particularly true of large edited volumes. I am indebted to the numerous secretaries who dealt so patiently with the production and later revision of manuscripts. Many cartographers also deserve thanks, since most contributors were able to arrange for the preparation of illustrations in their own departments. While this has resulted in some variation in cartographic style, it has not impaired quality, and it has ensured a level of illustration that would have been beyond the resources of a single department.

Thanks are also due to several support staff in my own department. By taking on many administrative jobs associated with our European Studies degree, which was temporarily under my wing, Mrs Ros Bryant made an invaluable contribution to enabling progress with the book to be maintained. More recently Sally Bishop and Kate Hopewell have similarly provided invaluable administrative support.

Although much of the artwork was provided by the contributors, some illustrations required minor modifications, and a number of maps and diagrams needed to be prepared from draft. This work was undertaken by our Cartographic Resources Unit, and most particularly by Brian Rogers and Tim Absalom. As always, the unit worked with great speed, efficiency and goodwill.

In addition I must acknowledge my wife's contribution. Throughout the entire process she has stoically accepted my abstraction and the advancing tide of paper that has flowed around the house. Only on one occasion – when she came home and found I had colonised the kitchen – were eyebrows raised. I may have worn her down, but I prefer to think that her patience and understanding remain unimpaired.

Finally, the publishers and I are grateful to the following copyright holders for permission to reproduce material: Aer Rianta and Finbarr O'Connell Photography, Figure 22.1; Associated British Ports, Southampton, Figures 1.7, 3.7 and 22.3; the Bridgewater Hall and Len Grant, Figure 23.5; British Petroleum plc, Figure 4.3; Dr Frank Broeze, Figure 1.4; Environmental Images, Figure 20.1; Eurotunnel, Figure 12.1; Dr Derek R Hall, Figures 10.1, 23.1 and 23.4; Hayes Davidson, Figure 10.11; *Journal of Transport Geography*, Figures 22.2 and 22.4; Professor Russell King, Figures 14.2, 14.4, 14.5 and 15.3; Lauenburgische-Akademie für Wissenschaft und Kultur, Figure 24.6; the New Millenium Experience Company, Figures 10.11 and 21.3; Professor David Pinder, Figures 1.2, 1.3, 2.3, 2.5, 8.1, 8.2, 8.3, 9.1, 10.2, 10.5, 10.6, 10.7, 10.12, 16.1, 16.2, 16.3, 16.5, 18.4, 21.2 and 22.5; the Stadium Group, Figures 9.3 and 9.4; Thamesport (London) Limited, Figure 1.6; Dr David Turnock, Figures 17.1, 17.4, 17.8 and 17.9; Dr Tim Unwin, Figures 19.2, 19.3 and 19.4; Brian J Woodruffe, Figures 24.1, 24.2 and 24.5.

David Pinder
Department of
Geographical Sciences
University of Plymouth
July 1997

Part I
Towards the New Europe

With the collapse of the socialism in central and eastern Europe in the late 1980s, the idea of a New Europe rapidly took root. This book explores this New Europe from three interrelated perspectives: the nature and direction of economic transition today; the social consequences of the powerful economic forces driving transition; and the direct and indirect environmental impacts of past and present economic development. Parts II, III and IV examine these perspectives in turn, each part being prefaced by a brief introduction outlining the rationale and coverage of the chapters which follow. Here, therefore, it is unnecessary to examine them at length.

Instead, Part I underpins the later sections by examining the New Europe from two key perspectives. First, David Pinder focuses on the New Europe concept itself, to emphasise that it is not simply since the late 1980s that this continent has changed dramatically. On the contrary, western, central and eastern Europe have all experienced turbulent economic and political histories over the last century or more. This has generated a whole series of New Europes, each of which has given way to a radically different successor. Although the influence of these earlier Europes has naturally waned with time, they remain relevant to current challenges, and some influence those challenges profoundly. To view the New Europe of today simply in terms of change wrought by the recent fall of socialism is, therefore, to adopt a very partial viewpoint.

Second, Mark Blacksell examines the political dimensions of present-day Europe, to highlight the marked mismatch between the current political situation and the supporting institutional infrastructures that have been developed since the Second World War. Political change has not simply been a matter of the demise of socialism and the proliferation of truly independent states. Throughout the continent there is a prevailing mood of uncertainty, which at its most extreme has sparked vicious nationalist wars in the name of ethnic and religious self-determination, most notably in the former Yugoslavia. Germany has re-emerged as the pivotal state at Europe's centre, and in the east new frontiers are being established between Europe and Russia, and Europe and the Muslim world. Against this radically altered background, Blacksell argues, effective institutional adaptation will be central to attempts to manage the new realities in the interests of economic and social progress.

1
New Europe or New Europes?

East–West development dynamics in the twentieth century

David Pinder

Department of Geographical Sciences, University of Plymouth, UK

With the collapse of socialism in central and eastern Europe in the late 1980s, the idea of a New Europe – generally encompassing the region shown in Figure 1.1 – rapidly took root. The popular scenario envisaged a Europe in which, as the ideologically enforced East–West dichotomy was consigned to the history books, new free-market economies would spring up and foster convergence on the successful Western development model. Already, however, it is evident that there are problems with this vision.

In part these problems relate to current conditions in central and eastern Europe, where it is now evident that the economic restructuring challenges were seriously underestimated at the outset. But it is also recognised that, while western Europe's economy remains far healthier than those of the former socialist states, it too faces many difficulties. Moreover, east and west of the former Iron Curtain, the issues are not simply those of *economic* development. Numerous *social* problems are both a reflection of current economic conditions and a legacy of the success or failure of

growth processes in earlier times. Similarly, a galaxy of *environmental* challenges must be overcome, again closely linked with past and present economic forces.

Against this complex background this book explores the New Europe from these three interrelated standpoints: economy, society and environment. Contributions are grouped under these broad themes in Parts II, III and IV, each of which is prefaced by a brief introduction (see pp. 43, 239 and 379). Part I, meanwhile, explores the emergence of the New Europe from two key perspectives. In Chapter 2 Blacksell focuses on the political dimension, examining in particular the nature and ramifications of change in Europe's political systems. Before considering this theme, however, the present chapter highlights the concept of the New Europe as an economic phenomenon, primarily to emphasise that it is not simply in the 1990s that Europe has changed dramatically. On the contrary, western, central and eastern Europe have all experienced turbulent economic histories over the last century or more,

Figure 1.1 *Territorial divisions in the New Europe*

generating a whole series of New Europes, each of which has given way to a radically different successor. Moreover, although the influence of these earlier Europes has naturally waned with time, they remain relevant to current challenges, and some influence those challenges profoundly. To view the New Europe of today in isolation, divorced from these powerful roots, is to adopt a very incomplete perspective.

New Europes, 1900–40

Landes (1969), analysing western Europe in the era of nineteenth-century industrial take-off, portrayed it as the "unbound Prometheus". As such it played a central role in establishing the nature and orientation of global development, but in the process a New Europe emerged

impressively as the rapid pace of change generated unparalleled economic, social and environmental contrasts between industrialised and unindustrial-ised areas.

Some of these contrasts were at the intra-national scale. Burgeoning industrial areas – based on resources such as coal, iron and the availability of labour reserves – became the economic leader regions of the day, leaving less well endowed regions trailing in their wake. Ports, too, became key elements in the system, providing vital links with commodity sources and markets overseas (Figure 1.2). But by 1900 major development contrasts had also emerged at the international scale (Bairoch, 1982). To some extent these differences were internal to western Europe itself. Thus industrialising countries such as the UK, Germany, France, Belgium and the Netherlands pulled ahead of those in the Mediterranean

Figure 1.2   *Links with the global economy: part of Liverpool docks in the interwar years*

5

periphery, of Ireland in the far west, and of the northern Scandinavian regions. Equally significant, however, was the development gap which emerged between western Europe, on the one hand, and central and eastern Europe on the other. Broad generalisations are naturally dangerous. Yet, as Aldcroft (1978, 47–8) has demonstrated, to a great extent central and eastern Europe remained essentially agrarian, while the west diversified and grew through industrialisation. Pockets of heavy industry – for example in parts of Poland and today's Czech Republic – were in many respects exceptions proving the rule. Although this spared many central and eastern areas from the environmental damage and social dislocation associated with the transition to industrial regions, it also ensured that large sections of the population continued to live in low-impetus economies with little prospect of economic take-off.

The First World War, economic disruption and East–West divergence

An early step towards a quite different New Europe was the outbreak of the Russian revolution in 1917, which led to the isolation of Russia from the remainder of Europe through the formation of the Soviet Union. However, this was a political development with only minor short-term consequences for the economic system. It was to be almost 30 years before the USSR's ideological divergence imposed far-reaching change on the economic development of large parts of Europe. Of far greater immediate significance was the impact of the First World War. Today this is primarily remembered, chiefly through archive film, for the appalling conditions in which the hostilities were conducted, and for the high death and injury rates suffered by the troops. But the war also had numerous short- and long-term consequences so far as European economic development was concerned.

Established trading relations were disrupted during the war itself, both within Europe and in the global market-place. With the leading European nations preoccupied with the hostilities, other countries – especially the USA and Japan – seized the opportunity to increase their shares of world trade (Aldcroft, 1978, 20–3). This had an obvious short-term effect on Europe's export earnings but, much more seriously, also created a situation in which many European industries found it impossssible to regain markets in the post-war period. In addition, many of the countries involved in the war borrowed heavily from outside Europe, to cover the lost export earnings and to maintain expenditure on the war effort. But these loans naturally had to be repaid later, draining away investment capital. And, as might be imagined, there were far-reaching changes in the scale and quality of industrial capacity. Activities unconnected with the war effort tended to become badly run down, while the industries supplying armaments, vehicles, ships, uniforms, etc. often expanded and exploited their investments to the limit. After the war, therefore, worn-out and surplus capacity was a common problem. In these ways Europe, and especially the more successful industrialised west, became permanently downgraded in the global economy and burdened by handicaps which would undermine post-war recovery.

Moreover, the end of the war brought new problems (Aldcroft and Morewood, 1995, 25). Some related to reparations, i.e. financial compensation exacted from Germany and her allies by the victors. Here the problem was that these payments severely reduced the capital available for recovery in the defeated countries, weakening their economies still further and creating conditions in which social instability could take root. Beyond this, the post-war peace settlements changed the political map drastically, especially in central and eastern Europe, as the decrepit Austro-Hungarian Empire was finally dismembered, and as valuable or potentially valuable regions were moved around the political chessboard. Aldcroft (1978, 29–33) provides a succinct summary of this complex reorganisation, the political effects of which were to create new countries (Finland, Estonia, Latvia, Lithuania, Poland, Czechoslovakia and Yugoslavia); expand an existing one (Romania); and severely curtail others (especially Germany, Austria, Hungary and Russia, but also Bulgaria and Turkey). A central feature of these far-reaching political changes was that they were imposed with very little thought for their economic consequences. No

Figure 1.3   *Crucial yet vulnerable industrialisation: Barrow-in-Furness steelworks in the interwar years*

effort was invested in attempting to create a situation in which the revival of prewar trading patterns would be encouraged. Some new frontiers cut through previously integrated economic regions, the classic example being the division of interdependent parts of the Austrian textile industry between Austria and Czechoslovakia. And a number of countries were faced with the problem of establishing economies based on contrasting social or ethnic groups, as in Poland and Yugoslavia.

The outcome of all this was that the New Europe of the interwar period was economically far less secure than the Europe it replaced. Rather than a return to prewar prosperity, in western Europe the early post-war years were marked by industrial slump and widespread unemployment; and recovery in the late 1920s was soon overtaken by the Great Depression. Traditional industrial areas – the former dynamic leader regions – were hit particularly badly as world markets collapsed and protectionism set in (Figure 1.3), but

economic malaise and its associated poverty left few localities untouched. Serious though the western experience was, however, circumstances in central and eastern Europe were such that the effects of economic crisis were even more profound.

There the already weak and largely agrarian economies relied on foreign borrowing to survive the economic problems of the early interwar period. This quickly created a situation in which further borrowing was necessary in order to repay existing debts. Then a key effect of the 1930s Depression was to cut off this credit as agricultural exports fell sharply and prices collapsed in the markets which survived. With a much-reduced flow of export earnings, bankruptcy overtook innumerable rural communities, making it impossible to modernise the still crucial, yet increasingly backward, farming sector. National economies, meanwhile, lost their creditworthiness in the international money markets. So severe was the crisis that responses included extreme measures such as the temporary closure of banks, the imposition of restrictions on debt repayments and draconian foreign exchange controls.[1]

Faced with this situation, some governments experimented with intervention to control and stimulate the industrial sector (Aldcroft and Morewood, 1995, 29–32, 76–82). Well before the socialist era, Poland began to engage in nationalisation and Hungary developed a five-year plan. However, these efforts were extremely modest compared with the economic forces at work, and in any case industrial export markets were at least as difficult as those for agricultural products. Consequently, while in Europe as a whole per capita incomes in the late 1930s averaged approximately $200, in central Europe only Czechoslovakia approached this figure, and in the poorest countries – Romania, Yugoslavia and Bulgaria – the averages were well below $100. By the end of the 1930s industry managed to generate half the national income in only one country in the region – Czechoslovakia. All this not only indicated the low standards of living endured by the vast majority of people, it also reflected the restricted nature of the more prosperous middle class. Car-usage figures are illuminating in this context. These naturally varied from country to country, but per capita car ownership in most central and eastern European states was between a tenth and a twentieth of the western European average (Aldcroft, 1978, 155, 118). While interwar conditions in western Europe may have appeared bleak, therefore,

> "down to 1939 eastern Europe remained a backward and predominantly agrarian-based region, and by every conceivable indicator it was less productive, less literate and less healthy than western Europe. . . . With the exception of Czechoslovakia, the countries of eastern Europe remained suppliers of food and raw materials and buyers of industrial goods. Politically, economically and socially they remained weak, . . . with little prospect . . . of solving their fundamental problems" (Aldcroft, 1978, 117).

New Europes, 1940–70: Ideology and the Changing Nature of Divergence

The Second World War naturally echoed the economic disruption brought about by the First,

but in reality was less devastating. Indeed, in some respects its immediate effects were economically beneficial since, on both sides, expenditure on preparations for war did much to ensure that national economies were pulled out of the Depression (Milward, 1970). Moreover, when peace came in 1945 attitudes were in general very different from those that had prevailed in 1918. Although the USSR imposed reparations on the central and eastern European countries which she overran at the end of the war, the Western allied aim was to ensure that (West) German economic recovery was as rapid as possible. More generally, Marshall Aid supplied by the USA was used to regenerate countries west of the Iron Curtain. There were, moreover, no wholesale revisions of national boundaries, such as those which had disrupted economic systems after the First World War. Even though these approaches helped to minimise the challenge of transition to peacetime conditions, however, the end of the Second World War ushered in a New Europe which in political, economic and social terms was to become scarcely recognisable compared with its interwar predecessor.

Socialist regimes and East–West divergence

In seeking to understand this transformation it is tempting to emphasise the stultifying effects of Soviet influence and socialism in central and eastern Europe, as opposed to the successful resurgence of economic activity throughout large parts of the democratic West. Yet from the earlier discussion of interwar circumstances it is apparent that the economic East–West divide did not arise simply through post-war political partition. It is a distortion to suggest that Western democracy succeeded in creating an environment conducive to economic success while, simultaneously, the handicaps of states east of the newly lowered Iron Curtain arose solely because of the economic damage caused by the imposition of Soviet-style planning.

Socialist approaches to economic development were not simply ideological; they were also a response to the severe economic and social problems that had become endemic under free-market conditions in the first half of the century.

Where state farms or, much more commonly, collective farms were created it was generally in the expectation that they would modernise agriculture where the market had failed, as Aldcroft and Morewood (1995, 118) note. New farming practices would end the diseconomies associated with the small-scale, highly fragmented and undercapitalised holdings which had previously predominated. Industrial planning, meanwhile, aimed to kick-start production, create large-scale employment, and lead to national self-sufficiency in each country, thus ending dependence on costly imports. Although there was no question of emulating the western European capitalist development model, the goal was to replicate certain outcomes of that model – above all manufacturing's domination of national income and the labour market – by other means.

What must also be recognised is that, at least in the early post-war decades, the socialist economies of central and eastern Europe did indeed achieve impressive growth. Assessing this growth accurately is difficult given the economic and political circumstances. It must also be remembered that expansion was occurring from a very low base. None the less, United Nations estimates quoted by Aldcroft (1978, 207–12) were that in the 1950s and 1960s total GDP increased by approximately 7 per cent a year, at least 2 per cent faster than the western European average. And although per capita growth rates were less than this because of population expansion, countries east of the Iron Curtain were generally 1.5–2 per cent ahead of the western European figure (a little under 4 per cent). To help maintain the pace of economic expansion, and to achieve more efficient growth, from the late 1950s onwards increasing emphasis was placed on co-operation between the socialist states. Thus the Council for Mutual Economic Assistance (CMEA, also known as Comecon) provided a framework within which economic plans were co-ordinated and the complementarity of national economies could be exploited.

Relatively good quantitative indicators, however, cannot conceal the fact that eastern and central Europe fell down with respect to the *quality* of growth. One reason for this was that central planning steered resources into basic industries, and especially into producer goods industries. This made activities such as iron and steel, oil refining, chemicals and engineering major investment targets. The rationale for this bias was that producer goods were essential if a proper foundation was to be established for the manufacturing sector. Also, although the trend was less marked than in the USSR, Cold War considerations meant that the defence sector was favoured. Meanwhile consumer demand, despite its potential for stimulating the manufacturing sector, was held in check by deliberately preventing the development of consumer goods industries. These industries could not, of course, be abandoned entirely. But where they were developed they were usually starved of the advantages of technological advance, often in sharp contrast to an industry such as armaments. Consequently, while the Czechoslovakian car industry could do no better than produce the Skoda, the country was also capable of manufacturing some of the world's best small arms.

Long-term economic development processes east of the Iron Curtain were also hindered by attitudes to labour productivity and the service sector. Because an important objective of the socialist economic system was to eliminate unemployment, little emphasis was placed on labour productivity. Consequently, while western European industries steadily improved their performance by replacing labour with capital and – very importantly – new technologies, east of the Iron Curtain productivity levels languished. In addition to having a quantitative effect, this impacted on the quality of products because new techniques were not employed to improve industrial design, the materials used and the standards of production processes. Similarly, the service sector came to be used as an effective "sponge" for absorbing surplus labour, but with little emphasis on quality (Maciejewicz and Monkiewicz, 1989). Perhaps most seriously from the viewpoint of long-term economic development, whereas producer *goods* were favoured, producer *services* were suppressed almost completely. In a world in which functions such as market research, advertising, competitive recruitment and strategic financial planning were either considered unnecessary or best delivered by bureaucratic channels, producer services had no need to exist. As Michalak argues in Chapter 8, what is now apparent is that this created one of the major obstacles to present-day attempts to place the central and eastern European economies on a competitive market-oriented basis.

In similar vein, other handicaps were imposed by attitudes to the physical infrastructure for economic development (Major, 1992). Because the economic system was not dependent on a host of competing companies seeking to market their products as swiftly and competitively as possible, the allocation of resources to create an increasingly efficient road network along the lines of western Europe's emerging motorway systems was not on the agenda. In the same way, rail system improvement was generally a low priority. And, while telecommunications systems in the western European market economies steadily became increasingly important to the trading of goods and services, in eastern and central Europe a failure to invest ensured that they remained technologically backward and of limited capacity. As with the absence of producer services, these limitations are now recognised as formidable obstacles to the process of economic modernisation.

Post-war western Europe: a cocktail for success

Meanwhile in western Europe, as we have already noted, growth was actually slower than in the new socialist states in the early post-war decades. Yet western per capita GDP rose, on average, by 4.4 per cent per year between 1950 and 1970, well above the world figure (3.0 per cent). Similarly, the annual average rate of increase in industrial production was 7.1 per cent, as opposed to a world figure of 5.9 per cent (Aldcroft, 1978, 161). Moreover, absolute growth outstripped that in central and eastern Europe because expansion was built on a much higher base. Also, as the discussion of socialist approaches to economic development has implied, economic success may be judged in terms of the quality and diversity of output, as well as the pace of change. Viewed in this light, western Europe's performance in this period easily overshadowed that of the socialist states (Boltho, 1982; Postan, 1977).

This achievement, of course, was closely associated with a cocktail of factors that were largely the mirror image of those handicapping the central and eastern economies. Although many western European governments experimented with economic planning, and commonly nationalised some basic industries and utilities such as gas and electricity, this did not amount to the adoption of rigid industrialisation blueprints (Hayward and Watson, 1975; Maunder, 1979; Shepherd, 1976). Investment in road networks – first at the intra-national scale and then increasingly in an international context – was impressive, especially if allowance is made for budgetary cutbacks which affected most countries from time to time.[2] From the late 1950s onwards, most western European governments invested heavily to upgrade both the capacity and the quality of telecommunications systems. And the market economy created the conditions for producer service development, although at that stage these services were often internalised by major corporations, and their importance to economic development processes was not yet fully recognised.

This was the era in which Fordist manufacturing, driven by major companies, based on assembly line mass production and frequently supporting an extensive network of suppliers, reached its zenith. There is no doubt that this exploitation of Fordist principles, which is well documented in the literature, made a substantial contribution to the growth that was achieved in western Europe. However, at this distance in time it is necessary to recall that other forces also had an important influence on the growth processes which distinguished the New Europe of the West from that of the East.

One was ability of the Western system to exploit technological change. Prewar industrial depression, severe though it was, had overlapped with an important period of innovation, especially in emergent industries such as electronics, aviation and road vehicles.[3] In many instances the Second World War acted as a forcing house for further development of these technological advances, and also as a spur to new innovations. In the post-war period many of the gains became available for exploitation in the civilian sector, in sharp contrast to central and eastern Europe, where advanced technologies were typically reserved for defence-related industries. To cite only three examples of this uptake in western Europe, the development of

Figure 1.4 *The* Labena, *one of the world's largest supertankers, in the mid-1970s*

radar for air, sea and land forces greatly enhanced post-war research and development capacity in the civil electronics industry; work on military jet propulsion, plus aerodynamic advances and the quest for high-altitude flying capabilities, paved the way for a revolution in airliner design; and the need to decipher military codes – particularly the advanced *Geheimschreiber* codes employed by the German forces – led to theoretical and technical advances of great importance for the development of the computer.

In addition, whereas eastern and central Europe generally drew on resources from fellow CMEA members within the socialist bloc, western European post-war growth was built on resource exploitation at the global scale. Although minerals such as iron ore and bauxite were (and still are) central to this global trade, in the pre-North-Sea era the truly vital imported commodity underpinning economic expansion was oil. In 1950 total oil refining capacity was less than 50 million t a year, yet by 1972 – on the eve of the first oil crisis – western Europe imported and refined 652 million t. Furthermore, this resource made a fundamental contribution to economic growth not simply because of its availability, but also because in real terms its price halved between 1950 and 1970 (see p. 69). In part this again reflected technological change, and particularly the development of the supertanker with its attendant economies of scale (Figure 1.4). But falling oil prices also resulted from a buyer's market, in which oil over-supply allowed western Europe – the world's dominant import region – to drive harder and harder bargains.

At this time, too, growth processes began to be stimulated by economic co-operation between western European states. In 1952 France, Germany, Italy, the Netherlands, Belgium and Luxembourg established the European Coal and Steel Community (ECSC), aiming to modernise and revitalise these essential yet war-depleted industries by making them much more open to the forces of market competition. This, it was argued, was an imperative if they were to continue to compete with other European producers and, increasingly, with more global competitors. Six years later these same countries established the European Economic Community, the direct ancestor of today's European Union of 15 member states. This Community aimed to extend the principles of the ECSC, based on competitive free trade within a Common Market, across the broad spectrum of economic activity. Although progress towards this goal has been far slower than originally anticipated – in the 1990s the much-enlarged EU is still struggling with single market issues, and especially the challenges of a single currency – this type of co-operation in western Europe has fuelled growth significantly by opening up wider markets for innumerable producers. By the mid-1990s almost two-thirds of member states' exports were destined for customers in other EU countries.

All this, however, should not be taken to indicate that post-war western European growth up to around 1970 was problem free. As Parts III and IV of this book demonstrate, many of today's social and environmental challenges took root or were intensified in this period. Similarly, although it was certainly not a new phenomenon, uneven development became an increasingly pressing political issue at this time. As early as the mid-1950s, Italy feared that her membership of the proposed European Economic Community might be disadvantageous because her lagging economy – and especially her southern regions – would be uncompetitive compared with those of other states. Concern led directly to the creation of the European Investment Bank (EIB) in 1958, and to the decision that its first priority should be the acceleration of economic growth in major lagging regions (Licari, 1970; Pinder, 1986; Honohan, 1995). With the accession of Ireland, the UK and Denmark to the Community in 1973, the scale of peripheral problem regions increased greatly, triggering the introduction of the European Regional Development Fund (ERDF) (Mawson *et al.*, 1985; Pinder, 1983; Wallace, 1977). This perceived need for intervention highlights an important and continuing paradox in western European development strategy in the post-war period, a paradox to which we will return at the end of this chapter. On the one hand there have been formidable political pressures to extend the economic union as widely as possible, to bind together through economic interdependence the interests of the maximum number of countries and avoid the resurgence of conflicts which focused two world wars on the region. Yet, on the other hand, political expansion which has progressed from core to periphery has led inevitably to greater contrasts in economic development levels, in turn making action to maintain cohesion an ever-present imperative.

Towards Today's New Europe: From Stability to Uncertainty

Viewed overall, the future of Europe in the early 1970s probably appeared more certain than at any other time since 1900. For all its shortcomings, the socialist economic system had produced industrialisation on an unprecedented scale, and was in any case firmly entrenched through the authoritarian regimes that were then in power. Western Europe had enjoyed 20 years of generally sustained growth, had laid the foundations of consumer societies, was substantially more stable politically than in earlier decades, and was beginning to reap the benefits of EEC development, at least for member states. If there was a danger it was that Cold War confrontation would degenerate into genuine war between NATO and Warsaw Pact forces on European soil.

But, if this could be avoided, there was every prospect that the two politically separate yet stable New Europes would maintain their independent development paths for the foreseeable future.

In practice circumstances have combined to break down this stable situation, creating instead the current New Europe in which conditions are far more fluid and the future is far less certain. And while this is obviously the case with respect to eastern and central Europe, in many respects – if for different reasons – the same is true of its western counterpart.

Transition to uncertainty in central and eastern Europe

Up to a point the current New Europe is the product of sudden, far-reaching, short-term change. In the mid-1980s radical political shifts in central and eastern Europe were not on the agenda, yet by late 1989 the demise of the socialist regimes was in full flood, and the ultimate coup, the disintegration of the Soviet Union, was in sight. Although the reversal was swift, however, it was the outcome of long-term forces. These were partly economic. Throughout the 1970s and 1980s the distorted economic systems that had been created east of the Iron Curtain, including the Soviet Union, functioned with increasing difficulty. While there were some spectacular

achievements, especially in connection with aerospace and defence, most industries stagnated because of the failure to prioritise investment in vital fields such as the application of new technologies to manufacturing and to research and development. Similarly in the service sector, although some countries provided very effective public services such as nursery schooling in East Germany, the range and quality of what was available often remained poor (Maciejewicz and Monkiewicz, 1989; Schneider, 1993).

Meanwhile, despite official control of the media and the low standard of communications, the populations of central and eastern Europe became more and more aware of the gaps in living standards and opportunities for choice which now divided East and West. This was particularly the case with younger age groups and those living in the main urban centres, who became increasingly intolerant of the status quo. Consequently a situation developed in which the frustrations and aspirations of important sections of society could not be met by the sclerotic national economies and their associated political and social systems. Earlier in the post-war period this mismatch might well have resulted in uprisings and repression by Soviet forces, as the experiences of Hungary and Czechoslovakia testify. But by the late 1980s conditions in the Soviet Union had also changed, the new priority in the era of *glasnost* and *perestroika* being to maintain political and

Table 1.1 *Agricultural employment and GDP in central and eastern Europe, 1993 (% of total)*

	Employment	GDP
Central + eastern Europe average	22	8.1
EU average	6	2.6
Albania	56	–
Bulgaria	22	9.2
Estonia	–	4.1
Hungary	9	6.4
Latvia	18	10.6
Lithuania	22	11.2
Poland	22	6.3
Czech Republic	7	6.0
Slovakia	9	6.7
Romania	36	20.6
Slovenia	10	4.5

Source: Eurostat (1995, 394–5).

economic stability at home, rather than support beleaguered central and eastern European governments by force.[4] Without the backing of the USSR, most regimes recognised the futility of resisting the popular pro-democracy movements which spread rapidly through the region, and as a result they were overthrown with virtually no bloodshed (Church and Hendriks, 1995, 115–26, 140–56).

Subsequent political developments are examined in Chapter 2, and need not be considered here. From this chapter's perspective, however, the long-term pressure for change, and the sudden translation of demand into reality by the peaceful revolutions of 1989, have plunged central and eastern Europe into what will almost certainly be a prolonged period of great economic uncertainty. Repressive regimes have been deposed, and the market economy has been embraced. But the reality now is that the painful process of economic reconstruction must seek to close a severe development gap that is the legacy of the socialist and presocialist eras.

Despite earlier industrialisation programmes, agriculture's contributions to employment and GDP remain more than three times the western European levels (Table 1.1). Much of the established industrial base is inappropriate to today's needs (Ernst *et al.*, 1996; Pickles, 1995). Although micro-businesses are springing up in an opportunistic fashion throughout the region, there is a general lack of entrepreneurial expertise in small firm development. Banking and legal systems need a good deal of refinement. As we have seen, the lack of producer services is by no means confined to banking and the law, and there is an urgent need to modernise economic infrastructures (Major, 1992). This need does not fit easily with either budgetary constraints or neo-liberal philosophies (Gowan, 1995), both of which work to restrain public investment rather than to encourage its expansion along unfashionable Keynesian lines. As demand grows it is essential to avoid exploitation and dependence on western Europe, where highly efficient producers might well view eastern markets as tempting targets,

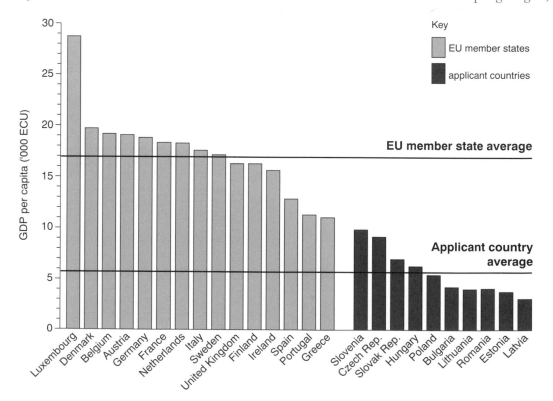

Figure 1.5 *Per capita GDP contrasts between the EU and former socialist states*

Table 1.2 *Life expectancy in central and eastern Europe, 1993 (yrs)*

	Men	Women
Central + eastern European average	66.8	75.1
EU average	72.7	79.1
Bulgaria	67.7	75.0
Estonia	64.1	75.0
Hungary	64.5	73.8
Latvia	61.6	73.8
Lithuania	63.3	75.0
Poland	67.4	76.0
Czech Republic	68.9	76.6
Slovakia	68.4	76.7
Romania	66.1	73.2
Slovenia	69.4	77.2

Source: Eurostat (1995, 394–5).

easily reached given the speed and flexibility of road transport. Foreign debt is already a significant problem (Gibb and Michalak, 1993), and rapidly rising car ownership has led to substantial tariffs to prevent petrol imports from western Europe, where refiners need new outlets for surplus products. Equally, it is important to be aware that, as growth in the central and eastern economies does occur, there is a danger that it will generate increasingly intense spatial and social polarisation. The signs in this respect are far from good. Between 1990 and 1994, for example, two-thirds of all foreign investment were attracted to Hungary and Czechoslovakia (where the region which is now the Czech Republic was the overwhelming beneficiary) (*The Guardian*, 1995; Ingham and Grime, 1994; Nemes Nagy, 1994).

This is not to argue that reconstruction leading to convergence on the Western economic model is impossible. Nor is it to deny that the leading economies will be spurred on by the prospect of progress being rewarded by accession to the EU (Gibb and Michalak, 1994). What must be acknowledged, however, is the magnitude of the challenges and uncertainties which have replaced the often dispiriting certainties of socialism (Jackman, 1994; Church and Hendriks, 1995, 199–203). Summarising these in terms of per capita GDP, only one central European country – the Czech Republic – comes close to matching the prosperity level of the EU's poorest member, Greece (Figure 1.5). Moreover, in six central and

eastern European countries per capita GDP is less than a third of the EU average. Linked with low prosperity – and the economic, social and environmental pressures associated with it – a man's average life expectancy in central and eastern Europe is six years less than in the EU; for women the gap is narrower, but is still four years (Table 1.2; Ellman, 1994). What must also be recognised is the slimness of the resources available to meet the challenges. And, despite current understandable enthusiasm for the free market (Gowan, 1995), it may also be salutary to recall the failures of that market earlier this century. State socialism produced many economic disasters yet, as the earlier discussion has emphasised, dire conditions in the interwar years resulted from the inability of markets to create stability out of highly unstable conditions.

New uncertainties for western Europe

Western Europe has not experienced a sudden reversal equivalent to the revolutions east of the former Iron Curtain, but long-term shifts have been as important here as in the East (Boltho, 1982). Since the early 1970s these have increasingly called into question the vision of a secure future. In 1973–74, and again in 1979–80, confidence in the region's ability to sustain growth was shaken severely by the two oil crises (Odell, 1986, 22–3). Following these shocks, western European nations were forced to grapple with rapid inflation as abrupt shifts in energy prices fed through the system, threatening competitiveness in the world economy. Yet while it may be a convenient shorthand to explain the end of sustained growth in terms of energy market upheavals, the reality has been much more complex. These oil shocks have intertwined with, and reinforced, other trends with long-term implications for the health and nature of western Europe's production and social systems.

Outstanding among these has been the intensification of global competition, to some extent from developing countries but also from advanced economies (Daniels and Lever, 1996; Henderson, 1995). Although this competition has recently generated a large globalisation literature, it is a long-established process which originated before the Second World War and spread in the post-war period to affect increasingly complex and technologically advanced sectors. Thus, while activities such as textiles came under great pressure in the 1950s, by the 1980s the electronics, automobile and aerospace industries were widely exposed to the new forces (Wells and Rowlinson, 1994). Ultimately this trend came to be

Figure 1.6 *The Thamesport container terminal, Isle of Grain, UK. Built on part of the former BP oil refinery site, one of the largest in Europe, the terminal illustrates recovery from industrial dereliction, as well as the globalisation of trade. (Photo: Thamesport (London) Limited)*

Figure 1.7 *A Wallenius Lines car transporter. (Photo: Associated British Ports, Southampton)*

interpreted as a major factor contributing to the crisis in Fordism and, therefore, a significant influence encouraging the shift to post-Fordist restructuring of the manufacturing sector. Much attention has been given to the role of transnational corporations in bringing about competitive globalisation, and rightly so (Nilsson *et al.*, 1996). Yet although these corporations were important contributors to the growing difficulties experienced by western Europe, they were by no means entirely responsible for creating the new competitive environment.

Government policies in industrialising countries were also of considerable significance, through the encouragement of import-substituting industries and, commonly, export-oriented activities. Good examples of the latter are the development of shipbuilding in South Korea, petrochemicals in Saudi Arabia and the Japanese car industry. In addition state-inspired East–West competition within Europe was in some instances significant. The decline of ship-

building was not simply a consequence of growing exports from first Japan and then South Korea. Heavy state subsidisation of this industry in Poland also had a major impact on the western European shipbuilding industry's competitive prospects.

Technological factors, and especially advances in communications and transportation, have similarly played an important role. Better telecommunications have done much to fuel international competition, but it is improved trans-portation – and, most importantly, sea transportation – that has made the global dispersion of production capacity physically possible. Two types of vessel, the container ship and the car transporter, have been crucial in this respect (Figures 1.6 and 1.7; Hayuth and Hilling, 1992).

Within western Europe technological change has exerted additional pressures as producers have aimed to remain competitive by reducing employ-ment, often investing instead in highly

Table 1.3 *Western European unemployment rates, 1995 (%)*

Spain	22.9
Finland	17.2
Ireland	12.4
Italy	11.9
France	11.5
EU average	**10.7**
Belgium	9.9
Sweden	9.2
Greece	9.1
UK	8.8
Germany	8.2
Netherlands	7.3
Denmark	7.1
Norway*	4.9
Austria	3.8

* Non-EU.
Source: Eurostat (1996, 156).

computerised automation. Also influential has been the questioning of Keynesian economic policies, and an associated shift towards neo-liberal approaches to the economy, which together have placed the public sector under a critical

Table 1.4 *EU youth unemployment* as % of total unemployment, 1995*

Italy	39.4
Spain	37.3
Portugal	33.6
Greece	32.1
Ireland	30.3
UK	30.2
Luxembourg	29.9
Netherlands	29.4
EU average	**27.6**
Belgium	26.8
Denmark	26.2
Sweden	25.3
France	25.0
Austria	23.2
Finland	18.0
Germany	12.6

* Unemployed aged under 25.
Source: Eurostat (1996, 155).

spotlight. Not least because of its tax burden, this sector is now seen in many quarters as a stultifying influence on economic development. Today, therefore, the rise in public employment has been reined in, deregulation has curbed the interventionist role of the state, and in many instances the privatisation of nationalised activities has resulted in large-scale job losses. While this has undoubtedly improved the efficiency of individual undertakings, it has also hit the labour market.

Elsewhere in the service sector, of course, there has been compensation. Despite the uncertain economic climate, total service sector employment in the EU's 15 member states grew by 2 per cent a year between 1989 and 1994, by which time it accounted for virtually two-thirds of all employment and 70 per cent of gross value added.[5] Such growth has been based chiefly on the increasing prosperity and rising expectations of western European societies, which have demanded an ever-widening range of personal, business, leisure and tourism services. As Chapters 9 and 10 stress, both the retailing and tourism sectors are now very powerful forces with far-reaching influence on both the nature and geography of economic development.

Even so, service-sector dynamism has been unable to offset completely the combined effects of continued contraction of the agricultural labour force and weak industrial employment growth, which between 1983 and 1992 amounted to no more than 3 per cent.[6] The labour force as a whole has expanded more rapidly than jobs, so that unemployment in today's EU has risen from 13.6 million in 1991 to 18.5 million in 1994, with only a modest improvement to 17.9 million in 1995. The average EU unemployment rate in the mid-1990s exceeded 10 per cent, substantially higher than in either the USA (less than 7 per cent) or Japan (only 2.5 per cent). Furthermore, in the mid-1990s individual national unemployment rates were as high as 22.9 per cent in Spain and 17.2 per cent in Finland (Table 1.3). Throughout western Europe as a whole, only Austria and Norway controlled the problem at "negligible" levels (3.8 and 4.9 per cent, respectively). Beyond this, unemployment has concentrated disproportionately on specific groups in society (Nicaise *et al.*, 1995; Symes, 1995). Thus high youth unemployment is a feature throughout the EU (Table 1.4), and immigrants too are frequently disadvantaged. In the Netherlands, for example, unemployment among the Dutch themselves was little more than 7 per cent in the mid-1990s; but for foreign workers it was 20 per cent, and for those from Turkey and Morocco – as opposed to other EU countries – it was almost certainly much higher. Finally, for those more fortunate, it is important to note an increasing emphasis on part-time labour, which grew by 60 per cent between the early 1980s and early 1990s. To some extent, of course, this type of work is attractive to employees; for many women, who fill nearly 85 per cent of all part-time jobs, there is the incentive of compatibility with household and family responsibilities. Yet part-time work is also closely associated with the wider phenomena of low pay, the need for families to have two incomes, casualisation of the labour force and increasing employment insecurity.

In response to such problems the European Commission has made efforts to re-establish economic impetus since the early 1980s (Batchler and Mitchie, 1994; Commission of the European Communities, 1981, 1983a, b). These efforts may be traced through to the Single European Act (Commission of the European Communities, 1986) and, as the problems have persisted, to renewed concern in the late 1980s and 1990s. Continuing anxiety was reflected in the creation of the Cohesion Funds for Spain, Portugal, Greece and Ireland, part of the long-running battle to ensure that uneven development does not become a destabilising force threatening the "European project" (Amin and Tomaney, 1995). But for the EU as a whole, concern is best represented by the Commission's 1994 Growth Initiative, which aimed to cultivate a return to buoyant economic conditions capable of sustaining progress towards goals such as continued integration and a single currency (Commission of the European Communities, 1994; Church and Hendriks, 1995, 162).

What must also be emphasised, however, is that the role of the EU has not simply been to take action to damp down uncertainty by counteracting stresses in the economic system caused by the powerful workings of the market. Instead today's widespread uncertainty has to a significant extent been brought about by the EU's own policies. For example, the long-established strategy of political

expansion, which has already posed major challenges by dramatically increasing the EU's list of less developed areas, now seems likely to lead to the accession of several former socialist states early in the twenty-first century (see p. 40). This will sharply increase demand for the development resources available to promote cohesion, with major implications for many regions currently receiving this support. Similarly, the convergence criteria adopted for the single currency have imposed severe constraints on government expenditure, impacting on public sector employment, investment and attitudes to leading budget commitments such as the social security safety net. Simultaneously, however, there has been great uncertainty as to whether the single currency would indeed become a reality. More-over, even though monetary union is now a strong probability for most member states, the ultimate political, economic and social consequences of the change, and of dividing the EU along currency lines, are still conjectural.

Conclusion

It is evident that the New Europe concept gains considerably from the adoption of a historical perspective. Changed circumstances do indeed justify the use of the term today, but it should be remembered that the last century has witnessed a series of shifts in the political and economic climate. Each of these created its own New Europe by establishing an alternative framework for the development process, so that New Europes have replaced each other with remarkable frequency.

Several observations are appropriate against this background. First, a central feature of the drama played out on the European stage has been long-run East–West economic divergence. Although it is tempting to ascribe the development gap to the socialist era, in fact it emerged in the Industrial Revolution, was exacerbated by interwar conditions, and was reinforced by post-war socialist regimes as they attempted to overcome backwardness in central and eastern Europe. Economic modernisers, therefore, are grappling with problems which partly predate the socialist structures they seek to transform or replace. Second, given the experience of western Europe, the omens for swift success in the battle to bridge the East–West development gap are not good. After decades of effort by national governments, and more recently the EU, economic development contrasts throughout the EU remain disconcertingly great. Third, linked with this observation, western European development is also fallible, even though it was quickly adopted as a role model in much of central and eastern Europe after 1989. Late-nineteenth-century success gave way to the economic malaise of the interwar years; and a resurgence of growth after the Second World War has in turn been replaced by a phase of weakened impetus. In the Europe of today, therefore, the economic challenges are not restricted to the promotion of eastern convergence on the west. Fourth, western Europe's current problems arose despite the best efforts of the EU, the most highly organised politico-economic grouping in the world today. While economic forces remain extremely powerful, however, finally it is legitimate to question whether some EU policies contribute to development problems, rather than resolving them. At the very least, uncertainty and weak impetus appear bound up with the combined effects of political expansion, market integration and the pursuit of monetary union.

As was indicated at the outset, subsequent chapters explore in greater detail a range of issues relating to economic development (Part II), social challenges closely related to development problems (Part III) and the environmental legacy of past development processes (Part IV). Before turning to these themes, however, deeper insights are necessary into Europe's political dynamics. How did the political map come to be redrawn, what are the current implications of the transformation, and what scenarios may be sketched for the future? Issues such as these are central to the remainder of Part I.

Notes

1. In order to maintain trade in this crisis situation, central and eastern European countries frequently resorted to barter arrangements. To a great extent, therefore, commodity imports were paid for in kind by exports of other goods, so that actual foreign exchange payments were only required in order to cover any difference between the values of the bilateral flows (Aldcroft, 1978, 111–12).

2. An unfortunate aspect of this is that rail networks tended to become the neglected Cinderellas of the transport system as demand swung rapidly towards road usage.

3. The emergence of such industries in a period of great economic difficulty can be related directly to Kondratieff's theory of long-wave development. See Freeman (1984).

4. An important financial attraction was that intervention would have been extremely expensive. Conversely, the possibility of withdrawing forces from areas such as Estonia, Lithuania and Latvia, as well as from the independent socialist states, offered great scope for economies.

5. For industry the equivalent figures were both around 30 per cent.

6. This figure was for the Community of 12 (i.e. excluding Austria, Sweden and Finland) and was equivalent to 1.3 million new jobs.

References

Aldcroft, D H (1978) *The European Economy, 1914–1970*, Croom Helm, London.

Aldcroft, D H and Morewood, S (1995) *Economic Change in Eastern Europe since 1918*, Edward Elgar Publishing, Aldershot.

Amin, A and Tomaney, J (1995) The challenge of cohesion, in A Amin and J Tomaney (eds) *Behind the Myth of the European Union*, Routledge, London.

Bairoch, P (1982) International industrialisation levels from 1750–1980, *Journal of European Economic History*, **11**, 269–333.

Batchler, J and Mitchie, R (1994) Strengthening economic and social cohesion? The revision of the structural funds, *Regional Studies*, **28**, 789–96.

Boltho, A (ed) (1982) *The European Economy: growth and crisis*, Oxford University Press, Oxford.

Church, C and Hendriks, G (1995) *Continuity and Change in Contemporary Europe*, Edward Elgar Publishing, Aldershot.

Commission of the European Communities (1981) A new impetus for the common policies, *Bulletin of the European Communities, Supplement* 4/81.

Commission of the European Communities (1983a) Increasing the Effectiveness of the Community's Structural Funds, *Bulletin of the European Communities, Supplement* 3/83.

Commission of the European Communities (1983b) Prospects for the development of new policies: research and development, energy and new technologies, *Bulletin of the European Communities, Supplement* 5/83.

Commission of the European Communities (1986) The Single European Act, *Bulletin of the European Communities, Supplement* 2/86.

Commission of the European Communities (1994) *Growth, Competitiveness and Employment*, Office for Official Publications, Luxembourg.

Daniels, P and Lever, W (eds) (1996) *The Global Economy in Transition*, Longman, Harlow.

Ellman, M (1994) The increase in death and disease under "katastroïka", *Cambridge Journal of Economics*, **10**, 329–56.

Ernst, M, Alexeev, M and Marer, P (1996) *Transforming the Core: restructuring industrial enterprises in Russia and central Europe*, Westview Press, Boulder, Colo.

Eurostat (1995) *Europe in Figures*, Office for Official Publications of the European Communities, Luxembourg.

Eurostat (1996) *Basic Statistics of the European Union*, Statistical Office of the European Communities, Luxembourg.

Freeman, C (ed) (1984) *Long Waves in the World Economy*, Pinter, London.

Gibb, R A and Michalak, W Z (1993) Foreign debt in the new East-Central Europe: a threat to European integration?, *Environment and Planning C*, **11**, 69–85.

Gibb, R A and Michalak, W Z (1994) The European Community and East-Central Europe, *Tijdschrift voor Economische en Sociale Geografie*, **84**, 401–16.

Gowan, P (1995) Neo-liberal theory and practice for eastern Europe, *New Left Review*, **213**, 3–60.

Hayuth, Y and Hilling, D (1992) Technological change and seaport development, in B S Hoyle and D A Pinder (eds) *European Port Cities in Transition*, Belhaven, London, 40–58.

Hayward, J and Watson, M (eds) (1975) *Planning, Politics and Public Policy*, Cambridge University Press, London.

Henderson, K (1995) *Europe and World Trade*, Pinter, London.

Honohan, P (1995) The public policy role of the European Investment Bank within the EU, *Journal of Common Market Studies*, **33**, 315–30.

Ingham, M and Grime, K (1994) Regional unemployment in central and eastern Europe, *Regional Studies*, **28**, 811–17.

Jackman, R (1994) Economic policy and employment in the transition economies of central and eastern Europe: what have we learned?, *International Labour Review*, **133**, 327–45.

Landes, D S (1969) *The Unbound Prometheus: technological change and industrial development in Western Europe from 1750 to the present*, Cambridge University Press, Cambridge.

Licari, J (1970) The European Investment Bank, *Journal of Common Market Studies*, **8**, 192–215.

Maciejewicz, J and Monkiewicz, J (1989) Changing roles of services in the socialist countries of eastern Europe, *Service Industries Journal*, **9**, 384–98.

Major, I (1992) Private and public infrastructure in eastern Europe, *Oxford Review of Economic Policy*, **7**, 76–96.

Maunder, P (ed) (1979) *Government Intervention in the Developed Economy*, Croom Helm, London.

Mawson, J, Martins, M R and Gibney, J T (1985) The development of the European Community regional policy, in M Keating and B Jones (eds) *Regions in the European Community*, Oxford University Press, Oxford, 20–59.

Milward, A S (1970) *The Economic Effects of the Two World Wars on Britain*, Macmillan, London and Basingstoke.

Nemes Nagy, J (1994) Regional disparities in Hungary during the period of transition to a market economy, *GeoJournal*, **32**, 363–8.

Nicaise, I *et al*. (1995) Pitfalls and dilemmas in labour market policies for disadvantaged groups – and how to avoid them, *Journal of European Social Policy*, **5**, 199–217.

Nilsson, J-E, Dicken, P and Peck, J (eds) (1996) *The Internationalisation Process: European firms in global competition*, Paul Chapman, London.

Odell, P R (1986) *Oil and World Power*, Penguin, Harmondsworth.

Pickles, J (1995) Restructuring state enterprises: industrial geography and eastern European transitions, *Geographische Zeitschrift*, **2**, 114–31.

Pinder, D A (1983) *Regional Economic Development and Policy: theory and practice in the European Community*, Allen and Unwin, London.

Pinder, D A (1986) Small firms, regional development and the European Investment Bank, *Journal of Common Market Studies*, **24**, 171–86.

Postan, M (1977) The European economy since 1945: a retrospect, in R T Griffiths (ed) *Government Business and Labour in European Capitalism*, Europotentials Press, London, 23–39.

Schneider, O (1993) The problems of the development of the service sector in Czechoslovakia, in P Daniels, S Illeris, J Bonamy and J Phillippe (eds) *The Geography of Services*, Frank Cass, London, 132–43.

Shepherd, W G (ed) (1976) *Public Enterprise: economic analysis of theory and practice*, D C Heath/Lexington Books, Lexington, Mass.

Symes, V (1995) *Unemployment in Europe: problems and policies*, Routledge, London.

The Guardian (1995) Eastern promise betrayed by latter-day Marshall Aid, 8 May, 14.

Wallace, H (1977) The establishment of the Regional Development Fund: common policy or pork barrel?, in H Wallace, W Wallace and C Webb (eds) *Policy-making in the European Communities*, Wiley, London, 137–63.

Wells, P and Rowlinson, M (1994) *The New European Automobile Industry*, Macmillan, London.

2
Redrawing the political map

Mark Blacksell

Department of Geographical Sciences, University of Plymouth, UK

As the twentieth century draws to a close it is becoming increasingly apparent that the political situation in Europe is out of line with the infrastructure of institutions that has been built up over the past 50 years. The cold war division of the continent is now a thing of the past and, in what was eastern Europe, the political and economic philosophy of Western democracy has taken over from the planned socialism that was the hallmark of the former Soviet Union and its client states (Cohen, 1991; Murphy, 1991; Nijman, 1992). The European Union, the *leitmotif* of western Europe's political and economic salvation after the Second World War, is struggling to come to terms with a wider Europe stretching as far east as the fertile prairies of the Ukraine, and the same is true of the major pan-European defence organisations, NATO and the West European Union. The urgency of the task of trying to fill the political vacuum is underlined by the demise of Comecon and the Warsaw Pact, the European Union's and NATO's Communist-inspired equivalents in the East, both of which died with the disintegration of the Soviet Union (Taylor, 1993; Luke, 1996).

Throughout the continent there is a prevailing mood of uncertainty which, at its most extreme, has sparked vicious nationalist wars in the name of ethnic and religious self-determination, most

notably in the former Yugoslavia. Germany has re-emerged as the pivotal state at Europe's centre, and in the East new frontiers are being established between Europe and Russia, and Europe and the Muslim world. This chapter will attempt to encapsulate these changes and clarify what has become an almost mesmerisingly complex situation, for the process of institutional adaptation through which politicians are trying to manage and contain the new realities is central to understanding what is still a key transition zone between West and East.

The Soviet Implosion and the Redefinition of Eastern and Central Europe

The collapse of the Soviet Union which began in 1989, and the emergence of Russia divested of most of its former European dependencies, has completely reset the scene for the political geography of Europe in the twenty-first century (Bradshaw and Lynn, 1994). A raft of new states has been created, or in many cases re-created, and even Poland, Romania, Bulgaria and Hungary – which were nominally independent and have retained their existing borders – have undergone complete internal transformations with the lifting

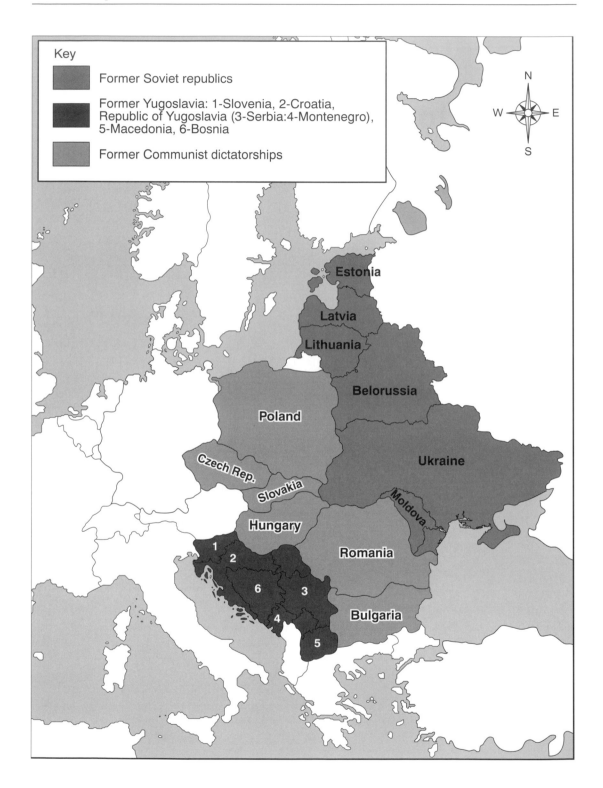

Figure 2.1 *Newly independent states in central and eastern Europe since 1990*

Table 2.1 *Independent European states (1996) which were former Soviet republics*

State	Area (sq. km)	Population (millions)
Belarus	207 600	9.4
Estonia	45 100	1.4
Latvia	63 700	2.5
Lithuania	65 200	3.3
Moldova	33 700	3.9
Ukraine	445 000	50.0
Total	**860 300**	**70.5**

Source: Hunter (1996).

of Soviet political and economic hegemony (Figure 2.1).

The size and strategic importance of the states that constitute the new map of eastern Europe vary enormously, but they stretch in an uninterrupted corridor for over 2000 km from the Baltic to the Black seas (Table 2.1). In the eastern Baltic, St Petersburg, the former Leningrad, is now the main port of entry to Russia, and Estonia, Latvia and Lithuania are all once again small independent states, a status they had previously enjoyed only briefly in the early years of the twentieth century between the two world wars. The last anomalous vestige of Russian influence in the European heartland is the Kalingrad enclave, lying between Lithuania and Poland. This is a part of the Russian state and an important military base, but its significance is steadily fading as Russia adjusts to its new geopolitical role and the states on its western frontier become more firmly established.

To the south of Latvia and Lithuania lies the very much larger land-locked state of Belarus, sandwiched between Poland, Russia and the Ukraine. Its area and population make Belarus potentially a major regional influence, though this has so far been somewhat constrained by its continuing dependence on Russia and the Ukraine, especially for energy supplies.

In political terms, however, all these newly independent states are dwarfed by Ukraine (area 445 000 sq. km; population 50 million). This covers the fourth-largest territory of any state in Europe, after France, Spain and Sweden, and has the third-largest population after Germany and the United Kingdom. Ukraine's enormous agri-

cultural potential and huge coal reserves, combined with its geographical position commanding the northern coastline of the whole of the Black Sea, make it a formidable force that will inevitably come to dominate the future of what is now eastern Europe. Ukraine has shared borders with Belarus, Poland, Slovakia, Hungary, Romania and the small land-locked former Soviet republic of Moldova (area 33 700 sq. km; population 3.9 million), so that all these countries will have to include Ukraine in their long-term political arrangements. This will make it a very significant, but as yet largely unknown, element in the geopolitical structure of Europe as a whole in the twenty-first century.

In the area that was previously identified as eastern Europe and is now central Europe, the collapse of the Soviet Union and the associated defeat of Communism have also led to substantial rearrangement of the political map (Grimm, 1994; Ivy, 1995). In 1994, after a referendum, Czechoslovakia divided peacefully into the Czech Republic in the west and Slovakia in the east (Pick, 1994). The original state, an outcome of the peace settlement at the end of the First World War, was always an uneasy alliance between two very different peoples, the Czechs and the Slovaks, each with their own language, and the period after 1989 was almost the first when true independence, without substantial foreign political interference, was a reality. Czechoslovakia was conceived by the USA and the other allied powers as part of post-war territorial rearrangements established by the Treaty of Versailles in 1919, but first German and, more recently, Soviet domination meant that external pressures precluded any serious examination by the people of the new state as to whether they could function as a single entity. Once they were brought face to face with this fundamental question, it quickly became clear that there was little will for a common political future on either side, and a largely amicable separation quickly followed.

Elsewhere, East Germany and Yugoslavia have both fallen victim to the changed political circumstances. The former, a country invented by Soviet Communist philosophy, was quickly absorbed into an enlarged, unified, Germany (Figure 2.3); while the latter, a Communist experiment for the most part outside the Soviet empire,

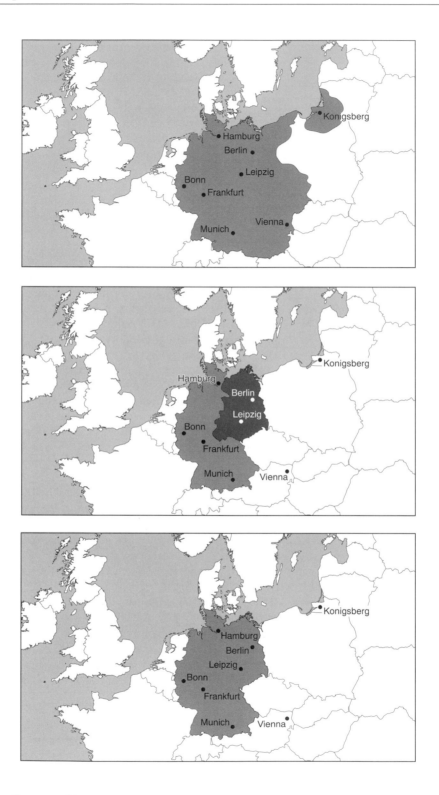

Figure 2.2   *Germany – 1938, 1945–90 and post-1990*

proved unable to survive the combined effects of the death of its charismatic founder and leader Josip Broz (Tito) in 1980 and the historic enmities between the religious and ethnic groups that comprised the federal state. The changes in Germany and the former Yugoslavia are so fundamental for understanding the geopolitical shape of the new Europe that each will be dealt with individually in separate sections below.

German (Re)unification

The formal unification of Germany on 3 October 1990 was a defining moment for Europe, ending an unwelcome and artificial cultural divide in the heart of the continent (Blacksell, 1995; Harris, 1991). The term "unification" is used in preference to "reunification" because the borders are substantially different from those of the Third Reich, the last previous unified German state (Blacksell, 1994) (Figure 2.2).

In the post-war era East Germany – the German Democratic Republic founded in 1949 – was a focus for the ideological and military division of the continent. West Germany – the German

Figure 2.3 *Vestiges of the Iron Curtain. The border between the former East and West Germanies is disappearing with remarkable speed. In most places it is merely marked by a strip of waste land, and watchtowers such as that shown are rare survivors. This particular tower has now assumed heritage status and is part of a* Grenzland Museum *(Border Museum). (Photos: D A Pinder)*

Federal Republic – never recognised East Germany and built into its constitution in 1948 the prospect of eventual unification; what is more, for a generation up until the early 1970s, West Germany also persuaded the rest of western Europe to follow its policy of non-recognition. In this way, East Germany became a symbol for an unbridgeable divide. Nowhere along its 1500 km length on mainland Europe was the so-called Iron Curtain more impenetrable and ruthlessly guarded, even allowing for the existence of the contested enclave of the divided city of Berlin (Breitfeld *et al.*, 1992; Friedlein and Grimm, 1995).

One of the most striking features of the division of Germany, and indeed the Iron Curtain as a whole, was the relative political stability it engendered (Ritter and Hajdu, 1989; Wild and Jones, 1993, 1994). The balance of power between, on the one hand, North America and western Europe in the guise of NATO and, on the other, the Soviet Union and its eastern European client states in the Warsaw Pact, by and large held for more than 40 years after 1948. The few attempts to challenge it, such as the uprising in Berlin in 1952, and the revolutions in Hungary and Czechoslovakia in 1956 and 1968 respectively, were all ruthlessly quelled and, crucially, did not provoke military intervention from NATO in the West. The explanation for NATO's lack of action is instructive: the organisation was conceived as a defensive alliance, committed to defending any of its members in the event of an attack by foreign power; it was not charged with protecting neighbouring states, or supporting their struggles for political change. As a result, NATO itself contributed more than any other organisation to sustaining the division of Europe, epitomised by the Iron Curtain.

In the early 1970s, as part of a new *Ostpolitik* (eastern policy), West Germany began to try to develop less confrontational relationships with its eastern neighbours, including East Germany. The change of attitude encouraged many of its NATO allies, though not West Germany itself, to break with their previous policy and to recognise East Germany, but the ensuing *détente* ultimately proved to have little real substance and the basic confrontation between East and West remained, even intensifying again in the 1980s.

The real change began to occur in 1989. A new openness towards the West promoted by the Soviet Union's then President, Mikhael Gorbachev, was accompanied by a withdrawal of support for the states in eastern Europe. This profound change of policy led directly to the rapid, and largely peaceful, overthrow of their Communist regimes (the only serious exception being in Romania); while in East Germany it initiated an aggressive move by West Germany to effect the unification of the country (Figure 2.4). The timing of this move was absolutely crucial, because at that point there had still been no formal end negotiated to the hostilities of the Second World War. Such a treaty was somewhat difficult to conclude because it required the assent of all the occupying Allied powers: France, the UK, the USA and – not least – the Soviet Union, which was itself under terminal threat. But, after protracted negotiations, the so-called Two plus Four Treaty was signed on 12 September 1990 by the four Allies and the two Germanies, formally bringing to an end the hostilities that had originally broken out in 1939.

The treaty included three provisions of seminal importance for the future political geography of Europe. First, it clearly defined the territory of a unified Germany as comprising the combined territories of East and West Germany, together with the whole of the city of Berlin. Second, it confirmed the Oder–Neiße line, the *de facto* boundary between Germany and Poland, as the *de jure* boundary, thus guaranteeing in international law Poland's sovereignty over its territory. Thirdly, it required that the united Germany renounce all other claims to former territories such as East Prussia in Poland and Bohemia in what has become the Czech Republic. In effect, therefore, the Two plus Four Treaty not only asserted the right of Germany to exist again as a unified state, it also brought to an end half a century of territorial uncertainty in central Europe.

Once unification had occurred on 3 October 1990, the new German government moved swiftly to conclude a peace treaty with Poland, enacting the provisions of the Two plus Four Treaty. The treaty was signed on 14 November 1990 and it enabled Germany to begin to normalise diplomatic relations more generally in Europe. This

process was of great importance, because in almost every sense Germany is central to the new Europe. It stretches over 500 km west to east from the River Rhine to the River Oder, and over 800 km north to south from the Baltic and North seas to the Alps; moreover, with some 80 million inhabitants, it is the most populous country in Europe. Although the unified state is only 70 per cent the size of the Second Reich at the turn of the twentieth century, which extended east to include much of present-day Poland and further along the Baltic coast into what is now Lithuania, Germany still retains common borders with nine other European states: Austria, Switzerland, France, Luxembourg, Belgium, the Netherlands, Denmark, Poland and the Czech Republic. If in 1999 the lower house of the German Parliament, the *Bundestag*, moves from Bonn to Berlin as planned, the latter will become the undisputed capital of the new Germany and the most important city in central Europe, drawing to it the public and private investment to make it the communications, economic and social hub of the continent (Figure 2.5) (Ellger, 1992; Smith, 1994).

Figure 2.4   *Symbols of unification. Sections of the Berlin Wall stand abandoned where they were stacked when the Wall was breached. In most of central Berlin the line of the Wall is now the scene of intense speculative building activity, generally for offices and high-value housing. The new building in the lower photograph advertises office space to rent, and stands on the strip of Wall-blighted land between Potsdamer Platz and the Brandenburg Gate. (Photos: D A Pinder)*

Figure 2.5   *Construction site for the new* Bundestag *building. (Photo: D A Pinder)*

The Break-up of Yugoslavia

If Germany stands for the positive and buoyant side of political change in Europe at the end of the twentieth century, the break-up of Yugoslavia represents the failure to bury ethnic, linguistic and religious rivalries in the interests of a common European ideal (Silber and Little, 1995). Throughout the nineteenth and early twentieth centuries the Balkan peninsula was riven by factional feuding and wars, as first the Turkish Ottoman Empire and later the Austro-Hungarian Empire collapsed. Notoriously, as a consequence of this feuding, the spark that ignited the outbreak of the First World War came in the Balkans with the assassination of the Austro-Hungarian Archduke Franz Ferdinand in the city of Sarajevo by a fanatical Serbian nationalist in 1914.

Right up until 1945 all attempts to bring political consensus and stability to the Balkans failed; indeed, the two largest ethnic and religious groups, the Croats and the Serbs, fought viciously against each other in the Second World War. Subsequently these and other differences appeared to be subsumed in a common determination to make a success of the Socialist Federal Republic of Yugoslavia led – as we have noted – by the charismatic former Communist partisan, Tito. The new federal state was unequivocally Communist, but Tito skilfully avoided it being absorbed by the Soviet Union, its huge eastern neighbour. Nor did he flirt, as was the case with another dissident Balkan Communist state, Albania, with closer links to the Chinese Communist Party. Indeed, every attempt was made to ally Yugoslavia to western Europe, in so far as this was possible without fundamentally compromising its status as a Communist state.

In the 1960s and 1970s Yugoslavia carved out for itself a unique position in western Europe as the acceptable face of Communism. However, the extent to which the state's future well-being was dependent on the force of one man's personality was increasingly exposed as Tito's powers began

Figure 2.6 *The break-up of Yugoslavia, showing the former federation; the approximate boundaries of a hypothetical Greater Serbia, governed from Belgrade; and the five independent republics in 1998*

to wane. After his death in 1980, national and religious feuding, with ever-more strident calls for the partition of Yugoslavia, became the dominant guiding force, fatally undermining the fragile political stability of the whole of the Balkan peninsula (Lendvai, 1995).

The political make-up of the region is really far too complex for it to be satisfactorily explained in simple terms, but five key elements give some indication of the dimensions of that complexity in the wake of collapse of the Socialist Federal Republic of Yugoslavia in 1991 (Figure 2.6).

Greater Serbia

At the forefront of the changes that have taken place in the former Yugoslavia since 1990 is Serbian nationalism and the desire to see it translated into a Greater Serbia. The Serbs are broadly speaking a Slav people, embracing Eastern Orthodox Christianity. As well as being fiercely nationalistic they also identify closely with other Slav peoples elsewhere in eastern Europe and in Russia. Serbs are mainly concentrated in the east of the former Yugoslavia, where Serbia was the largest of its republics, but important minorities also live in Kosovo in the south, Bosnia-Hercegovina in the west and Croatia in the north. The ideal of a Greater Serbia is that all these outlying minorities be drawn into a unified Serbian state, and the disintegration of Yugoslavia seemed to provide the opportunity for that ideal to become reality.

With nearly half the population, Serbs dominated the armed forces of the former federal republic and their initial tactic was to override the calls for national self-determination elsewhere by force of arms. However, it quickly became clear that this would be beyond them and, moreover, that it could actually jeopardise the realisation of a Greater Serbia. The first token of a change of tactic was the acceptance in 1991 that Slovenia, the smallest of the former republics in the north of the country bordering Italy and Austria, should be allowed to break away and become independent. Its population is predominantly Roman Catholic and ethnically distinct, so that Serbian interest in it remaining in a political union was relatively slight (Bebler, 1995).

In the other former republics the situation was much more fraught and less clear-cut. To secure its position, after acceding to the independence of Slovenia, Serbia joined forces with Montenegro, proclaimed itself the new Federal Republic of Yugoslavia and then set about expanding its borders to incorporate the Serbian minority populations living in the other former republics. This led, first, to the invasion of the newly independent Croatia to the north in 1991, and then to active support for a Serb-led insurrection in the western republic of Bosnia-Hercegovina in 1992. The ensuing war led to a massive, and brutal, forced redistribution of population in the name of so-called ethnic cleansing. Serbs from all over southern and western Croatia have flooded into both Serbia itself and the eastern parts of Croatia they have conquered, while Croatians have been driven out. To the south and west, Bosnia-Hercegovina still exists in name, but has effectively been partitioned between the Serbs, the Croats and the Muslims, with the self-styled Republica Serbska occupying the eastern half of the republic and now housing nearly all its Serb population. Meanwhile the Muslims and Roman Catholics have fled to the areas in the west that form the rump of the former republic.

The eventual political outcome of this latest attempt to create a Greater Serbia is still uncertain, although peace agreements have now been signed throughout the region (Glemy, 1995). Heavy international pressure was brought to bear on the government of Serbia and Montenegro, the new Yugoslavia, to pull back to its original borders, and in Croatia this was reinforced by that country's considerable military success against the Serbs in 1995 and 1996. Nevertheless, a substantial swathe of Croatian territory in the east remains in Serb hands. Meanwhile, in Bosnia-Hercegovina, although Republica Serbska has not been recognised by any other state, *de facto* it exists. In other words, an unstable military stalemate still confronts much of what was the core of Yugoslavia, with Greater Serbia a diminished prospect as a result of the wholesale redistribution of the population and the concentration of Serbs into their political strongholds in the east.

Historical links with the Axis powers

Croatia and Slovenia not only proclaimed their independence in 1991, they were also widely recognised more generally by the international community as legitimate states. The ready acceptance was partly simple *realpolitik*, but it also reflected deeply felt historical allegiances reaching back to the Austro-Hungarian Empire before the First World War. Both countries are overwhelmingly Roman Catholic; both had been part of Austro-Hungary, one of the two great nineteenth-century German-speaking European empires; and, crucially, both had fought alongside Germany and Italy in the Axis during the Second World War. The Serbs, on the other hand, formed the backbone of the Communist partisans and, more than any other single factor, it was the deep-seated bitterness and distrust between the two which doomed the long-term viability of the former Yugoslavia (Sobell, 1995).

The separation of Slovenia and Croatia from the rest of the former Yugoslavia is not, however, solely an internal matter. Considerable external political support was also forthcoming from other countries in western Europe, most notably Germany and the European Union in general. Germany was quick to extend formal recognition to both states and persuaded its partners to do the same. This immediately provided the new states with an enormously enhanced status, as well as removing any vestigial hopes of retaining the former Yugoslavia as a viable political entity.

Islam and the war in Bosnia-Hercegovina

If Roman Catholicism and the shadow of the Austro-Hungarian Empire played a part in the secession of Slovenia and Croatia from the former Yugoslavia, Islam and the shadow of the Turkish Ottoman Empire were equally significant in the unhappy emergence of Bosnia-Hercegovina. Islam is a widely practised religion in the southern Balkans, with a particularly large concentration in Bosnia-Hercegovina, where 40 per cent of the population are Muslims. Traditionally, there has been little tension between the Muslims, the Croatian Roman Catholics and the Serb Eastern

Orthodox Christians; all three groups have coexisted together in the republic with a high level of integration. Yet war has seen that coexistence shattered, causing the effective partitioning of the republic.

The causes of the collapse are very complex, but they strike at the heart of the wider Balkan rivalries. Having recognised Slovenia and Croatia, most European states were extremely reluctant to extend political recognition further, because to do so would clearly mark the abandonment of any pretence that a single central state could be sustained in the region. Germany, however, did recognise Bosnia-Hercegovina in 1992, thereby forcing the hand of a very reluctant European Union. Recognition also opened the way for a quite new dimension in the geopolitical situation. The international perception of a large Muslim minority being persecuted by a rapacious and expansionist Serbia evoked a wave of sympathy and assistance, most notably from other parts of the Muslim world, which chose to paint the war in Bosnia-Hercegovina as a front line in the wider struggle for Muslim ascendancy.

It is as yet impossible to say whether the *de facto* partition will be sustained in the face of considerable international efforts by the USA and its other NATO partners to try to reverse it, but it seems unlikely that anything more binding than a loose federation would ever be countenanced. A more probable outcome is that the Serb state of Republica Serbska will continue to exist in some form or other with close links to Serbia, and that a new, predominantly Muslim, state of Bosnia-Hercegovina will be formally established, thus further formalising the existing religious and ethnic political divides in the Balkan peninsula.

Albania and the Albanians

Albania is a small coastal state (28 750 sq. km; population 3.3 million) on the Adriatic Sea, which was never part of Yugoslavia, although it is entirely surrounded on its three landward sides by the former federation's republics. It is one of the poorest countries in the world, and for more than four decades after the end of the Second World War it was virtually a closed society, ruled by the idiosyncratic Communist dictator, Enver Hoxha. However, the economic and political conditions in Albania, together with the somewhat arbitrary way in which the original boundaries of the state were drawn, mean that there are as many Albanians again living in neighbouring states as there are in Albania itself.

Since Hoxha's death in 1985, and the subsequent collapse of the Communist government, Albania has rapidly become more outward-looking and more concerned for the fate of Albanians living outside its borders. This has had important repercussions in the south-western parts of the former Yugoslavia, especially in the semi-autonomous region of Kosovo, and in Macedonia, as well as further south in Greece. In Kosovo, 85 per cent of the population is estimated to be of Albanian origin and harbours a deep resentment at the way in which it is treated by the Serb minority that controls most senior administrative and political posts. The ethnic and linguistic differences are further reinforced by religion. More than 70 per cent of Albanians are Muslims, and this has been given new significance by the war and the growing political influence of Muslims in Bosnia-Hercegovina.

The tensions between Albanians and Serbs in Kosovo are extremely difficult to resolve, because Kosovo is revered as the historic birthplace of the Serb nation. It was from here that the Serbian leader Slobodan Milosevic launched the current wave of Serbian nationalism, and any question of relinquishing or sharing power with the Albanians awakens almost instinctive resistance, even though Kosovo now lies on the southern fringe of Serbia. There have been intermittent riots and an attempted rebellion against Serb rule, but so far the feared southward spread of the war in the north has not materialised.

Macedonia

Land-locked Macedonia (25 715 sq. km; population 1.9 million) was the southernmost republic of the former Yugoslavia and is entirely surrounded by Serbia, Albania, Greece and Bulgaria. Its small population speaks its own Macedonian language which has helped to emphasize its distinctness, but more than any

other of the emergent states in the Balkans it has been threatened by external pressures (Pettifer, 1995). Its independence was fiercely resisted by both Serbia and Greece, both of which, though for different reasons, still refuse recognition. Serbia wants to keep Macedonia in the new rump Yugoslavia because, with Greek connivance, it offers a convenient route for bypassing the economic blockade imposed in 1991 by the European Union. Greece is opposed for quite different nationalistic reasons. It too has a province called Macedonia across the border and sees an independent Macedonian state as a potential threat to the sovereignty of its northern territory, not to mention an end to its own territorial ambitions. As a member of the European Union, Greece was able to block general recognition for Macedonia but, as with so much else in the former Yugoslavia, events have overtaken rhetoric and the state does effectively exist. The concern is that Macedonia's intrinsic vulnerability, and the competing outside interests in its political future, could spark a war here as well. This could provide the flashpoint to widen the conflict in the north into the south, and to involve neighbouring states as well. It is significant that the government of Bulgaria has been almost as vocally supportive of Macedonia as that of Greece has been opposed. The seriousness with which the political situation is viewed is indicated by the fact the United Nations has stationed a pre-emptive peace force in Macedonia, so as to forestall any move to hostilities.

In the last years of the twentieth century the Balkans are as much a hotbed of political instability as they were a century ago. Nowhere else in Europe do so many competing political influences clash, and nowhere else are existing international agencies finding it more difficult to broker an accommodation. The relative calm of 1996 after five years of sporadic war is as yet no more than a stand-off, and it still remains to be seen whether it will develop into a durable peace. If it succeeds there will be new opportunities for much wider political integration in Europe; if it fails, the conflict could easily spread into eastern Europe and the eastern Mediterranean region, once again threatening the stability of the continent.

The Mediterranean: from Fulcrum to Frontier

It is hard for most Europeans to conceive of the Mediterranean as a frontier region. The home of both the Romans and the Greeks, the two classical civilisations that have done most to influence European culture, there is an almost inevitable tendency to invest the region with a greater importance than its present geopolitical status merits. However, for most of the twentieth century the main focus of power has been in western and central Europe, with the Mediterranean basin relegated to the fringes of European affairs. It is a situation that shows every sign of continuing into the next millennium, with considerable uncertainty among many of the smaller Mediterranean states as to whether their future lies inside or outside Europe. However, such uncertainty is as much a product of ambivalence among the states of the European core, as it is the result of the competing attractions of other geopolitical groupings in North Africa and the Middle East.

Nothing typifies the fractured state of relations more clearly than the position of Greece. A member of the Council of Europe since 1949, of NATO since 1952, and a full member of the European Union since 1981, in many ways it is a bastion of the European ideal, clearly signifying a commitment to the whole of the Mediterranean basin from east to west. On the other hand, the poor state of its relations with its neighbours in the eastern Mediterranean and Aegean seas has repeatedly undermined the stability of the region, and sometimes threatened an even wider breakdown (Veremis, 1996; Wilson, 1979).

The key to this instability has been Greece's relations with its historic enemy, Turkey. During the centuries of the Ottoman Empire, Greece was occupied by the Turks, only for the roles to be steadily reversed during the nineteenth and early twentieth centuries. By the end of the First World War the Greek government and Greek settlers were firmly established, not only on the western part of the Turkish mainland in Anatolia, but also on most of the hundreds of islands in the Aegean and the eastern Mediterranean. It was a situation fraught with tension, which was only heightened by the formation of the modern states of Turkey and Greece in 1922 and 1923 respectively. Nevertheless, the urgency of the situation created the conditions for a more permanent settlement, and in the Treaty of Lausanne (1923) the present borders were agreed, as well as an exchange of nationals residing on each other's territory.

Like most treaties, the Treaty of Lausanne solved only some of the outstanding issues between the two states and did little to assuage their mutual loathing for each other. Even though after the Second World War both were granted membership of NATO, so as to provide a common front against Communist expansion in the eastern Mediterranean, there have been repeated quarrels over sovereignty. In the Aegean, the relative share of territorial waters has been a constant bone of contention, sharpened further from time to time by the prospect of offshore oil and gas discoveries, though no substantial strikes have yet been confirmed. Similar disputes have also broken out over the rights to air space and, since 1974, it has been impossible to fly directly from Greece to Turkey, or vice versa.

The most serious disputes, however, relate to the sovereignty of islands (Figure 2.7). Virtually all the islands in the Aegean and the eastern Mediterranean are under Greek control, even though many are within a few kilometres of the Turkish coast. They provide a constant reminder to Turkey of the illogicality and apparent unfairness of the division, not to mention the threat posed by Greek forces on their very doorstep. By far the most serious of these disputes is that over Cyprus, which was a British colony until independence in 1960. The island lies some 800 km from mainland Greece, but less than 100 km from Turkey. Although the constitution allows for joint control by the two communities, it has a majority Greek population and throughout the 1960s and the early 1970s there were constant friction and growing demands for union with Greece. Turkey perceived this as a threat, not only to the Turkish community on Cyprus, but also to the Turkish mainland, and invaded and partitioned the island in 1974. Since then the partition has been supervised by United Nations troops, pending a settlement between the two communities. There is still little sign of this being achieved, and in the mean time the confrontation on Cyprus has become the front line in the wider dispute between Greece and Turkey.

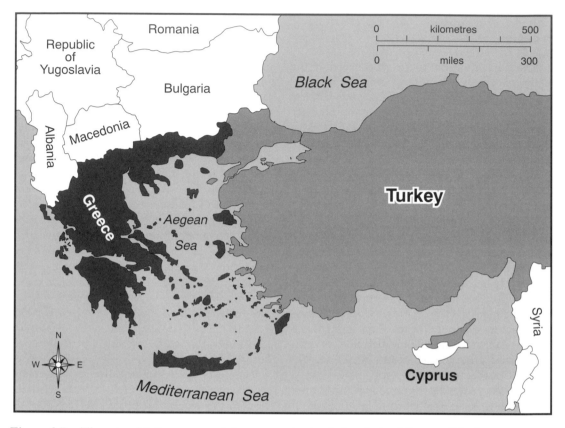

Figure 2.7 *The eastern Mediterranean and Aegean seas, showing the boundaries of Greece and Turkey*

The significance of this continuing quarrel is that it has made it virtually impossible to achieve any form of wider European integration in the region. Greece, as a member of the European Union, has effectively blocked Turkey becoming a member, despite the fact that both countries were granted Associate Member status as early as 1964, a move that was explicitly seen as the first step to full membership. Admittedly, Turkish applications have ostensibly been turned down on other grounds, including inadequate democratic institutions and a poor record on human rights, but Greece's implacable opposition has undoubtedly made negotiation on such issues virtually impossible. It is also the case that, were Turkey to join the European Union, it would completely unbalance the present structure. The country covers an area of 779 450 sq. km, making it half as big again as France, the next largest country in the European Union; similarly its 59.6 million citizens would make it second only to

Germany in terms of population. Partly as a consequence of the repeated rejections, Turkey has turned more towards the Middle East and begun to capitalise on the political power of its Muslim majority, despite the fact that it was founded as a secular state. In other words, the country has begun gradually to move away from Europe and is becoming more obviously its eastern frontier (Evreusel-Brown, 1992).

Elsewhere in the Mediterranean there has been a similar lack of decision. Hope of converting the European Union Associate Member status of Cyprus into full membership has been undermined by the continuing Turkish occupation of the island; and progress with Malta, which also has Associate Member status, has also been minimal, pending a wider regional settlement. As far as the rest of the Mediterranean is concerned, especially the countries on its North African and Middle Eastern shores, there has been little enthusiasm for developing anything more than preferential trade relations with Europe. For too many of these countries the memories of their recent colonial past are too fresh for close political union with Europe to be acceptable, even if it may be economically desirable.

Beyond the Nation State: Unions, Alliances and other Transnational Groupings

Europe, as defined in this chapter, comprises 38 fully independent nation states, not including at least a dozen micro-states, such as San Marino, Monaco and Andorra. Throughout the second half of the twentieth century the most important political project has been the succession of initiatives to try to simplify this mozaic into a more coherent structure. For the most part this was done against the backdrop of the Cold War and the consequent division of Europe, though since 1989 that context has completely changed and a new underlying logic of similar potency is urgently required to fill the vacuum created by the collapse of the Soviet Union.

It is worth remembering that much of the impetus for the international co-operation that did occur in Europe after the end of the Second World War came from outside in the form of superpower pressure from the USA and the Soviet Union respectively. Neither had much sympathy for the claims of the independent nation state to primacy in the political order, and both believed that their own interests would be best served by larger, quasi-federal, groupings. As we approach the twenty-first century, the main surviving results of this policy are the Council of Europe, NATO and the European Union, none of which has so far adapted particularly well to the political changes that have recently occurred.

The Council of Europe

The Council of Europe is the least formalised of all the major pan-European bodies, but it is important because, more than any other, it is a signal of a commitment to a common European ideal. Founded in 1949, its aim is to achieve a greater degree of unity among its members, by safe-guarding and developing their common heritage, and by encouraging economic and social progress. In this regard, the Council's greatest achievement is undoubtedly the establishment of the European Court of Human Rights in 1958 to protect individuals against the arbitrary acts of national governments. Over the ensuing years, this Court has defined basic standards of behaviour to which all the member states must be seen to adhere.

Throughout the Cold War, membership of the Council of Europe was confined to western Europe and even here not all states were permitted to join. Neither Spain nor Portugal was eligible until their dictatorships were replaced by democratic governments in the 1970s, and the membership of Greece was suspended during the period of the military junta between 1969 and 1974. But since the collapse of the Soviet Union, a succession of former Communist states in central and eastern Europe have applied for membership, most being accepted.

Finland, which had previously been severely constrained as to the western international organisations it could join by dint of its treaty arrangements with the Soviet Union, became a member in 1989. Hungary followed in 1990, Poland and the then Czechoslovakia in 1991, Bulgaria in 1992, Estonia, Lithuania, Romania and Slovenia in 1993, and Latvia in 1995. In five years the membership of the Council of Europe had grown by half, shifting the balance of its membership decisively towards the east. The most surprising development, however, happened in 1996 with Russia being accepted as a member. In terms of redefining the boundaries of Europe, and European political, social and economic culture, nothing could have greater symbolic significance. Russian membership also has to be seen in relation to the fact that acceptance is not necessarily a formality. Both Croatia and Belarus have been refused full membership for the time being, and the Ukraine and Bosnia are hesitating about lodging applications, presumably through fear of rejection.

In comparison with NATO and the European Union, the Council of Europe is a relatively low-key organisation. But unencumbered by their institutional and administrative paraphernalia, it has succeeded in carving out a role for itself as a touchstone for European values that is clearly much valued by the continent's wealth of independent nation states. Inadvertently, membership has also become an essential first step towards participation in the wider process of European integration.

The North Atlantic Treaty Organisation (NATO)

Of all the major European organisations, NATO is the one whose roots in the Cold War division of the continent are most obvious. Conceived in the aftermath of the Second World War as a bulwark against Communist expansion from the east, it is a partnership between North America and western Europe. Its members include the USA and Canada and 14 west European states, with the USA still very much the dominant partner.

Since the collapse of the Soviet Union in 1989, NATO has been going through a period of painful reassessment, trying to find a way of translating itself from an organisation geared primarily to maintain the balance of power against a clearly identified external military threat, to one able to assume unequivocal military leadership throughout Europe. It is proving a difficult transition, not least because of considerable debate within its membership about the advisability of abandoning its traditionally purely reactive defensive stance, in favour of a more proactive role. The dilemma has been brought into sharp focus since 1991 in the war in the former Yugoslavia. Initially, NATO's role was both tentative and ineffective, but since 1995 it has played an increasingly important role in bringing the hostilities in Bosnia-Hercegovina to an end, and in guaranteeing the subsequent peace. It is a crucial test, for if NATO fails in this theatre of European war its overall credibility and relevance will inevitably be brought into serious question.

In an attempt to adjust to the new political conditions in Europe, NATO has forged a formal relationship with most of the countries of central and eastern Europe through the Partnership for Peace initiative (Figure 2.8). Twenty-one countries, all of them (with the exception of Sweden and Finland) former Communist states or Soviet republics in Europe and Asia, signed partnership agreements in 1994 to liaise with NATO on defence

issues, but as yet these are still almost entirely paper commitments and of very limited real military or strategic significance. In many ways NATO's strongest suit is the weakness of any of the alternatives (Levan, 1995). The Western European Union (WEU), a subset of current European Union members that has come together intermittently since 1955 to try to develop a unified western European voice in defence matters, has promised more than it has actually achieved. Its future development is always compromised by the very different attitudes to military matters held by the EU member states. Four, Austria, Finland, the Republic of Ireland and Sweden, have neutrality written into their constitutions and are therefore totally forbidden from playing any part in such discussions; while others, such as Denmark, have fundamental differences on the most desirable direction for military strategy.

The situation in what is now eastern Europe is even less focused. The only formal institutional co-operation is through the Commonwealth of Independent States (CIS), which grew out of discussions between Russia, the Ukraine and Belarus in 1991. The CIS was founded in 1992 with 11 of the former Soviet republics as members. However, although the CIS has its headquarters in the Belarusian capital of Minsk, it does not even have a proper secretariat and only exists as a forum for the biannual consultative meetings of the member states. Moreover, Georgia and the three Baltic states, Estonia, Latvia and Lithuania, refused to have anything to do with it, although Georgia subsequently changed its mind in 1993.

The European Union

Without question the most important and developed of the pan-European organisations is the European Union. From its beginnings in 1952 as the European Coal and Steel Community (ECSC), it expanded first to incorporate the European Economic Community (EEC) and the European Atomic Energy Community (Euratom) in 1958, then merged the three into a single European Community in 1967, before finally emerging in its present form as the European Union (EU) in 1993.

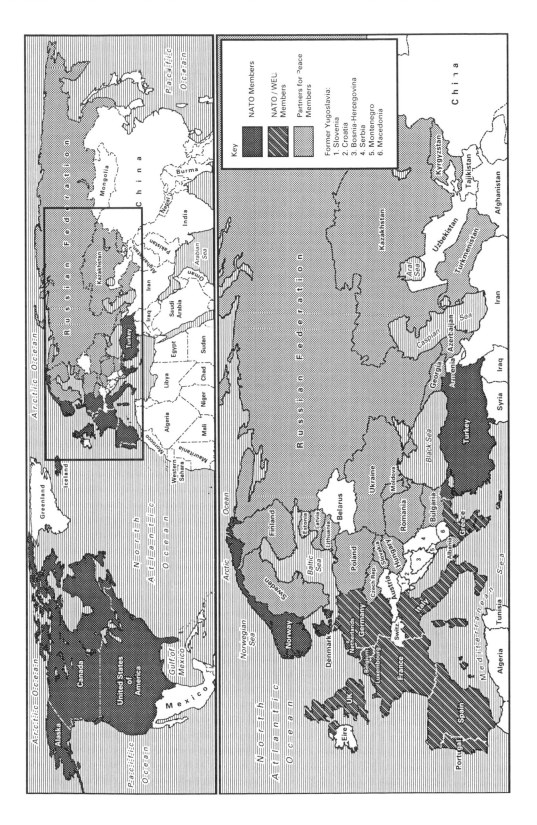

Figure 2.8 *The membership of defensive alliances in Europe, 1996*

Over the 40 years and more of its existence the EU has changed from being a small group of six industrial states in the heart of western Europe, jointly managing their heavy industrial resources through a customs union, into a group of 15 countries operating a single market embracing 355 million people (see Figure 3.8, p. 55). The original members were Belgium, The Netherlands and Luxembourg – which were already part of the existing Benelux customs union – together with France, West Germany and Italy. In 1973, after more than 20 years of steadily growing co-operation, they were joined by the UK, the Republic of Ireland and Denmark. This first expansion extended the EU northwards beyond its original core in continental western Europe, but did not fundamentally alter its direction and purpose. Indeed, the attempts by the UK, in particular, to achieve major policy changes on accession were notably unsuccessful.

The second phase of growth saw the inclusion of three Mediterranean countries, Greece in 1981, and Spain and Portugal in 1986. In all three cases, the reasons for their being admitted were rather different from those that drove the first expansion. Each had recently emerged from a period of right-wing dictatorship, and acceptance into the EU was as much about securing their nascent democracies as it was about extending the scope of the economic union.

The most recent phase of expansion was triggered mainly by the effects of the collapse of the Soviet Union. The unification of Germany meant that *de facto* a former Communist state became part of the EU. Moreover, the huge predicted costs of bringing its economy and infrastructure up to the standards of those in western Europe underlined how expensive, and politically difficult, it would be to admit any of the other fledgling democracies in eastern Europe, however desirable this might be in theory (Gibb and Michalak, 1993, 1994). It was clear that if any such expansion were to be entertained, then it would first be necessary to strengthen the EU's own economic base by encouraging other west European countries to join. There was some uncertainty as to which of them might be able and willing to do so, but in 1995 Austria, Finland and Sweden all eventually became members, thus providing precisely the kind of underpinning required.

In July 1997, as part of its agenda 2000 for the new millennium, the EU decided to invite applications for full membership from other European countries. Most are former Communist states, although the complex issues involving the countries of the eastern Mediterranean are also grasped. The first wave of five states – Estonia, Poland, the Czech Republic, Hungary and Cyprus – will probably join in 2002, with a further six states – Slovakia, Bulgaria, Romania, Latvia, Lithuania and Turkey – being admitted later. In most cases, the success of the applications will be dependent on specified political changes being implemented. These are mainly internal matters, but for Cyprus and Turkey a wider regional accommodation is required. The dispute over the division of Cyprus must be resolved, and Greece must be persuaded not to veto Turkish membership as it has repeatedly done in the past.

The EU itself is a complex body, which has steadily become more embedded into the political infrastructure of its member states as the range and depth of its activities have increased. It is a union governed by treaty and is, therefore, limited as to what it can do by the terms of its founding treaties, the Treaty of Paris which established the ECSC, and the two Treaties of Rome which established the EEC and Euratom respectively. By far the most comprehensive of these is the Treaty of Rome that created the EEC, and this has subsequently been substantially modified on two occasions. In 1986, the Single European Act, *inter alia*, introduced limited qualified majority voting, which meant that decisions within the union could be taken on the basis of a majority, rather than unanimity. For the first time, therefore, the absolute veto of member states was removed, albeit only to a very limited extent. The second modification was incorporated in the Treaty on European Union (the Maastricht Treaty) in 1993, which formally created the present union and also clarified the distribution of powers between the EU and its member states. The most important aspect of this was the concept of subsidiarity, which declared that decisions should always be taken at the political level as close to the people affected as possible. The intention, and effect, was to remove from the EU itself any areas of decision-making that could be undertaken at national and regional level, thus limiting federalist ambitions. The most recent modification was the 1997 Treaty of Amsterdam. This specifically wrote into the Treaty on European Union a requirement that member states uphold human rights, and also included the UK in the Social Protocol which governs employment rights and practices.

The most significant achievements of the EU have undoubtedly been the customs union in 1967 and the single market in 1993. The customs union established a free trade area among the member states and a common external trade policy towards third-party countries. It removed all trade tariffs and quotas, but did little to abolish the host of other restrictive practices, such as obscure technical requirements for manufactured goods, which can effectively inhibit free trade. The single market project addressed this much more difficult and diffuse problem, and has been largely successful in establishing uniform trading conditions and access to markets across the 15 member states.

The EU has been less successful at developing its own policies for specific areas of the economy. The best known of its initiatives is the Common Agricultural Policy (CAP), which has provided for a uniform system of public support for agriculture. Although necessary to remove what would otherwise have been substantial trade distortion in the food industries, the CAP has proved a hugely expensive and unpopular policy that, with some difficulty, has recently had to be amended (Vogeler, 1996; Young, 1993). The Common Fisheries Policy, although much less expensive, has proved similarly controversial; while the Common Environment Policy is frequently seen as an unnecessary intrusion by the EU in the internal affairs of member states. In some other areas, notably the Common Transport Policy, the EU has totally failed to devise an acceptable policy, despite a treaty commitment to do so. All three policies are examined further in Chapters 12, 18 and 21.

The difficulties that the EU has experienced in going beyond the single market stem largely from the lack of a consensus among its member states as to what kind of political body it should become. Some believe that it should be quasi-federal, much along the lines of the USA, while others do not want it to develop beyond an economic group of independent sovereign states. The results of this ambivalence are very much apparent in the EU's major institutions. It is still firmly controlled by the civil servants of the Commission, acting through the Council of Ministers, all of whose members are elected politicians in their own countries. Any kind of supranational power comes only as a result of the limited qualified majority voting that has now been introduced, or through the decisions of the European Court, which interprets the treaties. Here, however, it should be said that the latter does enjoy legal precedence over national jurisdictions and has become increasingly important as the EU has grown in complexity and the volume of case law has increased.

What is patently lacking in the EU is real direct accountability to its citizens. The European Parliament, which has been elected four times since 1979, has so far failed to bridge this democratic deficit. Its powers are extremely limited and the 626 MEPs have little influence in comparison with their counterparts at national level. Indeed, it is often accused of being little more than a debating chamber and seems likely to remain so unless the governments of the member states are prepared to cede to it real political powers.

At the moment there is little indication that this will happen, but much will depend on the outcome of the current negotiations on monetary union. If the proposals presently under discussion for a single European currency and a central European Bank to replace their national equivalents come to fruition, then the need for direct democratic controls at an EU level will become almost irresistible. It is the wider consequences of the adoption of a single currency and a central bank for the fundamental nature of the EU that make the debate so important. The outcome will undoubtedly have a decisive bearing on the future of the whole of Europe into the twenty-first century, for it will largely define the relative power of the nation states on the one hand, and the EU and other transnational political groupings on the other.

The Shape of the Future

The end of the Cold War has removed a major force for stability in political relations between European states and has initiated a fundamental reappraisal of the nature and geographical extent of Europe itself. The eventual outcome is still very far from clear, but many old antagonisms have been awakened and former alliances are being reforged (Tuathail and Lube, 1994). There is no longer so much certainty about the political pattern and already two states, Czechoslovakia and Yugoslavia, have fragmented. Others may follow, more or less peacefully. Claims for independence in, for example, Scotland, Corsica and the Basque country are growing rather than decreasing in intensity. The way ahead will depend much on developments within the EU, NATO and other international groupings in Europe. They could provide a strong framework within which a limited redrawing of political boundaries would be both possible and acceptable. On the other hand, if they fail to do so, through either their own weakness or the refusal of Europe's nation states to give them the necessary scope, then the political fragmentation, which at the moment is still geographically relatively confined, could spread much more widely through the continent.

References

Bebler, A (1995) Slovenia and Europe, *World Today*, **51**(5), 96–9.

Blacksell, M (1994) State and nation: Germany since reunification, in K Cameron (ed) *The Nation: myth or reality?* Intellect Books, Oxford, 11–12.

Blacksell, M (1995) Germany as a European power, in D Lewis and J R P McKenzie, *The New Germany: social, political and cultural challenges to unification*, University of Exeter Press, Exeter, 77–100.

Bradshaw, M J and Lynn, N J (1994) After the Soviet Union: the post-Soviet states in the world system, *The Professional Geographer*, **46**, 439–49.

Breitfeld, K *et al.* (1992) *Das vereinte Deutschland*, Institut für Länderkunde, Leipzig.

Cohen, S (1991) Global geopolitical change in the post-Cold War era, *Annals of the Association of American Geographers*, **81**, 551–80.

Ellger, C (1992) Berlin: legacies of division and problems of unification, *Geographical Journal*, **158**, 40–6.

Evreusel-Brown, A (1992) Turkey's membership in the EEC: obstacles to economic integration, *Tijdschrift voor Economische en Sociale Geografie*, **82**(4), 254–65.

Friedlein, G and Grimm, F-D (1995) *Deutschland und seine Nachbarn*, Institut für Länderkunde, Leipzig.

Gibb, R and Michalak, W (1993) The European Community and Central Europe: prospects for integration, *Geography*, **78**, 16–30.

Gibb, R and Michalak, W (1994) The European Community and East Central Europe, *Tijdschrift voor Economische en Sociale Geografie*, **84**, 401–16.

Glemy, M (1995) Heading off war in the southern Balkans, *Foreign Affairs*, May/June, 98–108.

Grimm, F-D (1994) *Zentrensysteme als Träger der Raumentwicklung in Mittel- und Osteuropa*, Institut für Landerkunde, Liepzig.

Harris, C D (1991) Unification of Germany in 1990, *Geographical Review*, **81**, 183–96.

Hunter, B (ed) (1996) *The Statesman's Yearbook 1996–1997*, 133rd edition, Macmillan, London.

Ivy, R L (1995) The restructuring of air transport linkages in the new Europe, *The Professional Geographer*, **47**, 280–8.

Lendvai, P (1995) Flashpoint Balkans, *World Today*, **51** (4), 78–80.

Leven, A (1995) Russian opposition to NATO expansion, *World Today*, **51**(10), 196–9.

Luke, T W (1996) Governmentality and contra-governmentality, rethinking sovereignty and territoriality after the Cold War, *The Professional Geographer*, **15**, 491–507.

Murphy, A B (1991) The emerging Europe of the 1990's, *Geographical Review*, **81**, 1–17.

Nijman, J (1992) The limits of superpower: the United States and the Soviet Union and World War II, *Annals of the Association of American Geographers*, **82**, 681–95.

Pettifer, J (1995) Macedonia: still the apple of discord, *World Today*, **51**(3), 55–8.

Pick, O (1994) The Czech Republic – a stable transition, *World Today*, **50**(11), 206–13.

Ritter, G and Hajdu, J G (1989) The East–West German boundary, *Geographical Review*, **79**, 326–44.

Silber, L and Little, A (1995) *The Death of Yugoslavia*, Penguin Books, London.

Smith, F M (1994) Politics, place and German reunification: a realignment approach, *Political Geography*, **13**, 228–44.

Sobell, V (1995) NATO, Russia and the Yugoslav war, *World Today*, **51**(11), 210–15.

Taylor, P (ed) (1993) *Political Geography of the Twentieth Century: a global analysis*, Belhaven Press, London.

Tuathail, G O and Lube, T W (1994) Present at the (dis)-integration. Deterritorialization and reterritorialization in the new wor(l)d order, *Annals of the Association of American Geographers*, **84**, 381–98.

Veremis, T (1996) Uncertainty on the Aegean fault line, *World Today*, **52**(3), 67–8.

Vogeler, I (1996) State hegemony in transforming the rural landscapes of Eastern Germany, *Annals of the Association of American Geographers*, **86**, 432–58.

Wild, T and Jones, P (1993) From peripherality to new centrality? Transformation of Germany's *Zonenrandgebiet*, *Geography*, **78**(5), 281–94.

Wild, T and Jones, P N (1994) Spatial impacts of German unification, *Geographical Journal*, **160**, 1–16.

Wilson, A (1979) *The Aegean Dispute*, International Institute for Strategic Studies, London.

Young, C (1993) A bitter harvest? Problems of restructuring East-Central European agriculture, *Geography*, **78**, 69–72.

Part II
Economic Transformation

The starting-point for Part II is recognition of Europe's role in the global economy, and of that economy's influence on Europe itself. Richard Gibb sets the scene with an analysis of Europe's significance and influence as one of the world's leading trading blocs. By emphasising the extent to which it is western Europe which dominates this trading bloc, his chapter also underlines the continuing economic gulf between east and west. Peter Odell continues the globalisation theme – without Middle Eastern oil, western European economic development would have been severely constrained, at least until the discovery of indigenous oil and natural gas resources. But Odell's chapter also demonstrates that the pendulum does not always swing inexorably towards globalisation. Because of the indigenous resources, Europe today is substantially less dependent on global oil supplies than in the 1970s. Moreover, despite the dire warnings of past commentators, the main challenges now facing the European energy economy are not related to resource shortages, but to the need to choose wisely between competing forms of energy. Odell also shows that, as these choices are made, the energy sector provides some of the clearest signs of economic convergence between eastern and western Europe.

The restructuring of manufacturing in western Europe and the new democracies is explored by Douglas Watts and Andrew Dawson in separate studies. The impact of globalisation naturally recurs as a theme in Watts' analysis of change in the west, not least in a discussion of inward investment. However, equally important issues are the effects of Single Market integration, and new forms of organisation under post-Fordist conditions. In this latter context Watts highlights the recognition now being given to regional specialisation, in which small and medium-sized firms play a leading role and are embedded into a specific local industrial culture. Dawson's main theme, meanwhile, is the multi-faceted nature of the problems to be faced following the collapse of the socialist industrial economies in central and eastern Europe. Despite some inward investment from western Europe and further afield, as well as a degree of indigenous growth, the dominant legacy of the old order is a lack of industrial impetus; ineffective transition to privatisation; endemic unemployment and underemployment; and widespread dependence on the black economy.

Peter Daniels and Wieslaw Michalak extend the discussion by focusing on the fundamental role of producer services in manufacturing growth and economic development more generally. In the process they expose one of the most significant contrasts in growth conditions currently dividing east and west. Daniels highlights the dynamism and constantly increasing sophistication of producer services in western Europe. Although the sector is a minor employer, and in the Single Market may exacerbate regional problems because of its bias towards Europe's leading urban centres, its quality and diversity are seen as central to the maintenance of economic success. Michalak, in contrast, argues that a key deficiency in central and eastern Europe is the paucity of producer services. For virtually half a century such services were officially deemed unnecessary, and the fact that it is impossible to re-create them quickly is likely to be a long-lasting impediment to east–west economic convergence.

The major role played by the service sector in modern economic development is also the underlying theme of chapters on retailing and tourism. Steve Burt and John Dawson emphasise the deep contrasts which continue to distinguish retailing in western and eastern Europe. While these contrasts partly reflect the stultifying influence of socialism on retailing, in very large measure they are also the outcome of economic, consumer, technological and policy changes in the west. These factors have combined to make retailing one of western Europe's most powerful and dynamic sectors – although, through its impacts on urban development, transport and the environment, it is increasingly seen as one which generates highly questionable externalities. Similarly, Allan Williams and Gareth Shaw portray tourism as a highly dynamic sector. As yet, much of the dynamism is centred on western Europe, where increasingly wealthy and demanding societies have led to the stagnation of mass tourism and a new post-modern emphasis on diversity of experience. But tourism also has the potential to become one of the powerful integrating forces in European development; western Europeans will certainly travel east in growing numbers in search of new experiences, and – as incomes rise in the former socialist states – significant flows from east to west may also be anticipated.

Two chapters concluding Part II simultaneously draw together much of the earlier discussion and highlight the importance of the social and environmental issues examined in Parts III and IV. In their analysis of uneven development in Europe, Michael Dunford and Adrian Smith paint a pessimistic picture. Despite some early post-war success, economic convergence in both western and eastern Europe gave way to divergence. In the west the failure of Fordism provoked the shift towards neo-liberalism. This failed to control unemployment, social exclusion, insecurity and inequality; yet, following the demise of socialism, neo-liberalism has also been embraced in central and eastern Europe, where it has provoked a massive collapse of economic potential. Finally, Vickerman questions the role of transport in promoting effective economic development at the European scale. Although investment in infrastructures such as trans-European networks has been given a high profile, the probability is that improved integration will polarise rather than spread development. This will not ameliorate social issues linked with spatially uneven growth. Moreover, while the environmental impacts of transport development are now widely recognised, Europe has scarcely begun to address the challenge of ensuring that transport is environmentally sustainable as well as efficient.

3
Europe in the world economy

Richard Gibb

Department of Geographical Sciences, University of Plymouth, UK

Introduction

The European Union (EU) is the world's largest trading bloc and plays a leading role, alongside the USA and Japan, in helping to determine the character, evolution and regulation of the world economy. At the same time, developments in that economy, and particularly the trend towards increasing international competition and globalisation, have an enormous impact on the character of the EU. The central aims of this chapter are to examine the nature and consequences of this two-way relationship, and to place the EU in a wider perspective by exploring international trade patterns and the institutional mechanisms and policies adopted by the EU in world trade talks. In addition the analysis seeks to confront the contentious issue of whether the EU promotes or erodes free trade and the multilateral process of liberalisation sponsored by the World Trade Organisation (WTO). And, underpinning the entire discussion, an important objective is to demonstrate that the EU cannot be understood in isolation from the world economy and its institutions.

Although this book is concerned with Europe as a whole, the chapter takes as its focus the EU. This reflects the fact that the EU is easily the most powerful economic and political organisation in the new Europe and is, moreover, set to expand geographically, economically and politically as the process of enlargement continues. The EU's economic dominance is illustrated by its share of world merchandise exports. Including EU intra-regional trade, the EU accounted for 40 per cent of world exports in 1992. In contrast, the equivalent figure for the Czech Republic, Slovakia, Poland and Hungary was just 0.9 per cent, and in the case of the Russian Federation it was 1 per cent. Even though east central European (ECE) states perceive membership of the EU as essential not only for successful transition to the free market, but also as a guarantee of long-term political stability, the reality is that the current EU is the global trading bloc with the greatest claim to attention.

Supranational Regionalism

To clarify the debate, and help elucidate the complex relationship between the EU and the world economy, it is useful to consider some of the principal conceptual frameworks surrounding the issue of international regionalism. The EU is an example, and is often regarded as a role model (Wise, 1994), of international regional integration. The success of the EU has led many

	Removal of internal quotas and tariffs	Common external customs tariff	Free movements of land, labour, capital and services	Harmonisation of economic policies and development of supranational institutions	Unification of political policies and powerful supranational institutions
Sectoral co-operation	◖				
Free trade association	●				
Customs union	●	●			
Common market	●	●	●		
Economic union	●	●	●	●	
Political union	●	●	●	●	●

Figure 3.1 *Levels of regionalism, from sectoral co-operation to political union*

commentators to suggest that it has promoted the cause of regionalism in other parts of the world (Gibb and Michalak, 1994). The process of regionalism intensified throughout the 1980s to such an extent that a number of respected economists (Bhagwati, 1991, 1992, 1993) now argue that trading blocs, by promoting protectionist tendencies, threaten the multilateral regulatory framework governing the world economy. In the latter stages of the GATT's[1] Uruguay Round of trade talks, coinciding with the EU's single market programme, regionalism experienced a particular revival with the GATT being notified of 33 new regional arrangements between 1990 and 1994 (WTO, 1995).

Regional trading arrangements take several forms and cover a multitude of different schemes, ranging from sectoral co-operation and free trade areas to political union (Figure 3.1). By definition, all trading arrangements involve an element of geographic discrimination in that various factors of production are subject to differing tariff barriers according to country of origin and destination (Gibb, 1993). The EU is, however, both quantitatively and qualitatively very different from other trading blocs. As Wise (1994, 75) observes: "... superficial descriptions of the Community [Union] as a 'common market' have

disguised the fact that it has always harboured political ambitions extending far beyond the free trading arrangements sought by other multistate regional economic organisations".

What makes the EU exceptional is the concept and practice of *supranationality* underpinning its institutional framework. Supranational institutions, above the level of the nation state, represent a level of authority and power absent in international fora such as the WTO, the GATT's successor. Member states of the EU voluntarily cede specific and well-defined elements of political sovereignty to supranational bodies, which then represent the collective strengths of the member states (Wise and Gibb, 1993). In certain areas the EU has the authority to create common policies and common legislation which applies to all 15 member states. In these specified areas, EU law is superior and transcends the laws of the member states. The level of supranationality within the EU should not, however, be exaggerated. The Council of Ministers, an essentially inter-governmental body comprising ministers from member states, is at the very heart of the EU decision-making process and has the power of deciding supranational legislation. None the less, once that legislation has been passed by the ministers of the member states it becomes genuinely European, in the sense that it is not vulnerable to member state veto and is applied throughout the EU.

As far as trade is concerned, supranationality has enabled the EU to present a common front to the world (Borchardt, 1995). The Treaty of Rome, which established the European Economic Community (EEC) in 1958, was concerned primarily with creating the economic framework of integration, focusing on a customs union and common markets in land, labour, capital and people. An important aspect of this integration framework in the international trade sphere concerned the creation of a Common Commercial Policy (CCP). Although the CCP is less well known than other common policies, such as the Common Agricultural Policy (CAP) or the European Regional Development Fund (ERDF), it nevertheless represents one of the core integrating common policies of the EU. Foreign trade is therefore an area of common policy governed by supranational laws, and member states cannot determine their own individual policies or act unilaterally. Although the Council of Ministers is responsible for key policy decisions with regard to the CCP, qualified majority voting on trade issues enables the Council to reach decisions more speedily than in many other areas of EU competence. Central to the workings of the CCP is the Common Customs Tariff (CCT), which sets EU tariff levels and quota restrictions on trade with non-member states. As well as managing the CCT, the EU has responsibility to conclude economic agreements; guide export policy; determine policies governing foreign direct investments into the EU; defend EU commercial interests overseas; and decide on trade protection measures where necessary (for instance against unfair trading practices such as dumping or subsidies).

As far as the rest of the world is concerned, the EU has a common and uniform set of trade policy instruments covering both exports and imports. In international negotiations over world trade held under the auspices of the WTO or the United Nations Conference of Trade and Development (UNCTAD), the EU has considerable authority to negotiate and conclude agreements on behalf of the 15 member states. However, in an increasingly globalised world economy, it is appropriate to question the role and effectiveness of the EU's ability to manage its trading environment.

Globalisation?

The trend towards globalisation, particularly in the economic sphere, is widely accepted in geography and throughout the social sciences more generally (Martin, 1994; Daniels and Lever, 1996; Thrift, 1996). Led by the internationalisation of the factors of production and consumption, particularly in finance where trade in financial instruments now exceeds that in material goods (Lever and Daniels, 1996), the process of globalisation is perceived to be eroding the sovereign powers of nation states. This has led a number of academics to suggest that the territorial state has lost its geographical primacy to uncontrollable market forces (Agnew and Corbridge, 1995). Central to this argument is the proposition that states are no longer able to manage or defend their national economies in the face of a truly globalised world economy. National economic development strategies and domestic policies designed to determine exchange and interest rates are seen as increasingly irrelevant (Hirst and Thompson, 1996). Agnew and Corbridge (1995, 5) identify the process leading to globalisation as "transnational liberalism" and observe that: "The contemporary world economy is shaped by pension funds and transnational companies, as well as by international organisations and often rather fragile nation states."

The globalisation of business through the spread of multinational companies, changing the fundamental relationship between markets and states, has led a number of scholars (O'Brien, 1992; Hopkinson, 1992) to take these arguments one step further and to predict "the end of geography"; in other words, a diminishing importance of the spatial dimension in the organisation of the world economy. A central question of relevance to the current chapter is, therefore, if the world economy has become dominated by uncontrollable market forces, what does this signify for regional integration generally and the EU in particular?

This chapter supports the contention that, somewhat paradoxically, the globalisation of business has promoted regional integration as states try to control at the regional level what they have increasingly failed to manage at the national or multilateral levels. Regionalism – in the form of groupings of nation states – may therefore offer a solution to the weakening of national powers associated with the globalisation process (Lever, 1996). This would, in part, explain why the appeal of regional integration, following the successful conclusion of the Uruguay Round of trade talks, shows no sign of abating (WTO, 1995). The deepening of EU integration throughout the 1980s and 1990s – epitomised by the 1987 Single European Act, the 1992 process, the Maastricht Treaty and efforts to create European Economic and Monetary Union (EMU) – can therefore be interpreted, in part, as a response designed to defend the territorial integrity of the EU and its member states. On this basis, regionalism can be seen as a new form of international regulation designed to accommodate the contradictory requirements of flexibility; that is, to preserve and intensify mobility in the factors of production (by eliminating barriers to trade within) while at the same time limiting the external threat (by reducing foreign competition). This argument was first advanced by Michalak (1994a) and Gibb and Michalak (1994, 1996) and is based on the premise that trading blocs, and in particular the EU, represent a new form of international regulation. Furthermore, when the association between regionalism and multilateralism is examined in relation to different systems of production, consumption and organisation, it may be possible to identify a fundamental change in the organisation of the capitalist world economy. Michalak (1994a) argues that Fordism and multilateralism are inextricably interlinked and mutually reinforcing. While there is no consensus over the precise reasons for its demise, it is generally accepted that the Fordist mode of regulation started to disintegrate in the 1970s (Gertler and Schoenberger, 1992), with the result that the principles and practices of multilateralism have been put in jeopardy (Gibb and Michalak, 1996).

The key to understanding the resurgence of regionalism and the success of the EU may therefore lie in identifying the successors to the Fordist and multilateral frameworks. In one respect this is no problem, since the importance of post-Fordism is widely acknowledged; yet there is no equivalent analysis of the successor to multilateralism as a mode of international regulation. Regional integration may, therefore, be replacing multilateral regulation as governments respond to the globalisation process by weakening their commitment to multilateral trade and, instead, ally themselves into regional trading blocs.

Having outlined some of the principal frameworks useful to an understanding of the EU's place in the world economy, we now consider the importance of EU regionalism through an examination of international trading transactions. Analysis focuses on the following questions: How large is the EU in the world economy? How does it compare with other trading blocs and its major competitors? Who are its principal trading partners? And what is the balance between intra-regional EU trade and EU third party trade?

European Union Trade

The EU is an economic superpower. In 1993, its share of world merchandise exports, excluding trade between member states, amounted to 20 per cent, compared to the USA's 16 per cent and Japan's 12 per cent. When intra-EU trade is included, exports from the EU accounted for approximately 40 per cent of all world merchandise exports. The EU's dominance in the commercial services market is even more pronounced. In 1992, including intra-EU trade, the EU accounted for 43 per cent of all world exports of commercial services, compared to the USA's 16 per cent and Japan's 5 per cent (Figure 3.2).

While these aggregate data highlight the economic importance and potential power of the EU, they are meaningful only if the EU acts as an effectively functioning and integrated market. In terms of population size, no individual member state can match the size of either the USA or Japan (Figure 3.3). Even Germany, the EU's most populous state with 81 million inhabitants in 1994, is approximately two-thirds the size of Japan.

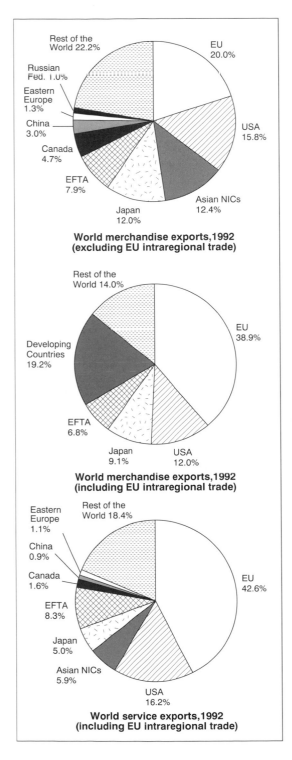

Rest of the World 22.2%
Russian Fed. 1.0%
Eastern Europe 1.3%
China 3.0%
Canada 4.7%
EFTA 7.9%
Japan 12.0%
Asian NICs 12.4%
USA 15.8%
EU 20.0%

World merchandise exports,1992 (excluding EU intraregional trade)

Rest of the World 14.0%
Developing Countries 19.2%
EFTA 6.8%
Japan 9.1%
USA 12.0%
EU 38.9%

World merchandise exports,1992 (including EU intraregional trade)

Eastern Europe 1.1%
Rest of the World 18.4%
China 0.9%
Canada 1.6%
EFTA 8.3%
Japan 5.0%
Asian NICs 5.9%
USA 16.2%
EU 42.6%

World service exports,1992 (including EU intraregional trade)

Figure 3.2 *Shares of world exports*

The EU, perhaps as a consequence of its partially fragmented "single" market (Wise and Gibb, 1993), lags behind the USA and Japan in respect of gross domestic product (GDP) per head of population. As Figure 3.4 illustrates, per capita GDP in Japan and the USA, measured in purchasing power standards (PPS), is 15 and 30 per cent higher than that existing in the EU. Collectively, however, the EU, having 378 million inhabitants in 1994, constitutes the largest market in the industrialised world and has a combined GDP of 5905 billion ECU, compared to 5346 billion in the USA and 3601 billion in Japan. However, the relative strength of the EU should also be judged alongside other regional trading arrangements, such as NAFTA (the North American Free Trade Area) and ASEAN (the Association of Southeast Asian Nations). This comparison of regional trading blocs is useful as there is evidence to suggest that the world economy is becoming increasingly dominated by a limited number of very powerful national groupings, focused on North America, Europe and the West Pacific Rim[2] (Gibb and Michalak, 1994). This triad of regional trading blocs may replace the multilateral system of international economic relations. As noted in Waites (1993, 190): "... the post-war multilateral system of international economic relations under US leadership could be, at least in part, in serious decline. ... In its wake, we are not seeing so much the emergence of a totally globalised economy as the emergence of a newly regionalising world economy".

The data presented here are for the EU 12 (before the 1995 membership of Finland, Sweden and Austria); NAFTA (comprising the USA, Canada and Mexico); and ASEAN+ (which includes the six countries belonging to ASEAN plus Hong Kong, Japan, South Korea and Taiwan). In 1991, intra-regional trade, that is exchange within the EU, NAFTA and ASEAN+, accounted for 38 per cent of the world's merchandise exports and imports. Inter-regional trade between the "triad" of trading blocs and between these blocs and third countries, represented 10 and 19 per cent of all merchandise exports and imports respectively. These figures demonstrate clearly the dominant role of regionalism in the world economy, with 67 per

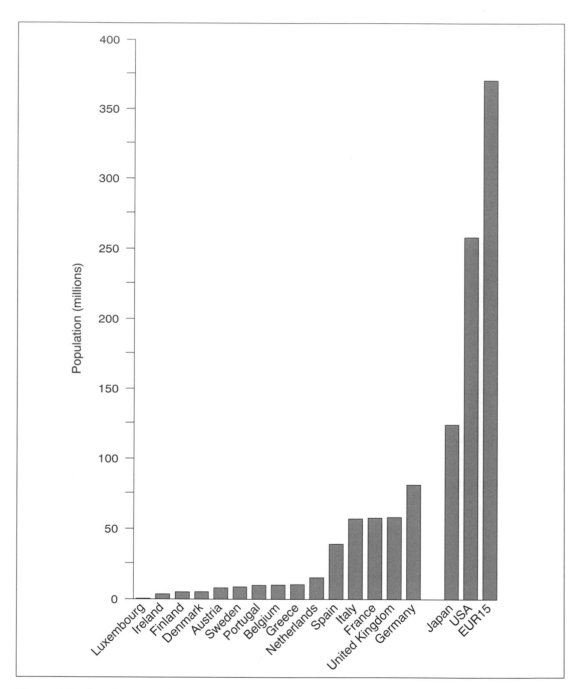

Figure 3.3   *Populations, 1993–94*

cent of global trade involving the EU, NAFTA and ASEAN+.

What distinguishes the EU from the other trading blocs, however, is the level of spatial discrimination promoted by its particular level of regionalism. Intra-regional trade within the EU is far more pronounced than elsewhere. The data presented in Figure 3.5 are calculated using 1994 members (so, in the case of the EU, trade figures for 1948 refer to the same 12 states that were

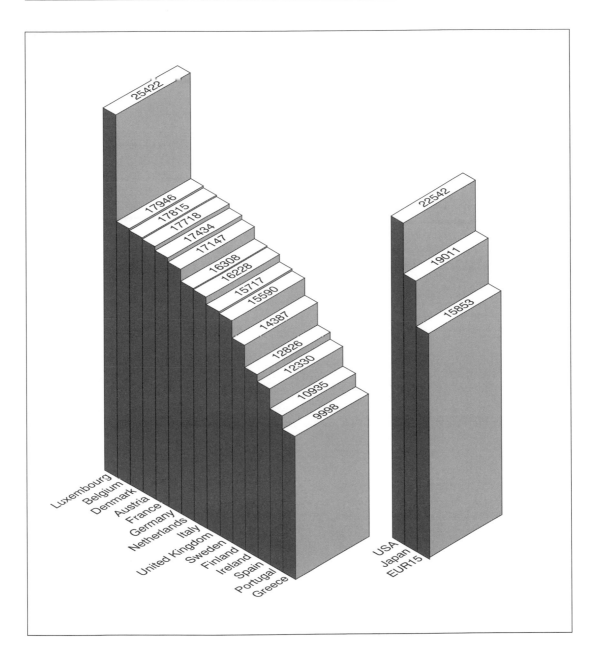

Figure 3.4 *GDP per head of population, measured in purchasing power standards, 1993*

members of the EU in 1994). Intra-regional trade grew from 35 per cent of all EU merchandise imports and exports in 1957 to 59 per cent in 1991. Clearly, EU regionalism has resulted in a geo-economic reorientation of trade towards intra-regional commodity flows promoted, in part, by the gradual removal of tariffs and quantitative trading restrictions within the EU. Conversely, inter-regional trade with other members of the "triad" is less important for the EU than for the other two blocs; 69 per cent of NAFTA exports go to the EU and ASEAN+; the latter markets 66 per cent of its exports in NAFTA and the EU; yet only 34 per cent of EU

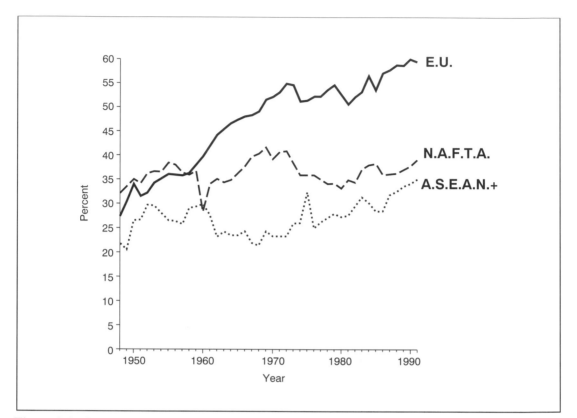

Figure 3.5 *Intra-regional trade: EU, NAFTA and ASEAN+, 1991*

exports are destined for NAFTA and ASEAN+ (Figure 3.6). This contrast helps to explain the perception of the EU, examined later in this chapter, as an inward-looking and protectionist trading bloc. But before proceeding to examine the idea of an emerging "Fortress Europe", two further issues concerning the level of intra-regional trade need to be discussed: first, the different trading patterns exhibited among member states and, second, the impact of enlargements on intra-regional trade levels.

The EU aggregate data conceal marked differences evident in the trading patterns exhibited by individual member states. In 1993, based on the EU of 12, intra-regional trade accounted for, on average, 62 per cent of exports by member states. However, for some states, most notably the so-called "big four" (Germany, France, the UK and Italy), the importance of non-EU trade is markedly higher than the EU average (Figure 3.7). Approximately half of Germany's and the UK's export trade is outside

the EU, while the corresponding figures for Italy and France are 47 and 39 per cent, respectively. By contrast, the smaller states of the EU typically trade with non-EU countries at a level between 25 and 35 per cent of their exports.

As Wise (1994) and Henderson (1995) point out, the spatial growth of the EU from 6 to 15 states (Figure 3.8) makes comparative analyses of intra-regional trade levels over time very difficult. Union enlargement may exaggerate the shift towards internally orientated trade as commodity flows that were once classified as "external" become treated as "internal". However, analysing the data presented in Figure 3.5, it can be seen that the fastest growth in EU intra-regional trade took place between 1957 and 1973, a period during which membership remained constant. In the period 1973–1992, during which time the EU expanded from 6 to 12, intra-regional trade experienced a relatively modest increase of approximately 10 per cent.

This section on EU trade patterns has demonstrated clearly that the EU is, in global

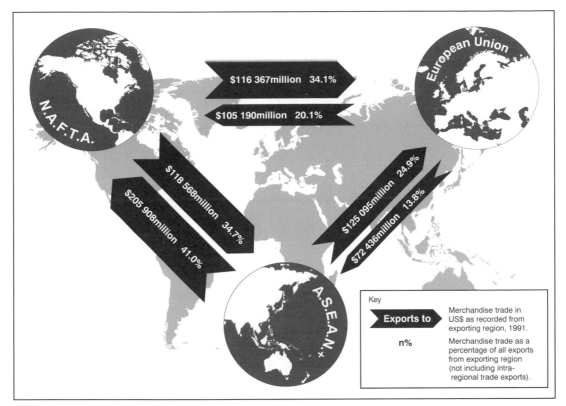

Figure 3.6   *Inter-regional trade: EU, NAFTA and ASEAN+, 1991*

terms, an economic superpower. Collectively, member states represent the largest single component of the world economy and, while intra-regional trade is greater than regional exports, the EU's trading relations are global in character. In addition there are marked differences between the trading patterns of individual member states: while the EU is often analysed as a homogeneous entity, there exists a noticeable difference between the export profiles of the "big four" and other member states. In the light of the trading patterns identified above, discussion now turns to the issue of an emerging "Fortress Europe".

Fortress Europe?

To most European citizens and their governments, the EU is perceived as an institution promoting, among many other things, free trade among member states. The phrase "common market",

which was an unofficial but widely accepted name for the European Economic Community (EEC), reflected this perception of free trade. However, countries outside the EU are often critical of its protectionist instincts, particularly in relation to agriculture. The restrictions imposed upon access to the EU market which, as the last section documented, represents the largest single market in the industrialised world, are often critical to the economic well-being of both developed and developing countries. Against this background, the term "Fortress Europe" developed in the run-up to the "1992" programme designed to create a Single European Market (SEM). Following the Single European Act (SEA) in 1987, the USA, Japan and the EFTA countries all expressed broadly similar fears that the EU was becoming inward-looking and protectionist. Fortress Europe was the phrase used to embody the fears of the EU's principal trading partners that it was intent on restricting access to the SEM. To most third countries, the EU's single market

Figure 3.7 *The internationalisation of trade in action: the Prince Charles container terminal, Southampton. (Photo: Associated British Ports, Southampton)*

commitment to eliminate internal frontier controls inescapably implied the reinforcement and strengthening of its common external trade policy. These fears, expressed in particular by the USA and Japan, focused on three aspects of the SEM programme: reciprocity, standards and rules of origin.

In the closing stages of the single market programme, the Commission established the reciprocity principle as a core organising philosophy underlying the formulation of external trade relations. Willey de Clercq, in his capacity as Commissioner responsible for external relations, stated in 1988:

> "... the benefits of our internal liberalisation should not be extended unilaterally to third countries. We shall be ready and willing to negotiate reciprocal concessions with third countries, preferably in a multilateral context, but also bilaterally. We want to open our borders, but on the basis of a mutual balance of advantages in the spirit of the GATT."

The USA, in particular, opposed the rule of reciprocity with two principal arguments. First, that it contravened the very foundations of the multilateral trading system based on the most favoured nation[3] (MFN) principle; and, second, that it would effectively force the USA to import EU practices and methods.

States outside the EU also expressed fears that the EU's new technical regulations and standards, necessary to enforce the SEM, were being drafted in isolation and without consultation. Again the USA objected, arguing that standards were being designed behind closed doors and in a manner likely to damage US exports. The USA therefore requested, but was subsequently denied, a "seat at the table" during the drafting of European standards. Another non-tariff barrier that alarmed third countries in the run-up to "1992" was the Commission's attempt to restrict the level of imported components destined for overseas manufacturing facilities established in the SEM.

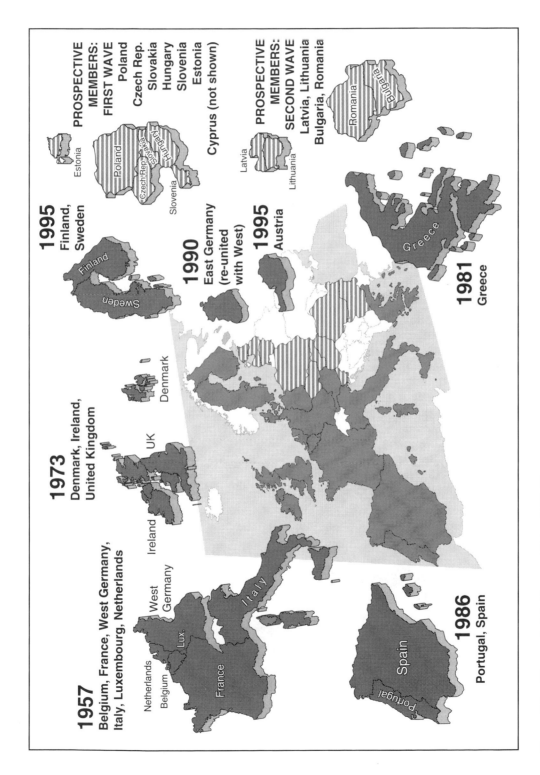

1957
Belgium, France, West Germany, Italy, Luxembourg, Netherlands

1973
Denmark, Ireland, United Kingdom

1986
Portugal, Spain

1981
Greece

1995
Finland, Sweden

1990
East Germany (re-united with West)

1995
Austria

PROSPECTIVE MEMBERS:
FIRST WAVE
Poland
Czech Rep.
Slovakia
Hungary
Slovenia
Estonia
Cyprus (not shown)

PROSPECTIVE MEMBERS:
SECOND WAVE
Latvia, Lithuania
Bulgaria, Romania

Figure 3.8 *The growth of the European Union, 1957–98*

By introducing "rules of origin" or "local content regulations", the EU hoped to persuade non-European manufacturers to locate within the EU and, furthermore, to purchase European components.

A key factor emerging from these protectionist worries, which has in turn influenced EU trading patterns, has been the dramatic growth in Japanese foreign direct investment (FDI) in the EU. Industry and capital from outside the EU, and in particular Japan, was persuaded to establish bases within the EU in order to exploit more fully the SEM (Wise and Gibb, 1993). The following brief overview of Japanese FDI activities directed towards the EU helps reiterate both the perception of the EU as protectionist and the importance attached to gaining access to the world's single most important market.

Compared to the FDI activities undertaken by the USA and EFTA countries, direct investment in the EU by Japanese manufacturing interests is a recent phenomenon. Between 1951 and 1988, the value of Japanese FDI invested in the member states of the EU stood at approximately US$6bn, representing 9 per cent of all Japanese FDI. In the same time period, US multinationals invested US$65bn, representing over 50 per cent of all USA direct investment (Wise and Gibb, 1993). This dissimilarity in investment priorities resulted in a marked difference between how the USA and Japan serviced the demands generated by the EU economy. Figure 3.9 illustrates that, in 1986, 70 per cent of the Japanese goods purchased in the EU were imported from Japan and only 16 per cent were produced, or licensed, within the EU. The pattern exhibited by the USA in servicing the demand for American goods was almost the opposite. The fact that Japan relied so heavily on exports to the EU economy explains why, during the mid-1980s, it was so concerned about the EU moving towards protectionism. This concern manifested itself in a sharp rise in Japanese FDI directed towards the EU. Between 1986 and 1988, the Japanese economy invested more in the EU than in the previous 35 years! There are, of course, many contributory factors leading to this growth in Japanese FDI, not least the benefits of investing in an expanding market and the disadvantageous impacts of the yen's appreciation. However, the single most important

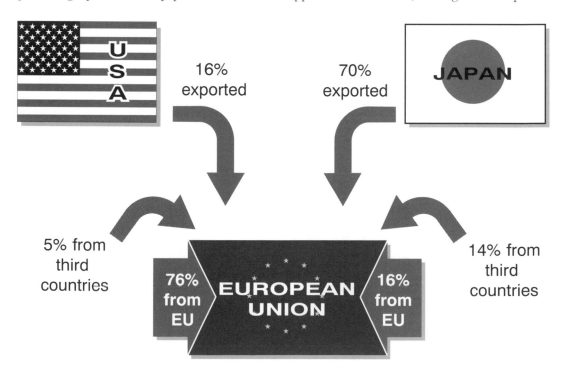

Figure 3.9 *The origins of American and Japanese goods destined for the EU market*

contributory factor was the perception of the EU moving towards protectionism in order to lessen Japan's massive trade surplus with the EU, which in 1988 stood at a staggering US$30bn.

Although fears of an emerging Fortress Europe may be very real, it is important to question whether they are soundly based. This may be done through closer examination of the outcomes of the Uruguay negotiations and, in particular, the confrontation which centred on the EU's protectionist Common Agricultural Policy (CAP).

The EU, the Uruguay Negotiations and the Fortress Europe Concept

Given the importance of extra-regional trade for the EU as a whole, and for the "big four" in particular, it is not surprising that first the EC and now the EU have played a supporting and influential role in successive GATT rounds. Since the Second World War, the GATT has eroded the importance of tariff barriers on manufactured goods, from an average of 40 per cent in the late 1940s to 6 per cent in the early 1990s. The Uruguay Round of the GATT, completed on 15 December 1993, promoted further tariff reductions cutting EU–US tariffs by approximately 50 per cent and world trade tariffs by 40 per cent (*The Economist*, 1993). Average tariff barriers among developed countries following the implementation of the Uruguay Agreement will be around 3–4 per cent. Although this figure is at first sight remarkably low, and would not in the majority of cases present an impediment to trade, throughout the 1970s and 1980s official and transparent tariff barriers were replaced by so-called non-tariff barriers. Such things as voluntary export restraints, quota restrictions in the form of semi-official bilateral agreements, orderly marketing arrangements, dumping fines and standards were erected in order to evade multilateral rules and prevent the free movement of trade. This, in addition to the fact that the service and agricultural sectors were largely outside the multilateral regulatory framework until Uruguay, meant that trade was far less free than official tariff figures suggested. Despite most industrialised countries belonging to and

benefiting from the GATT, its rules were frequently circumvented.

As a result of these shortcomings, the Uruguay Round was by far the most complex, ambitious and time-consuming, involving 28 separate accords extending multilateral principles of trade to agriculture, textiles, services, intellectual property and foreign investment. The EU is recognised to have played an influential role in the promotion and completion of the negotiations and, in so doing, has lessened the perception of an emerging Fortress Europe (Barnes and Barnes, 1995). Despite the last-minute decision by the French government to try to renegotiate the agricultural agreement and some high-profile trade disputes, most notably over the French and Italian decision to restrict Japanese car imports, the EU came out of the Uruguay Agreement with its free-market credentials intact. As Bainbridge and Teasdale (1996, 54–5) comment:

> "In spite of substantial national and political differences between Member States in trade policy, the Union has, on the whole, achieved a high degree of coherence and consistency in trade matters. . . . The Union has also largely succeeded in dispelling the fears of a Fortress Europe promoted by the single market programme, in spite of the recession still affecting the economies of many Member States."

Furthermore, de Clercq (1988) and Henderson (1988) argue that, far from advancing protectionism, the single market programme has assisted free-market principles and promoted liberal trade policies. By allowing overseas companies access to a truly integrated European market of 378 million people, without the cost penalties of nationally orientated non-tariff barriers, the SEM has been able to enhance the export potential of third countries. Member states are no longer able to impose national non-tariff barriers on imports from third countries and, as a consequence, once a product enters the EU it can move from one country to another with increasing ease (Wise, 1994). Indeed, because of this, many European companies now fear that the major long-term beneficiaries of the SEM will be the large Japanese and American multinationals. To support this contention, they refer to the EU's substantial balance of trade deficits with Japan and, at the start of the 1990s, with the USA (Eurostat, 1993).

On balance it would appear fair to conclude that the image of a fortified and protectionist Europe has been exaggerated and that, alongside the USA and Japan, the EU has a vested interest in promoting and sustaining multilateral trading arrangements. This is the case even though protectionist instincts and policies designed to circumvent the spirit of multilateral agreements linger on. As noted by Barnes and Barnes (1995, 358), "the EU's record on trade liberalisation is perhaps no better or worse than many others". There is, however, one issue over which the EU is perceived to have a far more protectionist policy than its principal trading partners: agriculture and the protective nature of the CAP. Because of the complexity of this issue, the following brief review focuses specifically on the conflict between the CAP and multilateralism.[4]

Agriculture is the most heavily protected sector of international trade, with the EU, the USA, Japan and many other states pursuing interventionist policies designed to stabilise domestic prices and guarantee security of supply. The first point to stress, therefore, is that the EU is not alone in protecting its agricultural industry. None the less, agricultural support is an extremely expensive business for EU taxpayers and consumers. In 1990 the overall cost of EU agricultural subsidies amounted to US$134bn, compared to US$74bn in the USA and US$59bn in Japan. The operational mechanisms adopted by the CAP are many and varied but, in its simplest form, the policy intervenes in international trade through a system of "Union preference" which supports tariffs on imported agricultural produce and subsidises exports.[5] It is this latter type of intervention, which enables the EU to export its surplus output at prices often below the costs of production, that has caused the greatest friction, particularly between the EU and the USA.

A remarkable feature of the agricultural industry is the extent to which it has remained unaffected by the GATT and pressures to promote free trade. However, the USA challenged the CAP in the Uruguay Round, arguing that the EU's support mechanism distorts world markets to an unacceptable degree. Ultimately, the Uruguay Agreement on agriculture only arose after bitter and acrimonious negotiations between the USA and the EU. The main proponent of agricultural liberalisation was the USA, supported by the 14 members of the so-called "Cairns Group" of agricultural exporters, including Australia, New Zealand, Canada and Argentina. Originally, the USA called for a 90 per cent reduction in EU export subsidies and a 75 per cent cut in domestic subsidies. These demands were met by determined EU resistance, led by France, Ireland, Denmark and the Netherlands. At times the stalemate over agricultural liberalisation threatened the very success of the entire Uruguay talks, but at the start of the 1990s – when collapse seemed imminent and with an immediate deadline to meet – the Blair House compromise was negotiated.[6] This led directly to the Uruguay Agreement on agriculture, which requires a prevention of new export subsidies; a reduction of 36 per cent in existing export subsidies; a "tariffication" of non-tariff barriers; and an overall reduction of 36 per cent in domestic tariff barriers. For the EU and other developed countries, tariff reductions are taking place over a six-year transition period. By introducing agriculture to the GATT in this way, the first tentative steps have been taken to liberalise the market.

The EU therefore negotiated an agreement that will see a substantial reduction in both import levies and export refunds. The Uruguay Agreement represents a significant step towards the liberalisation of trade in agricultural produce, not so much in terms of the absolute size of tariff reductions[7] but because multilateral principles have been applied successfully to the agricultural industry.

The EU, Lomé and East-Central Europe

Thus far, the EU's position and influence in the world economy have been discussed in relation to the developed and industrialised world. However, the EU has a number of preferential trading arrangements with developing countries that grant varying levels of non-reciprocal access to the single market. These agreements, sanctioned by the GATT, discriminate positively in favour of developing countries, with the principal objective of assisting Third World development.

Beneath this umbrella objective, however, the EU operates a hierarchy of discrimination between the ACP (African, Caribbean and Pacific) states, the Mediterranean basin countries, and certain countries in Asia and Latin America. The last two groups benefit from the EU's Generalised System of Preferences (GSP) designed to assist exporters of manufactured goods and some processed agricultural products. At the top of the hierarchy of privilege are the ACP states; these enjoy the lowest tariffs and highest quota restrictions.

The ACP states (Appendix 3.1) are signatories to the Lomé Convention, concluded in 1975 in Lomé, the capital of Togo. The Convention requires the ACP states to be given better access to the EU market than non-Lomé countries, and it is this which ensures that Lomé signatories are at the very top of the EU's complex hierarchy of preferential trading arrangements (Davenport *et al.*, 1995). The Convention aims: "to promote and expedite the economic, cultural and social development of the ACP states and to consolidate and diversify their relations in a spirit of solidarity and mutual interest".

How do these praiseworthy objectives translate into reality? The 70 states of Lomé enjoy guaranteed duty-free access for the export of manufactured products *originating* in ACP states. Strict rules-of-origin criteria are applied to prevent trade deflection and the possibility of goods gaining access to the EU market via ACP countries. In addition, ACP countries have duty-free access to the EU market for agricultural products *not* covered by the CAP. Lomé does not, therefore, extend to free trade in agriculture. However, the EU does guarantee access for certain ACP commodities, subject to strict quota limits, under a number of protocols covering beef, veal, bananas and sugar.

It is very difficult to evaluate accurately the impact of Lomé on the ACP states. Their trading performance is dependent on a whole range of additional factors that are local, national and international in character. However, despite being accorded wide-ranging preferences, ACP trade with the EU has been less than impressive. As Davenport *et al.* (1995) point out, the ACP share of exports in the EU market has declined quite markedly over the lifetime of the Lomé Con-

vention. In 1992, 3.7 per cent of the EU's total imports, excluding intra-regional trade, originated from ACP countries. In 1976, the equivalent figure was 6.7 per cent. One reason for this poor performance lies with the success of the GATT/ WTO multilateral process. As a result of international tariff barriers being reduced, the concessions offered by Lomé have, in relative terms, diminished over time. If tariff barriers on manufactured goods traded between industrialised countries rest somewhere between 3 and 4 per cent, duty-free access for the most underdeveloped countries is unlikely to compensate for their lack of comparative advantage.

As the relative importance of preferential trading arrangements has been undermined as a result of the multilateral process, the EU has come under increasing pressure to enhance its aid programme. However, there is considerable tension among member states over the issue of EU competence in this field. For example, the UK argues that, while preferential trading arrangements should be organised and negotiated at the EU level, aid programmes are better dealt with by individual member states. In practice this is what happens: in 1992, only 17 per cent of the EU's total overseas aid programme was diverted through the EU's European Development Fund (EDF).[8]

East-Central Europe

In addition to the preferential trading arrangements with developing countries, the EU has established trade agreements with the transition economies of ECE. The magnitude and speed of the "revolutions" that swept across ECE at the end of the 1980s took almost everybody, including the EU, by complete surprise (Gibb and Michalak, 1993a). The collapse of the Communist regimes in 1989–90 represented a start to the end of the post-war division of Europe and the industrialised world into two distinct and hostile political economies. Until then, East–West trade was of limited size and importance (Michalak, 1994b), and the EU had few official contacts with its Soviet-dominated equivalent, the Council for Mutual Economic Assistance (CMEA, also known as Comecon).

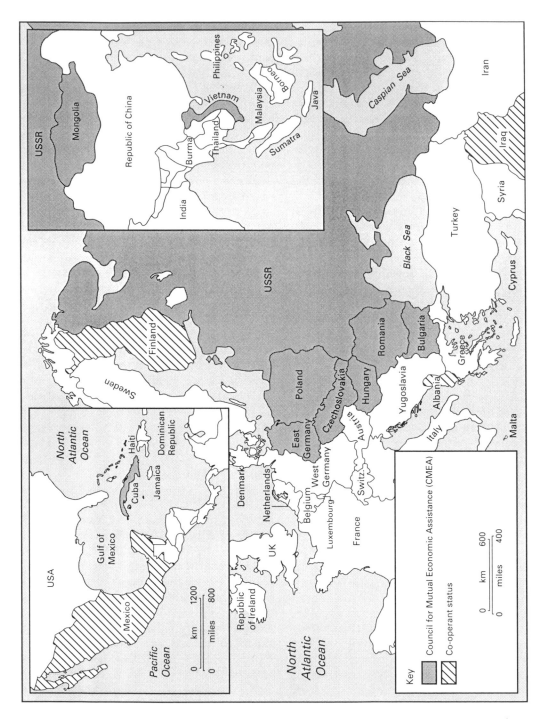

Figure 3.10 *Former members of the Council for Mutual Economic Assistance*

Although CMEA was from the start territorially much larger than the EU (Figure 3.10), it was never intended to be an evolving organisation with its own institutions and supranational powers. Instead it was an intergovernmental organisation whose official purpose was to stimulate *intra*-regional trade.

Relations between the EU and CMEA were tense, primarily as a result of the latter's reluctance to recognise the former. In the face of this non-recognition, the EU negotiated trade agreements with individual CMEA countries, but these agreements were at the very bottom of the EU's hierarchy of trading preferences. East–West trade was of minimal importance to both sides, reflecting political tensions; the difficulties of trading and pricing between free and command economies; the lack of hard currency in the East; and Western restrictions imposed on many export products, particularly high-technology goods.

The economic collapse of the Soviet Union in 1990 wholly discredited the Soviet model of economic management and dealt a terminal blow to the process of economic integration supported by CMEA (Wise and Gibb, 1993). As a result, in June 1991, its member states decided to dismantle the organisation. This decision to abandon CMEA-style integration and adopt hard currency transactions instead of soft currency and barter trade, resulted in an ECE trade reorientation re-establishing links with the West, and the EU in particular.

The EU's response to the unexpected political democratisation and economic liberalisation in ECE was slow to emerge. Shortly after the events of 1989–90, the ECE states made it very clear that their immediate goal was to apply for membership of the EU in order to guarantee the long-term economic and political security of the region. The EU's reaction was cautious, recognising the need for stability, but at the same time aware of the economic, social and political consequences of expansion to the East. The Centre for Economic Policy Research (1992) estimates that, in the event of enlargement, the net annual transfer from the EU to ECE would amount to over US$15bn per annum. Given the EU's already strained budget, such a flow would be politically unacceptable to many interest groups and member state governments. Through a series of "Europe Agreements" signed from 1991 onwards, the EU has recognised and accepted the legitimate desire for ECE membership of the EU, and in 1997 identified a group of countries as eligible for entry in the next enlargement (Figure 3.8).

The EU's principal policy response to the needs of ECE, the Europe Agreements, are trade and aid pacts designed to strengthen East–West commercial and political ties. The first were signed with Poland, Hungary and the then Czechoslovakia in 1991. In addition, the EU has established a number of aid programmes to support the transition economies, most notably through the creation of the European Bank for Reconstruction and Development, the PHARE Programme and loans via the European Investment Bank (EIB). Despite these measures, however, the level of access ECE goods have to the EU market remains a critical issue. Under the Europe Agreements, the EU has accepted an asymmetric reduction in tariffs in favour of ECE so that, in theory, most ECE goods should have unrestricted access to the single market. Yet the EU has also placed comprehensive restrictions on the import of so-called "sensitive" products from ECE, covering steel, iron, textiles and agriculture. These sectors, in which the ECE states have a comparative advantage when compared to the EU, are extremely important for the transition economies. In 1991 iron, steel, textiles and agriculture represented 47 per cent of Hungary's exports to the EU, 41 per cent of the (former) Czechoslovakia's and 33 per cent of Poland's.

Despite this friction, however, it must be acknowledged that political democratisation and economic liberalisation, plus the effects of the Europe Agreements, have resulted in a partial westwards reorientation of the transition economies (Figure 3.11). Notwithstanding the reluctance of the EU to open its market to ECE goods, this development is likely to be permanent and, indeed, to gain momentum for the foreseeable future.

Conclusions

This chapter has shown that the EU has emerged as the world's most powerful trading bloc, and is

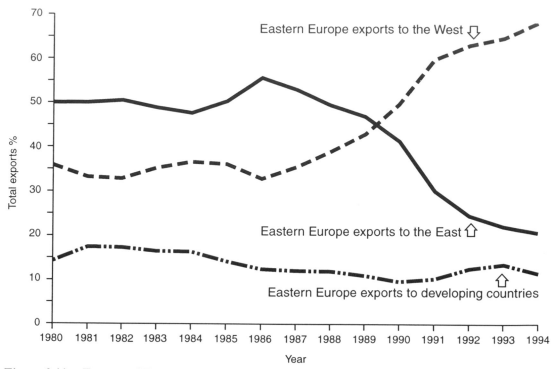

Figure 3.11   *East-central European exports by destination*

by far the strongest economic grouping in the new Europe. By virtue of its economic size, the EU has played an influential role in determining the character and regulation of the world economy. The EU's constructive negotiating stance in the GATT Uruguay Round of trade talks, and in particular its willingness to compromise over agriculture, helped contribute to the enhanced liberalisation of the world trading regime. The successful end to the Uruguay negotiations, signed in December 1993, would not have been possible without the support of the EU. It has therefore been instrumental in promoting a liberal trading regime covering material goods, services, intellectual property and foreign investments. Not only will the EU, alongside the USA and Japan, continue for the foreseeable future to play a leading role in helping to regulate the world economy, but in certain regions – particularly ECE and to a lesser extent the Lomé countries – it will be a key determining factor affecting economic well-being.

At the same time, the liberal world economy has an increasing influence on the EU. With tariffs on industrialised products averaging 3–4 per cent among industrialised countries, the ability of the EU to adopt protectionist measures in order to safeguard European industry and workers will be circumscribed. Multilateral measures designed to liberalise not only goods, but also services and agriculture, will have an enormous impact on the future character of the EU. The latest and most significant package of reforms affecting the CAP arose not from internal conflicts over the protectionist nature of this policy, but as a repercussion of international pressures to extend multilateral rules to the agricultural sector. The extent and nature of the EU's economic, industrial, commercial and social policies will, to an increasing degree, be determined by disciplines enforced by the multilateral framework. Clearly, the EU cannot be understood in isolation from the world economy.

However, the EU is as much a political organisation as it is an economic one, and for many Europeans and their governments economic integration is only one step, albeit a very important one, towards a deeper political unity of purpose and social harmony on the continent. Thus far, the multilateral liberal framework has not seriously threatened this objective. The willingness of member states to pool sovereignty, adopt supranational institutions and laws and establish common policies, has strengthened the economic well-being and authority of the EU. There is little doubt that the success of regional integration in western Europe is one of the most important reasons behind the present resurgence of regionalism in other parts of the world. Again, this is an example of the EU influencing developments in the world economy. The resurgence of regionalism being experienced in North America, Latin America, Africa, Europe and Asia (Gibb and Michalak, 1994) will in itself significantly influence future global developments. As suggested earlier in this chapter, regionalism may well turn out to represent one of the most fundamental restructuring processes affecting the multilateral trading system since the principles of international trade were established at the Bretton Woods conference.

The EU in the twenty-first century will continue to expand geographically, eventually incorporating ECE states, the Baltic states and some small Mediterranean countries as well. Furthermore, it is likely to deepen its level of political integration with the creation of EMU and a common currency. These actions will enhance still further the economic strength of the EU and its ability to influence developments in the world economy. Equally, the successful conclusion to the Uruguay Round, together with new WTO rules and regulations,[9] will undoubtedly extend the power of multilateralism. The challenge for the EU is to ensure that it continues to support multilateral liberalisation while at the same time defending European regionalism.

Notes

1. General Agreement on Tariffs and Trade.
2. There is no overall consensus on exactly how many trading blocs exist. Arguments have been advanced supporting two, three, five and eight regional groupings (Nierop, 1989; Petri, 1992). However, most analysts argue for the existence of a "tripolar" system of blocs, incorporating the EU or western Europe, North America and an ill-defined Asian grouping centred on Japan.
3. The most favoured nation (MFN) principle is the backbone to the GATT/WTO agreements. Its principal objective is to prevent discrimination by ensuring that any trading concession offered by a member state of the GATT/WTO is made available to all contracting parties.
4. For more detailed examination of the CAP, see Chapter 18 and also Barnes and Barnes (1995) and Swinbank (1995).
5. Notwithstanding the tariffs, the EU remains by far the world's largest importer of agricultural produce.
6. Although France later tried to withdraw its support for the compromise, it faced intense pressure from the EU to reach an agreement.
7. The EU will, for the foreseeable future, continue to subsidise and protect European agriculture.
8. The European Development Fund, established to assist the Third World, should not be confused with the EU's leading regional investment agency, the European Regional Development Fund.
9. These include acceptance of the rulings of a new WTO dispute settlement body.

Appendix 3.1 Developing Country Signatories to Lomé

Angola
Antigua and Barbuda
Bahamas
Barbados
Belize
Benin
Botswana
Burundi
United Republic of Cameroon
Cape Verde
Central African Republic
Chad
Comoros
People's Republic of Congo
Democratic People's
 Republic of the Congo (ex-Zaire)
Dahomey
Djibouti
Dominica
Equatorial Guinea
Ethiopia
Fiji
Gabon
Gambia
Ghana
Grenada
Guinea
Guinea-Bissau
Guyana
Cote d'Ivoire
Jamaica
Kenya
Kiribati
Lesotho

Liberia
Madagascar
Malawi
Mali
Mauritania
Mauritius
Mozambique
Niger
Nigeria
Papua New Guinea
Rwanda
Sao Tome and Principe
Senegal
Seychelles
Sierra Leone
Solomon Islands
Somalia
St Kitts and Nevis-Anguilla
St Lucia
St Vincent and the Grenadines
Sudan
Suriname
Swaziland
Tanzania
Togo
Tonga
Trinidad and Tobago
Tuvalu
Upper Volta
Uganda
Vanuatu
Western Samoa
Zambia
Zimbabwe

References

Agnew, J and Corbridge, S (1995) *Mastering Space: hegemony, territory and international political economy*, Routledge, London.

Bainbridge, T and Teasdale, A (1996) *European Union*, Penguin, London.

Barnes, I and Barnes, M (1995) *The Enlarged European Union*, Longman, Harlow.

Bhagwati, J N (1991) *The World Trading System at Risk*, Harvester-Wheatsheaf, Worcester.

Bhagwati, J N (1992) The threats to the world trading system, *The World Economy*, **15**, 443–56.

Bhagwati, J N (1993) Regionalism and multilateralism: an overview, in J de Melo and A Panagariya (eds) *New Dimensions in Regional Integration*, Cambridge University Press, Cambridge, 22–51.

Borchardt, K (1995) *European Integration: the origins and growth of the European Union*, Luxembourg, Office for the Official Publications of the European Communities.

Centre for Economic Policy Research (CEPR) (1992) Is bigger better? The economics of EC enlargement, *Monitoring European Integration*, CEPR Annual Report, London.

Daniels, P and Lever, W (eds) (1996) *The Global Economy in Transition*, Longman, Harlow.

Davenport, M, Hewitt, A and Koning, A (1995) *Europe's Preferred Partners? The Lomé countries in world trade*, ODI Special Report, London.

De Clercq, W (1988) The European Community in a changing world, speech given at the Fundación Jorge, Buenos Aires, 2 August 1988.

Eurostat (1993) *External Trade and Balance of Payments*, Statistical Yearbook, Luxembourg, Office for the Official Publications of the European Community.

Gertler, M S and Schoenberger, E (1992) Commentary: industrial restructuring and continental trade blocs: the European Community and North America, *Environment and Planning A*, **24**, 2–10.

Gibb, R A (1993) A common market for post-apartheid Southern Africa: prospects and problems, *South African Geographical Journal*, **75**, 28–35.

Gibb, R A and Michalak, W Z (1993a) The European Community and Central Europe: prospects for political economic co-operation, *Geography*, **78**, 16–30.

Gibb, R A and Michalak, W Z (1993b) Foreign debt in the new East-Central Europe: a threat to European integration? *Environment and Planning C*, **11**, 69–85.

Gibb, R A and Michalak, W Z (eds) (1994) *Continental Trading Blocs: the growth of regionalism in the world economy*, John Wiley, Chichester.

Gibb, R A and Michalak, W Z (1996) Regionalism in the world economy, *Area*, 446–58.

Henderson, D (1988) *1992: the external dimension*, Occasional paper No 35, Group Thirty, New York.

Henderson, K (1995) *Europe and World Trade*, Pinter, London.

Hirst, P and Thompson, G (1996) *Globalisation in Question*, Polity Press, Cambridge.

Hopkinson, N (ed) (1992) *Completing the GATT Uruguay Round. Renewed Multilateralism or a World of Regional Trading Blocs?* Wilton Park Paper No 61, HMSO, London.

Lever, W (1996) Market enlargement: the single European market, in P Daniels and W Lever (eds) *The Global Economy in Transition*, Longman, Harlow, 291–310.

Lever, W and Daniels, P (1996) Introduction, in P Daniels and W Lever (eds) *The Global Economy in Transition*, Longman, Harlow, 1–9.

Martin, R (1994) Stateless monies, global financial integration and national economic autonomy: the end of geography?, in S Corbridge, N Thrift and R Martin (eds) *Money, Power and Space*, Blackwell, Oxford, 253–78.

Michalak, W Z (1994a) The political economy of trading blocs, in R A Gibb and W Z Michalak (eds) *Continental Trading Blocs: the growth of regionalism in the world economy*, John Wiley, London, 37–64.

Michalak, W Z (1994b) Regional integration in eastern Europe, in R A Gibb and W Z Michalak (eds) *Continental Trading Blocs: the growth of regionalism in the world economy*, John Wiley, London, 111–28.

Nierop, T (1989) Macro-regions and the global institutional network, 1950–1980, *Political Geography Quarterly*, **8**, 43–65.

O'Brien, R (1992) *Global Financial Integration: the end of geography*, Pinter, London.

Petri, P A (1992) One bloc, two blocs, or more? Political economic factors in Pacific trade policy, in K Okwuizumi, K E Calder and G W Gong (eds) *The US–Japan Economic Relationship in East and South East Asia*, Centre for Strategic and International Studies, Washington, DC, 39–70.

Swinbank, A (1993) CAP reform, 1992, *Journal of Common Market Studies*, **31**, 3.

The Economist (1993) A guide to GATT, December 4, 25.

Thrift, N (1996) Shut up and dance, or, is the world economy knowable?, in P Daniels and W Lever (eds) *The Global Economy in Transition*, Longman, Harlow.

Waites, B (ed) (1993) *Europe and the Wider World*, Routledge, London.

Wise, M (1994) The European Community, in R A Gibb and W Z Michalak (eds) *Continental Trading Blocs: the growth of regionalism in the world economy*, John Wiley, Chichester, 75–110.

Wise, M and Gibb, R A (1993) *From Single Market to Social Europe: the European Community in the 1990s*, Longman, London.

WTO (1995) *Regionalism and the World Trading System*, WTO, Geneva.

4
Energy

Resources and choices

Peter R Odell

*Emeritus Professor of International Energy Studies, Erasmus University Rotterdam, The
Netherlands and Visiting Professor of Geography, University of Plymouth, UK*

Antecedents

Pre-1945 components

Current issues and future prospects in Europe's
energy sector emerge in part from a background
which has evolved over the more than 200 years of
the continent's modernisation and development.
From the mid-eighteenth to the mid-twentieth
century there was a slow evolution of the energy
market. Dependence on coal remained of the
essence and there was a high, though from the
late nineteenth century a slowly declining, share
of industrial activities concentrated on the
coalfields where most of the main centres of
population growth were also located (Pounds
and Parker, 1957; Foley, 1976). Even the late-
nineteenth-century discovery and application of
electricity made only slow headway in industrial
and residential energy use patterns over most
parts of the continent (Schumacher, 1985). It
was, indeed, only in a few regions, with advantageous physical conditions for the exploitation
of hydroelectric potential, that electricity established itself prior to the 1920s as the basis for
the location of some energy-intensive industries
and was cheap enough to secure widespread
application in the commercial and residential
sectors.

Elsewhere, much of non-urban Europe
remained beyond the local networks established
for the distribution of coal-based electricity until
the 1930s, or even into the post-Second World
War period. Even most industrial regions
remained relatively small users of electricity (for
lighting and machine power only), except for a
small number of locations in which more
sophisticated industrial production became
concentrated. Meanwhile, coal continued to
dominate the supply of primary energy to the
virtual exclusion of oil, let alone natural gas. In
contrast with the 27 per cent contribution of oil
to the total energy supply of the United States in
1937, the share of oil in the European energy
economy was less than 7 per cent, with even lower
figures of 6 and 2 per cent respectively in the
continent's two leading economies, the UK and
Germany.

The early post-1945 period

Pre-Second World War differences between
western and eastern Europe in respect of energy
provision and use were a matter of degree,
reflecting first, the generally greater availability
of coal resources in the West and second, the

mainly lower level of development in the East. There were, indeed, almost equally great differences within western Europe (as, for example, between the UK and Portugal) and even between regions within individual countries (as between northern and southern Italy). Post-1945, however, the difference became one of kind as a consequence of the imposition of Soviet-controlled centrally planned economies on the countries of eastern Europe. Over the next 40 years this political split between West and East led to the establishment of radically different energy economies between the two parts of Europe.

In western Europe economic rehabilitation and expansion after the Second World War was initially predicated on the basis of an "energy mixture" input as before the war, but with the anticipated eventual addition of nuclear-based electricity (Jensen, 1967). It is, indeed, significant that the first two European treaties, predating the Treaty of Rome whereby the Common Market of the Six was formed, were concerned with coal (plus steel) and with atomic power. These were the ECSC[1] and the Euratom treaties (Jensen, 1967; Lucas, 1977). In 1952 coal still provided 90 and 95 per cent, respectively, of the UK's and West Germany's primary energy, while in western Europe as a whole oil's share was still only 13 per cent. Among the larger countries, it was only in Italy, poor in coal resources, that oil had made any serious inroads into the industrial and power generation markets by the early 1950s.

Very considerable efforts – and investments – were made to stimulate western Europe's coal production so that the industry just about recovered to its pre-1939 size. In 1955 western Europe's own production of 476 million tonnes of coal, plus another 35 million tonnes of imports (largely from the United States), still supplied over 70 per cent of total energy needs. Thereafter, coal was dethroned by a combination of increasing depletion costs (e.g. through the exploitation of geologically more difficult coal resources) and rapidly rising real labour costs in the context of full employment. The process was quick and continuous as, with increasing speed, the industry lost its share of the then rapidly expanding western European energy market (Jensen, 1967; OEEC, 1960; Parker, 1994).

Meanwhile, there had been continuity in the other main pre-1939 thrust in western Europe's energy sector development, namely the steady growth of electricity use (Jensen, 1967). Networks of supply were expanded and intensified as part of post-war reconstruction so that virtually the whole of the region's population – except in the remote areas – secured access to electricity. In addition, the range of uses for this form of power also steadily expanded in the residential, industrial, commercial and agricultural sectors. By the early 1960s, after three-quarters of a century of slow but continuing development of the industry (Jensen, 1970), electricity finally became the norm across the whole of western Europe, not only for lighting, but also for power and other uses.

In Eastern Europe the adoption of Soviet-style centralised planning, including the maximum possible use of indigenous energy resources and the adaptation of the style of forced industrial-isation which had featured in the USSR's Marxist approach to economic development, brought rapid change in the region's energy situation (Dienes and Shabad, 1979; Park, 1979; Volochin, 1990). On the supply side, this included the expanded output of the region's coal, brown coal and lignite resources, and of what indigenous oil there was. The latter was largely restricted to Romania. In marked contrast with the decline in western Europe, eastern Europe's indigenous energy production by 1960 was 194 million tonnes of oil equivalent (mtoe),[2] over 30 per cent up on that of 1937 (Hoffman, 1985). Though imports – mainly of Soviet oil – did increase, these remained supplementary and largely complementary to national production; and they were not at the expense of indigenous energy resource develop-ment, as was the case with western European oil imports (Park, 1979; Hoffman, 1985).

Subsequent developments

Western Europe

Since the late 1950s the previous long and relatively non-traumatic evolution of western Europe's energy sector has been replaced by a period of highly dynamic and forceful develop-ments in which long-established structures have

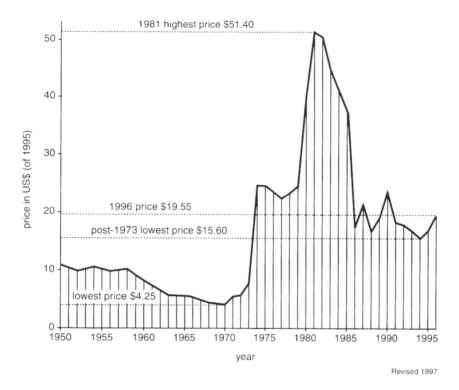

Figure 4.1 *The price of Saudi Arabian light crude, 1950--96 (in $ of 1995)*

been undermined not only by changing internal circumstances but also by the impact of external forces. First, there was a period from 1957 to 1973 in which oil from petroleum-exporting countries elsewhere in the world came to dominate almost the whole of the western European energy system (Jensen, 1970; Odell, 1975). A steadily declining real price for internationally traded oil during this period (Figure 4.1) was the outcome of an increasingly competitive supply system. This enabled oil products to take over residential, industrial and power generation markets from indigenous coal. (Parker, 1993). Simultaneously, specific markets for oil, particularly in the transport sector and in petrochemicals, enjoyed rapid expansion. In 1957 western Europe used only 115 million tonnes of oil (of which 85 per cent was imported). Fifteen years later, in 1972, western Europe's total oil use was over 700 million tonnes, of which all but some 20 million tonnes were imported. By then oil supplied over 65 per cent of the continent's total energy requirement, while coal had been pushed

back into a very poor second place, supplying no more than 22 per cent of the energy market.

Western Europe's ready and willing embrace of cheap oil between 1957 and 1973 was, however, a main factor in stimulating the continent's economy, which grew rapidly at an average annual rate of over 5 per cent for the 17-year period (Prodi and Clô, 1975). At the same time the rising use of oil was influential in changing the geography of western Europe's industry, particularly as it eliminated the energy cost disadvantages of the region's coal-less areas (Jensen, 1970), and also enabled the populations and economic activities of its cities to explode outwards in a welter of dispersal induced by motor transport (Odell, 1976).

Until 1973 there seemed to be no reason why these processes should not continue. Thus, most forecasts until then indicated continued – or even intensified – oil domination of the energy sector. There were confident expectations of 1000 million tonnes of annual oil use – and of oil imports – by western Europe by 1985 (OECD, 1974; Brondel and Morton, 1977); and of the need for over 2000 million tonnes a year by 2000 (Beale, 1972), with all that such volumes implied in terms of the proliferation of import terminals, refineries, petrochemical installations, and oil transport and distribution systems across the face of the continent. The dynamics of a development which had started in the late 1950s seemed to have become powerful enough to make the use of rapidly increasing volumes of oil western Europe over the rest of the century a near-certain prospect (Odell, 1976).

The dynamic of Europe's oil developments in particular, and the rapid expansion of the western European energy economy in general, were, however, halted virtually in their tracks by events in the international oil industry and market in 1973: by what has since become known as the first oil price shock, whereby the price of internationally traded oil increased in a matter of months by a factor of four (Ray, 1976). This was followed by a second oil price shock at the end of the decade, whereby the oil price again more than doubled. Thus, by 1981 crude oil delivered to western European refineries was over an order of magnitude more expensive (in real terms, after allowing for inflation) than it had been a decade earlier (Figure 4.1). This traumatic development not only helped to put the European economic system into recession, but also created gross uncertainty and a deep lack of confidence concerning future prospects. Moreover, the general perception at that time was of yet worse to come with respect to the price of oil (Manne and Schrattenholzer, 1984). There were, indeed, widely accepted forecasts that oil would, in the relatively short-term future, rise to $50, $60 or even $100 per barrel (compared with about $35 in 1981) and thus generate yet further adverse macro-economic effects in the western European economic and societal system.

The earlier expectations of a continued rapid growth in oil use were, of course, largely undermined by the massive rise in the price of the commodity. In response energy sector policies were introduced which deliberately sought to minimise oil use in favour of alternative energy sources (EEC, 1974; Taylor and Davey, 1984). Thus, growth in oil use first slowed down and then ceased. Post-1979 oil demand declined

sharply, while energy demand in general also turned down. By 1985 western Europe's energy use was somewhat less than it had been in 1973, and the contribution of oil to total energy supply had fallen back to only about 50 per cent compared with its contribution of almost two-thirds of the total only a decade earlier. Oil use declined in absolute terms from 750 million tonnes to only a little over 500 million tonnes, instead of continuing to grow as had been expected (Weyman-Jones, 1986). Nevertheless, in spite of this large reduction in consumption, there still remained a powerful perception of potential supply-side difficulties with this source of energy (EEC, 1974). Thus, there was an expectation of medium-term economic and other problems arising from the continued relatively high degree of dependence on imported oil – 80 per cent of which came from the member countries of OPEC, with this grouping's Middle East members supplying the lion's share. For the long term there was a widely held perception that global supplies of oil were approaching (or had even passed) their peak, so that competition for future limited supplies would become increasingly intense (British Petroleum, 1979). These powerful perceptions (though not based on a reasonable interpretation of the facts) encouraged energy conservation. Additionally – and increasingly – there was also another motivation for giving greater attention to the efficient use of energy, namely concern for the environmental impact of both the production and use of energy (European Environment Bureau, 1981; EEC, 1985).

As a result of these various factors the demand for energy over much of western Europe more or less stabilised at the level it reached in the late 1970s. The rapidly increasing concern for environmental impact questions has not, however, yet led to declining energy consumption, mainly because such concern has not stopped a continuing expansion in the most polluting sector of the economy, namely the use of private motor transport. Electricity demand has also continued to grow, largely as a result of the technical development of a range of new uses, notably in electronics. Nevertheless, contrary to the earlier widely held expectation, energy supply-side constraints on western Europe's prospects will be of little or no significance until well into the twenty-first century. Instead, choices between energy alternatives and supply sources will be of the essence over the next 25 years (Odell, 1995). This has implications not only for the future prospects of both traditional and newly developed indigenous energy resources, but also for western Europe's geo-economic and geopolitical relationships with the regions which supply its energy. Concurrently, under the stimulus of technological changes and of increased competition between energy suppliers, there are likely to be important organisational consequences for western Europe's energy industries over the next decade (Surrey 1990; Pouwels 1994; Mitchell, 1996). This will partly be the result of the Single European Act and its requirement for liberalisation.

Eastern Europe

For eastern Europe the process of increasingly energy-intensive economic expansion continued uninterruptedly through the 1970s, under the pressures of Soviet-style developments and in spite of severe limitations on the growth of private road transport. This region was, moreover, only marginally affected by the international oil price shock and its repercussions, because of the near-complete separation of the Western and Soviet economic systems (Hoffman, 1985). The latter was effectively insulated against the inflation of international oil prices, so that most energy in eastern Europe remained very low cost – and also, as a result, very inefficiently used. This applied as much to indigenous coal and lignite produced in Poland, East Germany and Czechoslovakia, etc. as to the oil and gas imported from the Soviet Union. Thus between 1973 and 1982 the use of energy in eastern Europe grew from 330 to 415 mtoe. As a result its total energy consumption rose to only a little under 40 per cent of western Europe's, even though the East's economy was less than 20 per cent of the West's, and car ownership was under 10 per cent of the western level (Hoffman, 1985).

Eastern Europe's energy use finally peaked in the mid-1980s, by which time the inefficiencies in use and the underpricing of energy were just being recognised. Thereafter, the renegotiation of

Soviet oil and gas prices led to significant price rises, and thus to the beginning of economic problems relating to energy and to an enhanced interest in energy conservation. The question of the degree and speed with which the eastern European centrally planned economies would or could have reacted to this challenge was raised because of the ingrained nature of the characteristics of energy supply and use patterns under Soviet-style central planning. These issues, however, were quickly overtaken by much more dramatic events, namely those leading to the collapse of the politico-economic systems of all the eastern European countries and their substitution by market-orientated regimes. In this process of radical adjustment the economies suffered severe recession, a significant range of activities were sharply reduced in size – or in some instances even closed down – and standards of living were adversely affected. As a consequence energy use fell sharply. From the peak of over 400 mtoe in 1986, it declined to 340 mtoe in 1990, to 269 mtoe by 1994, and to 252 mtoe in 1996.

Paradoxically, the falling use of energy has in many of the countries been accompanied by energy scarcity – particularly of electricity – arising in part from the disruption to organisational and infrastructure systems, but also from the difficulties in maintaining supplies of costly foreign exchange imports. These include oil and gas from Russia which, following its political storm in 1991, cancelled all the former favourable Soviet energy supply contracts with eastern Europe and began to price its energy exports at internationally orientated prices. Internally, the energy supply industries have suffered, first, from problems of sustaining production in the context of disorder and a lack of investment and, second, from problems of marketing their output in weak economies lacking purchasing power. Since 1988 total energy output has declined by almost 40 per cent, from 286 mtoe to under 180 mtoe. Coal overall, but most especially in Poland, has declined most emphatically in the context of an industry which was inherently uneconomic, as effective Western accounting methods have revealed (Coopers and Lybrand, 1991).

Needless to say, in the mid-1990s – less than 10 years on from the fundamental break with the previous 50 years' history of energy development in eastern Europe – the process of readjustment continues. The outlook remains highly uncertain, depending as it largely does on the speed and effectiveness of implementing Western-style approaches to both production and consumption decisions. These prospects, and the likelihood of integrating eastern Europe's energy systems with those of the rest of the continent, will be considered in the last part of this chapter.

Western Europe's Energy Resources: an "Embarras de Richesse"

Indigenous oil and gas

One of the important results of the two oil price shocks, and the associated deterioration in the security of supply of western Europe's almost entirely imported oil needs, was the stimulus given to the indigenous production of hydrocarbons (oil and gas). In 1967 the total western European production of natural gas and oil was a mere 40 mtoe. This came partly from a number of scattered and only locally important production centres in West Germany, Italy and France, partly from the initial exploitation of a new gas field in the Netherlands (the Slochteren field, later to be renamed the Groningen field) and partly from the first gas fields discovered in the southern sector of the UK's part of the offshore North Sea province (Figure 4.2). By 1972 gas production by the Netherlands and the UK had already grown significantly but, even so, total western European hydrocarbon output was still only 130 mtoe. This was equal to no more than 11 per cent of western Europe's energy use and was still much less than the already declining annual output of coal and lignite in western Europe. In 1972 this stood at 230 mtoe.

The North Sea basin

Moreover, even among those who were aware of the geological significance of the Groningen and North Sea finds of gas and oil – in terms, that is, of what they indicated about the potentially petroliferous nature of the North Sea basin stretching northward along the axis of the North Sea from Groningen to the latitude of the Shetland Islands (Figure 4.2) – there was a continuing tendency to discount the importance of the early finds (Chapman, 1976, 184–8). The potential for North Sea basin oil and gas was, indeed, generally portrayed as very limited. At best, it was widely argued, it could be the means whereby western Europe's incremental demand for oil and gas might be met for some years, but it would certainly not be a phenomenon which would enable large volumes of the then high and growing level of energy imports to western Europe to be substituted (Odell, 1973).

However, the enhanced motivation for oil and gas exploration that was generated by the international oil price shocks of the 1970s soon showed that the North Sea basin was a large, complex and potentially highly productive hydrocarbon province, the ultimate resources of which would take decades, rather than years, to be revealed in their entirety, even if there were a continuing exploration effort in all the national sectors (Figure 4.3). On the basis of the limited data available by the mid-1970s it was possible, with the help of a simulation study (Odell and Rosing, 1974), to indicate a 90 per cent probability of almost 11 000 mtoe of recoverable reserves, and a 50 per cent probability of reserves of more than 15 000 mtoe. Though the results of that study were generally disbelieved it is, nevertheless, proving to be a reasonable statement of the ultimate prospects. By the end of 1995 the hydrocarbon reserves already discovered totalled more than 14 000 mtoe – counting only the reserves of the fields already in production, in development, or for which an indication of development potential has been made by the companies concerned. There are additional, but still unknown, volumes of reserves in the many other fields which have been discovered, but for which development plans have not yet been announced (Nicholson, 1982; Norwegian Petroleum Directorate, 1993; UKOOA, 1996). Meanwhile, over 30 years on from the first North Sea discoveries, a continuing exploration effort for additional fields is still giving a high success rate, when measured against international norms (Department of Trade and Industry, 1996; Ministerie van

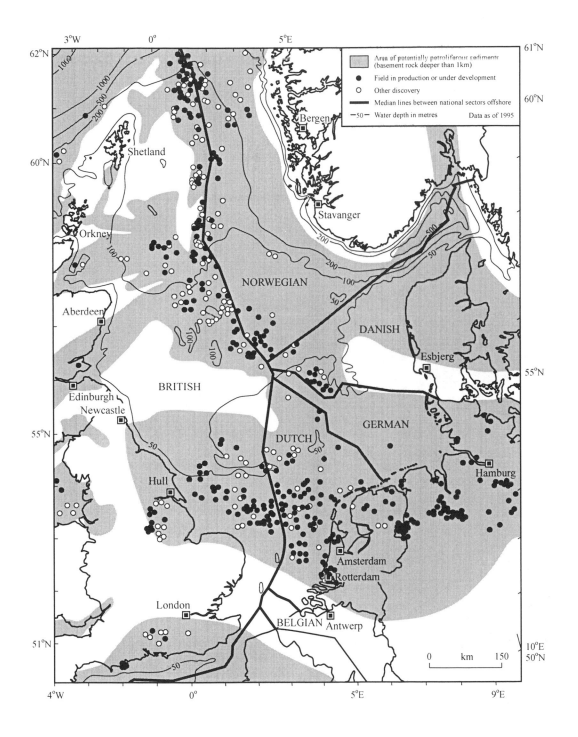

Figure 4.2 *Oil and gas fields and discoveries to December 1995*

Figure 4.3 *Production platform operating in BP's Magnus oil field, north-east of Shetland. Exploration and exploitation in deeper northern waters contributed graetly to known reserves and production. (Photo: BP PLC)*

Economische Zaken, 1996; Ministry of Industry and Energy, 1996). The average size of new fields is not, moreover, falling away as quickly as had been generally expected. There is thus a high probability that significant additional reserves will continue to be discovered for many years into the future (Odell, 1996a).

Simultaneously, the phenomenon of the "appreciation" (that is, the periodic upgrading of estimates of the declared reserves of fields which are in production) continues, so that output from most of these fields will go on for longer than was anticipated in earlier evaluations of their potential (County Nat West Wood-Mac, 1988; Odell, 1996a). One prime example of this appreciation process is the case of the Dutch Groningen gas field. Four years after its discovery, at the time of initial gas production in 1963, its recoverable reserves were declared as 1125×10^9 cu. m of gas (Odell, 1969). Since then more than 1500×10^9 cu. m of gas have been produced from the field, but the reserves which still remain to be recovered are now declared at almost another 1500×10^9 cu. m. Thus, compared with the 1963 figure, the latest estimate of the original recoverable reserves (3000×10^9 cu. m) has appreciated by over 265 per cent – and the process is not yet complete (Ministerie van Economische Zaken, 1996). Similarly, the first 13 oil fields brought into production in the British sector of the North Sea (prior to 1980) had initial declared reserves totalling 1072 million tonnes. Collectively, however, they had already produced over 1380 million tonnes by 1995 and the exploiting companies currently indicate that at least another 200 million tonnes remain to be recovered (Department of Trade and Industry, 1996). And, once again, it seems unlikely that the process of appreciation has fully run its course. Elsewhere in the oil world the phenomenon of appreciation of oil reserves has been noted as occurring over a minimum of 20 years (Halbouty, 1970; Energy Resources Conservation Board, 1971; Adelman, 1987, 1993). It would thus be surprising if the recoverable reserves of this set of fields does not eventually turn out to be at least double those that were originally declared, so that production will be sustained for much longer than originally expected and planned (Odell, 1996a).

The complexity of hydrocarbon development decisions

The continuity of the discovery of oil and gas reserves and of their production is, of course, dependent on very much more than the mere presence of resources. This is the case even though the first essential part of the development process is establishing the facts of their existence, and achieving recognition of their producibility (not only by governments, which make the decisions on granting concessions and production licences, but also by the companies whose investment funds have to be committed). In addition, there has to be evidence that adequate overall profitability can be secured from the volumes which can be produced (Robinson and Morgan, 1978). This is a prospect which depends on appropriate technology, markets, prices and tax regimes (Roland and Hann, 1987). These variables are individually difficult to evaluate, and collectively they constitute a complex background to the development decision-taking task for the companies concerned, especially as they are all subject to significant changes in value over time (Anderson, 1993).

For the development of a supply of North Sea hydrocarbons, in the heart of an energy-intensive industrial Europe, markets may perhaps be assumed; though even here, as will be shown below, in what is generally an open energy market, competition from alternative supplies in a period of easy supply/demand relationships cannot be excluded. The required technological inputs may also be assumed, especially given the high degree to which the technology of offshore oil and gas has been developed in western Europe (Lewis and McNicol, 1978; UKOOA, 1996). And, after a period in which European governments wrongly assumed that oil and gas production activities provided a "golden goose" phenomenon in respect of guaranteed high tax revenues (Kemp and Rose, 1984), there is now a general recognition that taxes can only be collected when an economic rent (i.e. a supernormal profit) can be earned on a project. The achievement of such rent depends, of course, on the market price of the product and thus, in an open economy such as western Europe, on the international price of energy in general, and of

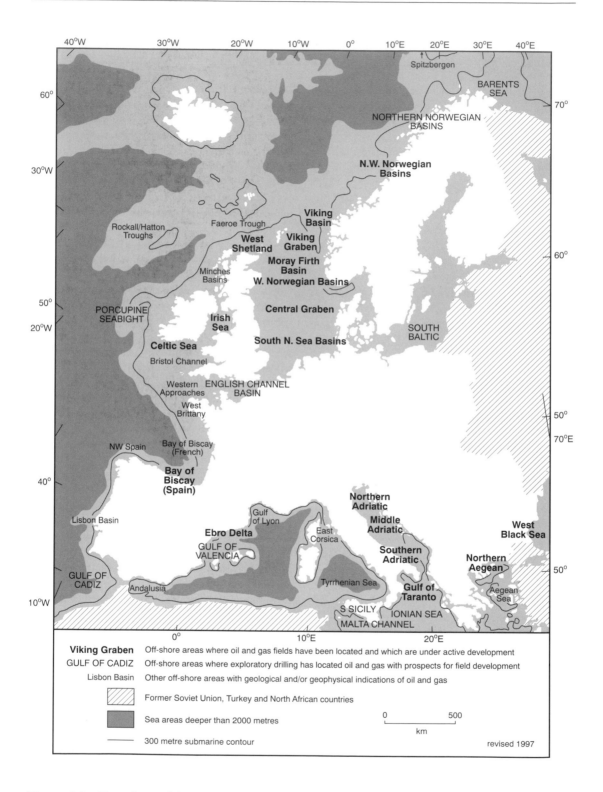

Figure 4.4   *Europe's petroliferous and potentially petroliferous offshore areas*

oil in particular. Earlier widely held expectations of continuing high, and even still rising, prices for oil have now been shown to be wrong (Figure 4.1) and replaced by the recognition that – for the rest of the century and beyond – prices will continue to be very much, lower than those of the late 1970s and early 1980s (Odell, 1991; Adelman, 1995).

Such uncertainty over price has, of course, raised doubts over the economic viability of continued oil and gas exploitation offshore in north-western Europe. Costs, however, have also declined significantly in real terms as a result of improved technology in both exploration and production activities (UKOOA, 1996). This phenomenon, together with the continuing adjustment of tax regimes so that post-tax returns on the oil companies' investments remain attractive, means that there is not likely to be much price-imposed constraint on potential western European oil production levels for the remainder of the century. Problems would arise only if international oil prices were to collapse to under $10 per barrel. Indeed, except in the event of such a price collapse, it now even seems less likely than just a few years ago that lower prices will slow down the geographical extension of oil and gas exploration and exploitation into other areas which show hydrocarbon potential around the coast of western Europe. As is demonstrated by current activity in Arctic waters to the north of Norway and in the deeper waters to the west of the British Isles – including Ireland – offshore technological developments are quickly pushing back the frontiers of hydrocarbon exploitation potential (Figure 4.4).

Coal resources: plentiful but uneconomic

In contrast with the continuing prospects for the further significant expansion of the region's oil and gas production, little of the rump which remains of western Europe's formerly widespread and productive deep-mined coal industry can be profitably exploited under existing or prospective cost, price and technological conditions (Manners, 1981; Gordon, 1987). Coal production has fallen year by year since 1986, following a decade of stability during the period of high oil prices, in spite of formal guarantees of markets

and/or continuing production-cost subsidies (Parker, 1993, 1994). The already long-employed alternative of using inherently lower-cost internationally traded coal from competing overseas suppliers has thus become increasingly attractive, not only for coal consumers, but also from the standpoint of national economic considerations. Until the mid-1980s, when concern for the environmental problems of coal use was at a lower level, there had been strong official encouragement for increased use of coal – related to the widely held (though erroneous) belief that hydrocarbons were inherently scarce. Thus energy policies were often orientated to their replacement by coal (EEC, 1974) and it was anticipated that imports would supplement a slowly growing availability of indigenous production. Now that the "belief" in hydrocarbon scarcity has been largely discounted, and as it is also generally accepted that oil and gas prices will not return to the early 1980s levels, greatly enhanced concern for the environmental dangers of burning coal (Schumacher, 1985) has enabled less emphasis to be given to encouraging its use. Thus, there is not only less encouragement for imports, but also a much-reduced willingness by governments – and the EU – to subsidise indigenous coal production. Consequently the share of coal in western Europe's energy supply seems set to fall even further from its 1996 contribution of only 17 per cent (British Petroleum, 1996). Until technology is developed such that the energy from deep coal resources in western Europe can be economically recovered as gas produced by underground combustion, most of the region's remaining millions of tonnes of coal will remain unutilised *in situ*.

Eastern Europe's Energy Resources: Over- and Under-exploitation

As already indicated above, the Eastern European centrally planned approach to energy use led to high inputs in highly inefficient modes. This energy-intensive process of development reflected the Soviet Union's own very large energy resource base, on which all east European countries came heavily to depend in the context of the integration of their economies with that of the

Soviet Union through Comecon (Park, 1979). Nevertheless, limitations on Soviet/east European exchange, and the strong national policies encouraging indigenous resource use, both meant that each east European country also sought the accelerated and maximum possible development of whatever energy resources it had to hand. Energy production potential within eastern Europe was thus exploited without much consideration of either economics or environmental issues (Hoffman, 1985).

Unhappily, eastern Europe's oil and gas prospects were viewed as extremely limited and, in competition with demands from the coal and lignite industry and from nuclear power, this branch of the sector's possible expansion was starved of funds (Hoffman, 1985). Moreover, the Soviet Union discouraged hydrocarbon developments among its allies (except Romania) in order to ensure it sustained its ability to export oil and gas to east Europe – given the absence of alternative acceptable exports in sufficient volume and value. Even the Romanian oil industry – dating back to the nineteenth century – was starved of investment and new technology, so that its output peaked as early as 1976 (Park, 1979). Thereafter, the country struggled to slow down the rate of production decline, but with little success. Production of oil is now little more than one-third of its peak level, while natural gas output halved between 1976 and the fall of Romania's centrally planned system.

In contrast, eastern Europe's coal industry has survived to a much greater extent than that of western Europe. By the early 1960s the latter's coal industry was already over the top, whereas that of eastern Europe then started to go through a period of rapid expansion (Hoffman, 1985). This took production above that of western Europe in 1980 and thereafter the industry continued to grow, albeit more slowly, for almost another decade – until 1988.[3] Its evolution was based on the centrally planned systems' "need" for energy, expressed essentially in volumetric, rather than economic, terms. Thus, by 1982, when coal and lignite output was approaching its peak, the six countries had a total production of 358 million tonnes coal equivalent, over 76 per cent of the total energy output of the region. This was

achieved in spite of difficult and worsening geological conditions, the exploitation of deeper horizons for deep-mined coal and increasing ratios of overburden to accessible reserves in the lignite/opencast coal industry. In addition, there was also a general fall in quality of product, while access to new supplies required the relocation of rivers, transport facilities and even villages and towns (Hoffman, 1985). Such development requirements not only seriously increased costs, but also led to deteriorating environmental conditions associated with mining and the use of such heavily polluting sources of energy. In brief, the solid fuel industry in eastern Europe continued to provide the lion's share of total energy required to keep the region's economies expanding – and there were physical resources enough to sustain the policy objective. However, in both economic and environmental terms, coal and lignite production and use increasingly imposed costs on the countries concerned, so that even before the change from the centrally planned systems, there were doubts as to the continuing wisdom of persisting with the policy of maximising the use of solid fuels (Hoffman, 1985).

This was one of the two main reasons which led all the east European countries (except Poland) to decide to build nuclear power stations. The second was the special relationship with the USSR, from which the nuclear technology and the know-how originated (Mounfield, 1991). Such nuclear developments (eventually totalling 30 reactors with a capacity of about 25 GW) supplemented the previously very high dependence on coal for power generation and so provided some help in the increasingly desperate attempt by the eastern European countries to sustain the high rate of increase in the use of electricity. In the process, output was priced, of course, at rates which did not reflect the scarcity inherent to the situation, but rather the Leninist philosophy of "socialism plus electricity equals communism!" (Lenin, 1966). However, the environmental impact of the Chernobyl accident in 1986 eventually led to a re-evaluation of the safety and other features of the Soviet-designed nuclear stations in eastern Europe and, after the political changes throughout the region, to even stronger reactions against the expansion of nuclear power. As in most of western Europe, so now in the east: nuclear power is on hold (Mounfield, 1991).

The new post-Communist regimes in eastern Europe have thus inherited a set of problems relating to the exploitation and use of energy resources that are as serious as those in any other sector of the new democratised countries; and they are certainly more difficult to resolve than the energy sector issues in western Europe at the beginning of the 1990s. The regional economic and social problems arising from the enforced run-down of the coal industries of east Europe have had their precursors in the West and, as their persistence in the West has shown, they will take decades to resolve properly. This is especially the case because they are, to a much greater degree than in western Europe, bound up with problems of environmental degradation and poor living conditions, to an extent which makes the former mining areas very unattractive for alternative activities. Coal still provides over 50 per cent of eastern Europe's total energy, but its contribution will continue to fall as the region adjusts to its sources of energy in the new environment of increasingly deregulated and privatised markets.

In contrast the use of oil, which fell in the aftermath of the political changes, seems now to have bottomed out under the influence of its rising use in transportation, as private cars and trucks become more widely owned in the changing societies. In similar fashion, although gas use also fell in the aftermath of change, it is now a preferred fuel for both economic and environmental reasons and its use is again increasing (Estrada *et al.*, 1995). In this case, the dynamics of the industry are such that it seems likely to expand quickly in ways which closely parallel those of only a few years previously in western Europe.

The future of electricity depends, first, on the speed at which per capita income increases and engenders demand through the more intensive electrification of households; and, second, on the evolution of a supply system which is reliable, economically attractive and capable of expansion in an environmentally acceptable and safe way. This seems more likely to emerge through the use of natural gas as the prime mover, rather than

through a resurgence of coal and/or the expansion of nuclear power (Stern, 1995; Estrada *et al.*, 1995).

Overall, eastern Europe's energy economy will grow steadily to resemble that of western Europe, so that the issues of resources and choices will become increasingly similar through the rest of the 1990s. By the year 2000 there seem likely to be far less significant East–West disparities than have existed for several decades. This convergence in the character of the energy sectors of eastern and western Europe in turn means that, in the rest of this chapter, Europe (up to the western boundary of the Former Soviet Union) can be treated as a whole.

Competition between External Suppliers for Europe's Markets

Import options

Within the context of a now-expected limited expansion of Europe's energy demand (as argued above), and given the continuing availability of indigenous energy in significant volumes (at more than 1000 mtoe a year, equal to about 60 per cent of total energy use in Europe in 1996), it is evident that potential exporters of energy to Europe will be obliged to compete for the markets available. Indeed, Europe has a greater number of options in respect of its now relatively limited energy import needs than is generally indicated in official forecasts (IEA, 1996; European Commission, 1996). The choice between the options is, however, of high-level geopolitical significance, and thus carries implications for Europe's external policies well beyond energy supply and supply security considerations alone (Odell, 1995; Mitchell, 1996). Apart from a wide choice of potential suppliers of imported coal – from which relatively small volumes are purchased to complement or to substitute indigenous production – the import options for oil and natural gas cover three large-scale supplying regions: North Africa, the Middle East and the former Soviet Union. With all three of these Europe needs, for one reason or another, to maintain close trading and economic relations (Odell 1996b).

79

Mediterranean basin prospects

In the 1980s, with the expansion of the European Union (EU) to include Portugal, Spain and Greece the centre of gravity of the Community's interests shifted southwards, so heightening the importance of the Mediterranean basin's affairs. These, of course, involve trans-Mediterranean relationships between the European countries on the northern side of the sea and the North African Arab nations on the southern side. Three of the latter (Egypt, Libya and Algeria) depend mainly, or in important part, on their exports of energy for their foreign exchange earnings, and some formal arrangements in respect of energy trade with their close European neighbours on the north side of the basin are already in place. These include the gas pipelines from Algeria to Italy and Spain (Figure 4.5) through both of which supplies have been contracted for 25 years (Stern, 1984, 1990, 1995; Estrada *et al.*, 1988, 1995); and also specific Libyan/Italian oil supply arrangements, including Libyan interests in the refining industry in Italy. In theory, the hydrocarbon resources of North Africa could supply much of Europe's medium-term energy import needs, while European markets constitute the only ones in which North African oil and gas have a transport cost advantage over supplies from elsewhere. In spite of current political difficulties, the mutual benefits from the development of European/North African energy interests seem likely to become increasingly important in the coming decade. A proposed gas line from Egypt to south-east Europe will be particularly significant in this respect, and there may also be a direct gas (and oil) pipeline from Libya to Italy and the Balkans. Expanded Mediterranean basin interdependence in the energy field thus provides an attractive option in both the short and medium terms.

Imports from the Middle East

The oil- and gas-rich countries of the Middle East proper (around the Persian or Arabian Gulf) are geographically more distant, but in terms of general historical, cultural and political contacts, as well as specific oil interests going back to the early part of the century, there exists a powerful relationship with a number of European countries (Schurr and Homan, 1971; Shwadran, 1977; Yorke and Turner, 1986). Recent western European energy policies, with their central emphasis on minimising dependence on oil – and especially dependence on oil imports, most of which in the 25 years of rapid demand growth from 1948 to 1973 originated from the oil-exporting countries of the Middle East – were at odds with this background. Nevertheless, EU/Middle East relationships in respect of oil have recovered markedly from their low point at the time of the Arab/Israeli War of 1973, when there was an Arab embargo on oil supplies to the Netherlands and the threat of reduced supplies for all other countries (Turner, 1978).

EU/GCC (Gulf Co-operation Council) and EU/OAPEC (Organisation of Arab Petroleum Exporting Countries) discussions on economic matters are well established and have already led to compromises on the perceived threat to Europe's refining and petrochemicals from the newly developed facilities in the Middle East oil- and gas-producing countries (EEC, 1988). Meanwhile, all the European-based oil companies have reached agreements over the valuation of their assets expropriated by Iran and other Middle East countries (in contrast with the pursuit of what appeared to be unrealistic claims for compensation by many US oil companies). Subsequently, Saudi Arabia and, even more noticeably, Kuwait have invested in downstream oil activities in a number of western European countries.

Meanwhile, oil transport links from the Middle East that are orientated to serving western European markets have been strengthened in recent years by the construction of new pipelines from the main oil-producing areas of the Gulf to, first, the eastern Mediterranean coast and, second, newly developed export terminals on the north-eastern coast of the Red Sea (*Petroleum Economist*, 1984). Such routes, specifically dedicated to securing and easing the oil supply routes to Europe, have served to reduce European importers' perception of the dangers of dependence on oil shipped from the Gulf, though from 1991 to 1996 the pipelines

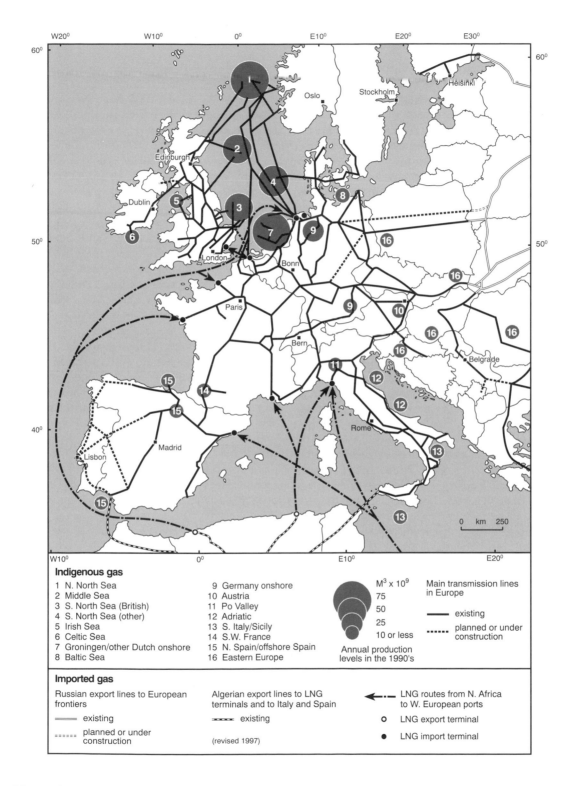

Figure 4.5 *Europe's gas production in the 1990s and the principal transmission lines for indigenous and imported gas*

from Iraq through Turkey were blocked as a result of the Gulf War.

The key countries in the further development of Euro-Middle East contacts are Egypt and Turkey, and it is not without significance that both have indicated a wish to be more closely associated with the EU. Membership seems out of the question as far as Egypt is concerned, but its wishes for closer relations with Europe can, nevertheless, be appropriately developed in its context as one of the Mediterranean basin countries with hydrocarbon resources (as discussed above). Turkey, on the other hand, has already submitted an application for membership of the EU and, though its accession will not be a near-future development, it could well become a formal associate before the end of the century. It thus has a strong and heightening motivation to enhance its role as the country through which Gulf oil and gas are transported to Europe. Such a development would assist its own economic growth and consolidate its relationship with the EU. Its role in this function would be particularly important – indeed, the critical component – in enabling natural gas from the extensive resources of the Middle East (notably from Qatar and Iran) to be piped to Europe. Turkey could thus make itself central to the potential expansion of the Middle East/Europe hydrocarbon trade. Moreover, from the European importers' viewpoint, Turkey's membership of the EU would take "Europe" right up to the frontiers of the world's main oil-producing region – both currently and for the foreseeable future – so helping to reduce the present strong perception of the inherent insecurity of supplies from the Middle East. For the Middle East oil and gas exporters, Europe – and especially eastern Europe – would become a "near neighbour", giving possibilities for the Middle East countries to increase their share of these markets. This would be at the expense of Russia, which currently dominates the energy trade of its former allies. Such a development would, in turn, help to undermine the validity of the "minimum Middle East" oil policies of the EU, whereby prospects for the oil exporters have been – and currently remain – so adversely affected; and it would also help to secure Middle East gas economically in other parts of Europe.

The Russian option

The large oil, and very large natural gas, resources of the former Soviet Union (FSU) (Dienes and Shabad, 1979; Jensen, 1983) have for a long time provided energy supplies to Europe. Both fuels have been marketed in large volumes and with exclusive rights in the economies of the FSU's former east European allies, but have also been sold to most western European countries in competition with other supplies, and in spite of political hostility. This export of oil and gas to the West was important as, in order to achieve a more efficient, productive and acceptable economic system, the Soviet Union needed to import large volumes of consumer, capital and investment goods and services. The only means it had to pay for these requirements (apart from borrowing) was by the export of large volumes of oil and natural gas (Stern, 1984; Odell, 1987; Estrada *et al.*, 1988). The only possible markets for these exports were in western Europe, from which a wide range of manufactured goods and services could be offered in return. The economic bargain struck between the USSR and the western European countries involved (notably) Germany, France and Italy and was thus a powerful one, with large potential benefits to both sides. It therefore appeared to override the hitherto well-rehearsed arguments in the West of strategic dangers from reliance on Soviet energy supplies (Maull, 1981; Adamson, 1985; Manne *et al.*, 1986), which involved broad geopolitical issues. One of the most important of these arose from the fact that the gas involved had to flow through eastern Europe, the economies of which the Soviet Union could no longer afford to sustain. Arguably, the oil-and-gas-for-goods-and-services bargain diverted the USSR's attention from its satellites, loosening ties with them and allowing them to become more closely involved with the rest of Europe. This political aspect of the large-scale Soviet oil and gas link with western Europe thus could have been even more fundamental than the purely economic considerations. Certainly, the combined economic and political changes, which were in part set in train by western Europe's willingness to import large volumes of Soviet oil and gas, led to a geopolitical change of fundamental importance, namely the detachment of the countries of eastern Europe from their alliance with the Soviet Union and, thereafter, the break-up of the USSR itself into its component national parts and their decisions to move towards democratic, market-orientated systems.

As already shown above, Russia's energy exports to eastern Europe have declined sharply since 1989, to the convenience of both parties. The eastern European countries' economies require reduced volumes of energy and are not able or willing to pay international prices for Russian supplies, preferring instead diversification from their previous near-complete dependence on Russian (Soviet) oil and gas. Russia, for its part, prefers to sell the reduced volumes of oil and gas available from its declining production to western Europe, for which payment at international prices is no problem (Stern, 1995).

Meanwhile, Western oil and gas companies have made tentative investments in Russian production prospects, in the rehabilitation of old fields and in the country's pipeline networks. Similarly they are investing in the oil and gas industries of other former Soviet republics, namely Azerbaijan, Kazakhstan and Turkmenistan. By the end of the century additional flows of oil and gas emanating from these Western enterprises in the FSU will be available to European customers, although the potential scale of the availability remains in doubt. This uncertainty in part reflects the fact that the international industry still has to get to grips with the realities of the Russian prospects. Currently there is pessimism on oil, but this may prove to be exaggerated, especially if the Russian/Ukrainian theory of a primeval (rather than biogenic) source for most hydrocarbons converts the sceptics in the Western world (Kenney, 1996). For natural gas the prospects are not disputed, but there are doubts concerning, first, the degree to which European markets can be connected into the potential supply system and, second, the amount of gas from Russia and other former Soviet republics that can be marketed in Europe (Stern, 1995; Odell, 1996b).

On the demand side, Russian oil and gas will no longer face the political limitations which inhibited their export to western Europe in the period to 1990. Instead, new limitations will be set by competition from other suppliers. The

opportunities in this new environment do, however, seem likely to generate exports additional to those already secured, purely on economic grounds in a competitive market. Moreover, Russian oil and gas – delivered through pipelines across the continent and thus safe from externally generated threats – may come to be viewed as more secure than most alternatives. This will be especially important if Western companies are successful in their upstream operations in Russia and other FSU states, and thus offer supplies in the context of their own integrated systems. Beyond this, the application of measures for encouraging development and trade between Europe and Russia under the terms of the European Energy Charter will also stimulate Russian oil and gas exports (Estrada *et al.*, 1995).

By contrast, eastern Europe, with its newly acquired independence, seems more likely to choose to diversify away from its previous overwhelming energy supply ties with Russia. Thus the latter's share of the east European oil and gas markets will fall to significantly lower levels; an adverse development for Russia even though, eventually, it may be offset by the region's increased demand for oil and gas at the expense of coal, lignite and nuclear power. For natural gas, part of this east European switch away from Russian supplies will be a result of gas flows from western Europe (notably Norway and the Netherlands) as closer integration is achieved between the energy systems of the hitherto strongly divided parts of the continent (Odell, 1996b).

Institutional and Technological Aspects of Europe's Energy Outlook

The impact of changes in the European political system

The changed energy demand outlook, and the wide range of options which now exists for supplying Europe's energy, together represent a significant challenge. The dynamics of the continent's energy sector will, however, be yet further intensified over the coming years by both political/legal changes within Europe itself and by technological developments which affect energy supply and demand. The impact of the latter will, moreover, be heightened in the more competitive environment which most of the political/legal changes are designed to create. These changes are arising not only from the creation of the EU and its geographical expansion, but also from various national moves to denationalise and/or to deregulate industries which have traditionally been in the public sector and thus subject to strong political control.

Reduced protection for coal

Most of the remaining European coal industry falls into this category. As shown previously, most of the industry which has survived competition from oil and gas has done so as a result of direct or indirect state support, usually in the context of state ownership in western as well as eastern Europe. Unhappily, no technological breakthroughs appear to be in sight for the European coal industry (such as the underground gasification of coal) which would help it to survive the increased competition from gas (for which there have been important technological advances, particularly in increasing the efficiency of its use) and from more freely imported and low-cost foreign coal. And an already bad situation and outlook for the remaining elements of Europe's coal industry are made even worse by the developing opposition to the continued use of coal because of its high specific contribution to the atmospheric CO_2 problem and, therefore, its perceived greenhouse effect on the world's climate (Grubb, 1995). Thus, a continuing decline in both coal production and use throughout Europe must be expected, though the process will necessarily be slowed by the social costs associated with reducing coal output in areas where large numbers are still employed by the industry (for example, southern Poland, the Czech Republic and former East Germany).

The reorganisation of the gas and electricity industries

Forthcoming politico-legal and technological changes will be of greatest significance for the future of Europe's gas and electricity industries.

In spite of some inter-European country trade in these commodities, the industries have remained essentially nationally organised and controlled. They have, moreover, often enjoyed a high (and sometimes complete) protection from competition. The advocates of the continuation of this situation argue that both the gas and the electricity industries are "natural monopolies", because of the high levels of fixed investment which go into their transmission, distribution and production systems, and of the long lead times and stability required for their expansion to meet requirements to give continuity of service.

The Single European Act threatens this structure for the member countries of the EU because it raises doubts as to the continued legality of, first, the essentially national monopolistic corporations which have been created, and, second, the current restraints on the trading of gas and electricity within the Community (Cameron, 1995). While few proponents of change in the present organisational structure envisage that competing electricity or gas companies will vie for business among residential and other small users, they do see scope for competition in the large-user market and in the operation of transmission systems – in ways that are not dissimilar from the UK government's privatisation of gas and electricity. Already, the domination of managerial aspirations in achieving technological efficiency has been substituted by economic efficiency objectives arising from competitive market conditions (Ministerie van Economische Zaken, 1995).

Once the changes are introduced it will be difficult to prevent customers from seeking their required supplies from other than the national suppliers. Thus, German industrial users of electricity, currently penalised by high prices created by subsidies to German coal producers may, for example, contract to buy their requirements from Electricité de France; or Dutch industrial users south of the Westerschelde may choose to buy their supplies from the Belgian electricity industry in which there is surplus capacity enabling spare electricity to be sold at prices related to short-run marginal costs. Similarly, in the gas sector, the national or regional monopolies, such as Gaz de France and Ruhrgas, will at the very least be obliged to accept a requirement that they offer so-called "third party access" to their pipelines at prices which reflect the costs involved.[4] Alternatively, other aspiring suppliers of gas will be able to build dedicated lines across the territories covered by the monopolistic organisations which, in effect, currently carve up the European market between them (Estrada *et al.*, 1995). As a result of these forces, the European electricity and gas systems will, on the one hand, become more complex but, on the other, will also become more integrated and offer much greater flexibility to both producers and users. What may also be anticipated is that the new systems will gradually be developed so as to encompass all European countries, both EU and non-EU members.

Technological changes favour gas

Meanwhile, a number of restraints that have served to inhibit the implementation of techno-logical breakthroughs in gas-using technology in Europe (Rogner, 1988) are likely to disappear.

The most important of these by far was the failure to expand gas use in high-efficiency power generation, either through combined-cycle technology, the efficiency of which is almost half as good again as the average 35 per cent efficiency achieved in standard coal and oil-based power stations, or through combined heat and power systems, in which overall thermal efficiencies in excess of 65 per cent can be achieved. In Japan, a 2000 MW natural-gas fuelled combined-cycle power plant has been operational for many years, together with a large number of other somewhat smaller units. By contrast, until very recently the largest combined-cycle power plant in operation anywhere in western Europe was only 230 MW. This represented a lack of interest by the monopolistic gas suppliers, and by the highly centralised, and usually monopolistic, electricity supply companies whose predilection was to build large centralised coal-fired or nuclear power stations, while neglecting the new technologies.

The freeing-up of the electricity and gas supply from monopolistic control in the UK has already produced a new organisational framework within which the cost-savings and the environmental advantages from using gas for combined-cycle

electricity generation have been recognised. This has already led to plans for the construction of 9000 MW of such generation capacity by the year 2000, a significant new development in the nature of the electricity production system which will spread across Europe as monopolies are broken up and markets liberalised. The ultimate result will be a much more geographically dispersed pattern of power production in which generation is brought closer to centres of demand. The long-distance transport element for the energy involved will then become that of the gas input, rather than the electricity output, so delivering energy to final consumers in a way which is much more cost effective and environmentally acceptable than that of the separate gas and electricity systems on which Europe has depended for half a century (Skea, 1988).

Towards competing systems

The politico-legal changes which are diffusing across Europe, together with the developing technico-environmental advantages of gas over coal, nuclear power and – to some degree – oil, will therefore serve to encourage the completion of a comprehensive and more integrated energy system in Europe. In this process natural gas will eventually become the single most important source of energy outside the transport sector, undergoing a rapid expansion of production and use. Meanwhile, national frontiers will become of decreasing significance in determining the pattern of supply. As a result many major consumers will achieve a wider choice of suppliers and the prospect of lower real prices.

Conclusions
The dominance of fossil fuels

Since the end of the Second World War, western Europe's energy system has undergone two dramatic changes. The first was in the 1950s and the 1960s, when imported oil replaced indigenous coal and when there was a continuing rapid rate of increase in energy use. The second was between 1973 and the mid-1980s, when much higher energy prices curbed demand growth to a near-zero rate, and when there was a massive development of western Europe's own oil and gas resources. However, in spite of the traumas associated with these changes, western Europe's present dependence on fossil fuels is very little less than it was in 1945. For 30 years nuclear power has promised much, but its overall contribution to total energy supply is still under 6 per cent (when the electricity produced in nuclear power stations is appropriately measured in terms of its heat value equivalent). Despite the huge long-term investments in its development, it was only in the late 1980s that this form of energy finally became more important than hydro-electricity. The latter, now contributing only 3 per cent to total supply, still remains the only significant source of benign (atmospherically non-polluting) energy in production in Europe. The other benign sources, such as wind, tide and wave power, and the direct use of the sun's energy, continue to contribute only a fraction of 1 per cent of western Europe's energy supply.

The apparent similarity between yesterday's energy sector situation and that of today is, however, superficial. Looking more deeply, there have been important changes in the relative use of the three hydrocarbon fuels in the West, together with developments in their sources of supply. These changes have, moreover, been accompanied by the evolution of energy sector institutional and organisational structure as the "belief" in "bigness", monopolistic centralisation and economies of scale on the supply side (Lovins, 1979) have been increasingly questioned. Centralisation and monopoly were, of course, also the hallmarks of the east European energy systems under the centrally planned regimes. As shown, however, their domination by indigenously produced coal and lignite persisted in the absence of any important openings to competition from imported oil. The limited volumes of oil required were automatically sourced from the Soviet Union and sold at administered prices into a system in which there was no competitive element. This formally controlled pricing process largely protected eastern Europe from the oil price shocks of the 1970s and the 1980s, but out of this rigidity there developed an increasing inability for indigenous coal and lignite to cope with either the demands of the energy system or the cumulative environmental impact of solid fuel production and use. The rigidities of the centrally planned energy system contributed to the failure of the politico-economic system to serve either the needs of the economy or of society and, in the crunch which followed (after 1989), the energy industries suffered from retrenchment in much the same way as the rest of the region's economic activities.

This recent change has led to large falls in energy use overall and to even larger declines in coal consumption. The slowly evolving moves towards relatively more oil and gas use are not unlike those which took place in western Europe up to four decades earlier. There seems little doubt, as eastern European markets continue to be opened up, that solid fuels there too will eventually fall towards the 20 per cent contribution to which they are now limited in western Europe. The lateness of the change to oil and gas domination of the eastern European energy economy seems likely, however, to lead to a relatively much greater role for natural gas far sooner than in western Europe. Modern gas transmission, distribution and consumption technologies will generate a preference for gas over oil in many sectors in which oil first replaced coal in the West, especially as the alternative options now available for gas supply to eastern Europe will make for a highly competitive pricing situation. Additionally, most east European countries have signed deals with experienced west European gas companies for the expansion and extension of natural gas systems and markets (Estrada *et al.*, 1995).

Though there remain major contrasts between west and east European energy systems and structures, these differences are unlikely to persist. Choices between energy sources, the moves towards liberalised and competitive markets, and concerns for the geopolitics of energy supply, will gradually apply equally to both parts of Europe. This will steadily reduce the differences which emerged out of the 40 years of separation under strongly contrasting political and economic systems. Such convergence, implying connectivity motivated mainly by commercial considerations but also by formal policies and structures of the EU and its potential eastern European members, seems likely to be achieved within a generation.

Thus, following the reduction in Germany's high level of support for its coal industry, and the rationalisation of the industry in Poland and the Czech Republic, the European coal industry seems likely to be down to little more than half its present size by 2010. Coal imports will continue to grow, though by no means as rapidly as has been expected and is still widely assumed. This is because increasing concern for environmental issues (or, put another way, the costs of achieving acceptably low pollution levels from coal use) will slow down the expansion of the market for imported coal. Conversely, natural gas will be the major growth element in Europe's energy supply for the foreseeable future – for a *mélange* of reasons. These include this fuel's ease of supply, its environmental advantages compared with other fossil fuels, technological advances and the emergence of a much more open and competitive situation for incorporating gas in a broader range of end uses (Odell, 1988, 1996b). In particular, natural gas use in high-efficiency generating plants will further reduce the level of fuel oil consumption in power stations and industry (especially in southern Europe), and also substitute what would otherwise have been nuclear- and coal-based capacity in most other countries. Soon after the turn of the century natural gas will most likely be Europe's single most important energy source, excluding transport fuels. Thereafter, on the assumption that compressed natural gas (CNG) becomes an accepted alternative automotive fuel within the next decade, natural gas use should replace oil as the overall top source of energy by about 2020. By then, only the most remote parts of Europe and low-populated rural areas will not be connected to the continent-wide, highly reticulated gas transmission and distribution system.

Prospects for alternative energy sources

Alternatives to coal, oil and gas will continue to be modestly developed and will still be dominated by hydroelectricity, for which slow capacity growth will continue. Nuclear power on the other hand seems likely to offer a slow-ly attenuating capacity (Beck, 1994). Its downside risk is, however, high, given that another major accident anywhere in Europe would produce an even stronger anti-nuclear response than did Chernobyl, leading to the cancellation of the few new facilities planned, as well as the closure of many existing stations. An accident in western Europe itself, at one of the stations of the PWR type that constitutes most of the existing capacity, would seem likely to lead to the near-instant close-down of the industry. This would have severe implications for electricity supply in general, but particularly in France and Belgium, which depend on nuclear electricity for, respectively, 70 and 60 per cent of their supplies. Nuclear stations in eastern Europe, meanwhile, will be either refurbished to meet acceptable safety standards, or closed down as alternative gas-fuelled power stations are built.

As for renewable energy sources, there will be continued, albeit modest, expansion of wind-powered generating capacity, and a few large-scale schemes for harnessing tidal or wave power could be under way by the turn of the century. Nevertheless, in spite of formal EU support, as well as national programmes for the promotion of renewable energy source development (EEC, 1987), major contributions to energy supplies from such new systems of power generation will be delayed until well into the twenty-first century, unless there is unequivocal and dramatic evidence in the meantime of a real medium-term threat of climate change from continued growth in the combustion of coal, oil and gas (Keepin and Kats, 1988; Grubb, 1990). Eventually, possibly by mid-century, fusion power and/or the underground gasification of coal may conceivably be competitors for meeting energy demand, especially as the price of oil – and of gas and coal – could by then at last be starting to rise once more towards the levels which were temporarily achieved in the early 1980s. If this happens it will be under the impact of so-called increasing "user costs", i.e. the costs of depleting reserves which might otherwise be saved for the future when they will fetch higher real prices (Adelman, 1993). At least until then, Europe's energy users seem likely to have a ready choice of alternative energy resources available to meet their demands (Odell, 1995).

Future strategic issues

Fundamental decisions seem likely to be required from time to time to determine how the choices of supply, technology and pricing shall be made. This will have to be done in the context of a broad range of economic and political factors which Europe will have to take into account in its relationships and dealings with its main external supplying regions, namely North Africa, the Middle East and Russia (plus other former Soviet republics). It will also be necessary to consider whether it may be appropriate to extend any degree of preference to ensure the production of indigenous oil and gas, the continued exploitation of which may otherwise be thwarted by competition from lower-cost imports (Odel, 1996). Continuing interest in such strategic issues seems highly likely in a world which will remain replete with energy problems of international and inter-regional significance, particularly as – at least until the first quarter of the twenty-first century – Europe will continue to be second only to Japan as the part of the world in which energy is used most intensively. Thus a strategy to limit post-2000 dependence on imported energy to no more than the current degree of "only" 45 per cent could be significant, not only for Europe's economic and political well-being, but also to avoid the need to "bend the knee" to energy-rich nations so as not to jeopardise the continuity of supplies.

Finally, though the environmental issue has not had centre stage over the last few years in the aftermath of the Kyoto Conference Europe may well have to face up to the fact that – through its high per capita energy consumption – it makes a disproportionately high contribution to the world's CO_2 emissions and thus to possible global warming, climatic change and a rising sea level (Grubb, 1990). The rise of this issue as a political imperative would require the whole energy debate in Europe to be reoriented to demand-side questions, compared with the supply-side options presented in this chapter. In particular it would be necessary to question the justification for, and to analyse ways of avoiding, the 20 per cent increase in energy use by 2020 that is currently expected under a "business as usual"

scenario. In that event the challenges of the next decade would be very different from those of the past, and could be even more demanding in terms of policy requirements.

Notes

1. The European Coal and Steel Community. Proposed in 1950 by the French foreign minister, Robert Schuman, it was formally created by the Treaty of Paris and came into existence on 1 August 1952. Its initial members were France, Germany, Italy, the Netherlands, Belgium and Luxembourg.
2. The conversion rates used in oil equivalence calculations are: 1 million tonnes of oil = 1.5 million tonnes of coal; 3.0 million t of lignite; and 1111 billion cu.m of natural gas (British Petroleum, 1996, 37).
3. Between 1982 and 1988, output rose by only another 5 per cent.
4. Organisations such as Ruhrgas, Gaz de France, Distrigaz in Belgium, etc. retain a *de facto* monopoly, not only over gas sold in regions in which they operate, but also over that moving in pipelines across "their territories" from a distant supplier on the one hand, to a distant consumer on the other.

References

Adamson, D M (1985) Soviet gas and European security, *Energy Policy*, **13**(1), 13–26.

Adelman, M A (1987) The economics of the international oil industry, in J Rees and P R Odell (eds) *The International Oil Industry: an interdisciplinary perspective*, Macmillan Press Ltd, London, 22–56.

Adelman, M A (1993) *The Economics of Petroleum Supply*, MIT Press, Cambridge, Mass.

Adelman, M A (1995) *The Genie out of the Bottle: world oil since 1970*, MIT Press, Cambridge, Mass.

Andersen, S S (1993), *The Struggle over North Sea Oil and Gas: government strategies in Denmark, Britain and Norway*, Scandinavian University Press, Oslo.

Beale, N (1972) The energy balance in the year 2000, in *Europe 2000: perspectives for an acceptable future*, Foundation Européene de la Culture, Amsterdam, 30–46.

Beck, P (1994) *Prospects and Strategies for Nuclear Power*, Earthscan Publications Ltd, London.

British Petroleum (1979) *Oil Crisis...Again?* BP Ltd, London.

British Petroleum (1996) *BP Statistical Review of World Energy*, BP, London.

Brondel, G and Morton, N (1977) The European Community: an economic perspective, *Annual Review of Energy*, **2**, 343–64.

Cameron, P (1995) *Gas Regulation in Western Europe*, Financial

Times Business Information, London.

Chapman, K (1976) *North Sea Oil and Gas: a geographical perspective*, David and Charles, Newton Abbott.

Coopers and Lybrand (1991) Energy in Eastern Europe, *Energy Policy*, **19**(9), 813–40.

County Nat West Wood-Mac (1988) *North Sea Report*, Edinburgh.

Department of Trade and Industry (1996) *The Energy Report: oil and gas resources of the United Kingdom*, HMSO, London.

Dienes, L and Shabad, T (1979) *The Soviet Energy System: resource uses policies*, Halsted Press, New York.

Doré, J and de Bauw, R (1995) *The Energy Charter Treaty: origins, aims and prospects*, Royal Institute of International Affairs, London.

Energy Resources Conservation Board (1971) *Reserves of Crude Oil, Gas, Natural Gas Liquids and Sulphur*, Annual Report, Calgary, Alberta.

Estrada, J, Moe, A and Martinsen, K D (1995) *The Development of European Gas Markets: environmental, economic and political perspectives*, Wiley, Chichester.

Estrada, J, Bergesen, H O, Moe, A and Sydnes, A K (1988) *Natural Gas in Europe: markets, organisation and politics*, Pinter Publishers, London.

European Economic Community (1974) Towards a new energy policy strategy for the Community, *Bulletin of the European Communities*, 4, Brussels.

European Economic Community (1985) *Energy in Europe*, **2**, 17–19.

European Economic Community (1987) *Energy in Europe*, **9**, 31–32 and 68–69 (December).

European Economic Community (1988) *Energy in Europe*, **11**, 15–18 (September).

European Commission (1996) European energy to 2020, *Energy in Europe*, Special Issue.

European Environment Bureau (1981) *The Milano Declaration on Energy, Economy and Environment*, Brussels.

Foley, G (1976) *The Energy Question*, Penguin Books, Harmondsworth.

Gordon, R L (1987) *World Coal: economics, policies and prospects*, Cambridge University Press, Cambridge.

Grubb, M (1990) *Energy Policies and the Greenhouse Effect*, Royal Institute of International Affairs, London.

Halbouty, M T (1970) World's giant oil and gas fields, *American Association of Petroleum Geologists*, Memoir 14.

Hoffman, G (1985) *The European Energy Challenge: East and West*, Duke University Press, Durham, NC.

International Energy Agency (1996) *World Energy Outlook*, OECD, Paris.

Jensen, R G (ed,) (1983) *Soviet Natural Resources in the World Economy*, University of Chicago Press, Chicago.

Jensen, W G (1967) *Energy in Europe 1945–1980*, G T Foulis and Co Ltd, London.

Jensen, W G (1970) *Energy and the Economy of Nations*, G T Foulis and Co Ltd, London.

Keepin, B and Cats, G (1988) Greenhouse warming: comparative analysis of abatement strategies, *Energy Policy*, **16**, 538–61.

Kemp, H G and Rose, D (1984) Investment in oil exploration and production: the comparative influence of taxation, in D W Pearce, H Siebert and I Walter (eds) *Risk and the Political Economy of Resource Development*, Macmillan Press Ltd, London, 169–96.

Kenny, J (1996) Impending shortages of petroleum re-evaluated, *Energy World*, **240**, June, 16–18.

Lenin, V I (1966) *Collected Works*, Vol 31, April–December 1920, Progress Publishers, Moscow.

Lewis, T M and McNicol, I H (1978) *North Sea Oil and Scotland's Economic Prospects*, Croom Helm, London.

Lovins, A B (1979) Re-examining the nature of the ECE energy problem, *Energy Policy*, **7**(3), 178–98.

Lucas, N J D (1977) *Energy and the European Communities*, Europa Publications, for the David Davies Memorial Institute of International Studies, London.

Manne, A S, Roland, K and Stephan, G (1986) Security of supply in the west European market for natural gas, *Energy Policy*, **14**(1), 52–64.

Manne, A S and Schrattenholzer, L (1984) International energy workshop: a summary of the 1983 poll responses, *The Energy Journal*, **5**(1), 45–64.

Manners, G (1981) *Coal in Britain: an uncertain future*, G Allen and Unwin, London.

Maull, H W (1981) Natural gas and economic security, *The Atlantic Papers*, 43, The Atlantic Institute for International Affairs, Paris.

Ministerie van Economische Zaken (1995) *Third White Paper on Energy Policy*, The Hague.

Ministerie van Economische Zaken (1996) *Oil and Gas in the Netherlands: exploration and production 1995*, The Hague.

Ministry of Industry and Energy (1996) *Fact Sheet: Norwegian petroleum activity*, Oslo.

Mitchell, J (1996) *The New Geopolitics of Energy*, Royal Institute for International Affairs, London.

Mounfield, P (1991) *World Nuclear Power*, Routledge, London.

Nicholson, J (1982) *Future Oil and Gas Developments in the UK North Sea: reserves of the undeveloped oil and gas discoveries and a commentary on their development options*, Midland Valley Exploration Ltd, Glasgow.

Norwegian Petroleum Directorate (1993) *Petroleum Resources – Norwegian continental shelf*, Stavanger.

Odell P R (1969) *Natural Gas in Western Europe: a case study in the economic geography of energy resources*, De Erven F Bohn NV, Haarlem.

Odell, P R (1973) Indigenous oil and gas developments and western Europe's energy policy options, *Energy Policy*, **1**(1), 47–64.

Odell, P R (1975) *The Western European Energy Economy: challenge and opportunities*, The Stamp Memorial Lecture delivered before the University of London, The Athlone Press, London.

Odell, P R (1976) *The Western European Economy; the case for self-sufficiency, 1980–2000*, H E Stenfert-Kroese BV, Leiden.

Odell, P R (1987) Gorbachev's new economic strategy: the role of gas exports to western Europe, *The World Today*, **43**(7), 123–25.

Odell, P R (1988) The west European gas market: current position and alternative prospects, *Energy Policy*, **16**(5), 480–93.

Odell, P R (1991) *Global and Regional Energy Supplies*, EURICES, Rotterdam.

Odell, P R (1995) europe's energy: panic over, opportunity knocks, *World Today*, **51**(10), 191–93.

Odell, P R (1996a) The exploitation of the oil and gas resources of the North Sea: retrospect and prospect, in G Mackerron and P Pearson (eds) *The UK Energy Experience*, Imperial College Press, London, 123–33.

Odell, P R (1996b) The cost of longer run gas supply to Europe, *Energy Studies Review*, **7**(2), 1–15.

Odell, P R and Rosing, K E (1974) *The North Sea Oil Province: an attempt to simulate its development and exploitation*, 1969–2029, Kogan Page, London.

Organisation for European Cooperation and Development (1974) *Energy Prospects to 1985*, OECD, Paris.

Organisation for European Economic Cooperation (1960) *Towards a New Energy Pattern for Europe*, OEEC, Paris.

Park, D (1979) *Oil and Gas in Comecon Countries*, Kogan Page, London.

Parker, M (1993) *The UK Coal Crisis: origins and resolution*, Royal Institute of International Affairs, London.

Parker, M (1994) *The Politics of Coal's Decline: the industry in Western Europe*, Royal Institute of International Affairs, London.

Pauwels J-P (1994) *Géopolitique de l'Approvisionnement Energétique de L'Union Européene au XXIᵉ Siècle*, Bruylant, Brussels.

Petroleum Economist (1984) *Map of Middle East Oil and Gas Export Routes*, Petroleum Economist Ltd, London.

Pounds, N J G and Parker, N W (1957) *Coal and Steel in Western Europe*, Faber and Faber, London.

Prodi, R and Clô, A (1975) The oil crisis in perspective: Europe, *Daedalus, Journal of the American Academy of Arts and Sciences*, **104**(4), 91–112.

Ray, G F (1976) Impact of the oil crisis on the energy situation in western Europe, in T M Rybczynski (ed) *The Economics of the Oil Crisis*, Macmillan Press for the Trade Policy Research Centre, London, 94–130.

Robinson, C and Morgan, J (1978) *North Sea Oil in the Future: economic analysis and government policy*, Macmillan Press, for the Trade Policy Research Centre, London.

Rogner, H-H (1988) Technology and the prospects for natural gas: results of current gas studies, *Energy Policy*, **16**(1), 9–26.

Rowland, C and Hann, D (1987) *The Economics of North Sea Oil Taxation*, Macmillan Press, London.

Schumacher, D (1985) *Energy: crisis or opportunity?*, Macmillan Publishers Ltd, Basingstoke.

Schurr, S H and Homan, P T (1971) *Middle East Oil and the Western World*, American Elsevier Publishing Company, Inc, New York.

Shwadran, B (1977) *Middle East Oil: issues and problems*, Harvard University Press, Cambridge, Mass.

Skea, J (1988) UK policy on acid rain; European pressures and alternative prospects, *Energy Policy*, **16**(3), 252–69.

Stern, J P (1984) *International Gas Trade in Europe: the policies of exporting and importing countries*, Heinemann Educational Books Ltd, London.

Stern, J P (1990) *European Gas Markets: challenges and opportunities in the 1990s*, Dartmouth Publishing, Aldershot.

Stern, J P (1995) *The Russian Natural Gas "Bubble": consequences for European gas markets*, Royal Institute for International Affairs, London.

Surrey, J (1990) Beyond 1992: the Single Market and EC energy issues, *Energy Policy*, **18**(1), 42–54.

Taylor, E and Davey W G (1984) Energy in Western Europe, *Energy Policy*, **12**(4), 409–24.

Turner, L (1978) *Oil Companies in the International System*, G Allen and Unwin, for the Royal Institute of International Affairs, London.

UKOOA (1996) *Towards 2020: future oil and gas production in UK waters*, London.

Voloshin, V I (1990) Electric power in the Comecon European countries, *Energy Policy*, **18**(8), 740–46.

Weyman-Jones, T G (1986) *Energy in Europe: issues and policies*, Methuen, London.

Yorke, V and Turner, L (1986) *European Interests and Gulf Oil*, Gower Publishing Company Ltd, Aldershot, for the Policy Studies Institute and the Royal Institute of International Affairs, London.

5

Restructuring of the western European manufacturing sector

H D Watts

Department of Geography, University of Sheffield, UK

Introduction

Although western Europe lost over 1.5 million manufacturing jobs between 1988 and 1993, the sector still employs 29 million people. This is significantly more than the 18 million manufacturing employees in the United States. In fact the west European economy, with a third of its workers in industry (defined here to include energy, mineral extraction, building and civil engineering as well as manufacturing) is substantially more dependent on these activities than the United States, where the proportion is only a quarter.

Even so, western Europe is steadily moving towards the North American pattern: as recently as 1980, employment in industry represented 38 per cent of the total west European (EU10) labour force. The decline in the numbers employed in manufacturing, and in industry's share of total employment, reflects responses to major changes in the west European economic environment. External pressures arise mainly from changes taking place in the global economy (see Chapter 3). Major internal pressures are the emergence of the new market economies in eastern Europe from 1989 onwards, the creation of the Single

European Market (SEM) from 1 January 1993 and the addition of Austria, Sweden and Finland to the EU in 1994. The nature of industrial restructuring in response to these external and internal pressures has varied from country to country and from region to region, and it has resulted in a complex pattern of geographical change within the largest concentration of manufacturing activity in the world. An exhaustive analysis of these changes is not possible within the scope of a single chapter, but an awareness of some of the key issues can be achieved by exploring selected themes.

It is clearly important to have an understanding of variations in manufacturing across western Europe. This can be attained through an examination of current patterns and recent changes in the number of manufacturing employees, in the mix of manufacturing activities and in the characteristics of the firms involved in the sector. A basic knowledge of the geography of manufacturing within western Europe provides a contextual framework for exploring the three themes which make up the remainder of the chapter.

The first of these highlights the fact that western Europe is a recipient of inward investment from firms based primarily in North America and the West Pacific Rim. It continues to receive new investment on a significant scale and, among long-established overseas-owned firms, the reorganisation of existing production activities also has an important effect on the geography of manufacturing. Second, within western Europe itself, there has been an increasing integration of the economy through stronger trade links and through the growth and development of firms who manufacture in a number of major countries. This internal reorganisation of the west European economy, like the inward investment from external sources, has naturally contributed significantly to the changing geography of manufacturing. Meanwhile, as the larger firms have been pursuing the integration of their activities across western Europe, there has been increased interest in the apparent dynamism of regional and/or local clusters of small firms. The nature, characteristics and patterns of change in these clusters make up the third theme.

In working through these topics, the chapter moves down from a global perspective, to a west European focus and finally to the local and regional scales. Although the three themes are treated separately they are interrelated. The closer integration of the west European activities of the larger west European firms is in part a response to the challenge from the very large North American multinationals, while some of the regional clusters gain their strengths from an ability to serve west European and, indeed, non-European markets.

The Geography of Manufacturing Employment

Although western Europe has lost manufacturing jobs over the last decade, such losses are not necessarily associated with loss of output. EU12 data for industrial production (which include the manufacturing and energy sectors but exclude construction) show that output was 15 per cent higher in 1992 than in 1985. This indicates labour productivity gains, without which western Europe's global competitiveness would have been very seriously undermined. Output growth in

western Europe was slightly better than the 13 per cent achieved by the United States but the EU lagged behind Japan, where production grew by 21 per cent (Eurostat, 1994, 189). Analysis of the manufacturing system in terms of changes in output would be an interesting exercise, but appropriate data disaggregated by region, country and industry are not readily available. Consequently, in western Europe as elsewhere, analyses of the geography of manufacturing activity are based on employment data. Reliance on these permits a direct link to be made between industrial change and its effect on employment, unemployment and regional inequalities (Chapter 17).

The new Germany (with almost 10 million employees in manufacturing) is the manufacturing centre of western Europe, while France, Italy and the UK share second place, with around 4 million employees each (Table 5.1). Spain, with 2.1 million workers, occupies an intermediate position between the larger centres of manufacturing and the other countries with over 500 000 manufacturing employees, such as Austria, Belgium, the Netherlands, Portugal and Switzerland.

The relative importance of industry (manufacturing plus the energy and construction sectors) varies from country to country around the EU12's mean of 33 per cent. Above-average dependence on industry is particularly characteristic of (west) Germany (with 39 per cent of its civilian employment in the sector), Austria (36 per cent) and Switzerland (34 per cent). The lowest dependence occurs in Norway (24 per cent) and in the Netherlands and Greece (25 per cent each). The remaining countries are spread evenly across a continuum from 33 per cent in Italy and Spain to 27 per cent in Denmark, Sweden and Norway (Eurostat, 1994, 139).

The west European economies experienced a fall of 6 per cent in their manufacturing employment in the five years from 1988 to 1993 (Table 5.1). There were no dramatic increases in employment and the labour-shedding process in manufacturing was characteristic of virtually all areas except the Benelux countries, Ireland and (west) Germany where manufacturing employment was stable or slightly rising. The greatest fall was in the former East Germany where, between

Table 5.1 *Western European manufacturing employment trends, by country, 1988–93*[*]

	1988 ('000)	1993 ('000)	Change ('000)	Change (%)	Notes
Austria	798	747	−51	−6	
Belgium	723	728	+5	+1	1991
Denmark	385	351	−34	−9	
Germany (West)	8 289	8 438	+149	+2	
Greece	489	467	−22	−4	1992
Finland	453	364	−89	−20	1992
France	4 424	4 089	−335	−8	
Ireland	185	194	+9	+5	1992
Italy	4 049	4 033	−16	−1	1992
Luxembourg	36	37	+1	+3	1991
Netherlands	1 067	1 076	+9	+1	Discontinuity
Norway	329	283	−46	−14	
Portugal	992	906	−86	−9	Discontinuity
Spain	2 229	2 062	−167	−7	
Sweden	528	375	−153	−12	
Switzerland	688	607	−81	−12	Estimated
UK	5 162	4 358	−804	−16	
Total	30 826	29 115	−1 711	−6	

* Because the definition of paid manufacturing employment varies between countries, the data in this table provide only broad indications of the size of the manufacturing workforce and must therefore be treated with caution.
Source: International Labour Office (1995, Table 5A).

1991 and 1994 alone, the manufacturing workforce shrank by almost 50 per cent (International Labour Office, 1995). Declines were much smaller elsewhere and only in Norway, Finland, Sweden, Switzerland and the UK were jobs lost at a rate equal to, or greater than, twice the west European average.

It will be recalled that employment loss cannot be equated necessarily with loss of output, and it may be that countries showing the highest losses are also showing the most rapid productivity gains and are thus adapting most rapidly to changes in western Europe's position in the world economy. Nevertheless, it is clear from these differing employment records that the impact of the external and internal pressures has varied significantly throughout this world region.

The manufacturing sector encompasses some 20 different "two-digit" industries (Table 5.2). Two sectors, each with around 2.3 million employees, account for almost one-quarter of the 21 million manufacturing jobs in the EU12. These two dominant activities are food, drink and tobacco (NACE 41 and 42) and electrical engineering (NACE 34).[1] The latter activity contains a number of subsectors with high-technology characteristics such as telecommunications equipment and consumer electronics. In a second group, with just under 2 million employees each and representing some 20 per cent of the total, are mechanical engineering (NACE 32) and the manufacture of metal articles (NACE 31). Mechanical engineering includes the production of items as large as complete steelworks, together with other individual products such as machine tools, conveyor systems and industrial robots. These products increasingly have major microelectronic components as part of their control systems. The metal articles sector is dominated by the production of tools, cutting edges, nuts, bolts, springs and chains. Chemicals and motor vehicles (each with just over 1.5 million employees) account for a further 16 per cent of manufacturing employment.

An analysis of spatial variations in industrial structure shows that the food, drink and tobacco industry is the largest source of employment in many countries (Belgium, Denmark, France,

Table 5.2 *Manufacturing employment trends (EU12), by sector, 1989–1994*

Sector	NACE	1989 ('000)	1994 ('000)	Change ('000)	Per cent
Production of metals	22	848	662	−186	−22
Non-metallic mineral products	24	1 051	919	−132	−13
Chemicals	25/26	1 781	1 584	−197	−11
Metal articles	31	2 425	1 987	−438	−18
Mechanical engineering	32	2 349	1 981	−368	−16
Office machinery	33	267	216	−51	−19
Electrical engineering	34	2 538	2 334	−204	−8
Motor vehicles and parts	35	1 726	1 614	−112	−6
Other transport equipment	36	900	650	−250	−28
Instrument engineering	37	333	308	−25	−8
Food, drink and tobacco	40/41	2 324	2 331	7	
Textiles	43	1 602	1 200	−402	−25
Leather	44	107	96	−11	−10
Footwear and clothing	45	1 559	1 278	−281	−18
Timber and wood articles	46	1 325	846	−479	−36
Paper and printing	47	2 009	1 350	−659	−33
Rubber and plastics	48	1 099	1 060	−39	−4
Other manufacturing	49	244	212	−32	−13
All manufacturing		24 487	20 628	−3 859	−16

Sources: 1989: Eurostat (1991); 1994: Commission of the EU (1995).

Ireland and the Netherlands). Clothing and footwear are the leading manufacturing sectors in Greece and Portugal, while the manufacture of metal articles is dominant in both Italy and Spain. Finally, the main source of manufacturing employment in (west) Germany is electrical engineering and in the UK mechanical engineering.

Not surprisingly, there are variations between industrial sectors in the rates of job loss. In the EU12 employment in manufacturing fell by 15 per cent in the five years between 1989 and 1994, and each sector had its own distinctive employment trend (Table 5.2). Only one sector, food, drink and tobacco, maintained its labour force, but a further four (electrical engineering, motor vehicles and parts, instrument engineering and rubber and plastics) lost less than 10 per cent. In contrast, four industries shed a quarter or more of their employees in the five-year period: textiles (−25 per cent), other transport equipment (−28 per cent), paper and printing (−33 per cent) and timber and wood articles (−36 per cent).

Manufacturing activities as a whole, and in each of the individual sectors, are guided in their day-to-day operations by the decisions of around 1.75 million enterprises (EU12, NACE 1–4). EU data recognise four different sizes of firm (or enterprise, which is the technical term): micro-enterprises with 0–9 employees (this includes self-employment represented by the zero value); small enterprises with 10–99 employees; medium enterprises with 100–499 employees and large enterprises with 500 or more employees. Micro-enterprises represent 11 per cent of manufacturing employment, small and medium-sized enterprises (SMEs) 46 per cent, and large enterprises 43 per cent. Spain, Italy and Portugal all had one-half or more of their employees in manufacturing in enterprises with less than 100 workers, while large enterprises accounted for over half the manufacturing employment in Greece, Germany and the UK. The latter in fact had the highest proportion with 55 per cent (Commission of the EC, 1991, 117).

The role of large firms in Germany and the UK is reflected in the distribution of the head offices of the largest 100 west European-owned manu-

Table 5.3   *The 10 largest western European-owned firms in manufacturing, 1992**

Firm	Head office	Main activity	Turnover (ECUm.)	Employment ('000)
1. Daimler Benz	Germany	Automobiles, Electronics	48,828	376
2. Volkswagen	Germany	Automobiles	42 315	282
3. Siemens	Germany	Electrical engineering	38 509	413
4. Fiat	Italy	Automobiles	37 237	285
5. Unilever	UK/Netherlands	Food	33 692	287
6. Nestlé	Switzerland	Food	29 997	218
7. Renault	France	Automobiles	26 220	147
8. Philips	Netherlands	Electrical engineering	25 752	252
9. Alcatel-Alsthom	France	Electrical engineering	23 621	203
10. Hoescht	Germany	Chemicals	22 727	178

* Excludes oil companies and diversified holding companies.
Source: Commission of the EU (1994, 83).

facturing firms. Germany leads the list with the head offices of 28 firms, while the UK has 21 and France 20. (These are estimates by the Commission of the EU, 1994, 94–6.) The pattern for the 10 largest west European-owned firms is rather different (Table 5.3). Germany has the largest share of headquarters with four firms, compared with two in France, one in each of Italy, Switzerland and the Netherlands and one joint UK–Netherlands operation. Despite the size of the UK's manufacturing sector, the largest firm in sole UK ownership, ICI, had a turnover 25 per cent smaller than the tenth largest west European firm. The sectoral mix among the top ten firms highlights again the significance of the electrical engineering and food industries, but the presence of several motor vehicle firms illustrates the high degree of concentration in the vehicle assembly sector, where around 10 firms account for virtually all output.

There have been major changes in the organisational structure of west European industry over the last decade. Evidence from the 100 largest firms (in all sectors not only manufacturing) indicates that their importance peaked in 1982 when they accounted for 36 per cent of EU output. This had fallen back to 27 per cent by 1990 (de Jong, 1993, 6) despite the increase in the number of mergers and acquisitions noted later in this chapter. Second, an equally important change has been an increase in the number of firms from smaller west European countries among the larger businesses: among the top 200 west European-owned non-financial concerns, the proportion of UK, French and German firms fell from 73 per cent in 1986 to 67 per cent in 1992. It is tempting to interpret this as an attempt by firms based in the smaller countries to exploit the gradual opening up of trade barriers which allowed them to serve wider markets (Commission of the EU, 1994, 88). Finally, the role of the UK in relation to France and Germany has changed markedly. In the mid-1980s it accounted for 39 of the top 100 manufacturing firms in western Europe (Geroski and Jacquemin, 1984, 359) compared with only 21 today.

Examination of the broad pattern of sectoral and organisational restructuring inevitably hides much of the detail of change that is taking place within individual sectors and firms. Some of that variety can be unpicked by examining particular sectors. Food and drink and electrical engineering have been selected because of their leading role as employers and because they have been relatively successful in maintaining their employment levels. Further, the largest firms in these sectors are well represented among the major west European firms listed in Table 5.3. However, despite this common ground, they also differ from each other in some important respects. Whereas the food and drink sector is characterised by slow growth, limited competition from inward investment and slow technological change, electrical engineering has a high growth rate, has to meet major challenges from inward investment and has to operate in a rapidly changing technological environment.

Food and drink

The food and drink industry includes within it some 436 000 employees involved in the manufacture of meat products, 242 000 producing dairy products and 456 000 engaged in the production of bread and flour. Smaller contributions to total employment in the industry come from, for example, pasta manufacture (19 000 employees), grain milling (36 000) and wine production (46 000).

The close association between food and drink production and the distribution of population means that there is a strong positive relationship between the size of the food and drink industry in a particular country and its population. Even the largest firms in this sector tend to locate their production units in the main markets because of the bulky low-value nature of many food products. This allows firms to minimise distribution costs. On average in the EU12 there are 9000 food, drink and tobacco employees per million people, and most countries lie within the range from 7000 to 11 000 per million. The two exceptions are Denmark where the rate is 19 000 per million (perhaps reflecting an export-oriented food and drink sector) and Italy, where the rate drops to 5000 per million (possibly due to a less industrialised food production system).

Larger firms are a particular feature of food production in northern Europe, as an examination of the development of the French firm Danone over the last two decades will underline later in this chapter. Nestlé (Switzerland) and Unilever (Netherlands/UK) have been consistently among the top 10 world food companies in recent years. Despite the existence of large west European food groups, geographical change in production systems has been slow. A major constraint is the continued variation in food consumption patterns throughout western Europe. A recent EU study contrasts Germany, Denmark and Benelux – where food consumption has a large traditional component of meat, chocolate, butter and biscuits – with Greece and Portugal, which have a high consumption of fresh products and use few prepared and convenience foods. Like Greece and Portugal, France, Spain and Italy have a high dependence on fresh foods, but this consumption goes side by side with the use of convenience products. These variations are a further factor encouraging the wide dispersal of production facilities as this allows firms to keep in touch with consumer preferences and tastes, a point discussed further by Dawson and Burt in Chapter 9. Despite these differing food consumption patterns throughout Europe, however, there is evidence that in all areas there has been a steady fall in the significance of traditional foods over the last decade (Commission of the EU, 1994, 13.4). As a result this cultural influence over food sector activities may be weakening. The growth of large west European food groups, and the declining significance of regional food consumption patterns, suggest this is a sector which may experience major changes in the geography of production in the near future.

Electrical engineering

This is a very diverse sector with outputs ranging from the production of insulated wires and cables, through electrical domestic appliances to electronic components such as semiconductors. Telecommunications equipment (881 000 employees) and consumer electronics (357 000) account for almost half the sector's labour force and, taken together, they employed as many people in western Europe as the assembly of motor vehicles (1.2 million). Overall, some two-thirds of sectoral output are sold direct to individual *consumers*, while the other third comprises intermediate products sold within and outside the *industry*.

The geography of this modern high-technology industry is dominated by Germany which, in 1992, accounted for 43 per cent of EU output. Its nearest rival, France, produces less than half the German total (18 per cent). It is also a sector with a high degree of concentration in that 4 per cent of the firms employ 80 per cent of the workforce. The geographical patterns of the different subdivisions of the industry can show very different features. For example, whereas there are only 10 factories producing primary batteries in western Europe, the production of insulated cables and wires takes place at over 250 production sites distributed among virtually all countries.

The important telecommunications sector (manufacturing, for example, mobile telephones and major switching and transmission equipment) is the one which has probably shown the greatest change in recent years as a result of technological innovation and trends in the market for the sector's products. Until the 1970s the firms tended to supply national public telephone systems with simple terminals (such as telephones and telex machines). Since the 1970s there has been a development of new products and increasing competition in the market-place. Although public switching systems are still the dominant market, there has been major growth in private networks, sophisticated terminals and mobile communications systems. Within western Europe by far the largest telecommunication equipment producer is Alcatel-Alsthom (France) with a market share of 28 per cent. Siemens, the second-largest firm, has an 18 per cent share, which is in turn much higher than that of other large companies in the sector such as GPT (UK), Ericsson (Sweden), Bosch (Germany) and Philips (the Netherlands). Alcatel-Alsthom grew primarily in the 1980s, first by acquiring another major French producer and then by taking over many of the private and public telecommunications facilities of the US producer ITT. It now has major activities in 21 countries and 60 per cent of its output is produced outside France. Despite its global orientation, however, Alcatel-Alsthom is one of the most markedly west European groups, even keeping its accounts in ECUs (Weinstein, 1992; Charles, 1996).

Inward investment from outside western Europe has been a major challenge to the electrical engineering industry. This can be seen both in the production of semiconductors and consumer electronics. Philips is the leader in the west European market for semiconductors (Commission of EU, 1994, 10.11) but in second and third place come two US firms (Intel and Motorola). In consumer electronics (TVs, radios, video recorders) Japanese producers control 27 per cent of western European production (Commission of EU, 1994, 10.28). It is to the more general characteristics of this market penetration by inward investment to which attention now turns as we examine the first of the three themes which comprise the remainder of the chapter.

Market Penetration

"One of South Korea's largest electronic groups looks set to invest more than £1 billion in South Wales, creating more than 4000 jobs.... Seventeen Korean companies have manufacturing plants in Britain, representing more than half South Korea's total investment in Europe" (*The Guardian*, 11 May 1996).

The dominant reason for non-EU manufacturing investment in western Europe is to gain access to the west European market. In some cases this is to avoid existing or anticipated trade barriers, but other factors include a desire for proximity in order to monitor and respond to local consumer tastes; to be accessible to other plants to which products are sold; and, especially in the case of acquisitions, to achieve proprietary expertise, technology or markets in which the acquired firm has particular skills. The selection of an individual country in which to make the investment can reflect further country-specific factors. The significance of inward investment within the EU mirrors the general openness of the west European economy towards inward investment and even France "which has been most suspicious of [inward investment] has adopted a more favourable attitude, especially towards investments which bring new technology, increase exports or create employment in depressed areas" (Dicken, 1992, 164–5).

There are two main forms of inward investment: acquisition of existing firms and the start-up of entirely new operations on greenfield sites. However, most data sets on inward investment do not distinguish between the two. The most striking feature of *all* inward investment in western Europe (which is replicated in the manufacturing sector) is the dominance of US firms, which owned a total stock worth 150 000 million ECU at the end of 1989. The significance of US firms is not unexpected as they have a history of inward investment since the late nineteenth century. The only other player of importance in the overall west European scene is Japan, but its total stock – a mere 44 million ECU – is minute compared with that of the US. Despite some initial hostility to inward investment by Japanese firms, a more encouraging attitude has developed as their plants are seen as preferable to market penetration by Japanese exports. It is important to note there is a marked difference in the sectoral mix of the Japanese and US investments. Whereas 50 per cent of the US direct investment stock was in manufacturing in 1989, this was true of only 18 per cent of the Japanese stock (Commission of the EC, 1991, 39–64), despite the high profile in the media of Japanese inward investment. This reflects the fact that much of Japan's inward manufacturing investment is in new factories on greenfield sites, whereas US investments are often acquisitions of existing west European firms.

The distinctive geography of US inward investment, relating to all inward investment and not only manufacturing, is shown in Figure 5.1. Forty per cent of the total stock is in the UK, the nearest competitors being (west) Germany with just 15 per cent, the Netherlands (11 per cent) and France (10 per cent). In terms of flows (more representative of current patterns) the UK dominance is even more marked. The UK received 10 times more US inward investment than any other country in 1989, although there were important flows into the Netherlands and France in 1987 and 1988. An EU commentator has correctly observed that the UK has always been the most important destination for US investment in western Europe and this share has changed little ... since the UK joined the Community" (Commission of the EC, 1991, 50).

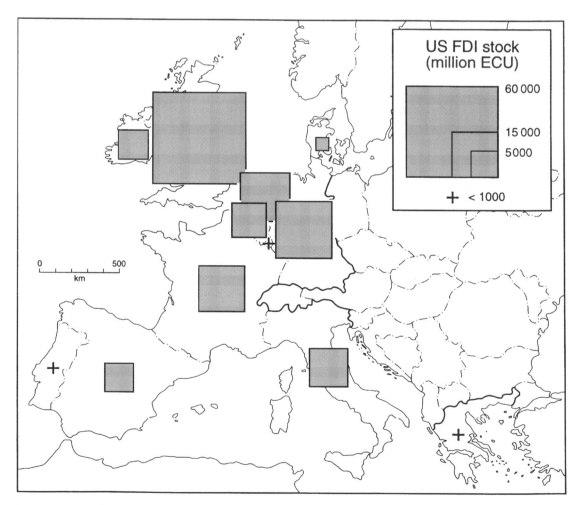

Figure 5.1 *US inward investment stock (in ECU) in western Europe, all sectors, end 1989*

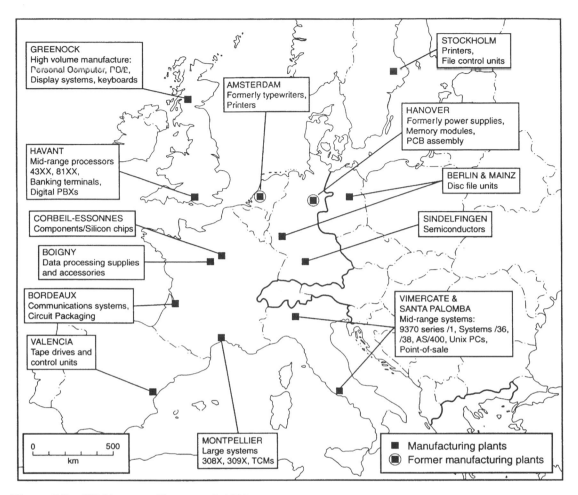

Figure 5.2   *IBM in western Europe, early 1990s*

Discussions of US investment in western Europe are normally dominated by descriptions of the activities of the major motor vehicle assembly plants owned by Ford and General Motors (Dicken, 1992, 301) but a further good example of a US firm with Europe-wide operations is provided by IBM (Kelly and Keeble, 1990, 28–54). The distribution of IBM manufacturing facilities in western Europe, which in the late 1980s employed 27 000 people, is shown in Figure 5.2. The firm's largest manufacturing operations were in Germany, France and the UK and these countries accounted for 77 per cent of its west European employment. The main German site near Stuttgart was opened as early as 1924, followed by a plant in France in 1925. The first UK site was not opened until 1951. Although

IBM activities are now concentrated in these three countries IBM also has important manufacturing facilities in Italy, Spain and Sweden. The Santa Palomba plant (Italy) and the Valencia plant (Spain) were both opened in the mid-1970s in southern European assisted regions, where incomes are low and unemployment high. Within IBM the pattern is for products to be manufactured in at least three different plants world-wide, with at least one each in the Americas, the West Pacific Rim and western Europe. Thus one western European plant is devoted to mainframes (Montpellier) and one to printers (Stockholm), while two are involved in the production of PCs (Greenock, Scotland and Vimercate, Italy).

Although inward investment is associated traditionally with the creation of new plants, the longer-established firms such as IBM have needed to make adjustments to their production systems to meet contemporary circumstances. Thus the late 1980s saw the restructuring of IBM's manufacturing operations. Plants in Amsterdam and Hanover ceased production, allowing the Amsterdam site to become the company's west European distribution centre and Hanover a software and service centre. It is perhaps significant that the plants from which manufacturing was withdrawn were well-established older sites in the high-wage areas of northern Europe. The long-established motor vehicle sector has seen adjustments too. General Motors announced in the early 1990s plans to reduce a 31 000 workforce by 6000 over the period to

1997 and, in the UK, employment at Ford's Halewood (Liverpool) plant is down to 7500 employees from a 1970s peak of 14 000 (Wells and Rawlinson, 1994, 55–6).

The geography of the Japanese-owned *manufacturing* affiliates is shown in Figure 5.3 and is similar to that of the USA. The main destination is the UK where, in 1990, there were over 20 000 jobs in plants owned by Japanese firms. However, both (west) Germany and Spain had over 10 000 jobs in Japanese manufacturing affiliates. Spain's high share partly reflects the fact that production there is more labour intensive, but it is also the consequence of the tendency of Japanese companies to follow the acquisition route in Spain and acquire firms with large workforces.

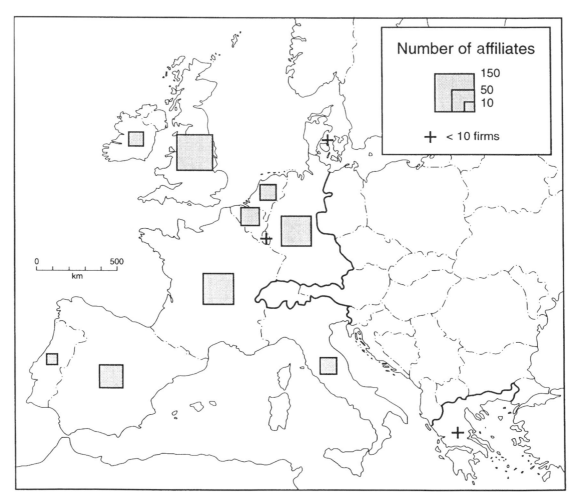

Figure 5.3 *Japanese manufacturing affiliates in western Europe, 1990*

Although France has one of the largest concentrations of manufacturing affiliates most are relatively small, and in total they provide only around 7500 jobs (Commission of the EC, 1991, 52). The bias towards the UK in Japanese investment is particularly evident in the assembly of motor vehicles: Nissan in Sunderland (£620 million) and Toyota at Derby (£700 million).

In explaining the variations in investment in different west European countries it can be argued that Europe's "... historically fragmented political structure, [and] differentials in regulationary policy towards international trade, foreign investment and industry have played an extremely important part in shaping current patterns of [inward investment] activity" (Dicken *et al.*, 1994, 10). The marked preference of US firms for the UK probably reflects long-standing cultural and linguistic links. Japanese investment there has been encouraged by strong political support from the UK government, low wages, a workforce less militant than in the past and, in some cases, direct financial assistance. The fact that English is the dominant second language in Japan may be relevant too. It is also important to recognise that there is often a major competition, between countries and between regions within them, for greenfield manufacturing investments.

Inward investment by Japanese firms has been more problematic than that by US companies, and they have been more tightly regulated by the EU than those from the USA. The most widely reported requirement placed upon Japanese firms is to meet "local content" targets, meaning a policy to ensure that at least a fixed percentage of inputs are purchased from local sources. In the EU context, local means from within the EU and not simply the country or region in which the plant is located. By insisting on a high local content, imports to the EU are reduced and, more importantly, there may be beneficial effects on EU producers who obtain contracts to supply the new facilities. A further side effect is to encourage Japanese suppliers to build their own plants in western Europe. However, these requirements do not necessarily engineer a situation in which investments have a substantial multiplier effect. For example, Nissan's Sunderland plant is highly vertically integrated with its own foundry and its own plastic injection moulding facility, thus reducing its demands for local suppliers (Wells and Rawlinson, 1994, 59–61).

Although in public debate considerable prominence is given to investment from non-European sources, it should be kept in perspective. Admittedly, it may be important in bringing into the EU new technologies and working practices which are transferred to domestic producers, but overall it accounts for only a small proportion of total employment. The UK provides a good example, with only 9 per cent of manufacturing employment in US-owned firms and little more than 1 per cent in Japanese-owned businesses (Central Statistical Office, 1995, 328). Consequently west European-owned operations, which are responsible for the vast majority of manufacturing within the EU, become the focus of interest as attention turns to this chapter's second theme.

West European Integration

"British Aerospace is to pool its own missile division with those of ... [the French group] Matra Hachette to create Europe's biggest missile supplier ... the new grouping will provide a powerful European competitor to US groups such as Lockheed Martin" (*The Independent*, 14 May 1996).

Since its formation the EU has seen the increasing integration of economic activities within western Europe, and the manufacturing sector is no exception. Such moves towards integration were given a further boost by the introduction of the Single European Market (SEM), but this is not the only factor of importance. Significant too is the need for west European firms to increase in size to achieve scale economies in order to meet competition in the global market-place, especially from firms based in North America. These two factors have contributed both to increases in the amount of intra-European trade and to a rise in the standing of west European companies in the global economy. No manufacturing sector has escaped totally from these changes.

The increasingly integrated nature of the west European economy is reflected in the growing significance of intra-European trade. As a proportion of total imports, this rose from 49 per cent in 1980 to 59 per cent in 1992. By 1994 (scarcely a year after the introduction of the SEM) one commentator was arguing that "cross-border deliveries are now as time and cost efficient as shipments within a member state" (Commission of the EU, 1994, 69) whereas in the mid-1980s the cost of border formalities alone equalled 2 per cent of the value of total intra-Community trade (Emerson, 1988, 49). The present stage of the SEM is witnessing a steady enforcement of the new rules, while the harmonisation of national technical standards is under way to create a more homogeneous Europe-wide market. What is evident, however, is that the harmonisation of technical standards has produced significant

problems. Attempts to remove the non-tariff boundaries have often been blocked because common standards would make it easier for North American and Japanese firms to penetrate the western Europe market. In addition, they have been opposed in some quarters because they may give advantage to west European countries whose technical specifications form the basis of the EU's standards.

The nature of cross-border investments (in all sectors, not only manufacturing) is shown in Figure 5.4. Almost half the inward investment in the UK from other parts of the EU comes from the Netherlands (reflecting the influence of Shell and Unilever on the aggregate data), while UK firms account for almost two-fifths of investment in both Denmark and Portugal. Meanwhile in the

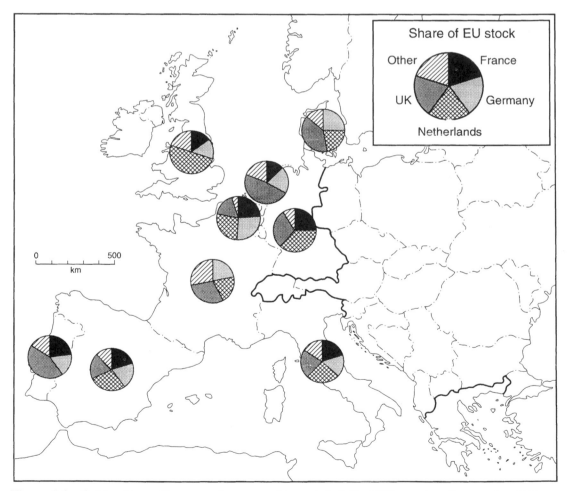

Figure 5.4 *Origins of inward investment from western Europe in individual EU countries, all sectors, late 1980s*

Netherlands, half the EU investment comes from Germany. To some extent the overall pattern reflects spatial proximity, but this is by no means a complete explanation since German and UK firms play a major role in Portugal and Spain. It is tempting to explain this investment in the south in terms of companies in high-wage countries, such as Germany, responding to an incentive to transfer labour-intensive operations to the Mediterranean fringe. This may be true in some cases, but market access is important too.

The pattern of cross-border investments is associated particularly with acquisitions and strategic alliances. Acquisition activity increased dramatically from the early 1980s onwards. The number of mergers by the largest 1000 EU companies (in all sectors) increased from around 200 a year at the beginning of the period to just over 800 in 1990. Manufacturing acquisitions mimicked the general trend, increasing from 200 per annum in 1984/85 to 622 in 1989/90 (de Jong, 1993, 4–7). The most active sectors were chemicals (525 mergers in 1984/85 to 1989/90) and foods (337) followed by paper and printing (244) and mechanical engineering (236). What must also be emphasised is that, apart from the high level of activity, "there is one very striking difference between previous takeover waves and that of the late 1980s; the late 1980s were characterised by an unprecedented number of cross border deals" (Commission of the EC, 1991, 66). A typical recent example of such cross-border activity is the purchase by Germany's BMW of the Rover Group (the last major UK-owned motor vehicle assembler) from British Aerospace.

Strategic alliances between firms often take the form of joint ventures, which have also increased in importance over the last decade. Between 1982 and 1990/91 the number of joint ventures by the 100 largest firms (in all sectors) increased from 46 to 125 per annum. These joint ventures were associated mainly with industries with undifferentiated products (such as primary metals and chemicals), but perhaps the best known example, originating before 1982, is the Airbus project discussed later in this chapter.

These cross-boundary mergers, acquisitions and joint ventures are of particular interest because they are a reflection of the greater integration of activities across the EU: cross-border reorganisation of this type now equals that within countries. France, Germany, the UK and the Netherlands have been the major *origins* of cross border investments and, of the large economies, only Italy has had limited involvement in this mode of restructuring. Meanwhile, the major *destination* for cross-border acquisitions has been the UK, where takeovers by other EU firms outnumbered those in France and Germany by four to one (Commission of the EC, 1991, 66–70).

An illustration of a west European firm which has grown primarily by acquisitions over the last 25 years is provided by Danone (BSN until 1994), the sixth largest west European-owned food firm. In the late 1960s this company was primarily involved in the manufacture of glass but, after an unsuccessful attempt to increase its market share, it switched attention to the food and drink sector. The first major acquisitions were Kronenbourg beers and Evian water in 1970, followed by the Gervais Danone dairy products group in 1973 (Ellis and Williams, 1995, 34–44). By 1982 it had divested itself of most of its glass-making activities (except the production of bottles) and by 1988 it was the world's largest mineral water producer, the third largest biscuit maker and, in western Europe, the second largest pasta maker. Growth by acquisition continued throughout the late 1980s and 1990s with, for example, takeovers of Imperial Foods and Huntley and Palmers in the UK in 1988 and 1990, and of the US firm Nabisco's western European biscuit manufacturing activities in 1989. Danone's overall strategy continues to be to acquire market share in core products such as dairy, grocery, biscuit, beer and mineral water brands. Further examples of growth by acquisition in the electrical engineering and pharmaceutical sectors are provided in Amin *et al.* (1992).

As noted above, since the early 1970s the best-known joint venture has been production of the various versions of the Airbus. France's Aerospatiale and Germany's Deutsche Aerospace (DASA) each hold a 38 per cent stake in Airbus Industrie, British Aerospace has 20 per cent and the Spanish partner (CASA) 4 per cent. The work is spread between the partners in relation to their share of the overall project. British Aerospace produces the wings, DASA the fuselage and

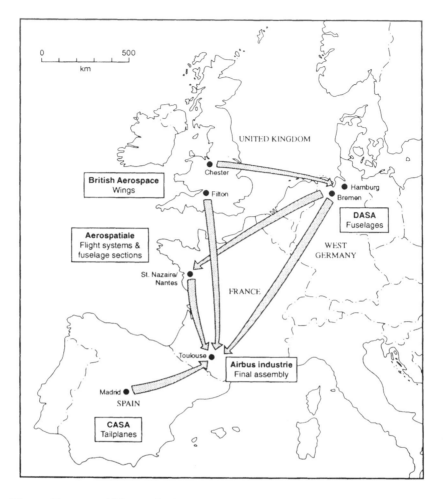

British Aerospace
Wings

Aerospatiale
Flight systems &
fuselage sections

DASA
Fuselages

Airbus industrie
Final assembly

CASA
Tailplanes

Figure 5.5 *The west European Airbus production system*

CASA the tailplane, while final assembly takes place in Toulouse (Figure 5.5). This joint operation has enabled west European producers to challenge US manufacturers in the production of large passenger jets and has significantly reduced Boeing's market share, a task probably beyond the scope of any single west European company (*The Economist*, 1988). However, one disadvantage of joint ventures can be the need for complex organisational structures which make it difficult to retain a competitive edge in the global market. One reflection of this is that the Airbus Industrie partners are currently considering the development of a more conventional corporate structure to enable Airbus to survive into the twenty-first century.

Although emphasis has been placed on cross-border activities and the increasing integration of the west European economy it is important to put this in context. Of the 10 biggest acquisitions in 1988, only two involved different countries (Commission of the EC, 1991, 47) and many European-owned firms operate mainly within their home country. This is particularly true of the steel industry. Multiple-country operations are more common in the automobiles sector, but even these are more marked among US-owned firms than those originating in western Europe. Similarly, in 1989 EU firms spent three times more on buying US companies than they did on cross-border purchases within the Community (Commission of the EC, 1991, 67).

Regional Specialisation

"Benetton handles in-house only those bits of manufacturing – mainly design, cutting, dyeing and packing – that it considers crucial to maintain quality and cost efficiency. It contracts out the rest to local suppliers. This devolved system reduces Benetton's risk and confers legendary flexibility". (*The Economist*, 23 April 1994).

The strengthening of both global and Europe-wide activities over the last decade may give the impression of an unrelenting trend towards standardisation and uniformity through the development of Fordist production systems. However, new technologies and flexible production systems are providing an opportunity for the revival and/or strengthening of regional/local specialisation. A discussion of these regional specialisations provides the third, and final, theme of this chapter. Such areas are usually associated with the spatial agglomerations of small firms linked to one or more leading industries, although the latter are often wider than a conventional industrial sector so that, for example, a textiles area would also include mechanical engineering (making textile machinery) and the chemical industry (producing dyes).

Within these regions, small firms are embedded into a specific local "industrial" culture characterised by intense and well-developed social and economic networks, generating information flows in many different directions and intersecting with one another in variety of ways. From this comes a technological dynamism derived from the spirit of co-operation and competition between small firms. The production process tends to be vertically disintegrated with different firms undertaking separate stages of the production process. Localities achieve the economies of large-scale production from external economies arising from the spatial agglomeration of activities, rather than from internal economies of scale based on concentration within one large plant. In the discussion of these areas, considerable emphasis is placed on the social and cultural milieu of the small firms, in which business and society "share a common mode of discourse about the production process" (Piore, 1990, 54). These areas are sometimes called "new industrial districts" but there is considerable debate as to whether they are in fact anything more than a modern form of the clusters of economic activity characteristic of many nineteenth-century industries. If there are substantial differences, however, they are that today they naturally use more advanced technologies and, to some extent, their strength comes from their flexible production systems which enable them to have a wide variety of products in response to an increasingly differentiated market.

Although these districts tend to be discussed together as a group, they take a variety of forms within the overall parameters described above. The term "new industrial district" tends to be applied to areas of markedly varying geographical extent. There are contrasts too between districts focusing on new industries and new markets (electronics) and those with an emphasis on new niche markets for old industries (textiles). Some serve intermediate demand (machine tools) while others supply final demand (clothing). Important too is the difference between districts where a limited number of large companies control the small firms' production activities through their subcontracting system (such as Benetton in the knitwear sector in the Veneto area of Italy), and those where co-ordination is achieved through the operations of a larger number of firms and local institutions (such as the Modena knitwear industry in Emilia-Romagna).

Although all kinds of areas in different countries have been, and are being, described as industrial districts, there does seem to be agreement that such districts exist in Baden-Württemberg (textiles, machine tools, autoparts and clothing), Jutland (textiles, furniture and machine tools), Rhône-Alpes (telecommunications and electronics) and Emilia-Romagna (textiles, furniture, ceramics and mechanical engineering). This list should be regarded as illustrative rather than exhaustive. The nature of the districts can best be illustrated by two brief examples, one from the traditional industries of the "Third Italy" and one from a high-technology development in France.

Figure 5.6 illustrates the 61 industrial districts of the Third Italy and the industries in which they specialise. All the districts have an above-average dependence on manufacturing (in most cases

105

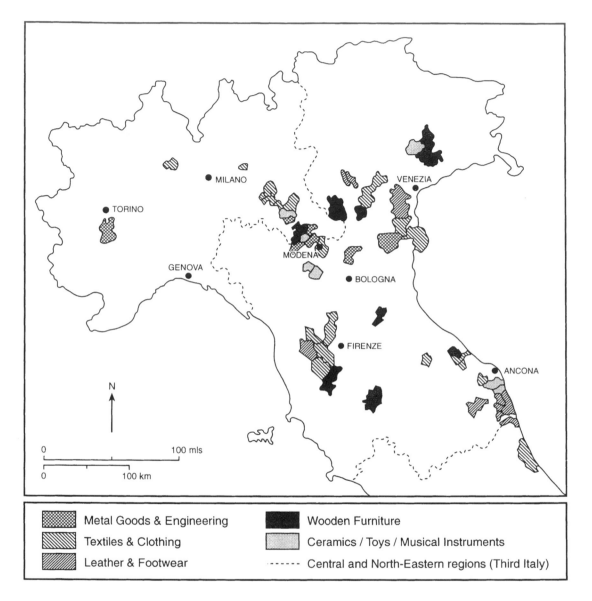

Figure 5.6 *Industrial districts in the Third Italy*

representing between 50 and 60 per cent of local employment) and on average the dominant industrial sector accounts for 50 per cent of the manufacturing labour force. The dynamic nature of these districts is reflected in the fact that they experienced the fastest increase in manufacturing employment in Italy between 1971 and 1981 (Sforzi, 1990).

The Modena knitwear district demonstrates the typical characteristics of these specialised regions. Modena is a province of 600 000 people and its knitwear sector is the third largest regional industry after mechanical engineering and ceramics. The sector employs 16 000 people and is represented by over 4000 firms with an average of just under four workers per firm, including owners and family help. Half the firms have just one worker. The vertical disintegration of the production system is evident in the different activities undertaken by the members of the

Modena National Confederation of Artisans. This organisation includes weavers (310 firms), complete assembly (224), partial assembly (374), laundry and pressing (282), embroidery (116) and button making (55). The vast majority of the larger firms in the industry rely on subcontracting for production, while they themselves concentrate on producing the prototype and organising the delivery of finished garments to buyers. Most manufacturers use a variety of subcontractors, all of whom work for a number of different manufacturers. Overall, the diverse production capacity of the subcontractors offers the manufacturers considerable flexibility to respond to demands for hundreds of different production orders which change after each season. The overall success of the district is reflected in the fact that the number of firms rose from 1590 in 1971 to 4291 in 1981 (Lazerson, 1990).

This dynamism is also evident in the second case study (Rhône-Alpes), where the number of firms doubled between 1977 and 1987. This is the largest French centre of communication and computing companies outside Paris, its nearest rival having less than half the number in Rhône-Alpes. In 1977 there were 305 computing companies in the region, a figure which rose to 439 in 1981 and almost 800 by the late 1980s. Over the same period employment in the relevant sectors grew by 40 per cent. The industry is characterised by sectoral diversity within the communications and computing sectors, small firms and a highly qualified labour force. Supporting activities within the area include important science-based educational facilities (Swyngedouw *et al.*, 1992). An important concentration of computing and communication industries within the wider Rhône-Alpes region is centred on Grenoble, which in the 1960s had already established itself as the most important centre for them outside Paris. Their large growth potential in Grenoble was recognised by the designation of one of the first technopoles, the ZIRST (*zone industrielle de recherche scientifique et technique*), in the 1970s at Meylan. (British readers would probably recognise this as a science park.) Here, building on the large pool of publicly funded research in Grenoble, a whole series of small firms became established. The ZIRST also includes two large research organisations, Merlin

Gerin and the Centre National d'Etudes des Télécommunications (CNET). As a group, these activities have been successful in developing research–industry links with entrepreneurs coming from the local institutes of higher education, and in participating equally in teaching and the supervision of doctoral studies.

Although the "new industrial districts" of western Europe might be seen as models for the typical pattern of manufacturing production in an age of flexible production systems, they cannot, however, be interpreted in an entirely positive light. For example, as Ganne (1989, 149) has highlighted, the Meylan ZIRST has generated "few relations of collaboration or complementarity between firms . . . but . . . on the contrary they seem to engage in acute competition, in order to preserve, in particular, the confidentiality of results". Also, from an analysis of recent changes in Baden-Württemberg and Emilia-Romagna, Cooke and Morgan (1994, 115) conclude "the exigencies of heightened global competition are creating significant challenges to the ingenuity and capability of the regional networks on which prosperity may increasingly depend". These regions are therefore not immune from wider forces operating in the western European economy, and evidence from Benetton hints of further changes to come. In 1995 this firm started replacing Italian subcontractors by those in Portugal for cotton garments, and in eastern Europe for outerwear (Morgan Stanley, 1995).

Conclusion

The picture that emerges of the geography of the west European manufacturing sector in the mid-1990s is that it is dominated by Germany and that the most important sectors are electrical engineering and food and drink. The largest absolute decline in manufacturing employment was recorded by the UK, which accounted for 47 per cent of the net jobs lost. Among the largest west European-owned firms those with head offices in Germany are most important, with France and the UK of equal significance. Non-European ownership of production facilities is concentrated in the hands of US firms and – as a result of pressures from these and other non-

European firms and the creation of the SEM – west European companies have increasingly sought to develop pan-European production facilities. However, set against this process of market penetration by global firms and the integration of formerly national production systems, there is some evidence of a resurgence of geographical clusters of small firms specialising in using new flexible production technologies to gain competitive advantage.

These trends create a picture of a dynamic and rapidly changing scene. Writing in the late 1980s Dunning and Robson (1987, 123) were of the view that "the process of the reorganisation of West European industry to West European integration is far from complete". This is still true today. Indeed, the EU continues to expand the number of countries within its orbit, to change its relationships with neighbouring countries and to increase the level of internal integration through moves towards a common currency. West European manufacturing industry is working within an increasingly turbulent environment.

Over the next decade it is not unreasonable to expect the number of employees in manufacturing to continue to fall and for the structure of the west European economy to move closer towards that of the United States. Services will become more important, and manufacturing less so, as sources of employment opportunities. Yet, despite the expected decline in the relative importance of manufacturing within western Europe, it is likely to remain the major centre of production in the global economic system.

With a current home market of 350 million consumers, and high GDP per head, the EU will continue to offer new opportunities for west European firms; it will also be served and exploited by multinational companies originating outside western Europe, especially those based in the West Pacific Rim. This clearly underlines the importance of west European progress towards more efficient production systems through the restructuring of existing operations. However, to some extent the significance of the overall globalisation of manufacturing may be tempered by the emergence of more localised production systems. As a result of the decreasing influence of international barriers within the EU, some would argue it is the region rather than the

country which will become the fundamental building block of the west European economy. Indeed, in the western Europe of the twenty-first century, it is quite possible that competition between regions for manufacturing investment may replace that which has traditionally occurred between nations.

Further Reading

Material used in this chapter can in many cases be updated from *Basic Statistics of the Community*. Issued annually, this series reports primarily on the EU, but also provides some data for Norway and Switzerland. More detailed information can be obtained from the main Eurostat statistical series and official publications of the EU. All major cities in the UK have an official collection of EU documents in one of the educational institutions. Unfortunately there is no one book which takes the geography of western European industry as its central theme, and contemporary patterns have to be pieced together from more general studies. Sectoral perspectives are provided by de Jong (1993) but perhaps the best source for sectoral analysis is the almost annual *Panorama of EC/EU Industry* (latest edition 1995–96, published in late 1995).

Case studies of the impact of multinationals on Ireland, Portugal, Spain and Italy will be found in Dicken and Quevit (1994) while analyses of the west European operations of major firms include studies of IBM, Philips (de Smidt and Wever, 1990), Alcatel-Alsthom, SmithKline Beecham, Thomson Consumer Electronics, Tootal and British Steel (Nilsson *et al.* 1996).

Note

1. NACE is the general industrial classification of economic activities in the EU.

References

Amin, A, Charles D R and Howells J (1992) Corporate restructuring and cohesion in the new Europe, *Regional Studies*, **26**, 319–31.

Central Statistical Office (1995) *Business Monitor PA 1002 1992*, HMSO, London.

Charles, D (1996) Alcatel: a European champion for a globalizing market, in J-E Nilsson, P Dicken and J Peck (eds) *The Internationalisation Process: European firms in global competition*, Paul Chapman, London, 13–37.

Commission of the EC (1991) *Panorama of EC industry 1991–2*, Office for Official Publications of the European Communities, Luxembourg.

Commission of the EU (1994) *Panorama of EU industry 1994*, Office for Official Publications of the European Communities, Luxembourg.

Commission of the EU (1995) *Panorama of EU industry 1995–6*, Office for Official Publications of the European Communities, Luxembourg.

Cooke, P and Morgan, K (1994) Growth regions under duress: renewal strategies in Baden-Württemberg and Emilia-Romagna, in A Amin and N Thrift (eds) *Globalization, Institutions, and Regional Development in Europe*, Oxford University Press, Oxford, 91–117.

De Jong, H W (ed) (1993) *The Structure of European Industry*, Kluwer, Dordrecht.

De Smidt, M and Wever, E (1990) *The Corporate Firm in a Changing World Economy*, Routledge, London.

Dicken, P (1992) *Global Shift: the internationalization of economic activity*, Harper and Row, London.

Dicken, P and Quevit, M (1994) *Transnational Corporations and European Regional Restructuring*, Netherlands Geographical Studies, 181, Royal Dutch Geographical Society, Utrecht.

Dicken, P *et al.* (1994) Strategies of transnational corporations and European regional restructuring: some conceptual issues, in P Dicken and M Quevit (eds) *Transnational Corporations and European Regional Restructuring*, Netherlands Geographical Studies, 181, Royal Dutch Geographical Society, Utrecht, 9–28.

Dunning, J H and Robson, P (1987) Multinational corporate integration and regional economic integration, *Journal of Common Market Studies*, **26**, 103–25.

The Economist (1988) Civil aerospace survey, 3 September, 9–10.

Ellis, J and Williams, D (1995) *International Business Strategy*, Pitman, London.

Emerson, M (1988) The economics of 1992, *European Economy*, **35**, 1–218.

Eurostat (1991) *Basic Statistics of the Community*, 28th edn, Office for Official Publications of the European Communities, Luxembourg.

Eurostat (1994) *Basic Statistics of the Community*, Office for Official Publications of the European Communities, Luxembourg.

Ganne, B (1989) Regional dynamics of innovation: a look at the Rhône-Alpes region, *Entrepreneurship and Regional Development*, **1**, 147–54.

Geroski, P A and Jacquemin, A (1984) Large firms in the European corporate economy and industrial policy in the 1980s, in A Jacquemin (ed) *European Industry, Public Policy and Corporate Strategy*, Clarendon Press, Oxford, 343–68.

International Labour Office (1995) *Yearbook of Labour Statistics*, Geneva, United Nations.

Kelly, T and Keeble, D (1990) IBM: the corporate chameleon, in M de Smidt and E Wever (eds) *The Corporate Firm in a Changing World Economy*, Routledge, London, 21–54.

Lazerson, M (1990) Subcontracting in the Modena knitwear industry, in F Pyke, G Becattini and W Sengenberger (eds) *Industrial Districts and Inter-firm Co-operation in Italy*, International Institute for Labour Studies, Geneva, 108–33.

Morgan Stanley (1995) *Benetton Group S.p.A*, Morgan Stanley & Co. New York.

Nilsson, J-E, Dicken, P and Peck, J (eds) (1996) *The Internationalisation Process: European firms in global competition*, Paul Chapman, London.

Piore, M J (1990) Work, labour and action: work experience in a system of flexible production, in F Pyke, G Becattini and W Sengenberger (eds) *Industrial Districts and Inter-firm Co-operation in Italy*, International Institute for Labour Studies, Geneva, 51–5.

Sforzi, F. (1990) The quantitative importance of Marshallian industrial districts in the Italian economy, in F Pyke, G Becattini and W Sengenberger (eds) *Industrial Districts and Inter-firm Co-operation in Italy*, International Institute for Labour Studies, Geneva, 75–107.

Swyngedouw, E, Lemattre, M and Wells, P (1992) The regional pattern of computing and communication industries in the UK and France, in P Cooke, F Moulaert, E Swyngedouw, O Weinstein and P Wells (eds) *Towards Global Localisation*, UCL Press, London, 79–128.

Weinstein, O (1992) The telecommunications equipment industry: the great transformation, in P Cooke, F Moulaert, E Swyngedouw, O Weinstein and P Wells (eds) *Towards Global Localization*, UCL Press, London, 152–77.

Wells, P and Rawlinson, M (1994) *The New European Automobile Industry*, Macmillan, London.

6

Industrial restructuring in the new democracies

Andrew H Dawson

Department of Geography, University of St Andrews, UK

The movers and shakers of the space economy of central and eastern Europe are so no longer. Manufacturing industry and mining, which for 50 years in central Europe, and 70 in the former Soviet Union, have been the engine of economic growth and spatial reorganisation, have lost their privileged position. Following political and economic reform, industrial restructuring has been the order of the day throughout the former Communist bloc; and mining and manufacturing, rather than being the commanding heights of the economy, have in many instances become its basket cases. Questions as to what is made and where have become of less importance than those concerning the distributional outcomes of what has become a continuous and rapid process of adaptation, involving owners of capital, entrepreneurs, workers, consumers, politicians and crooks, for many of whom the "best game" is no longer to be found in the industrial town, but elsewhere.

Such a sudden reversal of economic conditions would be traumatic for any country, but it has been the more so because it has affected all parts of central and eastern Europe simultaneously, engulfing not only one of the world's superpowers – the former Soviet Union – but also such other major industrial countries of the Communist period as Czechoslovakia and the former German Democratic Republic (GDR) (Table 6.1). The impact of economic reform on each of these would merit separate attention. There would also be merit in examining its effect elsewhere in the region: in Romania, where the country has been coming to terms with the dire legacy of Ceauşescu's idiosyncratic programme of economic development, or in the Balkans, which have been wracked by the wars of the

Table 6.1 *Industrial employment in the major economies of central and eastern Europe in the mid-1980s*

Country	Employees ('000)
Bulgaria	1650
Czechoslovakia	2890
GDR	3830
Hungary	1540
Poland	5290
Romania	3930
USSR	39 810
Yugoslavia	2210

Source: *National Yearbooks.*

Yugoslav succession. There is not, however, space to consider all of these interesting cases, and this chapter can do little more than outline the principal characteristics of the geography of industrialisation under Communism and the subsequent effect of economic reform in the region as a whole. It will, however, go on to explore the case of Poland, which was the largest of the industrial producers of the region after the Soviet Union, and the most important to have survived the revolutions which followed the fall of the Berlin Wall in November 1989.

Industrialisation under Communism

Looking back on Communist industrialisation, six characteristics stand out. Firstly, industry was awarded the highest priority among the sectors of the economy, with the consequence that, long before the end of the Communist era, manufacturing and mining had come to dominate the economies of all the countries in central and eastern Europe (Table 6.2). Furthermore, the Soviet Union had become one of the world's most important industrial powers, producing a wide range of minerals and manufactured goods, with Poland, the GDR and Czechoslovakia also achieving substantial outputs (Table 6.3). By the 1980s there were probably six major areas in the

region in which manufacturing and mining occupied an overwhelmingly important role in the local economy and made a major contribution to its industrial output as a whole. Four of these were in the Soviet Union – the Donbas, Kuzbas and Moscow regions, plus the southern Urals – while the other two lay in central Europe, in the Upper Silesian region of Poland and Czechoslovakia, and the Saxon area of the GDR. However, the role of manufacturing was also expanded in many other places, rendering ancient cities filthy and creating industrial cathedrals in rural landscapes.

Secondly, the economic geography of the region increasingly became that of a space plan, rather than of a space economy. Whereas before 1917 in Russia, and 1945 in central Europe, the map of manufacturing industry and mining had developed very largely in relation to the aims of profit-takers, thereafter it was determined by the priorities of the Soviet state, whose overriding need was for defence. This did not simply mean that, in both the Soviet Union and its central European satellites, greater emphasis was placed on the development of heavy industry and aeronautical and space technologies than almost anything else; in addition, industry was spread across the Soviet Union as strategic objectives were pursued. Coal-mines were sunk beyond the Arctic Circle; aircraft production was established

Table 6.2 *The changing role of industry in the major economies of central and eastern Europe, 1986–93*

Country	Percentage of employment in industry		Percentage of GDP generated by industry	
	1986	1992	1986	1993
Belarus		30*		43*
Bulgaria	37	40	58	35
Czechoslovakia	37	36	62	
Czech Republic				39
GDR	43		70	
Hungary	31	30	45	28
Poland	29	27	49	33
Romania	37	35	61	34
Russia		30		28
Ukraine		27*		43*
USSR	29		46	
Yugoslavia	24		43	

* 1991.

Sources: Muir-Carby (1995); *National Yearbooks*.

Table 6.3 *The production of selected goods in central and eastern Europe, 1986–92*

Country	Bituminous coal (m. tonnes)		Crude steel ingots (m. tonnes)		Electricity (m. kilowatt hours)		Cars ('000)	
	1986	1992	1986	1992	1986	1992	1986	1992
Bulgaria			3	2	42	36		
Czechoslovakia	26		15		85		185	
Czech Republic		19		7		59		173
GDR			8		115		218	
Hungary	2	1	4	2	28	32		
Poland	192	132	17	10	140	133	290	219
Romania	9	4	14	5	76	54	134	84
Russia		193		67		1008		1030
Ukraine		128		42		553		156
USSR	513		161		1599		1326	
Yugoslavia			2	1	77	37	210	

Source: United Nations (1994).

in Georgia and Kazakhstan; the Urals metallurgical complex was developed; and "closed" towns in central Russia concentrated on the building of nuclear and other weaponry. Although Soviet planners were encouraged to take account of the costs of production, including those of transport, in location decisions, industry was spread far and wide, leading to stories about wasteful cross-hauling on the Soviet Union's hard-pressed railway system.

Thirdly, Communist industrialisation was achieved through a rapid and substantial shift of capital and labour from other sectors of the economy, and especially agriculture. Countries in which more than half the working population was employed on the land in the 1930s, and less than a fifth in industry, had reversed the roles of the two sectors by the 1980s, at least in relation to their contribution to the gross domestic product (GDP). It was, in other words, an "extensive" form of economic development, not hindered by the fact that many of those who transferred from field to factory were obliged by shortages of urban housing to continue to live in their villages and spend hours commuting. However, in a situation in which many parts of central and eastern Europe were facing low birth rates,[1] growth by such a transfer was a once-for-all occurrence. Moreover, once the supply of surplus rural labour began to decline, the Communist system of central

planning, lacking personal incentives and brutally policed, failed to exchange this "extensive" form of economic growth for one based on innovation and increases in labour productivity.

Fourthly, industrial enterprises in Communist countries conducted their business very differently from private producers in a market economy. In particular, they paid neither the real rate of interest on the capital which the state had invested in them, nor the cost of the land which they used. Moreover, because of uncertainties of delivery by other enterprises, they produced many of their own specialist goods and services in support of their core business, despite the fact that they were often ill-suited to such activity. They also frequently avoided paying for the disposal of waste by-products, dumping them in rivers, lakes and seas, allowing them to seep into the soil or releasing them into the air: such actions reduced the productive potential of these natural resources and increased the demand for medical care from those whose health was subsequently injured (see also Chapter 20). Furthermore, they enjoyed what Kornai (1981) has called a "soft budget constraint": if they failed to pay their bills, they were not restructured or shut down, no matter how ill-located they were, how low their productivity or how unsaleable their products.

Fifthly, industrial enterprises were very large. Private firms, which usually start small, were not allowed to enter the market; and many of the plants established under central planning were huge. Many settlements were, as a result, not only one-industry, but in many cases one-plant, towns. The new town of Donaujvaros, which was built among the villages of central Hungary in the 1950s and 1960s, depended entirely on the large steel mill that was established there at that time, while the sleepy Polish market town of Plock, with a population of about 30 000 in 1950, tripled in size following the establishment of one of the country's chief oil refineries in it in the 1960s.

Lastly, the economies of the region were insulated to a very considerable degree from changes elsewhere. Despite a population of about 400 million, and a very high degree of industrialisation, the area only accounted for 7 per cent of international trade in 1988. There was very little trade in manufactured products with the rest of the world; little advanced technology was imported, not least because NATO's Co-ordinating Committee for Multilateral Export Controls (COCOM) policed exports to the region; and trade was managed by the Communist governments so that domestic industries were not subject to competition from producers in either the other countries of the Communist bloc or those outside it. On the other hand, some new patterns of spatial integration appeared within the region as, first, long-distance movements of raw materials and goods increased substantially within the Soviet Union and, later, new trading links were established between that country and its central European satellites. These links connected, for example, the coal and steel industries of Upper Silesia by wide-gauge railway to those of the Ukraine, while pipelines and electricity grids spun a further web of connections (Pinder and Simmonds, 1993). (It was this type of specialisation which led, for instance, to Hungary producing many of the buses for the region and the Soviet Union most of the aircraft.) As a result, 55 per cent of the international trade of the countries of the region in 1988 was with each other, and only about 20 per cent with western Europe. In the absence of competition, there was little pressure for either product or process innovation, and both the range of products and their quality were inferior to those available in the major market economies. Home-grown

technological development was highly concentrated in the defence and heavy industries, and even there – as the Chernobyl accident showed in relation to Soviet nuclear power stations – some of it proved to be of a dangerously low quality.

In short, Communist industrialisation was highly distinctive, and quite unlike that in North America, western Europe or the emerging market economies of eastern Asia. It was hardly surprising, therefore, that once the policies upon which it had been based were abandoned, the potential for change was very great.

The Impact of Reform

The reforms which have led to that change have everywhere been the same in principle (Ernst *et al.*, 1996) – privatisation and the creation of a free market – but have been complicated by the fact that the various countries of the region have implemented change at different rates. The Czech Republic, Germany, Poland and Russia led the way, while Belarus, Bulgaria, Romania and the Ukraine have lagged behind. Figure 6.1 conceptualises both the chief features of the Communist industrial era and the dominant shifts in the post-Communist phase.

Some of the earliest privatisations of publicly owned enterprises occurred even as the political revolutions which overthrew the Communist governments were taking place. Some managers, seeing an opportunity to transfer into their own hands assets whose value was not properly recognised by government, indulged in what became known as "wild privatisation". Potentially profitable parts of enterprises were bought at knock-down prices, leaving the state with those which were unsaleable; and existing contracts were rapidly exploited to make substantial personal fortunes. Not surprisingly, governments outlawed such activities, but not before some of the more valuable businesses had been moved into the private sector.

Almost all governments in the region have now embarked on more orderly privatisation programmes, though the form of privatisation, the range of economic activities to be included, and the speed at which they have been implemented have varied considerably. At one extreme, Germany established a state commission, charged with rationalising and selling all the former GDR's manufacturing and mining enterprises within a three-year period, while the Czech Republic moved quickly to implement voucher privatisation, in which citizens were given shares in a wide range of industrial enterprises. Elsewhere, several countries have allowed the transfer of substantial parts of enterprises to foreign, usually Western, firms. Thus, the Swiss firm Nestlé has taken over food-processing companies in Poland and Russia, Germany's Volkswagen has turned round the Czech Republic's car-making industry, the American firm General Electric has purchased a major holding in the Hungarian electric light-bulb industry, and South Korea's Daewoo has taken a controlling stake in Romania's Mangalia shipyard. Many other examples could be cited. There has, however, been widespread concern about the risks involved in allowing foreign capital to take decisive control of domestic industry. More recently, the Polish authorities, faced with the fact that nobody could be induced to buy many of the country's industrial behemoths, transferred them to consortia of banks, thus retaining them in the public sector for the present, but removing them from direct government control. This, the government hopes, will make their rationalisation politically easier. Meanwhile, many enterprises in Belarus, Bulgaria, Romania and the Ukraine remain in government ownership.

The second change has been the replacement of central planning with the market, exposing enterprises to the discipline of paying the real costs of their activities while having to produce goods at a price that customers can afford and of a quality which will persuade them to buy. Given the monetary "overhang"[2] in most of the economies of the region at the end of the Communist period, the abandonment of fixed prices led to rapid inflation and sharp falls in demand for all except essential goods. Industry has also been affected by the reform of the arrangements governing international trade. The restoration of the right of individuals and firms to own and run private businesses has been accompanied by that of their right to import and export. As a result, many people have taken the opportunity to import Western, brand-name products, selling them on the streets on the morrow of these reforms, and thus undermining the demand for locally produced goods. This is not to say that international trade is now unrestricted: import tariffs have been imposed on many products, and there are also export levies on Russian oil and gas. Nevertheless, trade is now conducted in a manner which is much closer to that in the rest of the world. At the same time, governments which in effect had been major consumers, especially of the products of industries supplying armaments and infra-structural goods, found that they did not need to spend as much on defence following the end of the Cold War. Consequently they reduced their demands substantially.

The effect of these changes on manufacturing and mining was marked, with levels of output falling sharply in many industries (Table 6.3), and enterprises laying off workers. Unemployment – an unheard of phenomenon under Communism – grew rapidly. Many of the enterprises which remained in the public sector did not, however, reduce their workforce in line with the fall in demand for their products, and bridged the gap by borrowing from banks or failing to pay their workers, suppliers or their taxes. Something of these changes is illustrated in Table 6.2, which also shows how substantial has been the fall in the sector's contribution to GDP.

Figure 6.1 *A model of the impact of economic reform upon the geography of manufacturing and mining. (Over the following two pages.) Figure 6.1a shows some of the features of the geography of manufacturing and mining in two centrally planned economies, Countries A and C, and in a mixed economy, Country B. Figure 6.1b shows some of the changes that have occurred since the collapse of central planning in A and C and the subsequent reform of their economies. In particular, it indicates the changes in the number, type, scale and ownership of enterprises in three types of location – the capital city, a major mineral-based industrial region, and in the more rural areas of each country. It also indicates changes in the scale and composition of trade between Country A and the others as a contribution of manufacturing and mining to that employment. It should be noted that, following the collapse of its Communist regime, Country C split into two new countries, D and E.*

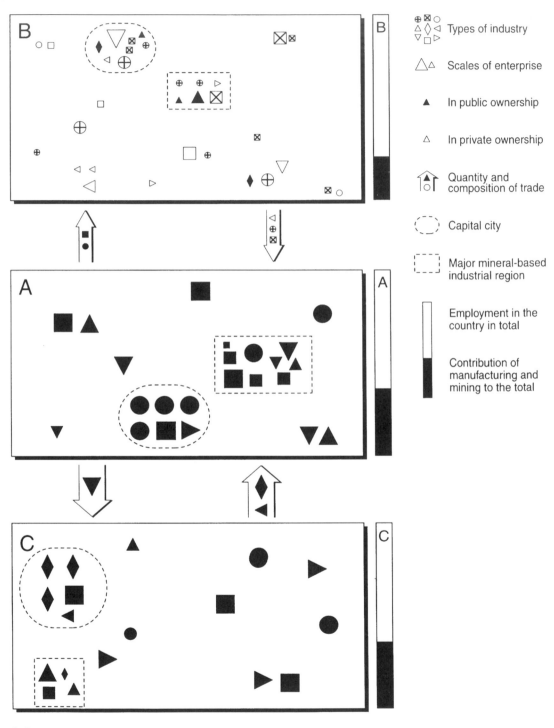

(a)

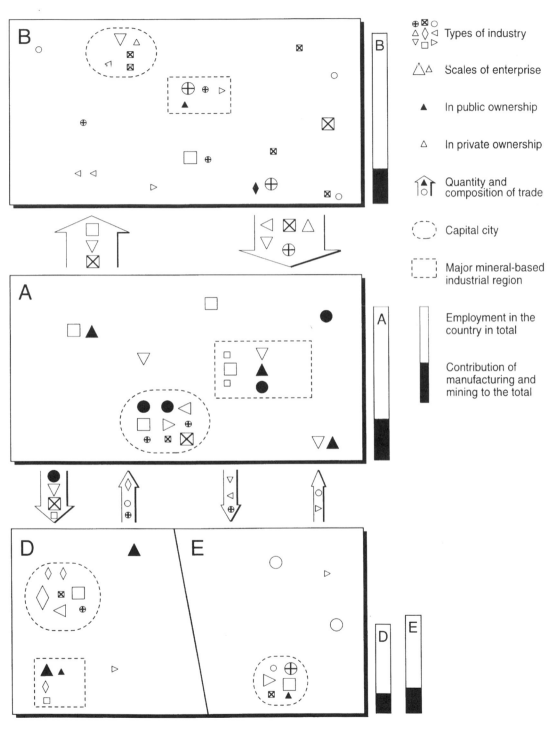

(b)

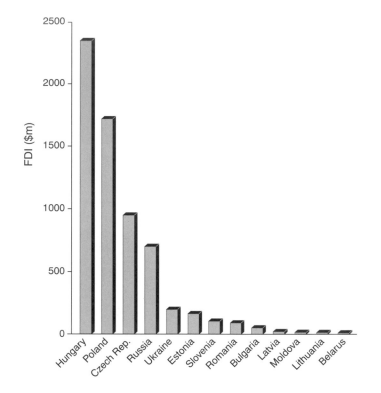

Figure 6.2 *Foreign direct investment in eastern and central Europe*

There have also been considerable changes in the trading patterns of the region. Given that there are now many more countries in central and eastern Europe than in 1989, it might have been expected that the amount of international trade would have increased, as what had formerly been internal transactions within the Soviet Union or Czechoslovakia became international. In the event, the economic disruption of the period far outweighed the effect of these changes, and by 1992 the region's contribution to world trade had fallen to 2.5 per cent of the total. Moreover, only about 20 per cent of that was between the countries of the region; almost half was with western Europe. Poland, in particular, reorientated its international trade to an even greater extent, conducting about two-thirds of it with western Europe by 1992.

Similar changes have begun to occur with regard to movements of capital. Despite some well-publicised licensed production of western European cars, long superseded by more modern models in their original markets, and a small number of joint ventures, Western firms invested very little capital in central and eastern Europe prior to 1989. Since then, however, several have bought enterprises, opened branch plants or entered into joint ventures with local firms. This has often led to investment in new plant, substantial improvements in both productivity and quality, and the introduction of new products. Such investments have been made, in part, to exploit local markets, where the opportunities are large: the Russian market, of 148 million people, has the potential to become one of the largest in Europe as standards of living rise. Similarly, those of the Ukraine and Poland, with populations of 52 and 39 million respectively, could both become significant. Investments have also been made with a view to exploiting the much lower labour costs of the region – an advantage which they are likely to retain for some years to come – through the production of goods for export to western Europe. However, only three countries – the Czech Republic, Hungary and Poland – had

Table 6.4 *Net foreign direct investment in selected former Communist countries in 1993 and in developing countries which received $1bn or more*

Country	GDP ($m.)	Net foreign direct investment ($m.)
Azerbaijan	5000	0
Belarus	27 500	10
Bulgaria	10 400	55
Czech Republic	31 600	950
Estonia	5100	160
Georgia	3000	0
Hungary	38 600	2349
Latvia	4100	20
Lithuania	4300	12
Macedonia	1700	0
Moldova	4300	14
Poland	85 900	1715
Romania	26 000	94
Russia	329 400	700
Slovakia	11 100	0
Slovenia	10 300	112
Ukraine	109 100	200
Argentina	255 600	6305
China	425 600	25 800
Indonesia	144 700	2094
Malaysia	64 500	4351
Mexico	343 500	4901
Portugal	85 700	1301
Thailand	124 900	2400

Source: World Bank (1995).

received significant quantities of foreign direct investment by the mid-1990s (Table 6.4 and Figure 6.2).

The Transition in Poland: Expectations versus Reality

Nowhere was economic restructuring adopted with greater official enthusiasm after the fall of the Communist regimes than in Poland. In 1989, some thought that a market economy could be created within five years (Sachs, 1994); Finance Minister Balcerowicz's "shock therapy" of 1990 was intended to do just that; and, in 1991, Blanchard offered a model of the likely trajectory that restructuring would take, made up of three stages. He foresaw an initial shake-out in the state sector, followed by the growth of private firms, leading to a third, equilibrium, stage during which the private sector would gradually expand at the expense of the rump of the nationalised economy.

The national picture

In the late 1980s about 30 per cent of the Polish workforce was employed in mining and manufacturing, and this sector produced almost half of the country's GDP. Poland was a major producer of coal, both bituminous and brown, and manufactured large quantities of metals, engineering products and textiles. Though much of this activity was located on the Upper Silesian coalfield and in Lodz, there was a substantial manufacturing sector in all the major cities, and most towns had been provided with at least one major industrial plant as part of the Communist development of the economy: Krakow's Nowa Huta steelworks was perhaps the most (in)famous example.[3] Even in the rural north-east of the country – an area with few mineral resources – a fifth or more of the labour force was employed in manufacturing. More than half the country's external trade was with other socialist countries, chiefly the other members of Comecon, with the most important exports being engineering products, coal, chemicals, metals and textiles, in that order. In this, the economy gave the appearance of being well adapted to the country's political and economic environment, providing its people with educational, housing, medical and social services, as well as the guarantee of employment. Standards of living had been achieved which differed little, either between one part of Poland and another, or from those in much of the rest of central and eastern Europe. It was not, however, so: in reality, Poland was overindustrialised (Sachs, 1994) with the result that standards of living were low, relative to those in western Europe, and declining. In addition, many Poles suffered from gross pollution of the atmosphere by manufacturing industry, and ordinary people chafed under the restrictions on their freedom of choice which accompanied the type of development that had been adopted.

Following the fall of the Communist government in 1989, institutional and policy change was rapid. Within a few months, much of the system of central planning had been abandoned, large-scale private enterprise had once again been allowed, most prices had been freed, and foreign trade had ceased to be a state monopoly. Import tariffs were cut to very low levels, other than on food, textiles and clothing. The privatisation of publicly owned enterprises was begun, and rigid budgetary discipline was introduced, including an end to most producer and export subsidies, with a view to achieving international currency convertibility and eventual entry to the EU. The role of the state as purchaser of much of the mining and manufacturing output was sharply reduced; that of a supplier of capital was terminated. Furthermore, following similar changes in several of the other countries of central Europe, Comecon collapsed; and Poland's pattern of trade was further disrupted by the break-up of the Soviet Union in 1991 and the end of the Warsaw Pact.

The impact was equally dramatic. Within two years, the country's GDP fell by a fifth, unemployment rose to 17 per cent, and standards of living declined, though not as sharply as these figures might suggest. Most, but not all, sectors of the economy were adversely affected. While there was a marked increase in employment in the distributive trades, and little or no change in education, health and social welfare, other sectors were severely hit, especially mining and manufacturing. Thus, between 1989 and 1990, the real value of sales by manufacturing fell by a quarter, and declined still further in 1991, while that of extractive industry continued to fall in 1992 and 1993 to two-thirds of what it had been at the end of the 1980s. Within this general picture, however, there was considerable variety of experience, both by industry and location. While sales and employment in engineering and textiles remained far below the levels of the late 1980s, the clothing and printing industries had returned to or exceeded those levels by 1993 (Table 6.5). Similarly, while employment in industry in a few voivodships[4] in 1993 was close to what it had been in 1986, most parts of the country experienced losses of at least 10 per cent, with falls of a fifth or more in a number of districts which previously had been highly dependent on industry. Prominent among these were Katowice, Kielce, Krakow, Lodz, Opole and Walbrzych. Overall, by 1993, manufacturing and mining employed only a quarter of those in work and contributed no more than a third to the country's GDP.

Enterprises were forced back upon their own resources. Large numbers of those in trade were privatised, while share offers and joint ventures

Table 6.5 *Polish industry, 1986–93*

Industry	Sales in 1993 in constant prices (1989 = 100)	Employment in 1993 (1986 = 100)	Percentage of sales by ownership in 1993	
			Public	Private
Coal-mining	62	76	99.3	0.7
Metallurgy	59	73	93.2	6.8
Engineering	64	58	65.6	34.4
Electrical engineering and electronics	90	58	47.7	52.3
Chemicals	78	83	61.5	38.5
Paper	88	73	49.1	50.9
Printing	127	83	25.9	74.1
Textiles	58	50	66.3	33.7
Clothing	96	107	12.0	88.0
Food	79	112	49.7	50.3

Source: Poland, Central Statistical Office (1994b).

with Western companies also removed a few factories from the public sector. Some closed. Meanwhile, many new, privately owned businesses appeared, partly in manufacturing but largely in the service sector. Thus, by 1994, the private sector accounted for more than half of the country's GDP. On the other hand, many of the mills and mines which had been so fundamental to the centrally planned construction of an industrial, proletarian society remained in public ownership, languishing outside the newly emerging space economy, isolated from the stimuli which were promoting growth within it, and cut off from the new and highly flexible sources of capital to which it gave access.

Engineering, mining and textiles

The pattern of change has, however, been a good deal more complex than this sketch might suggest, not least because it has been bound up with a move away from the political and economic certainties of the initial Balcerowicz plan, in an ongoing debate within the country about the rate at which reform should proceed. Three examples – the Ursus tractor factory, coal-mining and the Lodz textile industry – will demonstrate this complexity.

Ursus is a town of about 40 000 people on the south-western edge of Warsaw. Its tractor factory was founded in the late nineteenth century, destroyed during the Second World War and reconstructed during the 1950s. As a large-scale, state-owned, monopoly supplier of about 55 000 tractors per annum, not only to Poland, but also other Comecon countries, it then came to typify the industrial development of the post-war period. Moreover, with 25 000 employees, some of whom lived in dingy "worker hotels", it was the dominant economic and political force within Ursus. During the Gierek[5] period of limited economic opening to the West in the 1970s – in an attempt to attract capital investment – it had acquired a licence from the Canadian Massey-Ferguson company to build one of that firm's large tractors, and there was talk of raising output to 100 000 each year. This did not, however, happen; and the machine which it did produce was more suited to huge collectives than to the small, privately owned farms which accounted

for three-quarters of the country's cultivated land. Nor did the factory have a happy workforce, acquiring a reputation during the 1980s as one of the country's most important centres of anti-Communist agitation.

In the immediate aftermath of the fall of the Communist government, some Ursus directors showed that, contrary to Western views of Communist management, they were capable of considerable initiative, rapidly hiving off its more profitable activities by forming "private" companies which employed the factory's workers and "used" (that is, stole) its materials. That process, however, was quickly outlawed, and the plant remained in public ownership. By 1991, sales of tractors had fallen below 10 000, and the government, desperate to cut the wage bill, established a restructuring consortium to rid the enterprise of the most unproductive activities and halve the workforce. That consortium turned to the EU and British government for advice, advice which advocated even greater reductions in the number of jobs. But the fall of the reforming Bielecki government led to the removal of the consortium leader and the adoption of a less draconian plan, based on sales targets of 35 000 tractors by 1995 and 50 000 in 1996. In the event, these proved to be unattainable, not least because of the unsuitability of the factory's principal product for the domestic market. Production remained at very low levels; the enterprise's debts continued to grow; and such opportunities as existed for even such simple forms of diversification as the provision of spare parts for the existing production model were neglected. Workers, who took to the streets to demand more government subsidies, reduced still further the likelihood of attracting the foreign investment which will be required if new types of tractor are to be produced or the enterprise's debts restructured. Meanwhile, the management was urging the Polish government to hobble the private manufacturing of tractors by imposing swingeing tariffs on imported Belarusian parts – from which machines more suited to Polish conditions were being assembled, at much higher levels of labour productivity, by smaller private producers (Simpson, 1995). The government obliged, but only to the extent of noting that the manufacture of machinery, like that of food, textiles, furniture and pharmaceuticals, is deserving of special protection from foreign predators, and reversing its earlier policy of cutting tariffs. It was not prepared to go so far as to exclude imports. In other words, five years after the start of reform, the Ursus factory had proved to be too important to be allowed to founder, but too expensive to save. It was, however, being strangled by its debts.

In this it was like many of the other so-called industrial "dinosaurs" of the Communist period, which have proved to be so difficult to move from the public sector, in which they are of direct political significance to government, into the relative obscurity of private ownership. Most notable among these has been the coal industry. Under the Communist model of development, the highest priority was accorded to increasing the output of fuel, and Poland built up a large export market in bituminous coal, not only to other Comecon members, but also western Europe. Polish miners were among the country's highest paid workers. However, as with the Ursus plant, labour productivity was abysmal. Furthermore, several of the mines, including those which were being sunk in the 1970s and 1980s in the newly discovered Lublin coalfield, faced such difficult geological conditions that they could never have covered their costs in a market economy. The removal of government subsidies to the industry, the fall in demand from the country's heavy industries, the more efficient use of fuel brought about by economic reform, and the disruption of the industry's markets in the Soviet bloc, led to the closure of all the pits in the small Lublin and Walbrzych fields, a sharp fall in employment in the industry in general, and the promise of closures in Upper Silesia.

By the mid-1990s, however, no closures had occurred in that heartland of the industry, even though probably only a quarter of the Upper Silesian mines had been making any money, their contribution to the industry had been quite inadequate to offset losses in the other pits, the industry's debts had soared, and its taxes had remained largely unpaid. In 1990 the government was advised by the American consultants, Arthur Andersen, to close up to 15 pits; and in 1993 the World Bank offered to meet some of the social costs, if at least nine were shut. There has been talk

of halving the workforce over a period of 10 years. The government has, however, proved to be incapable of such action, let alone privatisation. Instead, it has fallen back on attempts to introduce some sort of internal market within the industry – attempts which have failed to balance its books – and has indicated that it does not intend to privatise industries, such as coal, which it considers to be "strategic". In short, Polish governments appear to have had no realistic answer to the fundamental problems which the initial Balcerowicz reforms created for the industry, and have proved politically unable to choose between radical restructuring (which would be necessary before private capital could be attracted) and a return to overt public subsidy.

Something similar has occurred in the textile industry. Poland's early industrialisation rested in large part upon textiles, and nowhere was the growth of industry and its associated urban settlements more spectacular than in and around Lodz. During the nineteenth century this settlement rose from the status of a hamlet to that of Poland's second city – a position which it has since maintained – partly on the basis of exports to other parts of the Russian Empire, to which central Poland then belonged. What is more, in the 1950s and 1960s, when the textile industries of the UK, France and Germany were in decline, that in Lodz increased its output and continued to dominate the city's economy; and several large new textile mills were built in the 1970s. About half of all employment in Lodz in 1980 was in manufacturing – itself a high proportion in Poland – and almost half of that was in textiles. Despite these apparent successes, however, in general the industry's plant remained old fashioned and its levels of productivity low, while its products became increasingly unattractive. In spite of the provision of export subsidies, and the transfer of some production to the new mills, Poland was already suffering from competition in its foreign markets in the 1980s. Several older premises were closed, and both output and employment in the city declined (Fierla, 1994; Paczka and Riley, 1992).

There has been a further massive decline in demand since 1989, as imports have risen and export subsidies removed. The effect has been that, whereas about 900 000 km of cotton cloth was woven in 1980 in Poland – about half of it in Lodz – the figure in 1993 was only 240 000. At the same time, the total number of people working in the city fell from 407 000 (or almost half of the population) to 250 000, with most of the fall concentrated in manufacturing. Some of those who have been thrown out of work in the textile mills have found jobs in the burgeoning retail sector; and some have since left the labour force: the population has not only fallen by about 1 per cent since the late 1980s, and aged, but the number of those engaged in higher education has risen by a half (Poland, Central Statistical Office, 1994a, b). Some of the unemployed are almost certainly conducting private businesses or being paid for work not registered with the authorities, but many remain among the officially jobless; and the city has had one of the highest urban rates of male unemployment in the country. A very few small textile enterprises have entered into joint ventures with west European firms; and a handful of the smaller, older premises in the city centre have been taken over by some of the many new banks and retail firms (Musial and Paczka, 1993). Others, however, stand idle; and almost all the big mills remain in public ownership. Neither Polish nor overseas investors appear to be willing to put large sums of money into the industry.

These three examples reveal the problems which have arisen as a result of "marketisation without privatisation"; problems which afflict not only enterprises in these industries, but also many of the 3000 which have remained in public ownership. Put another way, although the private sector has accounted for more than half the Polish economy since 1993, Table 6.5 indicates how little progress had been made to move the mining, engineering, chemical and textile industries out of public ownership by that year. It also indicates the nature of the problem which government faces: it is in precisely those industries in which improvements in labour productivity have been least, and which are therefore becoming decreasingly attractive to private investors, that privatisation has furthest to go. In 1994, Jackman commented that "The full force of structural adjustment has therefore yet to be felt in the labour market", and *The Economist* estimated that state agencies and firms employed about 1.5 million surplus staff. Consequently it should not be surprising that,

notwithstanding offers of financial support from the EU and World Bank, Polish administrations have been either unwilling or unable to break the log-jam which has existed ever since the original Balcerowicz privatisation package eschewed the mass, voucher-based approach of the Czechs (Ernst *et al.*, 1996). This is not to say that attempts to make progress have ceased. In one of the latest of these, in 1995, 505 of the largest enterprises which remained in government hands were taken over by 15 national investment funds, each managed by groups of Polish and foreign banks. This development has already led to some of the restructuring which has hitherto been put off. It is expected that some enterprises will survive, but others will be broken up. Eventually, some or all of the equity will be sold to the public (Simpson, 1996). And in 1996, the government announced a further cut of 18 per cent in the output of coal and the closure of 20 mines by the end of the century. It is, however, too early to say how radical the actual changes will prove to be.

Interaction with western Europe

Even if national capital does contribute to a solution of the problem of the large-scale, public-sector plant in Poland, it is unlikely that it will be able or willing to take on the entire legacy left by the country's central industrial planners. Nor has it ever been expected that it should, for the economic reforms of 1990 were not only perceived to be desirable in themselves, but to be an essential preliminary to the achievement of what most Poles have consistently considered to be their primary aim: to "rejoin Europe", in part by securing rapid admission to the EU.

In the event this has proved to be difficult, not least because other players in the European space economy game have also been jockeying for position. Prior to 1989, the European Community (EC) used a variety of tariff and non-tariff barriers, including quotas, to restrict the import of central and eastern European goods, and mounted a large number of anti-dumping actions against central European exporters. Many of the non-tariff barriers affecting Poland were removed in 1990, when the Generalised System of Preferences was applied in their place, putting Poland on a similar footing to that of many other non-EC market economies. Meanwhile, hard on the heels of the collapse of Comecon, the three central European countries which were generally considered to have the strongest case for admission to the EC – Poland, Czechoslovakia and Hungary – formed themselves into the Visegrad group and, later, the Central European Free Trade Association (CEFTA), in part to press their case in Brussels. The EC responded by signing Association Agreements with the group in 1991 – a preliminary step towards their eventual full admission. However, these agreements were not generous. They explicitly excluded free trade in chemicals, iron and steel, and textiles and clothing, all of which have been subject to continuing and only slowly declining tariffs, to severely limited quotas and to stringent "rules of origin". The full removal of tariffs on coal was delayed until 1996, on steel until 1997 and on textiles until 1998. Furthermore, the quota on textiles was granted not to Polish producers or EU retailers, but to EU textile producers, who thus have the opportunity to reimport goods whose manufacture began in the EU, but was subsequently continued in Poland. Messerlin (1993) has suggested that the maintenance of quotas, in combination with the removal of import tariffs, will have the effect of turning any previous EC tariff revenues into private rents which will not accrue to producers in Poland, but to those who import Polish goods into the EU. The effect will be "managed trade", managed in the interests of the Union, rather than those of Polish firms. It is doubtful whether such meanness of spirit on the part of the EU, and the distortions to which it will give rise, can be justified. Although half of CEFTA's exports go to the EU, they represent only a very small proportion of EU imports; if trade in manufactures between the group and the Union were to be completely free, the impact on industry within the EU would be slight.

Meanwhile, individual industries in the EU have also been attempting to manage the marketplace, and nowhere more so than in the case of the cement industry. This, like others, was strongly developed in Poland under Communism, chiefly in Chelm, Kielce and Opole voivodships, but suffered a sharp fall in demand after 1989. It was, however, one of those whose low labour costs

offered it the opportunity to switch its sales to western Europe, where it could undercut the prices set by a highly cartelised industry in spatially segmented markets. Not surprisingly, its growing sales were challenged. In 1994, the German Federal Association of Cement Industries – whose members were the most likely to be affected by Polish competition – filed anti-dumping charges against Polish, and also Czech and Slovak, producers before the European Commission, arguing that central European producers enjoy the unfair advantage of government-subsidised transport. It is not clear that the Association has a case: the Austrians earlier lodged, but then dropped, a similar complaint. The Austrians did, however, emerge with a voluntary agreement with Czech producers to limit exports. Nor may it really have been the aim of the Association to obtain a formal anti-dumping order against Polish cement makers for, by the mid-1990s, the major western European producers had developed their competitive strategy still further, by buying into Polish cement works.

Such investment is clearly what many Poles both expected and hoped would be the consequence of economic reform. But Poland is not the only available outlet for international funds, nor is it the only market into which the world's manufacturers wish to expand. The country must compete not only with others in central Europe, such as Hungary and the Czech Republic, which are proving attractive to foreign investors, but also with opportunities on the Pacific rim and in southern Asia. By 1995, when Polish GDP stood at about $100bn, foreign direct investment was running at $1.5bn per annum, half of which was going into manufacturing, and especially into food processing and electrical engineering (*Business Central Europe*, 1996). It should be noted, however, that this contribution to the Polish economy has been proportionately much less than that in many of the world's other former Communist and developing countries (Table 6.4).

Conclusion

Polish experience since 1989 has been similar, though not identical, to that in many of the former Communist states of central and eastern Europe.

Prior to that year, manufacturing and mining were the privileged sectors of the economy; those who worked in them were among the best paid; and the places in which they were located received most investment. The economic geography of the region was largely shaped by them. It is so no longer, for the impetus in economic development has now passed to the service sector and to capital cities. Five years after the overthrow of public ownership and central planning, many industrial conurbations, remote mining establishments and single-industry towns were still struggling to come to terms with their reduced role (Figure 6.1). Some of those who managed mills and mines under the former system have, by seizing selected assets, become millionaires. Some workers, finding themselves in the few enterprises which have been taken over by Western firms, have benefited from significant improvements in their conditions of employment. Some consumers, who not only have wealth, but flaunt it by, for example, the purchase of high-value imported goods, are widely suspected of having acquired it illegally. Many industrial workers, however, have been made redundant or cling to non-jobs in the remaining public-sector enterprises, making do with reduced standards of living or what they can get from participating in the large, unregulated sector of the economy, little of which is involved with manufacturing. Similarly, many of the new breed of voucher capitalists — those who now, in theory, own what were formerly public assets — are not noticeably better off than before. The scope for further change, through increased levels of international trade and a greater penetration of Western capital than has yet occurred, remains considerable. Under Communism, the countries of the region were known as "people's democracies". They had a distinctive economic geography. That of the new democracies has already become quite different. Its continuing evolution will prove to be a fruitful focus of research for many years to come.

Notes

1. The Muslim areas of Soviet central Asia and the Balkans, and Romania, with its anti-abortion policy, were exceptions to the pattern of low birth rates and ageing labour forces.

2. A monetary "overhang" occurs when savings build up for want of an opportunity to spend money. Towards the end of the Communist period, many prices and wages were raised, but the supply of goods and services did not increase, nor did increases in centrally determined prices reflect the severity of the shortages that existed. As a result, many people built up much larger savings than they wished, savings which they rushed to spend once prices were freed.

3. Following some opposition in Crakow in the late 1940s to the adoption of Poland's Communist constitution, the government ordered the construction of a major steel mill on the outskirts of the country's original capital and most historic city, in the hope that a large proletarian element would thus be added to its conservative and bourgeois society. This experiment in social engineering failed, but atmospheric pollution from the mill did enormous damage to the city's ancient monuments and the health of its citizens.

4. Poland is divided into 49 voivodships, or counties, for purposes of local government. These form the first tier of local administration below that of the national government.

5. Following a period of increasing economic stagnation in Poland during the 1960s, and riots in protest against price rises, Wladyslaw Gomulka, the Polish leader, was replaced in 1970 by Edward Gierek. Gierek attempted to reinvigorate the Polish economy through the purchase of Western technology and joint ventures between the country's publicly owned enterprises and Western firms. However, his plans were severely disrupted by sharp increases in the price of petroleum in the 1970s, and Poland became massively indebted to Western banks and governments. Facing the Solidarity crisis of 1980, Gierek fell from power.

References

Blanchard, O (1991) Notes on the speed of transition, unemployment and growth in Poland, Mimeo.

Business Central Europe (1996) **30**, 55.

Ernst, M, Alexeev, M and Marer, P (1996) *Transforming the Core: restructuring industrial enterprises in Russia and central Europe.* Westview Press, Boulder, Colo.

Fierla, I (1994) *Geografia Gospodarcza Polski*, PWN, Warsaw, 117–19.

Jackman, R (1994) Economic policy and employment in the transition economies of Central and Eastern Europe: what have we learned?, *International Labour Review*, **133**, 327–45.

Kornai, J (1981) *Economics of Shortage*, Elsevier, Amsterdam.

Messerlin, P (1993) The EC and Central Europe: the missed rendez-vous of 1992?, *Economics of Transition*, **1**, 89–109.

Muir-Carby, G (1995) *On The Road To Recovery: European/ Mediterranean developing markets*, Smith New Court, London.

Musial, W and Paczka, S (1993) Change of function of old

industrial and major residential buildings in Lodz as one of the forms of restructuring of the city, in S Paczka (ed) *Urban and Industrial Change in the New Economic Order in the Former Socialist Countries*, University of Lodz, 68–75.

Paczka, S and Riley, R (1992) Lodz textiles in the new Polish economic order, *Geography*, **11**, 361–3.

Pinder, D A and Simmonds, B (1993) Oil transport: pipelines, ports and the new political climate, in D R Hall (ed) *Transport and Economic Development in the New Central and Eastern Europe*, Belhaven, London, 49–59.

Poland, Central Statistical Office (1994a) *Poland: quarterly statistics*, II/3, Warsaw.

Poland, Central Statistical Office (1994b) *Rocznik Statystyczny 1994*, Warsaw.

Sachs, J (1994) *Poland's Jump to the Market Economy*, MIT Press. Cambridge, Mass.

Simpson, P (1995) Death by neglect, *Business Central Europe*, **23**, 25–6.

Simpson, P (1996) Birth pains, *Business Central Europe*, **30**, 59–60.

United Nations (1994) *1992 Industrial Commodity Statistics Yearbook*, New York.

World Bank (1995) *World Development Report 1995*, Oxford University Press, Washington, DC.

7
Advanced producer services and economic development

P W Daniels
School of Geography, University of Birmingham, UK

Introduction

In recent years much of the growth in market economies has been associated with the performance of the service sector. The broad geography of service employment, shown in Figure 7.1 for the EU9,[1] reveals significant disparities. While countries on the southern periphery, such as Greece and Portugal, have relatively small service sectors (less than 56 per cent of total employment), in others – e.g. the Netherlands, Belgium and Luxembourg – the sector's share is two-thirds or more.[2] These disparities are also reflected in variations in services trade, in which core economies like the UK again exhibit a strong performance.[3] The potential for trade in services has, of course, been enhanced by the single market programme. Not only is it now easier for a firm in one country to market services in other EU countries, but it is also much more feasible to trade the factors of production across national boundaries. Thus, especially through flows of human and physical capital, service establishments in one EU state are increasingly able to produce services in host countries elsewhere in the EU (Melvin, 1989; Ruane, 1993). This can be done by acquiring or merging with existing businesses in the countries that are being targeted, and also by establishing branches or subsidiaries. As will become apparent, the group of services on which this chapter concentrates – the advanced producer services or APS[4] – are in a particularly good position to take advantage of such trading opportunities. Because of this, and because of the key role of these services in current economic development processes, it is important to question how they will influence the EU's evolving economic geography. Examining this issue is this contribution's central aim.

Advanced Producer Services

The role played by services in the transformation of the European economy during the last quarter of the twentieth century has been shaped in particular by the dynamics of the APS (Daniels *et al.*, 1993; Marshall and Wood, 1995; Moulaert and Tödtling, 1995). These supply intermediate inputs to the production of a final good or service, and one of their most important distinguishing characteristics is the pivotal position of knowledge and information in the services they provide. This characteristic is embodied in the human resources

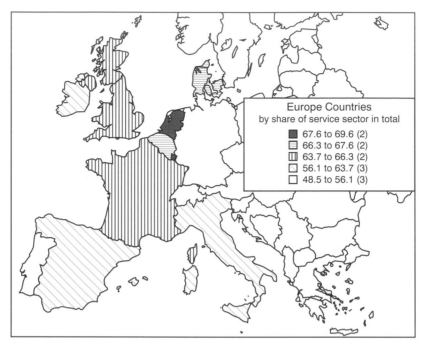

Figure 7.1 *Services as a proportion of total employment, selected European countries, 1991 (after European Commission, 1994b)*

and technologies that are made available by APS to other businesses that, for example, are striving to adopt or adapt their management, distribution, marketing or product lines in ways that will enable them to enter new markets, to attract new investors or to design and introduce new products. Many of these APS activities are therefore connected with some form of consulting, and the provision of specialised guidance and advice to businesses that themselves do not have the resources, time or expertise to perform such functions. These consultancies

Table 7.1 *Value of transactions between producer services and other economic sectors, the Netherlands, 1989 ('000 guilders)*

Sector	Producer services			
	Transactions to:	%	Transactions from:	%
Agriculture	2 514	2.7	20	0.1
Mining	487	0.5	0	0.0
Manufacturing	18 914	20.6	7 787	21.0
Construction	932	1.0	4 330	11.7
Utilities	23 555	25.6	312	0.8
Miscellaneous services	2 722	3.0	7 276	19.6
Imports	0	0.0	17 378	46.8
Exports	42 809	46.6	0	0.0
Total	91 933	100	37 103	100
Value of transactions between producer services		28 136		

Source: Derived from de Jong *et al.* (1992, 155).

typically operate in fields as diverse as human resource planning, information technology and computer systems, business development and planning, legal and tax matters, marketing strategy or assistance with floating a company on the stock exchange.

The importance of APS for other parts of the economy has been illustrated by de Jong *et al.* (1992) using data extracted from the National Accounts for the Netherlands (Table 7.1). These show that manufacturing does not dominate the pattern of transactions (at least by value); rather it is miscellaneous services and the producer services themselves that are the important consumers. It is also apparent that exports of producer services make a very significant contribution to the total value of transactions, exceeding the value of imports by producers by a ratio of more than two to one.

This basic, as opposed to the long-assumed non-basic, role of APS in urban and regional development is now becoming widely acknowledged. Over the last 10 years, studies in Europe (Bailly *et al.*, 1987; Sjoholt, 1994; O'Farrell *et al.*, 1993; Moulaert and Tödtling, 1995) and in North America (Beyers and Alvine, 1985; Beyers, 1991; Harrington *et al.*, 1991; Michalak and Fairburn, 1993) have consistently demonstrated that some APS are traded well outside the parent city or region, and that the share of these exports relative to their total output has been steadily increasing. Given that many of these services are embodied in people (i.e. they cannot be supplied unless individuals apply their specialist knowledge or skills to the needs of the client, often at the point of use) it is perhaps not surprising that they have been able to increase their basic role in economic development. While the reasons are to be found partly in the realms of improved transportation, such as the emerging trans-European high-speed rail network and the ever-improving networks of airline services (Hall, 1991), the dramatic improvements in information and tele-communications technology have also played a significant role by reducing the need for co-present interaction in the supply of APS (Miles, 1991; Goddard, 1995). Whereas the location of consumer services such as retailing is still very much determined by the location of their customers and relatively constrained within

national boundaries (see, for example, Myers 1995), that of APS is now much more flexible or footloose. Yet, as will be shown later in this chapter, the spatial distribution and dynamics of APS do not fully reflect the opportunities to be nearer market opportunities. The result is that the locational behaviour of APS is a crucial determinant of the relative performance of European cities and regions with respect to employment change, occupational restructuring, the internationalisation of economic activity and participation in the wider global economy.

Explaining the rise of APS

Explanations for the expansion of APS since the early 1980s can be linked to the factors that account for, first, the development of services in general and, second, those that are specific to APS. Martinelli (1991) identifies four main views on the emergence of service industries more generally. The earliest of these is demand-based (Clark, 1940; Rostow, 1966) with service activities and employment being a function of economic growth and, especially, rises in per capita income. These, it is argued, have the effect of releasing surplus expenditure (after housing, energy consumption and similar more or less fixed costs have been met) for the consumption of services that are more income elastic than the demand for many goods. Over time, this view has lost credibility in that it is too simplistic for the more complex and dynamic economic and social environment of Europe in the last quarter of the twentieth century. A second interpretation has been that the impact of the shift from manufacturing to service employment on rising unemployment levels, combined with the widespread introduction of welfare/social instruments in many European countries, has caused an expansion of the supply of public services such as health, education, social security and central/local government functions (Singelmann, 1978; Townsend, 1997). A third view, promulgated by – among others – researchers such as Walker (1985), Stanback (1979) and Gershuny and Miles (1983), is that the growth of services is not the result of greater final demand from households and individuals, but is instead a consequence of their emerging role as intermediate inputs to other production activities; herein perhaps lies the initial genesis of interest in APS. The fourth and final explanation reflects a recognition by policy-makers at local, national and European Commission levels that services should be the object of regulation, incentives or investment that will transform their role in economic development; in other words, services are now one of the preconditions for growth (Riddle, 1986).

Explanations that are specific to the demand for APS are essentially rooted in the twin processes of externalisation by firms and technological change. Together, these are usually presented as being fundamental to the rise of flexible production at the expense of Fordism (Wood, 1991; Coffey and Bailly, 1992). Flexibilisation, whether applied to manufactured goods or to services, has become the norm in response to market specialisation, reduced product life spans or, for example, more discriminating clients who are increasingly sensitive to price or quality. This presents significant new challenges to enterprises of all sizes and types. Moulaert and Tödtling (1995, 108) characterise this as APS profiling "themselves as the methodological champions in fighting the crisis of fordism at the level of the enterprise, as the creators of flexible production and distribution systems and as the conciliators of new technologies and strategic challenges in business". This is not to argue that enterprises are new to the notion of needing APS; insurance, legal or bulk transport services were already required before Fordist production methods really took hold early this century. The difference since that time has been that, while APS were originally provided via internal resourcing, the trend during the last quarter of this century has been to externalise the demand for them as they have become increasingly specialised, and therefore more difficult to support in-house.

The supply of APS has also extended significantly as a result of the internationalisation of European economies in general, and of the larger enterprises which provide them. The rapid emergence of service multinationals (MNEs) (Enderwick, 1989) is strongly dependent on the demand generated by their major clients, such as other MNEs and medium-sized to large firms operating at a national scale (Daniels, 1995). Thus the location of firms supplying APS is linked to

the pattern of control and production exhibited by these major clients. These are part of the agglomeration economies (Weber, 1929; Isard, 1956; Storper and Walker, 1989) that firms can share through clustering in relatively high density, diversified economic and social spaces (Moulaert and Gallouj, 1993).

Another important factor, affecting both the growth and the location of APS in Europe, has been the introduction of measures to harmonise the markets for services (Buigues *et al.*, 1993). There has been a long tradition of protecting national services from outside competition, so that there has been only limited movement of firms between European states (Sapir, 1993). Recently, however, one in six (50 out of 300) of the measures that form part of the internal market programme have been concerned with service industries, and the majority offer both opportunities and threats to APS in fields such as accountancy, advertising and personnel services. Some of the key features of the internal market likely to have an impact on the behaviour of APS are the harmonisation and mutual recognition of technical norms and professional qualifications; competition rules; the liberalisation of advanced telecommunications systems, capital movements and financial services; and reduced restrictions on the movement of human resources between the member states. Especially important is the principle of mutual recognition; each country accepts that an APS from another country may be available on an equal basis if they have been legally marketed in their country of origin. Such liberalisation has also been encouraged by changes in the supply of APS as a result of the developments in information technology (IT) and deregulation of telecommunications and financial markets by individual member states. In addition, the world-wide liberalisation of services trade under the 1995 General Agreement on Trade in Services (GATS) has had a similar effect.

While it is hoped that the net effect of these changes will be an improvement in the competitiveness of European APS (and services more generally) because markets and supply are less fragmented, it is also likely that they will have an impact on both the location of APS production and employment in the sector. The tradability of APS was already evident before the development of the internal market programme; now the new measures will enhance and facilitate greater centralisation of control functions, often through merger and acquisition activity in which small and medium-sized firms link up with similar firms in other member states or are acquired by some of the large business service MNEs. There is every reason to believe that this will continue as business services make increasing use of IT and information services more generally, especially if deregulation makes further progress. This change is taking place, however, in circumstances of very low business service market integration; in a sample of UK business service firms in 1991, 87 per cent of the turnover was derived from the national market, compared with only 6 per cent from clients in other EU member states, and 7 per cent from outside the EU (Service Industries Research Centre, 1992). Moreover, these shares had increased only slightly by 1994 (Daniels *et al.*, 1995). What may be relevant here is that, while the intentions of the internal market for APS are clear enough, they only comprise an initial step towards removing the obstacles to creating a truly trans-European market. The member states remain diverse in key respects including taxation policies, social and labour legislation, regulations relating to public sector competition, legal and corporate regulations, and access to occupations. APS firms wishing to operate in other EU countries must allow for these differences when devising strategies to service markets and match clients' expectations concerning the quality and appropriateness of their services (Daniels, 1995).

APS growth: empirical evidence

While there is general agreement that APS are among the fastest-growing sectors of economic activity in Europe (Moulaert and Tödtling, 1995; Vogler-Ludwig *et al.*, 1993; Daniels and Moulaert, 1991; Illeris, 1989), it remains difficult to compile good comparative statistics to demonstrate this fact. Thus, Vogler-Ludwig *et al.* (1993) relied largely on information provided by professional associations in their efforts to produce a profile of EU business services (a major component of APS) in 1988. Not only are the results riddled with uncertainty, they are also notable for the number of gaps, especially with respect to growth rates and forecasts. None the less, the data suggest that some 5 per cent of EU employment was in business services at the end of the 1980s with, interestingly, most of the jobs being for cleaning, security, temporary and vocational training staff, rather than for the knowledge-intensive experts such as accountants, engineering consultants, linguists and advertising or software specialists. This implies that APS can have an impact across the broad spectrum of the labour market.

Moulaert and Tödtling (1995) similarly attempted an inter-country comparison of the evolution of APS employment in Europe but concluded that it is extremely difficult. In order to trace changes over a reasonable period of time (1970–90) they had to compromise by re-aggregating APS with financial and insurance services for each country using labour force statistics published by the OECD (1992). They then compared the evolution of APS in European countries with the trends in North America and Japan (Figure 7.2). Between 1970 and 1990 the share of APS and financial/insurance services in total employment in 10 European countries almost doubled; only Sweden showed relatively slow growth during the 1970s.[5]

Once again, therefore, although APS has been growing strongly the evidence is that it represents a comparatively small proportion of all employment. What must be emphasised, however, is that the scale of the sector is not necessarily the big issue. As Moulaert and Tödtling (1995, 262) have stressed, the importance of APS firms "lies in their effects on other firms and economic activities. They play an active role in innovation and firm formation, technology improvement, market expansion and competitiveness."

What is more readily demonstrated is that the growth that has taken place has been divided between small firms, which numerically dominate the sector (Bryson *et al.*, 1993), and larger businesses (with more than 50 employees) that have been stimulated by EU integration measures and more general expansion of world trade in APS. These larger enterprises are frequently engaged in activities such as accountancy (Leyshon *et al.*, 1988), advertising (Daniels, 1995), engineering consultancy, market research, and cleaning and security services (Henry and Allen, 1995). Because

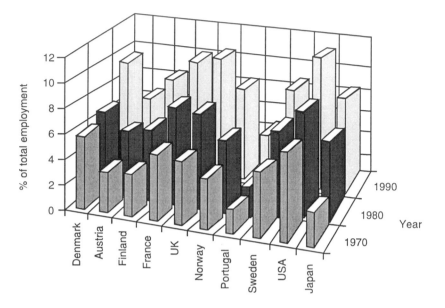

Figure 7.2 *Share of total employment in FIRE and business services, European countries, USA and Japan 1970–90 (after Moulaert and Tödtling, 1995, 262)*

the majority of growth has been stimulated by these larger firms, the net effects on the supply side have been increased concentration of APS; the availability of a wider range of more sophisticated APS, especially in locations with strong demand from the more advanced industry sectors; and the development of transnational networks of APS, either via direct establishment of new branches or through acquisitions, mergers or co-operation with existing firms in target markets.

It is also evident from Figure 7.2 that, in common with service industries as a whole, the evolution of APS is far from uniform across Europe. In the "core" countries that were early participants in the restructuring process that produced more tertiarised economies, APS was already more prominent in 1970 compared with the less developed and, usually, more peripheral countries in Europe, such as Portugal, Norway and Finland. The subsequent expansion of APS has not only sustained these initial differentials, if anything they have become more pronounced. In 1990 the difference between the highest and lowest shares of APS in total employment (in the UK and Portugal) was 5.8 per cent; in 1970 it was only 3 per cent (Denmark highest, Portugal lowest).

At the same time, however, there are also signs that this situation may be changing. The most recent statistics cited by Townsend (1997) show that the highest growth rates for producer services (including APS) between 1986 and 1994 have taken place in countries with low shares of services in total employment: Portugal (130 per cent), Italy (100 per cent) and Spain (86 per cent) (Figure 7.2). There is undoubtedly a "catching up" process going on as these economies engage in a transition from their above-average dependence on agriculture, manufacturing and services such as tourism. Yet, despite these differential growth rates, these economies are of course building from a low absolute and proportional share of services, so that countries with slower growth rates, such as Luxembourg, the Netherlands or the UK, have been able to maintain their position as the core concentrations of APS.

City/regional orientation of APS

The national statistics for APS disguise a high concentration of these activities within their principal metropolitan areas and the most diversified regions of each country. This clearly

Table 7.2 *Concentration of APS in European capital cities and other major cities*

Country	City	Share of national APS employment (%) (1981)
Portugal	Lisbon	56
	Oporto	18
Norway	Oslo	50
Denmark	Copenhagen	50
Austria	Vienna	46
United Kingdom	London	43
France	Paris	41
Sweden	Stockholm	40

Source: Moulaert and Tödtling (1995, 264–5).

emerges in the comparison by Moulaert and Tödtling (1995) of the intra-national patterns of APS location in Europe (Table 7.2), even though the problem of obtaining consistently comparable data means that the analysis must relate to 1981.

Senn (1993) suggests that the location of APS is a function of the position of an individual city within its regional and national hierarchy; of the levels of connectivity (networks) between the city and its regional or national counterparts; and of its human resource characteristics (see also Wegener, 1995). In general, the larger the city the more diversified will be the human resources available, and this will tend to pull APS towards the upper reaches of the urban hierarchy. That said, concentration is certainly by no means a universal phenomenon. In some countries, notably Germany and Italy, with a large number of significant urban agglomerations and more decentralised patterns of government, APS are more widely distributed. Rome, for example, only accounted for just under 9 per cent of the national total in Moulaert and Tödtling's analysis of 1981 data. Moreover, while the evidence may not be conclusive, and the pace of such change is variable between European countries, deconcentration of APS has in fact been a notable feature since the 1970s. The regions and intermediate-sized cities adjacent to the major urban concentrations of APS have been gaining, often at the expense of both the dominant regional city and peripheral/ problem cities or regions. Assisted by the enabling role of IT and the increased tradability of services; by improvements in the personal mobility of the labour force; by the lower cost commercial accommodation; and by improved quality of life in less central locations, many APS firms have been able to decentralise. This has enabled them to escape some of the negative externalities (congestion, high rent and labour costs) of major city locations, without forgoing the advantages of agglomeration or lowering the quality of service to their clients.

The resulting pattern of change is most usefully characterised as "concentrated decentralisation" or the creation of more extensive, lower density but highly interconnected networks of APS and dependent activities, focused on the long-standing primary concentrations in each country. Examples include the south-east region around London, the Ile de France around Paris, the Lombardy region adjacent to Milan, and the polynuclear Randstad region incorporating Amsterdam, the Hague, Rotterdam and Utrecht. Similarly, in Austria, whereas in 1980 almost 46 per cent of APS employment was focused on Vienna (42 per cent of it in the city itself), by 1989 the equivalent statistics were 44 per cent of the national total with 40 per cent in the city (Tödtling and Traxler, 1995). Using data for business services,[6] van Dinteren (1990) shows the growth rate of employment in these activities to be higher in the intermediate zone between the Randstad cities and the Netherlands' peripheral regions (e.g. Groningen province). As a result, between 1975 and 1983 the Randstad reduced its share of business services from 64 to 61 per cent while the intermediate zone expanded its share from 22 to 24 per cent, chiefly through city-based growth. What van Dinteren's analysis also demonstrated, however, is that this decentralisation extends in some circumstances to benefit peripheral regions. Thus, the Dutch peripheral provinces increased their share of business services, a phenomenon that has also been occurring elsewhere. Gaebe *et al.* (1993) show how the regions of France well away from the Ile de France have achieved slow but positive gains in, for example, business and computer services (Britanny, Midi-Pyrénées or Languedoc-Roussillon), legal advice (Alsace, Limousin) or advertising which reveals a more general relative regional spread.

A further development identified by Moulaert and Tödtling (1995) is the evolution of urban/ regional specialisation in APS. As APS themselves become more specialised, the benefits of networking and clustering that confer the advantages of the untraded interdependencies become more significant. Building also on initial regional differences in client demand and regional economic structure, some examples of specialisation include services related to high technology firms in Rhône-Alpes, engineering consultancy in Paris, shipping certification services in Oslo, environmental services in Copenhagen and banking/financial services in London. This specialisation tends to reinforce the established positions of the major city regions where APS are primarily located, even though their relative share of national APS employment may be falling in most EU countries.

Inward investment and APS location

Changes in the structure of inward investment to Europe during the 1980s have strengthened these patterns of APS location and development. In contrast to earlier periods, some 60 per cent of direct investment into the EU between 1984 and 1991 was in service activities, many of which have been engaged in internationalisation of their organisation and markets. Examples include business services, banking, insurance, and retail distribution (Enderwick, 1989; European Commission, 1994a). In pursuing internationalisation they invariably follow their clients and, because of the introduction of the internal market and the consequent reduction of differences in tax, employment and other regulations, they are able to provide services to several countries from a limited number of locations. Since many of the clients of APS are themselves primarily located in the large city regions, and because these locations are also well connected to other parts of Europe, direct investment by multinational APS organisations will gravitate towards them, and further strengthen them. Notable beneficiaries are London, Amsterdam, Paris, Frankfurt and Brussels (where many large international firms have located in part to be near to the major EU institutions). The net effect is to enable the "core" or central regions of the EU to attract a disproportionate share of all inward investment and APS growth.

APS and Research and Development

Many of the themes discussed above can be explored through further examination of two mainstream APS activities: research and development (R&D) and management consultancy. It has already been stressed that APS are increasingly vital to the capacity of the economic activities in cities and regions to innovate and upgrade their products and services so that they can become more competitive and raise regional output via increased inter-regional or even international trade. R&D is one example of an APS which has an important role to play in this process; it contributes to product improvement, better processing methods, greater flexibility of production, improvements in quality of product or service, lower costs and the introduction of methods enabling a quicker response to changes in market demand (European Commission 1994b, 1995). The difficulty, of course, is that all the factor inputs conducive to R&D – such as the managerial, technical, financial and organisational requirements – are grouped together in the core cities and regions in the way already outlined. The result is a significant "technology gap" between the member states of the EU (Figure 7.3) as measured by the number of R&D workers per thousand employees. Germany, France and Ireland had more than 5 R&D scientists and engineers per 1000 employees in 1989 compared with just 1.1 in Portugal, 1.4 in Greece and 2.2 in Spain. In addition, more than two-thirds of R&D in Portugal and Spain is undertaken by the public sector, whereas in the more advanced countries the position is reversed. Recently, it is true, there have been signs of greater convergence at this broad European scale. In Ireland and Spain the share of R&D undertaken by the private sector is growing, which may be seen as a crude measure of modernisation in their APS infrastructure, while R&D employment during the 1980s grew fastest in Spain at some 9 per cent per annum (European Commission, 1995). Yet, although the gap is narrowing, it remains large.

With R&D involving an element of risk, the availability of venture capital is a further influence on its development; again the less developed regions suffer from inadequate access to such funds because the financial environment also tends to be less innovative and open to new ideas.

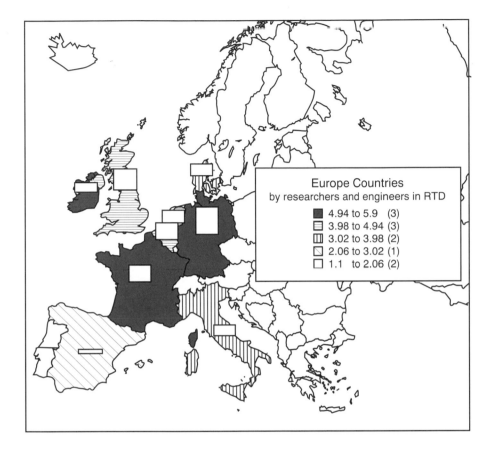

Figure 7.3 *R&D scientists and engineers per '000 employees in the entire economy and in the private sector (bar graphs), selected European countries 1989*

Consequently, there is a heavy dependence on the core regions for risk capital and/or technology transfer. It therefore comes as no surprise that a recent study of the pattern of R&D activity in the EU found that there are 10 major "islands of innovation" that are relatively small, and mainly urban, areas comprising tight networks of R&D laboratories and enterprises devoted to new product development and processes of production (Hilpert, 1992). These are Greater London, Rotterdam/Amsterdam, Ile de France, the Ruhr, Frankfurt, Stuttgart, Munich, Lyon/Grenoble, Turin and Milan (Figure 7.4). All are in the more developed member states; and this theme of favoured developed areas is maintained by the fact that the R&D that is located in Spain,

Portugal or Greece is primarily concentrated in the regions in and around the capital cities.[7] It has been estimated that some 75 per cent of all public research contracts are undertaken by enterprises and laboratories located in the innovation centres; they also function as a closely knit network with which research laboratories located elsewhere in Europe (especially in the peripheral regions) have very weak links (European Commission, 1994b).

Management Consultancy

A major function of many APS activities is to make specialist knowledge and advice accessible,

135

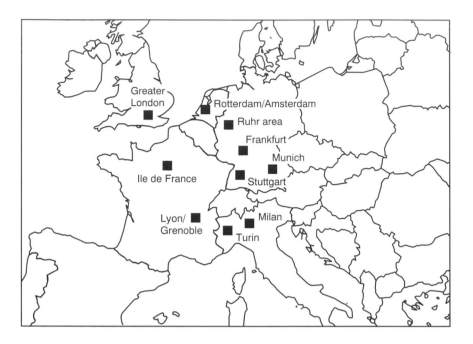

Figure 7.4 *"Islands" of science-based innovation, EU9, 1991 (after Hilpert, 1992, reproduced in European Commission, 1994b)*

for a fee, to private and public sector clients. Thus management consultants[8] provide advice on, for example, how to develop business development strategies, introduce more efficient organisational or management practices, or incorporate new technology into organisations effectively. The market is more easily defined than the sector because firms other than "pure" management consultants are involved (auditing companies and market research firms, for example) so that statistics on the size and growth of the sector must be treated cautiously. However, Vogler-Ludwig *et al.* (1993) cite data indicating that in 1989 there were more than 115 000 consultants and supporting staff employed by 11 900 management consultant enterprises (excluding Italy and Spain).[9] The fact that this was equivalent to less than 0.1 per cent of total employment well illustrates the point made earlier that the importance of APS activities may be out of all proportion to their scale.

Advice on corporate strategy and development of organisations is the most important source of fee income, followed by advice on human resource management and the introduction of IT systems.

The market for management consultants is shaped by the degree to which clients choose to transfer activities performed in-house to specialised external firms. Cost is also a factor because the demand for such services is often one-off and therefore unlikely to be easily supported in-house. But users of management consultants do not necessarily make an either/or choice between external and internal provision. Some clients use a combination of these (European Commission, 1988) and, furthermore, the balance between the choices varies in relation to the kind of service required (Figure 7.5). The EC study found that general management consultancy was obtained from external sources by 45 per cent of the firms surveyed, compared with only 18 per cent for financial management. It also noted that the demand for external management consultants did not just result from a switch from internal production, but also arose from a tendency by firms to use external suppliers to perform services that had never been performed internally. More recent research by O'Farrell *et al.* (1993) has also shown that the balance between external and internal provision of APS is constantly changing as the

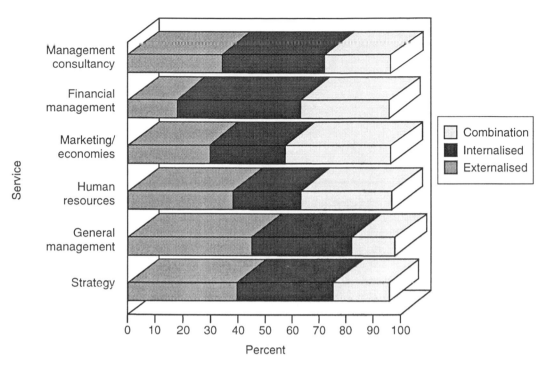

Figure 7.5 *External versus internal provision of management consultancy services, EU firms, 1987*

needs and competencies of firms change; thus it is a mistake to assume that there is a constant trend towards externalisation.

As with R&D, the geographical concentration of management consultants is an important feature: four out of five enterprises are found in Germany, France and the UK. The largest firms (measured by the number of consultants per firm) are located in the UK and the Netherlands. Beyond this, in a study of the evolving organisation and structure of consultancy services in primate, second-tier and third-tier European cities that included management consultants[10] (Daniels *et al.*, 1992) it has been shown that primate cities (Paris, Amsterdam, London, Zurich, Madrid, Milan) are the focus for their activities. The headquarters of large management consultancies (more than 50 employees) with significant national or international markets are found in these cities, where they function as control centres for the regional and branch offices of the large firms, cither within the same

European country or elsewhere in the EU and beyond. The clients of management consultants in the primate cities tend to be the head offices of other manufacturing and service firms, as well as public sector activities such as central or local government or the utilities. In second- and third-tier cities management consultancies are not only smaller, they are likely to be autonomous firms (without branches) servicing clients that reflect the economic characteristics of the immediate locality or region. This does not mean, however, that these consultancies are excluded from national or international markets; in fact in the 1992 study more than 30 per cent had at least some international clients. Furthermore, 42 per cent of the establishments serving mainly regional markets had some control over a network of branches. Thus, the propensity of APS in general to locate in the primate, functionally diverse, European cities need not mean that smaller, often more peripheral, cities cannot participate in wider markets. Provided that APS firms in lower-order cities can set up their own networks or link with existing ones they will enhance the economic development of their locality by increasing the scope for exporting their services and for improving the quality of the knowledge and expertise accessible to local or regional market firms.

Conclusion

This chapter has underlined the key role of APS in economic development, but has also demonstrated that – as these services are becoming more specialised – they require locations strategically positioned relative to markets. In the same way, APS wishing to retain competitive advantage or innovative capacity must choose locations within or near places with easy access to diversified economic activity, finance, state-of-the-art telecommunications, international transport services and highly skilled human resources.

Although these imperatives naturally reflect the workings of the market, their impact in western Europe is intensified by EU policy. The single market has encouraged the gravitation of investment towards the more favoured locations, and infrastructure policy is similarly fostering mobility. Further investment in trans-European road and rail networks (European Commission, 1992) will work in this way, as will the harmonisation of information and communications networks across the EU. In similar vein, the Commission's Bangemann Group, established to formulate policies and strategies for telecommunications networks, has identified 10 priority programmes, all of which will impact on producer services and spatial development. One survey of 500 large enterprises (cited in Commission of the European Communities, 1994a) revealed that 59 per cent considered high-quality telecommunications services to be an important determinant of where to locate. Where such firms settle, APS will follow.

While the response of APS to the EU's single market and infrastructure policies is complex, not least due to sectoral differences and varying circumstances in member states, changes are taking place. The liberalisation of markets is increasing the attractions of agglomeration economies and,

therefore, the inherent magnetism of large cities, especially in the core (northern) countries which already have some of the largest conurbations with environments very suitable for the development of high-level services (Buigues *et al.*, 1993). Thus London, Frankfurt and Paris have been at the forefront for investment in banking and financial services; Brussels, London and Amsterdam have been preferred by non-European MNEs establishing European headquarters; and Rotterdam, Amsterdam and Antwerp have attracted transport and distribution MNEs seeking locations with good links within Europe (via the road, waterway and rail networks) as well as outside (via Schiphol Airport). As Europe's APS markets become more global – for example, through the provision of services to clients in North America and Asia – the attractions of core locations such as these are highly likely to grow.

As the EU's economy evolves, therefore, there is increasing evidence – and concern – that policy initiatives are reinforcing rather than counteracting the free-market tendency of APS to favour core cities and regions. Moreover, this echoes the tendency of manufacturing to shift production away from the peripheral member states and towards dominant market areas and concentrations of good communications. On the one hand, this may serve the EU's aim of economic efficiency but, on the other, it cuts across the long-held political goal of more even development throughout an expanded EU. Whether this circle can be squared remains a major, and very open, question.

Notes

1. EU9: Belgium, Denmark, Germany, Spain, France, Italy, Luxembourg, Portugal, UK.
2. In the southern and less-developed member states there are relatively high shares (relative, that is, to the EU9 average) of employment in distribution, hotels/catering and other tourism-related services, while the northern group have an above-average share of communications, financial and business services employment. These are also the sectors that generally experienced the fastest growth throughout the 1980s, especially in Luxembourg, the UK, Belgium and Denmark (Ilkovitz, 1993). Put another way, high-skill, high-productivity and information-intensive services are primarily supplied from the northern (core) member states while lower skill,

less-productive services are primarily supplied by the southern (peripheral) group.

3. During 1987–89 the UK, France, Belgium and Luxembourg dominated the EU9's banking and insurance markets (>70 per cent of the total); in business services France, Germany, the Netherlands, Belgium and Luxembourg were dominant (>80 per cent); while in tourism France, Ireland and Spain had more than 60 per cent of the market.

4. Defined as: R&D, services auxiliary to finance and insurance, legal services, accounting and fiscal consulting, technical and professional services, advertising and public relations, marketing services, organisational consulting, electronic data processing and related services (computer services), typing, photocopying and other paper processing services, rental of production equipment, and other business services (cleaning, security, etc.).

5. By comparison, the rate of growth was slower in the USA over the same period, but it already had a larger share of APS and financial/insurance services in all employment in 1970 than its European counterparts (4–5 per cent). APS employment in Japan trebled after 1970 but started with a very low share (2.6 per cent) and was still behind some of the European countries as well as the USA by 1990.

6. Including banking, insurance, real estate and professional services.

7. Strong regional imbalance in R&D is not unique to Europe; approximately 75 per cent of the $145 billion R&D budget in the USA in 1991 was expended in just 10 states (California, New York, Michigan, New Jersey, Massachusetts, Pennsylvania, Texas, Illinois, Ohio and Maryland) (European Commission, 1995).

8. Others include: legal consultancy, market research, auditing, technical services, advertising, accountancy.

9. These estimates are for the EU12, excluding Italy and Spain. The inclusion of these countries and the expansion of the EU to 15 member states would clearly take the employment estimate to nearer 140 000.

10. Engineering consultants and computer software consultants were also included.

References

Bailly, A S, Maillat, D and Coffey, W J (1987) Service activities and regional development: some European examples, *Environment and Planning A*, **19**, 653–68.

Beyers, W B (1991) Trends in the producer services in the US: the last decade, in P W Daniels (ed) *Services and Metropolitan Development: international perspectives*, Routledge, London, 146–72.

Beyers, W B and Alvine, M J (1985) Export services in post-industrial society, *Papers of the Regional Science Association*, **57**, 33–45.

Bryson, J R, Keeble, D and Wood, P A (1993) Business networks, small firm flexibility and regional development

in UK business services, *Entrepreneurship and Regional Development*, **5**, 265–77.

Buigues, P, Ilkovitz, F, Lebrun, J-F and Sapir, A (eds) (1993) *Market Services and European Integration: the challenges of the 1990s*, European Economy Social Europe, No 3, Commission of the European Communities, Brussels.

Clark, C (1940) *The Conditions of Economic Progress*, Macmillan, London.

Coffey, W F and Bailly, A S (1992) Producer services and systems of flexible production, *Urban Studies*, **29**, 857–68.

Daniels, P W (1995) The internationalisation of advertising services in a changing regulatory environment, *The Service Industries Journal*, **15**, 276–94.

Daniels, P W, Bryson, J R and Churchward, S (1995) The performance of UK business services during a period of recession, 1991–94, Service Sector Research Unit, University of Birmingham (mimeo).

Daniels, P W, Illeris, S, Bonamy, J and Philippe, J (1993) *The Geography of Services*, Cass, London.

Daniels, P W and Moulaert, F (eds) (1991) *The Changing Geography of Advanced Producer Services: theoretical and empirical perspectives*, Belhaven, London.

Daniels, P W, van Dinteren, J H J and Monnoyer, M C (1992) Consultancy services and the urban hierarchy in Western Europe, *Environment and Planning A*, **24**, 1731–48.

De Jong, M W, Machielse, K and de Ruijter, P A (1992) Producer services and flexible networks in the Netherlands, in H Ernste and V Meier (eds) *Regional Development and Contemporary Industrial Response: extending flexible specialisation*, 147–62.

Enderwick, P (ed) (1989) *Multinational Service Firms*, Routledge, London.

European Commission (1988) The cost of non-Europe for business services, in *The Cost of Non-Europe (Vol 8)*, Office for Official Publications of the European Communities, Luxembourg.

European Commission (1994a) *Europe 2000+: co-operation for European territorial development*, Office for Official Publications of the European Communities, Luxembourg.

European Commission (1994b) *Competitiveness and Cohesion: trends in the regions*, Office for Official Publications of the European Communities, Luxembourg.

European Commission (1995) *Research and Regional Development*, Office for Official Publications of the European Communities, Luxembourg.

Gaebe, W, Strambach, S, Wood, P and Moulaert, F (1993) Employment in Business-related Services: an intercountry comparison of Germany, the United Kingdom and France, Report for the European Commission, Stuttgart (unpublished).

Gershuny, J and Miles, I (1983) *The New Service Economy: the transformation of employment in industrial societies*, Frances Pinter, London.

Goddard, J (1995) Information and communication technologies, corporate hierarchies and the new Europe, in J Brotchie, M Batty, E Blakely, P Hall and P Newton (eds)

Cities in Competition: productive and sustainable cities for the 21st Century, Longman, Melbourne, 108–26.

Hall, P (1991) Moving information: a tale of four technologies, in J Brotchie, M Batty, P Hall and P Newton (eds) *Cities of the 21st Century: new technologies and spatial systems*, Halstead Press, New York, 1–22.

Harrington, J W, MacPherson, A D and Lombard, J R (1991) Interregional trade in producer services: review and synthesis, *Growth and Change*, **22**, 75–94.

Henry, N D and Allen, J (1995) Growth at the margins: contract labour in a core region, in C Hadjimichalis and D Sadler (eds) *Europe at the Margins: new mosaics of inequality*, Wiley, Chichester, 149–66.

Hilpert, U (1992) *Archipelago Europe: islands of innovation*, FAST, Brussels.

Ilkovitz, F (1993) Sectoral/country dimension, in P Buigues *et al.* (eds) *Market Services and European Integration: the challenges for the 1990s*, Report No 3, Commission of the European Communities, European Economy/Social Europe, Brussels, 41–62.

Illeris, S (1989) *Services and Regions in Europe*, Gower, Aldershot.

Isard, W (1956) *Location and Space Economy*, MIT Press, Cambridge, MA.

Leyshon, A, Daniels, P W and Thrift, N J (1989) Large accounting firms in the UK and spatial development, *The Service Industries Journal*, **8**, 317–46.

Marshall, J N and Wood, P A (1995) *Services and Space: key aspects of urban and regional development*, Longman, Harlow.

Martinelli, F (1991) A demand-oriented approach to understanding producer services, in P W Daniels and F Moulaert (eds) (1991) *The Changing Geography of Advanced Producer Services: theoretical and empirical perspectives*, Belhaven, London, 15–29.

Melvin, J (1989) *Trade in Services: a theoretical analysis*, The Institute for Research on Public Policy, Victoria, BC.

Michalak, W Z and Fairburn, K J (1988) Producer services in a peripheral economy, *Canadian Journal of Regional Science*, **11**, 353–72.

Miles, I (1991) Telecommunications: abolishing space and reinforcing distance, in J Brotchie, M Batty, P Hall and P Newton (eds) *Cities of the 21st Century: new technologies and spatial systems*, Halstead Press, New York, 73–93.

Moulaert, F and Gallouj, C (1993) The locational geography of advanced producer service firms: the limits of economies of agglomeration, *The Service Industries Journal*, **13**, 91–106.

Moulaert, F and Tödtling, F (eds) (1995) The geography of advanced producer services in Europe, *Progress in Planning*, **43** (2–3), 90–274.

Myers, H (1995) The changing process of internationalisation in the European Union, *Service Industries Journal*, **15**, 42–56.

OECD (1992) *Labour Force Statistics*, OECD, Paris.

O'Farrell, P N, Moffat, L A R and Hitchens, D N W N (1993) Manufacturing demand for business services in a core and peripheral region: does flexible production imply vertical disintegration of business services?, *Regional Studies*, **27**, 385–400.

Riddle, D I (1986) *Service-led Growth: the role of the service sector in world development*, Praeger, New York.

Rostow, W W (1966) *The Stages of Economic Growth*, Yale University Press, New Haven.

Ruane, F (1993) Internationlization of services: conceptual and empirical issues, in P Buigues *et al.* (eds) *Market Services and European Integration: the challenges for the 1990s*, Report No 3, Commission of the European Communities, European Economy/Social Europe, Brussels, 109–24.

Sapir, A (1993) The structure of services in Europe: a conceptual framework, in P Buigues *et al.* (eds) *Market Services and European Integration: the challenges for the 1990s*, European Economy/Social Europe, Brussels, Commission of the European Communities, 83–97.

Senn, L (1993) Service activities' urban hierarchy and cumulative growth, in P W Daniels, S Illeris, J Bonamy and P A de Ruijter (eds) *The Geography of Services*, Cass, London, 11–12.

Service Industries Research Centre (1992) *Pilot Survey of Business Services in the United Kingdom and Republic of Ireland: final report*, Service Industries Research Centre, University of Portsmouth.

Singelmann, R K (1978) *From Agriculture to Services: the transformation of industrial employment*, Sage, Beverley Hills, CA.

Sjoholt, P J (1994) The role of producer services in industrial and regional development: the Nordic case, *European Urban and Regional Studies*, **1**, 115–30.

Stanback, T M (1979) *Understanding the Service Economy*, Johns Hopkins University Press, Baltimore, MD.

Storper, M and Walker, R (1989) *The Capitalist Imperative: territory, technology and industrial growth*, Blackwell, New York.

Tödtling, F and Traxler, J (1995) The changing location of advanced producer services in Austria, *Progress in Planning*, **43** (2–3), 185–204.

Townsend, A R (1997) *Making a Living in Europe*, Routledge, London.

Van Dinteren, J H J (1990) Producer services and medium-sized cities, *Netherlands Geographical Studies*, **20**.

Vogler-Ludwig, K, Homann, H and Vorloou, P (1993) Business services, in P Buigues *et al.* (eds) (1993) *Market Services and European Integration: the challenges for the 1990s*, European Economy/Social Europe, Brussels, Commission of the European Communities, 383–400.

Walker, R A (1985) Is there a service economy? The changing capitalist division of labour, *Science and Society*, **49**, 42–83.

Weber, A (1929) *Theory of Location of Industry*, University of Chicago Press, Chicago.

Wegener, M (1995) The changing urban hierarchy in Europe, in J Brotchie, M Batty, E Blakely, P Hall and P Newton (eds), *Cities in Competition: productive and sustainable cities for the 21st Century*, Longman, Melbourne, 139–60.

Wood, P A (1991) Flexible accumulation and the rise of business services, *Transactions of the Institute of British Geographers*, **16**, 160–77.

8
Producer service development problems in the new democracies

Wieslaw Michalak

School of Applied Geography, Ryerson Polytechnic University, Ontario, Canada

Introduction

Restructuring in eastern and central Europe (ECE) has gone through one major phase since 1989 and is now in a second. The first introduced radical political, social and economic reforms which provided at least some of the foundations for the development of a modern market economy. For many, this "refolutionary" phase (revolution by reform) was the pinnacle of an extended struggle to introduce a long-term strategy aimed at fundamental restructuring of the centrally planned variant of the socialist economy (Davis, 1996). Although the radicalism of these reforms was not uniform throughout the region – many countries, including Slovakia, Russia and Ukraine, opted for a more gradual approach – on aggregate the outcome of this first phase was a qualified success. This was despite unfortunate social side-effects: as huge state-owned factories and industrial complexes collapsed (Figure 8.1), thousands were thrown out of work while those depending on state benefits and pensions found themselves unemployable and, often, below the poverty line. One consequence of this was widespread discontent with the pace and direction of the reforms, which in turn meant that elections in Hungary, Poland, Slovakia, Bulgaria and Lithuania were all marked by a significant "ex-Communist" vote signalling a possible retreat from the early radicalism.

Despite this swing of the pendulum, the second phase of restructuring is now in progress – albeit in a less radical fashion – and is maintaining the transformation towards market economies. It is in this phase that the past systemic neglect of services, and producer services in particular, has been exposed as a major cause of the industrial sector's low productivity, inefficiency and economic decline (Bicanic and Skreb, 1991). Producer services have been identified by many researchers as one of the key ingredients in the successful mix of the competitive market economy (Winiecki, 1988; Maciejewicz and Monkiewicz, 1989; Daniels *et al.*, 1993; Marshall and Wood, 1995). Western economists and geographers have frequently pointed out that inputs of innovation and high technology, new management and organisational methods, legal and banking services, investment and financial instruments are crucial competitive stimuli. Yet when the "velvet revolution" occurred at the end of the 1980s the condition of these services in ECE countries left almost

Figure 8.1 *Abandoned works in East Germany. (Photo: D A Pinder)*

everything to be desired. This deficiency naturally has serious implications for future economic development processes.

Against this disconcerting background, this chapter seeks to explore four central issues. What is the role of producer services in highly developed economies, i.e. the role that ECE must now attempt to cultivate? Why are producer services in the former Communist countries in such a parlous state? What policy instruments may be deployed to retrieve the situation? And what problems are likely to confront the effective use of these instruments?

What must be emphasised finally by way of introduction is that any attempt to answer these questions, and particularly those relating to policies for improvement, cannot avoid major difficulties. Above all, this is because relevant and reliable quantitative data are scarce in the extreme. None the less, the picture is becoming sufficiently clear for a provisional analysis – which will inevitably evolve in the next few years – to be proposed.

The Role of Producer Services

Although there is as yet no wholly adequate interpretation of contemporary advances in the capitalist economic system, most geographers agree that the last two decades have witnessed a number of significant changes in industrial structures and production processes (Marshall and Wood, 1995). At the forefront of these changes is the rise of the service sector as the largest employer, and potentially the largest contributor of GNP, of all capitalist economies. The significance of this development is increasingly acknowledged not only in geography (for example, Coffey and Polése, 1989; Harvey, 1989; Wood, 1991a; Daniels, 1991; Beyers, 1991; MacPherson, 1991; Ley and Hutton, 1991) but also in the economic literature (Stanback *et al.*, 1981; Gershuny and Miles, 1983; Piore and Sabel, 1984; Hansen, 1990). Of course, not all service activities are of equal importance in the economic process. In fact the so-called "service sector" comprises myriad activities collectively labelled "services" simply because they do not fit into the classificatory schemes designed in the past to accentuate the leading role of manufacturing as the prime engine of growth and determinant of living standards in industrial societies.

Among these diverse activities, however, producer services – which supply intermediate resources to other establishments rather than final consumers – have been singled out as the leading activities in the economic transition from a "Fordist" to a "post-Fordist" form of industrialisation. Producer services lie at the heart of the modern production system because they are the main suppliers and distributors of innovation and technologies (Michalak and Fairbairn, 1988, 1992; O hUallachain and Reid, 1991; MacPherson, 1991) and they also accommodate an increasingly complex and expanding division of labour (Christopherson, 1989; Hansen, 1990; Sayer and Walker, 1992). Both functions, it is argued, ultimately translate into productivity increases and comparative advantage throughout key sectors of the economy.

Precisely how this is achieved remains, it must be admitted, a matter of debate. However, subcontracting and the externalisation of service functions are often identified as the main mode through which efficiency and innovation are transmitted to other sectors. Thus these processes are also frequently viewed as major driving forces behind the recent growth of producer services. Meanwhile, improved competitive advantage and capital accumulation in modern capitalist economies are believed to be related to the shift from labour directly involved in the production process to inputs supplied by independent producer service enterprises employing highly specialised personnel. Such firms are an integral part of the modern mode of production in these economies, with a range of specialisms spanning strategic planning, research and development, the allocation and management of capital, purchasing and franchising, product development, market research and advertising. In other words, by exploiting the division of labour, these firms provide services which promote innovation, efficiency, productivity and ultimately comparative advantage among their clients and, therefore, within regional, national and international economies (Nusbaumer, 1984;

Walker, 1985; Harvey, 1989; Goe, 1990; Marshall and Wood, 1995).[1]

While the externalisation of producer service purchases has been a high-profile development, it is important to recognise that this shift towards the vertical disintegration of activities has not been the sole mode of producer service growth. Despite a gradual retreat from the Fordist mode of production, large firms continue to generate some services within the corporate organisation and to distribute these services through intra-firm channels as inputs to the production process. For example, Northern Telecom, a large Canadian manufacturing firm producing communication systems, employs only one-fifth of its workforce in genuine production processes. The rest are engaged in designing, planning, programming, marketing and problem-solving. In other words, four-fifths of the entire workforce of what is officially a manufacturing enterprise are in fact involved in what may be broadly defined as producer service activities.[2] Precisely how much reliance any one firm will place on in-house provision, as opposed to external purchasing, will of course, be largely determined by the financial incentives and strategic implications of outsourcing.

The growing demand for producer services in market economies is chiefly the result of two processes. First, it is the outcome of changing organisational and institutional arrangements in the private and public sectors. At the forefront of these changes have been shifts towards more complex and advanced managerial, administrative and planning structures and functions, manifested in the growing scale and complexity of operations. Associated with this, the greater technical, spatial and social division of labour within the modern economic system, and at the level of the individual firm, have increased the need for co-ordination and integration (Howells and Green, 1987; Wood, 1991b). Thus growing demand has been dependent partly on the division of labour and partly on the number of interconnected elements at the operational level of the production system (Christopherson, 1989). In this scenario, the increasing burden of administrative and development functions has imposed new and urgent demands for specialised producer services. These demands may have been met initially within the firms themselves but then, as certain thresholds were exceeded, they were often satisfied in the market, stimulating the creation and expansion of specialist suppliers. Among other things, this highlights one of the fundamental roles of producer services in modern economies, that of integrating or binding together the increasingly differentiated and specialised parts and functions of business organisations.

Second, rising demand in highly developed economies has been caused by the increasing pace of product innovation and market segmentation in response to quickly changing market conditions and a shortened product life-cycle. "In large measure the expansion [of producer services] has resulted from a growing need for intermediate services and human capital in an economy characterized by an increased sophistication in terms of *what* it produces and *how* it carries out production" (Stanback *et al.*, 1981, 1). This has led directly to greater utilisation of such services as research, design and development, marketing, specialised training and the provision of finance and investment expertise. In this way, producer services have become a "strategic economic activity", not least because they have enabled their consumers to make non-routine adaptations such as new product development and marketing, expansion into new markets and growth through mergers or takeovers. In addition, however, the more diverse range of producer services has also become important as a facilitator of more constant adaptation. For example, services such as advertising, public relations, strategic planning, forecasting and management consultancy often contribute in this way. Similarly, new "managerial technologies" – enabling the adoption of a host of techniques such as inventory control, market analysis, just-in-time delivery, sophisticated product testing programmes and financial control and capital investment analysis – facilitate day-to-day functioning and cost control with a degree of sophistication that was previously impossible.

In the centre of these developments is *competition*. In the modern world this forces firms to be adaptive and responsive, compelling them to seek greater flexibility and responsiveness to change. "Ability to see new opportunities and to seize them rapidly is the most valuable ability we have. And nearly all the occupations relevant to the development and rapid adaptation of technical and managerial change are service occupations" (Marquand, 1983, 128). This, clearly, has stimulated demand for producer services. But, in addition, competition has affected the structure of producer service delivery through the overwhelming pressures it places on most business organisations to reduce overhead costs and introduce ever-shorter customised product lines. Thus, as demand has grown, the externalisation of many producer service purchases has been intended to reduce key overhead costs such as wages, benefits and capital requirements.

Viewed from these perspectives, producer services are arguably the most important phenomenon in the development of contemporary economies. Understandably enough, during the initial phase of industrial restructuring in ECE, they received relatively little attention. In the early 1990s considerable emphasis was placed on the creation of legislative and political environments conducive to the development of modern market economies. Thus the major priorities of virtually all countries in the region included currency convertibility, opening up the market to foreign trade and investment, and establishing legal frameworks for private enterprise. Simply put, at that early stage there were more pressing matters than the state of producer services. Increasingly, however, the new relative openness of these economies to foreign competition is exposing an urgent need for mechanisms that will promote improved productivity and competitiveness in domestic industries. This inevitably not only underlines the shortcomings of the current producer services sector, but also indicates the importance of understanding how these shortcomings were able to become so widespread and so severe.

Producer Services in ECE: Causes of Neglect

Before the spectacular collapse of the Communist regimes in 1989, and the reforms that followed in the 1990s, ECE's service sector was vastly undercapitalised and underdeveloped. This was true not only of the high-end producer services examined in the previous section, but also of virtually every branch of the sector, including transport, communications, retailing, finance, public administration, health, education, welfare, legal and leisure services.

This woeful state could be blamed on many factors, not all of them the result of the Communist era. As is well known, the service sector was relatively undeveloped in most of ECE before the Second World War. This was not because capital stocks in services were particularly low relative to other sectors (Major, 1992), but instead reflected structural factors – especially a bias towards labour-intensive, low-level personal services. Also, the higher-end activities such as finance, banking, trade and communication were penetrated to a significant degree by foreign capital (Michalak, 1993). In fact the great depression of the 1930s had catastrophic consequences for most of these countries in this respect. Although in Czechoslovakia foreign-held assets were relatively low – around 15 per cent[3] – in Poland in the early 1930s they stood at around 25 per cent and in Hungary they reached a

staggering 70 per cent. To make matters worse, the lion's share of the profits was often transferred to headquarters in the West with little regard for the capital and investment needs of the region.

Above all, however, the retarded development of advanced services was a post-war phenomenon, fundamentally embedded in the ideological and theoretical dogma of state socialism (Ofer, 1973; Major, 1985). According to the official ideology of Marxism-Leninism imposed throughout ECE by the Soviet Communist regime, services do not create or contribute anything to GDP and are, therefore, *unproductive* and entirely *redistributive* in character. As a result the official economic policy was to limit these activities to the bare and essential minimum, allowing economic priorities to be directed almost entirely towards manufacturing, mining, construction and agriculture.[4] Moreover, in the planned economy based on the central allocation of resources, there was no theoretical or practical requirement for banking, insurance and social welfare (Kornai, 1992). In states where work was compulsory and

Figure 8.2 *The celebration of socialist labour. Stained glass windows in the headquarters of the former East German government. The heroic slogan* "Trotz Alledem!" *translates as* "Despite everything!" *(Photo: D A Pinder)*

– at least officially – employment full, where was the need for social security nets (Figure 8.2)? In sharp contrast to this underdevelopment of private and welfare services, however, the government sector was vast, powerful and very influential, politically and in terms of employment and investment (Figure 8.3). This sector, too, bears a large degree of responsibility for the low productivity and inefficiency of the ECE economies. It is not only the restricted share of private services in the industrial make-up of the pre-1989 economies which contributed to the crisis, but also the poor quality of what little was available.

In the case of construction and engineering services, it is true, the picture was slightly different, mainly because the socialist economies required these to support industrialisation, housing programmes and infrastructure investment. One result of this was that they were able to develop to the point at which significant service exports became possible (Major, 1992). Usually the competitive edge in these instances was based on traditional linkages or political affinity with countries experimenting with the

socialist model of development, but the availabilty of low-cost skilled labour was also significant. This was especially the case when the competition for business came from Western companies demanding payment in hard currencies rather than barter – the most common form of trade transaction in the centrally planned economies. In the defence sector, too, different circumstances prevailed, chiefly because extensive research and development were required by the military complex. But much of this research was concentrated in the Soviet Union, and the fruits were not allowed to filter through to improve consumer-based industries.

Elsewhere in the producer services sector systemic distortion was the rule, one of the most important examples of this being provided by the finance "industry", which by the start of the transitional phase required very urgent and radical reform. The functions of financial services in the planned economy were defined as *passive*. That is, money followed the decisions determined in the material or "productive" sphere of the economy, and there was no need for competitive financial institutions, stock exchanges or other financial

Figure 8.3 *Seats of power. The headquarters of the East German government (page 146) and the* Palast der Republik *or the parliament building (above). The vast* Palast *was popularly known as "Erich's lightbulb shop". Erich was Erich Honecker, the head of state; the innumerable lights in the glass-walled* Palast *shone out on a country in which production system deficiencies often made it virtually impossible to obtain basic items such as bulbs. (Photos: D A Pinder)*

services. Credit and distribution were decided by the central planning office, which produced elaborate plans and blueprints of investment priorities and production targets. International banking and finance – the backbone of modern, highly developed industrial economies – were especially badly neglected. Moreover, the capitalist economy was despised in the official propaganda for creating the "middleman deviation" – the entire class of bankers and financial "parasites" reaping fortunes on the backs of the proletariat.

This caricature of the financial sector in the modern market economy was extrapolated to cover most high-end services, with catastrophic results as the systematic ideological bias that was adopted against them produced their near-complete absence in the socialist economies. In official interpretations of pre-socialist Russia and

the states of ECE, consultants, accountants, insurers, lawyers, advertising professionals, traders and bankers were all treated with suspicion and blamed for the plight of the working class. Since these "unproductive" and "parasitic" activities coincided with what could broadly be described as the middle class, it was no wonder that the ideological fervour of the Communist Party succeeded not only in attaching a pejorative stigma to producer services, but in some cases in exterminating those involved in them – for example in the Stalinist Soviet Union. Needless to add, the few surviving producer service professions, and government departments performing similar functions, were kept under close supervision and no private firms were permitted. Consequently, even in the relatively developed East Germany, which inherited a substantial industrial base from the Third Reich,

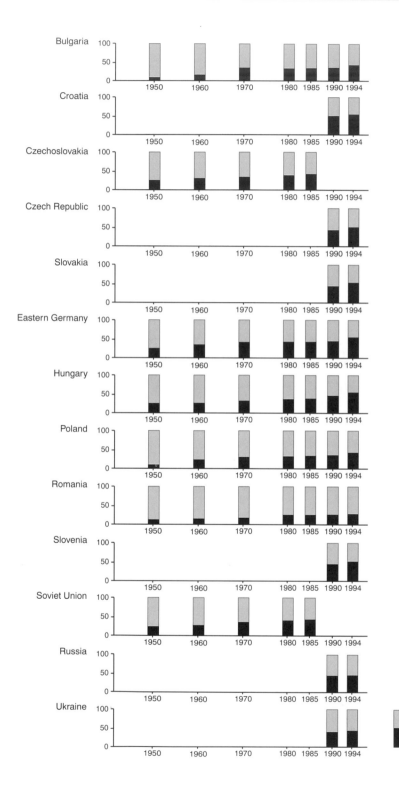

Figure 8.4 *Services' share of employment, 1950–94*

there were only 10 certified accountants per 100 000 inhabitants in 1992. In fact even these figures are misleading since, strictly speaking, there was no profession in East Germany – or the rest of ECE for that matter – which was comparable with that of the certified accountant in western Europe. Although there were approximately 140 people working under this title, they were all employees of the Ministry of Finance and various state industrial complexes, and in reality they were responsible for planning and control tasks, not independent auditing. This peculiar arrangement was introduced by the Soviet Union throughout most of ECE (Gaebe, 1995; Schamp, 1995).

Under such conditions, the efficiency of the service sector in general was limited for decades to, essentially, prewar levels. Ironically, since the state monopolised all services, contrary to official ideology it was possible for state planners to impose relative high profit margins. Yet, despite this, in the end the quality and availability of services declined even further. This was not unconnected with the fact that service-sector salaries – including those for high-order services – were significantly below the national average. For Western observers, one of the most striking features of the ECE economic system was the low remuneration of physicians, academics, teachers, researchers, etc. In practical terms there was little difference between the salary of, say, a physician and a postal worker. Even if genuine producer services had existed, therefore, it is highly probable that their employees would have been extremely poorly paid, with implications for quality.

These problems mean that the limited service-sector employment estimates that are available must be treated with extreme caution. It is true that after the war, in association with the policy of "extensive economic growth" significant service-sector expansion occurred. Figure 8.4 reveals a marked upswing in all countries, with growth in Bulgaria and Romania being particularly impressive. Overall, the unweighted average share that services had of total employment in all six ECE states rose from 19.6 per cent in 1950 to 31.8 per cent in 1970.[5] Superficially, this trend echoed that in the West, but there was a very significant difference between East and West in terms of the reasons for, and the nature of, the expansion of service-sector employment. In the market economies expansion was to a great extent a response to growing demand for ever more sophisticated services, some of which were already increasingly infused with innovation and high technology. Planned economies, in contrast, expanded their service sectors primarily to deal with the lack of capital stocks in other activities, compensate for archaic technologies and achieve statutory full employment. This artificially expanded the low-order services while simultaneously, for the reasons discussed above, the emergence of advanced producer services was stifled.

What may be added is that, in the later Communist period, this control of the service sector introduced another contrast with the West. While services in western Europe continued to develop rapidly in the 1970s and 1980s, in ECE their expansion was restricted, and in Bulgaria the sector actually declined slightly (Figure 8.4). By this time, after some initial prewar success, the socialist model of the economy was flagging, and able to generate nothing more than a very moderate increase in services. Thus, for the six ECE states as a whole, the share of total employment held by services only rose from 31.8 per cent in 1970 to 35.9 per cent in 1985.[6] And, within this unimpressive performance, the development of almost all producer services continued to be held back.

Towards a Producer Service Development Strategy

The implementation of radical reforms in the early 1990s has had a clearly accelerating effect on most ECE economies. In particular, Poland, the Czech Republic and Slovakia have experienced a minor boom, with annual economic growth rates of between 5 and 10 per cent (Andrzejewski and Szczepaniak, 1995). Associated with this, perceptible – and sometimes substantial – expansion of the service sector has occurred (Figure 8.4). As a result, although Romania – for decades plagued by fanatical ideologues and ethnic and national tensions – still has very restricted service employment, on average in the remaining ECE countries services accounted for 50 per cent of total employment by 1994.[7]

Expansion to this level is one factor that has cultivated a widespread belief that, particularly in central Europe, the formerly state-planned economies are achieving successful transition towards the market. Moreover, within the producer service sector *per se*, this view is encouraged by significant changes such as the replacement of dominant central banks by a decentralised system of private or hybrid (private/public) financial institutions. For example, Hungary now has more than 40 banks; over half of these are private and many have a foreign owner. By 1994, Poland had over 80 private banks, none of which existed before 1989. Some of the largest banks in the region – such as the Bank Handlowy in Warsaw, the Bulgarian Foreign Trade Bank, the Komerčni Banka in Prague or the Orszagos Takarekpéntzar Bank in Budapest – are hybrid institutions with joint state and private ownership. In addition, approximately 15 Western financial institutions have made substantial investments in ECE. Two in particular – Citibank from the United States and ING from the Netherlands – have purchased minority stakes in private banks created since 1989, while several others have established a strong region-wide presence. Thus the Austrian bank Creditanstalt has subsidiaries and branches in Budapest, Prague, Warsaw, Bratislava, Ljubljana, Sofia and Moscow; France's Société Générale has invested in joint ventures in a very similar range of major cities; and other Western giants, such as Commerzbank, Crédit Lyonnais, Deutsche Bank or Bank Austria, are all represented in the region's major capitals (*Business Central Europe*, 1994). Western investment and expertise in this sphere have therefore been accepted by all countries in the region, and ECE today offers a very liberal approach towards trade in services and capital. This is the case even though, because of the sensitivity of the financial sector, a number of regulations and conditions have had to be put in place.

Despite some appearances, however, the powerful influence of the past means that producer services remain extremely limited, in terms of their absolute scale, their degree of sophistication and their geographical distribution. As might be anticipated, the services which are emerging are tending to concentrate in the upper reaches of the urban hierarchy, leaving access to them very variable, both within and between countries. What must now be considered, therefore, is the way forward. How may more rapid development of the sector be encouraged? The analysis offered here is that much is likely to depend on infrastructural improvements, on cultivating appropriate skills in the labour market, on assistance made available through Western aid and – not least – on the impact of foreign direct investment (FDI). But what is also argued is that, although ways forward may be proposed, there remain substantial obstacles to their implementation.

A very significant force restraining the producer services sector today is the exceptionally low quality and density of the infrastructure, particularly with respect to telecommunications (Schneider, 1993). There are many reasons why this is so, including technological backwardness induced by systemic neglect, and Western embargoes on the transfer of new technologies to countries east of the Iron Curtain. Above all, however, backwardness in this field reflects the paramount importance the Soviet Communist regime attached to exerting political control of its ECE satellite states. To maintain the climate of repression in these countries, an efficient and modern communication network could not be allowed because of the serious threat it would pose to the monopoly of information held by the state. The lack of verifiable information – particularly on the state of the economy, political events and the world outside the "socialist brotherhood" – was crucial to maintaining the grip on these societies.[8]

In spite of political propaganda to the contrary, therefore, few resources and little effort were put into securing the foundations for an "information society". As a result, it is now necessary to make telecommunication services a central component in infrastructural investment. Progress in this direction is certainly being assisted by the West, partly through aid (Table 8.1), but also through loans. Between 1990 and 1994, for example, a quarter of all lending in ECE by the European Investment Bank (EIB) was for telecommunication projects, and in 1994–96, 585

Table 8.1 *Composition of aid commitments by type of aid, 1990–93 (million $)*

	Visegrad Four*	The Balkans	Western ex-republics	Southern ex-republics	Russia	Total
Agriculture and education	871	229	–	–	1034	2134
Manufacturing and energy	1952	395	185	59	–	2591
Transport, telecom and roads	2330	843	85	–	9	3267
Banking and services	1601	245	7	–	49	1902
Social security and retraining	100	13	–	–	70	183
General	567	73	10	177	40	867
Macroeconomic restructuring	2299	1032	290	311	690	4622
Emergency assistance and environment	18	–	–	–	–	18
Total	9738	2830	577	547	1892	15 584

* Poland, the Czech Republic, Slovakia and Hungary.
Source: UNECE (1994).

million ECU were committed. Welcome though this assistance is, however, so far the beneficiaries of these network improvements have been limited to the Visegrad Four plus Bulgaria (Figure 8.5), and it is certain that even here the upgrading programmes will be protracted.

Second, the earlier policy of repressing producer services has naturally meant that in the new climate of the 1990s there is a severe shortage of appropriately qualified human capital. The necessary expertise and skills are seriously deficient within the region, and the situation is made worse by the more general lack of entrepreneurial experience. While one way of overcoming this obstacle may be to exploit FDI, a strategy that is discussed further below, it can also be suggested that the education and training arena is one in which Western aid institutions – such as the European Bank for Reconstruction and Development, the International Monetary Fund and the European Union – could well play an important role. Unfortunately, sectoral lending is only rarely reported by bilateral institutions (Michalak, 1995) with the result that only a generalised picture of aid recipients can be drawn. However, Table 8.1 summarises this multilateral assistance by type of aid between 1990 and 1993, and from this two important observations may be made. First, within ECE there are considerable international variations in the spatial targeting of aid, variations which in general work in favour of the "Visegrad Four" countries (Poland, the Czech Republic, Slovakia and Hungary). Second, although some of the assistance is certainly highly relevant to producer services (e.g. with respect to telecommunications and banking) the subventions destined for education and retraining are in comparison currently limited. Despite the need and potential, therefore, this does not suggest that at present aid is significantly addressing the sector's expertise and skills deficit.

Third, not least because of the vacuum left by aid, it is arguable that there is a particular place for the expansion of FDI. One of the principal roles which this could play in ECE is that of import substitution. Massive foreign debts (e.g. in Hungary and Poland) are in part caused by trade deficits with the West, which are in turn partly a consequence of imported producer services (Gibb and Michalak, 1993). Indeed, in the mid-1990s, most high-end producer services are simply imported to ECE from the highly developed economies. Clearly, FDI could substitute for at least some of these imports. In addition, as ECE governments have quite openly recognised, in the absence of sufficiently large domestic savings, foreign capital can provide a major source of alternative finance. But beyond this, foreign producer service firms locating in ECE countries would provide local employees with valuable experience, thereby helping to bridge the expertise gap and create a skilled workforce from which new entrepreneurs should emerge. Similarly, incoming firms could exert a catalytic

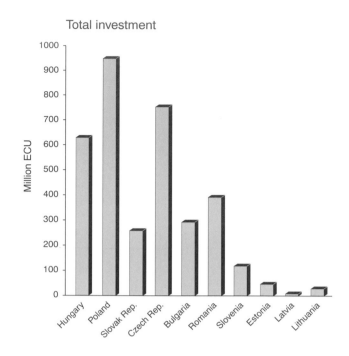

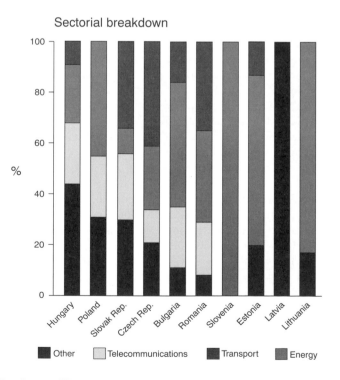

Figure 8.5 *Sectoral distribution of European Investment Bank loans in eastern and central Europe, 1990–94*

demonstration effect stimulating new firm formation, while there is also scope for them to make a significant contribution to the reduction of the continuing technology gap between firms in eastern and western Europe. Elsewhere in the world, it is well recognised that FDI is becoming not simply one of the major sources of capital, but also an effective way of transferring technology, know-how and organisational management skills. Indeed, the economies of South East Asia consider FDI highly desirable because of the influx of new technologies and skills rather than of capital itself. Against this background, all newly elected governments in ECE recognise the potential significance which FDI could have for their economies and, in response, have introduced wholly new and very liberal regulations since 1989. With few exceptions, foreign investors now enjoy very similar legal frameworks to those usually taken for granted in western Europe.

Once again, however, there are obstacles to the effective exploitation of this pathway. First, as was noted earlier in this chapter with respect to the interwar period, there are potential pitfalls in the FDI strategy. External control of key activities such as producer services is not necessarily good for emerging market economies. There may be, for example, a tendency for incoming investors to increase excessively their net profits and to transfer outdated technology to the recipient countries. Second, although ECE governments are currently highly receptive to FDI, their primary target for investment is the manufacturing sector rather than producer services. As Table 8.2 shows for some of the leading countries, although investments in the tertiary sector are quite numerous, the lion's share of the finance is destined for manufacturing. In this context it is arguable that the key role of these services is still not properly appreciated in political circles, where emphasis is placed too heavily on boosting current production, and too little attention is given to establishing an appropriate foundation for future competitive economic development. Despite many other changes, in this respect the earlier bias of Communist governments appears to persist in post-Communist times. More perceptive political perspectives on development mechanisms is certainly necessary.

Third, in spite of the economic and legal reforms, and in spite of the high hopes of the new regimes, so far Western firms have not translated the new economic climate into substantial cross-border investment flows (Murphy, 1992). This is probably the case even in Hungary, the most advanced country in terms of the economic

Table 8.2 *Foreign investment in Czechoslovakia, Hungary and Poland by sector, 1989–90*

Sector	Czechoslovakia*		Hungary*		Poland[†]	
	% number	% value	% number	% value	% number	% value
Primary	**4.0**	**7.8**	**0.9**	**0.2**	**4.4**	**9.9**
Secondary	**37.7**	**65.9**	**45.7**	**63.5**	**77.8**	**69.4**
Manufacturing	32.0	64.5	39.7	58.8	73.3	67.0
Construction	5.7	1.4	6.0	4.7	4.5	2.4
Tertiary	**58.3**	**26.3**	**53.4**	**36.3**	**17.8**	**20.7**
Trade	19.7	0.4	22.5	7.0	3.2	2.0
Transport and communication	6.6	15.2	5.5	1.3	2.5	5.0
FIRE	2.2	0.1	2.7	18.7	0.7	0.2
Computer and data processing	6.1	0.6	3.2	0.4	1.1	0.5
R&D	0.4	0.2	0.6	0.1	0.3	0.2
Business services	12.3	1.1	13.7	5.4	2.9	1.3
Other public and final services	11.0	8.7	5.2	3.4	7.1	11.5
Total	100.0	100.0	100.0	100.0	100.0	100.0

* Data for 1990.
[†] Data for 1989.
Sources: UNECE (1990, 1991); Scott (1991); SFIA (1992); FAFI (1992); MIER (1992).

Table 8.3 *Change in foreign investment in Hungary by sector, 1989–90*

Sector	1989		1990		% change 1989–90	
	Number	$m.	Number	$m.	Number	Value
Primary	**9**	**2.0**	**9**	**1.9**	**0**	**−5**
Secondary	**310**	**329.5**	**460**	**538.0**	**48**	**63**
Manufacturing	268	299.3	399	498.0	49	66
Construction	42	30.2	61	40.0	45	33
Tertiary	**263**	**152.4**	**537**	**307.8**	**104**	**102**
Trade	92	30.7	226	58.7	146	95
Transport and communication	34	10.5	55	11.0	62	5
FIRE	18	81.2	27	158.8	50	96
Computer and data processing	13	1.5	32	3.2	146	113
R&D	3	0.5	6	0.9	100	80
Business services	67	12.7	138	46.0	106	262
Other public and final services	36	15.3	53	28.2	47	84
Total	**582**	**483.9**	**1006**	**847.7**	**73**	**75**

Sources: UNECE (1990, 1991); MIER (1992).

transition from a planned to a market economy. On the one hand, in the early transition period a third of this country's FDI was invested in services, and mostly in trade, business services and FIRE (finance, insurance and real estate). This association between progress with transition and producer service investment suggests the importance of the latter. But, on the other hand, at least in these early years, the absolute scale of investment was modest (Table 8.3).

For ECE as a whole this partly reflects the difficulties in the process of economic integration with the West. The initial optimism, following the fall of the Berlin Wall in 1989, has been replaced by a more cautious attitude. Not least, the costs of German unification, which have proved to be much higher than originally estimated, have dampened the initial momentum of the process. In addition, however, it is probable that the slow growth of FDI reflects a fear among Western businesses that they may give away their competitive advantage. The combination of newly obtained expertise, high technology and a well-educated but relatively low-wage labour force could not only undermine Western exports of producer services to ECE, but also introduce new low-cost entrants in western European markets. In reality this threat is probably exaggerated, at least while ECE countries remain outside the EU. If the

protectionist measures introduced by the EU to limit imports of eastern European steel, coal and agricultural imports are anything to go by, the EU is well able to safeguard its interests and there is little chance of a radical threat to Western producer services. But if cautious producer service decision-makers are discounting the potential effectiveness of protection, reluctance to engage in FDI on a significant scale would be an understandable outcome.

Conclusion

As has been demonstrated, the development of the producer service sector in ECE has been severely handicapped by its political and economic heritage. Moreover, the nature of transition from centrally planned to market economies, combined with the unprecedented pace of change in political and social spheres, is imposing additional stresses. In the short time that has elapsed since 1989, radical shifts have occurred in all dimensions of ECE economies, and it has naturally been difficult for stunted key activities such as producer services to respond. To some extent the problem is alleviated by the fact that, thus far, demand for producer services has been relatively small by comparison with Western economies (Gaebe,

1995). No doubt this reflects the still-antiquated state of the former Eastern Bloc economies.

All the same, restructuring will result in growing demand for producer services as traditional industrial linkages and complexes are disbanded, and as the ECE economies are gradually integrated into Western and global markets. As this occurs, two dangers are likely to arise. First, the lack of adequate producer services within the region may well impair the emergence of advanced competitive economies and, second, a state of dependency may emerge as the vacuum created by the weakness of endogenous producer services is in many instances filled by purchases from western Europe. Either outcome would be highly unsatisfactory, and there is no doubt that – if ECE's own producer service sector is to fulfil its important role in the vanguard of transformation – there is a need to bring into focus both the fundamental significance of producer services and the requirement for strategies to develop them.

Notes

1. Because of this fundamental relationship with production, it can be argued that producer services should not be regarded as "services" in any conventional sense, but rather as indirect inputs to the production process.
2. One implication of the fact that corporations may have significant numbers of producer service employees who are classed as production workers is that official estimates of total producer service employment may be deceptively low.
3. This low proportion was partly a consequence of the fact that Bohemia, Moravia and, to a lesser extent, Slovakia were relatively highly industrialised before the formation of the Czech and Slovak Federal Republic. In addition, a very successful industrial development programme in Bohemia enabled the Czechoslovak government to reduce foreign-owned equity significantly through a policy of "nostrification" during the 1930s.
4. Even the "productive" sectors were chosen in accordance with "socialist" principles of class warfare. Thus heavy industries and mining had higher priority than construction; the latter's status placed it above the chemical sector and cement production; agriculture came below these, and so on. Metal and processing industries were the principal suppliers of the class-conscious proletariat – the core of the socialist state and Communist dogma.
5. If the Soviet Union is included, the equivalent figures for 1950 and 1970 are 20.1 and 32.5 per cent.

6. In this case the figures with the inclusion of the Soviet Union are 32.5 per cent (1970) and 36.6 per cent (1985).
7. When Russia and Ukraine are included, the equivalent figure is 49 per cent.
8. This point is underlined by the fact that rising levels of awareness of conditions and developments in the democratic countries, usually gained despite the dilapidated telecommunications infrastructures, ultimately contributed significantly to the collapse of the Communist regimes.

References

Andrzejewski, P and Szczepaniak, M (1995) Państwa grópy wyszehradzkiej – obraz gospodarczy (Visegrad group – an economic overview), *Przegląd Zachodni*, **4**, 57–84.

Beyers, W B (1991) Trends in the producer services in the USA: the last decade, in P W Daniels (ed) *Services and Metropolitan Development: international perspectives*, Routledge, London, 146–72.

Bicanic, I and Skreb, M (1991) The service sector in East European economies: what role can it play in future development?, *Communist Economies and Economic Transformation*, **3**, 221–33.

Business Central Europe (1994) Banking survey, *Business Central Europe*, **1**, 37–59.

Christopherson, S (1989) Flexibility in the US service economy and the emerging spatial division of labour, *Transactions of the Institute of British Geographers*, **14**, 131–43.

Coffey, W J and Polése, M (1989) Producer services and regional development: a policy-oriented perspective, *Papers of the Regional Science Association*, **67**, 13–27.

Daniels, P W (1991) Service sector restructuring and metropolitan development: processes and prospects, in P W Daniels (ed) *Services and Metropolitan Development: international perspectives*, Routledge, London, 1–25.

Daniels, P W, Illeris, S, Bonamy, J and Philippe, J (1993) *The Geography of Services*, Cass, London.

Davis, N (1996) *Europe: a history*, Oxford University Press, Oxford.

FAFI (Federal Agency for Foreign Investment) (1992) Foreign investment in Czechoslovakia (in Czech), Federal Agency for Foreign Investment, Prague, mimeo.

Gaebe, W (1995) The significance of advanced producer services in the new German Länder, in F Moulaert and F Tödtling (eds) *The Geography of Advanced Producer Services in Europe*, Pergamon, London, 173–84.

Gershuny, J I and Miles, I D (1983) *The New Service Economy: the transformation of employment in industrial societies*, Pinter, London.

Gibb, R A and Michalak, W Z (1993) Foreign debt in the new East-Central Europe: a threat to European integration?, *Environment and Planning C*, **11**, 69–85.

Goe, W R (1990) Producer services, trade and the social division of labour, *Regional Studies*, **24**, 327–42.

Hansen, N (1990) Do producer services induce regional economic development?, *Journal of Regional Science*, **30**, 465–76.

Harvey, D (1989) *The Condition of Postmodernity: an enquiry into the origins of cultural change*, Blackwell, Oxford.

Howells, J and Green, A (1987) *Technological Innovation, Structural Change and Location in UK Services*, Gower, Aldershot.

Kornai, J (1992) *The Socialist System: the political economy of communism*, Princeton University Press, Princeton.

Ley, D F and Hutton, T A (1991) The service sector and metropolitan development in Canada, in P W Daniels (ed) *Services and Metropolitan Development: international perspectives*, Routledge, London, 173–203.

Maciejewicz, J and Monkiewicz, J (1989) Changing role of services in the socialist countries of eastern Europe, *Service Industries Journal*, **9**, 384–98.

MacPherson, A (1991) Interfirm information linkages in an economically disadvantaged region: an empirical perspective from metropolitan Buffalo, *Environment and Planning A*, **23**, 591–606.

Major, I (1985) Les services en economie planifié: l'exemple de la Hongrie, *Revue d'Etudes Comparatives Est-Ouest*, **16**, 51–72.

Major, I (1992) Private and public infrastructure in Eastern Europe, *Oxford Review of Economic Policy*, **7**, 76–92.

Marquand, J M (1983) The changing distribution of the service employment, in J B Goddard and A G Champion (eds) *The Urban and Regional Transformation in Britain*, Routledge, London, 99–134.

Marshall, N and Wood, P (1995) *Services and Space: key aspects of urban and regional development*, Longman, London.

Michalak, W Z (1993) Foreign direct investment and joint ventures in East-Central Europe: a geographical perspective, *Environment and Planning A*, **25**, 1573–91.

Michalak, W Z (1995) Foreign aid and Eastern Europe in the "New World Order", *Tijdschrift voor Economische en Sociale Geografie*, **86**, 260–77.

Michalak, W Z and Fairbairn, K J (1988) Producer services in a peripheral economy, *Canadian Journal of Regional Studies*, **11**, 353–72.

Michalak, W Z and Fairbairn, K J (1992) The location of producer service firms in Edmonton, *Canadian Geographer*, **36**, 2–16.

MIER (Ministry of International Economic Relations) (1992) Foreign investment in Hungary, Ministry of International Economic Relations, Budapest, mimeo.

Murphy, A B (1992) Western investment in East-Central Europe: emerging patterns and implications for state stability, *Professional Geographer*, **44**, 249–59.

Nusbaumer, J (1984) *Les Services – Nouvelle Donne de l'Economie*, Economica, Paris.

Ofer, G (1973) *The Service Sector in Soviet Economic Growth: a comparative study*, Harvard University Press, Cambridge, Mass.

O hUallachain, B and Reid, N (1991) The location and growth of business and professional services in American metropolitan areas, 1976–1986, *Annals of the Association of American Geographers*, **81**, 254–70.

Piore, M and Sabel, C (1984) *The Second Industrial Divide*, Basic Books, New York.

Sayer, A and Walker, R (1992) *The New Social Economy: reworking the division of labour*, Blackwell, Oxford.

Schamp, E W (1995) The geography of advanced producer services in a goods exporting economy: the case of West Germany, in F Moulaert and F Tödtling (eds) *The Geography of Advanced Producer Services in Europe*, Pergamon, London, 155–71.

Schneider, O (1993) The problems of the development of the service sector in Czechoslovakia, in P Daniels, S Illeris, J Bonamy and J Philippe (eds) *The Geography of Services*, Frank Cass, London, 132–43.

Scott, N (1991) The implications of the transition for foreign trade and investment, *Oxford Review of Economic Policy*, **8**, 44–57.

SFIA (State Foreign Investment Agency) (1992) Permits granted by Foreign Investment Agency for establishment of companies with foreign participation in Poland, 1989–1992, Ministry for Foreign Economic Co-operation, Warsaw, mimeo.

Stanback, T M, Bearse P J, Noyelle T J and Karasek R A (1981) *Services: the new economy*, Allanheld and Osmund, Totowa, NJ.

UNECE (United Nations Economic Commission for Europe) (1990) *Economic Reforms in the European Centrally Planned Economies: proceedings of a symposium conducted in association with the Vienna Institute for Comparative Economic Studies*, United Nations Economic Commission for Europe, Geneva.

UNECE (1991) *Statistical Survey of Recent Trends in Foreign Investment in East European Countries*, United Nations Economic Commission for Europe, Geneva.

UNECE (1994) *Economic Survey of Europe in 1993–1994*, United Nations Economic Commission for Europe, Geneva.

Walker, R (1985) Is there a service economy? The changing capitalist division of labour, *Science and Society*, **49**, 42–83.

Winiecki, J (1988) *The Distorted World of Soviet-type Economies*, Kegan Paul, New York.

Wood, P A (1991a) Conceptualising the role of services in economic change, *Area*, **23**, 66–72.

Wood, P A (1991b) Flexible accumulation and the rise of business services, *Transactions of the Institute of British Geographers*, **16**, 160–72.

9

European retailing: dynamics, restructuring and development issues

John Dawson and Steve Burt

Department of Business Studies, University of Edinburgh, Management School, UK and Institute for Retail Studies, University of Stirling, UK

Introduction
Antecedents

For many decades, widespread social changes involving consumers and companies have been instrumental in moulding the retail sector at both the structural and operational levels (Dawson, 1982; Burt, 1989). The development of nineteenth-century industrial society, in which consumers simply wanted more products, enabled the expansion of retailing and the emergence of capitalist chains and consumer co-operative societies to provide for the basic needs of rapidly growing urban populations. Demand for fashion goods also grew at this time, and was met by the development of department stores. This occurred first in major cities – including London, Paris, Berlin and St Petersburg – and subsequently in provincial towns and cities.

In the twentieth century, the schism of Europe into socialist and capitalist societies split the sector, creating in its place two structurally contrasted retail systems. Retailers in western Europe gradually evolved marketing concepts in response to consumer demand, and in the process established new patterns of retail location, differentiated their product ranges, adopted innovative approaches to promotion and actively competed for consumers through price and service differentials. In socialist central and eastern Europe, in contrast, retailing was deemed an unproductive use of capital. Central direction therefore downgraded it into a passive activity which merely distributed what was made in the productive sector. Product availability was dictated by bureaucratic decisions rather than the market, just as centralised decision-making determined the location of shops and restricted the expansion of retail space (Figure 9.1).

In the 1990s the sector is again changing dramatically. In central and eastern Europe, privatisation of retailing has opened up innumerable opportunities. In response, medium-sized chains – often owned by foreign investors – have begun to emerge; and, although the retail network is still very sparse as a legacy of many years of the non-market economy (Meyer, 1992; Seitz, 1992), there has been an explosion in the number of locally owned small firms. Thus in Poland 160 000 additional sales outlets were

Figure 9.1 *Former branch of the Konsum chain. Konsum shops sold foodstuffs throughout East Germany. (Photo: D A Pinder)*

created between 1990 and 1994, while for Hungary the equivalent figure was 110 000. Meanwhile in western Europe, a late-twentieth-century shift to a post-industrial "anything goes" society (Brown, 1995a, b), in which consumers require different products rather than simply more of them, has generated an almost mesmerising variety of structures, operations and values to which retailers are responding.

Although intensive change is affecting all parts of Europe, for two reasons this chapter focuses primarily on change in the west. First, in most of central and eastern Europe, the retail sector is as yet in the early stages of development, and considerably more research is necessary before even these early years can be properly understood. Second, there is every prospect that developments in western Europe will ultimately spread to the former socialist economies, either through the activities of foreign investors, or as consumer demand converges on western "norms". To explore and understand western Europe, therefore, may well be to gain insights into the future of the former socialist countries. What should also

be emphasised is that, although the spatial consequences of retail sector development are certainly considered, a central aim of the analysis is to highlight and explore the dynamism and consequences of the processes currently shaping this vital component of the economy. To this end the chapter is structured around three themes: the forces of change in retailing, the industry's responses in terms of structural reorganisation, and the social and environmental issues raised by the combination of these forces and responses.

The Forces of Change in Retailing

Retailing accounts for the major share of consumer expenditure across Europe. In 1990–91, the latest year for which reliable estimates are available (Eurostat, 1993), retail sales in the 12 European Community countries (the EU12) were over £950 bn. In addition, sales worth a further £90 bn were generated by the five other western European countries in the European Economic Area (EEA). More informal estimates would

Table 9.1 *Estimates of key statistics on retailing (including motor trades)*

	Number of enterprises ('000)	Per cent of all enterprises	Persons employed ('000)	Per cent share of GVA[*]	Number of outlets ('000)	Outlets per 10 000 inhabitants
Belgium	127.8	14.8	274.7	15.4	140.0	141
Denmark	48.1	11.1	199.7	13.4	51.5	100
Germany	439.0	19.0	2353.0	10.1	533.7	85
Greece	175.0	34.5	338.2	12.4	184.9	184
Spain	454.9	30.2	1434.0	13.8	523.2	134
France	461.8	21.4	2090.0	13.2	546.2	97
Ireland	29.3	25.5	131.4	10.4	31.7	90
Italy	929.7	30.3	2410.0	15.8	983.0	171
Luxembourg	3.5	19.5	18.1	13.5	4.4	116
Netherlands	95.0	15.2	637.5	13.7	119.4	80
Portugal	173.3	34.0	366.3	17.3	190.0	192
United Kingdom	348.2	19.4	3030.0	12.8	466.7	81
Austria	40.9	11.8	256.4	12.8	52.5	69
Finland	29.5	36.0	157.2	9.2	38.5	77
Iceland	1.5	11.0	8.0	10.8	1.7	67
Norway	32.0	10.0	123.4	12.0	38.8	92
Sweden	50.0	20.2	314.0	9.5	80.5	94
Switzerland	42.0	16.6	380.5	13.7	55.1	83
Poland				8.9	227.0	43[†]
Romania				5.9	58.8	23[†]
Former Czechoslovakia				10.7	62.8	36[†]
Hungary				10.8	63.7	50[†]
Bulgaria				8.8	44.0	38[†]

[*] Gross value added in economy of all distributive trade (including wholesale).
[†] Fixed shops only.
Source: Eurostat (1993); figures relate to various years 1988–91.

suggest that by 1996, across all 17 countries, sales were close to £1500 bn. Moreover, although there are significant international contrasts in the retail sector (Table 9.1), as a whole it accounts for 25 per cent of firms in the entire economy and 12 per cent of gross value added.

Increases in personal consumption associated with higher living standards naturally generate a growing volume of retail sales; consequently the real increase of 20 per cent in the EU12 between 1985 and 1993 was a significant development. Just as importantly, however, growth in consumption creates increased variety across the sector. This finds expression partly in the diversification of products and services which are offered by retailers and purchased by consumers. New product development is now at a higher level than ever before, while fashion cycles are shorter than at any time in the past. But variety is also

characteristic of the stores and non-store operations through which products and services are marketed, and this diversity is increasing through innovations such as self-checkout stores, new locations for shops, multimedia sales-kiosks, and virtual shops on the Internet (Rowley, 1996). A cryogenic shopper of the 1960s, suddenly revived in the late 1990s, would find a very different pattern of shops, many unfamiliar names and products, and substantially altered retail operations from those of the 1950s and 1960s.

An appreciation of the structural changes which have occurred – and are still occurring – in the "channel of distribution" is vital for understanding the present patterns of retailing in Europe. Originally this distribution channel was a conduit through which manufacturers pushed goods to consumers. Each of the various participants in the channel – manufacturer, wholesaler, import agent, retailer, etc. – had individual functions. Today, however, movement through the channel is driven by consumers who pull goods through it from the manufacturers. Moreover, as this switch has occurred, many individual functions have been blurred, so that many retailers now take responsibility for aspects of wholesaling, for example physical distribution, and may even be involved in traditional manufacturing functions such as new product development. Equally, some wholesalers have expanded into retailing, with all that this entails in terms of shop ownership, promotion, product display and sales to the final consumer. A good example of this is the UK's Alldays chain of convenience stores, which emerged from the activities of a wholesaler.

While the functions which are performed in the channel have largely remained the same,[1] the responsibility for their performance has shifted significantly. Retailers today are just as likely to design and brand goods as are manufacturers, as the product lines offered by retailers such as Marks & Spencer, IKEA, Casino, and Hennes & Mauritz readily demonstrate. Because of the blurred boundaries between functions, it may even be difficult to categorise a firm as a retailer, wholesaler or manufacturer. This shift is clearly a major departure for the distribution channel and, as will be demonstrated, it is central to explanations of many of the changes in retail structure and operations discussed below.

The changing environment

A major influence on the changing structure, performance and location of retailing is the operational environment in which retail firms must function. This environment encompasses social, economic, technological and political elements which generate a culture to which retailers respond with managerial decisions. From a retailing perspective some aspects of this environment are converging across Europe, but others show increasing differences and divergence. With these more complex patterns of change, and the increased speed at which change occurs, the commercial environment is becoming more turbulent and unpredictable.

There are some strong convergent tendencies. Demographic trends towards more and smaller households, an ageing population, later marriage, and lower fertility are common to the various western European countries, although each is at a different stage. Some shifts in consumer values, for example increased concern with the natural environment, are converging across much of Europe. Similarly, technological innovations – for example, as applied in domestic and household goods, or information and communication technologies – are acting in a convergent way to make the operating environment more similar. This may be illustrated by progress towards Europe-wide television channels, increased (although as yet far from perfect) integration in road transport, and easier electronic networking of information for business uses. By looking for convergent trends, some commentators have suggested that they dominate the business environment, and that there is emerging a single market characterised by powerful Euro-brands (Lanon, 1991) produced in a few strategically located plants and distributed though a Euro-network of large integrated distribution centres.

In reality, however, not all the trends are towards convergence. Some aspects of the retail environment remain strikingly contrasted in different parts of western Europe (Wierenga *et al.*, 1996) and many aspects of life style underline diversity. Quite apart from cultural differences based on language, European tastes in food and drink, styles and colours of clothes and furnishings, music choice and architecture all remain highly varied – not only nationally but in some cases regionally. Indeed, regional patterns and proclivities are in some respects becoming increasingly accentuated and divergent (Usunier, 1996). Similarly there is little evidence for political convergence, given the existence in the operating environment of strong subnational political forces in Spain, Italy, the former Yugoslavia and the former Czechoslovakia; nationalistic tendencies in, for example, the UK, Denmark, Switzerland and Poland; and an inclination towards supranationalism elsewhere, as in Belgium and the Netherlands. Some economic trends also show divergence, as pockets of economic stress or success reveal greater polarisation than was typical 10 or 20 years ago.

160

Table 9.2 *Strategic and managerial issues associated with levels of turbulence in the retail environment*

| | Turbulence level | | | | |
	1	2	3	4	5
Environmental turbulence	Repetitive	Expanding Slow Incremental	Changing Fast Incremental	Discontinuous Predictable	Full of surprises Discontinuous Unpredictable
Strategic aggressiveness	Stable Based on precedents	Reactive Based on experience Incremental	Anticipatory Based on extrapolation Incremental	Entrepreneurial Based on observable opportunities	Creative Based on creativity Discontinuous Novel
Organisational responsiveness	Stability seeking Rejects change	Efficiency driven Adapts to change	Market driven Seeks familiar change	Environment driven Seeks related change	Environment creating Seeks novel change
Manager type	Custodian	Controller	Growth leader	Entrepreneur	Creator
Leadership	Political	Rational	Inspirational	Charismatic	Visionary
Key knowledge	Internal politics	Internal operations	Historical markets	Global environment	Emerging possibilities
Typical retail marketing responses	Standard store and ranges. Use wholesalers Seasonal ranges	Conforming stores Regular range reviews Format franchising	Bigger stores Expand ranges Low cost or focus strategy Retailer advertising Cosmetic designs	New formats Frequent range changes More new product development Non-domestic suppliers POS promotion	Highly differentiated stores NPD by retailers High service – low cost strategy Direct promotions Time as part of marketing mix .

Source: Based on Ansoff (1991).

These signs of divergence have provoked some commentators to see in western Europe an increasingly fragmented retail operating environment in which strong regional cultures demand regional brands and product ranges, produced in regional plants supplying the market through regional distribution networks. The emergence of strong regional retail grocery chains – for example Eroski in the Basque country, Morrisons in northern England, Cora in Alsace, Savia in Silesia and Kathreiner in Bavaria – underpins this view. Such a pattern is argued to be one of the spatial manifestations of the retreat from mass-marketing and the emergence of micro-marketing, the aim of which is satisfaction of the consumer as an individual. Here we may identify strong parallels with the emergence of postmodern tourism markets, discussed by Williams and Shaw in Chapter 10.

In practice the conflicts between convergence and divergence within retailers' operating environments generate discontinuous change, while simultaneously many of the processes of social, economic and technical adaptation are accelerating. This combination of discontinuous and faster change has generated greater turbulence for European retailers, in the sense that there is increasing unpredictability. Some implications are shown in Table 9.2, in which different levels of turbulence are posited and linked with the suggestion that the higher levels of disturbance are becoming more characteristic of retailing.

The changing consumer

One aspect of the more turbulent environment is the considerable change occurring in consumer demand, attitudes and behaviour. Demographic shifts underpin some of these consumer changes. Across the EU12 countries, for example, the proportion of people in the older age groups is increasing significantly. In 1950, 10 per cent of the population were over 65; now the comparable figure exceeds 15 per cent (Eurostat, 1995; de Jouvenal, 1989), and since 1980 there has been an absolute increase of 12 million in this age group (see also Chapter 13). A similar trend is evident in other European countries, both east and west, while in some instances – e.g. Poland – birth rates are below natural replenishment rates. The types of product required by older people constitute a major influence on retailers, partly because of the simple factor of age but also due to relationships. For example, there are more people in grandparent–grandchild relationships as a result of longevity and rising divorce and remarriage rates. The increase in older people, however, is not evenly spread across all regions. In most countries there are areas which, for various reasons, have concentrations of the elderly (Findlay and White, 1986). As a result, the effects of shifts in age structures are compounded by spatial changes which often have an income factor within them; spatial concentrations of the older affluent and of the older poor are becoming a notable demographic feature in Europe. Because older consumers tend to have high levels of brand and store loyalty, and often also expect high levels of service, retailers are having to respond to such demographic change with regionally – and even locally – specific retail merchandising programmes.

Alongside demographic developments there is also change in the relationship between the residence and workplace of many consumers

Changing work practices.

Table 9.3 *European food shopping occasions and store types*

Food shopping occasion	Corresponding store format
Major purchase visits for domestic stock replenishment	Warehouse Club Hypermarkets Food superstores
Primary (weekly) purchase visits for revolving domestic stock replenishment	Hypermarkets Food superstores Discount stores
Secondary purchase visits, short life domestic stock purchase and convenience food items	Town centre supermarkets Discounters Neighbourhood supermarkets Convenience stores Superettes
Top-up purchase visits for domestic unanticipated out-of-stock items	Convenience stores Garage stores Town centre supermarkets Superettes Corner shops
Specialist items purchase; visits for comparison-food items	Specialist food shops Food halls in department stores Internet and mail order

(Kinsman, 1987). More women work outside the home; there is an increase in travel-to-work times; and both are important influences on consumers' preferred shopping behaviour. Conversely, there is now emerging a shift towards home-based working which potentially reverses the trends of the last 40 years, even though numbers are still small. As a result workplace and "homeplace" become indistinguishable for some consumers, while worktime and hometime overlap. As this trend develops, retail strategy must interpret the new meanings of convenience, ease of shopping and the various price–quality–time trade-offs held by the resident-workers in these home-workplaces.

Another feature of today's consumers is that social change has altered the way they value and use time (Bergadaá, 1990). Time is now seen as a commodity which can be saved or consumed. It has a value and hence a price, and retailers have to adapt their activities to provide consumers with either more time or more effective ways to use their time. However, this challenge also means that there are new ways to generate consumer loyalty (Pashigian and Bowen, 1994). In effect, consumers are creating new opportunities for retailers to innovate through the management of time, as is clearly seen in food shopping behaviour patterns. Various types of food store have been developed in response to consumers' contrasting behaviours at different times. These outlets have very specific operational characteristics and locations, and a single retail company often operates several different types of outlet (Burt and Sparks, 1995). Table 9.3 illustrates this match between behaviour and store format. Over a 12-week period western European shoppers typically visit three to five different types of store.

There are many other ways in which consumer changes affect shopping behaviour. Among them are:

- a more active search for individualism in life style and, in consequence, in the products and services sought. This results in local differences being enhanced as part of a shift away from a uniform pattern of mass demand across Europe, so that post-modern interpretations are again relevant in this context

- growing personal mobility both in physical terms, through increased car ownership, and also in perceptual terms as distance is decreasingly seen as a barrier
- higher-quality expectations, reflecting new views on what constitutes quality in a product, service or shopping environment
- more non-price promotional responsiveness as consumer awareness and knowledge of advertising and other promotional methods develop[2]
- less price knowledge as product ranges grow and as retail brands make direct price comparisons impossible across some product areas

Studies of these, and related, issues are reported by Cathelat (1991), Minnee and de Boer (1990), Opinion Research Corporation (1992), ESOMAR (1991) and Harris and O'Brien (1993). All the changes impact simultaneously on retail operations and present them with opportunities for new competitive activity. Even though their intensity varies considerably from country to country, they are widely observable across Europe.

Changing technologies

Technology of various types has been central to the efficient operation of retailing and to shaping consumer behaviour for many decades. The early department stores in Paris in the nineteenth century depended on new technologies for their construction; they also relied on the emergent mass transport technologies to bring customers to the city centre. The modern hypermarket is similarly enabled by, and dependent on, various transport, material-handling, communications and control technologies to move products to the store; manage stock and finance; control security and the in-store climate; and – not least – bring customers to the site. The relationship between technology and retailing is a close one and, because it is equally applicable to different cultures, it is a significant force for European convergence.

A notable change in the application of technology in European retailing is its use to change business cost structures and meet new

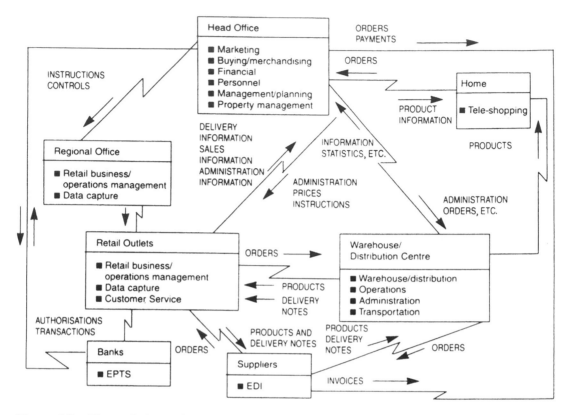

Figure 9.2 *The supply chain cycle*

consumer demands (Dawson, 1994a). For example, the use of bar-code scanning systems at point of sale enables the collection of detailed data on sales; these data are then transmitted electronically to the retailer's head office, distribution centre and product suppliers, facilitating the flow of replacement products from distribution centre to store; the ordering of additional products by the head office; and the manufacture of replacement products by the supplier. At the same time information about orders, invoices and payment is communicated through electronic data interchange (EDI) systems. The integrated system (Figure 9.2) reduces the costs associated with the spatial disaggregation of activities: transport costs are lowered through efficiencies in logistics; transaction costs across space are cut; and depot numbers (together with the associated costs of land, labour and capital) are minimised. For large food and grocery retailers, for example, total logistics costs have been

halved over the last decade and now are typically less than 3 per cent of the value of retail sales. Moreover, while the food sector has been in the vanguard of this change, other sectors – such as clothing and DIY – are rapidly following its example.

There are also implications for retailers in a further area of technological change: personal and household technologies. Car ownership is a very important influence on consumer demand and behaviour, and therefore on the location and trading policies of retailers. Within rural Europe car ownership is a major factor underpinning the decline of rural shops and the concentration of retailing into medium-sized towns. Within urban Europe it encourages the decline of traditional city centres by making possible the decentralisation of retailing to suburban and out-of-town locations. This issue is discussed further towards the end of this chapter. Meanwhile, although home-based working and home-based shopping at present have a low level of penetration, they are likely

e-commerce Amazon.com,
— launch of Topman.co.uk

to increase – albeit at varying rates across Europe. And new household information and communication technologies (ICT), which combine television, telephone and personal computer, promise to have impacts on consumer behaviour in the future as they diffuse through populations. Although the demise of the fixed shop is not likely, in the long run extensive exploitation ICT could well change the spatial structure of retail provision.

end of essay!

There are several other innovations in materials handling and biotechnology which affect consumer demand and also change cost structures and spatial structures in the sector. Advances in material-handling technologies are resulting in changes in the location, number, size and configuration of depots and warehouses required by retailers. The acceleration of material-handling processes means that less inventory (i.e. stock) is required, and so less warehouse space is needed. This can be accommodated by fewer depots, or in some cases by smaller ones. At the end of 1994 Casino, a French grocery retailer, serviced a national chain of 106 hypermarkets, 489 supermarkets and 2304 small stores from only 13 depots. Seven of these dealt with dry and fresh products, two with fresh products, two with dry products, one with non-food items and one with products with very long rotation times.

In addition the new handling technologies influence retail systems by responding to the specific requirements of products. For example, the emergence of a logistics system and material-handling technologies for chilled food had a major impact on UK supermarket operations in the 1980s, widening the range of chilled products on offer, not least through the advent of "foreign" foods. These technologically based changes are now being adopted in other parts of Europe – notably in France, Germany and Spain – and it is likely that similar consequences will follow. Meanwhile, advances in biotechnology are starting to affect product ranges, for example as novel foods and advanced textile products appear. These advanced products are acultural and do not reflect national, regional or local patterns of consumer demand. While their influence is as yet small, it is likely to increase substantially over the next decade.

Changes in government policy

The widespread philosophy of deregulation over the last 20 years has changed the nature of governmental involvement in Europe's retail sector. On the one hand there has been a general relaxation of government competition policy and trading hours legislation in many countries, including the UK, France, Spain and Germany. But, on the other hand, there has been no relaxation in controls over the right to establish new shops. While these controls differ considerably across Europe, in all countries they are a significant influence on the spatial structure of retailing (CEC, 1991).

The mechanisms for the control of new shop development remain highly varied, and attempts are not being made to bring them into a common European framework (Davies, 1995). Within the UK they are part of the general legislation associated with land-use planning (Guy, 1994). The mechanisms include both the implementation of structure plans which relate to particular districts, and the application of development controls based on Planning Policy Guidance Notes issued for England and Wales, and Scotland, by the Departments of the Environment in London and Edinburgh. These guidance documents indicate preferred policies for the location of new large shops and shopping centre schemes. During the 1980s the policies for England and Wales, but not for Scotland, indicated a willingness to allow out-of-town and edge-of-town locations for new stores. However, policy review in the early 1990s has resulted in new guidance which makes it more difficult to obtain permission for large stores and shopping centres other than in town-centre sites.

In other countries very different mechanisms are in operation. Thus in Italy a licensing system requires any new store to obtain product-related licences to enable it to trade. These are granted by a local agency in which local retailers are represented, with the result that grass-roots politics and inter-community competition become important in the licensing decisions. In 1973 a similar system was introduced in France, but within a regional rather than a local framework. Regional committees comprising various interest groups made decisions on applications for large stores, subject to a national appeal board. Government intervention in 1996, however, amended this framework through the *loi Raffarin*, which in effect placed an embargo on all new large stores. Policy in Spain has followed a similar route, including national government intervention in 1995 to limit the powers of regions to permit new large stores in out-of-town and edge-of-town locations. In several major countries, therefore, government controls have become tighter. As will be argued later, this reflects increasing recognition of the urban development, social and environmental consequences of retail decentralisation.

Achieving the balance between national and local government in respect of policies towards retailing has been – and remains – difficult. Local policy tends to address issues such as access to stores by consumers with low mobility or income, local environmental pressures, or the need to reconcile opening hours with local circumstances, for example in tourism areas. National policy, in contrast, often concentrates on questions of competition, monopoly control and corporate fiscal policy. Difficulties arise particularly when permission is sought for new large stores and shopping centres which raise issues transgressing the traditional local and national areas of concern. Thus, while a new hypermarket proposal is likely to affect local consumers through access to shopping provision, local employment, competition and, perhaps, local environmental concerns, it can also raise issues of sectoral concentration and the emergence of monopolies, control of price inflation, or tax relief on capital investments. National governments therefore tend to have a history of selective intervention in local retail location policies, highlighting an uneasy balance between central and local government responsibilities.

Organisational Restructuring

In response to changes in the operating environment, managerial decisions are resulting in widespread structural shifts within the sector. Notable developments examined in this section are:

- a decrease in the numbers and market power of small independent firms

- fewer but more powerful large firms
- an increase in the proportion of retailing owned by financial institutions
- the widespread implementation of formal corporate strategies
- increased international product sourcing and retail operation
- and a tendency for simple inter-firm transactions (purchases and sales) to give way to strategic business relationships and partnerships

Small firm decline

Small independent retail firms, which once dominated retailing, are declining in numbers and market power in all parts of western Europe.[3] The downward trend became established in the UK, the Benelux countries and Scandinavia during the 1960s, in France and Germany in the 1970s and more recently has spread to Spain and Italy. Typically it initially affects the independent general food sector and then the non-food sector. Specialist retailers are hit later than others, but the trend is now clearly seen among specialist outlets in the UK and is becoming apparent in France and Germany. Reasons for the demise of the small retail firm are complex, but they include consumer demand for a wider choice of product; diseconomies carried by small organisations, particularly in terms of product sourcing costs; the difficulties faced by small firms in keeping up to date with new marketing and managerial ideas; problems of succession in small family firms; and the high cost of capital for business improvements.

Large firms, market power and financial institutions

In contrast, the increased market power of a few large firms is substantial. Within almost all sectors of retailing, national sales concentration ratios for the largest 5 and 10 firms are rising.[4] One important reason for this is that the number of these large firms across Europe is falling due to merger and take-over activity that is often international. For example, in the Iberian context, the three largest corporately owned grocery chains in Spain (Pryca, Continente and Alcampo) are all

French owned; the Dutch retailer Ahold, and the French firms Auchan, Carrefour and Promodès, have all established a substantial market presence in Portugal through mergers and take-overs.

The finance required for mergers and acquisitions, as well as for new stores and for ICT infrastructure, is large and requires firms to go to the capital markets. This provides opportunities for the major pension and insurance funds, which often operate internationally, to invest in large-scale retailing. One important result is that the retailers are now being required by their institutional shareholders to implement short-term strategies to ensure the continuous growth of investment returns. This encourages the large firms to develop new stores, create additional floor space and to devise new types of retailing to produce increased profits through greater sales. Admittedly, a few privately owned large firms survive. Several of the largest are in Germany, notably Aldi (discount food), Tengelmann (food and groceries) and Metro, a mainly German-based[5] food and general merchandise retailer. Similarly, in some firms family interests still retain a substantial shareholding, as with Sainsbury, Casino and Carrefour. Across much of Europe, however, the largest firms are now public companies.

Formal corporate strategies

This growing domination of large-scale retailing has been associated with the implementation of more formal strategies by large firms. As will be demonstrated, the objectives are to achieve differentiation to suit the local market, minimise the cost of operations and maximise consumer choice.

Differentiation to suit the local market

This has been the traditional approach of local retailers and convenience stores, the objective being to seek competitive advantage derived from knowledge of local conditions. Today, even though the small retail business is in decline, this strategy continues to have considerable appeal, especially where there are strong local and regional cultures. Product range, price policy, promotions and other variables such as opening hours are adjusted to respond to consumer demand and behaviour in the locality, and success depends on accurate knowledge of local circumstances. This knowledge is most easily obtained by local management which, in consequence, has retained a high level of decision-making authority. Buying is in relatively small quantities in order to suit local needs, so purchasing economies are minimal. Margins, on the other hand, are relatively high because customers' precise requirements are well matched by the products sold.

Minimising the cost of operations

In this strategy the search is for scale economies, particularly at the organisational level. Widely used in western Europe, it is also being employed to penetrate emergent markets in the former socialist states. It involves increasing the scale of buying activities so that volume- and power-related discounts, as well as other favourable trading terms, are obtainable from suppliers. The low cost of procurement is passed to the consumer through low prices (Colla, 1994), encouraging sales growth from price-responsive consumers and generating a high level of stock-turn. Cash flow in the company is positive, allowing expansion of the store network to be funded out of internal finance. Expansion in turn increases sales and buying volumes, allowing costs to be driven down by further economies of scale as the chain gets larger. Product ranges are tightly controlled and often restricted to focus maximum buying power on a limited number of products. Store size may be relatively small, to accommodate the limited range, so that expansion of the store network is facilitated by the low cost of individual shops. Alternatively, if larger stores are employed, the use of space is tightly planned, enabling each shop to be operated as a group of small units each covering a product department. The similar nature of the firm's stores reduces costs and allows replication economies to be achieved. This strategy is used in the food (CIRP, 1993) and non-food sectors by companies such as Aldi, Netto, Lidl & Schwarz, Zeeman, Rimi, What Everyone Wants, the Edinburgh Woollen Mill and Superdrug.

Maximising consumer choice

This has been the traditional key strategy employed by European department stores, many leading grocery retailers, dominant specialist retailers such as IKEA, Fnac and Virgin, and some of the more traditional specialists (e.g. the Burton Group, Hennes & Mauritz and Cortefiel). Some multi-sector companies, operating several store formats, have also adopted this approach, including Magazine zum Globus and El Cortes Inglés. In contrast to the previous strategy, in this approach the objective is to exploit "economies of scope" associated with wide or deep product ranges which may complement or interact with each other. Customers may make a specific purchase because there is a deep range of products on the items they seek. Alternatively, broad combinations of products can also attract potential customers who may then make a wide cross-section of purchases, either in a single visit (as in shopping at a large supermarket) or over several visits (as in department store shopping). Because this strategy of consumer attraction is based on non-price factors, it is well suited to western Europe's high purchasing power.

Internationalisation in the retail sector

The increasing internationalisation of retailing – for product sourcing and sales – is widespread (Burt, 1993; Dawson, 1994b; McGoldrick and Davies, 1995). All the major European retailers now have international operations within Europe and, often, beyond. Increasingly, of course, substantial proportions of these firms' sales come from non-domestic operations, as the British case shows (Table 9.4). To quote just four examples at the level of the firm, Ahold generates over half its sales through activity outside its domestic Dutch market, via chains in the USA, Portugal, the Czech Republic and Poland; Hennes & Mauritz (based in Sweden) makes two-thirds of its sales in Norway, Denmark, Germany, Belgium, the Netherlands, the UK, Austria and Switzerland; Hachette, the world's largest newspaper and magazine retailer, has approximately 60 per cent of its outlets outside its French home market; and Carrefour (the leading hypermarket operator in France and Spain) has

Table 9.4 *Overseas sales of selected UK retailers, 1995*

	Overseas sales (£m.)	Percentage of total sales
J Sainsbury	1334.0	11.7
Kingfisher	1157.9	22.1
Marks and Spencer	974.9	14.3
Thorn EMI	885.0	20.6
GUS	729.3	27.4
Signet	555.7	56.2
Tesco	446.0	4.4
Body Shop	351.2	70.2
W H Smith	223.3	14.2
Courts	178.6	60.1
Laura Ashley	177.4	55.0
Granada	100.0	4.7
Wickes	97.6	13.3
C & J Clark	95.0	14.5
Kwik Fit	66.5	22.3
Sears	53.5	2.5
Fine Art	43.6	12.8
Storehouse	41.8	4.0
Tie Rack	34.7	41.4
MFI	27.0	4.1
French Connection	26.8	41.9
Church & Co	18.3	23.9
Liberty	17.3	20.6
Austin Reed	11.3	15.8
Thorntons	10.5	11.4

Source: Company accounts.

developed a substantial market presence in Argentina, Brazil and Taiwan, and also has new stores in Portugal, Italy, Turkey, Malaysia, Thailand and Mexico. In addition it is actively planning hypermarkets in China in a joint venture with the Chinese retailer Li Huan. Meanwhile, the appearance in Europe of non-European firms over the last decade is exemplified by The Gap, Toys R Us, Blockbuster, Disney Store and The Museum Shop.

Increased internationalisation partly reflects continual pressure by the financial institutions for retailers to increase their sales – and therefore profits – annually. To achieve this, new commercial opportunities are pursued at the international scale. But it is also a response to spatial differences in operating environments and costs, together with retailers' belief that they can exploit these differences by expanding into new areas offering more opportunities than the domestic market (Pellegrini, 1994). Thus, for example, Carrefour and Promodès expanded into Spain and then other European countries when government legislation limited the growth of large stores in France; Marks and Spencer believe that their particular retail formula can tap profitable demand in France, Spain, Belgium, Greece, Turkey, Hungary, the Czech Republic and Germany; and IKEA, Virgin Megastore, Zara, Body Shop and others similarly judge that the transfer of their particular trading style to different operating environments is preferable to creating new styles of trading in their home country.

New transactional relationships

A final aspect of change in the organisational structure of retailing is the relative decline of simple transactional relationships between firms (Crewe and Davenport, 1992; Dawson and Shaw, 1990, 1992; GEA, 1994). Traditionally, retailers and suppliers negotiated "deals" for the supply of goods; similarly, the consumer and retailer struck a "deal" in the shop or at the market stall. These were simple individual transactions, and when they were concluded each party moved on to another transaction with little reference to the earlier deal. Recently, however, many alternative forms of relationship – depending on innovations such as extended supply contracts and consumer loyalty programmes (Sopanen, 1996) – have become more important, as Table 9.5 demonstrates (Kaas, 1993). Diverse though the range is, the general aim is to build firmer links between retailers and suppliers and retailers and customers, in order to ensure for the retailer greater stability and control in the turbulent retail environment.

Moves towards different types of relationship have also resulted in more collaborative liaisons between firms through, for example, the joint development of new locations. Thus the Spanish hypermarket company Pryca has developed shopping centres in co-operation with various

Table 9.5 *Examples of new relationships in the retail system*

Retailer–supplier relationships

Franchise relationships	Long-term links are generated which cover not only products but also the whole method of retailing
Extended supply contracts	Agreements are made between retailers and suppliers for supplies over a whole season, e.g. between farmers and retailers or clothing manufacturers and retailers
Administered relationships	Retailers stipulate product specifications and quality control standards and, in return, suppliers have rights to repeat contracts. Many of the sourcing arrangements made by Marks and Spencer are of this type
Voluntary chain relationships	Retailers agree to place orders with particular wholesalers in return for help in various aspects of marketing and operations management. Spar retailing and wholesaling operates this way throughout Europe

Retailer–consumer relationships

Consumer loyalty reward schemes	Consumers qualify for incentives if they remain as shoppers with a particular retailer or at a particular store (Rayner, 1996)
Mail or telephone retailing	Retailers attempt to create longer-term relationships with customers through direct contact
Increased consumer credit	Store credit cards encourage repeat visits by consumers

large non-food retailers. In the UK Marks and Spencer, Tesco and a number of other food retailers have jointly financed out-of-town shopping centres, while Safeway are co-operating with BP to create shops at petrol stations. There has also been extensive retailer collaboration to establish buying groups, sometimes operating Europe-wide (e.g. Intersport and Spar), but often at the national level (Täger and Weitzel, 1991; Bailey *et al.*, 1995). For example, in Italy the buying groups of Crai and Conad both have networks of over 6000 shops; in France the Leclerc group has become France's second-largest retailer with over 500 stores; in Spain the combined sales of members of Euromadi exceed those of the largest food retailer; in Germany there are 29 significant buying groups operating in the clothing sector; and Rewe has used this type of arrangement to become Europe's second-largest retailer measured in terms of sales.

Implications

The implications of these interrelated changes in organisations are several and complex. Not only is the spatial structure of retailing changing but so are the theories and concepts which provide the framework for understanding the spatial patterns and processes involved. Rent theory based on a small business economy does not explain the new forms of decision-making by large organisations; neither do the traditional central-place and interaction models. New approaches are therefore being developed using ideas of game theory, market positioning concepts (Hooley and Saunders, 1993), sunk costs (Clark and Wrigley, 1995; Wrigley, 1996) and transaction costs. In more practical terms, the frictional and cost effects of the spatial separation of activities are changing within the new organisational structures. Managerial perceptions of space and distance have shifted with the emergence of new managerial ideas such as just-in-time distribution and the real-time scheduling of activities. As will be shown, these changed perceptions translate into decisions within organisations which not only alter substantially the established spatial structures of retailing, but also raise significant issues relating to the sector's development.

Conclusion: Sectoral Restructuring, Store-level Operations and Development Issues

The adaptation of retail organisations and systems to the very powerful forces discussed above has inevitably imposed new demands and constraints at the level of the individual store. Thus, as we shall see, the total number of shops has fallen markedly, superstores of all types have developed impressively, and "controlled retail environments" have become common. However, any conclusion which focused solely on the consequences of restructuring within the sector would certainly be incomplete. Instead, it is now recognised that internal restructuring along these lines should also be seen as the source of significant externalities, particularly with respect to social, planning and environmental problems.

Despite growth in consumer numbers and retail sales, the total number of shops has decreased in parallel with the decline in the number of firms in the industry. Table 9.6 shows the very large reductions which have occurred over the last 30 years for selected countries, and elsewhere the trends are similar. In Spain, for example, surveys by Nielsen indicate a decrease of 34 000 in the number of traditional food stores between 1988 and 1995 to 58 600, while over the same period the number of supermarkets and hypermarkets rose from 5300 to 7800. Today the decrease in shop numbers is particularly marked in Spain and Italy, having been strong in northern Europe during the 1970s and 1980s.

The reasons for the contraction relate to the long-term economic viability of small units, which are only profitable if they have a clear marketing focus to their product ranges; provide specialist products or services; and have efficient systems for stock management, financial control and personnel management. In general, the small units that fulfil these conditions are limited to specialist food and fashion clothing shops, those with a clear focus on the target consumer group (e.g. Shell Shop, Parfümerie Douglas, Oddbins, Schlecker drug stores and the discount food retailer Dia) and those with membership of a franchise-type organisation able to provide the management systems needed (such as Interdiscount, Benetton and Body Shop).

Table 9.6   *Estimated changes in the number of shops**

	Change in number of shops		Change in number of food shops 1971–91
	1961–71	1971–91	
Belgium	−40 000	−28 000	n/a
Denmark	−10 500	−7000	−8000
France	−55 000	−54 000	−105 000
Germany (West)	−90 000	−75 000	−115 000
Ireland	−5000	+2000	+1000
Italy	+15 000	−40 000	−80 000
Luxembourg	0	−800	n/a
Netherlands	−35 000	−43 000	−25 000
United Kingdom	−70 000	−137 000	−120 000

* Excludes motor trades. Dates are indicative because annual data are not available.
Sources: Distributive Trades EDC (1973), Eurostat (1993).

As has already been noted with respect to small retail firms, the decline in economic viability and consequent closure of small shops has several socio-spatial implications. These include the decreased attractiveness of mid-suburban shopping areas, which historically have been locations favoured by small shops; commercial blight on the edges of the central commercial area of large towns; and the disappearance of retailing from small rural communities. All of these spatial changes can result in difficulties of access to essential retail services by sections of the community having low levels of mobility. Here, therefore, we have clear indications that retail sector development, which in itself is so impressive, may instigate significant social and urban planning problems.

The decline of small shops has been partly offset by the growth of superstores in all product areas. Within the food sector this has been a feature of change since the early 1970s, but during the 1980s superstore concepts were applied to the retailing of DIY products, furniture, garden products and electrical goods. More recently the same concepts have become accepted and widely used in clothing (Matalan in the UK and La Halle aux Vêtements in France), shoes (Shoe City with 60 UK stores), toys (Toys R Us operates 205 shops in 12 European countries), sports goods (Decathlon in France, Germany, Spain and Italy), pet supplies (Pet World), and office supplies (Office Centre, Office Depot, Office World). The economic benefits of scale and scope discussed earlier, coupled with

consumers' preference for a wide choice of products at a single location, have strongly encouraged retailers to make investments in this type of retailing.

Coupled with these shifts, there has been significant evolution in the form of retailing, particularly through the growth of shopping centres (Reynolds, 1993). Defined as purpose-built and managed complexes containing several shops and owned and operated as an integrated retail environment, these have a long history in Europe dating back to the nineteenth century.[6] Major developments took place in the 1950s, 1960s and 1970s as city centres were reconstructed and redeveloped after war damage. Also influential was government sponsorship of "new towns", in which retailing was planned within a hierarchical spatial system, notably in Sweden, the UK and the Netherlands. More recently different types of centre have emerged, while approaches to their management have become considerably more complex. Thus the early simple focus on maintenance and security was replaced by an emphasis on managing the mix and location of shops allowed to trade in a centre, which has in turn given way to control of the entire sensory environment (Figure 9.3). This includes the introduction of aromas and sounds, the control of atmospheric conditions and the creation of a planned visual environment. While the techniques involved in all this are similar across Europe, if the environment created is to be successful it has to reflect the local culture of consumers. Precise outcomes

Figure 9.3 *The CentrO retail centre, Oberhausen, Germany. Adjacent to the largest shopping mall in Europe is Adventure Island, part of a complex designed to cultivate the concept of shopping as a leisure activity. (Photo: the Stadium Group)*

Table 9.7 *Types of shopping centre development*

Major city-centre renewal schemes	Provide a wide range of shopping facilities adding to the provision of the existing town or city centre
Small in-town schemes	Usually provide specialist shopping facilities
Non-central-city centres (district and neighbourhood centres)	Comprise several stores and sometimes a superstore or hypermarket targeted at everyday consumption needs
Edge-of-town and out-of-town centres (retail parks, factory outlet centres)	Typically based around one or two large superstores and containing retailers in a variety of product areas
Large out-of-town regional shopping centres	Create the equivalent of a new city centre outside the city
Centres associated with transport nodes	Built, for example, at sites such as railway stations (often within the urban area) and airports (outside it)

Figure 9.4 *CentrO and the environment. Although it relies heavily on the car, CentrO contrasts with many shopping centres in that it demonstrates that environmental impacts can be mitigated. The tram line in the foreground links the centre with nearby towns, while the futuristic tram station provides virtually direct access to the shopping mall beyond. Built on a derelict steelworks site, CentrO also exemplifies local environmental improvement through land reclamation. (Photo: the Stadium Group)*

consequently vary from country to country, and sometimes from region to region.

Some individual superstores and shopping centre developments involve intra-urban investment and, not uncommonly, redevelopment. Other types of centre, however, result in the decentralisation of retailing, either to the edge of towns and cities, or to the countryside beyond (Table 9.7). Critical to the economic success of this decentralisation process is the centres' accessibility by private car, which has expanded their catchment areas impressively, plus the development of shopping as a recreational activity (see Chapter 10). The distances which consumers are willing to travel by car to use a large centre can now be over 100 km, even for regular visitors. The increase in the number of centres, coupled with willingness to travel, means that more of them are potentially accessible to any one consumer, so that for many

individuals choice is enhanced. However, such developments often reduce the relative attractiveness of the more traditional forms of retail provision in town centres and high streets, posing the threat of physical decline and more limited choice for those without cars. Potentially, therefore, without a commensurate investment in town centre redevelopment, decentralisation driven by shopping centres may militate against the interests of important interrelated groups, including the elderly, the young and the poor.

To a great extent, the growing trend towards government intervention to restrict decentralisation, noted earlier in the chapter, is a reaction to these urban and social problems. Increasingly, however, decentralisation is considered problematic because of its global environmental implications. Just as new roads are now known to cause traffic growth (see Chapter 23), there is no

Table 9.8 *European retailers with WWW in mid-1996*

Company	Address of site	Company	Address of site
Ahold	http://www.ahold.nl/	John Lewis	http://www.johnlewis.co.uk/
Argos	http://www.itl.net/go/to/argos/	John Smith	
Asda	http://www.asda.co.uk/	& Son	http://www.johnsmith.co.uk/
Austin Reed	http://www.austinreed.co.uk/	Lands End	http://www.landsend.com/
Austrian Home		La Redoute	http://www.redoute.fr/
Shop	http://.www.austrian-homeshop.co.at /homeshop/	La Rinascente	http://www.rinascente.it
		London Mall	http://www.londonmall.co.uk/
Barclay Square	http://www.itl.net/barclaysquare/	Louis Vuitton	http://www.ac95.org/30/30.3.27.html
Benetton	http://www.benetton.com/	Mac 'n Maggie	http://www.dds.nl/~mnm/
Bertelsmann	http://www.bertelsmann.de/	Neckermann	http://www.neckermann.de
Blackwells	http://www.blackwell.co.uk/bookshops/	Otto Versand	http://eunet.bda.de/bda/int/otto/index .html
Blockbuster	http://www.blockbuster.co.uk/		
Body Shop	http://www.the-body-shop.com/	Promodès	http://www.promodes.fr
Boots	http://www.boots.co.uk/	Quelle	http://193.83.204.3/Quelle/index/.html
Carrefour	http://www.carrefour.fr/	Shopping	http://www.Austria.EU.net/sca/Shop
Co-op	http://www.coop.co.uk/	center	/index.html
Decathlon	http://www.decathlon.com/	Supsa	http://www.plusfresc.es/supsa/
Eroski	http://www.mondragon.mcc.es/ english/grpemp.html	Tesco	http://www.tesco.co.uk/
		Texas	http://www.emporium.turnpike.net:80
FNAC	http://www.fnac.fr/	Homecare	/texas/index.html
Galeries		The Galleria	
Lafayette	http://www.glparis.com	Outlet Centre	http://www.factory-outlets.co.uk/
Great Universal		UK Internet	
Stores	http://www.shoppersuniverse.com/	Florist	http://www.mkn.co.uk/
Holland &		UK Shops	
Barrett	http://www.holland-and-barrett.co.uk	Directory	http://www.ukdirectory.com/shop/
Innovations	http://www.innovations.co.uk/ GiftPoint/welcome.html	Unipalm Pipex	http://www.worldserver.pipex.com /affectionet/
Internet		Virgin Records	http://www.vmg.co.uk/
Bookshop	http://www.bookshop.co.uk/	Waitrose	http://www.waitrose.co.uk/
Intersport	http://www.intersport.co.uk/	Wehkamp	http://www.wehkamp.nl/
J Sainsbury	http://www.j-sainsbury.co.uk/	West Orchards	http://www.hiway.co.uk/westorchards
James Thin	http://www.jthin.co.uk/	S.Centre	/index.html

doubt that shopping centres induce movement on an appreciable scale. While this is beneficial for the stores (which make enhanced profits), and for individual consumers (who gain from choice and competition), it may well be that the price paid is greater externalities imposed on the environment: noise, congestion and exhaust emissions associated with more and longer car journeys. Thus the significance of the decentralisation debate, and of attempts to control the phenomenon, could be considerably wider than was initially appreciated (Figure 9.4).[7]

Given advances in information technologies, it might be argued that the environmental impacts of retail sector development can be reduced by fostering electronic shopping from home and work. Several small-scale, often experimental, schemes already use either cable-type communications or the World Wide Web (Table 9.8). Although these electronic shopping schemes are at an early stage of development, they may certainly point to future changes in the shopping environment in which, from the consumer's perspective, the location of retailing becomes virtual as movement is eliminated.

Even so, electronic retailing is unlikely to result in the rapid death of the fixed shop, as is sometimes forecast. On the supply side, the large retail and financial firms have substantial and growing investments in buildings, real estate and systems which they will undoubtedly use their power to protect. Meanwhile, on the demand side, there is an inherent conservatism, and an important social component, in consumer shopping behaviour. Indeed, as has already been indicated, in this postmodern world there are signs that the shopping experience is becoming more important to individuals, especially when there is significant overlap between shopping and leisure activity. For the foreseeable future, therefore, the question will not be whether we travel to shop, but how far we go and how we make the journey. Based as it is on market principles, the retail sector will in all probability press for maximum individual choice in these respects. But if it does so we may anticipate increasing tensions between, on the one hand, the interests of the industry and the individual consumer and, on the other hand, the broader concerns of society and the environment. Resolving these tensions will be a considerable challenge for the planning and regulatory systems of the new millennium.

Notes

1. These functions are, in essence: design, make, brand, price, promote, buy, stock, display, sell and deliver.
2. This has occurred, for example, through supranational advertising of the type used by Benetton.
3. Conversely, independent firms have increased in number in eastern and central Europe as state-owned retailers have been privatised. Europe-wide, however, the growth has been insufficient to offset the substantial annual decrease in the west.
4. The only exceptions are in situations where levels are so high that further concentration is difficult. For example, in Finland the top five firms in the food and grocery sector already have over 90 per cent of the market, and so further increase is unlikely.
5. Although it retains a large German sales network, Metro has relocated its head office to Switzerland.
6. Examples are to be found in the central city shopping arcades of Brussels and many British cities, the commercial schemes around London and Berlin associated with the expanding suburban railways, and commercial property redevelopments in Paris and Milan (Dawson, 1983).
7. Conclusive research, however, has yet to be undertaken on the relative environmental impacts of spatially centralised and decentralised retail provision.

References

Ansoff, H I (1991) Strategic management in a historical perspective, *International Review of Strategic Management*, **2**(1), 3–69.

Bailey, J, Clarke-Hill, C M and Robinson, T M (1995) Towards a taxonomy of international retail alliances, *Service Industries Journal*, **15**(4), 25–41.

Bergadaá, M M (1990) The role of time in the action of the consumer, *Journal of Consumer Research*, **17**(3), 289–302.

Brown, S (1995a) *Postmodern Marketing*, Routledge, London.

Brown, S (1995b) Postmodernism, the wheel of retailing and the will to power, *International Review of Retail, Distribution and Consumer Research*, **5**(3), 387–414.

Burt, S L (1989) Trends and management issues in European retailing, *International Journal of Retailing*, **4**(4), 1–97.

Burt, S L (1993) Temporal trends in the internationalization of British retailing, *International Review of Retail, Distribution and Consumer Research*, **3**(4), 391–410.

Burt, S L and Sparks, L (1995) Understanding the arrival of limited line discount stores in Britain, *European Management Journal*, **13**(1), 110–19.

Cathelat, B (1991) *Panorama des Styles de Vie 1960–1990*, Les Editions d'Organisation, Paris.

CEC (Commission of the European Communities) (1991) *Towards a Single Market in Distribution*, Com 91.41, Commission of EC, Brussels.

CIRP (1993) *Discount Food Retailing in Europe*, Corporate Intelligence Research Publications, London.

Clark, G and Wrigley, N (1995) Sunk costs: a framework for economic geography, *Transactions of Institute of British Geographers NS*, **20**, 204–23.

Colla, E (1994) *I Discount*, Etaslibri, Milan.

Crewe, L and Davenport, E (1992) The puppet show: changing buyer-supplier relationships within clothing retailing, *Transactions of Institute of British Geographers NS*, **17**, 183–97.

Davies, R L (ed) (1995) *Retail Planning Policies in Western Europe*, Routledge, London.

Dawson, J A (1982) *Commercial Distribution in Europe*, Croom-Helm, London.

Dawson, J A (1983) *Shopping Centre Development*, Longman, London.

Dawson, J A (1994a) Applications of information management in European retailing, *International Review of Retail Distribution and Consumer Research*, **4**(2), 219–38.

Dawson, J A (1994b) Internationalisation of retailing operations, *Journal of Marketing Management*, **10**, 267–82.

Dawson, J A and Shaw, S A (1990) The changing character of retailer–supplier relationships, in J Fernie (ed) *Retail Distribution Management*, Kogan Page, London, 19–39.

Dawson, J A and Shaw, S A (1992) *Inter-firm Alliances in the Retail Sector: evolutionary, strategic and tactical issues in their management*, University of Edinburgh, Department of Business Studies, Working Paper, 92/7.

De Jouvenal, H (1989) *Europe's Ageing Population*, Butterworth, Guildford.

Distributive Trades EDC (1973) *The Distributive Trades in the Common Market*, HMSO, London.

ESOMAR (1991) *The Growing Individualisation of Consumer Lifestyles and Demand: how is marketing coping with it?*, ESOMAR, Amsterdam.

Eurostat (1993) *Retailing in the European Single Market*, Eurostat, Luxembourg.

Eurostat (1995) *Demographic Statistics – Annual,* Eurostat, Luxembourg.

Findlay, A and White, P (1986) *West European Population Change*, Croom Helm, London.

GEA (1994) *Supplier–retailer Collaboration in Supply Chain Management*, Coca-Cola Retailing Research Group – Europe, London.

Guy, C (1994) *The Retail Development Process*, Routledge, London.

Harris, F W and O'Brien, L G (1993) The greening of shopping, in R D F Bromley and C Thomas (eds) *Retail Change*, UCL Press, London, 229–46.

Hooley, G J and Saunders, J (1993) *Competitive Positioning*, Prentice-Hall, Hemel Hempstead.

Kaas, K P (1993) Symbiotic relationships between producers and retailers in the German food market?, *Journal of Institutional and Theoretical Economics*, **149**(4), 741–7.

Kinsman, F (1987) *The Telecommuters*, Wiley, Chichester.

Knee, D (1988) *City Centre Retailing in Continental Europe*, Longman, Harlow.

Lanon, J (1991) Developing brand strategies across borders, *Marketing and Research Today*, **19**(3), 160–8.

McGoldrick, P J and Davies, G (eds) (1995) *International Retailing*, Pitman, London.

Meyer, G (1992) Retail development in East Germany: the example of the city of Jena, *International Review of Retail Distribution and Consumer Research*, **2**(3), 245–61.

Minnee, S and de Boer, M (1990) Individualisation and women in the nineties, *Marketing and Research Today*, **18**(2), 116–21.

Opinion Research Corporation (1992) *Trends in Europe: consumer attitudes and the supermarket*, Food Marketing Institute, Chicago.

Pashigian, B P and Bowen, B (1994) The rising cost of time of females, the growth of national brands and the supply of retail services, *Economic Inquiry*, **23**(1), 33–65.

Pellegrini, L (1994) Alternatives for growth and internationalization in retailing, *International Review of Retail, Distribution and Consumer Research*, **4**(2), 121–48.

Rayner, S (1996) *Customer Loyalty Schemes*, Pearson, London.

Reynolds, J (1993) The proliferation of the planned shopping centre, in R D F Bromley and C J Thomas (eds), *Retail Change: contemporary issues*, UCL Press, London, 70–87.

Rowley, J (1996) Retailing and shopping on the Internet, *International Journal of Retail and Distribution Management*, **24**(3), 26–37.

Seitz, H (1992) Retailing in eastern Europe: an overview, *International Journal of Retail and Distribution Management*, **20**(6), 4–10.

Sopanen, S (1996) *Customer Loyalty Schemes in Retailing across Europe*, Oxford Institute of Retail Management, Oxford.

Täger, U and Weitzel, G (1991) *Purchasing Organisations*, CEC, DGxxiii, Series Studies, Commerce and Distribution, 19.

Usunier, J-C (1996) *Marketing across Cultures*, Prentice-Hall, Englewood Cliffs.

Wierenga, B, Pruyn, A and Waarts, E (1996) The key to successful Euromarketing: standardization or customization? *Journal of International Consumer Marketing*, **8**(3/4), 39–67.

Wrigley, N (1996) Sunk costs and corporate restructuring: British food retailing and the property crisis, in N Wrigley and M Lowe (eds) *Retailing Consumption and Capital: towards the new retail geography*, Longman, Harlow, 116–36.

10
Tourism and economic development

Allan M Williams and Gareth Shaw
Tourism Research Group, Department of Geography, University of Exeter, UK

Introduction

Tourism plays an important role in both reshaping and maintaining economic spaces in Europe. The European Commission (1994, 1) gives some notion of the pervading importance of tourism, estimating that the sector accounts for 5.5 per cent of GNP in the EU, with Spain and France reaching almost double this level. Moreover, Europe also accounts for about 60 per cent of international tourist arrivals, world-wide, and 53 per cent of global tourism revenues.

Tourism spaces are complex economic and cultural entities, not least because tourism services involve intense face-to-face contacts between consumers and producers, wider host–guest interrelationships, the creation and consumption of cultural and natural objects of the tourist gaze (Urry, 1990), and seasonal and spatial polarisation (Shaw and Williams, 1994, 3–8). They are subject to revision and reconstruction in response to cultural changes in consumption and to competitive pressures, a notion which is illustrated – in a simplified form – in Butler's (1980) resort cycle model. At a more macro scale, changes in the "map" of European tourism can be seen as the outcome of long historical processes of

tourism development which reflect shifts in cultural practices, technology and the geography of production (Claval, 1995).

The outstanding feature of the twentieth-century evolution of the sector has been the emergence of mass tourism, characterised by a high degree of internationalisation (Marchena Gómez and Rebollo, 1995). This can be understood in the context of the emergence of mass consumption. Mass tourism is not, of course, a single homogeneous product. There are important variants such as the differences between coastal and winter sports resorts, or between Mediterranean, Black Sea and North Sea coastal resorts. However, despite the fact that the very notion of tourism is predicated on place differences, mass tourism is a remarkably uniform cultural and economic phenomenon (Shaw and Williams, 1994, 185–90). Furthermore, it is subject to a high degree of standardisation in design, marketing and production, as well as to the dictates of economies of scale and external dependency.

There have been important changes in tourism demand in the late twentieth century, and these have influenced and been influenced by tourism investment. There has, for example, been growing interest in mega events, in cultural tourism, in heritage tourism and in rural tourism. To some extent these developments reflect broader societal changes in consumer culture (Lury, 1996), and the exploitation of place differences rather than similarities (as in mass tourism). These new forms of tourism also involve shifts away from the mass production of tourism services, and they can, to some extent, be understood in terms of Lash and Urry's (1987) conceptualisation of "disorganised capitalism". These "new" forms of tourism usually involve a greater degree of flexibility in production, and smaller-scale and more spatially diffuse patterns of consumption, than is the case with mass tourism. Much of the emphasis on sustainable tourism has also focused on these smaller-scale and more flexible forms of tourism.

While there has been a shift in the production and consumption of tourism services, these are tendencies and reality is far more complex. First, as Williams and Montanari (1995, 4) argue, "care must be taken not to oversimplify the changes in the mode of production of tourism services. There was no simple linear and universal shift from Fordism to post-Fordism." Even at its peak in the 1970s and early 1980s, mass tourism coexisted with other forms of more individualised tourism. Second, mass tourism areas were differentiated in terms of their labour markets and capital structures (Shaw and Williams, 1994, 186–96). Third, even though the growth of mass tourism markets has abated, and perhaps even stagnated in much of northern Europe, there is still strong absolute and relative growth in markets in southern and eastern Europe. Fourth, many of the demands for more individualised holidays, for greater quality and for more environmentally sustainable tourism are leading to modifications of the mass "product", rather than to entirely new forms (and locations) of tourism. The renewed demand for rural tourism is particularly symptomatic of this shift.

The changes in central and eastern Europe have also grafted a layer of complexity on to the map of European tourism. In the early years of the command economies, tourism was essentially seen as an important element in collective consumption; "the social dimension of state socialism emphasised the well-being of the working population, and to this end enterprise and trade-union-sponsored facilities were developed for domestic, group-orientated tourism and recreation" (Hall, 1991a, 80). In the post-Stalinist period there was a growth of international tourism within the Council for Mutual Economic Assistance (CMEA) block. At the same time, Yugoslavia – pursuing its own distinctive economic strategy – developed a Mediterranean mass tourism industry, reliant on Western markets. From the 1960s, the need for hard currencies to finance their expanding trade with the West led most of the central and eastern European countries – with the exception of Albania – to foster inward international tourism. In contrast, outward international tourism remained the preserve of a small trusted political elite.

Since 1989 – at varying speeds – the central and eastern European economies have become increasingly linked to western European markets, while also experiencing a loss of traditional markets within the CMEA block and growing outwards flows of tourists (Hall, 1995). The destinations of international tourists within the region have also changed. While arrivals in the Black Sea and the Mediterranean areas have declined (particularly following the crisis in the former Yugoslavia), cities in central Europe – especially in Hungary, (former) Czechoslovakia and Poland – have proved attractive destinations in the context of the new forms of tourism consumption. Rural tourism has been slower to take off in central and eastern Europe, but there are some important foci such as the Tatra Mountains in Slovakia and the Danube Delta in Romania.

Irrespective of how these shifts in both the West and the East are conceptualised, it is clear that important changes are occurring in the geography of European tourism; existing resorts are subject to restructuring while new tourism products and spaces are being created. This has important implications for the European map of production and employment, as well as for local, regional, cultural and environmental systems. Within the confines of this chapter we concentrate on economic shifts while acknowledging that, in the case of tourism, the economy, environment and culture are strongly interrelated.

It is inevitable that an industry with such major economic, cultural and environmental implications should be subject to state intervention.

Two features of this intervention are particularly notable. First, there was relative neglect of tourism as a policy object during the early post-war years; there were, of course, examples of intervention, particularly state promotion of incoming international tourism, and municipal land-use planning. However, these were limited in scope and ambition. The second feature is the "discovery" of tourism as an object of state economic policy in recent decades, together with increasing awareness of its cultural and environmental impacts. This has led to the universalisation of tourism policy across most levels of state intervention, from the EU to the local.

In the remainder of this chapter we investigate the principal themes outlined above. The discussion is divided into three sections, dealing respectively with tourism demand, the economic impacts of tourism, and state intervention.

Changes in Tourism Consumption

Mass tourism

Mass tourism is a form of mass consumption and, as such, is characterised by standardised products, dominance by producers not consumers, the domination of markets by individual producers, and little differentiation of commodities (Urry, 1990, 14). The growth of mass tourism can be traced from the late nineteenth century, but in much of Europe the golden era of domestic mass tourism was in the 1950s and that of international mass tourism in the 1960s and 1970s (Figure 10.1; see also Shaw and Williams, 1994). The standardisation of tourism services is most clearly evident in the cases of domestic North Sea resorts and international Mediterranean, Black Sea and Alpine tourist resorts, but is not exclusive to them.

The timing of the boom in mass tourism can partly be explained by the removal of constraints in the 1950s. Workplace and worktime conventions were relaxed so that not only did the majority of workers in northern Europe have more free time, but changes to its structure allowed them to spend longer away from their home areas (Shaw and Williams, 1994, 175–6). In addition, there was a marked increase in real disposable incomes in northern Europe in the early post-war

decades as a result of sustained economic growth and a one-off redistribution of income. Extensions to the right to paid holidays also encouraged tourism, while another important factor was massive state investment in transport infrastructure, particularly airports, which facilitated long-distance travel.

The demand for tourism emanated from a diverse set of motivations, including the desire for relaxation, for "escape" and for stimulation. However, the growth of the mass market in this period was also encouraged because tourism is a positional good, i.e. one of the commodities which "are actively used as markers of social position and cultural style by consumers who seek to define their position *vis-à-vis* other consumers" (Lury, 1996, 46). Foreign holidays became positional goods for large segments of the population during the 1960s and the 1970s. There were also shifts in the popularity and significance of particular resorts, and sometimes countries, as positional indicators in response to the development of new resorts and to fashion changes. Urry (1995, 138) further argues that mass tourism rests upon the collective gaze which requires the presence of large numbers of other people – as at the English seaside – to give atmosphere to a place; this is "... indicative that this is *the* place to be and that one should not be elsewhere". The presence of masses of other people is also required to provide a market for the types of accommodation, entertainment and other services that most mass tourists wish to purchase as part of their tourism experiences.

The general consumption of mass tourism was translated into demand for holidays in a specific set of resorts or destinations by the interplay between the tourist gaze and the image makers who direct that gaze to particular tourist "signs", associated with specific places. This is what Krippendorf (1987, 10) terms "the promise of the paradise seekers". Urry (1995, 132) writes that:

> "Places are chosen to be gazed upon because there is an anticipation, especially through day dreaming and fantasy, of intense pleasures, either on a different scale or involving different senses from those customarily encountered. Such anticipation is constructed and sustained through a variety of non-tourist practices, such as film, newspapers, TV, magazines, records and videos which construct that gaze."

Figure 10.1 *Icon of mass tourism: Benidorm. (Photo: D R Hall)*

In the 1960s and the 1970s the mass tourist gaze was directed unequivocally at Europe's Mediterranean coastline, before being shifted (in relative terms) to the southern and eastern Mediterranean shores in the 1980s (Williams, 1997), as well as to the Alpine winter playgrounds.

Despite this perception factor, it is unlikely that the phenomenon of international mass tourism would have occurred without a series of interrelated developments in the economics of travel and tourism. There was a mutually reinforcing set of links between transport technology changes (Figure 10.2), the increasing oligopsonistic powers of small groups of tour companies, and economies of scale related to the expansion of effective demand.

Not all forms of mass tourism were dominated by international tour companies (ITCs), but these were particularly strong in the short- and medium-haul air-travel inclusive holiday sector. One of the particular advantages of selling *inclusive* air holidays was that it allowed tour companies to internalise market transactions (Dunning, 1977), that is to realise profits on the different components of the total holiday package. In addition, they were able to benefit from "a distribution system enabling production to be marketed before completion and capital savings obtained by utilising the investments of carriers and hoteliers and the down payments of customers" (Ascher, 1985, 57).

ITCs are not in equally dominant positions in all the main European markets; they are strongest in northern Europe, particularly in Germany, the UK and Scandinavia. In terms of the 50 largest ITCs in Europe, 12 are German and 10 are British (Figure 10.3). Such data understate their true importance, for 7 of the 10 largest companies are either British or German. TUI of Germany is the largest ITC in Europe, and carried over 3 million holidaymakers in 1991–92.

There are important differences in the structures and linkages of ITCs, even among those tour companies operating in the two main national markets (Williams, 1995). German companies have the advantage of serving the largest market in the world, but they have also extended their market reach by large-scale investment abroad; some 30

Figure 10.2 *The holiday jet: essential tool of the tourism industry. (Photo: D A Pinder)*

per cent of TUI's sales, and more than 50 per cent of those by ITS, are made outside Germany. They have also developed strong vertical linkages, particularly with the hotel sector. In contrast, the three largest UK tour companies have concentrated almost exclusively on air travel and on the UK market. Consequently, although they too are strongly vertically integrated and own or have important alliances with travel agencies and airlines, their linkages with the hotel sector are much weaker. Taken together with the fact that in both countries the top three companies control more than one-half of the air holiday industry, the tour companies have strongly influenced the shape of mass tourism. In the UK, in particular, they have exercised strong downwards pressure on prices, thereby extending the market to lower-income groups.

The growth of mass tourism has underpinned the present geography of European tourism activity, as is evident in the distribution of nights spent away from home (Figure 10.4). Care is required in interpreting these data (see OECD, 1995), not least because they grossly underestimate the real totals for some countries, particularly Spain and Italy. It should be noted that, in terms of numbers of *arrivals*, France, Italy and Spain continue to be the three leading European destinations. However, the data on overnight stays do demonstrate the main patterns of domestic and international tourism in Europe. In terms of nights spent in all types of accommodation, the main international destinations are countries with well-developed mass tourism industries – Spain, Austria, Greece, Italy, Portugal and, to a lesser extent, Switzerland – or those with major cultural attractions and/or business tourism sectors, such as the UK, France and Germany. The national differences in terms of domestic tourist nights should also be approached cautiously, but the strength of the German, Italian, British and French home markets does reflect the size and prosperity of their populations. The data in Figure 10.4 are probably most useful for comparisons between the relative importance of domestic and foreign tourism in each country. There are four main groups, those where:

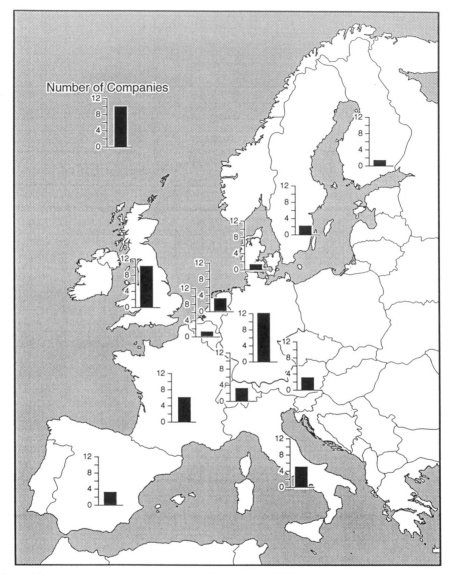

Figure 10.3 *Major international tour companies (after Bywater, 1992)*

- international tourism is strongly dominant: Austria, Greece, Hungary, Poland and Turkey
- domestic tourism is dominant: Finland, Germany, the Netherlands, Norway, Poland, Slovakia and Sweden
- domestic tourism is dominant, but there is also a large international tourism segment: France, Italy and the UK
- domestic and international tourism are in approximate balance: Belgium, Bulgaria, Denmark, Switzerland and Spain

(Not all European countries are included in this classification due to data limitations.)

The patterns of nights spent are particularly significant given the focus of this chapter on the relationship between tourism and economic development. These data also reveal the growing importance of the domestic markets of the southern European countries, particularly Spain with its large population and gradual convergence on EU average income levels.

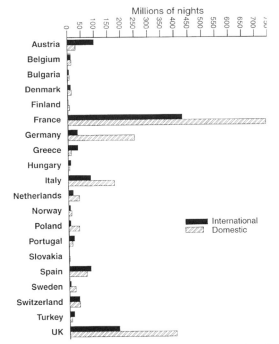

Figure 10.4 *Nights spent by international and domestic tourists*

The patterns of tourism in central and eastern Europe are best considered separately, partly because of data deficiencies, and partly because their historic structures are still in transition. Table 10.1 shows the numbers of rooms available to let and also the numbers of international arrivals in

Table 10.1 *Tourism in central and eastern Europe, 1994*

	No. of rooms	No. of international tourists ('000)
Albania	1 573	28
Bulgaria	54 560	4 055
Czech Republic	66 965	17 000
Hungary	35 878	21 425
Poland	52 393	18 800
Romania	84 475	2 796
Slovakia	16 000	902
Former Yugoslavia		
Croatia	85 169	2 293
Slovenia	16 566	748
TFYR Macedonia	28 899	185
Yugoslavia	37 577	91

Source: World Tourism Organisation.

1994. On the basis of these statistics we can suggest a threefold classification:

1 Bulgaria, Romania and the former Yugoslavia were the principal foci of mass coastal tourism in central and eastern Europe prior to 1989. Subsequently, they have suffered from adverse public images, the conflicts in the Balkans (Carter *et al.*, 1995) and the loss of traditional markets within the former CMEA block. Hence they have relatively modest levels of international arrivals compared to the large stocks of accommodation available.

2. Slovakia and Slovenia occupy intermediate positions and have quite limited accommodation stocks and international arrivals. Neither figured large in pre-1989 international tourism, but they are gradually establishing small niches in international cultural and rural tourism.

3. Hungary, Poland and the Czech Republic have by far the largest numbers of international tourist arrivals, while they also have medium to high levels of accommodation stocks. In the immediate aftermath of the events of 1989, Hungary was first to benefit significantly from new tourism growth, given its previous partial opening to Western trade and tourism. Subsequently, Poland and the Czech Republic have registered high growth rates. All three countries have been particularly successful in attracting urban tourism, and in establishing niches in the market for new forms of consumption.

Albania does not easily fit any of these categories; it was virtually closed to tourism prior to the 1990s and only now is seeking to establish a place in international markets. Progress is being retarded by a severe lack of infrastructure, although the country has ambitions to become an important player in the market for Mediterranean mass tourism.

New forms of tourism consumption

In recent decades there have been discernible shifts away from mass consumption. According to Lury (1996, 94), there have been three main interrelated changes. First, there have been shifts in production to greater flexible specialisation. Second, there has been a greater range of commodities on offer, each of which has had a shorter life-cycle, as a result of more rapid changes in fashion and greater differentiation by market segments. And third, consumers have become increasingly specialised, with more individualised and hybrid consumption patterns. Consumer preferences have also become more volatile, with a "fluidisation" of consumption. One of the major forces behind these changes has been the growing influence of the new middle class, whose tastes have led the (relative) rejection of mass consumption. Featherstone (1991, 86) argues that "the new heroes of consumer culture make life style a life project and display their individuality and sense of style in the particularity of the assemblage of goods, clothes, practices, experiences, appearance and bodily dispositions they design together into a lifestyle". The cultural tastes and holiday preferences of these "new heroes" are not, of course, invariable across Europe and, for example, the German middle classes showed an earlier and stronger interest in "green tourism" than did their counterparts in the UK or France (Figure 10.5).

There are naturally links between the (relative) shift from mass tourism and the growth of more flexible and individualised tourism (Urry, 1995, 151). Increasingly, the individuality of holiday products has been stressed, there has been proliferation in the numbers and types of tourism products available, and there have been more volatile consumer preferences. This is evident in the rapid expansion (and often short lives) of new theme parks, museums, and other tourism attractions. There have also been fewer repeat visits, the provision of more information about alternative holidays and attractions through the media, the growth of "green tourism", and the de-differentiation of tourism from leisure, culture, retailing, education and sport (Figure 10.6). The net result, in terms of the locations of tourism activities, has been the decline, both absolutely and relatively, of traditional mass tourism resorts, and the proliferation of new sites of tourism. Three types of site are considered below: rural tourism, urban tourism and theme parks.

Figure 10.5 *Green tourism in action. Free walkers' buses in the Paznaun valley, Austria, encourage reduced reliance on cars in a popular mountain holiday region. (Photo: D A Pinder)*

Figure 10.6   *Tourism, leisure and sport. A cliff abseiling lesson for an activity holiday group. (Photo: D A Pinder)*

Rural tourism is long established and has been of considerable importance in many European societies. Cavaco (1995, 130) sees rural tourism as a "meeting place where rural culture encounters an urban culture that is extremely sensitive to nature and the bucolic". In the more recently industrialised European countries, rural tourism had become a highly polarised form of activity; city owners of large estates took holidays in the countryside alongside first- and second-generation urban migrants who returned to spend one or two weeks in the summer with their extended families. In some regions – such as the Alps and the Scottish Highlands – there was also continuation of the romantic tourist gaze upon Europe's "wilder" rural landscapes (Figure 10.7).

In recent years, there has been a notable expansion of rural tourism. This has been propelled by a series of changes. On the consumption side, there has been a re-evaluation of cultural and natural landscapes, led by the new middle class (Urry, 1990). Changes in the organisation of free time (allowing more shorter breaks) and in personal mobility (based on increased car ownership) have also facilitated the growth of rural tourism. At the same time, there have been supply-side changes as farmers and others have sought to diversify their businesses in response to the crisis in agricultural production (see Chapter 18). Tourism has also featured strongly in the rural regeneration strategies of many local development agencies, as well as in EU programmes such as LEADER. Cavaco (1995, 130–1) sees the growth of rural tourism as a direct response to the increasing negative reaction to mass provision:

> "This is, in effect, a flight from the summer-holiday resorts of mass tourism and, instead, more middle-class tourists are choosing to visit rural areas. They are looking for alternatives to the sun and the beach and prefer isolation, privacy, rest, peace and quiet, personalised service, warm human relations, something that, above all, is different and special.

Figure 10.7   *Ridge walk on the Austria–Switzerland border, Silvretta Alps. (Photo: D A Pinder)*

In essence, they are looking for well-protected, 'pure', unspoilt nature; for grand, varied landscapes; for archaeological, historical, memorial and cultural heritage; for novel architecture with its roots in regional folklore; for festivals and feast days; for traditional music, dancing and folklore; and for traditional gastronomy. ... In other words, they are giving new value to traditional destinations previously cast aside in the great summer stampede to the beach."

Some idea of the relative importance of rural tourism in Europe is given by a survey of holiday destinations in the EU10 (excepting the UK) in the early 1980s. The countryside and the mountains were the destination of more than one-third of all tourists in all countries except Greece, and for more than one-half of all tourists in France, the Netherlands and Germany (Commission of European Communities, 1986; Williams and Shaw, 1990). The impact of rural tourism on farm structures is also evident, with more than one-fifth of farmers in Austria, Switzerland and Sweden providing tourist accommodation (Requena and Aviles, 1993). In time, central and eastern Europe can be expected to figure more prominently in European rural tourism. There were important international destinations prior to 1989, such as the Danube Delta and the Tatras Mountains, while there were also well-developed specialist market segments such as hunting (Hall, 1991b). However, since 1989 these areas have been relatively slow to attract international tourists from the West due to a lack of quality infrastructure and services, and instead have become more reliant on domestic markets.

Urban tourism has also increased in importance in recent years. This is a complex sector which has significant business, cultural, sporting and retailing dimensions (Law, 1994; Page, 1995). In terms of leisure tourism, its growth is linked to

changing market segmentation and, in particular, to age structure changes which have led to the expansion of demand from elderly couples and single persons rather than from families. As with rural tourism, changes in the structure of free time have also facilitated growth in the short-break market. The widening of educational access is also considered to have generated an increase in urban culture, as has the fascination with heritage tourism. De-differentiation, with tourism being combined with retailing and with various leisure activities, has also been instrumental in the rapid growth of urban tourism.

The implications of growth are seen at both the national and international scales (Law, 1994; Page, 1995). In the UK, for example, Manchester,

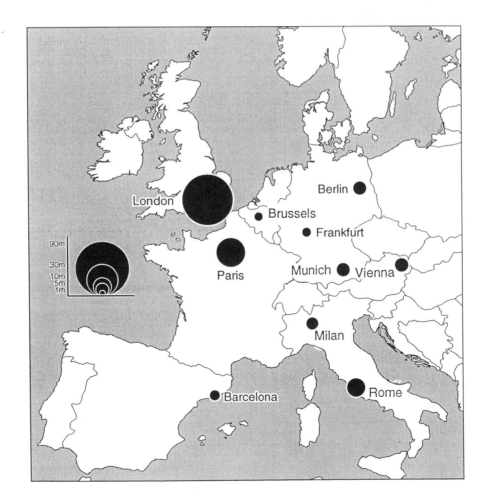

Figure 10.8 *Major urban tourism areas (after van den Berg et al., 1994)*

Bradford, Wigan and other cities are now important domestic tourist destinations, while improvements in rail and air transport have allowed places such as Florence, Amsterdam and Bruges to become significant *short-break* centres. Shachar (1995, 156) stresses that cultural tourism is helping to determine the emerging ranking of urban tourism destinations: the "geographical patterning of the performing arts in the culture industries gives urban tourism a strong metropolitan character, with an emphasis on the world cities which occupy the highest level of the global urban hierarchy". In terms of nights spent in major metropolitan areas by all forms of tourists, London, Paris and Rome are the leading destinations, followed by Munich, Vienna and Berlin (Figure 10.8). This reflects a combination of cultural and business activities. Barcelona has been particularly successful in marketing its cultural and heritage attractions, and has been aided in this by skilful exploitation of the promotional opportunities provided by the 1992 Olympic Games (Carreras i Verdaguer, 1995).

Central Europe has also been successful in the market for international urban tourism. Much of the sector's growth in Hungary, the Czech Republic and Poland in particular has been dependent on the attraction of their capital cities and other urban destinations such as Karlovy Vary (Hall, 1991b). These have been the sites of greatest

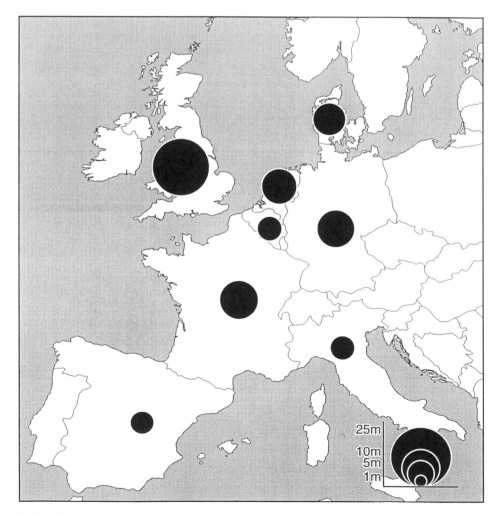

Figure 10.9 *Attendances at major theme parks (after McEniff, 1993)*

interest to international capital, which has invested in new hotels and acquired existing ones in these cities (Hunt, 1993). The outstanding success story has been Prague which, by the 1990s, was a major pole of attraction for international tourists drawn by its cultural and architectural features. It already has more than 50 000 bed spaces available (Ministry of Economy of the Czech Republic) and is continuing to attract the interest of international chains such as Four Seasons Hotels.

A third type of leisure attraction which has grown significantly in popularity in recent years is theme parks. Day visitors constitute an important element in their markets, but several of the larger examples have developed their own overnight tourism market segment. Theme parks are particularly important in demonstrating how capital investment, allied to new technologies, can create new, and rapidly changing, "extraordinary" objects for tourists to "gaze" upon. Urry (1990) argues that they have contributed to demystifying traditional coastal resorts, making their attractions seem ordinary.

Theme parks already constitute a major economic sector in their own right, and it is estimated that in 1994 they attracted 58 million visitors with a spend of £1 bn (*Financial Times*, 1995). Over time their size has increased in order to secure the economies of scale which are required to support the high costs of technological development, and of mass-marketing. Figure 10.9 shows the distribution of attendances at Europe's major theme parks (those with more than 1 million visitors) in 1992. At that date, the UK, France, the Netherlands and Germany had the most substantial theme park sectors. The largest traditional theme park was Blackpool Pleasure Beach, with 6.5 million visitors, and other major UK attractions included the Palace Pier at Brighton, and Alton Towers. The most important German theme park was Phantasialand with 2.2 million visitors, while Tivoli gardens in Denmark attracted more than 4 million. In recent years, the market has been transformed with the opening of several new destinations such as Port Aventura near Tarragona, and planned new parks such as Warner Brothers' "Movies World" in Germany. However, the most significant development has been investment in Euro Disney, near Paris, which attracted more than 11 million visitors in 1993 and has a series of hotel complexes.

Tourism and Economic Development
Differences and structures

The economic impacts of tourism are particularly complex, but their inherently uneven nature is not in question. This is dictated by the nature of the tourist gaze (Urry, 1990), which seeks out the extraordinary and emphasises place differences. The economics of tourism – particularly mass tourism – serve to underline this unevenness; concentration is required for the provision of some tourism services, including entertainment and low-cost air travel. In addition, concentration supplies the atmosphere and the reinforcing signifiers provided by the presence of others at a tourist site. Seasonality serves to reinforce further the highly polarised effects of most forms of tourism (Shaw and Williams, 1994, 184), although the geographical patterns of polarisation have changed over the long term. Claval (1995), for example, outlines what he terms mega changes in the geography of European tourism which have accompanied shifts from romantic tourism to mass tourism to new forms of tourism; he relates these to changes in the geography of production, in transport technology and in culture and fashion.

These major shifts provide the broad canvas against which the economic implications of tourism are worked out. Just as the mega shifts are shaped by place and locality differences, so their economic implications are contingent. In particular, they are dependent on the nature of tourism consumption, the organisation of production and differences in local economic structures.

In the late twentieth century there has been a fundamental divide between mass tourism and the new forms which are variously labelled post-Fordist or post-modernist. This can be illustrated by reference to spatial form and to the nature of competition. Mass tourism is highly spatially polarised but, in contrast, many of the "new" types of tourism are spatially diffused (although still regionally selective). This applies, for example, to rural tourism, to non-metropolitan heritage sites, to gastronomic tourism and to many recreational activities. However, not all forms of post-modernist tourism are spatially diffused; for example, urban tourism based on cultural and industrial heritage involves spatial polarisation of

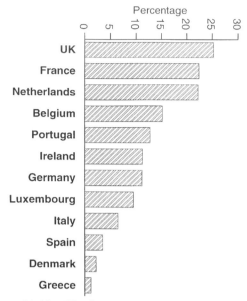

Percentage

UK
France
Netherlands
Belgium
Portugal
Ireland
Germany
Luxembourg
Italy
Spain
Denmark
Greece

Figure 10.10 *Hotel ownership: proportions operated by chains and quoted hotel companies (after Slattery and Johnson, 1993)*

large numbers of tourists. There is also differentiation in terms of the nature of competition. Whereas mass tourism emphasises generalised tourism attractions (such as sunshine or snow), post-modernist tourism emphasises place differences. As a result, compared to post-modernist tourism, competition in mass tourism tends to be in terms of prices, with costs being driven down via a double squeeze on both profit margins and payments to subcontractors (Williams, 1996). Prices may also be reduced by increased self-provisioning (within hotels, or through a shift to self-catering accommodation), a strategy which has distinct economic implications.

The second set of mediating influences relates to company structures, which differ by sector and by locality. For example, mass tourism which is reliant on international tour companies tends to be characterised by oligopsonistic relationships (Williams, 1996), with the result that small firms acting as local subcontractors tend to become dependent and to lack capacity for independent action and innovation (Williams and Montanari, 1995, 3). Differences in company structures can be readily illustrated by reference to the hotel sector. Europe has a small-scale hotel industry

with a fragmented ownership structure. An estimated 70 per cent of firms are independents, while only 19 per cent are in domestic chains and 11 per cent are in foreign ones (Pizam and Knowles, 1994, 284). In contrast, 85 per cent of North American hotels belong to chains. Within this widespread picture of fragmentation there are considerable national differences, with the UK, the Netherlands and France having stronger elements of chain ownership, and also of quoted hotel companies (Figure 10.10). In addition, there are differences in business culture, with the "innkeeping" tradition of Switzerland contrasting with the "management and business" orientation to be found in the UK (Pizam and Knowles, 1994, 285; Go and Pine, 1995). However, not all sectors of the hotel industry are similarly affected by such differences in ownership structures. The leisure hotel section is largely dominated by independently owned enterprises, and surprisingly this applies almost to the same extent to mass tourism as to, say, rural tourism (Williams, 1995). In contrast, large hotel chains are mostly present in major towns and cities and play a more significant role in urban tourism, particularly in the business segment. Such ownership differences are important for a number of reasons, including the way that they affect the propensity and capacity to internationalise (Beattie, 1991). This in turn influences the distribution of tourism income, not only between localities but also between countries. Size and ownership structures also have labour-market implications because smaller enterprises are often only able to survive via self- or family-exploitation (Shaw and Williams, 1994, 148).

The tourism sector in central and eastern Europe is markedly different, having largely been in state ownership for most of the post-war period. It is now subject to change due to two linked processes: privatisation and inward investment. Hungary was one of the first of these countries to experiment with privatisation and, indeed, the Ibusz tour company was the country's first privatised company (Hunt, 1993). There has also been progress in privatising the national airline, Malev, and smaller accommodation and catering establishments. Privatisation is also relatively well advanced in Poland and the Czech Republic, and latterly in Slovakia; as in Hungary, tourism has been at the forefront of privatisation in these countries, but has tended to be restricted to small and medium-sized establishments. Where there have been international sales of the shares of the larger companies, Western investors have been attracted particularly to the Visegrad Four group of countries; for example, by 1993 Alitalia had taken a 30 per cent share in Malev, and Groupe Air France had taken a 20 per cent holding in the Czech airline CSA (Hunt, 1993). The hotel sector has been most attractive to foreign investors. For example, more than 20 companies were reported to have been interested in purchasing a 51 per cent share in the Hungar Hotels chain when it was put on sale (Hall, 1995, 237).

The third element which mediates the impacts of tourism development is the structure of the local economy. There are obviously major differences between those localities wherein tourism is the dominant sector (most but not all mass tourist resorts) and those where it is only one segment of the economy (as in most forms of rural and urban tourism). There is also differentiation in terms of the development of local capital structures. In Spain, for example, there are contrasts between coastal resorts in Catalonia, which were developed by local capital, and those in Andalucia, which were dependent on non-local investment (Shaw and Williams, 1994, 186–92). Similarly, high-level, purpose-built Alpine resorts tend to rely on external entrepreneurs and employees, while those at lower altitudes are generally more integrated into local capital and labour markets (Barker, 1982).

Labour-market differences are one of the most significant mediating influences on the economic impacts of tourism. Tourism services have to be provided at specific places and times, so that the demand for labour is inherently uneven. Capital therefore requires particular strategies, both to control labour costs and to assemble labour at particular points in time and space. There is no single strategy but, instead, depending on local contingencies, various forms of informalisation and flexible labour contracts may be used (Shaw and Williams, 1994, 142–9). Gender is frequently deployed to achieve labour-market segmentation, in order to reduce overall labour costs. Many jobs are socially constructed as being "female jobs", such as cleaning, making beds and, in some

countries, cooking. There is, of course, nothing inherently female in the skills requirements of these jobs. Instead, women carry over into the paid labour market their domestic roles which, in turn, are also socially constructed (Williams and Montanari, 1995, 10).

International migration can also be used to structure labour markets. King (1995) reports that international migrants are particularly important in the tourism industries in Switzerland and Luxembourg, are of lesser importance in France, Belgium and Germany, and are of least importance in the UK and Netherlands. There are, in turn, gender and national differences within those labour-market segments occupied by international migrants (King, 1995, 184):

> "In both Spain and Italy, chambermaids and cleaners from the Philippines and some Latin American countries are widespread in hotels and apartment complexes. Hotels in big cities in Italy, especially Rome, employ kitchen and portering staff from many Third World countries such as Somalia, Eritrea, India and Morocco. Street-hawkers, a highly visible component of the street scene and beach life of Mediterranean tourist resorts, are mainly from Senegal and other West African countries."

Economic impacts

There are considerable difficulties involved in estimating the economic importance of tourism, not least because the industry is poorly represented in most statistical sources. As a starting point, however, we can take the EU's own estimate that tourism accounts for approximately 5 per cent of GDP and 6 per cent of jobs in the EU12. Over time, Europe's share of the world market has been declining, reflecting changes in the geography of production (and thereby disposable incomes), as well as European tourists' increasingly global scan for holiday destinations. As a result, the EU and EFTA's positive balance-of-payments travel account declined by two-thirds between 1985 and 1991 (Commission of the European Communities, 1995, 68). In addition, the World Travel and Tourism Council (1995) – using a different set of definitions – estimates that Europe's share of world gross tourism will decline from 44 to 38.4 per cent between 1992 and 2005. Given that eastern Europe's share is predicted to increase in this period, this means that the EU/EFTA share is set to decline sharply. However, in practice this will be contingent on political conditions and it must also be remembered that these data are relative. In absolute terms, western Europe is expected to experience continued steady, modest growth in both tourist arrivals and the economic importance of tourism. This is evident in the prediction that tourism's share of total employment will rise from 10.3 to 11.6 per cent during these years.

In terms of the contribution of tourism to the national economies of Europe, there are significant if largely predictable variations reflecting both the sizes and natures of the individual tourist industries and their strength relative to other sectors. Table 10.2 summarises the OECD data for international tourism, which unfortunately exclude Ireland, Italy and the UK for key indicators, as well as central and eastern Europe. There are three groups of economies:

(a) Those where tourism accounts for a relatively large share of employment, GDP and exports: Austria, Greece, Portugal, Spain and Switzerland. All five have mass tourism indus-

tries, although they are also actively engaged in promoting sustainable tourism.

(b) Those where tourism is relatively unimportant in terms of all three economic indicators: Belgium, Denmark, the Netherlands and Norway. They have relatively small-scale international tourism industries and diversified industrial and service economies.

(c) Those where tourism is of modest importance in terms of at least one of the economic indicators: France, Germany, Luxembourg and Turkey. Turkey stands out in this group because its emerging mass tourism industry makes a relatively significant contribution to the current account, compared to the limited weight of other international trade in the economy.

These data serve to underline four main points. Firstly, tourism is important in all the European economies, but especially in the Alps and the Mediterranean countries. Secondly, the current accounts of the Mediterranean countries and of Austria are highly dependent on the industry. Thirdly, it is most important in those countries with mass tourism industries. And, fourthly, it is a particular concern of national trade-related policies because, quite simply, its receipts help to fund the visible trade deficits of several countries.

Table 10.2 *Economic importance of tourism in national economies, 1993*

	Share of total employment	Share of GDP	Travel account receipts as a % of all exports of goods and services
Austria	13.9	14.0	17.6
Belgium	2.0	4.0	1.8
Denmark	2.6	2.5	4.2
France	4.8	2.6	6.1
Germany	6.5	5.6	2.0
Greece	10.0	8.0	23.4
Luxembourg	6.4	5.0	6.3
Netherlands	2.8	2.1	2.5
Norway	3.4	2.9	3.9
Portugal	5.6	8.0	15.5
Spain	9.1	8.0	19.9
Sweden	3.4	6.0	3.8
Switzerland	8.2	5.6	6.4
Turkey	0.7	3.4	14.4

Source: OECD (1995).

In addition, the role of tourism in employment explains its increased interest to policy-makers in the recessions of the 1980s and 1990s.

The economic role of international tourism in central and eastern Europe is summarised in Table 10.3. The data used here are different from those deployed by the OECD, so that they cannot be compared directly with those for western Europe. Nevertheless, the picture is relatively clear and echoes the pattern of international arrivals observed earlier. In absolute terms, the role of tourism in 1995 was greatest in Poland; to some degree this reflects its larger population and economy (and hence business trips) compared to other central and eastern European countries. Poland is followed in importance by the Czech Republic, Hungary and Slovakia (with their booming economies and important niches in urban tourism) and by Croatia and Slovenia, which have been experiencing modest recoveries from the effects of the crisis in the former Yugoslavia. Perhaps of greater interest is the pattern of change in the net tourism balance between 1990 and 1995. In particular, this shows strong advances in the tourism industries in all these countries, but particularly in Poland, Slovakia and the Czech Republic, where negative balances were converted to healthy positive accounts. A fuller discussion of the economic impacts of tourism in central Europe can be found in Balaz (1996).

Table 10.3 *The economic role of tourism in central and eastern Europe ($m.)*

	Tourism receipts	Tourism balance	
	1995	1990	1995
Albania	7	3	2
Bulgaria	400	131	166
Czech Republic	1966	−36	1245
Hungary	1428	347	749
Poland	6400	−65	900
Romania	574	3	−121
Slovakia	620	−111	290
Former Yugoslavia			
Croatia	1584		813
Slovenia	1163		841
TFYR Macedonia	30		
Yugoslavia	42		

Source: World Tourism Organisation.

While there are significant economic differences at the national level, these can only hint at the sector's importance to particular regional and local economies, many of which – such as the Costa del Sol, the Greek islands, the Bernese Oberland and Florence or Venice – are dominated by tourism. Given the selectivity of the tourism gaze and the economics of mass tourism, the industry's regional and local distribution is inevitably highly uneven. Of course, there are also contrasts in the experiences of individual countries. For example, the degree of concentration is greater in Spain than in the UK, while there are also differences between types of tourism, with the foreign variety usually being far more polarised than the domestic form (Williams and Shaw, 1994).

A more difficult question to answer is whether tourism encourages overall economic convergence or divergence. In other words, how does it contribute to the generation and redistribution of capital and income between rich and poor regions? Williams and Montanari (1995, 6) argue that "The social construction of tourism – with an emphasis especially in mass tourism on the 'flight' from the pressures of working and urban life – have meant that 'peripheral' areas (in contrast to [the] dominant and prosperous 'core') have been important tourist destinations." They qualify this argument to stress that not even large-scale international tourism inevitably privileges the peripheral regions, as is shown by the experiences of Catalan coastal tourism, and of mass urban tourism to Paris or London. The evidence from Hungary and the Czech Republic, where tourism is massively concentrated in the capital cities, highlights this picture of tourism reinforcing the advantages of the richer regions. Slovakia presents a more mixed pattern; although Bratislava dominates the tourism scene, there are also important concentrations in the relatively poorer Tatra and Fatra mountain regions (Balaz, 1994). Returning to western Europe, we can also note that the emergence of new forms of tourism has produced an increasingly complex map of economic impacts, not least because localities in both rich and poor regions have pursued tourism development strategies in the face of rising unemployment in the 1980s and the 1990s. It would therefore be more accurate to argue that, at present, "there are many different forms of tourism and that each has distinctive regional implications which do not necessarily conform to any simplistic periphery–centre or centre–periphery model" (Williams and Shaw, 1994, 308).

Some of the different regional outcomes of traditional and more recent tourism development are illustrated by the examples of the UK and Austria. In the UK, mass tourism has traditionally favoured poorer regions, but recent changes in tourism markets and investments have benefited richer areas. This is partly related to the continuing internationalisation of UK tourism markets, which has tended to privilege London and the southern regions, both in terms of gains from incoming visitors and relative losses to outgoing tourism. In addition, compared to mass tourism, the rapid expansion of less spatially polarised post-modernist tourism has also favoured these regions. The fact that many of these new forms of tourism – such as theme parks and urban, cultural, heritage and sporting tourism – depend more on short-break markets than on the traditional long summer holiday, also favours those destinations which are relatively accessible to major metropolitan areas. Similarly in Austria, tourism income has in the past contributed to reducing regional disparities. In particular, the expansion of GDP was greater between 1970 and 1992 in the winter tourism-dominated areas of Tyrol, Salzburg and Voralberg than in most other Austrian provinces, especially Carinthia where the summer industry peaked in the 1960s and early 1970s. However, there has been an important shift in recent years and the richer regions, such as Vienna and Lower Austria, have experienced more rapid tourism growth due to the increasing importance of international visitors drawn to the capital, and to the short-break markets provided by the recreational needs of the Viennese population (Zimmerman, 1995, 38)

Tourism and State Intervention

There are two main reasons for state intervention in the industry in Europe in the 1990s. The first is that the private sector cannot guarantee the reproduction of the tourism industry, due to its inability to bridge the gap between individual capital's realisation of profits and the requirement for investments in common goods (particularly infrastructure) which are not in themselves profitable. Therefore, there has been a long history of collective or social investment by the state to underpin the activities of individual tourism capitals. The examples extend from early municipal investments in piers, promenades and public gardens in British coastal resorts in the nineteenth and early twentieth centuries, through the construction of airports such as that at Malaga to open up the Costa del Sol to international tourism, to public investment to facilitate such mega events as the Barcelona Olympics or the planned Millennium exhibition at Greenwich (Figure 10.11).

The other principal motivation for state investment in tourism is the desire to use this sector as an instrument of wider macro-economic policy. International tourism has been promoted since the 1950s by most European governments because of its potential contribution to the current account. In Spain, for example, the surplus on the balance-of-travel account helped to finance a visible trade deficit and to fund imports of capital and intermediate goods for the modernisation of manufacturing in the 1960s and 1970s. Since the 1970s, weaker and more volatile economic growth, combined with persistent structural unemployment, have led to renewed public sector interest in tourism as one of the few sectors with consistent current and future employment-generating capacity. This has been evident at all levels of public sector policy, but has been particularly pronounced in the proliferation of local and regional economic development strategies in the 1980s and the 1990s.

As a result of this renewed interest, tourism has lost its "Cinderella" status in the field of economic policy and has instead moved centre stage in discussions about economic regeneration and international competitiveness. The economic logic behind such a shift has been reinforced by the growing realisation of the key role played by tourism in shaping Europe's environmental and cultural systems (Williams and Shaw, 1994). To explore the policy effects, in this final section we consider state intervention in tourism at three levels: the EU, the national and the regional/local.

The EU has been a late convert to the need for Europe-wide tourism policies, and there was a gap

Figure 10.11 *Computer simulation of the completed New Millennium Experience site at Greenwich, UK. Behind the site itself (foreground) lie a large part of the redeveloped London Docklands and (background) central London. (Photo: Hayes Davidson and the New Millennium Experience Company)*

of 25 years between the Treaty of Rome and the first attempt to draft a comprehensive European tourism policy. There were a number of reasons for this. First, the economic importance of tourism was not realised, particularly as much of the early EU emphasis was on reshaping industrial trade through the common external tariff and the customs union, and on establishing a framework for agricultural expansion via the Common Agricultural Policy (Williams, 1994, 34–56).

Second, even when there was a greater realisation of the importance of tourism in the 1970s and early 1980s, attempts were made to subsume tourism within other policy initiatives such as those for regional development, agricultural diversification and the environment; this meant that EU tourism policy was weak and fragmented. Finally, there was national resistance to EU interventionism as tourism was seen as part of the competencies of the member states.

The first comprehensive attempt to produce a specific strategy for tourism came only in 1982, when "pressure from public opinion, particularly on the question of the environment, and from the European Parliament on the issue of the protection of Europe's cultural heritage . . . combined with a growing realisation of the scale of tourism's importance" (Robinson, 1993, 13) to encourage the production of the "Initial Guidelines on a Community Policy on Tourism". These identified five main areas of interest which reflected the Community's broader concerns with internal trade liberalisation and with evolving common policies: freedom of movement of tourists, working conditions in the industry, impact on transport policy, safeguarding the European heritage, and regional development (Williams and Shaw, 1994, 314–15).

Publication of the 1982 guidelines was followed by more than a decade of debate over European tourism policy which also became entwined with discussions over the single market and the Treaty on European Union. One of the landmarks in this period was the European Tourism Year 1990; although a minuscule programme costing no more than 5 million ECU and achieving a very low level of public recognition (Williams and Shaw, 1994, 315), this did raise awareness of tourism at the European policy-making level (Robinson, 1993, 15–16). One tangible effect of this higher profile was the EU's 1991 Action Plan for Tourism, which provided modest resources for a number of distinctive initiatives related to improving the quality of tourism, promoting European tourism to the rest of the world, and policy co-ordination. In common with some other sectoral initiatives, for example in respect of technology, these initiatives were based on public – private co-funding and on constructing international partnerships. This repositioning of tourism in the EU policy framework culminated in 1992 with the sector's recognition as a separate entity in the Treaty on European Union. This ensured continuing activity in the fields of environmental and consumer protection, as well as new activities in the areas of education, training, culture and transport. More significantly, Declaration 1 of Article 3 of the Treaty opened the possibility of tourism having its own "title", allowing the EU to implement specific tourism decrees and acts.

This proposal was subject to a consultative green paper in 1995, setting out alternative strategies for EU involvement and non-involvement, and it was one of the subsidiarity issues considered at the 1996–97 Inter-governmental Conference (IGC) held to review the Treaty.

Irrespective of any revision of the Treaty on European Union, the EU will continue to intervene in tourism through policy initiatives under its other titles. The European Regional Development Fund (ERDF) and the environment are particularly important in this respect (Williams and Shaw, 1994) and the former is considered here in relation to economic development. The ERDF has had two broad tourism objectives: the use of the sector as an instrument of regional economic development (Figure 10.12), and diversification to assist those regions which are excessively dependent on tourism or suffer from acute seasonality effects. Reflecting increased recognition of the sector's role, its importance within the ERDF has increased, so that a comparison of actual expenditure on tourism projects up to the mid-1980s, and of planned funding within the Community Support Framework for 1989–93, demonstrates both increased underpinning for the industry and changes in the geography of regional aid. Between 1975 and 1984 tourism accounted for only 1.4 per cent of all ERDF expenditure (Pearce, 1988), but by 1989–93 it was expected to absorb 5.5 per cent of the Fund's investment in Objective 1 regions, and 7.5 and 6.8 per cent in Objective 2 and Objective 5b areas. Tourism has become particularly important in ERDF programmes in southern Europe and the UK (Figure 10.13).

Despite the increased role of the EU in tourism intervention, this remains largely the preserve of national governments. Having said this, it must be recognised that the industry has achieved a far lower profile in national economic policies than have other economic sectors. There are a number of reasons for this, including the general neglect of the service sector, continuing strong growth in tourism which has belied the need for an effective national strategy, and the fragmented and competitive nature of the industry which has militated against effective pressure group activity within the state. However, as was emphasised earlier, the recurrent crisis of unemployment has

Figure 10.12 *Big Pit, Blaenavon, UK. With the closure of the South Wales coalfield, mining is now exploited as heritage. ERDF investment has helped turn the Big Pit into a visitor attraction offering an underground experience. (Photo: D A Pinder)*

contributed to giving tourism a higher policy profile in recent years.

National tourism policies continue to be dominated by economic concerns (Table 10.4), and two of the four top-rated objectives – according to interviews with staff in national tourism organisations – are to increase foreign tourists' expenditures and numbers. Most of the other more highly rated objectives also concern economic goals such as employment creation, and increasing the size of the industry. Not surprisingly, this is reflected in the relative importance that is attached to particular policy instruments, with provision of information via international offices being ranked first, and destination and joint marketing occupying two of the other four top positions. In general terms, marketing seems to be the principal role of the

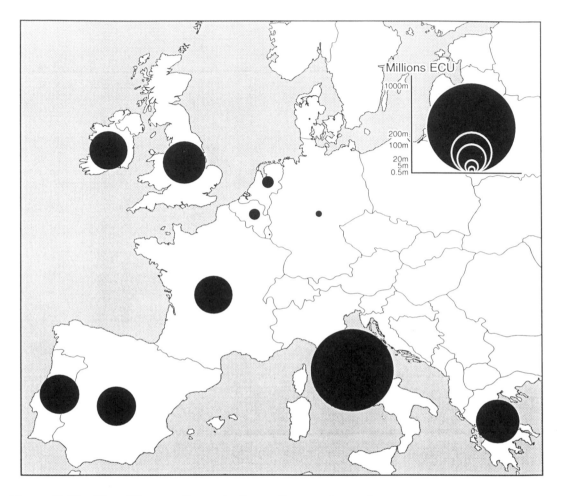

Figure 10.13 *Planned European Community Support Framework expenditure on tourism, 1989–93*

national tourism organisations, although national governments may also support the industry via other channels, such as investment in transport infrastructure. In keeping with the recent political emphasis on rolling back the frontiers of the state, relatively little weight is attached to direct state investment or subsidies to the private sector. In general, national tourism policies are most important in those countries where a relatively large proportion of GDP is accounted for by tourism, and where governments have a general interventionist rather than a *laissez-faire* approach to economic policy, as in Greece or Portugal (Akehurst *et al.*, 1993).

Finally, we turn to the role of tourism in local and regional development strategies, which have

mushroomed in the 1980s and 1990s. This growth has been based on three interlinked processes: the substitution of local for central government initiatives in response to the scaling down of (national) regional policies, the need to generate jobs in response to deindustrialisation, and the potential for exploiting the economic value of place differences in response to the growth of new forms of tourism consumption.

Local tourism development strategies have become commonplace throughout Europe's rural and urban spaces. For example, although the EU's LEADER programme was introduced to facilitate integrated rural development strategies rather than specifically to promote tourism, the latter was a leading sector in 71 of the first 271

Table 10.4   *National tourism policies*

Ranking of policy objectives (Max. value − 5)		Ranking of policy instruments (Max value = 5)	
Increase foreign expenditure	4.7	Provision of information via international office	3.8
Improve product quality	4.2	Destination marketing	3.6
Reduce seasonality	4.0	Research planning	3.4
Increase number of foreign visits	3.8	Joint marketing	3.3
Redistribute tourism	3.6	Provide printed information to foreign visitors	3.3
Increase industry size	3.5	Environmental improvement	3.1
Create employment	3.3	Training and employment policies	2.5
Provide expert advice	3.2	Disseminating good practice	2.5
Encourage joint initiatives	3.2	Provide printed information to domestic tourists	2.2
Improve training and professionalism	3.2	Capital grants to tourism enterprises	1.9
Promote environmental tourism	3.1	Regulating enterprises	1.7
Increase domestic expenditure	2.4	Development of tourism facilities	1.6
Regulate industry	2.0	Provision of information through local offices	1.5
Increase numbers of domestic tourists	1.8	Subsidies to tourism enterprises	1.2
Assist restructuring	1.7	Provision of soft loans	0.8
Diversification to tourism	1.5		

Note: Scores based on ratings given by staff of national tourism organisations.
Source: Akehurst *et al.* (1993, 40, 42).

local programmes (Cavaco, 1995, 145–6). Among the measures financed by the programme were training, capital grants and advice to accommodation and handicrafts ventures, as well as improvement of the value added of farm produce. Tourism has also become a mainstay of many urban development strategies, which have sought to capitalise on the transport links, the existing accommodation and commercial facilities, and the cultural resources of cities.

One very specific form of urban tourism promotion is the hosting of mega events. Carreras i Verdaguer (1995, 196) writes that "The end objective of the organisation of such mega-events is to reinforce local economic activities; so as to mark the position of each locality on the world map, in order to attract foreign capital, foreign investors and foreign visitors. Local strategies are designed to try and extend temporally what would otherwise be [their] purely momentary effects." There are many different types of mega event, but two of the more important are the summer Olympics and the Universal Exhibitions. Both are world events, and Europe has hosted a disproportionate share of them. For example,

London has twice been host to both the Olympic Games and to Universal Exhibitions, while Paris has been the venue for two Olympics and three Exhibitions. The Barcelona Olympics vividly illustrate the benefits of hosting such events; these Games attracted 10 500 athletes, 11 000 journalists and an estimated television audience of 3.5 billion. This is place marketing on the mega scale. At the other end of the spectrum there are, of course, far more modest yet well-established policies to develop tourism as part of local economic strategies in most European cities (Law, 1994).

Conclusions

This chapter has reviewed some of the major features of tourism and development in western Europe. It is clear that in the context of a general internationalisation of tourism activities, there has also been a major shift in consumption which can be characterised in terms of the relative stagnation of mass tourism and the growth of new forms of post-modernist products. This has meant not only that there is an increasingly complex map of tourism destinations, but also that the economic benefits of tourism are more evenly spread. While there are important national contingencies in this, there seem to be two major locational implications: the production of an increasingly diffuse map of economic impacts, which is also overlain by a *relative* shift of tourism destinations away from Europe's poorer and less-developed regions.

This pattern is likely to be modified by three important developments in the near future. First, the recent polarisation of incomes in western Europe is likely to lead to disproportionate increases in demand from the more wealthy segments of society; this in turn will probably add to the stagnation of mass tourism and to the demand for new tourist activities and destinations both within and outside Europe. Second, economic convergence within the EU may well contribute to the growth of tourism markets in southern Europe, and this may both reinforce domestic mass tourism destinations and generate new international tourism flows counter to the dominant north–south movements of the post-war period. Third, there will be the growing presence of central and eastern Europe on the wider European tourism scene (Hall, 1995). One of the immediate implications of this is that the opening up of new competing destinations is likely to go beyond today's urban tourism in cities such as Prague and Budapest, to include mass tourism products such as winter sports in the Tatra Mountains. In addition, rising and polarising incomes in central Europe may provide new sources of tourism demand which, at least for the medium term, may serve to bolster the uncertain demand for mass tourism.

Whatever the long-term implications of these trends, it is clear that the European and world tourism industries are experiencing an extended process of change. Further changes can be expected in consumption, in the organisation of tourism as more subsectors become internationalised, and in the role of tourism in economic policies. Moreover, pressures to expand the industry for economic purposes will be contested by those with growing concerns about the sector's cultural and environmental impacts. In the 1990s, possible "solutions" to these impacts have focused on the concept of "sustainable" tourism, but it is already clear that this approach

is not free of contradictions. Even when one is dealing with an economically buoyant activity, achieving balanced, socially and environmentally acceptable development may prove a challenging long-term goal.

References

Akehurst, G, Bland, N and Nevin, M (1993) Tourism policies in the European Community member states, *International Journal of Hospitality Management*, **12**, 33–66.

Ascher, F (1985) *Tourism Transnational Corporations and Cultural Identities*, UNESCO, Paris.

Balaz, V (1994) Tourism and regional development in the Slovak Republic, *European Urban and Regional Studies*, **1**, 171–7.

Balaz, V (1996) *International Tourism in the Economies of Central European Countries*, Discussion Paper No. 9, Tourism Research Group, University of Exeter, Exeter.

Barker, M L (1982) Traditional landscape and mass tourism in the Alps, *Geographical Review*, **72**, 395–415.

Beattie, R M (1991) Hospitality internationalisation: an empirical investigation, *International Journal of Contemporary Hospitality Management*, **3**, 14–20.

Bywater, M (1992) *The European Tour Operator Industry*, Economist Intelligence Unit, Special Report 2141, London.

Butler, R W (1980) The concept of tourist area cycle of evolution: implications for management of resources, *Canadian Geographer*, **14**, 5–12.

Carreras i Verdaguer, C (1995) Mega-events, local strategies and global tourist attractions, in A Montanari and A M Williams (eds) *European Tourism: regions, spaces and restructuring*, Wiley, Chichester, 193–206.

Carter, F, Hall, D R, Turnock, D and Williams, A M (1995) *Interpreting the Balkans*, Royal Geographical Society, Intelligence Paper No. 2, London.

Cavaco, C (1995) Rural tourism: the creation of new tourist spaces, in A Montanari and A M Williams (eds) *European Tourism: regions, spaces and restructuring*, Wiley, Chichester, 127–50.

Claval, P (1995) The impact of tourism on the restructuring of European space, in A Montanari and A M Williams (eds) *European Tourism: regions, spaces and restructuring*, Wiley, Chichester, 247–62.

Commission of the European Communities (1985) *Tourism in Europe*, DG XXIII, Commission of the European Communities, Brussels.

Commission of the European Communities (1986) *Les Européens et les Vacances*, General Directorate of Transport, European Omnibus Survey, Brussels.

Dunning, J H (1977) Trade, location of economic activity and the MNE: a search for an eclectic approach, in B Ohlin, P O Hesselborn and P M Wijkman (eds) *The International Allocation of Economic Activity*, Macmillan, London.

European Commission (1994) *Tourism Policy in the EU*, European Commission, London.

Featherstone M (1991) *Consumer Culture and Postmodernism*, Sage, London.

Financial Times (1995) Investors sing the theme song, *Financial Times*, 15, 16 August.

Go, F and Pine, R (1995) *Globalization Strategies in the Hotel Industry*, Routledge, London.

Hall, D (1991a) Evolutionary patterns of tourism development in Eastern Europe and the Soviet Union, in D Hall (ed) *Tourism and Economic Development in Eastern Europe and the Soviet Union*, Belhaven, London, 79–118.

Hall, D (1991b) Tourism opportunities in Eastern Europe and the Soviet Union, in D Hall (ed) *Tourism and Economic Development in Eastern Europe and the Soviet Union*, Belhaven, London, 29–48.

Hall, D (1995) Tourism change in Central and Eastern Europe, in A Montanari and A M Williams (eds) *European Tourism: regions, spaces and restructuring*, Wiley, Chichester, 221–43.

Hunt, J (1993) *Foreign Investment in Eastern Europe's Travel Industry*, Economist Intelligence Unit, London.

King, R (1995) Tourism, labour and international migration, in A Montanari and A M Williams (eds) *European Tourism: regions, spaces and restructuring*, Wiley, Chichester, 177–90.

Krippendorf, J (1987) *The Holiday Makers*, Heinemann, London.

Lash, S and Urry, J (1987) *The End of Organized Capitalism*, Polity, Cambridge.

Law, C (ed) (1994) *Urban Tourism*, Mansell, London.

Lury, C (1996) *Consumer Culture*, Polity, Cambridge.

McEniff, J (1993) Theme parks in Europe, *EIU Travel and Tourism Analyst*, **5**, 52–73.

Marchena Gómez, M J and Rebollo, F V (1995) Coastal areas: processes, typologies and prospects, in A Montanari and A M Williams (eds) *European Tourism: regions, spaces and restructuring*, Wiley, Chichester, 111–26.

Ministry of Economy of the Czech Republic (1996) *Tourism in the Czech Republic 1995*, Prague.

OECD (1995) *Tourism Policy and International Tourism in OECD Countries 1992–1993*, OECD, Paris.

Page, S (1995) *Urban Tourism*, Routledge, London.

Pearce, D G (1988) Tourism and regional development in the European Community, *Tourism Management*, **9**, 133–51.

Pearce, D G (1992) Tourism and the European Regional Development Fund: the first fourteen years, *Journal of Travel Research*, **30**, 44–51.

Pizam, A and Knowles, T (1994) The European hotel industry, in C P Cooper and A Lockwood (eds) *Progress in Tourism, Recreation and Hospitality Management*, Wiley, Chichester, 283–95.

Requena, J C and Aviles, P R (1993) O agriturismo, uma forma de turismo rural a considerar, *Leader Magazine*, **4**, 13–15.

Robinson, G (1993) Tourism and tourism policy in the European Community: an overview, *International Journal of Hospitality Management*, **12**, 7–20.

Shachar, A (1995) Metropolitan areas: economic globalisation and urban tourism, in A Montanari and A M Williams (eds) *European Tourism: regions, spaces and restructuring*, Wiley, Chichester, 151–60.

Shaw, G and Williams, A M (1990) Tourism and development, in D A Pinder (ed) *Western Europe: challenge and change*, Belhaven, London, 240–57.

Shaw, G and Williams, A M (1994) *Critical Issues in Tourism: a geographical perspective*, Blackwell, Oxford.

Slattery, P and Johnson, S M (1993) Hotel chains in Europe, *EIU Travel and Tourism Analyst*, **1**, 65–80.

Urry, J (1990) *The Tourist Gaze*, Sage, London.

Urry, J (1995) *Consuming Places*, Routledge, London.

Van den Berg, L, van der Borg, J and van der Meer, J (1994) *Urban Tourism*, EURICUR, Erasmus University, Rotterdam.

Williams, A M (1994) *The European Community: the contradictions of integration*, second edition, Blackwell, Oxford.

Williams, A M (1995) Capital and the transnationalisation of tourism, in A Montanari and A M Williams (eds) *European Tourism: regions, spaces and restructuring*, Wiley, Chichester, 163–76.

Williams, A M (1996) Mass tourism and international tour companies, in M Barke, J Towner and M T Newton (eds) *Tourism in Spain: critical issues*, CAB International, Wallingford, 119–35.

Williams, A M (1997) Tourism and uneven development in the Mediterranean, in R King, L Proudfoot and B Smith (eds) *The Mediterranean: environment and society*, Edward Arnold, London, 208–26.

Williams, A M and Montanari, A (1995) Introduction: tourism and restructuring in Europe, in A Montanari and A M Williams (eds) *European Tourism: regions, spaces and restructuring*, Wiley, Chichester, 1–16.

Williams, A M and Shaw G (1990) Tourism and regional economic development: perspectives on western Europe, in S Hardy, T Hart and T Shaw (eds) *The Role of Tourism in the Urban and Regional Economy*, Regional Studies Association, 1–10.

Williams, A M and Shaw, G (1994) Tourism: opportunities, challenges and contradictions in the EC, in M Blackwell and A M Williams (eds) *The European Challenge: geography, development and the European Community*, Oxford University Press, Oxford, 301–20.

Williams, A M and Shaw, G (1995) Tourism and regional development: polarization and new forms of production in the UK, *Tijdschrift voor Economische en Sociale Geografie*, **86**, 50–63.

World Tourism Organisation (1994) *Compendium of Tourism Statistics*, World Tourism Organisation, Madrid.

World Travel and Tourism Council (1995) *Travel and Tourism: a new economic perspective*, World Travel and Tourism Council, Brussels.

Zimmermann, F M (1995) The Alpine region: regional restructuring opportunities and constraints in a fragile environment, in A Montanari and A M Williams (eds) *European Tourism: regions, spaces and restructuring*, Wiley, Chichester, 19–40.

11
Uneven development in Europe

Michael Dunford and Adrian Smith
School of European Studies and School of Social Sciences, University Sussex, UK

Introduction

As the twentieth century comes to an end, the character of Europe is changing dramatically. At its heart lie two interconnected geopolitical realities: the European Union (EU) and a Greater Germany. The EU is a single market in the making in which legislative power will increasingly lie in the hands of intergovernmental organisations. Geographically it is centred on a core of major international cities and advanced city regions, most of which lie along a vital axis (Figure 11.1). This axis extends from Greater London through the Rhinelands in the western half of Germany to northern Italy. Near this corridor are two major foci: in the north-west lie the historic capitals of Europe's major colonial powers (Paris, London and Randstad-Holland); in the south-east are located a number of major German, Swiss and Italian cities (Stuttgart, Munich, Zurich, Milan, Turin and Bologna) whose faster recent economic growth has pulled the centre of gravity of the axis to the south-east. The new Germany is a more recent development that stems from German unification and from Germany's re-establishment of economic and political ties with areas in eastern and central Europe (ECE). This geopolitical and economic influence has expanded after the collapse of Communism; the break-up of the Soviet Union and its sphere of influence carved out at German expense at the end of the Second World War; the division of Czechoslovakia; and the German-sponsored secession of Slovenia, Croatia and Bosnia-Hercegovina from the former Yugoslavia.

These changes in the geopolitical map of Europe coincide with a working out of powerful forces leading towards much greater international economic interdependence and a significant reconfiguration of the map of global development. These new features of the international order are primarily a result of economic expansion in Japan and East Asia, and the emergence of this region as a third major trading bloc alongside Europe and North America (see Chapter 3). Greater interdependence and the challenge of East Asian industrialisation have been stimuli to a redefinition of modes of governance. In Europe greater economic and political integration is a part of this redefinition, which is not just a consequence but also a cause of economic globalisation. At a fundamental level the European project is aimed at reinforcing the economic potential of Europe and at creating a platform for the internationalisation of European companies. The creation of an internal market, and the moves towards a single currency, are designed to reduce costs to European companies and to produce scale economies allowing European firms to compete more

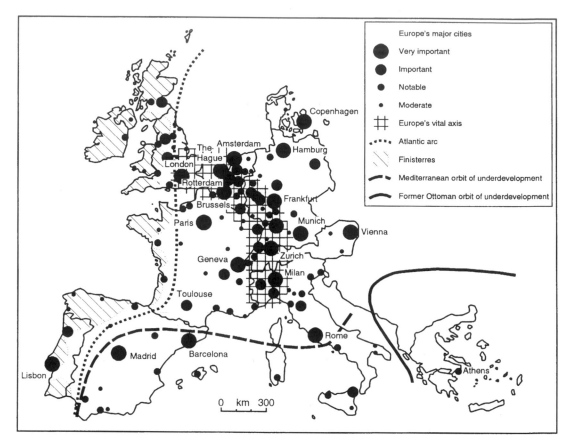

Figure 11.1 *Europe's vital axis*

effectively in global markets. The chosen model of integration is that of a liberal market in which deregulation, competition and privatisation are implemented in order to open up opportunities for profitable private investment and to increase European competitiveness.

Similarly, since 1989 the economies of ECE have witnessed the imposition of various liberal market programmes aiming to secure a transition to capitalism and away from centrally planned modes of governance. These programmes, while having distinct characteristics in each economy, focus on the privatisation of state property, the deregulation of economic activity and the encouragement of new forms of entrepreneurship through government support programmes. While national governments in the region have been the main agents of change, they have been subject to considerable pressure from international organisations such as the World Bank and the

International Monetary Fund (IMF), which have placed "conditionality" on credit and support in a similar manner to the structural adjustment programmes implemented in the Third World.

The dominance of a liberal model of integration goes hand in hand with a transformation of the socio-economic character of Europe: in the West the social settlement in the mixed and managed economies and societies that was established after the Second World War, and which underpinned the unparalleled increases in prosperity of the post-war "golden age", is changing in the face of the liberal challenge. A consequence is the return of mass unemployment, which has placed increasing strains on the Welfare State, as has the challenge of East Asian industrialisation. In the East the former Communist economies are undergoing a rapid transition to capitalist market economies and representative democratic politics which have similarly produced social dislocation.

Finally in both West and East new information and communications technologies are leading to profound changes in the organisation of work, travel and consumption through increasing mobility and the interaction of goods, money and people in a context of what Harvey (1989) has called "time-space compression".

It is in these new conditions of globalisation and liberal market integration, economic and political transition, and technological change that the positions of places in wider divisions of labour are changing. At the centre of this change are processes of competition between localities. Competition is a contest between rivals whose outcome depends on the prevailing set of rules and on the strengths and weaknesses of the rivals who take part. Not all places and not all people are equally able to compete. A consequence of any competitive struggle is therefore the existence of winners and losers, though in the EU various measures aimed at increasing social cohesion[1] through the Structural and Cohesion Funds help check the negative consequences of integration and competition and assist places that are weak to adapt (European Commission, 1995; Bachtler and Michie, 1994. See also Chapter 13). While such cohesion programmes have not been a part of the attempt to reduce widening regional and social differences in ECE after 1989, there has been an attempt to implement Western-style regional policies with the help of the EU's main assistance programme – PHARE.

The aim of this chapter is to outline and explain some of the unevenness of this adaptation of places to the changing economic and political order. First, it outlines the scale of the contemporary disparities in Europe and its immediate neighbours, and indicates how these disparities have evolved. It also shows that disparities and their evolution can be divided into two elements: one that depends on differential trends in productivity and another that reflects differences in the employment rate or in the capacity of economies to mobilise their human potential. Second, some of the mechanisms that explain these disparities, and in particular that illuminate the contrasting performance of regional economies, are indicated. Attention is paid initially to determinants of the differential dynamics of the productive and regulatory orders in global cities,

industrial districts and old industrial areas in different parts of Europe,[2] and then to the structure and organisation of the market for labour. In the conclusion we argue that the trajectories of regional and urban economies reflect not just their structures and strategies, but also the nature of the "rules of the game" which are set by the prevailing modes of globalisation and integration. What must also be noted is that our focus on the determination and extent of regional economic disparities in Europe means that we do not consider the complex set of policies developed to attempt to deal with these inequalities. (However, for introductions to these issues see Barnes and Barnes (1995) for western Europe and Jessop (1995) and Smith (1997) in the context of eastern Europe. See also Chapter 13.)

The Map of Geographical Inequality in Contemporary Europe and its Neighbours

At present there are marked differences in levels of development and the economic performance of regional and urban economies. Some regions have been much more successful than others. The aims of this section are to identify some of the winners and losers of the late 1970s, 1980s and early 1990s, and to identify some of the trends in regional inequality since the early 1960s and their relation to economic performance.

Differential development in the new Europe and its neighbours

Europe and the zones that border it are at present divided into a series of nation states which differ significantly in the size and strength of their economies. These nations are themselves made up of mosaics of cities and regions with different resource endowments, productive structures and economic capacities. If economic potential is measured not in terms of the size of economies, but of the value of the goods and services produced per inhabitant, a clear hierarchy emerges.

Figure 11.2 records per capita gross national product (GNP) in 1993 for groups of European countries and their neighbours. The data provide

205

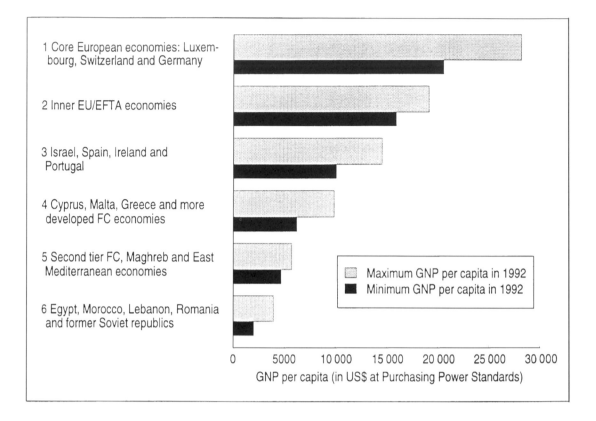

1 Luxembourg, Switzerland, Germany

2 France, Denmark, Austria, Belgium, Norway, Italy, Sweden, Netherlands, Iceland, United Kingdom, Finland

3 Israel, Spain, Ireland, Portugal

4 Cyprus, Malta, Greece, Czech Republic, Belarus, Estonia, Russian Federation

5 Algeria, Hungary, Slovakia, Turkey, Bulgaria, Tunisia, Ukraine, Syria, Poland, Kazakhstan, Latvia, Jordan

6 Turkmenistan, Moldova, Lithuania, Egypt, Morocco, Kyrgyzstan, Lebanon, Romania, Azerbaijan, Uzbekistan, Armenia, Georgia, Tajikistan

Figure 11.2 *Orbits of development and underdevelopment in Europe and its neighbours*

a hierarchical relief "map" of economic development. In rank order, the group at the top of this hierarchy comprises Luxembourg, Switzerland, Denmark and Norway, with 1993 per capita GNP of US$25 960–US$37 100. Next comes a cluster of EU and EFTA countries with figures of US$18 050–US$24 900. Around these cores lie zones made up of countries that are either EU members or potential members who are already part of EFTA. First there are four southern and western peripheral EU member states, plus Israel, Malta and Cyprus, the last two being Mediterranean economies seeking to join the EU. Per capita GNP for this group ranges between US$7 480 and US$13 920. What we may also note about them is that these countries belong to wider areas of relative underdevelopment. The Republic of Ireland and Portugal are parts of a maritime Atlantic arc of regional and national economies, stretching from the Shetlands to Gibraltar, with low population densities, high rates of unemployment, and levels of GDP per head that are at best around the EU average and at worst just over half of it. Similarly, the least-developed regions of Spain are part of a zone of Mediterranean regional economies where (with the exceptions of Catalonia, the French Midi and northern Italy) the share of income from low-productivity agricultural sectors is large, unemployment is high, and incomes per head are less than 75 per cent of the EU average.

Meanwhile, a second arc comprises Turkey and a number of more developed former Communist countries, with per capita GNP figures between US$1970 and US$3520. In the former Communist countries included in this group, historical patterns of backwardness have re-emerged on the pan-European stage indicating that – while the Communist experience transformed economic and social life in profound ways, and especially through industrialisation – there was general failure to catch up with developments in western Europe.[3] Finally, beyond this arc lies a further tier encompassing several Arab Mediterranean countries, Bulgaria, Romania, some former Soviet republics and Albania. GNP per head here ranged between US$340 and US$1770 in 1993, and in some countries there has been profound economic collapse and extreme social marginalisation.

As distance increases from the core areas of Europe, therefore, economic wealth declines quite rapidly, with a particularly sharp divide separating the EU from (1) the semi-developed countries of the Preferential Interest Agreement that stretch around the southern rim of the Mediterranean from Morocco to Turkey and (2) the less-developed ECE countries and former Soviet republics. In many of the countries to the south a number of key structural problems exist. Jobs are in short supply, the land cannot feed its inhabitants, water is scarce, debt and external dependence are widespread, there are strong propensities for emigration and uncontrolled urbanisation, frontiers are contested and governments face challenges from Islamic movements. Together these signal the failure of earlier strategies of economic and social modernisation. In several of the former Communist countries economic collapse has gone hand in hand with the rise of nationalism. All of them have long histories of relative underdevelopment, whether as areas in which a second serfdom prevailed or as

former Ottoman countries (see Chapter 1). There were, however, some areas of early industrial development in the extraordinary patchwork quilt of economies and nations that made up the Austro-Hungarian Empire, in the eastern half of Germany and in the Russian Empire. After the rise of Communism, industrialisation at first accelerated – as is reflected in the fact that the Soviet Union closed the development gap with the United States quite significantly in the period up to 1973 (Table 11.1). No country, however, made a successful transition from extensive to intensive growth and, as with most other less-developed nations, none in the end closed the gap between themselves and the advanced capitalist world.[4] Since 1989 the transition to various forms of market capitalism has seen dramatic falls in output, a slump in industrial production, job losses, a sharp rise in joblessness – especially among women and in less-developed areas – social polarisation, crime and, in extreme cases, tragic ethnic and nationalist conflicts. The IMF, for example, suggested that output fell by 3.6 per cent in 1990, by 10.1 per cent in 1991 and by 15.5 per cent in 1992 (IMF, 1992, 129, 138).

The experience of "transition" after five years or so has been one of economic collapse, rationalisation, an onslaught on labour and social and political disorientation, with collapsing birth rates and increasing death rates suggesting a deep-seated social and psychological crisis (Ellman, 1994). The results include profound increases in poverty and inequality. Milanovic (1994), for example, argues that poverty now affects some 58 million people in ECE, or 18 per cent of the region's population. Real wages have dropped dramatically throughout the region and, alongside increased inequality, there has been a rise in homelessness, declining health levels and other social problems associated with polarisation. Furthermore, the emergence of poverty and inequality has been a breeding ground for two forms of activity. The first is the increased reliance of household survival strategies (Pirainen, 1994) on activities such as the exchange of household production (food and other basic items) between friends and in networks established in the workplace, leading to a burgeoning of the informal economy. The second is the rise of illegal, semi-legal and criminal activities embodied in the

Table 11.1 *Comparative economic development: GDP per head, 1820–1992 (1990 prices; US = 100)*

	1820	1870	1900	1913	1950	1973	1992	GDP per head in 1992 in 1990 US$
Austria	101	76	71	66	39	68	80	17 160
Belgium	100	107	89	78	56	72	80	17 165
Denmark	95	78	71	71	70	81	85	18 293
Finland	59	45	40	39	43	65	68	14 646
France	95	76	70	65	55	78	83	17 959
Germany	86	78	77	72	45	79	90	19 351
Italy	85	60	43	47	36	63	75	16 229
Netherlands	121	107	86	74	61	77	78	16 898
Norway	78	53	43	43	52	62	81	17 543
Sweden	93	68	63	58	70	81	79	16 927
Switzerland		88	86	79	93	108	98	21 036
United Kingdom	136	133	112	95	72	72	73	15 738
United States	100	100	100	100	100	100	100	21 558
Greece				31	20	47	48	10 314
Ireland	74	72	61	51	37	42	54	11 711
Portugal		44	34	26	22	46	52	11 130
Spain	83	56	50	42	25	50	58	12 498
Turkey				18	14	16	21	4 422
Bulgaria				28	17	32	19	4 054
Czechoslovakia	66	47	42	39	37	42	32	6 845
Hungary	0	52	41	40	26	34	26	5 638
Poland					26	32	22	4 726
Romania					12	21	12	2 565
USSR	58	42	30	28	30	36	22	4 671
Yugoslavia				19	16	26	18	3 887
7 Latin American countries		32	32	33	36	30	28	5 949
of which								
Argentina		53	67	72	52	48	35	7 616
Brazil	52	30	17	16	17	24	22	4 637
Mexico	59	29	28	28	22	25	24	5 112
11 Asian countries	47	26	19	16	9	15	25	5 294
of which								
Japan	55	30	28	25	20	66	90	19 425
South Korea			21	18	9	17	46	10 010
10 African countries					9	8	6	1 331
of which								
Egypt			12	10	5	6	9	1 927
Morocco					17	10	11	2 327

Source: Based on Maddison (1995).

so-called East European "Mafia" (Varesse, 1994).

In the case of Yugoslavia relatively fast economic growth occurred in the 1970s. In 1980, however, there was a sharp reversal with rapid relative economic decline leading finally to violent national disintegration and civil war. As Woodward (1995, 6) argued, "a critical element of the failure was economic decline caused largely by a programme intended to resolve a foreign debt crisis. More than a decade of austerity and declining living standards corroded the social fabric and the rights and securities that individuals and families had come to rely on." Austerity measures designed by Western lending institutions exacerbated inter-republican rivalries and animosities. The result was an increase in social tension through the deprivation and desperation the programmes created, which in turn generated a layer of unemployed or underemployed angry and frustrated young men of war-making age who were easily mobilised by nationalist ideologues.

Winners and losers: indicators of regional performance over time

Data on long-term trends in territorial inequality in the EU suggest that disparities in national and regional GDP per head and in the distribution of income – all of which diminished in much of the

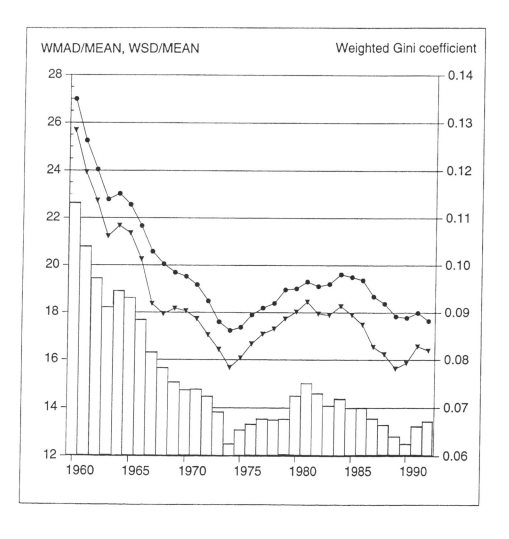

Figure 11.3 *National disparities in per capita GDP of EU member states at current market prices (EC12=100)*

1960s and early 1970s – have subsequently increased. Figure 11.3, for example, shows several indicators of inequalities in GDP per inhabitant in the first 12 member states. The graph shows strong convergence until the mid-1970s, giving way to divergence up to the early to mid-1980s, depending on the indicator used. From the mid-1980s until 1990 member states again converged, yet once again there there was an upturn in most measures of inequality in the 1990s. This reversal almost returned disparities to the 1974 levels, so that between the early 1970s and the early 1990s there was no overall improvement.

Similar trends towards convergence and divergence can be seen in ECE, although their causes are different. Zaniewski's (1992) analysis of economic and social disparities in ECE has shown that after the Second World War there was a significant reduction in the economic differences between regions. Similarly, Smith (1996) has argued that Slovakia saw convergence with the western Czech lands (today the Czech Republic) as the "forced industrialisation" of backward rural peripheries transformed economic and social life. However, since 1989 the implementation of liberal marketisation programmes has resulted in the emergence of a significant shift towards regional fragmentation. The competitive conditions imposed as part of the rules of a liberalisation game mean that regions are increasingly competing for access to scarce investment and support. The main result has been that some regions are beginning to emerge as highly competitive, often as a result of the short-run impacts of foreign direct investment (FDI), while others that were often "late industrialised" have suffered from deindustrialisation and local economic collapse (Smith, 1995).

Regional disparities in Europe

To identify some of the variations in resource endowments, productive capabilities and development at a finer geographical scale, 1992 data from the REGIO database for NUTS II regions can be used for the European Union.[5] What do these data show? In spite of recent revisions in the methods used to estimate regional and national GDP for the REGIO database, which resulted in increases

in Greek, Portuguese and Irish per capita GDP (as well as increases for Luxembourg), and in spite of the fact that the GDP of the unified Germany in 1991 was 14 per cent less than for West Germany, disparities remain large. The latest purchasing power estimates of regional per capita GDP are plotted in Figure 11.4 for 15 member states ranked from left to right according to their national per capita GDP. Most countries had strong inter-regional contrasts, and even in those with less striking disparities the differences were not negligible. In Spain, for example, the best region scored slightly above the EU average, but the worst was only half the average. Moreover, the countries where inter-regional contrasts were least marked were also generally those with national averages lagging behind the remainder of the EU. Summarising this more quantitatively, GDP per head in the NUTS II regions varied from 196 to 37 per cent of the EU average. The 10 least-developed regions had average incomes which were about one-quarter of those of the 10 most advanced regions.[6] And almost a quarter of regions recorded indices below 75 per cent of the EU average.

While a database of comparable quality does not exist for the countries of ECE, there are recently published data on a number of national economies which indicate significant regional differentiation. Recent data for Slovakia, for example, show that, in terms of purchasing power parity, per capita GDP dropped from 32.4 per cent of the US level in 1987 to 24.3 per cent in 1992 (World Bank, 1994). Data for regional GDP suggest that there is significant regional variation from these national figures (Figure 11.5). For example, the poorest region – the rural hinterland of Košice (Košice-vidiek) – recorded a per capita GDP of only US$631, 31 per cent of the national average. In contrast the wealthiest region, Bratislava, achieved US$8123, about four times the average. Between these two extremes, only four regions had above-average figures, whereas 18 areas recorded between half and a quarter of the average. These latter areas are regions where industrial restructuring has had a generally negative impact upon economic life, and similar forms of uneven development are evident in most other post-Communist economies (Nemes Nagy, 1994; Csefalvay, 1994; Gorzelak, 1996).

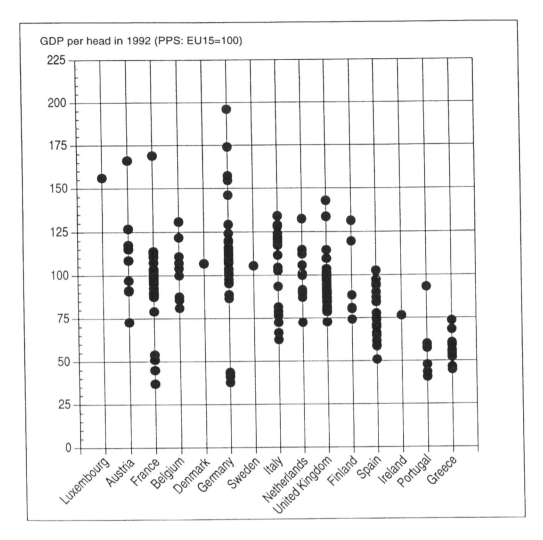

GDP per head in 1992 (PPS: EU15=100)

Figure 11.4   *Per capita GDP variations for NUTS II regions, 1992*

These figures indicate that any further enlargement of the EU to include ECE countries will probably see a significant increase in disparities. The January 1996 expansion saw the accession of three member states (Austria, Finland and Sweden) whose per capita GDP is close to the EU average. However, the new candidates for membership include not just Cyprus and Malta, but also Poland with a population of 38.2 million people and a per capita GDP of 36.4 per cent of the EU average; Hungary with 10.6 million and 40.5 per cent; the Czech Republic with 10.3 million and 45.7 per cent; the Slovak Republic with 5.2 million and 34 per cent; Romania with 23 million and 23.7 per cent; and Bulgaria with 9 million and 32.9 per cent. Short of a change in EU regulations and a considerable strengthening of the Structural and Cohesion Funds, further enlargement will therefore have far-reaching consequences for populations in areas currently benefiting from these important sources of regional assistance. In particular the 132 million people who reside in the most assisted Objective 1 areas,[7] and the 63 million inhabitants of the four Cohesion countries (Greece, Portugal, Spain and the Republic of Ireland), may experience a significant decline in regional aid as enlargement is likely to lead to a descheduling of a substantial number of assisted

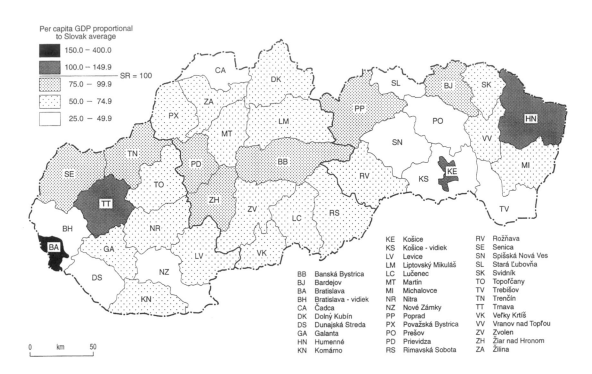

Per capita GDP proportional
to Slovak average

150.0 – 400.0
100.0 – 149.9
75.0 – 99.9   SR = 100
50.0 – 74.9
25.0 – 49.9

BB	Banská Bystrica	LC	Lučenec	RV	Rožňava
BJ	Bardejov	MT	Martin	SE	Senica
BA	Bratislava	MI	Michalovce	SN	Spišská Nová Ves
BH	Bratislava - vidiek	NR	Nitra	SL	Stará Ľubovňa
CA	Čadca	NZ	Nové Zámky	SK	Svidník
DK	Dolný Kubín	PP	Poprad	TO	Topoľčany
DS	Dunajská Streda	PX	Považská Bystrica	TV	Trebišov
GA	Galanta	PO	Prešov	TN	Trenčín
HN	Humenné	PD	Prievidza	TT	Trnava
KN	Komárno	RS	Rimavská Sobota	VK	Veľký Krtíš
KE	Košice			VV	Vranov nad Topľou
KS	Košice - vidiek			ZV	Zvolen
LV	Levice			ZH	Žiar nad Hronom
LM	Liptovský Mikuláš			ZA	Žilina

0   km   50

Figure 11.5 *Inequality in Slovakia: per capita GDP, 1993. (Source: Statistical Office of the Slovak Republic)*

areas and the identification of new priorities for Cohesion policies. Many Objective 1 areas, for example, will no longer qualify for this status as they will lie above the critical borderline, 75 per cent of EU per capita GDP. Similarly there will be a change in the relative position of the Cohesion countries which at present have a per capita GDP equal to 72.8 per cent of the EU average. The existence of problems of this kind, and the extent of the East–West disparities, have led to calls for a "tiered" implementation of an easterly expansion of the EU, enabling the former Communist countries to be part of a greater Europe, without being eligible for regional assistance from existing programmes (Smith *et al.*, 1996).

Towards an Explanatory Framework: (1) Supply-side Approaches

To help identify the causes of disparities, differentials in development can be divided into two elements: productivity differences and variations in the employment rate (the percentage of the population in employment) (Dunford,

1996). More formally

$$\frac{\text{Gross Domestic Product}}{\text{Resident Population}}$$

$$\equiv \frac{\text{Gross Domestic Product}}{\text{Employed Population}}$$

$$\times \frac{\text{Employed Population}}{\text{Resident Population}}$$

Differences in productivity reflect discrepancies in physical productivity, prices and earnings. These differences may result from variations within a single sector or in sectoral/functional specialisation. Differences in the employment rate (defined as the share of the population in employment) reflect variations in the capacity of an economic system to mobilise its human potential. In this section we focus on factors underlying high and low productivity in European regions; in the next we look at the question of the use of an area's human potential.

Much of the recent geographical literature on the dynamics of cities and regions has focused on two sets of areas that are thought to have won in the 1980s and 1990s as a result of being highly productive. The first and most studied group comprises strong industrial economies and industrial districts in Switzerland, Germany and northern Italy. The second is made up of global cities. To these groups it is important to add a number of areas that have had quite high rates of growth, including regions where expansion was closely related to large inflows of inward investment, areas (other than global cities) whose growth is related to increases in output and employment in services, and localities that have developed around tourist-related activities.

To explain the relative success of different areas, most attention is paid to supply-side factors such as the transformation of the productive system, the creation of a framework for co-operative industrial relations, the development of transport and telecommunications infrastructures, the establishment of synergies between public research and industry, the implementation of strategies for technology transfer and investment in education and skills.

Global cities and metropolitan growth

Empirical research on comparative growth suggests that large cities and, in particular, some global cities (of which the main European examples are Greater London and Paris) have significantly reinforced their position in economic league tables. At present metropolises have two significant economic advantages. First, large cities are major concentrations of highly qualified people. Today the importance of this factor is reinforced as the geography of the job market for executives with technical skills has become a major locational factor. As Daniels emphasises in Chapter 7, the increased importance of these skills is a result of the growth of skilled, white-collar jobs in research and development, management and marketing and a corresponding decline in direct production workers. Second, major cities gain because strategies of economic integration, and the development of networks, favour locations that are on key computer and telecommunications networks and are near major road, (high-speed) rail and air transport infrastructures. What results is a polarisation of high-level activities in well-resourced nodes with high levels of connectivity and connectedness, and an increase in the relative rental values of metropolitan properties and land. The polarisation of activities further creates the economic potential required to justify additional improvements in infrastructures.

The French case is a good example of these phenomena. In France the location of advanced sectors, high-status occupations, command functions and modern infrastructures reinforces the growth of a metropolis-network headed by Paris (Table 11.2). In the late 1980s, with just over 18 per cent of the French population (10 million people), the Paris *Zone de Peuplement Industriel et Urbain* (ZPIU) accounted for over 50 per cent of all of the "abstract functions" and high-tech jobs in France (Beckouche, 1991). At the same time low-skilled jobs were strongly under-represented, thereby exacerbating the problems of unemployment of those with few skills. The Paris ZPIU did not just specialise in sectors with a large share of skilled workers. Within each group of industries it accounted for a high proportion of jobs in research and marketing, and much lower proportions of production jobs. The car sector epitomises the contrast: it is, as Beckouche (1991) points out, at one and the same time a high-technology sector concentrated in Paris and a sector that depends on price-competitiveness and the employment of low-paid direct production workers located in the provinces.

In the western part of Germany there is a lesser — but none the less high — degree of centralisation of management and control functions in major cities. In the UK the marked dominance of Greater London rests to a large extent on its role as a centre for high-status jobs and the provision of financial and producer services. While this metropolis provides 15 per cent of the country's total GDP, it generates almost 30 per cent of financial and business service output, a figure which rises to nearly 60 per cent for London plus the remainder of the south-east. This bias is of considerable significance for a country in which these types of activity account for around 35 per cent of total GDP, particularly as the growth of global cities and their metropolitan hinterlands is closely

Table 11.2 *The share of the Paris ZPIU in national industrial employment by sectors and functions of production (%)*

Sector*	Design and research	Sales and marketing	Administration and management	Various services	Storage and transport	Manufacture	All sectors
Technicien sectors							
T1	54	66	58	48	32	29	44.6
T2	31	56	37	28	18	14	24.0
Vehicles	49	66	54	37	32	24	30.4
Non-*technicien* sectors							
Q1	15	38	22	19	11	12	14.4
Q2	14	31	20	6	6	5	8.0
Unskilled sectors							
S1	10	34	20	12	10	8	10.9
S2	13	27	18	16	8	6	8.8
Construction	37	28	34	30	15	22	23.3

* Industrial sectors were classified on the basis of the share of very skilled jobs (engineers, executives and technicians) into a number of groups. The T1 industries, with a high proportion of high-skilled *techniciens*, include defence electronics, telecommunications, computers, automation equipment, aerospace and high-power electrical equipment. The T2 group includes basic chemicals, parachemicals, machine tools, industrial equipment, precision instruments and equipment, and consumer electronics. The Q activities are still characterised by the presence of a large share of skilled manual workers: iron and steel, motor and commercial vehicles, rail equipment, Linotype printing, general engineering and metal manufacturing. The S activities have a high proportion of unskilled workers: food processing, textiles, leather goods, shoes and furniture. The construction of private vehicles and vehicle equipment forms a separate class.
Source: Beckouche (1991).

related to the expansion of services. In the UK's case, this was the only sector in which employment increased between 1981 and 1991. Moreover, the 10 travel to work areas (TTWAs) with the greatest employment growth were almost all near Greater London, and in these areas 24 per cent of the expansion came from distribution, 43 per cent from financial services and 23 per cent from other services. What is also significant is that this structural shift was linked with a dramatic change in the gender composition of employment and in the role of part-time work. While 1.3 million men lost full-time jobs in the country as a whole, 71 per cent of the new opportunities were part-time, while 83 per cent were taken up by women.

While the metropolitan economies of ECE have not achieved global city status, there are clear tendencies in this direction, and these tendencies for metropolitan markets to grow, and for large urban economies to expand, help explain the regional divergence discussed earlier. Much of the economic strength of these metropolitan regions (often capital city regions) is derived, as in the UK, from the existence of financial and control functions. The most dynamic financial

markets are in Budapest, Prague and Warsaw (Hutton *et al.*, 1994). For example, in 1994 the Budapest, Prague and Warsaw stock markets closed the year, respectively, some 29, 96 and 787 per cent higher than the year before (Commission of the European Communities, 1994).[8] Capital market development has been associated with the growth of a host of financial and producer services, suggesting the emergence of metropolitan areas potentially similar to the global cities of the "advanced" capitalist world. Furthermore, the increasing synchronisation of trading between capital markets in the Visegrad countries has led to a rapid "speed up" in capital flows, increasing the volatility of these markets which may undermine any attempt to construct long-term sustainability – a kind of regionalised compression of space and time (Harvey, 1989).

A further aspect to metropolitan dominance in ECE is the role of large urban areas in attracting much sought-after foreign capital. Prague, Bratislava, Budapest and Warsaw all dominate the geographical distribution of FDI in their respective countries. Some 60 per cent of Slovakia's total investment is concentrated in

Bratislava, and around one-half of Hungary's in Budapest. Finally, in both Slovakia and the Czech Republic, where privatisation of state industries has been led by a coupon method, control over company shares is dominated by investment privatisation funds. Most of these are concentrated in the capitals of Bratislava and Prague and are closely linked to major national banks (Kenway and Klvačová 1996), thereby consolidating the control of these two capitals over their respective national economies.

Industrial districts

The industrial district model was inspired by Alfred Marshall's idea that geographical proximity and sectoral specialisation could create a particular economic advantage for certain regions. In areas where there is a thick local texture of interdependencies between small and medium-sized enterprises (SMEs) and a local community, a concentrated local experience in the design and production of specific commodities, and a strong dynamic of localised innovation and learning by doing, external and agglomeration economies exist at the level of the district. These economies reduce transaction costs (especially in the presence of mutual knowledge and trust), are said to facilitate the accumulation of skills and know-how (what Marshall called the "industrial atmosphere") and stimulate the innovation process at the individual and collective level. SMEs will, however, only maximise the use of their specialised means of production if the production process is decomposed and divided among the system's firms. Effective specialisation therefore requires each firm to specialise in one or more phases of the production process. In practice, some firms sell their products directly on the market, while others are involved in the production of the component parts of a product. Moreover, the same firm can be a sub-supplier at one time, and a final seller at another. As a result, exchange relations and hierarchical relations are interwoven, and competition and co-operation coexist.

As Watts has highlighted in Chapter 5, in the 1980s there was a renewal of interest in industrial districts. Two factors explain this increase in attention. First, there was an observed economic dynamism in such areas in the Third Italy and in a range of other places in Europe (including parts of Germany,[9] Switzerland, Denmark and France). Second, these areas became identified as exemplars of a new model of flexible specialisation which Piore and Sabel (1984) thought offered a way out of the crisis of the Fordist model (defined as mass production of standardised goods with dedicated machines and unskilled workers) that had dominated post-war western European industrial growth.

While industrial districts did provide a basis for regional economic expansion in the 1970s and 1980s, the small-firm industrial district and flexible specialisation models are presently coming under increasing criticism. A large number of small-firm districts currently face major problems of adjustment to shifts in wider market and production conditions. The models are also criticised for their failure to recognise that the districts might themselves change, and that their relative success was a result of particular external conditions (Harrison, 1994). Any shift towards craft production of design-intensive goods for niche markets will support fewer firms. Major investments in research and development and in expensive productivity-increasing technologies are required, as are greater cost-competitiveness, and greater quality and security of supplies, yet large investments are beyond the scope of many independent SMEs. A model centred on small and medium-sized family firms with an extensive local social division of labour is perhaps less viable than it was. Greater specialisation, the development of collective services and greater co-operation perhaps offer the districts a way forward, though in some districts there is evidence of financial centralisation and greater vertical integration. Sometimes successful firms evolve into leaders that flex their economic muscle and impose hierarchical rules, due to the take-over of leading firms by large financial groups or as a result of intensified competition. In the case of the woollen textile district of Prato, for example, performance declined as customers of Prato firms sought more diversified output and shorter delivery times, as large competitors recovered, as large enterprises increased sourcing from low-wage countries and as cheap imports grew.

What is ironic about these criticisms of small-firm industrial districts is that the model has been used as a basis for the practice of local economic restructuring in ECE after 1989. Arguments centred on the experiences of the Third Italy and other industrial districts in western Europe have been used explicitly as ways of moving away from the dominance of "Fordist" production and towards locally integrated, industrial agglomerations. These arguments have been put particularly forcefully because of the dominance of large firms in the industrial economies of ECE (Newbery and Kattuman, 1992), and in response to the view that the slowdown and crisis of state socialist economies reflected their inability to increase the flexibility, or reduce the size, of production units. The break-up of the large combines, and the development of new entrepreneurial small enterprises, were accordingly seen as the basis for an effective transition to capitalism (Bianchi, 1992; Murray, 1992).

These ideas have had an important impact on regional development policies. European Union enterprise support programmes such as the PHARE SME programme have stressed the use of SMEs in the reconstruction of regional economies. In Slovakia, as elsewhere in ECE, one of the central components of economic policy – and the focus of a large proportion of foreign economic assistance – has been the attempt to create a base of new, private SMEs. The creation of a small-scale entrepreneurial economy is seen as a way of counterbalancing the dominance of large enterprises, diversifying local economies by providing alternative employment, and creating more dynamic, flexible, regional industrial economies. However, in the context of national economies dominated by large enterprises, this steering of resources into a new area of activity can be criticised for neglecting the existing economic strength. Also, recent evaluations of the industrial district model suggest that it often amounts to an over-romanticised vision of democratic local development (Smith, 1997).

Old industrial areas

New technologies, the saturation of affluent markets and new competition have had devastating consequences for areas dependent on employment in traditional industries. The collapse of employment in industries such as coal, chemicals and metal production, and the consequent restructuring of old industrial areas, raise questions not just about the reorganisation of production but also about the nature of employment. These we highlighted earlier in the chapter, and we shall return to them towards the end. A fundamental problem is the failure to reintegrate those who lose their jobs back into employment. An important example is provided in a study by Beatty and Fothergill (1995), which examined the impact of job loss in TTWAs in England and Wales through employment decline in the coal industry. What it showed (see Table 11.3) was that for every increase of 100 in the supply of male labour due to (1) the loss of jobs in coal and (2) the net increase in the size of the workforce (the difference between the number of young people who joined the job market and the number of workers who reached retirement age), 37 moved permanently out of the area; 31 either found alternative work, commuted to work outside the area or were employed on a government scheme; and 33 dropped out of the workforce altogether with many being classified as "permanently sick". Almost no increase in unemployment was registered, but there was a significant growth in male non-employment.

This reduction in labour-force participation is important because it will add to disparities in development, other things being equal. What it also indicates, however, is that the characteristic measures designed to reconvert old industrial areas (attempts to develop SMEs and an enterprise culture, attract inward investment, develop tourism and heritage industries, encourage property-led regeneration and develop retail complexes) have so far failed to offer alternative employment to those displaced by industrial decline (Hudson, 1994).

The economic crisis that has hit ECE has also resulted in the decline of industrial output and employment. Consequently, a report for the European Commission has argued that "[t]he closure of particular industrial plants, or the decline of production, with redundancies as a natural consequence, are likely to cause some of the most serious regional problems" (Commission

Table 11.3 *Labour market accounts for coalfield areas in England and Wales, 1981–91*

	Absolute values	Values as % of increase in supply of labour	Values as % of economically active males aged 16–64 in 1981
Job loss in coal industry (*A*)	159 400		13
Natural increase in workforce (*B*)	96 900		8
Increase in supply of labour (= *A* + *B*)	256 300	100	
Net outmigration	94 400	37	8
Increase in net out-commuting	4 500	2	0
Reduction in labour-force participation	84 600	33	7
Increase in jobs in other industries	44 900	18	4
Government schemes	27 300	11	2
Increase in unemployment	500	0	0

Source: Beatty and Fothergill (1995).

of the European Communities, 1992, 108). Deindustrialisation has affected industries and regions which have only a weak ability to respond to rapid liberalisation. The old regional dependencies, with enterprises dominating local economies cut off from the operation of the law of value, have been devastated. In particular, areas dominated by one-sided industrial structures – the classic model of forced state socialist industrialisation – and areas with concentrations of armaments, heavy engineering, mining, and the steel and chemicals sectors have fared badly. Clear comparable data on the extent of deindustrialisation are limited, yet work on particular countries has highlighted the extent to which industrial collapse is one of the key experiences of "restructuring".

Data published by the Russian government, for example, suggest that between 1991 and the end of 1994 industrial production fell by some 41 per cent (*Russian Economic Trends*, 1994, 63–4) while employment in industry declined from 21.5 million in 1992 to 19.1 million in mid-1994 (*Russian Economic Trends*, 1994, p. 91). In Slovakia research has shown that deindustrialisation has been particularly apparent in areas with high concentrations of armaments production; in regions more recently industrialised through branch plants where the system of vertically integrated industrial associations has collapsed; and in peripheral regions where industrial

expansion did not occur until the mid-1980s and had only a limited transformative impact upon local social relations (Smith, 1994, 1995, 1996). Plant closures, however, have been relatively limited. What has predominated is large-scale employment and output decline and shifts to unpaid holidays. These changes have clear implications for local economic life as personal consumption declines.

A similar situation has been experienced in Hungary where, for example, the crisis of iron and steel production in the north-east (Research Institute of Industrial Economics, 1992) has led to the re-emergence of profound east–west inequalities in the Hungarian space economy. This polarisation revolves around the continued concentration of economic development in Budapest and the northern Transdanubian region (Cséfalvay, 1994; Nemes Nagy, 1994). In Ozd, one of the key centres of ferrous metallurgy, in 1991 there were 7 vacancies for every 1000 unemployed persons.

Another example is provided by Bulgaria where Pickles (1995) found that the almost complete dislocation of the national economy particularly affected the most marginal areas. As he argued (Pickles, 1995, 8–9):

"The regional allocation of production under central planning has given way since 1991 to widespread branch plant closure as state industries seek to maintain benefits and labour in core plants.

The core plants of the formerly multi-plant state enterprises have closed branch plants, labour has been shed, and the semi-autonomous enterprises have withdrawn from the workshop economy of peripheral, low-wage, often female based factories . . . The result has been devastating in the peripheral localities and regions of the branch plant economies."

In some of the most peripheral areas unemployment rates have soared to a staggering 90–95 per cent. Core–periphery competition has therefore emerged, leading to struggles between managers, labour and communities all dependent upon large plants for survival. Thus the regional industrial structures of large enterprises dominating local economies – what Illner (1992) has called "industrial paternalism" – have not given way to new forms of dynamic capitalist growth. The intersection of the "old" local dependencies with the "new" law of value has meant that the "other side" of capitalist practice (economic decline and closure) has been all too prevalent. Indeed what lies behind the experience of uneven development discussed above is the eradication of economic capacities and livelihoods as new economic relations devastate institutional structures weakened by economic decline.

Towards an Explanatory Framework: (2) the Mobilisation of Human Resources

Development does not just depend on the productivity of an area's activities. Inequality and trends in economic performance, as measured by a region's GDP, are also a function of the degree to which human potential is mobilised. A systematic explanation of variations in employment rates requires an analysis of a number of factors beyond the scale of unemployment itself. These include the age profile of an area's population, conventions concerning retirement, schooling and learning; the proportion of working age adults who are inactive or whose work is hidden because of different gender roles; the scale and character of child care provision and welfare support; the extent of early retirement, sickness and hidden unemployment; and the scale of the informal sector.

As a first step we shall consider just one of the issues that require attention. Earlier some of the major disparities in GDP per head in the EU in 1992 were sketched out. Differences in labour-force mobilisation are a proximate cause of these disparities, partly because of the existence of very sharp variations in unemployment. In April 1992 EU unemployment stood at 9.4 per cent but differed markedly from one region to another. In southern Italy and Spain there were many areas with unemployment rates in excess of 20 per cent. At the same time, less than 5 per cent of the workforce had no job in the south of Germany, Luxembourg, some parts of northern Italy and Portugal – at least outside the Lisbon area and the Alentejo. What were also marked, however, were the contrasts in employment prospects between different social groups. In the EU as a whole, 8 per cent of men were out of work, compared with 11.5 per cent of women and 18.1 per cent of people under 25. Moreover, these inter-group contrasts had their own regional dimensions. For example, among the under-25s, unemployment exceeded 50 per cent in many parts of the Italian Mezzogiorno; indeed, in Napoli, Enna and Agrigento it exceeded 60 per cent and in Caltanissetta it was 73 per cent. Similarly, youth unemployment was over 30 per cent in two-thirds of Spanish NUTS II regions, averaged 26 per cent in Ireland and reached 25 per cent in certain Belgian and French regions (Eurostat, 1993).

This focusing of unemployment on specific social groups in disadvantaged areas is discussed further by Samers and Woods in Chapter 13. Here we must note that, at any point in time, contrasts in unemployment help to explain variations in GDP per head. Exploration of this point requires that attention be paid to the dynamics of unemployment. Figure 11.6 accordingly records the evolution of this indicator in four western European countries from 1964 onwards, i.e. since the final years of the post-war "golden age" of full employment and comparatively high growth. This figure underlines the way in which unemployment has varied with the economic cycle. The trend for Germany, for example, shows how unemployment has risen, and then fallen somewhat, on three occasions since the mid-1960s. What is also evident from the five curves is that – except in Sweden until very recently – the level around which

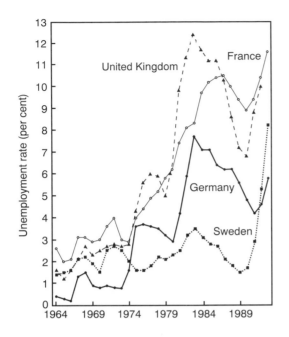

Figure 11.6 *Unemployment trends in Sweden, Germany, France and the UK, mid-1960s to the early 1990s*

unemployment has fluctuated has increased in all countries after each of the major economic shocks. This clearly points to the conclusion that, although unemployment levels differ significantly from one country and one region to another, market societies do not automatically restore full employment after economic recessions. Unemployment does, however, have a negative effect on regional economic performance: secular increases on the scale illustrated by Figure 11.6 certainly generate inequalities and have a depressive effect on regional growth.

The degree of mobilisation of human resources is also undergoing an important shift in ECE. Liberal arguments over transition posit that economic globalisation and reconstruction must occur through enterprises restructuring by shedding labour. Indeed in the absence of developed capital markets, the prime mechanism for enterprise restructuring has not been through borrowing for new investment in plant and equipment, but through "downsizing" by shedding labour and reducing its price (Gowan, 1995). Consequently, employment loss has been a universal yet uneven experience (Table 11.4). Bulgaria, Hungary, Poland and Slovakia stand out as the worst examples. The Czech Republic and Russia seem to have fared better, yet what lies behind the relatively low levels of decline in these countries is complex. In the case of the Czech Republic labour has been retained (up until 1992) in industrial enterprises. This suggests that the perceived success of the Czech model was *initially* based upon limited intra-enterprise restructuring which has only recently begun to make an impact. Furthermore, relatively low levels of unemployment and labour-force reductions have been achieved through encouraging large-scale retirement of workers past retirement age, notably women (Paukert, 1995). In Russia the continued and clear commitment to the enterprise "labour collective" is still in operation (Clarke, 1993). For example, a recent International Labour Office report argued that some 35 per cent of Russian employees had no job to do, thus producing high levels of "hidden unemployment" waiting to be "shed" (Williams, 1994).

The key result of employment change in ECE has been the growth of unemployment (Ingham and Grime, 1994), often within the context of only

Table 11.4 *Percentage employment change in selected ECE countries, 1990–92*

	Total	Agriculture	Industry	Services
Bulgaria	−28.7	−31.2	−37.1	−16.8
Czech Republic	−8.8	−29.5	−14.2	2.7
Hungary	−12.1	−34.3	−17.7	−0.5
Poland	−12.6	−13.3	−20.4	−5.7
Slovakia	−13.5	−27.5	−22.6	1.8
Russia	−4.2	−3.7	−6.9	−1.7

Source: UNECE (1994, 85).

limited social security provision and in societies in which, up until 1989, employment was a social right and commitments to full employment were a fundamental part of the model of development. Official unemployment has been particularly severe in Albania, Bulgaria, Croatia, Poland and Slovenia, where levels reached over 15 per cent in 1994 (UNECE, 1994, 86). Furthermore, female unemployment rates have tended to be higher than those for males as the commitment to "equalising the sexes" has given way to mass lay-offs differentially affecting women; and, although official figures do not exist, ethnic minorities – and particularly Romanies – have suffered badly (Ladanyi, 1993). Unemployment has also been regionally concentrated, with areas of Slovakia, for example, seeing rates of up to 25 per cent. Cursory evidence suggests, as we have argued for the EU, that unemployment has a key relationship to regional buoyancy. It is in those regions where economic decline is greatest that unemployment and the lack of mobilisation of human potential are also greatest.

Conclusions

We have noted that there was a change of direction in economic growth in the early 1970s in western Europe when growth slowed down and convergence gave way to divergence. The change of direction stemmed from the breakdown of the (Fordist) post-war model of development and was reflected in decreased rates of output and productivity growth and an increased globalisation of economic life. A delayed yet similar pattern of change is seen in eastern Europe where initial economic expansion immediately after the Second World War gave way to increasing stagnation leading to the eventual collapse of the centrally planned system. The response to both of these crises was the rise of a neo-liberal economic and political project. Evidence to date suggests that this project has proved a complete failure, particularly in comparison with the order it sought to replace in the West. Rates of growth have remained at less than one-half of those of the post-war golden age, unemployment has soared and earlier tendencies for inequalities to diminish have been thrown into

reverse gear. In eastern Europe the neo-liberal project has resulted in a massive collapse of economic potential, with the likelihood that it will be well into the next century before economic growth returns these countries to levels of development attained in the late 1980s. As indicated in the last section, mass unemployment and widespread social exclusion have returned, insecurity and inequality have increased and the performance of regional economies has often diverged in both parts of Europe.

What we have also shown is that disparities depend first of all on productivity differentials reflecting not just variations in productivity in particular industries, but also differences in the economic structure of regional economies. Productivity is greater, in other words, in areas that specialise in high-value-added activities, or products that can command high prices and incomes, than it is in areas that specialise in low-productivity activities. At the same time, however, disparities also depend on differences in the capacity of a region to mobilise its human potential as measured by its employment rate. This particular partition of GDP per head is important for two reasons. First, it makes it possible to identify the impact which disparities in productivity, specialisation and the speed of endogenous growth have on differences in regional performance. Second, it demonstrates that, other things being equal, the differential impact of the dramatic crisis of unemployment and exclusion in Europe is a critical determinant of disparities in development and in regional economic performance. Areas that achieve high rates of employment have consequently performed far better than those that have not, suggesting that it is necessary to rethink the neo-liberal project of competitive globalisation.

Notes

1. Cohesion implies the existence of economies which offer equal access to what is valuable in life to all, irrespective of their social, geographical or ethnic origin, or of their gender, talents or preferences. Cohesion implies, therefore, a relatively equal social, national and regional distribution of employment opportunities, wealth and income, as well as improvements in the quality of life to satisfy increasing expectations.

2. Space forces us to omit a discussion of the evolution of rural areas or of Europe's remoter and underdeveloped peripheries.

3. In recent years there have been rapid changes in World Bank estimates of GNP for former Communist countries. These changes are a result in part of revisions to the methods used to estimate GNP, but they also reflect the sharp decline in output associated with the transition to capitalism and the fact that some of the new economic activities are not picked up in economic survey data. At present there is a new International Comparison Programme aimed at establishing comparable purchasing power standard-based estimates of GDP for most countries in the world. These new estimates, which are based on consumer surveys for 1993, will be reflected in the *World Bank Atlas 1997* as well as the *World Development Report 1997*. The new estimates are not systematically higher than the old ones, though for some countries (-including Belarus, Estonia and Latvia) they are substantially lower.

4. The countries that were initially successful in closing the gap with the United States were in western Europe, where there were major productivity gains after the Second World War. Later Japan and then South Korea also caught up, not least because their development was fostered by the United States as part of its Cold War policy of containing expansion of the Communist world.

5. REGIO is a geographical database for the EU created and maintained by Eurostat (the Statistical Office of the EU) in conjunction with national statistics offices in each member state. The database includes a wide range of demographic, economic, labour market, agricultural, transport, energy and research and development indicators. The data are provided at a range of geographical scales starting with the EU and member states and proceeding to the increasingly detailed NUTS I, II and III geographical scales. NUTS stands for *Nomenclature des Unités Territoriales Statistiques* and is a hierarchical classification of administrative areas in the EU. NUTS I areas include, for example, the UK standard regions and the German *Länder*. NUTS III areas include UK counties and French *départements*. NUTS II areas include the French regions and, in the case of the UK, counties or aggregations of counties.

6. The weakest regions were located mainly in Greece, Portugal, the French overseas departments and the former GDR, where GDP fell dramatically after the unification of Germany. The 10 strongest were Hamburg, Darmstadt (including Frankfurt), Ile de France, Vienna, Oberbayern (including Munich), Luxembourg, Bremen, Stuttgart, Greater London and Lombardia (including Milan).

7. For a discussion of EU regional assistance, see Chapter 13.

8. The astonishing expansion of the Warsaw exchange was in part due to the important role of foreign investment, accounting for one-quarter of average daily turnover.

9. In Germany the districts were often organised around large firms.

References

Bachtler, J and Michie, R (1994) Strengthening economic and social cohesion? The revision of the Structural Funds, *Regional Studies*, **28**, 789–96.

Barnes, I and Barnes, M (1995) *The Enlarged European Union*, Longman, Harlow.

Beatty, C and Fothergill, S (1995) *Registered and Hidden Unemployment in Areas of Chronic Industrial Decline: the case of the UK coalfields*, Centre for Regional Economic and Social Research, Sheffield Hallam University, Sheffield.

Beckouche, P (1991) French "high-tech" and space: a double cleavage, in G Benko and M Dunford (eds) *Industrial Change and Regional Development*, Belhaven, London, 205–25.

Bianchi, G (1992) Combining networks to promote integrated regional development, in T Vaško (ed) *Problems of Economic Transition: regional development in central and eastern Europe*, Avebury, Aldershot, 89–105.

Central Statistical Office (1994) *Economic Trends*, HMSO, London.

Clarke, S (1993) The crisis of the Soviet system, in S Clarke, P Fairbrother, M Burawoy and P Krotov *What About the Workers? Workers and the transition to capitalism in Russia*, Verso, London, 30–55.

Commission of the European Communities (1992) *Socioeconomic Situation and Development of the Regions in the Neighbouring Countries of the Community in Central and Eastern Europe*, Regional Development Studies 2, Brussels and Luxembourg, CEC.

Commission of the European Communities (1994) Private capital flows to CEECs and NIS, *European Economy*, Supplement A, no 3, March.

Csefalvay, Z (1994) The regional differentiation of the Hungarian economy, *GeoJournal*, **32**, 351–61.

Dunford, M (1996) Disparities in employment, productivity and output in the EU: the roles of labour market governance and welfare regimes, *Regional Studies*, **30**, 339–57.

Ellman, M (1994) The increase in death and disease under "katastroika", *Cambridge Journal of Economics*, **18**, 329–56.

European Commission (1995) *Grants and Loans from the European Union*, European Commission, Brussels.

Eurostat (1993) Unemployment in the regions of the Community in 1992, *Rapid Reports: regions*, no 2.

Eurostat (1995) Per capita GDP in the European Union's regions, *Statistics in Focus: regions*, no 1.

Gorzelak, G (1996) *The Regional Dimension of Transformation in Central Europe*, Regional Studies Association/Jessica Kingsley, London.

Gowan, P (1995) Neo-liberal theory and practice for Eastern Europe, *New Left Review*, **213**, 3–60.

Harrison, B (1994) *Lean and Mean: the changing landscape of corporate power in the age of flexibility*, Basic Books, New York.

Harvey, D (1989) *The Condition of PostModernity*, Blackwell, Oxford.

Hudson, R (1994) Institutional change, cultural transformation and economic regeneration: myths and realities from Europe's old industrial areas, in A Amin and N Thrift (eds) *Globalization, Institutions and Regional Development in Europe*, Oxford University Press, Oxford.

Hutton, B, Denton, N and Bobinski, C (1994) Foreign tidal wave hits eastern markets, *Financial Times*, 4 February, 3.

Ingham, M and Grime, K (1994) Regional unemployment in central and eastern Europe, *Regional Studies*, **28**, 811–17.

Illner, M (1992) Municipalities and industrial paternalism in a "real socialist" society, in P Dostal *et al.* (eds) *Changing Territorial Administration in Czechoslovakia: international viewpoints*, Instituut voor Sociale Geografie, Amsterdam, 39–47.

International Monetary Fund (1992) *World Economic Outlook*, International Monetary Fund, Washington, DC.

Jessop, B (1995) Regional economic blocs, cross-border cooperation, and local economic strategies in postsocialism, *American Behavioral Scientist*, **38**, 674–715.

Kenway, P and Klvacová, E (1996) The web of cross-ownership among Czech financial intermediaries: an assessment, *Europe-Asia Studies*, **48**, 797–809.

Ladanyi, J (1993) Patterns of residential segregation and the gypsy minority in Budapest, *International Journal of Urban and Regional Research*, **17**, 30–41.

Maddison, A (1995) *Monitoring the World Economy 1820–1992*, OECD, Paris.

Milanovic, B (1994) A cost of transition: 50 million new poor and growing inequality, *Transition*, **5**, 1–4.

Murray, R (1992) Flexible specialisation and development strategy: the relevance for Eastern Europe, in H Ernste and V Meier (eds) *Regional Development and Contemporary Industrial Response*, Belhaven, London, 197–217.

Nemes Nagy, J (1994) Regional disparities in Hungary during the period of transition to a market economy, *GeoJournal*, **32**, 363–8.

Newberry, D and Kattuman, P (1992) Market concentration and competition in eastern Europe, *World Economy*, **15**, 315–31.

Paukert, L (1995) Privatization and employment: labour transfer policies and practices in the Czech Republic, *International Labour Office Labour Market Papers*, no 4.

Pickles, J (1995) Restructuring state enterprises: industrial geography and eastern European transitions, *Geographische Zeitschrift*, **2**, 114–31.

Piore, M and Sabel, C (1984) *The Second Industrial Divide*, New York, Basic Books.

Piirainen, T (1994) Survival strategies in a transition economy: everyday life, subsistence and new inequalities in Russia, in T Piirainen (ed.) *Change and Continuity in Eastern Europe*, Dartmouth, Aldershot, 89–113.

Research Institute of Industrial Economics (1992) *Regional Patterns of Structural Adjustments in Hungary: the case of the iron and steel industry in an international comparison*, Hungarian Academy of Sciences, Budapest.

Russian Economic Trends (1994) Incomes and the social safety net, **3**, 48–53.

Smith, A (1994) Uneven development and the restructuring of the armaments industry in Slovakia, *Transactions of the Institute of British Geographers*, **19**, 404–24.

Smith, A (1995) Regulation theory, strategies of enterprise integration and the political economy of regional economic restructuring in central and eastern Europe: the case of Slovakia, *Regional Studies*, **29**, 761–72.

Smith, A (1996) From convergence to fragmentation: uneven regional development, industrial restructuring and the "transition to capitalism" in Slovakia, *Environment and Planning A*, **28**, 135–56.

Smith, A (1997) Constructing capitalism? Small and medium enterprises, industrial districts and regional policy in Slovakia, *European Urban and Regional Studies*, 4.

Smith, A, Holmes, P, Sedelmeier, U, Smith, E, Wallace, H and Young, A (1996) *The European Union and Central and Eastern Europe: pre-accession strategies*, Sussex European Institute Working Paper no 15, University of Sussex, Brighton.

UNECE (1994) *Economic Survey of Europe in 1993–1994*, United Nations, New York.

Varesse, F (1994) Is Sicily the future of Russia? Private protection and the rise of the Russian Mafia, *Archives Européennes de Sociologie*, **35**, 224–58.

Williams, F (1994) ILO warning on Russian jobless, *Financial Times*, 1 November, 3.

Woodward, S (1995) *Balkan Tragedy: chaos and dissolution after the cold war*, Brookings Institution, Washington, DC.

World Bank (1994) *Slovakia: restructuring for recovery*, World Bank, Washington, DC.

World Bank (1995) *World Tables*, World Bank, Washington, DC.

Zaniewski, K (1992) Regional inequalities in social wellbeing in Central and Eastern Europe, *Tijdschrift voor Economische en Sociale Geografie*, **83**, 342–60.

12

Transport, communications and European integration

Roger Vickerman

Centre for European, Regional and Transport Economics, University of Kent, UK

Introduction

Transport is a major sector in the European economy and fulfils two functions. First, it is a vital link in the spatial economy which affects the efficiency of all other markets. Second, it is a major sector in its own right, as an employer and as a producer of output. Altogether it contributes around 7 per cent of European Union GDP and employs, directly and indirectly, over 8 million people. In some senses this is wasted output, because a proportion of the production value is consumed in transporting it to its end user. A reduction in the costs of transport would free these resources for use in more productive activities. However, increasing integration leads to increased trade, and we must expect increased transport from increasing integration; the key, therefore, is to ensure that the minimum resources are devoted to transport for a given volume of trade. This clearly underlines the fact that transport is a vital sector which should be as efficient as possible in order to maximise its contribution to European development and economic integration.

Transport is also characterised by the need to provide large and expensive infrastructure. The emphasis on a policy of creating trans-European networks has dominated recent policy-making. This has focused attention on new networks of high-speed railways and completing key missing links in the European networks, such as bridges and tunnels in Scandinavia and across the Alps, as well as the Channel Tunnel and its connecting links (Figure 12.1). The provision of infrastructure is essentially a "lumpy" activity, varying considerably in time and space, in which scale economies are likely to be significant. Moreover, despite these economies, it can be extremely expensive to construct. The proposed Channel Tunnel Rail Link, for example, has an average cost of about £27.7m. per kilometre, with even the non-tunnel sections estimated at £12m. per kilometre. This leads to an argument for infrastructure investment to be treated as a natural monopoly, since only organisations with some protection from competition will be able to justify the risks of such large-scale projects.

Until the relatively recent emphasis on privatisation, it was assumed that responsibility for this natural monopoly lay primarily with the public sector. As a result a principal aim of this chapter is to explore how European-level policies in the EU are grappling with the legacy of national infrastructure programmes in order to create a

Figure 12.1   *Channel Tunnel terminal, Folkestone, Kent, UK. (Photo: Eurotunnel)*

transport framework capable of promoting EU goals such as integration-related growth and cohesion. Because, for 40 years, ambiguity and confusion have surrounded not only the role of the transport sector in the integration process but also the appropriate policy framework needed to optimise that role, it is important that these themes are explored. Beyond this, however, the chapter has two further goals. One is to provide a critical analysis of EU policy by highlighting a range of major issues associated with current strategy. The latter, it will be argued, has considerably more

potential pitfalls and contradictions than is commonly supposed. The other is to examine, from both a conceptual and a practical standpoint, the changing role of transport in an integrating market. Although discussions of European transport have often neglected this dimension of the subject, it is in fact fundamental and is therefore considered first.

There is a further dimension of European transport policy which is of increasing importance. While much of our policy analysis is, of necessity, limited to the EU and hence to western Europe, the opening up of Europe to the east is a key element in the future development of the EU's trading pattern and process of integration. Since trade requires transport, this sector's development in central and eastern European countries is becoming a matter of increasing concern, especially in terms of the need to ensure that improved standards of infrastructure, together with policies towards pricing, regulation and environmental control, conform to EU standards in the interests of free and competitive trade. Thus an important subtext is the potential of western European experience to inform transport policy development for the former socialist states.

Transport in an Integrating Market

In a simple model, transport is presented as a derived demand. It is needed in order to meet the needs of a spatial economy in which activities have been located according to the distribution of either naturally occurring raw materials or markets. Hence, transport is provided to satisfy the potential demand for linking these two. It only affects the demand for goods and services requiring transport by imposing the cost of overcoming space. If there are two alternative sources of a product in a particular market, each with identical costs of production, then the one with the lower transport costs will gain a comparative advantage and a larger share of that market. In turn, lower transport costs may be the result of either a closer location, or more efficient transport. Thus the key elements in the equation will be accessibility and the internal efficiency of the transport sector.

In a more complex modern world, it has become clear that most industries are footloose in the sense that they are not tied to specific locations by material inputs or markets. Assembly industries, for example, usually have a much greater choice of potential locations, regardless of transport quality, than traditional heavy industries such as steel or textiles. Similarly those industries which are traditionally tied to the market because of the need for direct contact with the final consumer, such as many financial services, are becoming much less tied through the growth of telecommunications; these enable home-based

banking, insurance, etc., to operate effectively using remote back offices. In such a world the role of transport becomes much more intricate.

Theory tells us that it is the existence of space, and hence of non-zero transport costs, which interacts with production scale economies to determine the geographical concentration or deconcentration of economic activity (Krugman, 1991a, b). As a result of this interaction, instead of using transport just to move predetermined quantities of goods, improved transport provision can lead to one production location serving a larger market. The latter enables firms to exploit available scale economies and consequently more than offset the greater transport costs of serving more distant consumers. This balance between transport costs and production scale economies is a major element in determining the extent to which greater economic integration leads to a concentration of economic activity, and thus potentially to either the divergence or greater convergence of local economies (Krugman and Venables, 1990). This can clearly be of major significance within individual countries and at the broader European scale.

Given the importance of the relationship between transport costs and scale economies, it is tempting to assume that it is the average cost of transport that is of central significance for firms. In practice, however, this usually is not the case. Typically the average cost is only 3–4 per cent of gross value added, and a much more important factor is the potential variance in that cost, which depends on reliability. Variations in transport costs caused by unreliability will typically have a substantial impact on profits and, more seriously, affect future markets. To a considerable extent this is because the direct cost of transport is not as important for most firms as the cost of inventories, which can be kept small by good, reliable transport services. This is the case, for example, with just-in-time production techniques. Similarly in the tertiary sector, large supermarket firms have reduced the number of central warehouses from which they supply their branches, as Dawson and Burt have demonstrated in Chapter 9. Well-situated distribution depots, typically at major motorway interchanges, now deliver to branches two to three times a day. In a sense a branch's stock is kept in delivery vehicles, thus reducing the need for large – and expensive – branch inventories. Logistic costs are estimated to account for 32 per cent of the final price of consumer goods, of which transport costs amount to some 25 per cent. There is, therefore, no doubt that it is not just the existence of transport which has a key influence on economic activity, but how efficiently that transport system serves the specific needs of the local economy.

Efficiency is, in turn, dependent on both the sector's technical quality and the competitive structure of the transport market. Although thus far we have treated transport as a generally homogeneous commodity, in reality there are marked differences between and within the various transport modes. Thus we must now examine characteristics of the supply and delivery of transport services.

With respect to the efficiency benefits to be gained from more competitive transport markets, progress has in general been slow. Largely state-owned, monopolistic and highly regulated markets – in whatever sphere – are not always the most responsive to change, and transport has been no exception. Failure to progress has been attributed to obstacles such as the perceived problems of inefficient and bureaucratic management in state-owned companies and, particularly in recent years, the challenges posed by increasingly constrained public budgets which have prevented both new investment in, and maintenance of, vital networks. Whatever the precise causes, however, there has been mounting frustration in EU circles with the slowness of change, and not least with the associated problems of reaching international agreement on the development of genuinely European networks, especially for air and rail systems. This has been a factor contributing to the search for greater competitive efficiency through deregulation and privatisation, a departure to which we shall return later in the analysis.

In contrast, so far as technical quality is concerned, the sector has undergone a free-market technological revolution since the Treaty of Rome was signed. For goods transport, the increased size and tractive efficiency of the lorry have changed the nature of long-distance freight almost beyond recognition. Above all this reflects the development of the efficient and flexible diesel-powered

truck. This technical advance was a major factor enabling road freight transport – measured in terms of tonne kilometres – to increase by nearly 120 per cent between 1970 and 1990 in the 16 member states of the European Conference of Ministers of Transport (ECMT). In contrast, total freight movements – measured simply in tonnes – rose by only around half that figure.

Meanwhile, with respect to the quality of personal mobility, since the mid-1950s we have seen car ownership in western Europe metamorphose from the prerogative of the rich to the expected norm of most. This has been achieved through an eightfold increase in the level of car ownership, giving current figures of 350–450 cars per thousand population. Moreover, within this overall growth there has been a marked rise in the number of multi-car households, which in the UK's case increased from 2 per cent in 1966 to 23 per cent by 1990. The particular significance of this trend is that people in multi-car households travel much further (and this distance has been increasing much faster) than those in other households. In 1990 the average weekly distance travelled was 296 km per capita (up 40 per cent compared with 1966) against 197 km in one-car households (up 28 per cent) and 85 km in those without cars (up 27 per cent) (Department of Transport, 1992).

Similarly in the air, we have seen first the universal adoption of the jet engine and, later, the development of wide-bodied jets. These innovations have enabled business to exploit bigger markets and have also brought flying for leisure purposes within reach of the large majority, causing air passenger kilometres to quadruple between 1970 and 1990 (ECMT, 1994). Finally, the widespread adoption of high-speed rail is leading to a renaissance of railways for medium-distance travel (i.e. between 400 and 800 km) (Vickerman, 1994a; Ross, 1994). At present this development is being led by France, which first introduced high-speed trains in 1981, and still has Europe's most extensive network. Here passenger kilometres by rail increased by 17 per cent in the decade 1980–90. However, as high-speed rail networks continue to expand in other countries, and are also welded into a genuinely European network, it can be anticipated that increased rail usage will result more widely. Among other things, this should in turn help to overcome increasing congestion, both on the roads and in the air.

What is also relevant in this context is the influence of telecommunications on transport demand. For many years there have been predictions that the twentieth century as the age of mass transport would gradually give way to an era in which physical communication would be rendered less and less necessary by the growth of telecommunications. The information highway would supplant the road to a significant extent, even though the growth of modern telecommunications could not replace all physical transport. Particularly in the passenger transport sector, the growth of telecommuting would overcome the constraints faced by urban commuters, while the need for longer-distance movement would be curtailed by the use of innovations such as teleconferencing to replace the business meeting (Capello and Gillespie, 1993).

In practice, however, the indications are that in many instances telecommunications do not act as a substitute for physical transport, but rather as a complement to it. Indeed, much telecommunications activity is associated with increased demand for transport. Because people learn about more meetings, and can plan more efficient itineraries between appointments, the result is often a net expansion of the amount travelled. Similarly, although the assumption is that telecommuters sharply reduce the number of journeys between home and the employer, the reality is that this is often not the case. Many simply plan their work more efficiently by avoiding travel at peak periods, with the result that more efficient use of the available transport system may not be linked with a reduction in the total volume of travel. Meanwhile, as we have noted, when companies use telecommunications as part of their total logistic systems, their primary concern is for reliable delivery of goods to ensure the minimisation of inventory costs. In many instances this encourages them to source their materials from further afield, thus increasing the total transport associated with a given production process (Ruijgrok and Bus, 1997).

The outcome of these major developments is that traffic growth is not just a simple expansion of each type of traffic. Instead there have been profound changes in the nature of both freight and passenger traffic, in the direction of flows on the networks and in the mode that is most appropriate for specific types of movement. Table 12.1 summarises western European surface transport trends between 1970 and 1991 to give an overview of the changing situation, and includes for comparison data on some central and eastern European countries. In the case of freight, the relatively restricted inland waterway system held its own, while the pipeline network – chiefly handling crude oil, refined oil products and gas – achieved modest growth despite crises in the refining industry (Pinder and Simmonds, 1994). In contrast, even though total freight tonne kilometres for all modes rose by 162 per cent, rail freight fell by almost a tenth as road haulage captured the lion's share of the growth and therefore more than doubled. In the passenger market rail fared better, chiefly through greater metropolitan commuting, long-distance national travel and increasing international movement. Indeed, the railways' performance almost matched

Table 12.1 *Traffic trends in western and eastern Europe (1991 as % of 1970)*

Freight (tonne km)	Rail	Road	Inland waterways	Pipelines	Total
Western Europe	91.2	223.6	101.8	123.7	161.6
CEFTA[*]	70.3	224.0	96.9	150.0	97.5

Passenger (passenger km)	Rail	Car	Bus and coach	Total road	Total
Western Europe	131.9	202.5	140.6	193.9	184.9
CEFTA[*]	95.5	643.8	167.1	215.8	175.3

[*] Central European Free Trade Agreement: Poland, Slovakia, Czech Republic, Hungary.
Source: ECMT data in Voigt (1995).

that of their public transport competitor, bus and coach travel. But, as might be anticipated, both bus and rail developments were easily outstripped by escalating car usage, which doubled over the period.

The increase in freight transport is clearly related to rising levels of economic performance making additional demands on the transport system. Voigt (1995) cites sources indicating annual average freight growth of around 2.2 per cent over the period 1970–91. Compared with the rise in GDP, this implies an income elasticity only a little less than unity. Such average freight growth rates are expected to continue in the foreseeable future but, impressive though they are, they should not be allowed to disguise the fact that passenger transport has risen at a rate indicating an elasticity that is actually greater than unity. In fact, over the 1980s, personal mobility increased about 50 per cent faster than GDP, producing the substantial contrast in passenger and freight growth indices in Table 12.1. Perhaps the most surprising feature of this expansion is that it has not shown the degree of saturation previously expected. Admittedly, current forecasts predict a rather lower growth rate of the economy, for most countries of the order of 1.5–2 per cent per annum, but in the least economically advanced nations substantially higher rates are still anticipated. Above all, rising per capita incomes have been the major determinant of increased use of the private car as a dominant means of personal transport (CERTE & TecnEcon, 1994).

This is where the data on central and eastern European countries are of particular relevance, since they show clearly that, while there have been rather different experiences in the immediate past, the potential for widespread rapid change is undoubtedly there. The relatively rapid growth of road transport has been constrained by poor infrastructure and lack of private vehicles, but now these constraints are being quickly removed. At the same time the public sector transport system – rail, urban bus and tram – is increasingly unable to compete, given its years of severe underinvestment. This suggests that there will be a particularly great upsurge in private car traffic and in road haulage in these states, and between them and western Europe, a probability that should be a matter of concern to both sets of countries.

Transport Policy in the EU: Approaches and Issues

Against this background of a rapidly expanding and evolving transport market, how is EU activity encouraging further development, and what issues arise from the EU's policy stance? The history of the development of transport policy in the EU is not a particularly happy one. Although transport was designated as requiring a common policy in the Treaty of Rome, until the late 1980s very little progress was made towards resolving more than a limited number of technical, social and fiscal harmonisation issues. This partly reflected the different pulls within the Community at various times, with transport being a classic case of a policy area torn between regulation and harmonisation in one direction, and deregulation and the promotion of free markets in the other. We shall not review this full history here, but rather concentrate on the recent years in which transport has come to have a much more central role.

It will become apparent, however, that the primary concern has been to use transport to achieve largely economic and political aims, rather than to develop an integrated EU transport policy in its own right. This has been the case despite the publication in 1992 of a White Paper on *The Future of the Common Transport Policy* (European Commission, 1992). This identified the chief concerns as sustainable mobility; the internal market and free movement; the development of coherent, integrated transport systems; environmental controls (especially carbon dioxide) and safety. The preoccupation with goals other than transport policy *per se* is, of course, natural given the role of transport in the economy which we have already identified. But it is important to bear in mind the possibility that the use of policy to achieve non-transport ends may produce results in the transport sector which are less than desirable.

The main theme which entered much of the policy debate in the early 1990s was that of trans-European networks (TENs). Here the overt idea was to define a series of high-level networks in both transport and communications which would help to foster the integration process through the twin aims of *competitiveness* and *cohesion*. Competitiveness in this context is largely a matter of reducing the costs of European business through more efficient transport, and the chief method identified to achieve this has been through the construction of new infrastructure intended to integrate national economies more effectively. In other words, to a great extent TENs are about providing new – rather than improved – links, although new network sections can naturally bridge the gaps left by existing infrastructures. Beyond this it is also argued that network improvements serve to reduce differences in the quality of infrastructure between different parts of the EU, and hence promote cohesion by removing congested bottlenecks in the network and eliminating missing links. The extension of this argument is that infrastructure investment will improve economic convergence between the EU's peripheral and core regions.

The legal basis for the creation of TENs was provided by the Treaty on European Union (Maastricht Treaty) of 1992. Among many other things, this identified the key role which TENs have the potential to play in EU development; stressed a range of network issues of common interest to all EU members; emphasised the need for network interoperability (based on the removal of technical and bureaucratic obstacles to movement between member states); and highlighted the fundamental role of finance in TEN development. Subsequently the 1994 White Paper on *Growth, Competitiveness and Employment* (European Commission, 1994a) has offered a definition of which schemes are the most relevant, and has gone beyond this by exploring the question of transport, integration and employment creation. Although this White Paper makes claims for the convergence properties which better infrastructure will produce, its general tenor is to give prominence to competitiveness issues over cohesion. Conversely, however, cohesion receives a considerably higher profile in the 1994 statement on *European Spatial Development Policy* (European Commission, 1994c), in which the key objectives are defined as development (competitiveness again), improved spatial balance (cohesion related) and more effective environmental protection. Of special significance for the present discussion is the fact that, with particular reference to the problems of peripherality, this policy document emphasises the importance of an efficient and environmentally acceptable infrastructure which

displays parity of access. Included in this is the "infostructure" controlling the physical infrastructure, a perspective which highlights the complementary importance of communications and transport networks (Nijkamp *et al.*, 1994).

The TENs are principally about creating a European-level infrastructure to promote integration (and hopefully cohesion). They represent the most visible type of activity, but are far from being the only type of involvement in infrastructure provision. The European Regional Development Fund, from its inception in 1975, has spent around 80 per cent of its total assistance to regions on infrastructure, mainly transport (Vickerman, 1994a). Most of this expenditure has been on the poorer regions of the Community, and this bias towards the peripheral member states has been increased since the redesignation of the Structural Funds in 1989, although the proportion of a much larger fund now spent on infrastructure has decreased to around 30–50 per cent in the eligible member states. In addition substantial European Investment Bank activity has supported even more new projects. As Pinder *et al.* (1995) have demonstrated, an impressive increase in European Investment Bank (EIB) lending since 1986 has largely resulted from rising allocations to Spain and Portugal following their accession to the Community.

The growth of this concern to promote cohesion through infrastructure investment is related to major variations in the provision of infrastructure across the EU, variations that are predominantly the outcome of past government funding policies. Table 12.2 illustrates the situation with respect to road and railway provision in the Community of 12 (EU12). These data give both an indication of variations in the crude provision of capacity per unit of area or population, and insights into the quality of that infrastructure. From this it is clear that provision is best in the heavily congested areas towards the geographical centre of the EU, while the regions most poorly served are those in the periphery.

These disparities in the provision of infrastructure are much greater than those in either incomes or employment. Total road length per square kilometre ranges from 23 per cent of the EU12 average in Spain and Greece to 238 per cent in the Netherlands and 328 per cent in Belgium.

Table 12.2 *Selected indicators of transport infrastructure provision*

	Road surface per km^2 (Index EU12=100)	Road surface per 1000 inhabitants (Index EU12=100)	Road accident deaths per 100 000 inhabitants	Length of rail lines per km^2 (Index EU12=100)	Length of rail lines per 1000 inhabitants (Index EU12=100)	Percentage of rail lines electrified
Belgium	328	145	45	205	91	66
Denmark	51	62	33	100	122	11
Germany (West)	176	101	24	195	112	43
France	107	152	38	113	157	37
Italy	107	81	23	96	73	59
Luxembourg	222	224	35	189	187	73
Netherlands	238	88	23	123	49	70
UK	185	115	22	125	77	29
Greece	23	45	69	34	65	0
Spain	23	43	43	51	97	48
Ireland	76	211	50	51	145	2
Portugal	42	58	69	63	87	15

Source: European Commission (1994b).

Per capita provision extends from 43 per cent in Spain to 224 per cent in Luxembourg. Similarly for rail, although per capita line lengths do not give clear-cut core–periphery contrasts, track density (km per unit of area) is 34 per cent of the EU12 figure in Greece, compared with 205 per cent in Belgium. Turning to some, albeit crude, indicators of quality, we find similar variations. Motorway provision is only 5 per cent of the EU12 figure in Ireland and 9 per cent in Greece, but 266 per cent in Belgium. Railway electrification ranges from nothing in Greece to 70 per cent in the Netherlands; and while automatic block signalling has yet to be introduced to Ireland, in Belgium it has been installed on 65 per cent of the network. Differences in telecommunications provision are not so marked, but the number of lines per capita still varies from 61 per cent of the EU12 average in Portugal to 132 per cent in Denmark. Quality again varies in this context: only 8 per cent of subscribers are connected to digital exchanges in Greece, as opposed to 75 per cent in France (European Commission, 1994a).

Variations in infrastructure are also about how effectively the infrastructure works. In telecommunications, for example, there are only 0.09 faults per line per year in France, but the corresponding figures for Portugal and Greece are 0.50 and 0.53. In other words, lines in these countries develop faults five or six times as often. And, while the quality of roads is not the only cause of accidents, it is still instructive to examine accident rates. Once again, the worst road death rates are found in the southern peripheral countries, where Greece and Portugal have figures over 220 per cent of the EU12 average, compared with a UK figure of only 70 per cent.

Data such as these appear to present a strong case for continuing investment in infrastructure development designed to stimulate upward economic transition in the periphery through improved integration. However, as the following section demonstrates, this type of strategy raises a range of issues suggesting that current approaches should not be accepted uncritically.

Critical Policy Perspectives

Obvious though the geographical differences in infrastructure provision are, we should be careful about drawing too simplistic a conclusion from them. This is primarily because there is a temptation to argue that low levels of economic performance in these countries are a consequence of the low levels of infrastructure. That there is an association between the lagging economies and weak infrastructures is undoubtedly the case, at least in part; but in which direction is the causality? Low levels of economic performance lead to low levels of demand for transport, and hence infrastructure (Munnell, 1992), so that providing new infrastructure would not automatically lead to an increase in traffic. Moreover, there is evidence that pressures on the existing infrastructure are typically least in the poorer countries. This can be demonstrated by comparing data for Ireland, Spain, Portugal and Greece (the four cohesion countries) with those for the remainder of the Community of 12. (Information for the current 15-member Union is not as yet available.) In the Cohesion Four, rail freight carried per kilometre of track was only 40 per cent of the level achieved in the other eight states. For passenger traffic the equivalent figure was 60 per cent. Moreover, while it is difficult to provide an equivalent measure of road usage, congestion levels again appear to be much higher on average in the "EU8" countries than in the Cohesion Four.

Despite this, however, in recent years the cohesion countries, partly due to the enhanced availability of EU funds, have increased the share of GDP going into transport infrastructure investment, and especially into roads. The immediate short-term impact of such construction is usually beneficial to economies since it produces a typical Keynesian investment boost. Construction is a valuable lead sector with low leakages and high local multiplier impacts. But there is a concern that public infrastructure expenditure may crowd out private investment, and thus reduce the longer-term productivity improvement which is essential to foster overall economic growth (Aschauer, 1989). In a major study for the European Commission, Biehl (1986, 1991) identified the way in which infrastructure acts as a public good by enhancing private productivity. However, as Gramlich (1994) and Vickerman (1995) have noted, this study also demonstrated clearly that a simple aggregate relationship between infrastructure expenditure and economic performance does not exist. In many cases the serious infrastructure constraints identified lay not in the peripheral regions, but in the EU core.

From this it is evident that the emphasis in recent policies on the development of TENs could be counter-productive because it may fail, first, to generate cohesion and, second, to stimulate accelerated development in core regions. Improved accessibility resulting from implementation of the proposed high-speed rail network can be shown to increase both absolute and relative accessibility in the major metropolitan regions, but this will be achieved at the expense of peripheral regions and, indeed, regions which lie between metropolitan nodes in the European core (Vickerman, 1996; Spiekermann and Wegener, 1996). Accessibility may be a rather crude measure of the actual change in economic welfare, but as a measure of transport cost it is clearly relevant to the economic outcome. Firms in core regions may be able to exploit these reductions in transport cost better than those in peripheral regions since, as transport costs fall, differences in production costs due to scale economies become more relevant. This suggests that, if peripheral regions are to receive more effective assistance, greater note should be taken of evidence that the "domestic" infrastructure of a region is more important than the inter-regional infrastructure (Martin and Rogers, 1995). It is necessary to continue to invest within regions as well as between regions to improve the efficient working of the economy but, as in so many policy areas, this indicates the need for one set of measures to undo the potential distortions introduced by another.

Beyond this, new questions are emerging with respect to who should provide new infrastructures. Traditionally the public sector has been responsible for construction, typically treating it as the creation of a public good for which users pay a right of access, such as a licence fee, which entitles them to unlimited use. The argument has been that consumers will not be served efficiently by the market in what is essentially a natural monopoly. But over the past two decades the traditional assumption of public sector provision has become to be questioned more and more, leading to both deregulation and privatisation. This is chiefly due to three factors: increased questioning of the use of scale economy considerations to justify the natural monopoly argument; public sector expenditure restraint; and a belief that investment by a deregulated private sector will achieve lower costs of operation which

231

can outweigh any possible risk of destructive competition.

This process has been taken further in the UK than in most other European countries. The rail infrastructure has been transferred to an organisation independent of the service operators, Railtrack, which was subsequently privatised in 1996, while the provision of roads has been made the responsibility of an arm's-length organisation, the Highways Authority. In addition there have been important attempts to bring private capital into new construction projects, the main examples being the Channel Tunnel, the Dartford and Second Severn crossings, a number of road schemes such as the Birmingham Northern Relief Road (BNRR), and now the Channel Tunnel Rail Link (CTRL). These projects have had various degrees of success. Some have been successfully completed (the Dartford Bridge is a good example); others, and in particular the Channel Tunnel, have been completed but have proved financially problematic; and some have failed to make much headway (e.g. BNRR and, thus far, CTRL). A key issue has been the need for the public sector to underwrite income, usually by the provision of revenue streams from existing infrastructure during the construction period and/or the transfer of other assets.

In other European countries a similar, but typically slower, path is being followed. Even so some countries, including France, Italy and Spain, have long experience with the use of directly tolled highways. Sweden has fully separated the provision of rail infrastructure and services, and is using a franchising method on certain routes. Germany is similarly separating the control of infrastructure and services and is also transferring responsibility for local rail services to regional authorities. New construction, for example of the proposed Transrapid Maglev between Hamburg and Berlin, is being canvassed using the private sector, but with the state providing the loan finance. Private sector capital, albeit with some public sector guarantees, is, however, being involved in some major infrastructures such as the Great Belt and Øresund projects in Denmark and Sweden.

On the one hand, this trend to involve a growing number of private investors is consistent with the EU ethos of fostering an environment conducive to private sector initiative. But, on the other, there is already a greater need to recognise that network policy based on the provision of infrastructure as disconnected links on a national or regional basis cannot deal effectively with the current network integration issues. Privatisation, with its capacity to complicate both the range of vested interests and their priorities, clearly has the potential to increase the problems of achieving the development of coherent TENs. To date, of course, most infrastructure provision has been kept firmly within public sector control in most European countries. Yet, as privatisation continues, it may well increase the argument for regulation and co-ordination at the European level. It is important that investments are appraised on a consistent basis to create consistent networks, as well as to ensure that service operators are able to respond to a consistent set of signals, in whatever market they have their home base.

While privatisation may cause problems, so too may national and local governments. The emphasis on new road schemes in many peripheral regions is primarily driven by the short-term employment effects associated with construction and the availability of cheap EU finance. The longer-term economic benefits may be more questionable and the fiscal burden their construction and maintenance impose on both the national and local governments may prove problematic. Beyond this a key criticism relating to the EU in general concerns the means chosen to designate the TENs. In many instances, governments have proposed bottom-up defined lists in which the regions or member states attempt to include as much as possible of their own infrastructure in order to maximise their external funding from Europe. While this is may serve subsidiarity, and also be in line with a long-standing EU principle of providing infrastructure funding in response to demand (Pinder *et al.*, 1995), there is no guarantee that in the long term it will foster rational network development.

Similarly, it is important to question the emphasis placed by governments on big prestige projects which catch the headlines and are thus considered likely to attract private finance. Here the problem is that this approach frequently neglects the need to identify a region's transport requirements. The obsession with high-speed rail, for example, has often led to a disproportionate investment in this mode, including instances in which it is not the most appropriate form of investment on either economic or environmental grounds. The scope for private finance has also tended to distort both the selection and timing of projects. Thus, for example, the TENs projects adopted following the Corfu and Essen European Council meetings are dominated by high-speed rail projects (Figure 12.2), largely because these were the most advanced and were seen by governments as the most likely to provide an identifiable rate of return to private investors.

What must also be recognised is that, even if TEN development were to proceed smoothly, there are other obstacles to effective integration which must be overcome. Moreover, it is likely that privatisation and deregulation will increase rather than reduce their significance. To a great extent, these obstacles relate to what has become known as *interoperability*. It has long been recognised that there is a need for technical harmonisation to ensure that transport can flow smoothly between EU countries, the best-known example being the question of lorry weights. But while this is a high-profile problem (not least because of its environmental links) there are also significant social and fiscal issues which need resolution before there can be a single market in transport. Examples include drivers' hours regulations, as well as fuel and vehicle taxation. Moreover, achieving interoperability also requires consistent investment planning to ensure similar treatment of similar modes. This is not just a matter of reaching agreement on rates of return, levels of subsidy or accounting practices, all of which have been issues at various times. Instead there are major questions to be resolved on, for example, how to incorporate in project evaluations the environmental costs of transport and the implied value of life used in safety analyses.

In similar vein, serious competition questions remain, not least as a result of the uneven progress with privatisation. Recent experiences in the airline industry, including attempts to introduce an open-skies policy, are relevant here. When one country has a heavily subsidised state-owned airline, and another has a number of aggressively competitive private operators, there is likely to be a clear problem of conflict within the market. This conflict will extend to cover access rights, fares and new market developments. However, it goes further than this, since the presence of a competitive airline market has impacts on other modes of transport as well. Thus the state-controlled airline may be subsidised, but also regulated to protect the rail industry, and this may in turn bias mode use in one country relative to that in another.

The conceptual and practical issues arising from the triangular relationship between EU transport policy and the goals of competitiveness and cohesion are therefore considerable. However, many present-day observers would argue that the greatest problem facing the sector is that of its environmental impact. The promotion of mobility in the interests of economic growth and cohesion has inevitable environmental implications, not simply for the choice and use of transport modes, but also – and more fundamentally – for the proper size of the transport sector. In other words, the sustainability issues stemming from growth policy are now becoming more central.

Transport and the Environment

Transport is a major contributor to Europe's environmental problems. Most forms of transport depend ultimately on the production of energy from carbon-based fuels, either within the vehicle itself or, in the case of electrified railways, from a static power generation plant. The only exception is where electricity is generated from nuclear or hydroelectric plants. It is thus clear that the growth of transport from a developing and integrating economy will lead to an intensifying environmental problem. The simple statistics demonstrate the size of this problem: the transport sector consumes about 30 per cent of all energy in industrialised countries (over 80 per cent of which is accounted for by road transport) and generates 22 per cent of carbon dioxide emissions. But this is not the only concern. Transport also produces 78 per cent of carbon monoxide, 60 per cent of nitrous oxides and is a major generator of volatile organic compounds and particulates. Estimates of the total cost of these environmental concerns are always difficult, but some of the higher figures, including accidents, give an average for European countries

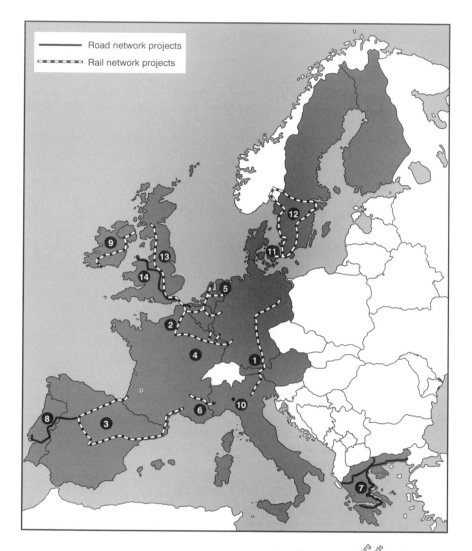

		Austria	Belgium	Denmark	France	Germany	Greece	Ireland	Italy	Luxembourg	Netherlands	Norway	Portugal	Spain	Sweden	UK
1	High-speed train/combined transport North-South	●			●	●			●							
2	High-speed train North		●		●						●					●
3	High-speed train South			●										●		
4	High-speed train East				●	●				●						
5	Rail/combined transport, Betuwe line					●					●					
6	High-speed train/combined transport, Lyon-Turin				●				●							
7	Greek motorways						●									
8	Motorway, Lisbon-Valladolid												●	●		
9	Rail, Cork-Dublin-Belfast-Larne							●								●
10	Malpensa Airport Milan								●							
11	Oresund fixed link, Denmark-Sweden			●											●	
12	Nordic Triangle (rail/road)			●								●			●	
13	West coast main line (rail)															●
14	Benelux-Ireland road corridor		●					●								●

Figure 12.2 *Priority projects in the trans-European transport networks*

of about 4.6 per cent of GDP. These estimates vary from 3 per cent to over 10 per cent, and are highest in the least developed countries (Peirson *et al.*, 1995; Mauch and Rothengatter, 1995; Maddison *et al.*, 1996).

Early attention in the traffic/environment debate centred on the link between carbon products and global warming, and there are still major fears about this relationship, which remains an inadequately measured and evaluated phenomenon. But more recently additional concern has focused on the local air pollution problems caused by particulates. Above all this is because there is now evidence of serious and immediate direct linkages between poor air quality in congested urban areas and increasing medical problems. Conditions such as asthma, for example, have become considerably more common (Maddison *et al.*, 1996).

This shifting concern generates a problem for policy-makers. Early indications suggested that the greater efficiency of the diesel engine, plus its lower emission of greenhouse gases, should lead to an effort to switch fuel uses. Now the importance attached to particulates suggests that diesel engines are less environmentally efficient, certainly as presently developed.

However, it is not just global warming and local air pollution which are affected by transport. Noise is a major problem for those living close to major transport corridors or in large cities. Accidents, particularly road accidents, impose a substantial cost on society, and are frequently the biggest source of potential benefits from new road construction schemes. And congestion, extending beyond the traditional peak-hour urban problem to include the all-day congestion experiences of many of the major inter-urban roads in the core of Europe, is the greatest source of external cost.

Although there is general agreement on a need for policy to address the environmental effects of transport use, and to ensure that transport users pay the full cost of the environmental damage they cause, there are substantial political obstacles to such a reorientation. Vested interests and lobbies in the transport sector are powerful. But such political problems are not the only difficulty confronting would-be reformers. Most evidence suggests that a simple pricing policy might not be sufficient to effect a large enough shift in transport use to have much impact, unless parallel policies were introduced to address the land-use and other implications of any major reduction in the amount of transport needed to sustain a given level of economic activity (Peirson and Vickerman, 1997). Some would wish to argue further than this, that it is growth itself which is the problem, and that only by inflicting a penal pricing regime on transport will the economy be restructured into a more sustainable condition (Whitelegg, 1993). Sustainability is thus seen to be critically linked with transport.

Those wishing to avoid substantial restructuring frequently put their faith in continuing technological improvement, as exemplified by the catalytic converter, the development of electric road vehicles and greater reliance on electric trains to replace less environmentally efficient road vehicles and aircraft (Royal Commission on Environmental Pollution, 1994; Office of Science and Technology, 1995). Others, and not least the vested interests, argue the case for alleviation through the construction of new transport infrastructure: roads, rail lines and airports. This is said to have numerous benefits, including diverting traffic from areas where it causes noise and pollution, and also boosting job creation through construction projects. But in reality this approach generates further problems. First, because the creation of new infrastructure is usually additional to existing infrastructure, it increases the total land area devoted to transport, with consequent effects on both the market for land and on the natural environment. Many of the most strident protests against transport have come from its perceived destruction of natural habitats. The problem here is that any development of land is irreversible and this generates a major question of economic evaluation. Second, there is clear evidence that new infrastructure is not simply a means of reducing the costs of existing traffic; it actually creates additional movement. If this new traffic enables the generation of additional economic wealth there is an argument in favour; but as yet our appraisal techniques are not usually good enough to identify whether new activity associated with transport improvements arises from genuine growth or is just a relocation phenomenon (Rietveld and Nijkamp, 1993; Vickerman,

1994b). Moreover, even if there is aggregate economic gain, with it will come transport-related environmental penalties. Against this background, the Commission's 1995 Green Paper on *Fair and Efficient Pricing* is of considerable significance (European Commission, 1995b). This highlights the three key areas in which transport imposes external costs (congestion, accidents and the environment), and emphasises the need for much greater transparency in this respect, even though a consequent move to pricing externalities would be dependent on new technological breakthroughs.

While these concerns arise from western European experience, it should be emphasised that many of them are perhaps even more relevant in central and eastern European countries. In part this is because the stock of vehicles is generally older and less environmentally efficient than in western Europe, implying that the more rapid expansion of mobility expected will be even more environmentally damaging. In addition, the backlog of infrastructure investment which is now being addressed in these countries also has severe environmental implications, especially the emphasis in most plans on new highways and high-speed rail. There is a difficult balance which has to be struck between the need to provide an infrastructure appropriate for the anticipated economic growth of these countries, and to allow levels of mobility consistent with that growth, but to avoid repeating the many mistakes which have been made in western Europe. This is a policy which is of concern to all Europe and not just the countries in transition.

Conclusion: Towards Policy Adaptation

Increasing concern with the growing problems of environmental impacts and the provision of adequate, but efficient, public transport, led in 1995 to two much more specific and directly transport-related policy documents from the European Commission. These reflect not so much the failure of earlier policies, but simply the difficulty of making tangible progress with the enormous tasks of reshaping transport networks for Europe as a whole and its urban system. The Green Paper *The Citizens' Network* is subtitled

"fulfilling the potential of public passenger transport in Europe" (European Commission, 1995a). This goes beyond TENs to the local level and addresses much more directly the role of public transport and the problem of congestion. There is perhaps an old-fashioned ring to the call for integrated systems of transport in local areas, but it recognises that this may be a more effective way of achieving a genuine local level input to the transport policy process in Europe. The real problem with TENs is that they have become too much an open invitation for local interests to put in claims for infrastructure as a solution to perceived transport problems, rather than viewing both use, and hence pricing, as just as essential as the construction of new infrastructure.

The other Green Paper, *Fair and Efficient Pricing*, represents one of the first attempts in a policy document to move to a recognition of the need for a system of consistent and transparent prices for different transport modes which adequately reflect the true cost of transport (European Commission, 1995b). Only if pricing in the transport sector is correctly identified can we hope to implement a satisfactory set of policies to guide the spatial development of the EU and tackle the key balance between competitiveness and cohesion. This cannot be achieved quickly, however, because an immediate adoption of "correct" transport prices would have disastrous consequences for both individual regional economies and that of the EU as a whole. For the immediate future, therefore, the key policy issues are how to start making the transition and how fast the economy can be expected to adjust towards one that is consistent with a sustainable transport system.

The principal argument addressed here is that at all levels transport policy has too often in practice been devoted to ends other than those of improving the efficiency of the transport sector itself. This may occur because transport is seen as a useful way of achieving certain macro-economic goals. In particular, there is a bias towards major construction projects which, if nothing else, provide essentially Keynesian employment gains in the short run. TENs are dressed up as instruments of improving *competitiveness*, but the real objective is a short-run boost to an economy in recession. On the other hand, the *cohesion* argument may be flawed because relative accessibility is not improved. There has even been an increasing polarisation of accessibility and hence economic activities into big cities from the twin effects of airports and high-speed rail with the areas in between or outside these major cities suffering the environmental costs.

Further development of policy also has to recognise three important dimensions of the economics of transport which we can term location, logistics and regulation. Transport has to be related to the spatial structure of the economy, and to its transport needs, but in the context of regulation which applies to both the transport sector *per se* and to the economy's spatial organisation. Transport policy should therefore be designed both to effect control of the transport market and of spatial development. However, behind both will be the context of macro-economic policy, an integral part of which must be transport policy itself. The likely outcomes of these interrelationships, in terms of the twin objectives of sustainability and spatial development, can be seen as a series of potential conflicts already identified above: centralisation versus decentralisation; concentration versus deconcentration; and sustainable transport versus sustainable development.

Transport is trapped in the middle, expected to deliver improvements in both macro-economic performance and its distribution. The problem is that it may be able to do neither effectively, with the result that both improved sustainability and better balanced spatial development may be lost. Moreover, the various dimensions and impacts of transport and transport policy give rise to conflicts which may dominate the execution of both policy and specific projects. Such conflicts arise between private agents, between private agents and public agencies and between public agencies at different levels. How to resolve these opposing standpoints is a major issue on which future research and policy need to focus.

References

Aschauer, D A (1989) Is public expenditure productive?, *Journal of Monetary Economics*, **23**, 177–200.

Biehl, D (ed) (1986) *The Contribution of Infrastructure to Regional Development*, Office for Official Publications of the European Community, Luxembourg.

Biehl, D (1991) The role of infrastructure in regional development, in R W Vickerman (ed) *Infrastructure and Regional Development*, European Research in Regional Science vol. 1, Pion, London, 9–35.

Capello, R and Gillespie, A (1993) Transport, communications and spatial organisation: future trends and conceptual frameworks, in G Giannopoulos and A Gillespie (eds) *Transport and Communications Innovation in Europe*, Belhaven, London, 24–56.

CERTE & TecnEcon (1994) *Future Evolution of the Transport Sector: implications for regional planning*, Final Report to European Commission, DG XVI, Centre for European, Regional and Transport Economics, University of Kent & TecnEcon Ltd, forthcoming, Office of Official Publications of the European Communities, Luxembourg.

Department of Transport (1992) *National Travel Survey 1990*, HMSO, London.

European Commission (1992) *Future of the Common Transport Policy*, White Paper, COM(92)494, Office for Official Publications, Luxembourg.

European Commission (1994a) *Growth, Competitiveness and Employment*, Office for Official Publications, Luxembourg.

European Commission (1994b) *Competitiveness and Cohesion: trends in the regions*, Fifth Periodic Report on the Social and Economic Situation in the Community, Office for Official Publications, Luxembourg.

European Commission (1994c) *European Spatial Development Policy*, Office for Official Publications, Luxembourg.

European Commission (1995a) *The Citizens' Network*, Green Paper, COM(95)601, Brussels.

European Commission (1995b) *Towards Fair and Efficient Pricing in Transport*, Green Paper, COM(95)691, Brussels.

ECMT (European Conference of Ministers of Transport) (1994) *Trends in European Transport and Infrastructure Needs*, ECMT, Paris.

Gramlich, E (1994) Infrastructure investment: a review essay, *Journal of Economic Literature*, **32**, 1176–96.

Krugman, P (1991a) *Geography and Trade*, MIT Press, Cambridge, MA.

Krugman, P (1991b) Increasing returns and economic geography, *Journal of Political Economy*, **99**, 483–99.

Krugman, P and Venables, A J (1990) Integration and the competitiveness of peripheral industry, in C J Bliss and J Braga de Macedo (eds) *Unity with Diversity in the European Community: the Community's southern frontier*, Cambridge University Press, Cambridge, 56–75.

Maddison, D, Johansson, O, Pearce, D, Calthrop, E, Litman, T and Verhoef, E (1996) *Blueprint 5: the true cost of road transport*, Earthscan, London.

Martin, P and Rogers, C A (1995) Industrial location and public infrastructure, *Journal of International Economics*, **39**, 335–51.

Mauch, S P and Rothengatter, W (1995) *External Effects of Transport*, Report by IWW, Karlsruhe and INFRAS, Zürich, International Union of Railways (UIC), Paris.

Munnell, A H (1992) Infrastructure investment and economic growth, *Journal of Economic Perspectives*, **6**, 189–98.

Office of Science and Technology (1995) *Technology Foresight 5: Transport*, HMSO, London.

Peirson, J, Skinner, I and Vickerman, R W (1995) Estimating the external costs of UK passenger transport: the first step towards an efficient transport market, *Environment and Planning A*, **27**, 1977–93.

Peirson, J and Vickerman, R W (1997) Environmental effects of transport: a model of optimal pricing and investment for the UK, *International Journal of Environment and Pollution*, **7**, 343–56.

Pinder, D A, Edwards, J B and Wise, M (1995) The European Investment Bank, transport investment and European Union objectives: an exploratory analysis, *Journal of Transport Geography*, **3**, 167–77.

Pinder, D A and Simmonds, B (1994) Crisis intensity, industrial restructuring and the West German oil refining industry, *Erdkunde*, **48**, 121–36.

Rietveld, P and Nijkamp, P (1993) Transport in regional development, in J Polak and A Heertje (eds) *European Transport Economics*, Blackwell, Oxford, 130–51.

Ross, J F L (1994) High-speed rail: catalyst for European integration?, *Journal of Common Market Studies*, **32**, 191–214.

Royal Commission on Environmental Pollution (1994) *Transport and the Environment, Eighteenth Report*, Cm 2674, HMSO, London.

Ruijgrok, C J and Bus, L (1997) Infrastructure quality and freight flow scenarios, in E Quinet and R W Vickerman (ed) *The Econometrics of Major Transport Infrastructures*, Macmillan, London, 69–82.

Spiekermann, K and Wegener, M (1996) Trans-European Networks and unequal accessibility in Europe, *EUREG*, **4/96**, 35–42.

Vickerman, R W (1994a) Transport infrastructure and region building in the European Community, *Journal of Common Market Studies*, **32**, 1–24.

Vickerman, R W (1994b) Regional science and new Transport infrastructure, in J Cuadrado Rouro, P Nijkamp and P Salva (eds) *Moving Frontiers: economic restructuring, regional development and emerging networks*, Avebury, Aldershot, 151–65.

Vickerman, R W (1995) Location, accessibility and regional development: an appraisal of Trans-European Networks, *Transport Policy*, **2**, 225–34.

Vickerman, R W (1996) Restructuring of transport networks, *EUREG*, **3/96**, 16–26.

Voigt, U (1995) Traffic flow trends, in *Transport: new problems, new solutions*, Proceedings of the 13th International Symposium on Theory and Practice in Transport Economics, Luxembourg, ECMT, Paris.

Whitelegg, J (1993) *Transport for a Sustainable Future: the case for Europe*, Belhaven, London, 289–339.

Part III
Social Stress in the New Europe

Economic development – or the lack of it – creates many social stresses for European peoples. Part III therefore begins with a discussion by Michael Samers and Robert Woods of major social issues arising from development problems in western Europe. While the growth of trade has been impressive, and there has been an absolute rise in employment, the link between economic expansion and employment creation has been weak. Labour supply has outstripped demand, causing chronic unemployment problems; and important spatial and social dimensions of these problems have emerged. Spatially, unemployment and low output have remained associated with weaker parts of the EU, generating considerable challenges to cohesion policy. Socially the issues relate chiefly to the impacts of labour flexibilisation and welfare reform on disadvantaged groups – particularly women, the young, older workers and immigrants.

Russell King pursues the theme of disadvantaged groups in two chapters focusing on international migration. The first is concerned with the consequences of large-scale labour immigration from western Europe's Mediterranean periphery in the post-war era of Fordist industrial growth. 'Guest workers' from this period, and their descendants, have typically been confined to the lower echelons of the employment and housing markets, to a life of low social mobility and to social exclusion. In many instances, of course, members of these groups wish to maintain their cultural identity. But this does not mean that, compared with their host country counterparts, it is equitable for them to have lower incomes, higher unemployment rates, poorer educational attainment and a higher incidence of physical and mental illness. King's second chapter, meanwhile, highlights the revolution in international migration that was initiated by the oil crises and reinforced by the fall of Communism. In this era the keynote has been increasing complexity, as ordered patterns of movement from periphery to core have been replaced by more complex flows of asylum-seekers and clandestine immigrants. Despite expectations in the early 1990s, large-scale east–west migration has not developed, and current immigration issues revolve around relationships with developing countries. Whatever the origin of would-be immigrants, however, they face widespread hostility from European governments and – whether their entry is legal or illegal – almost guaranteed economic and social exploitation.

While King's concern is social stress arising from migration at the European scale, Paul White takes the analysis down to the urban level. The highly segmented urban underclass bears the brunt of economic, social and demographic change, to which the political response has all too often been inadequate or inappropriate. Western European welfare states, one of the glories of the post-war period, have been shown to be insecurely based and liable to underperform just when they are needed most. In central and eastern Europe, welfare regimes were broken by the fall of socialism, and new forms have yet to emerge. This has created a hiatus of uncertainty as many aspects of earlier provision have evaporated. And changing ideologies, particularly the New Right political discourse, have strengthened the stigmatisation and marginalisation of disadvantaged groups in urban societies. While the details vary from country to country and from city to city, the overall picture comprises strikingly similar elements.

Three further chapters return us the broader spatial scale. David Turnock's analysis of social stress in the new democracies confirms the importance of appreciating the segmentation of society. Unemployment, ethnicity, gender, housing status and access to transport are all shown to have emerged in the 1990s as key determinants of social deprivation in central and eastern Europe. Their differential impact is generating complex patterns of deprivation at the interregional and international scales throughout the former socialist bloc; and in the neo-liberal environment there is every prospect that corrective measures – such as nascent regional policies and cross-border co-operation – will require a long time-scale to stand a chance of success.

Finally, the contributions by Brian Ilbery and Tim Unwin look specifically at changing rural circumstances and hardship in western and eastern Europe. Ilbery's concern is the post-productivist shift in the EU's agricultural system and its implications for farming communities. Farmers are learning to adopt various pathways of farm business development as state support for agriculture is reduced. Yet uneven development is deepening, with immediate consequences for the prosperity and life prospects of individuals and families. These consequences are particularly severe in the remote and economically marginal agricultural regions, where survival mechanisms contrast sharply with the accumulation strategies that are often typical of lowland farming communities. Unwin's analysis, meanwhile, is that – following the upheavals linked with the collapse of socialism – the agricultural economies of central and eastern Europe are likely to experience increasingly rapid change. As attempts are made to modernise the agricultural sector to match western Europe, mechanisation will increase; the tiny privatised farms which have become commonplace will prove to be unviable; and these powerful forces will cause intense labour-shedding in the agricultural sector. While one outcome will be increased deprivation among former farm workers, another will be intensified rural–urban migration by young adults repelled by rural conditions. And this is in turn likely to lead to the interrelated challenges of unbalanced rural community structures and intensified demands on urban economic and social systems that are already under severe strain.

13

Socio-economic change, EU policy and social disadvantage

Michael Samers and Robert Woods
Department of Geography, University of Liverpool, UK

Introduction

Earlier chapters in this book have examined major economic developments which are currently transforming Europe. What they have not explored, however, are the social implications of these changes. Issues arising from these implications therefore provide the focus for Part III, starting in this opening chapter with an analysis of consequences arising from the complex interactions between demographic change, economic restructuring and the labour market. As a starting point we review several important "facts" which everyone knows, or should know, about the demography of Europe in the 1990s. The discussion then turns to trends in growth, employment and unemployment, which in turn leads to consideration of policy responses and related issues. Then, to emphasise the importance of understanding the segmented nature of the labour market, we consider the circumstances of a range of vulnerable social groups: women, the young, older workers and immigrants. Here our principal concerns include how they are treated by restructuring welfare regimes and EU policy. Before we begin one final point must be made:

with limited space, and a major topic, it has been necessary to restrict our analysis to the EU. Eastern and central Europe are considered later in Part III, and particularly in Chapter 17.

Contemporary Demographic Trends

At the outset it is important to recognise seven key and defining characteristics of Europe's contemporary demography.

1. The rate of European population growth has slowed in recent decades and is unlikely ever to return to levels once achieved in the nineteenth century. Europe's population may come close to being stationary early in the twenty-first century, although national and regional differences will of course persist to some extent. Currently the EU has a population of nearly 370 million, compared with almost 500 million in the wider Europe outside the former USSR (Noin and Woods, 1993; also Table 13.1).
2. Slow to zero growth has come about because fertility and mortality have both declined to near replacement levels and, furthermore, there has been a high degree of inter-regional convergence

Table 13.1 *Demographic characteristics of selected western European countries, early 1990s*

	Population (millions)	Male life expectancy at birth (years)	Female life expectancy (years)	Infant mortality rate (per '000)	Total fertility rate
Austria	7.83	73	79	6.5	1.51
Belgium	9.98	72	79	8.0	1.54
Denmark	5.20	72	78	5.6	1.68
Finland	5.01	71	79	4.4	1.79
France	57.06	73	81	7.3	1.77
Germany	80.00	72	78	6.2	1.44
Greece	10.20	72	76	8.5	1.39
Ireland	3.52	76	81	6.0	2.11
Italy	56.80	72	80	7.4	1.25
Luxembourg	0.39	71	78	8.5	1.89
Netherlands	15.10	74	80	6.3	1.59
Portugal	9.90	70	77	9.3	1.51
Spain	39.03	73	80	7.6	1.30
Sweden	8.62	75	81	4.8	2.09
UK	57.80	74	79	6.6	1.79
EU15	370.30	–	–	–	–
Non-USSR Europe	495.10	–	–	–	–

Sources: United Nations *Demographic Yearbooks*.

in birth and death rate levels and trends. Thus in Italy, Greece and Spain – previously countries with high birth rates because of the Catholic tradition – the total fertility rate was less than 1.4 in the early 1990s, and only in Ireland and Sweden was it above 2.0.

3. Chiefly through medical progress, life expectancy has improved significantly. For example, the infant mortality rate per thousand live births is almost down to 8 in Greece and Portugal and to 7 in France, Italy and Spain, while in Sweden and Finland it is already less than 5. In most EU countries life expectancy at birth is now 72–74 years for males and 6 years higher for females. With the exception of the Japanese, western Europeans experience the highest survival chances in the world and – although there remains scope for greater social equality – it is difficult to see how average life expectancy can be substantially improved.

4. The continued decline in fertility, and the increase in life expectancy, have led to the ageing of the population. This has created several important challenges for the European economies, especially in terms of the labour force structure, the rising dependency ratio, the gender balance within adult society, and the demands on health and welfare programmes. In most of the EU15, some 18–20 per cent of the population are now aged 60 or older, the full range being from 15 per cent in Ireland to 24 per cent in Sweden (United Nations, 1993). Projections into the early decades of the twenty-first century suggest that, although roughly two-thirds of the population are likely to remain in the working age category (15–64), the proportion under 15 will fall to less than 18 per cent by 2010. This compares with 25 per cent in 1970, and will naturally result in fewer school leavers entering the job market.

5. The structure of the European labour force has also changed because – across the entire economically active age range – higher proportions of women are entering the labour force. The persistent decline of agriculture and manufacturing industry, and the rise of the service sector, have encouraged this trend, which is often accompanied by an increase in part-time and casual employment, as we shall see later in the chapter.

6. New patterns of family formation and living arrangements have developed which also tend to have certain implications for the labour market. The Europe-wide increase in divorce, cohabitation, single-parenthood and living alone all pose challenges for social cohesion, welfare programmes and the economic organisation of society. The problems posed by increasing demands for pre-school child care and nursery education, combined with the rising female labour-force participation rate, exemplify the kind of challenges to be faced under this heading (Hall, 1993).

7. Immigration to Europe, and international or inter-regional migration within it, reflect structural shifts in the labour market, but also set additional challenges for EU states (Rees *et al.*, 1996). In the case of immigration there has been a socio-political-legitimation crisis in most countries, especially where vacancies and employers' inducements originally drew labour into the metropolitan centres from ex-colonies or the south and east of Europe. The post-1960s economic recession, the increasingly competitive market for unskilled labour, and racist and discriminatory reactions to migrants have made the effects of immigration an important matter in several states.

We are not, of course, the first to offer this type of analysis of western Europe's changing demography; Bourgeois-Pichat (1981) and van de Kaa (1987), for example, have both provided their own short summaries. But our résumé covers most of the issues that others have suggested and also encourages readers to consider the wider implications of demographic change, especially for the economy of the EU. Before turning to some of these issues, however, we must first consider recent developments with respect to economic growth, employment and unemployment in the EU.

Growth and the Labour Market: Key Indicators

At first sight, several key economic indicators for the EU appear good. For example, in 1990 the EU accounted for only 7 per cent of the world's working-age population but, on a dollar basis, member states produced 30 per cent of global output. They were also responsible for 40 per cent of total global trade, and 45 per cent of world exports. Moreover, whereas the value of exports rose modestly in the late 1980s (at about 1.5 per cent a year), this figure climbed to 10 per cent in 1994, and was still 8.5 per cent in 1995 (CEC, 1996a). In addition, manufactured products have typically accounted for some 60 per cent of all exchanges of goods and services and, perhaps contrary to widespread opinion, the proportion of manufactured goods in EU exchange has recently increased.

Recent GDP data, however, project a rather different picture. Despite upward trends in per capita GDP in some countries, growth has in general been absent (Figure 13.1). Taking the EU as a whole, in real terms average annual GDP grew by 3.3 per cent in the second half of the 1980s, but the rate then fell to 1.2 per cent in 1991–92 and GDP actually declined (by −0.6 per cent) in 1993. Moreover, although in 1994 the growth rate recovered to 2.8 per cent, by 1995 it had settled back to 2.5 per cent (CEC, 1996a, b). We must, of course, be wary of assuming the existence of a close correlation between fluctuating GDP and the demand for labour; many other factors influence the latter, and there is considerable debate as to their relative importance. None the less, the mixed economic performance highlighted by GDP figures was certainly echoed by unemployment trends.

Problems with measuring unemployment across the EU abound, but as a starting point we will attempt to minimise them by examining the official Eurostat data. According to these, total unemployment fell from 10.8 per cent in 1985 to 8.3 per cent in 1990, but then rebounded to 11.3 per cent in the recesssion of 1993–94. By that time the number of people unemployed exceeded 16 million (Begg, 1995; CEC, 1993, 1994, 1996a; Dunford, 1995). Moreover, although the rate subsequently declined once more, to 10.7 per cent in 1994–95, it then levelled off and was still 10.9 per cent in the first quarter of 1996 (CEC, 1996b).

Regional data, meanwhile, highlight the strong spatial contrasts inherent in growth and unemployment. Thus in the 10 EU regions with the lowest GDP, average unemployment reached

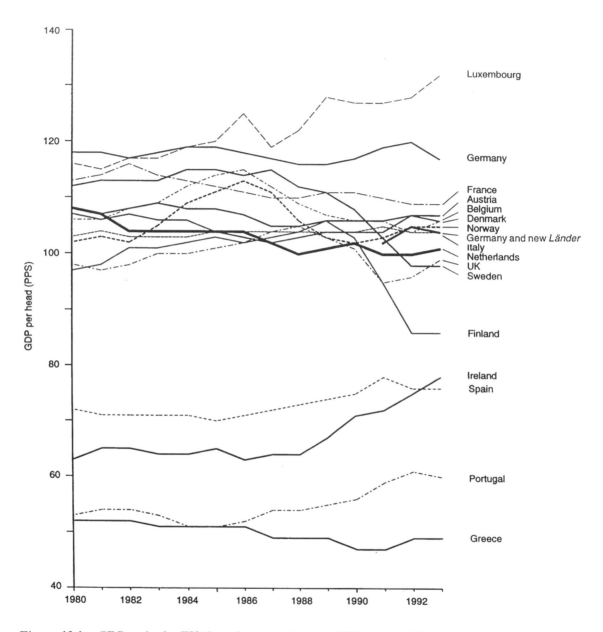

Figure 13.1 *GDP per head in EU15 member states, 1980–93 (EU average = 100)*

slightly more than 25 per cent in 1993. In the 10 wealthiest regions the equivalent figure was 4 per cent, and their GDP was around 4.5 times that of the least affluent group (Dunford, 1995; Dunford and Perrons, 1994; Michie, 1995). In the case of Italy, which has the highest spatial variation in employment prospects, southern unemployment was 20.7 per cent in July 1995, compared to 6.4 per cent for the north (CEC, 1996a).

One criticism of the statistics quoted above is that they may actually underestimate the true levels of unemployment. For example, they do not reflect those in "informal employment", the marginally unemployed, discouraged seekers and those involved in youth and other training schemes. Thus many researchers consider them insufficient to measure the gap between the numbers of jobs and job seekers, and argue that a more appropriate barometer is the ratio of employment to the working-age population (Green and Owen, 1995; Vandermotten, 1993). This approach indicates that in 1993 approximately 60 per cent of Europe's working-age population actually had paid employment, a proportion that had changed little since the late 1980s (Dunford, 1995; Michie, 1995; CEC, 1994). When the data are broken down, however, sharp spatial contrasts again emerge: in the EU's economically weak Objective 1 regions (Table 13.2) only half the potential labour force was actually in work, compared with 62 per cent in more prosperous areas.

Moreover, this contrast is reiterated when absolute employment change is considered. Despite relatively high unemployment, the total number of jobs has continued to rise; indeed, employment has grown in most EU countries, with the strongest expansion occurring in Ireland, Denmark, Luxembourg, Sweden and Finland. Yet the average growth rate in Objective 1 regions (1.5 per cent a year in the late 1980s) has been only half that in more prosperous areas (Green and Owen, 1995).

What can be generally drawn from this analysis is that the EU has recently experienced, somewhat contradictorily, small gains in employment and a continued – though fluctuating – rise in the number of unemployed. The links between accumulation and job growth prove to be only distant, giving rise to the widespread fear of "jobless growth". And, while this is the overall picture, strong regional disparities persist with respect to both unemployment and the creation of new jobs. From the Commission's viewpoint, these disparities are particularly serious, because they are perceived to pose a threat to the goals of cohesion and successful progress towards greater integration, including monetary union. At this point, therefore, it is appropriate to consider the EU's chief policy responses, before turning to the issues surrounding employment, unemployment, monetary union and vulnerable social groups.

EU Intervention: the Role of the Structural and Regional Funds

The EU's main institutional mechanisms for regulating unemployment are provided by the Structural Funds. Initially created to address rising socio-spatial inequalities, Brussels revised these funds in 1988, and doubled the amount of funding between 1989 and 1993. This revision came primarily as a response to growing unemployment, and its threat to political and economic cohesion, but it was also a reaction to the lack of co-ordination among the original bodies responsible for these measures (Casey, 1993; CEC, 1994). Under the so-called Delors II package (1994–99), the current structural and regional funds include the European Regional Development Fund (ERDF), the European Social Fund (ESF) and the European Agricultural Guidance and Guarantee Fund – Guidance Section (EAGGF-GS).

Originally the Structural Funds were allocated in relation to five Objectives, of which Objectives 1, 2 and 5b are regionally oriented, while 3, 4 and 5a are structurally based. (Summaries of the aims, coverage, etc. of these Objectives are provided by Table 13.2, while Figure 13.2 summarises the populations covered by a selection of them.) More recently, in the light of Sweden and Finland's accession to the EU, a sixth Objective has been added to address areas of sparse population, and a Cohesion Fund of 13.6bn ECU has been introduced for states whose national GDP is less than 90 per cent of the EU average. This fund operates by part-financing environmental projects and trans-European networks in the weaker states, and is currently targeted at Greece, Ireland, Portugal and Spain (Amin and Tomaney, 1995; CEC, 1995). In addition, under the Delors II package, Objective 3 now combines the tasks of Objectives 3 and 4.

Figures 13.3 and 13.4 detail the regional and structural funding allocated under Objectives 1 and 2 in 1989–93, while Table 13.3 compares anticipated levels of spending on these policies for 1994–99 with the budgets for other EU programmes. Because the EU is concerned especially with what it calls "concentration" (in other words, the focusing of funds on specific problems), Objective 1 funding as a percentage of Structural/Regional Funds will increase from 65 per cent in 1994 to 73 per cent in 1999. This is particularly significant because it is these non-industrial Objective I regions which have witnessed the highest rates of population growth and the inability of labour markets to absorb new entrants

Table 13.2 *EU regional and structural intervention measures*

Instrument	Aims	Geographical coverage	Population coverage
Regionally orientated			
Objective 1	Assists regions whose GDP is 75% or less of the community average, and in general whose development is "lagging". Also, since 1993, some industrial regions experiencing economic decline	Covers most of Spain and the former GDR, all of Ireland, Northern Ireland, Portugal, Greece, Corsica, north-west Scotland, Merseyside in the UK, part of the region bordering France and Belgium, southern Italy, Sardinia and Sicily	92 million (25% of the EU population). Because the new German *Länder* receive Objective 1 funding, more than 20% of Germany's population (or 16.4 million people) are now covered
Objective 2	Focuses on regions undergoing industrial restructuring	Examples: South Wales, Teeside and Tyneside, much of the Pas de Calais and Picardy, parts of Catalonia, and the area around Turin	60.5 million (16.4% of the EU population).
Objective 5b	Concerns the adjustment of vulnerable rural areas and involves the revision of the CAP. Policies are aimed at the alleviation of low incomes, under- and unemployment	Primarily north-eastern Spain, southern and central France, central and northern Wales, Cornwall, northern England, central Italy and south-eastern Germany	32.8 million (8.8% of the EU population, as opposed to 5% in 1989).
Objective 6	Aims to promote the development of lagging regions of the new Scandinavian member states (Finland and Sweden)	Sweden: large majority of land north of latitude 60°. Finland: large majority of land north of latitude 62°	1.3 million (5% of Swedish population and 16.6% of Finnish).
Cohesion Fund	Created by the Treaty on European Union, this fund provides financing for environmental upgrading and trans-European networks in states with GDP less than 90% of the EU average.	Greece, Portugal, Spain, Ireland	Cohesion country populations total 63 million

Instrument	Aims	Geographical coverage	Population coverage
European Social Fund (ESF)	Provides training and employment measures; support for SMEs using "local resources"; support for certain technologies through technical and innovation-producing training; the promotion of tourism through training/employment aid and environmental improvements. Cities undergoing severe forms of industrial restructuring also receive special funding, regardless of whether they are situated outside Objective 2 regions	Has especially targeted "lagging" and declining industrial regions (Objectives 1 and 2)	More than 100 million

Structurally orientated

Instrument	Aims	Geographical coverage	Population coverage
Objective 3	Addresses the long-term unemployed and improves employment chances for young people. Now combines the tasks of Objectives 3 and 4 under the Delors II package	n/a	n/a
Objective 4	Provided training and other measures for labour-force adaptation to industrial restructuring	n/a	n/a
Objective 5a	Aims to accelerate the adaptation of production, processing and marketing structures in agriculture and forestry and to help modernise and restructure the fisheries and aquaculture sectors	n/a	n/a

Sources: Eurostat (1995; 1997); CEC (1996c)

and to improve the disastrous effects of long-term unemployment (Begg, 1995; Symes, 1995).

Within this framework the current principal goals of the European Social Fund (ESF) are to support initiatives for the long-term unemployed and young people, and especially for young or unemployed members of "vulnerable" groups (disabled people, migrants and women). In providing this assistance, the ESF has targeted "lagging" and declining industrial regions. ESF funding in these areas is (in theory anyway) combined with other EU institutional financing provided partly by the other Structural Funds, but also by the European Investment Bank (EIB). For

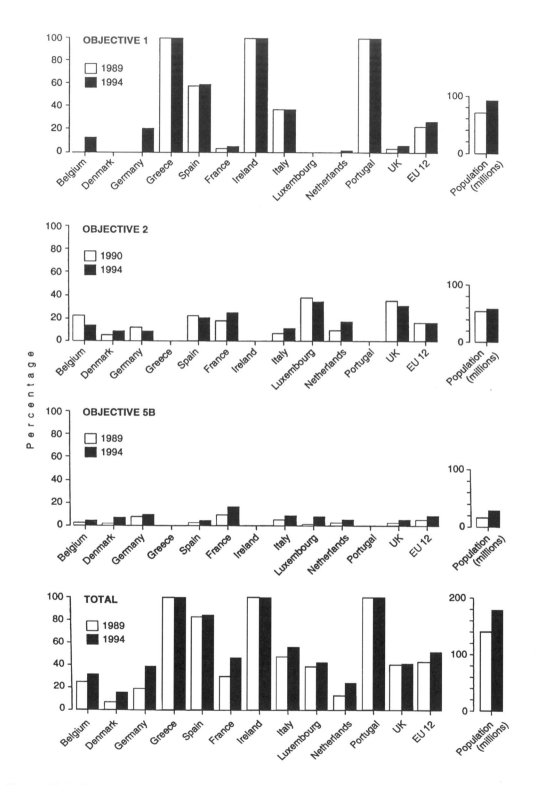

Figure 13.2 *Proportions of member states' populations covered by the regional objectives of the Structural Funds*

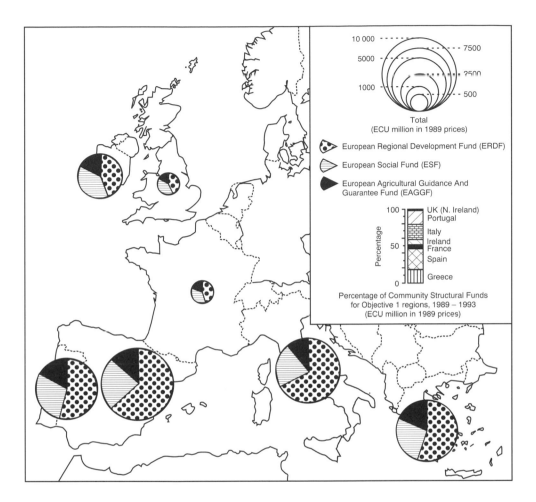

Figure 13.3 *Assistance from the Structural Funds for Objective 1 regions, 1989–93*

example, the EIB might invest in high-technology projects, environmental improvements, small and medium-sized enterprises (SMEs) and the like, with aid for training and skill adaptation, etc. coming from the ESF (Symes, 1995).

Alongside the Structural/Regional Funds there are initiatives which focus on managing industrial restructuring, fishing, urban areas, peripheral regions, rural development and inter-state co-operation. Total allocated resources for the period 1994–99 amount to 13.45bn ECU. Some of the more notable initiatives are INTERREG for trans-state co-operation on energy development; RECHAR to assist regions hit by the decline of the coal, steel, textile and defence industries; URBAN, which provides funds and resources to micro areas suffering from particularly high levels

of deprivation in and around cities; ADAPT to assist those made redundant by industrial restructuring; and programmes such as NOW (for women), HORIZON (for the disabled and long-term unemployed) and YOUTHSTART (for those under 20) (CEC, 1994; Lloyd *et al.*, 1995; Symes, 1995). Table 13.4 shows funding for each of these programmes.

For the European Commission the importance of these initiatives, and of the Structural Funds, is to address socio-spatial inequalities that stem from uneven development across the EU and have been exacerbated by what might be considered a collapsed mode of regulation. In effect, the EU measures represent a sort of spatial-workfarism[1] combining both Keynesian and "trickle-down" policies. This in turn constitutes a nascent

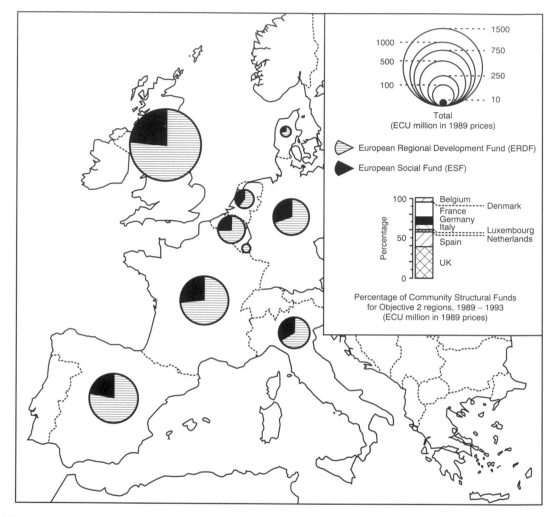

Figure 13.4   *Assistance for Objective 2 regions, 1989–91*

economic and social mode of regulation to complement an uncertain combination of national and international regimes of accumulation.

Several issues relating to the effectiveness of this funding must be identified at this point. The first is the relatively small scale of the budget. Overall, the Structural/Regional and Cohesion Funds amount to only 21bn ECU and represent no more than 0.3 per cent of EU GDP, or 1.6 per cent for Objective 1 regions. This is modest, even though between 1994 and 1999, under the Delors II package, an increase of 40 per cent has been agreed (CEC, 1994, 1995). Second, considerable variability in funding has meant that some initiatives such as RECHAR have been far

more effective than others (Lloyd *et al.*, 1995; Symes, 1995). Such problems in utilising EU funding extend to all sorts of projects both large and small, and often reflect the difficulties of governance, co-ordination and EU priorities (see for example Lyberaki, 1996, for the case of Greece; Lloyd and Meegan, 1996, with respect to Merseyside). Third, the EU requirement for so-called "additionality" (i.e. the principle that EU funding can only be "added" to national matching funds) often favours the wealthier countries with lower unemployment rates. This is because more prosperous member states can allocate larger sums of money to combat unemployment, thus securing an equally large financial package from Brussels.

Table 13.3 *Community budget resources, 1993–99*[*]

	1993		1996		1999	
	bn ECU	%	bn ECU	%	bn ECU	%
Agriculture	35.2	50.9	36.4	48.4	38.4	35.7
Structural actions *of which:*	21.3	30.8	25.0	33.2	30.0	35.7
Cohesion Funds	*1.5*	*2.2*	*2.3*	*3.1*	*2.6*	*3.1*
Structural Funds	*19.8*	*28.6*	*22.7*	*30.2*	*27.4*	*32.6*
Internal policies	3.9	5.6	4.5	6.0	5.1	6.1
External action	4.0	5.8	4.6	6.1	5.6	6.7
Other	4.8	6.9	4.8	6.4	5.0	5.9
Total commitments	69.2	100	75.2	100	84.1	100
Payment appropriations	65.9		71.3		80.1	
Payment appropriations as % of EU GNP	1.2		1.2			1.3

* In 1992 prices.
Source: CEC (1994, 126).

Fourth, ESF promotion for training may be of little effect because, generally speaking, the main problem in Europe is the availability of jobs and not a skills mismatch (Symes, 1995). It is therefore commonplace for people to be trained with little

Table 13.4 *EU initiatives, 1994–99 (bn ECU)* *

INTERREG	2.9
Rural Development (LEADER II)	1.4
REGIS	0.6
Employment	
NOW	na
HORIZON	1.4
YOUTHSTART	na
Industrial change	
ADAPT	1.4
RECHAR	0.4
RESIDER	0.5
KONVER	0.5
RETEX	0.5
Portuguese textiles industry	0.4
SMEs	1.0
Urban policy	0.6
PESCA (fisheries)	0.3
Reserve	1.6
Total	13.5

* At 1994 prices.
na = not available.
Source: CEC (1994, 189).

prospect of subsequent employment. Finally, the Structural/Regional Funds are often hampered by other EU policies which reinforce rather than abate spatial inequalities (Amin and Tomaney, 1995; Dunford and Perrons, 1994). This has been the case, for example, with those designed to support regions which have, or have the potential to develop, high-technology profiles; and, as will now be demonstrated, it is very much a current concern with respect to monetary union.

The EMS and monetary union

One of the less discussed *European-scale* institutional frameworks that governs employment levels is the role of the European Monetary System (EMS). The creation of the exchange rate mechanism (ERM) within the wider EMS in 1978–79 initially sought to address widely fluctuating exchange rates by introducing a more fixed structure of parity limits in which currencies could operate. At first the ERM allowed a certain space for macro-economic manoeuvring among individual states, commonly known as the "adjustable peg system", but the institution of a more rigid mechanism in 1987 eliminated much of this autonomy (Bordes *et al.*, 1995). The

251

intended results were price stability and the elimination of threats to European political and economic cohesion. Yet narrow parity bands – combined with the lifting of regulations on capital movements in 1990 – in fact led to problems of monetary autonomy (Begg and Mayes, 1993; Carchedi, 1991). Scope was reduced for controlling inflation and public deficits; for de- or revaluing currencies; and for adjusting interest rates. Individual countries thus gave up control of policy levers previously used to influence growth; and, in the neo-liberal climate of the time, many national policies were adopted that were anathema to countervailing programmes that might have stimulated job growth or protected those excluded by labour markets. This became a particular issue for the economically weaker states and those prone to higher inflation rates, e.g. Italy and Spain.

An extension of this problem is that European governments are now under considerable pressure to meet the monetary union convergence criteria (Begg and Mayes, 1993). Once again, these criteria are essentially concerned with low inflation, stable exchange rates, low interest rates and reduced budget deficits (CEC, 1994). Although considerable efforts are being invested to achieve the convergence goal, when the Commission surveyed progress in 1994 only France and Luxembourg had managed to approach the EU criteria; Italy, Portugal and Greece had "0" scores; and even Germany remained "unprepared" for convergence by Commission standards (Table 13.5). Moreover, in some respects this situation subsequently deteriorated. By 1997, for example, the ability of Germany and France to meet the criteria was being questioned, although they were the two central actors in the project. From the viewpoint of this chapter these problems of achieving convergence have been of great significance, chiefly because many policies in many member states have been tightened in response. This has involved severe constraints on public expenditure, which have in turn created significant obstacles to the attack on unemployment.

So far we have regarded the unemployed as a homogeneous group but, as was indicated at the

Table 13.5 *Maastricht convergence criteria and member states' performance*

	Inflation rate (%)	Budget deficit (%)*	Debt ratio (%)[†]	Long-term interest rate (%)[‡]	Exchange rate stability[§]	Total score
Maastricht criteria	3.3	3.0	60.0	10.7	–	–
Belgium	2.8	7.0	138.4	8.7	Yes	3
Denmark	1.4	4.4	90.6	9.0	Yes	3
Germany	3.4	4.2	48.9	8.0	Yes	3
Greece	13.7	15.5	121.2	16.6	No	0
Spain	4.7	7.2	55.9	12.1	No	1
France	2.3	5.5	44.1	8.6	Yes	4
Ireland	2.0	2.3	99.0	9.1	No	3
Italy	4.4	9.4	118.1	11.9	No	0
Luxembourg	3.6	2.5	10.0	7.9	Yes	4
Netherlands	2.1	4.0	81.4	8.0	Yes	3
Portugal	6.7	8.1	66.4	13.2	No	0
UK	3.4	7.6	48.8	9.1	No	2
EU12 average	3.8	6.0	65.9	10.2	–	–

* Government deficit as % of GDP;
[†] Government debt as % of GDP;
[‡] Long-term rates in 1992;
[§] Yes indicates that a country had not devalued in the preceding two years and had remained within the ± 2.5% fluctuation allowance for the European ERM.
Source: CEC (1994, 147).

outset, this is not a realistic representation. Some groups in society have many more advantages than others, and it is to this issue that we now turn via the concept of "flexibilisation".

Employment Flexibilisation and Disadvantaged Groups

The period since the mid- to late-1980s has been associated with the flexibilisation of employment in the EU as Fordist-Keynesianism has declined. Major influences have been continuing high unemployment in many areas, declining unionism and widespread feelings of uncertainty and insecurity among workers. In addition, the process has been encouraged by the growth of part-time work, service sector expansion and the "feminisation" of the labour force (especially in services). Part-time and casual work have progressed furthest in the UK and the Netherlands (Bruegel and Hegewisch, 1994), but have increased across most of Europe, with a concomitant "rolling-back" of welfare benefits. Moreover, while the balance of forces has often been very complex, flexibilisation has in many instances become an employer strategy, rather than simply an outcome of labour demand–supply relationships.

One important consequence of flexibilisation is that it has resulted in the intensified segmentation of workers in terms of gender, age, etc., causing a range of vulnerable groups to account for disproportionate shares of the unemployed (Figure 13.5). At this point, therefore, it is appropriate to examine key groups to identify their problems more specifically and to question how – in the interests of social, economic and political cohesion – European policy-makers have reacted to their emergence by targeting policies directly at them (Symes, 1995; Nicaise *et al.*, 1995).

Gender differentials and unemployment

Under pressure from EC/EU law, which has sought to improve opportunities for women, welfare regimes have moved away from the traditional "male breadwinner model". However, as will be demonstrated, this development has had contradictory implications for women's roles in European labour markets. Categorisation of welfare regimes is highly complex, but Esping-Andersen (1990) provides perhaps one of the most widely encountered analyses. His typology envisages:

- the "social democratic model", which supports a universal system in which the provision of benefits and services rests on citizenship and full employment (as in Sweden and Denmark)
- a liberal, means-tested benefit system, with only a residual (i.e. basic needs) role for the state (e.g. UK)
- a (Catholic)–conservative–corporatist model which supports and maintains a strict division between men as workers and women as wives, and between adults and children. Austria, Belgium, France, Germany and the Netherlands exemplify this approach. Here the state has supported this ideological structure through a system of "subsidiarity" in which it intervenes where the family cannot provide

These, of course, are only "ideal types" and there are significant variants. Italy, Portugal, Spain and Greece, for example, share many of the elements of countries like Germany, but their welfare regimes tend to be more "clientelistic" with the provision of support regulated by male-dominated contacts (Lewis, 1993b). Moreover, the models naturally evolve, and Esping-Andersen's conceptualisation is flawed because women are brought into the analysis only as waged labour, whereas they are often unpaid workers. None the less, it is helpful to examine some of their general implications for labour markets. Esping-Andersen (1990) argues that the corporatist model discourages female participation through tax disincentives to two-earner couples, insufficient child care provision, etc. Meanwhile, liberal regimes (e.g. the UK) display a lack of publicly funded child care that has favoured part-time rather than full-time female participation. And the southern "Catholic" model stands apart in that domestic unwaged labour and high youth unemployment are masked by the already high registered unemployment levels.

Moving on from Esping-Andersen's categorisation, Germany may be argued to have a "neutral" approach to women's entrance into the labour market, under which the nature of benefits

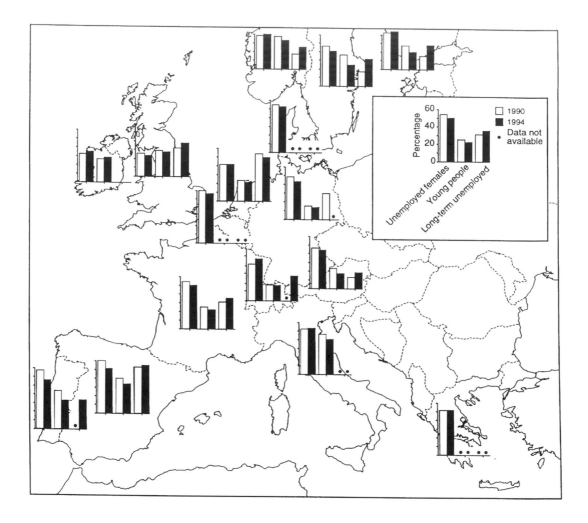

Figure 13.5 *Unemployment by sex, age and duration in western Europe*

allows them to "choose" whether to work. Once the decision to do so is made, however, there is little support for their integration. The German tax system is heavily biased in favour of married, one-earner couples, although the state admittedly also provides substantial child care benefits. The UK, as we have seen, is noted for its poor child care provision, while Italy's attitude to women's participation is ambiguous. On the one hand patriarchal family laws and a lack of coherent social services place a burden on women as carers, and make it difficult for lone mothers to obtain benefits. On the other hand, recent legislation has provided rather generous protection for lone mothers at work, and child care provision is similar

in structure to that of Germany. France has maintained a generally favourable attitude to women at work, including generous maternity leave for working mothers, and strong publicly funded child care. Indeed, it sets itself apart from other countries in providing so many benefits for lone mothers that it may actually discourage them from entering the labour market. Most recently the French system has served to penalise married women's work, yet favour women in low-income families entering the labour force. The Irish state actively promotes adult women as wives and mothers – which may explain married women's very low participation in the workforce – but since 1990 has provided special benefits for lone mothers. In contrast, Sweden has a highly progressive tax system which has encouraged women to enter the labour market, treats all adult women as workers, couples this with generous guaranteed levels of child care, and offers strong parental leave entitlements.

What can be generalised from this complex picture? Above all, from Ireland on the one extreme to the Scandinavian countries on the other, three characteristics mark the relationship between welfare regimes and women's work. First, as Lewis (1993b) and Dunford (1996) argue, women tend to "fare better" under the social-democratic model epitomised by Sweden, and this may actually improve the employment rates of specific regions. Second, all countries have modified the male breadwinner concept, although it still very much prevails in Germany, Ireland and the UK. Third, restructuring of welfare systems has for many countries involved a "neutral" approach to work, offering women both "independence" and "dependence". Thus, despite what might be argued to be "post-Fordist" tranformations of national welfare regimes, or the decline in the male breadwinner model, its replacement outside Scandinavia by more neutral policies seems to have exacerbated the problems which women face in the labour market (Kennett, 1994; Lewis, 1993b).

Beyond this, women's (and thus men's) participation in the labour force is governed by a host of factors: their share of the population of working age (15–64); their marital status; the number of children they have; their involvement in unpaid work; society's cultural expectations and norms (including men's attitudes to child-rearing); and the structure of work (part-time, full-time, casual employment, etc.) (Lewis, 1993b). EU statistics regarding participation have to be read with extreme caution, but it is generally agreed that female rates have been increasing since 1975, and have grown dramatically in recent years for the age group 25–54. Part of this shift has been much greater participation for married women with children, except in Ireland. By 1991, 84 per cent of childless single women, and 67 per cent of childless married women between the ages of 25 and 49, were in work or looking for work.

These aggregate figures naturally mask substantial national variations. For example,

female participation was particularly high in Denmark, but well below average in Ireland, Greece and Spain (CEC, 1993). Beyond this it is also clear that gender equality in employment is still far from complete (Mossuz-Lavau, 1992; Symes, 1995). In part this is evident in gender biases which exist in pension schemes, welfare systems and family institutions. The restructuring of the Welfare State – and especially its social security systems – has meant that women are increasingly being treated as individuals, rather than as dependants of men, which has also worsened their poverty risks (Ginn and Arber, 1994; Leira, 1994; Scheiwe, 1994). Most obviously, however, gender bias is a major feature of unemployment. Female unemployment rates remain much higher than those for men in all EU countries except the UK (CEC, 1993; Green and Owen, 1995; United Nations, 1995). Women constitute half the long-term unemployed, and gender segmentation is still firmly rooted in women's disproportionate absence from industry. In Spain, Greece and Italy about 33 per cent of women under 25 were unemployed in the early 1990s, although it is true that this level was far lower than a decade earlier, when the figure hovered around 80 per cent (CEC, 1993).

How has the EU responded to such developments? The ESF first acknowledged the disadvantaged position of women within European labour markets in 1977, and training initially targeted "typically male" sectors to address the gender imbalance. In 1984 Brussels revoked these special funds, hoping there would be a drift towards gender equality, but research then found that women tended to be trained for positions which were becoming obsolete, and men for emerging technologies. Indeed, training for some sectors legally excluded women. In 1989, therefore, the EU once again recognised the necessity of a specific programme aimed at training women for more permanent (and not simply low-skilled part-time) jobs. Even so, the funding made available has remained restricted. Special pro-grammes designed to address these issues received only 5.8 per cent of the total funding for Objectives 3 and 4 in the last ESF calculation (1990–92). Furthermore, national allocations within these grants varied considerably from country to country (Table 13.6).

Meanwhile, EU initiatives such as NOW (mentioned earlier), have also attempted to redress gender inequalities, by promoting women's qualifications and business initiatives, and by providing counselling and support services for women re-entering the labour market after a long absence. In Objective I regions, for example, the EU allocated 120m. ECU in 1991 for the provision of child-care schemes and crèches to allow more women to enter the labour market. This type of action is complemented by local employment initiatives, which are similar in some respects to NOW, and offer grants to female-owned businesses which promise to hire "more disadvantaged" women such as migrants, the disabled and the long-term unemployed (Symes, 1995). However, beyond a very localised arena, whether these programmes have played a substantial role in boosting women's employment is doubtful, if only because of the insufficient scale of the funding (though this is increasing). Perhaps a more important effect is the role that they have in changing women's and men's attitudes towards the place of women in the labour force.

Youth unemployment

With the exception of Germany, youth unemployment in the EU remains on average higher than for all other working-age categories. (The youth category covers the age range 15–24.) After falling from 23.3 per cent in 1985 to 16.8 per cent in 1990, the rate has subsequently climbed once again, in sympathy with overall unemployment (CEC, 1993, 1994). By May 1993 the incidence among young men reached 19 per cent in the EU as a whole, while the equivalent figure for young women was 20 per cent. At over 40 per cent, Italy clearly has the highest proportion of young people looking for work (Figure 13.5). Meanwhile Finland, Spain, France, isolated parts of the UK and Greece also have high rates, whereas the lowest levels are concentrated in Luxembourg, Germany, Denmark and the Netherlands. In general, therefore, youth unemployment is highest in the agricultural regions of southern Europe (which may be related to technological innovation in agriculture, and the lack of opportunities in urban areas) and also in districts undergoing severe forms

of industrial restructuring, such as southern Belgium, north-eastern France and parts of the UK (CEC, 1993). What we should also note, of course, is that it is strongly associated with social groups who are also disadvantaged in other ways (e.g. in terms of race).

While the determinants of youth unemployment levels remain as elusive as those for general unemployment, contributory factors include the number of people entering the labour market; the difficulty which young people with little experience or few qualifications face in finding work during economic recessions (CEC, 1993; Symes, 1995); the extent to which employers can or cannot benefit by hiring young workers on low wages; the degree to which older workers nearing retirement are retained or released; the scale and effectiveness of training and apprenticeship policies; and the structure of technological change, which naturally can create employment opportunities for those with appropriate skills.

Policy responses generally assume two forms: education and training. As youth unemployment climbed rapidly during the 1980s, ESF funding increasingly targeted this problem through Objective 4 funding. Allocations rose from 609.5m. ECU in 1980 to over 2.7bn in 1989. The majority went to the UK, Italy, Spain, France and Portugal. After 1989, 75 per cent of ESF finances were directed into programmes for people under the age of 25. Most of these programmes included vocational education for specific labour markets, apprenticeships in firms, training for high technologies, incentives for employers to hire young people, and measures to help them into stable forms of self-employment (Symes, 1995). Table 13.6 shows for a number of member states the funding directed towards policies specifically affecting young people.

Such Europe-wide initiatives have often been complemented by specific national benefit schemes, although their breadth has varied enormously – from simple discounts and subsidies on transport (most notably in France) to tax allowances and small business schemes. Spain is one of the least supportive countries in this respect, offering as it does few benefits combined with a low minimum wage rate. In sharp contrast, considerable advantages are given to young people in the Netherlands, Belgium, France and Italy. In

Table 13.6 *European Social Fund financing plan, selected member states, 1990–92 (m. ECU)*

	France	Germany	Netherlands	Spain	UK
Objective 3 – Long-term unemployment					
Training	259.1	104.1	36.0	121.8	325.0
of which:					
Technological	*13.0*	–	*12.4*	*10.0*	–
Basic	*246.1*	–	*23.7*	*111.8*	*325.0*
Recruitment subsidies	39.1	14.3	35.0	22.2	71.0
Disadvantaged groups	101.2	118.2	42.8	25.4	118.0
of which:					
Women	*19.2*	*22.3*	*28.5*	*16.0*	*56.0*
Disabled	*66.8*	*57.2*	*8.1*	*8.7*	*56.0*
Migrants	*15.2*	*38.7*	*6.2*	*0.7*	*6.0*
Other	–	*35.1*	–	–	–
Total Objective 3	399.4	271.1	123.5	169.4	514.0
Objective 4 – Youth unemployment					
Training	370.4	33.3	52.6	293.0	405.5
of which:					
Technological	*74.0*	–	*37.0*	*11.7*	*96.5*
Basic	*296.4*	–	*15.6*	*281.3*	*309.0*
Recruitment subsidies	29.6	–	16.4	74.2	–
Disadvantaged groups	37.8	231.9	19.5	20.9	64.5
of which:					
Women	*1.9*	*11.4*	*8.3*	*13.5*	*22.5*
Disabled	*35.6*	*69.6*	*4.3*	*5.6*	*40.5*
Migrants	*0.4*	*31.7*	*7.0*	*1.8*	*1.5*
Other	–	*25.8*	–	–	–
Transnational/innovatory	–	5.2	8.3	–	–
Total Objective 4	437.8	296.2	96.8	388.1	470.0
Total Objectives 3 and 4	*837.2*	*567.9*	*220.3*	*557.5*	*984.0*
Article 1	34.9	5.2	9.7	5.6	41.0
Total European Social Fund	*872.1*	*573.1*	*230.0*	*563.1*	*1025.0*

Source: Symes (1995, 48).

1994 the Italian government instituted tax credits for employers recruiting first-time job seekers and other disadvantaged workers into permanent positions. In Belgium the employment prospects for young people have been improved through the *Plan d'Embauche des Jeunes*, and in the 1980s France also instituted a range of measures to combat youth unemployment (Petit, 1987).

As we noted earlier, however, the issue is chiefly the supply of jobs, rather than a skills mismatch (Symes, 1995), and because of this the effect of these programmes on unemployment has probably been minimal relative to other forces (United Nations, 1995). Moreover, the presence of a large pool of unemployed young workers, willing to work for depressed wages, may have hindered international competitiveness by acting as a disincentive to innovation. In the absence of job-led European economic growth, therefore, it seems that the future improvement of youth unemployment might only come at the expense of other categories of workers.

"Older workers" and unemployment

"Older workers", generally understood to be in the 50–64 age category, cannot and should not be taken as a homogeneous group. Clearly, there are differences based on class, ethnicity, gender, skills, experience, etc. Nor should it be assumed that they are always at the mercy of the labour market. For example, provided older workers constitute a significant proportion of workers in the firm, they may be able to resist organisational and technical innovations, although often at the risk of declining productivity. Similarly, technological change does not always have an adverse effect on the employment possibilities of older workers, as their skills and experience may prove more useful than obsolete.

Nevertheless, it is undeniable that industrial restructuring in particular has had a massive effect on men employed in "traditional" manufacturing (steel, coal, textiles and automobiles), through the well-known phenomena of voluntary redundancy, early retirement packages and, of course, forced redundancies. To a significant extent, in the late 1970s and early 1980s this reflected the rise of youth unemployment, which meant that – in the interests of political stability – European governments promoted all manner of youth training schemes, apprenticeships and the like, while simultaneously pressing for older workers to retire. Because these workers have typically been trapped in regions dependent on specific declining industries, they have naturally found it difficult to gain alternative jobs, resulting in either long-term unemployment or a complete withdrawal from the labour market (Dunford, 1996).

Meanwhile, as we have seen, female employment prospects have been boosted by the general shift from economies largely based on industrial employment to those based predominantly on the service sector. Once again, however, we may identify problems for older workers connected with this change, especially in northern Europe. Here there have been apparent recruitment difficulties, perhaps because young workers are wary of problems of job security, weak benefits, low pay, etc. As a result, employers have increasingly turned to older single or married women, recruiting them into jobs that are disproportionately part-time. In the EU in 1991,

for example, 35 per cent of women aged 50–64 worked part-time, compared to 26 per cent of those aged 25–49 (CEC, 1993). And in the Netherlands and the UK the equivalent proportions were 54 and 72 per cent respectively. Today, therefore, older women constitute a large proportion of those working part-time in the service sector, and notably in the UK and the Netherlands where such jobs have represented the overwhelming majority of newly created employment. In many instances, of course, this causes no problems, especially when women have opted for this type of work. But often – because of the weaknesses of existing pension and welfare schemes – these women are in the labour market either to supplement the income of a husband or partner who is unemployed, retired or low paid, or to support themselves in straightened circumstances. In the UK, where poverty levels for older single women are higher than anywhere else in Europe, this is a particular concern (Ginn and Arber, 1994).

Immigration

Although this theme is considered by King in later chapters, brief consideration is none the less appropriate here. Immigration has expanded across European states since the mid-1980s, after a long slow-down following economic crisis in the mid-1970s. From a government perspective, if only in the short term, immigration may improve international competitiveness by depressing wage levels. EU governments therefore have considerable interest in encouraging it, at least at a modest level. This, however, has to be set against the danger that low wages may discourage technological change; and it must also be reconciled with socio-political-legitimation crises that often confront states. Immigration is all too easily seen as a threat to the jobs of nationals even though, for a wide range of reasons, the correlation between actual immigration levels and labour demand created by production imperatives is in reality weak.

Against this background, European immigration policies are too numerous and complex to review in detail. However, two central features must be highlighted: the European Commission, and to some extent national governments, appear to be increasingly committed to the harmonisation of policies which will satisfy for them the conditions of a "social Europe", while ensuring that the anticipated effects will not disrupt political and economic cohesion. Reconciling these objectives has proved extremely difficult, but the preferred approaches can now be identified. First, given that migrants face discrimination in the housing and employment spheres, the EU is committed to policies of "integration" and non-discrimination for foreign workers and their dependants in all member states (CEC, 1991). Second, because more people wish to enter the EU than is currently legal, immigration policies have tended to converge as individual member states have sought to ensure that they are no more attractive to migrants than other countries. Of course, this process has been by no means perfect; for example, practices are far more restrictive in the northern and western states of the EU than elsewhere. Moreover, the restrictive trend may be contradictory to the implications of demographic slow-down in northern and western EU countries (Convey and Kupiszewski, 1995; King, 1993; *Les Echos*, March 1995, 24–5). Even so, the "race to restriction" is well established, and it is possible that it may ultimately have repercussions for labour markets, technological change and social security systems.

Conclusion

Western Europe has recently experienced significant demographic and broad socio-economic changes: decreased population growth rates, longer life expectancy, an ageing of the population, greater female participation in paid employment, and shifts in reliance on immigrant labour. At the same time, some indicators have suggested that economic performance has been good, but others have been much less encouraging. Thus, while trade development has in some respects been impressive, and there has been absolute growth in employment, the link between economic expansion and employment creation has proved weak. Labour supply has continued to outstrip demand, causing chronic unemployment problems; and unemployment and low output have remained strongly associated with weaker parts of the EU.

At a time of increasing emphasis on integration and cohesion, the spatial dimensions of these problems have posed a considerable challenge for the EU. The main policy response has been extension and development of the Structural/ Regional Funds, which are now much more elaborate than in the 1970s. For a whole range of reasons, however, the effectiveness of these funds may be doubted, and an additional obstacle to progress is that some of the EU's own policies – such as the EMS and monetary union – may intensify rather than reduce inequalities.

While it is important to consider these broad issues, it is also necessary to recognise that – only a little beneath the surface – labour market and unemployment problems remain highly significant for a whole range of disadvantaged groups. Indeed, these problems have intensified through processes such as the flexibilisation of labour, the feminisation of employment and the restructuring of welfare regimes. Once again, the EU's policy response is relevant in this context, and it may be claimed that some modest successes have been achieved, for example with respect to youth employment. However, structural biases which disadvantage specific groups have certainly not been ended, and it can be suggested that EU policy has only "repaired", rather than cured, this structural discrimination.

Despite this widespread failure, it is striking that the greatest publicity is not given to these issues, but to what is becoming known as the "ageing timebomb" – the need to support through social security and pension schemes an expanding elderly population that is economically inactive. We would argue, however, that the threat posed by this phenomenon is exaggerated. Employment is likely to continue to grow and, although Europe's unemployed may be reluctant to migrate to other countries in search of work, immigration could be increased to fill jobs and, therefore, social security coffers. Alternatively, if immigration policy harmonisation were to block off this route, the supposed "crisis" could be averted by revising current political attitudes to taxation. Conversely, however, the problems of disadvantaged regions and social groups are far more difficult to eliminate, and it is with these issues that we should be primarily concerned.

Note

1. By this we mean a combination of "neo-Schumpterian workfare" and supranational and national Keynesianism which aims to stimulate economic growth – and thus employment – at the regional level.

References

Amin, A and Tomaney, J (1995) The challenge of cohesion, in A Amin and J Tomaney (eds) *Behind the Myth of the European Union*, Routledge, London, 10–47.

Begg, I (1995) Threats to cohesion, in A Amin and J Tomaney (eds) *Behind the Myth of the European Union*, Routledge, London, 110–24.

Begg, I and Mayes, D (1993) Cohesion, convergence and monetary union in Europe, *Regional Studies*, **27**, 149–65.

Bordes, C, Girardin, E, and Me'litz, J (eds) (1995) *European Currency Crises and After*, Manchester University Press, Manchester.

Bourgeois-Pichat, J (1981) Recent demographic change in Western Europe: an assessment, *Population and Development Review*, **7**, 19–42.

Bruegel, I and Hegewisch A (1994) Flexibilization and part-time work in Europe, in P Brown and R Crompton (eds) *A New Europe? Economic restructuring and social exclusion*, UCL Press, London, 33–57.

Carchedi, G (1991) *Frontiers of Political Economy*, Verso, London.

Casey, B (1993) Employment promotion, in M Gold (ed) *The Social Dimension: employment policy in the European Community*, Macmillan, London, 172–83.

CEC (1991) *Policies on Immigration and the Social Integration of Migrants in the EC*, Commission of the European Communities, Brussels.

CEC (1993) *L'emploi en Europe*, Commission of the European Communities, Brussels.

CEC (1994) *Competitiveness and Cohesion: trends in the regions*, Commission of European Communities, Brussels.

CEC (1995) *EC Regional Policies*, Commission of European Communities, Brussels.

CEC (1996a) Annual economic report for 1996, *European Economy*, No 61.

CEC (1996b) Supplement A: economic trends, *European Economy*, No 56.

CEC (1996c) *Structural Funds and Cohesion Fund, 1994–99: regulations and commentary*, Commission of the European Communities, Brussels.

Convey, A and Kupiszewski, M (1995) Keeping up with Schengen: migration and policy in the European Union, *International Migration Review*, **4**, 939–63.

Dunford, M (1995) Cohesion, growth and inequality in the European Union, in A Amin and J Tomaney (eds) *Behind the Myth of the European Union*, Routledge, London, 125–46.

Dunford, M (1996) Disparities in employment, productivity and output in the EU: the roles of labour market governance and welfare regimes, *Regional Studies*, **30**, 339–57.

Dunford, M and Perrons, D (1994) Regional inequality, regimes of accumulation and economic development in contemporary Europe, *Transactions of the Institute of British Geographers*, **19**, 163–82.

Esping-Andersen, G (1990) *The Three Worlds of Welfare Capitalism*, Polity Press, Cambridge.

Eurostat (1995) *Europe in Figures*, Office for Official Publications of the European Communities, Luxembourg.

Eurostat (1997) *Basic Statistics of the European Union*, Office for Official Publications of the European Communities, Luxembourg.

Ginn, J and Arber, S (1994) Gender and pensions in Europe, current trends in women's pension acquisition, in P Brown and R Crompton (eds) *A New Europe? Economic restructuring and social exclusion*, UCL Press, London, 58–85.

Green, A E and Owen, D (1995) The labour market aspects of population change in the 1990s, in R Hall and P White (eds) *Europe's population: towards the next century*, UCL Press, London, 51–68.

Hall, R (1993) Family structures, in D Noin and R Woods (eds) *The Changing Population of Europe*, Basil Blackwell, Oxford, 100–26.

Kennett, P (1994) Exclusion, post-Fordism and the "New Europe", in P Brown and R Crompton (eds) *A New Europe? Economic restructuring and social exclusion*, UCL Press, London, 14–32.

King, R (1993) *The New Geography of European Migrations*, Belhaven, London.

Leira, A (1994) Combining work and family: working mothers in Scandinavia and the European Community, in P Brown and R Crompton (eds) *A New Europe? Economic restructuring and social exclusion*, UCL Press, London, 86–107.

Les Echos, March 24–5, 1995.

Lewis, J (ed) (1993a) *Women, Work, Family and Social Policies in Europe*, Edward Elgar, Aldershot.

Lewis, J (1993b) Introduction: women and social policies in Europe, in J Lewis (ed) *Women, Work, Family and Social Policies in Europe*, Edward Elgar, Aldershot, 1–24.

Lloyd, P and Meegan, R (1996) Contested governance: European exposure in the English regions, *European Planning Studies*, **4**, 75–97.

Lloyd, P, Meegan, R and Samers, M (1995) *Prior appraisal of the New Generation of Community Initiatives: URBAN*, Final report to Directorate-General XV, Commission of European Communities, CRED Research Unit, Department of Geography, University of Liverpool.

Lyberaki, A (1996) Greece–EU comparative economic performance at the national and regional levels: why divergence?, *European Planning Studies*, **4**, 313–29.

Michie, J (1995) Unemployment in Europe, in A Amin and J Tomaney (eds) *Behind the Myth of the European Union*, Routledge, London, 83–109.

Mossuz-Levau, J (1992) European women in 1992: in transformation, in Commission of the European

Communities (ed) *Women of Europe*, Commission of the European Communities, Brussels, 12–21.

Nicaise, I, Bollens, J, Dawes, L, Laghaei, S, Thaulow, I, Verdié, M and Wagner, A (1995) Pitfalls and dilemmas in labour market policies for disadvantaged groups – and how to avoid them, *Journal of European Social Policy*, **5**, 199–217.

Noin, D and Woods, R I (eds) (1993) *The Changing Population of Europe*, Basil Blackwell, Oxford.

Petit, P (1987) Heurs et malheurs de l'état face au rapport salarial: la France, in R Boyer (ed) *La flexibilité au travail en Europe*, Editions la Découverte, Paris, 35–64.

Rees, P H *et al.* (1996) *Population Migration in the European Union*, John Wiley & Sons, New York.

Scheiwe, K (1994) Labour market, welfare state and family institutions: the links to mothers' poverty risks. A comparison between Belgium, Germany and the United Kingdom, *Journal of European Social Policy*, **4**, 201–24.

Symes, V (1995) *Unemployment in Europe: problems and policies*, Routledge, London.

United Nations (1993) *Demographic Yearbook, Special Issue: population, ageing and the situation of elderly persons*, United Nations, New York.

United Nation (1995) *Economic Survey of Europem 1994–95*, United Nations, New York.

van de Kaa, D (1987) Europe's second demographic transition, *Population Bulletin*, **42**(1), 3–57.

Vandermotten, C (1993) The geography of employment, in D Noin and R Woods (eds) *The Changing Population of Europe*, Basil Blackwell, Oxford, 135–50.

14

From guestworkers to immigrants

Labour migration from the Mediterranean periphery

Russell King
School of European Studies, University of Sussex, UK

Migration is not only a human link between one place and another, it is also a link between economic and social geography. The majority of long-distance migration, including international migration, takes place primarily for economic motives. A growing economy, such as north-west Europe in the 1950s and 1960s, needs additional workers to sustain its growth and in particular to perform certain types of jobs; migrants move from poor to rich economies in order to increase their incomes and improve their life chances. But migrants, self-evidently, are also human beings and hence economically motivated migration is also a social process, the protagonists of which endure social stress of various kinds.

This chapter, and the next, provide important links between Part II of this book, on economic transformation, and Part III on social stress. In this chapter international labour migration within and from outside Europe will be shown to have functioned as a fundamental component of the industrial development of Europe between the end of the Second World War and the first oil crisis. In particular, mass migration was an important structural element of the Fordist system of organised labour and mass industrial production.

Chapter 15 will examine the new geographies of international migration and social stress in the post-Fordist and post-Communist eras.

The material presented in this chapter moves progressively from the political and economic context of migration to its social and cultural aspects. We will mainly concern ourselves with international migrants – the "guestworkers" and "immigrants" in the title of the chapter – but will also make brief reference to some large-scale migrations within countries, such as that between the south and north of Italy. The geographical structure of the chapter will follow the main axis of the migrants' moves from the Mediterranean periphery of Europe to their destinations in the industrial countries of northern Europe. But the story would not be complete without some mention of other migrant-sending countries such as Ireland and Finland, as well as the important immigrations from former colonial territories of European powers in the Caribbean, Africa and South Asia, so these migrations are fitted into the picture too.

The chapter consists of six sections.[1] The first provides a brief overview of geographers' contributions to research on European labour migration and maps out the main spatial patterns of flows between countries. The following section discusses the political economy of labour migration during and after the formation of the European Community: it stresses the importance of labour demand as the principal variable governing the migration of workers, and evaluates the relevance of the EC's "free movement of labour" policy. The third part of the chapter examines the employment of immigrants, which is also a key to understanding their social position and mobility. In the fourth section, on the housing and residential characteristics of immigrant populations, parallels will be noted between immigrants' positions among the lower echelons of both the employment and the housing markets, and between their social and spatial mobility. The penultimate part of the chapter looks at a range of social and cultural issues mainly focused around questions of social integration and social exclusion. Finally, we follow those migrants who have returned to their home countries to see how they have reintegrated in their native societies and whether they are acting as a dynamic force for the development of their home regions.

To a large extent this chapter is written in the past tense. It concerns a remarkable period in western Europe's post-war economic history when migrant workers were recruited in their millions from a wide range of source countries. This period came to an end in 1973. But its legacies live on in the lives of those migrants and of their children and, now, grandchildren. As the chapter moves from the economic geography of labour migration to the social and cultural geography of established immigrant or ethnic populations, so the tense shifts from the past to the present.

Of Flows and Stocks: Geographers and Migrants

"Flows" and "stocks" are regrettably dehumanising terms to use for migrants, treating them as if they were an industrial product or a quantity of merchandise to be stored or moved. Yet, in a sense, this is entirely appropriate since employers, governments and the entire apparatus of the Fordist system regarded them in exactly this way: as a factor of production. Flows and stocks are also a shorthand for distinguishing between two aspects of migration which in practice are often treated quite separately and which have generated distinct literatures: the migration *process*, and the *consequences* of migration in terms of the formation of ethnic minorities. However, even these terms can be questioned: "minorities" for instance not only implies a numerical inferiority to the "majority" population (whatever that may mean) but also signifies some kind of cultural subservience which must be overcome by adjusting to the majority's norms – the process of assimilation. It also fails to acknowledge the diaspora view of migrant populations from the perspective of their societies of origin.

Before this chapter turns into an essay on deconstruction, let us return to the distinction between migration and the formation of ethnic populations and note that geographers (and sociologists) have done much more research on the latter than they have on the former. West European geographers have a well-established tradition of studying "minority groups". These studies are far too numerous to be listed here, for in addition to the many investigations of ethnic populations in the UK there are also rich literatures in French, German, Dutch and Swedish. These recount the experience of individual countries, cities and regions, and have now moved on from the rather sterile discourse of segregation indices to the exploration of migrants' everyday lives. Much of this multi-lingual material has been expertly summarised by Paul White (1984, 97–133, 1993a, b; see also Chapter 16 of this volume). Perhaps more important to note here is the relative lack of geographical studies which take a Europe-wide or comparative view of the *processes* of labour migration: despite the work of Fassman and Münz (1994) and King (1993) the pioneering set of essays edited by Salt and Clout (1976) have yet to be fully updated.

Data problems

The totals of foreign workers residing in host countries are a function of three main factors: the annual inflow of migrant workers; their mean length of stay; and the proportion who return to their home countries. Many data sets relating to these parameters are available: they may appear superficially accurate because of their detail, but in practice migration statistics are notoriously imprecise, due for instance to sampling errors or to the different ways in which the act of migration is defined and measured. Sometimes the differences between estimates of the same flow that are produced by host and sender countries are enormous: one may be 5 or 10 times as large as the other. A particular problem with UK statistics on immigrants is that census and other official figures refer only to "foreign-born", which is no guarantee of a particular nationality.[2] On the other hand, "nationality" creates its own inconsistencies: in the Netherlands Surinamers have Dutch nationality, and in France the residents of overseas *départements* such as Guadeloupe and Réunion have French citizenship. In certain countries a significant number of foreign migrants have become legally naturalised or have taken up citizenship of the host country – many more in France than in Germany for instance. Clandestine migration has been an awkward problem for many countries. The majority of migration between Portugal and France during the 1960s and early 1970s was believed to be clandestine. Finally, return flows are particularly poorly monitored.

Despite these grave difficulties, several estimates of western Europe's immigrant population in the early 1970s, on the eve of the oil crisis, converge on a figure of around 12–13 million. The majority of these were workers rather than dependants, although this ratio was in the process of changing as "family reunion migration" was increasingly permitted. And the majority came from Mediterranean countries – Spain, Portugal, Italy, Yugoslavia, Greece, Turkey, Morocco, Algeria and Tunisia.

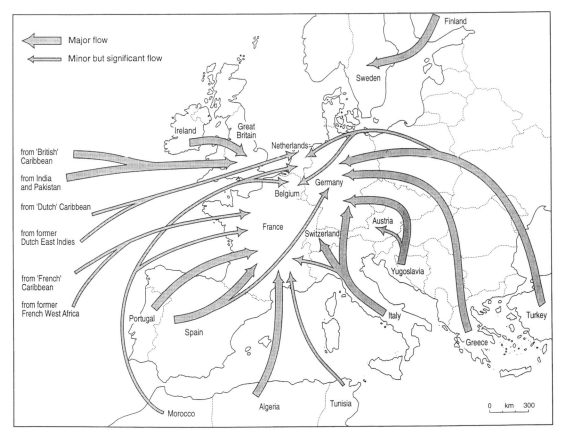

Figure 14.1 *Main international labour migration flows to western European countries, 1945–73*

Spatial patterns

The global figure of 12 or 13 million masks a complex situation with varying numbers of migrants moving to different destination countries. To try to map all the flows would produce a picture resembling a plate of spaghetti – an appropriate analogy seeing that Italians have been the most diverse in their migratory destinations. In simplifying the picture by focusing on the major flows, Figure 14.1 shows there to be a broad spatial symmetry to the pattern of movement between 1945 and 1973. France took migrant workers mainly from the south-western segment of the Mediterranean Basin (Spain, Portugal, Algeria, Morocco, Tunisia), Switzerland received mainly Italians, and West Germany recruited migrants from countries to the south-east (Yugoslavia, Greece, Turkey). Moving north from the Mediterranean sources of supply, the spatial coherence of the periphery-to-centre pattern was maintained by the migration of large numbers of Irish into the UK and of Finns into Sweden. Of course, there are some exceptions to this overneat, simplified pattern. For instance, Belgium recruited first from Poland and Italy, then from Morocco and Turkey. Reflecting its imperial heritage, the UK has incorporated many migrants from the Caribbean and South Asia; by 1971 these immigrants from the "New Commonwealth" numbered 1.1 million, including 302 000 West Indians, 313 000 from India and 230 000 from Pakistan and Bangladesh.

The intra-European migration scene during the period covered by Figure 14.1 was largely built around the rise and fall of Italy as a key supply country, a fact not brought out by the map. In the immediate post-war years, Italy provided the first Mediterranean emigration on any scale, particularly to France, Belgium and Switzerland, but also to the UK. West Germany started taking Italian workers in the late 1950s, and became the main destination for emigrant Italians in the early 1960s. Throughout this period most Italian emigrants came from the south, where poverty, unemployment and poor social conditions were widespread (Figure 14.2). However, during the 1960s southern Italians came to be increasingly in demand for the growing industries of northern Italy, so their need to migrate abroad tailed off.

Thus, by the late 1960s, after the short-lived German recession of 1966–67, Yugoslavs and Turks replaced Italians as the main labour migrants to West Germany, while in France the Italian migration flow had already started to fade in the 1950s, supplanted by Portuguese and Algerian immigrants.

From the broad patterns of flows described above, it is clear that the national characteristics of the immigrant workforce came to have a different composition in each receiving country. Moreover this composition was not static but changed

Table 14.1 *Distribution of foreign workers by nationality, selected countries, 1976*

	Foreign workers (million)	Principal nationalities (%)
West Germany	2.17	
Turkish		27.2
Yugoslav		20.1
Italian		14.3
Greek		9.2
France	1.90	
North African*		35.1
Portuguese		22.8
Spanish		12.9
Italian		12.6
Switzerland	0.55	
Italian		47.7
Spanish		11.5
French		10.7
German		10.1
Sweden	0.23	
Finnish		43.7
Danish or Norwegian		13.3
Yugoslav		11.5
Greek		5.3
Belgium	0.20	
Italian		32.0
Spanish		10.0
North African†		9.3
Turkish		5.0
Netherlands	0.18	
EC (Nine)		30.1
Turkish		21.1
North African‡		16.6
Spanish		8.8

* Mainly Algerian.
† Mainly Moroccan.
‡ Nearly all Moroccan.
Source: SOPEMI (1977).

Figure 14.2   *The emigration setting: a scene in a peasant household in Basilicata, southern Italy, in the 1960s. Emigration has removed the younger elements of the population, leaving mainly the elderly*

through time. Table 14.1 sets out data for six destination countries for 1976, after the migrant "stocks" had become stabilised by the cessation of mass labour migration in 1973–75. The figures are from SOPEMI, the agency responsible for monitoring migration trends in OECD countries, and all the caveats about the quality and comparability of the statistics mentioned earlier should be borne in mind.[3] Turks predominated in West Germany, Algerians in France, Italians in Belgium and Switzerland, and Finns in Sweden. In general, the Mediterranean flavour of this mass migration is confirmed, although in the Netherlands, Switzerland and Sweden there is evidence of sources of workers which are closer at hand and reflect the intensity of relations between neighbouring countries. Particularly relevant here is the common Nordic labour market, established in 1954 to facilitate the mobility of workers between Sweden, Norway, Finland and Denmark.

Guestworkers and immigrants

During the early phase of post-war migration, most international flows comprised mainly workers – either single men or single women, usually the former. Towards the end of the 1960s (earlier in some countries, notably the UK and France), "family migration" was allowed, and the composition of the flows began to change, with more women and children involved. At that time the so-called "guestworkers" (*Gastarbeiter* in German parlance), whose presence had been thought of as temporary, started the trans-formation into permanent or long-term immigrants, settling abroad with their families or forming new family nuclei in their new countries of residence. In other words, parroting the title of two books which reviewed this transition period, the "guests" had come to stay: they were "here for good" (Castles *et al.*, 1984; Rogers, 1985). Some, on the other hand, preserved their originally assigned status as temporary migrant workers and returned home, perhaps to re-emigrate a few years later.[4]

As noted earlier, the overall migration situation changed in the mid-1970s with the halt to new foreign labour recruitment. For the next decade – until the rise of asylum migration in the second half of the 1980s – the south–north migration flows that took place were mainly dominated by moves for family reunification. To illustrate the point with a specific example, in 1970 France took in 174 000 foreign workers and 81 000 family members; in 1980 the respective figures were 17 400 and 51 000. A good deal of return migration also took place during the 1970s and early 1980s:

we shall pick up the story of these returnees towards the end of the chapter.

The changing composition of migrant flows also changed the balance in the "stocks" of migrants living abroad: fewer workers, proportionately, and more family members. This trend is confirmed particularly clearly in West Germany, the classic west European country of guestworkers-turned-immigrants, where the number of foreign workers remained static between 1970 (1 839 000) and 1985 (1 824 000) but the total foreign population increased from 2 725 000 to 4 379 000. In other words, foreign workers made up 67.5 per cent of the total foreign population in 1970, but only 41.7 per cent in 1985. In the next part of the chapter we examine the political and economic background both to post-war labour migration, and to the shift from labour migration to family migration.

Political Economy of Labour Migration

It is important to understand the macro-economic and international political contexts of European labour migration, and equally important to understand that these structural factors do not explain everything about the size and direction of these flows – indeed in some cases migration flows have behaved in a way that is counterintuitive to the structural "explanation". Take, for example, the EEC's free movement of labour provisions which, on the basis of Articles 48 and 49 of the Treaty of Rome, were put into operation during the 1960s to facilitate the mobility of workers from labour-surplus to labour-deficit regions within the Six.

According to Böhning (1972) this "liberal-capitalist prescription" for free labour movement had negligible effects. It facilitated some Italian migration to France, Belgium and West Germany but, as we have already noted, Italian emigration was already declining from the early 1960s as internal migration took over. In fact, this is not the whole story as Italian emigration to Switzerland, a non-EEC country, continued to grow and for most years in the 1960s more Italians migrated to Switzerland than to the five Community states![5] What the free movement scheme failed to do was to prevent the continuation of a statistical trend that was already established by the early 1960s, namely the decline of intra-EC migration as a proportion of all international migration to EC countries. For at the same time as the free movement policy was being pushed within the EC, individual labour-recruiting countries (all EC states except Italy) were concluding bilateral agreements with an ever-widening set of emigration countries around the Mediterranean basin. By 1974 a total of 33 such bilateral links had been agreed, two-thirds of them involving France or West Germany (Salt, 1976). These extra-EC links provided the channels along which most of the millions of labour migrants flowed during the 1960s and early 1970s.

EC policy-makers maintain that "free movement" was never intended to unleash mass migration, merely to remove the barriers that existed to movement. The division of expectation between politicians and policy-makers continued with subsequent Community enlargements. With the UK, for instance, Conservative politicians promoted the expectation that the UK would be flooded with European, and especially Italian, immigrants when the UK joined the Community in 1973. In saying this they displayed an appalling ignorance of European migration trends. Again when Greece, Spain and Portugal joined, further mass emigration was anticipated – and forestalled by lengthy transition periods. Now that the transition periods have expired, there has been some upturn in emigration from Portugal and Greece to France and Germany, but nothing approaching "mass" proportions.

There is less room for argument over the fundamentally economic nature of European labour migration. By definition, the migrants were "employment-seeking" and hence tended to move from countries with weak economies to those with strong ones. But while the "push factors" of unemployment, poverty and poor career prospects were important at the behavioural level, the movement as a whole was demand-driven by the recruitment countries. The causes of labour

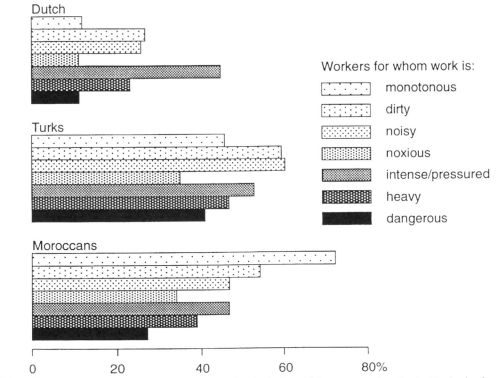

Figure 14.3 *Characteristics of work performed by Dutch, Turkish and Moroccan workers in the Netherlands. (Source: Pinder, 1990, 13)*

269

shortage in the advanced industrial economies included the lack of further labour-shedding in agriculture, fertility decline, increasing rates of participation in higher education (hence delayed entry to the labour market), a rapid rate of economic growth creating full employment, and the upward mobility of indigenous populations. This last trend led to particular labour-supply difficulties in jobs that were perceived as undesirable.

These low-status jobs – unpleasant, insecure, menial and poorly paid – nevertheless presented opportunities to many unemployed and destitute workers from the Mediterranean countries and former European colonies. As guestworkers poured in, the native workers of countries like West Germany, Switzerland and France were relieved of the necessity of doing these jobs and thus enjoyed an upward shift in their aspirations and social status. Figure 14.3 provides a graphic illustration of the contrast in working conditions in the Netherlands between Dutch workers and the two main immigrant groups.

Furthermore, economists, manpower planners and employers in the more prosperous countries realised that temporarily employed foreign workers could provide a cushion for the indigenous workforce against the effects of economic cycles – the so-called *Konjunkturpuffer* effect. West Germany and Switzerland – the most ruthless exponents of this strategy – kept their guestworkers in a system of constant rotation by only employing them on short-term contracts.

However, by the early 1970s, as the competition for migrants intensified and as the longer-term need for migrant labour was finally accepted, the "rotation" systems were liberalised, allowing more permanent settlement and the reunification of families by the arrival of dependants. Labour migrants, and their families, had become a permanent structural feature of north-west European workforces and societies.

Employment

Let us examine a little more closely the jobs performed by immigrant workers who moved north from Mediterranean and ex-colonial countries during the 1950s, 1960s and early 1970s. Three employment sectors concentrated the vast majority of immigrant workers during this period. First, heavy manufacturing industry recruited large numbers of male migrants. Within this broad area of employment two further trends could be noted: the disproportionate presence of immigrants in unskilled rather than skilled jobs; and their over-representation in industrial sectors and processes where the quality of the working environment was unpleasant and dangerous – for instance in mining, iron and steel or chemicals. The second key employment sector comprised low-grade tertiary occupations such as refuse-collecting, office-cleaning and menial work in hospitals; some of these activities employed mainly female migrant labour. Third, the

Table 14.2   *Employment sector and nationality of male foreign workers in France, 1968 (%)*

	Italian	Spanish	Portuguese	Algerian	Moroccan	Tunisian
Agriculture, forestry	10.3	17.4	8.0	1.3	11.7	2.4
Extractive industries	3.9	1.2	11.6	2.4	13.4	0.7
Metal production	6.9	2.3	1.4	5.7	2.0	0.8
Engineering, electrical goods	10.7	12.8	7.9	17.4	18.7	12.2
Building, public works	41.6	34.6	58.2	37.0	26.2	28.8
Commerce	6.4	7.7	3.3	9.7	7.7	15.8
Total, six sectors	*69.8*	*76.0*	*80.4*	*73.5*	*79.7*	*60.7*
Total	100.0	100.0	100.0	100.0	100.0	100.0
No. of workers ('000)	20.5.0	198.5	156.3	242.9	53.9	24.5

Source: Castles and Kosack (1985, 64).

building and construction industry came to be very dependent on foreign labour. The tough, precarious and geographically mobile nature of construction work made it unattractive to native labour seeking secure and stable employment.

Within these three broad occupational sectors, variations may be noted between destination countries and among the various immigrant nationalities. These have been analysed in detail by Castles and Kosack (1985, 57–115) and Salt (1976) for the late 1960s and early 1970s. Tables 14.2 and 14.3 are drawn from these sources and refer to France and West Germany respectively. Although the data in these two tables are not strictly comparable (the years are different, the French data are only for males, and the percentages are calculated on the basis of different totals), they nevertheless indicate some interesting features. A first contrast can be noted between the German case, where most immigrant employment was linked to manufacturing industry, and France where construction and the service sector were relatively more important. Second, a hierarchy quickly developed whereby workers from southern Europe (especially Italians and Spaniards) acquired better jobs than North African and Turkish workers, who were relegated to the very bottom of the socio-occupational ladder. This distinction is only hinted at by the tables, but was clearly evident from other studies and from more disaggregated employment data (Castles and Kosack, 1985).

This differentiation could be explained partly by length of stay (hence Italians, recruited earliest, had more time to progress up the job ladder), partly by initial educational qualification (European immigrants having higher standards of basic education), and partly by employer prejudice against non-European immigrants.

Tables 14.2 and 14.3 also show interesting examples of national specialisation which occurred independent of this hierarchy. In France, extractive industries were especially reliant on Moroccans and Portuguese, the Spanish were prominent in seasonal agricultural work, the Portuguese and Italians were over-represented in the construction industry, and the Tunisians made the biggest impact in the field of commerce. In West Germany, according to Salt (1976, 110–12), employers often tended to recruit from single nationalities in order to minimise language problems and facilitate job instruction. This explains the specific distribution of national groups in different German cities – for example in Cologne where Turks were recruited into the car industry and Spaniards into the postal service. In West Germany as a whole, Yugoslavs were found particularly in construction, Greeks in manufacturing and Turks in mining and basic industries such as iron and steel (Table 14.3).

The ending of mass labour migration in 1973, and the shift to more permanent migrant settlement, did not change the basic patterns of employment of those workers who migrated during the Fordist period. Migrant workers

Table 14.3   *Employment sector and nationality of foreign workers in West Germany, 1973 (%)*

	Italian	Spanish	Portuguese	Greek	Yugoslav	Turkish	Other	Total
Agriculture, forestry	18.7	10.7	4.3	2.9	16.5	21.6	25.3	100.0
Mining	15.7	5.6	2.5	4.3	11.4	46.0	14.5	100.0
Iron and steel production	13.2	8.4	3.3	13.7	9.7	41.4	10.3	100.0
Iron and steel fabrication	23.1	11.0	3.1	16.0	14.1	21.6	11.1	100.0
Vehicles	16.7	8.7	2.7	16.1	13.5	32.2	10.1	100.0
Chemicals	21.2	10.3	2.4	19.7	9.6	15.2	21.6	100.0
Textiles	19.7	7.5	7.7	15.3	12.9	29.0	7.9	100.0
Construction	20.5	3.6	1.8	2.8	35.0	19.3	17.0	100.0
Transport	20.4	15.2	5.3	4.6	11.9	22.4	20.2	100.0
Total foreign workers (%)	17.5	7.6	2.9	11.4	20.0	22.5	18.1	100.0
Total foreign workers ('000)	409.7	177.5	69.0	268.1	466.1	528.2	426.5	100.0

Source: Salt (1976, 113).

continued to be seen, not least by their employers, as a source of low-status and relatively cheap labour. Moreover most of them lacked the education, training and language skills to compete for higher-status jobs. West German data on the employment profile of the foreign labour force reveal very little change during the decade of the 1970s (Castles and Kosack, 1985, 495–6). In 1972, 79 per cent of males were employed in metal production, engineering, manufacturing and construction; 74 per cent in 1980. Female migrant employment did shift somewhat from manufacturing (74 per cent in 1972, 56 per cent in 1980) to services (21 per cent in 1972, 40 per cent in 1980), but this does not necessarily signify an upward status move. In fact, taken as a whole, 81 per cent of foreign workers in West Germany were still manual workers in 1978 (compared with 40 per cent of Germans), 14.5 per cent were non-manual workers (Germans 37.5 per cent), and only 4 per cent were employers, self-employed or civil servants (Germans 18.5 per cent).

French data do point to some occupational progress on the part of immigrant workers during the 1970s (Table 14.4) – an indication, perhaps, of the more open nature of the French labour market and of French society as a whole, which has tended to encourage assimilation. On the other hand, Table 14.4 confirms that the various manual worker categories remained the main areas of immigrant employment, accounting for 93.6 per cent of total employment in firms with more than 10 employees in 1971, and 85.5 per cent in 1979.

There is no doubt that the "Fordist crisis" of the 1970s impacted negatively, and disproportionately so, on immigrant workers. In many cases they were among the first victims of deindustrialisation, and consequently suffered high rates of unemployment and return migration. Most immigrants from the Mediterranean, however, decided to stay on. After so many years, and with children in local schools, their new roots were already too deep to be easily transplanted back home. Their continuing progress (or lack of it) into the 1980s and 1990s is assessed in Chapter 15.

Housing and Residential Distribution of Immigrant Communities

The extensive literature on the evolving social geography of immigrant groups in European cities[6] reveals that, despite the varying mixes of different nationalities in different cities, their role in the dynamics of the housing market and in the demography of inner-city areas is fairly consistent. This role exhibits interesting parallels with the labour-market situation discussed above. Just as guestworkers and immigrants replaced the lower strata of the indigenous population in the occupational hierarchy, so they have acted as a replacement population in the older neighbourhoods of the inner city which have been abandoned by the native population (or by earlier waves of immigrants).

In the early years of their settlement, guestworkers and immigrants were housed in a variety of different types of accommodation. Company hostels were prevalent in West Germany and Switzerland; many large industrial firms in these countries had to build hostels before being allowed to recruit guestworkers (O'Loughlin, 1980). Life in these hostels is well captured in the photographs in Berger and Mohr (1975): crowded, single-sex dormitories, the ultimate in residential and social segregation. When family reunification and other policies allowed movement out of the hostels to take place, migrants generally settled in adjacent low-grade private tenancies.

Company housing for migrant workers was less common in other countries, although in France it had some importance in the building industry where construction gangs have often been housed in caravans and huts on building sites, and in the company-owned *foyers-hôtels* organised by firms

Table 14.4 *Occupational status of foreign employees in French industrial and commercial firms with more than 10 employees, 1971–79 (%)*

	1971	1973	1976	1979
Supervisors	1.1	1.3	1.7	2.1
Forepersons, technicians	1.7	1.7	2.1	2.6
Clerical	3.6	5.1	6.7	9.2
Skilled manual	20.8	30.5	34.8	37.9
Semi-skilled manual	46.1	42.6	38.2	34.5
Unskilled manual	26.7	18.8	16.1	13.4

Source: SOPEMI (1983).

for their workers. More common in France have been the *garnis* or *hôtels-meublés* (privately run inner-city "hotels" occupied by immigrants) and the peripheral squatter settlements known as *bidonvilles*. The growth of these shanty towns around the edge of major French cities was a feature of the 1950s and 1960s, corresponding to the massive influxes of North African and Portuguese immigrants. Although a law was passed in 1964 providing for the clearance of the *bidonvilles* and the re-housing of their inhabitants, some shanties were slow to disappear, notably those around Marseilles which remain to this day.

After hostels and *bidonvilles*, the third residential environment settled in by immigrants was the low-quality end of the private housing market. After the dismantling of the hostels and squatter districts in the late 1960s and 1970s, the inner city came to be the favoured destination, although the element of

choice open to the immigrants was minimal. In fact, the limitations on immigrants' choice of housing were several. The most important initial constraint had to do with their low-paid work, which gave them poor bargaining power in the housing market and left them concentrated, at least for some years until their savings built up, in the worst housing and the most run-down neighbourhoods. Critics held immigrants responsible for initiating a spiral of deterioration, deprivation and social malaise in these areas, but this is a harsh and even mistaken judgement: in many cases immigrants gave life to areas which were decaying anyway, and they created lively ethnic neighbourhoods with their own shops, cafés, religious and community institutions (see Figure 14.4).

Another source of disadvantage for immigrants in the housing market has been their exclusion

Figure 14.4   *Ethnic communities and their institutions gave new life to many inner-city areas. This scene is of the early 1970s in Bedford, a British town with large numbers of immigrants from southern Italy, the Caribbean and Asia*

from public housing. Allocation mechanisms often placed immigrants at the bottom of the priority list, except where they were rehoused through slum clearance schemes. In the UK, where some entry of Afro-Caribbeans into public housing has taken place, a tendency has been noticed for them to be allocated the least desirable estates and dwelling-units (Peach, 1982). Racial discrimination constituted a third arena of disadvantage for immigrants seeking adequate housing. Castles and Kosack (1985) have amassed a wealth of evidence to show how landlords ruthlessly exploited immigrants, denying them access to good properties, charging them excessive rents for substandard accommodation, and taking advantage of their lack of knowledge of the language and of their rights.

The residential distribution of immigrant workers and their families has become an important element of urban structure in north-west Europe, where already by the early 1970s most large cities had at least one-tenth (and often a much larger share) of their populations of foreign origin (White, 1984, 110). In spite of the decrease in migrant worker entries after 1973, many cities increased their foreign populations during the 1970s as family members arrived to turn guestworker districts into settled immigrant communities. Hence West Berlin's foreign population grew during the decade by 63 per cent, Munich's by 75 per cent, Frankfurt's by 80 per cent and Vienna's by 49 per cent. However, immigrant concentrations in European cities have rarely reached the "saturation" status of the black ghettos of American cities; even in well-known cases of ethnic segregation, such as Berlin's Kreuzberg district, less than half the population is of one minority – in this case Turkish (Huttman, 1991, 21).

Once established in inner-city areas or in districts close to industrial employment, immigrant concentrations have tended to remain stable over time, partly because of ethnic cohesiveness and access to ethnic shops and institutions, and partly because of the diminishing residential attractiveness of immigrant areas for the indigenous population. However, processes of residential change – both intra-urban and inter-regional – have occurred among immigrant populations.

First, there is an upward movement of immigrants within the housing market due to increasing well-being achieved by the savings accumulated over many years of work. This process leads to a shift to better-quality and more spacious property, often in the owner-occupied sector, and towards suburbanisation and desegregation. White (1993a) notes that ethnic segregation indices have been falling over recent years in several European cities, often as a result of family reunion and resulting housing adjustments. Suburbanisation has been greatest among long-established immigrant groups such as Italians in France and Germany, Spanish and Portuguese in France, and the Irish in the UK. In Paris, for instance, Italians, Spanish and Portuguese have made moves into the suburbs in the same way as the French, and they have moved through the same sectors of the housing market, although they have not reached owner-occupation in such large numbers (White, 1996). Whether this process of "natural dispersion" will happen for more recently arrived and culturally distinct migrants is debatable: Gans (1990) found that Turks in some German cities became *more* concentrated during the 1980s, due partly to the tightening of housing markets and decreasing scope for immigrants to move to better areas. Different again is the experience of Asian immigrants in the UK who have achieved high rates of owner-occupation (higher in fact than the British population as a whole) and yet remain highly concentrated spatially in inner suburbs of towns like Bradford and Leicester.

Second, immigrants have been affected by the instruments of housing policy and urban planning, notably slum clearance and access to social housing. Where inner-city rented tenements have been cleared, public rehousing has often taken place to new estates on the city peripheries, leading to a sudden and marked suburbanisation of ethnic populations. However, decentralising inner-city immigrant communities to ex-urban housing estates such as the French *grands ensembles* has not generally proved to be a satisfactory outcome. In the UK, access to public housing for Afro-Caribbeans has not involved dispersion but their relocation into inner-city high-rises. Throughout western Europe, immigrants' improved access to public housing was mainly associated with major rehousing schemes in the 1960s and 1970s. Since then housing and redevelopment policies have slowed; as a result the public role in managing ethnic housing change has been greatly reduced.

This return to the logic and power of the private property market has also had impacts on inner-city concentrations of migrants who have been displaced by pressures for gentrification and commercial development. This is the third trend to affect immigrants' residential locations. Amsterdam provides a good illustration (Cortie and van Engelsdorp Gastelaars, 1985). In the early 1970s the city's Mediterranean and Caribbean immigrants were virtually all concentrated in the old, inner districts. Ten years later they had been displaced from the inner city to newer districts outside the central residential area, including some public housing. These were still areas of predominantly cheap housing, but perhaps more suited to family living than the overcrowded boarding-houses and bedsits of the inner city. Meanwhile the central area has become increasingly the preserve of young Dutch people, either students in bedsits or high-income professionals who are buying and restoring dwellings formerly in multiple occupation.

Socio-cultural and Political Issues: Steps towards a Multicultural Europe

At the beginning of this chapter, the point was made that migration provides a link between economic transformation and social stress. In the intervening pages we have seen how labour migrants – initially guestworkers, later settled immigrants – made a fundamental contribution to the economic development of post-war western Europe while bearing many of the social and human costs – poor housing, discrimination, isolation – on their own shoulders. Now, in an era of industrial restructuring and high unemployment, migrants are victims of socio-economic change; but they are not the primary cause of social stress, as some political groups would make us believe. Such political forces, appealing to social groups who can see no further than their own self-interests, have inflamed racial tension by portraying immigrants as "invaders" of

job markets, housing and welfare provisions, to the detriment of indigenous workers and their families. Enoch Powell (in the UK), James Schwarzenbach (in Switzerland) and Jean-Marie le Pen (in France) are the best-known figures in this racist political lineage which, in one way or another, has taken root in most European countries since the 1960s. Yet in 1963, in one of the first and most thorough analyses of an immigrant group in UK, the sociologist John Jackson (1963) pointed out that social problems were not caused by the immigration of the Irish or West Indians or Pakistanis, but that their presence served only to expose the inadequacies in social provision for society at large. In the UK it is apparent that the black population, particularly those whose origins lie in Africa and the Caribbean, have inherited decay for which part of the political and social system is now blaming them; and the same may be said of the North Africans in France and the Turks in Germany.

It is very difficult to pass a clear judgement about what is happening with regard to cultural adaptation and social integration of what are now long-standing immigrant populations in Europe. This is not only because the experiences of individual nationalities differ, both among themselves and between the various destination countries, but also because there are deep moral uncertainties about what *should* happen. Germany's stubborn insistence that it is not a country of immigration, and its denial of naturalisation and many civic rights to immigrants who have been there for 35 years or to persons who were born in Germany of non-German parents, is one normative model which has many critics both outside and within the country (Blotevogel *et al.*, 1993). Another is France's assimilationist model, whereby large sections of the immigrant population are allowed to become French provided they go a long way towards renouncing their cultural origins. Both these models have been applied less strictly in recent years. Within Europe, only Sweden comes close to the multicultural models of Canada and Australia. But the ethical dilemma of exclusion versus assimilation versus multiculturalism does not end there: how far should respect for the values of immigrants' cultures go if this involves rigid suppression of women or female circumcision? And how far should one welcome the birth of new cultures such as the specific culture of British-born blacks with its roots in alienation and rejection by the host society?

If these are not easy questions to resolve, some comfort can be taken from the fact that millions of immigrants *have* settled successfully in Europe, trading their Mediterranean villages and hillsides for a very different future in the towns and factories of the north. Of course, the nature of the accommodation they have had to make between their two worlds and identities varies from individual to individual. More systematically it varies according to the "cultural distance" separating the origin and destination countries, and it also differs across generations – nostalgia will tend to be greater for the primary migrants, whereas their foreign-born offspring will know mainly, even exclusively, the culture of their birthplace.

Nevertheless the picture should not be depicted as too rosy. By whatever measure adopted, most immigrant groups (at least those whose origins lay in the post-war labour migrations that are the core of this chapter) have continued to remain worse off than their host country counterparts: they still suffer lower incomes, higher rates of unemployment, poorer housing, lower rates of educational achievement, and higher incidence of physical and mental illnesses. Recent unemployment data for immigrant groups are analysed in Chapter 15.

But statistics and indices only capture a part of the "migrant experience". The real experts on migration are the migrants themselves. Only they can tell what it is like to be a migrant in a foreign and often unwelcoming land. The testimonies of migrants through in-depth interviews, autobiographies and other primary documents are now being appreciated as invaluable accounts. Of course, they have to be interpreted carefully and critically, but they yield a level of insight which in many ways is far superior to the cold statistics of censuses and surveys. Recent reviews of *Gastarbeiter* literature (Fischer and McGowan, 1995), of the writings of Algerians in France (Hargreaves, 1995) and of Asian British fiction (Bald, 1995) have demonstrated what rich veins of material exist to be analysed by scholars interested in getting closer to the human meaning

of post-war European migration – the fear, hope, pain and triumph of lives lived in other places. Such material embraces also poetry and symbolic language. Thus in a few key words the Moroccan Tahar Ben Jelloun (1976, 136) sketches out the life of an expatriate worker from the Maghreb: "local misery – passport – corruption – humiliation – medical – emigration office – journey – long crossing – condemned housing – work – metro – suitcase – holidays – money order – return – customs . . .". [7]

Back to the Mediterranean

Ben Jelloun's sketch of the stages and emotions of the migration cycle closes with the return home. For some temporary migrants the return home too is temporary, to be followed by another departure. The interaction of emigration and return produces a variety of migration types which are rarely identifiable as such in migration statistics, but which are important components of the space-time variety of European international migration.

Probably the most common type is long-term emigration without return or with deferred return. These are the guestworkers-turned-immigrants who have progressively extended their stays abroad and who are now unlikely to return except for holidays and perhaps eventually on retirement. For many of those migrants who moved as young men and women during the great migration boom of the 1950s and 1960s, this decision is now drawing nigh, or has already taken place. Hence there is now a "return of retirement" of significant numbers of migrants to their Mediterranean homelands. However, it is also becoming clear that the majority of long-stay migrants will not return when they retire: they will prefer to stay with their foreign-born children and grandchildren. This gives rise to another new phenomenon: the ageing of ethnic populations, already clearly apparent with the earliest post-war arrivals such as the Italians in France and Belgium and the Irish and Caribbeans in the UK.

At the other end of the migration spectrum are seasonal migrants who manage to combine two lives and two types of work in two places. Typically they are migrants from rural areas of the Mediterranean who move north every year to take temporary jobs, for instance in the tourist trade or construction industry, while still retaining a link to agriculture in their home villages. Switzerland, with its tightly regulated immigrant labour market,[8] depends greatly on seasonal migration from countries such as Italy and Portugal, while there is also a strong seasonal migration tradition from Morocco to various European destinations. In such cases the migrant remains socially and psychologically anchored in his or her home community, where the earnings from migration are integrated with other household sources. Migrant income may be a key ingredient in modernising the farm as well as helping to support family members and improve the standard of housing.

In between retirement migrants and seasonal migrants are others who return after several years living and working abroad and who are still potentially economically active at the time of their return. Some of these are migrants for whom the "emigration project" was always intended as a purely temporary affair. Others return because of unemployment, nostalgia, the need to look after ageing parents, the desire to have their children educated in their "home" language, or because of their wish to launch a new "return project" such as a small business – with the money saved from working abroad. For this group the decision to return is often a very difficult and finely balanced one, in which the feelings of different members of the family – mother, father, children – have to be carefully considered. In many cases there is a "reverse culture shock" in which a painful readjustment has to be made to the different pace of life and way of doing things. Some returnees fail to come to terms with the social structures, clientelism, corruption and gossip of Mediterranean village life. Socially excluded abroad because of their background and ethnicity, they are also socially excluded back home, where they seek solace in the company of other returnees who thus form a marginal group within village society (Bernard and Ashton-Vouyoucalos, 1976). Special problems await the return of foreign-born children who have to cope with new

Figure 14.5 *Return migration rarely leads to investment in local productive activities because returnees tend to spend most of their savings on status symbols such as large new houses, like this example in the south Italian region of Abruzzo*

school systems and, perhaps, language difficulties. Women who worked abroad may not be able to do so on return, because of the shortage of jobs or social disapproval.

Economically, have returned migrants brought a new stimulus for the development of their home regions? During the great emigration boom, migration planners, government policy-makers and some economists argued that the real benefits of labour migration would accrue when the migrants returned home with money and skills to invest in their countries of origin (Griffin, 1976). Twenty or 30 years later, it is difficult to see much evidence of this having happened. While migrant remittances have been an important item of invisible earnings in the balance of payments in all Mediterranean sending countries, at the local and regional levels the developmental impact has been diluted by the spending and investment behaviours of returnees which have tended to be directed towards highly visible status symbols (new houses and consumer durables) rather than at the long-term productive capacity of the locality (Figure 14.5). Where a "productive return" has taken place, it is usually where the area has developed new economic activities since the emigrants' departure; hence returnees have been able to invest in tourism, fishing or intensive agriculture (Mendonsa, 1982). The problem is that most emigrants left from overcrowded, hilly, marginal areas of the Mediterranean where these possibilities are lacking. For these returnees, perhaps forced back through the failure of their emigration project or by family obligations, there is little future beyond some part-time farming, occasional work on public projects such as road-mending, or an attempt to set up a small shop or bar in a declining rural community already saturated with such services (Rhoades, 1979). For them the migration cycle has come full circle and the benefits are hard to see; only the realisation of having been born in the wrong place at the wrong time.

Notes

1. This chapter reuses some material from my corresponding chapter in the book which was the precursor to this volume (King, 1990). However, the earlier material has been summarised, rearranged, reinterpreted and augmented as appropriate, so that the present chapter presents a substantially new account.

2. An ethnic self-assessment question was introduced in the 1991 census.

3. The SOPEMI Annual Reports, issued since 1973, are an invaluable aid to geographers and Europeanists interested in international migration trends. It needs to be stressed, however, that these reports are compilations of individual country submissions and hence the data are not likely to be comparable between countries. For further evaluation of SOPEMI data, see Salt (1987).

4. These re-emigrants do not show up in the migration statistics as such; instead they are merely recorded as "new" emigrants. From my various field surveys among European migrants, a surprisingly significant minority turn out to be repeat migrants. Sometimes they have emigrated and re-emigrated to different countries – for example, to Belgium or France in the 1950s, and then to Germany in the 1960s (King *et al.*, 1986).

5. This is not an entirely fair comparison since much emigration to Switzerland comprised seasonal and annual migrants who moved several times and were therefore recorded in each year's statistics. See also note 4.

6. In addition to the work of White cited earlier (1984, 1989, 1993a, b), see Glebe and O'Loughlin (1987) and Huttman *et al.* (1991).

7. Quoted in Sporton (1996) whose essay on Moroccan community development in France emphasises the role of social networks in the migration process.

8. Switzerland admits four types of migrant, subject to tightly controlled quotas: permanent, annual, seasonal and frontier.

References

Bald, S R (1995) Negotiating identity in the metropolis: generational differences in South Asian British fiction, in R King, J Connell and P White (eds) *Writing Across Worlds: literature and migration*, Routledge, London, 70–88.

Ben Jelloun, T (1976) *La Réclusion Solitaire*, Denoël, Paris.

Berger, J and Mohr, J (1975) *A Seventh Man: the story of a migrant worker in Europe*, Penguin, Harmondsworth.

Bernard, H R and Ashton-Vouyoucalos, S (1976) Return migration to Greece, *Journal of the Steward Anthropological Society*, **8**, 31–51.

Blotevogel, H H, Müller-ter Jung, U and Wood, G (1993) From itinerant worker to immigrant? The geography of guestworkers in Germany, in R King (ed) *Mass Migrations in Europe: the legacy and the future*, Belhaven, London, 83–100.

Böhning, W R (1972) *The Migration of Workers in the United Kingdom and the European Community*, Oxford University Press, Oxford.

Castles, S, Booth, H and Wallace, T (1984) *Here for Good: Western Europe's new ethnic minorities*, Pluto Press, London.

Castles, S and Kosack, G (1985) *Immigrant Workers and Class Structure in Western Europe*, Oxford University Press, Oxford (2nd edition).

Cortie, C and van Englesdorp Gastelaars, R (1985) Amsterdam: decaying city, gentrifying inner city? in P E White and B van der Knaap (eds) *Contemporary Studies of Migration*, Geo Books, Norwich, 129–42.

Fassmann, H and Münz, R (eds) (1994) *European Migration in the Late Twentieth Century*, Edward Elgar, Aldershot.

Fischer, S and McGowan, M (1995) From Pappkoffer to pluralism: migrant writing in the German Federal Republic, in R King, J Connell and P White (eds) *Writing Across Worlds: literature and migration*, Routledge, London, 39–58.

Gans, P (1990) Changes in the structure of the foreign population of West Germany in the 1980s, *Migration*, **7**, 25–49.

Glebe, G and O'Loughlin, J (eds) (1987) *Foreign Minorities in Continental European Cities*, Steiner, Wiesbaden.

Griffin, K (1976) On the emigration of the peasantry, *World Development*, **4**, 353–61.

Hargreaves, A (1995) Perceptions of place among workers of Algerian immigrant origin in France, in R King, J Connell and P White (eds) *Writing Across Worlds: literature and migration*, Routledge, London, 89–100.

Huttman, E D (1991) Housing segregation in Western Europe: an introduction, in E D Huttman, W Blauw and J Saltman (eds) *Urban Housing Segregation of Minorities in Western Europe and the United States*, Duke University Press, Durham, NC, 21–42.

Huttman, E D, Blauw, W and Saltman, J (eds) (1991) *Urban Housing Segregation of Minorities in Western Europe and the United States*, Duke University Press, Durham, NC.

Jackson, J A (1963) *The Irish in Britain*, Routledge and Kegan Paul, London.

King, R (1990) The social and economic geography of labour migration: from guestworkers to immigrants, in D Pinder (ed) *Western Europe: challenge and change*, Belhaven, London, 162–78.

King, R (1993) European international migration 1945–90: a statistical and geographical overview, in R King (ed) *Mass Migrations in Europe: the legacy and the future*, Belhaven, London, 19–39.

King, R, Strachan, A and Mortimer, J (1986) Gastarbeiter go home: return migration and economic change in the Italian Mezzogiorno, in R King (ed) *Return Migration and Regional Economic Problems*, Croom Helm, London, 38–68.

Mendonsa, E L (1982) Benefits of migration as a personal strategy in Nazaré, Portugal, *International Migration Review*, **16**, 635–45.

O'Loughlin, J (1980) Distribution and migration of foreigners in German cities, *Geographical Review*, **70**, 253–76.

Peach, C (1982) The growth and distribution of the Black population in Britain 1945–1980, in D A Coleman (ed) *Demography of Minority Groups in the United Kingdom*, Academic Press, London, 23–42.

Pinder, D (1990) Challenge and change in Western Europe: an overview, in D Pinder (ed) *Western Europe: challenge and change*, Belhaven, London, 1–16.

Rhoades, R E (1979) From caves to main street: return migration and the transformation of a Spanish village, *Papers in Anthropology*, **20**, 57–74.

Rogers, R (ed) (1985) *Guests Come to Stay*, Westview, London.

Salt, J (1976) International labour migration: the geographical pattern of demand, in J Salt and H Clout (eds) *Migration in Postwar Europe: geographical essays*, Oxford University Press, Oxford, 80–125.

Salt, J (1987) The SOPEMI experience: genesis, aims and achievements, *International Migration Review*, **21**, 1067–73.

Salt, J and Clout, H (eds) (1976) *Migration in Postwar Europe: geographical essays*, Oxford University Press, Oxford.

SOPEMI (1977) *Annual Report 1976*, OECD, Paris.

SOPEMI (1983) *Annual Report 1982*, OECD, Paris.

Sporton, D (1996) Migrant networks and community development: Moroccan migration to France, in M L Gentileschi and R King (eds) *Questioni di Popolazione in Europa: una prospettiva geografica*, Pàtron, Bologna, 53–66.

White, P (1984) *The West European City: a social geography*, Longman, London.

White, P (1989) Immigrants, immigrant areas and immigrant communities in postwar Paris, in P E Ogden and P E White (eds) *Migrants in Modern France*, Unwin Hyman, London, 195 211.

White, P (1993a) Immigrants and the social geography of European cities, in R King (ed) *Mass Migrations in Europe: the legacy and the future*, Belhaven, London, 65–82.

White, P (1993b) The social geography of immigrants in European cities: the geography of arrival, in R King (ed) *The New Geography of European Migrations*, Belhaven, London, 47–66.

White, P (1996) The intra-urban mobility of ethnic minorities, with special reference to the Paris agglomeration, in M L Gentileschi and R King (eds) *Questioni di Popolazione in Europa: una prospettiva geografica*, Pàtron, Bologna, 39–51.

15

Post-oil crisis, post-Communism

New geographies of international migration

Russell King
School of European Studies, University of Sussex, UK

During the 1980s, a new map of European migration unfolded, with new patterns and forms of movement. Gone were the south-to-north labour migration flows from the Mediterranean basin countries to industrial Europe; already in the 1970s they had been replaced by return migration flows, as we saw at the end of the previous chapter. Instead new economic realities, together with an increasingly overt anti-immigration policy on the part of the European Community, led to three major new forms of migration. The first was skilled international migration within the EU and between EU countries and other poles of the global economy. This reflected the increasingly high-tech nature of European industry and the rise of advanced producer services as multinational phenomena. The second was the sharp rise in the number of asylum-seeking migrants, especially after the mid-1980s, and the third was the expansion and diversification of clandestine migration into Europe. Both of these last two reflected the process of closing off "normal" channels of entry into Europe and both also reflected the gathering strength of push factors for migration from the source regions of the world. At the end of the decade the East–West divide – which had been very much a barrier against migration – dissolved and new types of east–west movement appeared.

Hence the new typology of European international migration over the last 15 years consists of three main forms of migration – skilled, asylum, clandestine – overlapped with the two major "compass migrations": East–West and South–North (Salt, 1992a). South–North in this context does not mean south–north within Europe, but employs the global meaning of the South as the less developed world and the North as containing all of western Europe including southern Europe. In fact, southern Europe, up to the 1970s a source of mass emigration, has become a major destination for immigrants both from the global South and from eastern Europe.

This chapter is in five parts. The first looks at the impact on migration of the new economic structures which replaced the Fordist system in the wake of the oil crisis. In this "post-Fordist" Europe two migration-related phenomena are singled out for detailed treatment: the rise of new opportunities for ethnic enterprise in a Europe dominated increasingly by small firms and deregulated labour markets, and the expansion of skilled international migration both within and from outside Europe. Section two examines the geography of asylum migration and the increasingly negative policy towards asylum-seekers put in place by the target states of western Europe in the 1990s. The third section documents the rise of southern Europe as a major migration destination since the mid-1980s; it will be seen that mainly clandestine migration flows originate from a great variety of countries and pose challenges for migration policy to which responses are only slowly emerging. The fourth part of the chapter is on East–West migration since 1989. Accurate data on these movements are scarce, not least because some of the mobility, such as long-distance commuting, questions the conventional definition of migration. The main conclusion, however, is that mass transfers of population have failed to occur. Two cases of East–West migration are singled out for detailed examination: migration into (West) Germany, both before and after unification; and the Albanian exodus of 1991. The concluding section of the chapter, on the future of international migration in Europe, will pick up and integrate a number of themes such as the global context of migration, demographic trends, migration policy and changing concepts of migration.

Recession and Restructuring: the Impact on Migration

In the previous chapter it was briefly pointed out that immigrant workers suffered dispro-portionately from the industrial closures and rationalisations of the late 1970s and early 1980s. The phenomenon of high rates of immigrant unemployment as a fall-out from the Fordist crisis is hardly surprising, since in many cases migrant workers had been recruited specifically to staff the expansion of manufacturing industries in the previous two decades. Immigrant workers were also vulnerable because of their over-repre-sentation in the construction industry, a sector which fluctuates widely according to market confidence. And they suffered when some public sector activities (transport, postal services, care services) were rationalised, automated and privatised during the 1980s and 1990s.

Unemployment

Table 15.1 shows that this trend of high and rising foreigner unemployment was common to many western European countries of immigration during the 1980s and 1990s. Only in the Benelux countries did the rate of unemployment of foreigners fall during 1983–93. It should be pointed out, however, that unemployment is recorded in different ways in different countries and therefore cross-country comparisons in Table 15.1 may not be valid. We should also remind ourselves that "foreigners" and "immigrants" are measured differently in various European countries: for instance, in the Netherlands most Antilleans and Surinamers are regarded as Dutch

Table 15.1 *Unemployment of foreigners in selected European countries, 1983–93 (%)*

	Foreigners' share of labour force		Foreigners' share of unemployed		Unemployment rate of foreigners		Unemployment rate of native workforce	
	1983	1993	1983	1993	1983	1993	1983	1993
France	6.7	6.3	12.3	11.3	14.6	20.7	7.5	10.8
Germany	8.3	10.6	14.4	23.3	11.3	12.7	6.1	4.9
Belgium	8.2	8.4	15.3	20.0	21.9	19.4	10.8	7.1
Netherlands	3.9	3.9	8.0	12.3	24.5	19.7	11.4	5.8
Luxembourg	30.4	38.6	37.0	46.2	3.8	2.8	2.8	2.0
UK	3.9	3.6	4.9	5.6	14.0	16.0	11.1	10.1
Sweden	5.3	5.1	9.7	12.9	5.9	20.9	3.1	7.6

Source: SOPEMI (1995, 32–3).

Table 15.2 *Unemployment rates by age, sex and ethnic group in the Netherlands according to two sources (%)*

	Native Dutch	Surinamers	Antilleans	Turks	Moroccans	North Mediterraneans*	Others (refugees)
Ministry of Social Affairs 1987							
Male	12	27	21	40	41	18	35
Female	16	25	27	58	49	21	38
Total	13	27	23	44	42	18	36
Unemployment register 1986							
15–24	26	31	20	45	47		
25–44	14	27	20	36	35		
45–64	9	25	25	39	36		
Total	16	28	20	40	38		

* North Mediterraneans comprise Italians, Greeks, Spaniards and Portuguese.
Source: Penninx *et al.* (1994, 114–15).

citizens and are therefore excluded from Table 15.1.

Where disaggregated data are available, it is apparent that unemployment rates vary among immigrant ethnicities, and also by age and gender. Table 15.2 shows official data from the Dutch Ministry of Social Affairs and Employment and from the Dutch Unemployment Register broken down by age and sex. Immigrant-origin women generally suffer higher rates of unemployment than men (this is also true of the native Dutch); and there is a bimodal age pattern of unemployment for ethnic groups, with higher rates at 15–24 and 45–64 than at 25–44 (this is not the case for the Dutch). Another trend evidenced from Table 15.2 is for the highest rates of employment to be recorded by the Turks and Moroccans, with somewhat lower rates for Surinamers and Antilleans and the lowest rates (but still above those for the Dutch) for the "North Mediterranean" group of countries. It should be pointed out that the rate of "ethnic" unemployment in the Netherlands is higher than in any other western European country, and that the ratio between ethnic group and native Dutch unemployment – the former more than three times the latter – is also the highest.

In a discussion of the characteristics of foreigner employment and unemployment in European OECD countries in the 1980s and early 1990s, SOPEMI (1995, 36–7) points to a number of general trends. Unemployment of foreign workers derives particularly from their concentration in declining mining and manufacturing sectors where, because of their lack of training and mature ages, it is difficult to convert to other employment. Their spatial concentration in declining industrial regions further limits their options. In fact there is a "double unemployment squeeze" on foreigners because, while the first generation are handicapped by their age and lack of skills, young (second-generation) ethnic minority workers are vulnerable because they generally have lower educational qualifications than indigenous youngsters. The age-specific unemployment data in Table 15.2 lend support to the hypothesis of the double unemployment squeeze. For all workers of immigrant origin, including the second generation, discriminatory practices further penalise their chances in the job market. Finally, the recent arrival of many new immigrants through family reunion, asylum and other means contributes to swelling the numbers of unemployed foreigners. The top part of Figure 15.1 summarises the effects of deindustrialisation on three migrant subgroups – first-generation, second-generation and new immigrants.

Employment data show that immigrants and foreign workers are tending to move out of those sectors where they are over-represented (mining, manufacturing, heavy engineering, construction) and into those sectors where they are under-represented (notably the services, but excluding public administration for which there is usually a

RESTRUCTURING PROCESSES	FIRST-GENERATION IMMIGRANTS	SECOND GENERATION	NEW IMMIGRANTS
Decline of Fordist industries	Unemployment; return migration	Lack of work opportunities	Not relevant; no opportunities
Rise of high-tech industries	Access blocked because of age and lack of education, training and language	Restricted access dependent on educational qualifications	SIM within Europe and from advanced countries; some brain-drain
Expansion of SMEs	Strong involvement *ab initio*, and transfer in after unemployment	Selective entry dependent on qualifications and entrepreneurial traditions	Limited impact
Expansion of informal sector, especially in southern Europe	Some involvement of established ethnic businesses	Some involvement in some countries, e.g. France	New demands for cheap flexible labour; strong influx of new immigrants into informal labour market

Figure 15.1 *Links between economic restructuring and migrants*

nationality criterion). Table 15.3 shows that, for most countries, the annual rate of employment growth for foreigners is higher in economic sectors where they are under-represented than in sectors where they are over-represented. The net result is that the "disparity indicator" – the percentage of foreign workers who would need to be reallocated from the over-represented to the under-represented sectors to achieve parity in employment distribution with the native workforce – falls between 1983 and 1992, indicating an overall evening-out of immigrant employment distribution (SOPEMI 1995, 38–41). Only two countries do not conform to this pattern. The Swedish situation is static and in the British case foreign workers have become sectorally more concentrated.[1]

The role of education

Moving down Figure 15.1, the restructuring of the western European production system into high-tech industries and advanced producer services creates demands for rigorously qualified labour which largely exclude established first-generation migrants, especially those who were hired to work in factories and on building-sites

Table 15.3 *Changing employment pattern of foreign workers in selected European countries, 1983–92 (%)*

	Annual rate of employment growth				Disparity indicator*		Foreign share of total employment	
	Sectors where foreign workers are over-represented		Sectors where foreign workers are under-represented					
	Nationals	Foreigners	Nationals	Foreigners	1983	1992	1983	1992
Belgium	0.4	0.2	1.8	3.0	21.7	20.2	7.2	7.2
France	−0.8	−2.8	0.9	1.1	24.2	18.9	6.2	5.6
Germany	0.9	1.9	1.6	5.8	22.9	17.9	7.8	9.3
Denmark	0.9	0.3	1.0	7.6	16.3	9.7	1.6	1.9
Sweden	0.6	1.6	1.2	2.0	15.4	15.7	5.2	5.5
UK	1.2	0.3	1.1	0.7	11.3	13.6	3.8	3.5

* For "disparity indicator" and other explanations, see text.
Source: SOPEMI (1995, 39).

in the 1950s and 1960s. Second-generation workers can gain access to these jobs only if they have the formal qualifications – usually a university degree and/or professional training. Most sources of information on the educational performance of children and students of ethnic minority background in Europe show that they fall well below the standards achieved by local indigenous young people (see, for example, Frey and Mammey, 1996, 48–61 for Germany, and Penninx *et al.*, 1994, 130–41 for the Netherlands). Various reasons are suggested for this, such as poor linguistic preparation, different cultural background, limited family support for studying, low expectations on the part of teachers, and the poor quality of facilities and education in the inner-city schools which tend to be overcrowded with ethnic minority children.

However, as time goes by there are clear signs that children from immigrant backgrounds are performing closer to the national average standards, and in some cases are exceeding the results of the indigenous children. Data from the UK are very illuminating in this regard, not only with respect to the basic statistics on educational attainment but also as to how the data are interpreted. Already in the late 1970s statistics collected by the Rampton Committee showed that "Black (i.e. Afro-Caribbean) pupils performed consistently worse than Asian or white [ones] in public examinations and were less represented amongst those pupils who went on

to university." Only 3 per cent of Afro-Caribbean school-leavers obtained five or more passes at O level, compared to 18 per cent of Asian and 16 per cent of other (i.e. predominantly white) pupils. There was a similar trend at A level, where 2 per cent of Afro-Caribbean pupils gained one or more passes, compared to 13 per cent of Asian and 12 per cent of others (data quoted in Thomas-Hope, 1994, 56). The pattern of Asian "success" and Afro-Caribbean "failure" seemed clear. However, critics of these figures (Cashmore and Troyna, 1983) maintained that some ability tests, such as ritualised examinations, may not be adequate for assessing the progress of ethnic minority groups. It was also pointed out that crude ethnic examination data do not control for social class and other social factors: if the Rampton Committee figures had been analysed along class as well as ethnic lines, the results would have shown that black pupils performed at a similar level to white working-class school-leavers.

More recent British data, while confirming the broad ethnic performance pattern noted above, are also more sensitively contextualised within the social backgrounds of the various ethnic groups. If anything, the Asians (especially the Indians) have drawn significantly ahead of the white school-leavers in terms of O level (or GCSE) and A level performance, while the Afro-Caribbeans, still lagging, reveal a gender contrast as girls outperform boys (see the discussion in Drew and

285

Gray, 1991). It is also apparent that there are wide variations between the three main Asian groups: Indian children generally perform best, followed by Pakistanis and then Bangladeshis. The pre- and post-migration background of the parents is now considered a highly relevant factor in helping explain these differences. The Indians are longer established in the UK and, with their more urban, Westernised backgrounds and strong business involvement, have attained middle-class status. The Pakistanis and (especially) Bangladeshis are more recent arrivals, come from rural, peasant backgrounds and have mainly manual jobs in factories or low-grade services. The best exam results of all are achieved by pupils of Chinese and African parentage: the former come from a business background and the latter from a largely professional class of immigrants.

The relevance of this discussion on educational attainment is that it is very closely related to patterns of employment opportunity and ethnic social mobility in the UK – and the same goes for western Europe as a whole (Cross, 1993). Some groups are "making it", some are not. In an analysis of the "ethnic question" in the 1991 British census, Peach (1996) mapped out two routes to social mobility: a "Jewish model" which is being followed by the Asian groups in the UK, and an "Irish model" followed by Caribbeans. In a field as delicate as race relations such labelling was regarded by some as insensitive,[2] although Peach no doubt intended his Jewish and Irish models as heuristic devices to make a vast amount of data and trends accessible to his readership.

The Jewish model is characterised as white-collar, professionally qualified, self-employed, suburban, owner-occupying and upwardly mobile. It is being followed most clearly by Indians and Chinese. A variant of it is the Hasidic community – more enclosed, inner-city, traditionally orthodox; this trajectory is being followed by Pakistanis and Bangladeshis, according to Peach. The Irish model is presented as more working class, with a higher percentage of manual workers, less self-employment and business involvement, lower educational achievements and a greater presence in council housing. Although there are scant data on the Irish beyond the first generation – with the result that Peach's stereotype may well be inaccurate – this

appears to be the trajectory being followed by the Caribbean communities in the UK.

Ethnic enterprise

There has been a considerable amount of recent research on ethnic businesses and self-employment in Europe, especially in the UK. (For useful introductions and case studies see the collections edited by Waldinger *et al.*, 1990 and Ward and Jenkins, 1984.) Three explanatory models can be identified: the niche model, the cultural model and the reactive model. These are not necessarily to be seen as exclusive, and in practice are often complementary to each other. The niche model develops out of the special demands of the ethnic community for goods and services – food shops, import/export concerns linked to the home country, cafés, restaurants, even accountants and estate agents. The market is provided within the "parallel economy" of the ethnic enclave and is especially well developed where there are large ethnic communities in major cities like London and Paris. While it is generally true that the ethnic radius limits the scope for expansion of these niche firms (both in terms of their number and their individual scale), sometimes they can "break out" and supply wider markets. This is especially the case with certain catering activities – Italian ice-cream, Chinese take-aways and Indian restaurants. In fact the relentless search of the European middle classes for ever more "interesting" and "exotic" cuisine has given a tremendous fillip to the proliferation of ethnic restaurants.

The cultural model is based on the idea that some cultures give their members particular encouragement to engage in business. Sometimes this is expressed concretely through ethnic credit co-operatives for financing business development, but in other cases it may be less tangible – for example, the recognition that certain groups possess an "entreprenurial spirit". Following Peach's typology discussed earlier, the Irish and Caribbean communities in the UK are thought not to be business oriented, whereas the Asians are.[3] The most successful Asian businesses in the UK are generally those run by Asians who came from East Africa, where they had a strong involvement in business and the professions.

Table 15.4 *Self-employed foreigners in Germany, 1972–93*

Year	Total self-employed foreigners ('000)	As % of all self-employed in Germany	As % of all foreign workers in Germany	Breakdown by nationality (no. = '000; % = of total workforce of that nationality)								
				Italian		Greek		Yugoslavian		Turkish	
				no.	%	no.	%	no.	%	no.	%
1972	44	1.7	1.9	9	2.1	–	–	–	–	–	–
1980	86	3.8	4.1	17	5.5	11	8.3	9	2.5	7	1.2
1987	121	5.1	7.6	26	14.3	14	13.9	10	3.4	16	3.1
1993	213	8.2	9.8	25	12.9	24	19.9	20	4.8	31	4.9

Source: Frey and Mammey (1996, 96, 142); some data recalculated because of errors in original table.

Pakistani and Bangladeshi self-employed are usually engaged in more small-scale and economically marginal activities like corner-shops and taxi-driving. In fact these latter groups are closer to being examples of the third model, whereby self-employment is seen as a defensive reaction to unemployment and discrimination in the labour market.

While ethnic communities may differ with regard to their "flair for business", the countries of immigration also vary in terms of the encouragement given to foreign-owned enterprises. For example, the UK and France have provided favourable climates for ethnic enterprise to flourish, whereas in Germany and the Netherlands – until recently at least – there have been significant institutional and legal barriers. Despite the influence of national setting, however, everywhere in western Europe the growth of ethnic business formation has been faster than for native-run concerns. Thus in France the number of self-employed foreigners rose by 50 per cent during 1983–89 to 5.6 per cent of the total immigrant labour force. Some German data are set out in Table 15.4. These show a fivefold increase in foreign self-employed over the period 1972–93, during which time there was no increase in total foreign worker numbers. In 1993 self-employed foreigners accounted for 8.2 per cent of all self-employed workers in Germany and nearly 10 per cent of all foreign workers. The Italians and Greeks have higher rates of self-employment than the other major immigrant groups, but there has been a rapid expansion of Turkish self-employment since obstacles to the running of businesses by non-EU nationals were removed in the 1980s. Various studies quoted by Frey and Mammey (1996, 98–9) indicate that more than three-quarters of Italian enterprises and more than half of Greek concerns are in the catering sector and have predominantly German clienteles. Turkish businesses, on the other hand, are more widely spread in different sectors – food shops, electrical goods, wholesaling, import/export, restaurants, travel agents – but service mainly the Turkish ethnic market in Germany. Turkish business owners are younger on average than the other main groups (including the Germans), indicating a substantial involvement of the second generation.

Finally, the precise nature of the relationships between economic restructuring and ethnic business expansion need to be drawn out (Blotevogel and King, 1996). On the one hand there is a causal link running from deindustrialisation through unemployment to the growth of small, usually one-person concerns – the reactive model described above. In the UK taxi-driving seems to be the classic occupation of redundant Asian factory workers in those cities where industrial closures have hit hard. On the other hand the strong growth of small and medium enterprises (SMEs) owned by ethnic minorities is part and parcel of the process of restructuring itself (Figure 15.1). Such firms often employ family and ethnic labour in flexible, deregulated ways – long and unsocial hours, piece-rates, etc. Exploitation of female and even child labour in sweatshop conditions in some of these enterprises is probably more widespread than commonly acknowledged. In this way international migration has imported the working practices of the less developed world into Europe, giving a new twist to the New International Division of Labour.

Skilled international migration

Appreciation of the growing importance of skilled international migration (SIM) within an overall declining quantity of recorded intra-European migration dates from the early 1980s. At that time it was seen largely in the context of the restructuring and globalisation of the European economy (Figure 15.1) and, at the individual scale, as a function of the spatially mobile nature of professional career paths (Salt, 1984). Further research demonstrated the role of international mobility within the internal labour markets of large multinational enterprises; the increasing use of international recruitment agencies and contract systems for channelling skilled labour to locations of demand; and, outside the strict world of business, the importance of international organisations – not least the European Community itself – in stimulating professional migration within Europe (Findlay and Garrick, 1990; Salt, 1992b; Tarrius, 1992). These various processes give a clue to SIM's heterogeneity, a characteristic which is further complicated by the elusiveness of the concept of "skill" and by the statistical elusiveness of the phenomenon of SIM. In fact Findlay (1995) finds it difficult to pin down any convincing data which show that SIM has indeed increased over the past 10–15 years. This failure is closely related to the fact that, in a European Community with virtually no internal frontiers, business and élite migrations are impossible to monitor with any degree of accuracy. What we must do here, therefore, is to describe SIM intuitively, concentrating on its general patterns and conditions rather than on its measurement.

First, the patterns. Reflecting the increasingly integrated nature of the European and world economies, most SIM occurs as relatively balanced two-way flows among the most advanced countries of Europe, and between Europe and the other global economic poles, notably Japan and North America. Within these countries the key nodes defining the movement patterns are the capital cities; the financial and business centres (London, Paris, Frankfurt, Randstad, etc.); the bureaucratic capitals where EU institutions and international organisations like OECD or the World Health Organisation are headquartered (Brussels, Strasbourg, Paris, Geneva, etc.); and newly emergent industrial areas such as Bavaria, Rhône-Alpes, northern Italy and Catalonia (dominated by Munich, Grenoble, Milan and Barcelona). However, given the spatially variable nature of supply and demand for professionally qualified and highly skilled workers, there are also asymmetric flows. Ireland, Spain, southern Italy and Greece suffer from youth unemployment rates of 20–35 per cent, even higher in some regions like Extremadura and Sardinia. Unlike the past, many of these unemployed are highly educated. Hence today's emigrant from southern Italy, Greece or Spain is unlikely to be a poorly educated *Gastarbeiter*, but may well be a computer technician, engineer, translator or doctor. Research on Irish graduate emigration has revealed not only the high propensity of this group to emigrate but also a growing trend away from traditional Irish emigration destinations (the UK, North America, Australia) in favour of continental Europe (Shuttleworth, 1993).

Two other SIM flows into western Europe can be recognised. The first of these comes from eastern Europe and is considered later in the chapter. The other consists of "brain drain" flows from developing countries and is largely patterned according to the relationships created by former colonial empires, including similarities of language and educational systems, and prior migration ties. The main movements are from francophone Africa to France and from anglophone Africa and South Asia to the UK, and many of them result from students staying on after completing their university training in the metropole.

Widening the scope of SIM to include migration of "élites" involves students, artists, researchers and wealthy retired persons who act as both gatekeepers and pioneers for high-status migration. Student migration within Europe is particularly important, not only because of the large numbers involved but also because studying in another country sets the scene for future migration through work or marriage. In the late 1980s only 2 per cent of university students in the EC lived in countries other than their own: it is the objective of the Socrates programme of student exchange to increase this to 10 per cent. Student migrations obviously take place among the university towns of Europe. Very different are the international migration paths of Europe's wealthy retired who mainly move south to picturesque rural or coastal environments such as Tuscany, the Dordogne or the Côte d'Azur. Following on from Spain's experience of encouraging mass international tourism since the 1960s, retirement migration to the Spanish *costas* has evolved from an élite to a broader class phenomenon.

The growth of student migration, the increasing importance of professional, technical and managerial work in the European economy, and the general process of European economic and cultural integration are all factors which presage further growth in SIM, yet there are also opposite trends to be observed. For companies responsible for stimulating SIM, the movement of skilled personnel is expensive, involving costly relocation packages and high salaries as incentives. Most European managers and business personnel are highly selective as to the places they are willing to work in; hence extra compensation is necessary to lure them elsewhere. Interviews with European professional élites reveal a tiredness with perpetual mobility and a desire to establish a more sedentary base and hence a "local" identity (Tarrius, 1992). As a result of these constraints on SIM, some large firms are now "localising" and subcontracting their recruitment and deployment of skilled labour instead of moving their established staff. There has also been a switch to shorter-term business or "trouble-shooting" visits of a few days rather than longer-term relocation; in this way SIM shades imperceptibly into business travel. Finally the enormous growth in the sophistication of telecommunications makes "live" and "real-time" communication, including problem-solving over long distances, increasingly feasible as a substitute for travel or migration.

Asylum-seekers

After the cessation of mass labour migration in 1973, the only legal means of entering western Europe for those would-be immigrants not able to take advantage of family reunification provisions or the special permits accorded to highly skilled workers and students has been the asylum route. As Fassmann and Münz (1994, 19) point out, refugees, displaced persons and asylum-seekers form a nexus of overlapping categories with a previous history in Europe, especially with regard to East–West moves. Between 1945 and 1950 some 8 million displaced persons moved into the territory of West Germany (as defined during 1949–90), and between 1945 and 1961 another 4 million people emigrated from the former East Germany. It was in this largely European end-of-war context that the United Nations regulations for refugee recognition were drawn up, applying to groups and territories rather than individual cases. Over time the UN Geneva Convention relating to the status of refugees – i.e. those who have "a well-founded fear of being persecuted for reasons of race, religion, nationality, membership of a particular social group or political opinion" has proved to be increasingly unworkable in practice. One reason for this has been the sheer weight of refugee numbers; since the mid-1980s escalating requests for protection, and the rising costs of processing applications, have threatened the very institution of asylum. Another has been the changing

circumstances by which asylum-seekers are "produced": the overwhelming majority of those seeking asylum in Europe in the last 10 years do not satisfy the UN Convention criteria of persecution, even though most have been forced to leave their countries because of war, famine, ethnic strife or environmental disaster. Yet while there is a strong feeling among governments and scholars of migration that a growing number of asylum-seekers have been merely "economic migrants in disguise", it must also be recognised that the distinction between economic migrants and those escaping dangerous and unbearable conditions at home has become increasingly difficult to make.

Table 15.5 shows the annual numbers of applications for asylum in the main European receiving countries since 1983. From relatively low levels in the 1970s and early 1980s (generally below 20 000 per year), requests grew to 75 000 in 1983, reached a peak of 693 000 in 1992, and then fell to 319 000 in 1994. Germany has consistently been the most important receiving country. Table 15.6 shows the distribution of main nationalities of asylum-seekers for eight receiving countries in the 1980s. Most applications for asylum in Germany and Austria were from eastern and central Europe, whereas countries in the less developed world dominated the pattern in other European states.

Interpreting asylum statistics is problematic (Black, 1994, 88–92). Issues of inconsistency and non-comparability arise because of differences in the definition and treatment of asylum-seekers by different countries. Germany, Switzerland and Sweden have traditionally had liberal stances towards them, allowing residence while their cases are being considered. The UK has evolved a harsher policy, including immediate repatriation to the country of arrival or transit. The most significant interpretation problem, however, is that the number of applications cannot be equated with actual arrivals. Many requests are made before or after arrival; and some applicants make simultaneous approaches to two or more countries (Hovy, 1993). Finally asylum data are often hyped by political interests and the media to portray a "crisis" – in reality most refugees move *between* countries of the developing world, especially Africa, rather than to Europe (UNHCR, 1995).

Behind the bare statistics of Tables 15.5 and 15.6 lie a variety of geopolitical factors and a

Table 15.5   *Asylum applications to western Europe, 1983–94 ('000)*

Country	1983	1984	1985	1986	1987	1988	1989	1990	1991	1992	1993	1994
Germany	19.7	35.3	73.8	99.6	57.4	103.1	121.3	193.1	256.1	438.2	322.6	127.2
France	22.3	15.9	25.8	23.4	24.8	31.6	58.8	54.8	46.7	26.8	27.6	26.0
Sweden	3.0	12.0	14.5	14.6	18.1	19.6	30.4	29.4	27.4	84.0	37.6	18.6
Switzerland	7.9	7.4	9.7	8.5	10.9	16.7	24.4	35.8	41.6	18.0	24.7	16.1
UK	3.6	3.3	5.4	4.8	4.5	5.3	15.5	26.2	44.8	24.6	22.4	32.8
Austria	5.9	7.2	6.7	8.6	11.4	15.8	21.9	22.8	27.3	16.2	4.7	5.1
Netherlands	2.0	2.6	5.6	5.9	13.5	7.5	13.9	21.2	21.6	17.5	35.4	52.6
Belgium	2.9	3.6	5.3	7.6	6.0	5.1	8.1	13.0	15.2	17.7	26.9	14.4
Italy	3.0	4.6	5.4	6.5	11.0	1.3	2.2	4.7	23.3	2.5	1.5	1.4
Denmark	0.8	4.3	8.7	9.3	2.7	4.7	4.6	5.3	4.6	13.9	14.4	6.7
Spain	1.4	1.2	2.4	2.3	2.5	3.3	2.8	6.9	7.3	12.7	12.9	12.0
Greece	0.4	0.8	1.4	4.2	6.9	8.4	3.0	6.2	2.7	2.0	0.8	1.3
Norway	0.2	0.3	0.8	2.7	8.6	6.6	4.4	4.0	4.6	5.3	12.9	3.4
Western European total	75.0	101.6	167.7	201.3	181.7	233.7	345.8	434.3	560.0	692.7	549.4	318.9

Sources: Hovy (1993, 211); UNHCR (1995, 253).

multitude of human dramas. Several types of movement can be recognised (Hovy, 1993; Koser, 1996). "Quota refugees", such as those originating in Vietnam, were important in the 1970s and early 1980s but have dwindled since. A second type consists of people from outside Europe who arrive independently and claim asylum "spontaneously". The scale of these flows escalated considerably during the 1980s. Sri Lanka, Turkey and Iran have been constant suppliers of spontaneous asylum-seekers, many of whom are from minority groups like the Kurds and Tamils. Other asylum events are more truly spontaneous, concentrated in space and time, like the sudden arrival of more than 20 000 Albanian "boat people" who were given refugee status in Italy in 1991. Some asylum movements reflect earlier colonial relationships; other links, like that between Turkey and Germany, build on a history of previous labour migration.

Two other types of refugee movement originate closer to western Europe – from eastern Europe and the Balkans. Both before and after the removal of the Iron Curtain, refugees have moved from eastern Europe and the former Soviet Union, following the general line of those resettlement migrations which occurred after the Second World War. Before 1989 Hungary,

Czechoslovakia and Poland were the principal sources; more recently Romania has become significant. The geography and nature of East–West migration are described in more detail presently. From the point of view of asylum migration, the most important development has been the reclassification of many central and east European states (Poland, the Czech Republic, Slovakia, Hungary, Slovenia and Croatia) as "safe countries" because they have become signatories of the Geneva Convention. This means that western Europe has effectively created a "buffer zone" to the east against overland immigration, with the further result that countries like Hungary have now become important destinations for asylum-seekers (Collinson, 1996).

A major eruption of refugees and asylum-seekers occurred with the break-up of Yugoslavia in the early 1990s. Refugees from the conflict have tended to be dealt with outside the normal national asylum procedures, and have been given the status of "temporary protection". Also, internal displacement to so-called "safe havens" has contained some of the movement within the boundaries of the former Yugoslavia. Nevertheless, by the end of 1993 it was estimated that more than 4.2 million people were displaced and

Table 15.6 *Citizenship of asylum applicants in selected European countries, 1983–90 (%)*

Germany		France	
Poland	14.7	Turkey	19.4
Turkey	12.8	Zaire	11.9
Yugoslavia	9.9	Sri Lanka	8.0
Iran	8.8		
Sri Lanka	7.1	Belgium	
Romania	6.6	Ghana	20.0
Lebanon	6.5	Turkey	12.9
		Zaire	8.6
Austria		India	8.5
Romania	27.9	Pakistan	6.4
Czechoslovakia	15.9	Iran	5.2
Poland	15.0	Poland	5.1
Hungary	13.7	Yugoslavia	5.0
Turkey	6.4		
		Netherlands	
Switzerland		Sri Lanka	9.1
Turkey	36.8	Turkey	8.7
Sri Lanka	14.4	Ghana	7.8
Lebanon	7.6	Iran	7.2
Yugoslavia	6.9	Somalia	5.9
United Kingdom		Sweden	
Sri Lanka	16.7	Iran	23.9
India	12.3	Chile	9.0
Turkey	10.6	Lebanon	7.9
Somalia	8.7	Ethiopia	6.0
Ethiopia	5.4	Iraq	5.8
Iraq	5.1		

* Source countries with at least 5 per cent of total.
Source: UNHCR data in Hovy (1993, 219).

had received United Nations High Commissioner for Refugees assistance: 1.6 million internally displaced, 1.8 million assisted war victims and 820 000 refugees living abroad (Koser, 1996, 153).

In the early 1990s a consensus emerged within western Europe on the need to contain the escalating numbers of asylum-seekers, especially those who were using asylum as a cover for economic migration. The Dublin and Schengen Accords, signed by several EU states in 1990, signalled a more restrictive and more unified Community stance. One of the more controversial measures introduced was that of "carrier liability", which made airlines responsible for ensuring that their passengers have all the necessary documentation to enter an EU country. Since 1992–93 countries such as Germany, Sweden and Austria, once known for their liberal asylum policies, no longer admit applicants who have already transited a "safe country" (such as Poland or Hungary). Compulsory visas for most non-European nationals, a severe tightening of asylum criteria and procedures, and more stringent border controls including troop deployment along the old Iron Curtain (this time by the West and not by the East) are other measures which have been introduced in the last few years.

These have been backed up by national legislative change. For instance, in Germany, which received over half of all asylum applications made to European countries in the late 1980s and early 1990s, a new Asylum Procedure Act implemented in 1993 led to both an immediate drop in numbers (Table 15.5) and a declining application approval rate. The latter was below 5 per cent by the early 1990s (compared with 29 per cent in 1985). In the UK there has been intense interaction between government policy, the courts and bodies representing the interests of refugees and asylum-seekers. In 1991 the British government announced changes to its asylum law in response to a tenfold growth in asylum claimants over the previous three years: the system of processing applications was speeded up but also toughened, and the fine on airlines bringing in improperly documented asylum-seekers was doubled to £2000. In February 1996 the Home Office withdrew benefits and housing rights from asylum-seekers who had not filed a claim for asylum at the point of entry, and also from those whose cases were under appeal. The Court of Appeal ruled against this measure in June 1996 but was immediately outmanoeuvred by the government's July amendment to the Asylum and Immigration Bill, which put the cuts policy on a legal footing. Opening a night shelter for homeless refugees in London in September 1996, Cardinal Basil Hume, leader of the Catholic Church in Britain, said "It seems to me that the reception given to those applying for asylum is an illuminating indicator of a society's moral health." Referring to the government's overruling of the Court of Appeal judgement on the illegality of the benefit withdrawals, he went on to stress that "the moral and practical force of the court's judgement still stands".[4]

Southern Europe and the New Immigration

The hardening climate against asylum-seekers and most other forms of immigration in north European countries has been one of the factors behind the rapid growth of immigration into southern Europe in recent years. In Chapter 14 we saw how Spain, Portugal, Italy and Greece had been among the major exporters of labour migrants during the 1950s and 1960s. Already by the 1970s immigration flows had started, especially to Italy, and these influxes have subsequently accelerated.

Apart from the diversion effect noted above, several reasons help to explain the boom in immigration into southern Europe (King and Rybaczuk, 1993). They include ease of entry into countries with massive tourist influxes; geographical proximity to many of the major supply countries of the "new immigrants" in North Africa, the Middle East and the Balkans; strong southern European economic growth, especially in Italy and Spain; and the strength and dynamism of the informal sector, into which migrant employment can easily be incorporated.

As the bottom part of Figure 15.1 suggests, the last factor has been particularly important. A number of recent analyses have begun to reveal the extent to which the south European "model" of economic development, based on minimal government intervention in the labour market (or avoidance of those regulations which exist), is bolstered by immigrant workers who – as well as contributing a new source of profit for their employers – are also ingenious in creating employment and income for themselves. According to Montagné-Villette (1994), illegal work is part of a well-established tradition and is virtually part of the national culture in southern European countries. It has therefore proved easy to absorb undocumented immigrant workers, although the extent to which this has been a deliberate act of recruitment strategy driven by employers seeking to reduce their labour costs, or has resulted almost by chance because of a lack of immigration control policies at the national level, remains an open question. The precise circumstances vary from country to country and from one immigrant group to another; indeed they vary at the locality level according to how different immigrant groups are incorporated into the local urban and rural labour markets. At a general level, however, there has been a dynamic and mutually reinforcing relationship between the massive inflow of undocumented workers into southern Europe since the early 1980s, and the growth and adaptability of the black economy in these countries.

Most estimates put the total number of immigrants in the four southern European countries at around 3 million, made up of 1.2–1.5 million in Italy, 500 000–700 000 in Spain, 300 000–500 000 in Greece and 200 000–250 000 in Portugal. The imprecision of these estimates is based on the weak statistical hold the southern European countries have over their immigrant populations and the high proportion of undocumented immigrants. Census, residence permit and work permit records give much lower totals, while regularisations of clandestine immigrants have been only partially effective in "fixing" a highly fluid and mobile migrant situation.

Two things account for the difficulties these countries have in enumerating their immigrant populations and in facing up to the attendant policy issues. The first is that immigrants are attractive to employers, and therefore to the economy as a whole, *precisely because they are illegal*. Employers can exploit their illegal status by not paying any social insurance or other benefits, by paying wages which are below the legal minimum, and by hiring and firing at will. Migrants cannot complain to the authorities because to do so would reveal their illegal presence in the country, resulting in fines, imprisonment or deportation.

The second important characteristic is the heterogeneity of immigration: it involves a multitude of nationalities and a great variety of job types. This is in contrast to the situation in the earlier post-war migrations described in Chapter 14, where migrants from a well-defined set of Mediterranean basin and ex-colonial countries took up mainly factory and construction work. For southern Europe in the 1980s and 1990s, a diverse and overlapping set of source countries is involved: for Portugal mainly lusophone countries of the former Portuguese Empire (Brazil, Cape Verde, Angola, Mozambique); for

Table 15.7 *Main immigrant communities in Italy, 31 December 1994*

Country of origin	no.	Country of origin	no.
Morocco	92 617	Brazil	19 589
Ex-Yugoslavia	89 444	China	19 485
USA	56 714	Poland	18 929
Tunisia	41 105	Sri Lanka	18 689
Philippines	40 714	Switzerland	17 775
Germany	37 050	Spain	16 395
Albania	31 926	Somalia	16 325
UK	26 435	Greece	14 282
France	25 723	India	13 336
Senegal	24 615	Ex-USSR	13 329
Egypt	21 230	Ghana	12 626
Romania	20 220	Argentina	10 681
		Ethiopia	10 145

Source: Caritas di Roma (1995, 90).

Spain a variety of countries in Latin America plus the Philippines, Morocco, Senegal, Gambia and Poland; and for Greece a similarly diverse catchment including Albania, Poland, Egypt, Iraq and the Philippines.

In Italy the range of source countries is so extensive it is best set out in tabular form. Table 15.7 shows these to be distributed across all three continents of the developing world, together with important new source countries in eastern Europe as well as migrants and settlers from advanced countries who are part of skilled migration flows, or who have come to Italy for marriage, residence or retirement. It should be stressed that the figures are based on official records of *permessi di soggiorno* or "permits to stay". They exclude undocumented migrants whose numbers are by definition unknown. The table is limited to the 25 largest communities – those of at least 10 000. Excluded from the table are several groups who are, in one way or another, prominent in Italy's increasingly multiracial scene – Nigerians, Cape Verdeans, Bangladeshis, Pakistanis, Colombians, people from the Dominican Republic, and many more. Total permit-holders on 31 December 1994 numbered 922 706, a number which has been more or less static for the last few years (1991, 859 571; 1992, 925 172; 1993, 987 407).

The national distribution and employment of immigrants in Italy exhibit considerable regional variation (King, 1993; Montanari and Cortese,

1993). Overall, as Figure 15.2 shows, there are relative concentrations in northern regions which are economically strong (Lombardy, Veneto) or are border regions (Trentino, Friuli) traversed by routes from over the Alps or beyond Trieste. In central Italy Latium stands out because of Rome (the largest single concentration of immigrants in the country), while the high density in Umbria is partly explained by the "University for Foreigners" at Perugia. The south of Italy has a greater concentration of undocumented migrants who are excluded from the map and from the figures in Table 15.7.

Most immigrant communities in Italy have employment specialisms, which also tend to define their spatial distribution. Senegalese and some other African groups are mainly street-hawkers in the big cities and (in summer) the seaside resorts (Figure 15.3). The Moroccans have a wider distribution as market traders and travelling salesmen, including coverage of the rural areas. Tunisians dominate the fishing industry in Sicily. Other Africans, mainly from Africa south of the Sahara, are seasonal agricultural workers in areas of specialised farming such as the Neapolitan Plains and Apulia. The Chinese run restaurants all over Italy, as well as the leather trade in Tuscany. Filipinos and Cape Verdeans – mainly women – work in domestic service as cleaners, nannies and care assistants. The Nigerians and the Albanians are the main immigrant groups involved in prostitution.

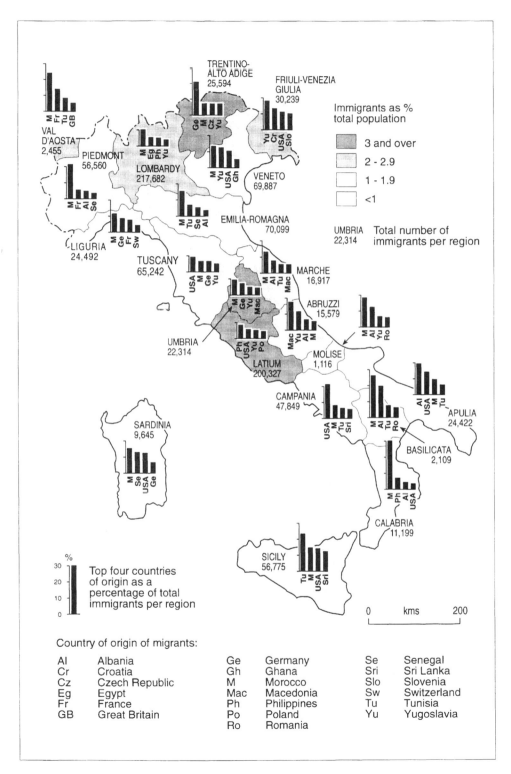

Figure 15.2 *Regional distribution of immigrants in Italy, 31 December 1994, based on "permits to stay" data*

Figure 15.3 *African street-hawkers on the Ponte Sant' Angelo, Rome*

Southern Europe shows how migration history repeats itself and comes full circle. A region of Europe which only 30 years ago was a great reservoir for outmigration has turned into a magnet for immigration within one or two decades. As yet it is too early to see if the "guestworkers-turned-immigrants" model of north-west Europe will apply to the south. The nature of the migration processes, the connections of the immigrants to the labour market, and the importance of illegal immigration are all differentiating factors between the old and the new migrations. But already among some communities, such as the Cape Verdeans in Portugal and the Filipinos and Somalians in Italy, there are signs of a settling-down process with family migration and the birth of the second generation.

East–West Migration

In the last decade, the most significant event to change the migration map of Europe has been the removal of the Iron Curtain. The importance of this barrier for migration, in both real and symbolic terms, can hardly be overstressed. It was the Berlin Wall which graphically symbolised the bipolar division between East and West; restriction on people's movement went hand in hand with protecting the ideological foundations of state socialism. During the Cold War the West made endless political capital out of decrying the restrictions on personal freedom in the East – including the freedom to emigrate. Those who did "get out" were almost automatically welcomed as refugees by west European governments.

And it was migration which breached the Iron Curtain in 1989, setting in motion forces leading to the ideological collapse of the "Second World". Hungary's decision to open the border with Austria in summer 1989 (thus allowing East Germans to migrate to West Germany) triggered other incipient migration flows and helped to create the domino effect of political conversion throughout eastern Europe and the former Soviet Union.

Soon after the "iron barrier" to migration was removed, however, alarm bells started ringing. While the West was ecstatic about the removal of bipolar geopolitics in Europe, it was less prepared for some of the practical implications, in particular the spectre of mass immigration from the East. The threat of a mass East–West exodus was inflamed by media images of encampments of East Germans in Hungary waiting to cross to the West, by people swarming over the Berlin Wall as it was being torn down, and later (in 1991), by striking pictures of the Albanian boat people arriving in southern Italy. These images were fanned by surveys, many of them based on unscientifically small samples, which suggested that millions wanted to emigrate from the former Eastern Bloc countries. Further fuel was heaped on the fire by neoclassical economists who hypothesised that East–West imbalances in the distribution of capital and labour could be corrected by the annual migration of 5 million people for 20 years – equivalent in 2010 to about half the population of eastern Europe and the European parts of the former Soviet Union![5]

According to Papademetriou (1994) Europe's near-hysteria about massive, spontaneous East–West migration lasted for about three years, after which realisation began to dawn that such movements were unlikely to occur, with a few exceptions – the mass movement of East Germans and ethnic Germans into West Germany, the Albanian flight, and the war-induced refugee movements in Yugoslavia. The Yugoslav displacements have been mentioned already; the German and Albanian migrations will be covered shortly. Papademetriou (1994, 20) explains the failure of mass westward migration to materialise by reference to "the one still valid law of migration [which] is that immigrants follow in the footsteps of earlier immigrants, taking advantage of familial, village and ethnic networks ...". Large-scale migration flows tend to build up momentum slowly, except when extreme conditions are present such as a civil war (as in Yugoslavia) or the virtual breakdown of society and the economy (the case of Albania in the early 1990s).

The problem of assessing the quantity of East–West migration that has taken place since 1989 is the perennial one of paucity of data. East European countries count only those emigrants who leave officially, which means the acquisition of some kind of emigration permit. In reality, the majority of emigrants have simply acquired a tourist passport and have emigrated as non-returning tourists or "overstayers". While registers of foreigners in destination countries such as Germany and Austria give some idea of the scale of westward migration, especially of those who apply for asylum or a work permit, these sources shed little light on the magnitude of clandestine or illegal movements (Kupiszewski, 1996, 13–15).

Although 1989 was the watershed year for the creation of a new East–West migration system, it also needs to be appreciated that significant flows across the Iron Curtain had been taking place since the mid-1980s. White and Sporton (1995) list four such flows: from East to West Germany (61 000 mainly elderly people during 1987–88); ethnic Germans from Poland, Romania and the Soviet Union (1.2 million during 1970–89); Soviet Jews to Israel (98 000 during 1987–89); and ethnic Greeks from the Black Sea regions of the Soviet Union to Greece (around 15 000 per year). Post-1989, these movements expanded and new ones started. Total East–West migration in 1989 was estimated by Salt (1993) at over 1.2 million, including 720 000 Germans, 320 000 Turks from Bulgaria (many of whom subsequently returned to Bulgaria) and 235 000 Soviet citizens. In 1990 emigration from the USSR rose to 450 000, including 200 000 Jews, 145 000 Germans, 55 000 Armenians and 20 000 Greeks.

Large-scale East–West migration continued during the early 1990s but by 1993 it seemed the boom was over. The extent to which the post-1993 decline has been due to increasingly rigid control policies from the West, as opposed to a "natural" decline in supply, remains debatable. However, continuing increases in temporary migration, some of it illegal, suggest that supply is far from exhausted. Three main types of legal temporary movement have evolved – contract workers, seasonal migration and cross-border commuters (Kupiszewski, 1996, 23–4). Contract migration provides Germany with quotas of workers for one to two years; currently the quota is for 73 000 workers, mainly from Poland, Hungary and Romania. Seasonal workers are allocated 3- to 12-month permits for work in a limited number of sectors – tourism, agriculture and forestry. In 1992 there were 212 000 seasonal workers from Poland, the Czech and Slovak republics, Hungary and Romania. Cross-border commuters are allowed to work in Germany from adjacent parts of Poland and the Czech Republic, provided they do not spend more than one night in Germany.

Illegal immigrants come mainly from the former Soviet Union, Poland, Romania, Bulgaria and Albania. Most are aiming at Germany or the easy-to-enter southern EU countries, but there is also a growing in-movement to the richer east European states such as Hungary, the Czech Republic and Slovenia from poorer countries further east and south. Movement over difficult boundaries – such as into Germany, Austria or the new migration buffer-states – is increasingly organised by professional guides who demand large fees.

We now examine two specific East–West migratory phenomena. The "ethnic" dimension of immigration into (West) Germany is remarkable both for its selectivity and for its scale. The second migration, the Albanian exodus, is much smaller in size but notable as the one instance of what was feared in the early 1990s: an uncontrolled and unexpected "invasion" into the EU "fortress".

German immigration: the ethnic imperative

In 1989 West Germany received a record net influx of 1 million persons: 383 000 Germans from East Germany, 377 000 ethnic Germans from eastern Europe and the USSR, and 250 000 foreigners of whom 121 000 were asylum-seekers. The following year saw the overall scale maintained: 359 000 East Germans, 397 000 ethnic Germans and 193 000 asylum-seekers. While the number of asylum-seekers continued to increase to a peak in 1992 (Table 15.5), after 1990 the number of East German migrants (*Übersiedler*) and ethnic Germans from eastern Europe (*Aussiedler*) declined. The former fell away rapidly after German unification at the end of 1990, while the latter flow stabilised at around 22 000 per year throughout the five years 1991–95 (Table 15.8). However, behind this stability of the *Aussiedler* stream lay a shifting balance of origins: the drastic decline of Poland and Romania after 1989–90, and the compensating rise of ethnic migrants from the former USSR, who during 1993–95 accounted for more than 90 per cent of the ethnic inflow.

The outflow from East Germany, both before and after unification, indicates strong selectivity processes. Outmigrants are disproportionately made up of young adults. Based on an age analysis of the 1989 flow, 64.3 per cent are aged 18–45, compared to only 40.5 per cent of the West German population; and only a tenth are aged over 45, as opposed to 41.2 per cent of West Germans (Table 15.9). Children, too, are somewhat over-represented among the *Übersiedler*. Other data show that East German outmigrants are strongly concentrated in certain employment categories,

Table 15.8 *Immigration into (West) Germany, 1987–95*

	Net migration between former East and West Germany (*Übersiedler*)	Immigration, and countries of origin, of ethnic Germans (*Aussiedler*)						
		Total no.	Poland		Romania		USSR	
			no.	%	no.	%	no.	%
1987	20 424	78 523	48 419	61.7	13 900	17.8	14 488	18.5
1988	40 806	202 673	140 226	69.2	12 902	6.4	47 572	23.5
1989	383 261	377 055	250 340	66.4	23 387	6.2	98 134	26.0
1990	359 126	397 073	133 872	33.7	111 150	28.0	147 950	37.3
1991	169 476	221 995	40 129	18.1	32 178	14.5	147 320	66.4
1992	78 825	230 595	17 742	7.7	16 146	7.0	195 576	84.8
1993	53 285	218 888	5431	2.5	5811	2.7	207 347	94.7
1994	27 260	222 591	2440	1.1	6615	3.0	213 214	95.8
1995		217 898	1677	0.8	6519	3.0	209 409	96.1

Source: Frey and Mammey (1996, 147).

notably the service sector, building trades and the medical profession. In 1989 alone, 11 per cent of doctors left, forcing some hospitals to close (Kemper, 1993).

The age structure of the *Aussiedler* population is different again: they have a higher proportion of children than either the *Übersiedler* or the native West Germans; twice as many old people as the *Übersiedler* group, but only half as many over-45s as the West German population (Table 15.9). More important than these demographic comparisons, however, are the social and economic aspects of this "gathering in" of the "German race". These have to be understood against a long history of the eastward expansion of the German peoples over several hundred years (for details, see Jones, 1994). Within the former USSR the Germans were distributed, and redistributed, far and wide – from the Baltic states to Crimea, Azerbaijan and far into Siberia. The number of ethnic Germans still living in eastern Europe and beyond can never be known: Frey and Mammey (1996, 10, 44) give a wide-ranging estimate of 4–10 million and suggest that 2.6 million of them (mainly from the Soviet Union) might immigrate to Germany by the year 2010.

The key point about ethnic Germans is that, according to "blood law" (*jus sanguinis*), they are entitled to take up residence in the Federal Republic and be granted full citizenship and naturalisation rights. There are, however, contradictions between their privileged status and the realities of their everyday lives in German society. A further contradiction exists with the rights of the descendants of the *Gastarbeiter* phase of immigration. With a note of exasperation, Jones (1994, 30–1) explains that German law grants automatic citizenship to the Russian-speaking

descendants of Germans who migrated to Russia at the time of Catherine the Great, but not to the German-born, German-speaking children of Turkish immigrants who have been living in Germany for more than 30 years!

Several problems hinder the full social integration of the ethnic Germans (Jones, 1994; Kemper, 1993). The first, especially for those originating in Poland and the Soviet Union, is poor or non-existent knowledge of the German language. A second, related difficulty is their tendency to stick together with family and friends from the same background. While this network of social contacts helps them to cope with life in new surroundings, it undoubtedly hinders their wider assimilation, and sets up negative reactions among the indigenous population. Housing is a third problem. *Aussiedler* have generally started in emergency hostel accommodation in the major cities and from there have moved into the cheapest end of the privately rented sector, sharing the same urban neighbourhoods as Turkish and other Mediterranean immigrant populations. Entry into the labour market has been hampered by their poor knowledge of German and lack of other relevant qualifications: they have become over-represented in marginal jobs and are three times as likely as other Germans to be unemployed. The spatial allocation of *Aussiedler* to all German *Länder* according to the principle of burden-sharing has not helped to maximise employment possibilities, especially for those assigned to the *Länder* of the former GDR (Jones, 1996). Socially the *Aussiedler* are intermediate between native Germans and the Mediterranean immigrant populations; "their self-identification and aspirations lie firmly with the former, but ... their real-life experiences are more similar to the latter" (Jones, 1994, 44). The best chances of integration are held by ethnic Germans from Romania, where the German communities were able to hold on to their language and where a high proportion of those migrating have high levels of education and German culture.

The Albanian exodus

The suddenness of emigration from Albania after 1990 differentiates it from the recent emigration experience of other former socialist countries.

Table 15.9 *Age distribution of West Germans, immigrants from East Germany and ethnic Germans, 1989 (%)*

Age groups	Population of West Germany	Immigrants from East Germany (*Übersiedler*)	Ethnic German immigrants (*Aussiedler*)
0–18	18.2	25.2	31.5
19–45	40.5	64.3	49.4
45+	41.2	10.6	19.1

Source: Kemper (1993, 262).

Much of the drama centred on the Albanian "boat people" who left in flotillas of overcrowded craft in 1991, heading for the coast of southern Italy, but the really significant Albanian exodus has been across the mountains to Greece where the number of Albanian immigrants has been estimated at anything between 150 000 and 400 000. Taking the median band of these estimates (250 000–300 000), this represents a very significant proportion of Albania's total population of 3.2 million, and a not insignificant addition to Greece's population of 10.2 million.

The push factors expelling emigrants from Albania were basically the same as those for other eastern European states during the transition to democracy and capitalism, except that in the Albanian case they were more concentrated, reflecting the greater degree of isolation of Albania in the past and the speed of the transition. Indeed "transition" is hardly an appropriate term to describe the chaos into which the political and, even more dramatically, the economic system descended during 1990–92.

The main factor which breached the otherwise virtually complete socio-spatial isolation of Albania was television. Although tuning in to foreign radio and television broadcasts was regarded as an "act of agitation or propaganda against the state", most Albanians were avid watchers of television programmes transmitted from Italy, Greece and Yugoslavia (especially the Albanian language service from Kosovo). In this way Albanians, most of whom had access to small black-and-white sets, could witness the events unfolding elsewhere in eastern and central Europe.

The arrival of the boat people received enormous media coverage around the world. As the bedraggled Albanians massed on the quaysides at Brindisi, it seemed as if they had stepped out of history from another world – even if this other world was only 70 km away. Yet little is known about the subsequent settlement and lives of this "first wave" of Albanian immigrants who were taken into Italy in the spring of 1991, except that they were granted special refugee status and temporary work permits and dispersed mainly to rural settlements. This was to facilitate their insertion into local labour markets, but it could also be seen as a tactic to defuse a potentially explosive situation (dell'Agnese, 1996).

Further drama occurred in August 1991 with the arrival of the "second wave" of Albanian boat people, again triggered by political instability in Albania (administrative elections and the continuing tension between Communist and democratic forces). This time the Italian government's attitude had changed and, after some days of indecision during which 20 000 refugees languished in the ports in boiling temperatures, they were brusquely repatriated. Widespread condemnation surrounded the inhuman way in which the would-be immigrants were treated, but no western European government lodged an official protest. Indeed with Italy struggling to meet its obligations as a member of the Schengen group, the EU was undoubtedly pleased that this "back door" for the entry of non-EU citizens was so firmly shut (Brochmann, 1993).

Albanians turned instead to Greece. During 1991–93 some 300 000 are estimated to have entered the country clandestinely, most of them across the mountains, some via Corfu. Unlike the policy of Italy, which swung from acceptance to rejection within five months, the Greek government's reaction to a much higher level of Albanian immigration has been one of constant ambiguity. Periodic mass deportations are used to appease public opinion and to prevent new arrivals from augmenting the total already in Greece. According to the Ministry of Public Order, more than 700 000 Albanians were expelled during 1991–94, a number which indicates that very many pursue a constant cycle of emigration, repatriation and re-entry. While reasonable treatment is accorded to the ethnic Greek Albanians who originate from the Orthodox Christian villages of southern Albania, the majority are at best tolerated and at worst reviled. Like earlier generations of immigrant workers elsewhere in Europe (including the Greeks themselves in Germany in the 1960s), Albanians are regarded as an "underclass" and stereotyped as dirty, lazy, crafty and with a tendency to criminality (Laziridis, 1996).

In Greece the vast majority of Albanians are engaged in unskilled, low-paid precarious jobs in the informal economy. They constitute, in other words, a flexible and cheap labour force willing to work in seasonal jobs and in harsh conditions. Normally they are paid rates which are around half or two-thirds the pay a Greek worker would get for equivalent work. But the real costs of Albanian immigrant labour to employers may be as little as one-third the standard rate since the Albanians, as illegal immigrants, cannot be paid any social insurance or health contributions. Albanians are undoubtedly exploited and discriminated against in all sorts of ways. They endure this treatment because of their illegal position and because their levels of income are still three to six times higher than in Albania (Fakiolas and King, 1996).

The Future of Migration in Europe

East–West or South–North: which future for European migration? Are the Albanians in Greece – criminalised, socially excluded, racially abused – the harbingers of new forms of immigration into Europe, or is it an old story in a new setting? How can a "socially just" migration policy be rationalised with the evident need to preserve (or even enhance) some degree of control over the immigration flows entering (or wanting to enter) Europe? In a Europe of high and seemingly permanent unemployment, is there still a need for labour migration? On the other hand, will scenarios of European demographic decline early in the next century create the need for immigration to rejuvenate the population? These are just some of the questions that this chapter, and the previous one, have left unanswered. This conclusion cannot provide all the answers, not least because some of the questions are so intractable, but it will attempt to integrate a number of important themes and suggest pointers to the future.

The first pointer to stress is the global setting. As Castles and Miller (1993) emphasise in their landmark volume *The Age of Migration*, the world is entering a new phase of mass population movements in which migration to Europe can only be understood in a global context. This context has many dimensions, including new levels of competition based on new divisions of labour and technology; a new willingness to "use" immigrant labour in an unregulated way to boost growth and mop up the least desirable jobs (the USA or Californian model now being reworked in the southern European "California"); and continued push pressures for emigration from

the developing world driven by population growth, war and environmental crisis. Hence one conclusion is clear: the real long-term migration pressures will emanate from the South and not from the East, which is already being incorporated into the European space of migration control. Quite apart from the transformed political and migration policy contexts of eastern Europe, several other factors suggest that, by and large, the "crisis" of East–West migration is over. Contrasts in demographic behaviour are relatively insignificant, except in Albania where fertility is still high. The main structural variable framing migration continues to be economics. However, countries like Hungary, the Czech Republic and Slovenia are approaching the per capita income levels of Greece and Portugal, so that parts of central and eastern Europe are evolving into a semiperiphery of the EU – a trend reinforced by patterns of inward investment, political and economic integration and reduced emigration. Much less easy to predict is the potential for migration arising out of ethnic conflict and the non-coincidence of national and ethnic boundaries. A long list of these exists: Hungarians in Slovakia, Romania and Vojvodina; Greeks in Albania; Albanians in Kosovo and Macedonia; Turks in Bulgaria; plus a whole series of ethnic and nationalist tensions in the former Soviet Union (Öberg and Boubnova, 1993). Wherever possible, the West's policy will be to contain these crises, if and when they occur, in their local settings and prevent geopolitical and migration overspill. None the less, Soviet emigration potential remains an enigma, both because of the scale of the old union and its political and economic instability. It is known, for example, that Finland, the EU's "frontline state" with Russia, has created a network of skeleton camps stockpiled with food along the Karelian frontier in case of emergency immigration (White and Sporton, 1995, 148–9).

Another pointer is that previous distinctions between types of migration, and between migration and other forms of mobility, are becoming increasingly difficult to draw. Let us summarise these "marginal" types of migration: East–West commuting; skilled international movement that shades into business travel; student migrations and exchanges; working holidays in ski resorts, picking fruit or as au pairs; travelling traders who shuttle between markets in East and West; illegal immigrants who move around the interstices of the informal economy. Most of these movements are motivated by work and income. Then there are other migrations related to leisure, environmental factors and retirement. International retirement migration brings British and other northern Europeans south to the warmer temperatures and attractive landscapes of the Mediterranean. Some are seasonal migrants, spending summer in the north and winter in the south. Whether temporary or permanent they are creating new forms of multicultural Europe in regions like Provence, Tuscany, and the Spanish coasts and islands.

Such heterogeneity of types of movement – differentiated by length of stay, motivation, nationality, social status, age, means of arrival, legality/illegality, etc. – undermines the formulation of coherent government policies, which as a result have become increasingly complex and contradictory (Castles, 1993). There are no comprehensive joint European policies on migration and refugees. Where there are moves towards common policies, as with Schengen, the emphasis is on restriction and exclusion rather than on the rational planning of a more humane approach. Exclusion and criminalisation of migrants, and forms of migration which do not fit EU criteria lead to new forms of racism which are added to those long-established forms deriving from colonialism and the egoism of the nation state.

Finally, is a new rationale for immigration provided by a European population that is becoming ever more elderly and, according to some scenarios (see Chapter 13), is likely to shrink in the next century? No European country facing stagnating or declining population trends has made this "logical" connection to increased immigration. While there are obvious political reasons for this, the argument also has its moral traps: to view migrants as a kind of "parachute" for declining European populations is to assign them a demographic functionalism which is dehumanising. If a guess has to be made, it is probably more likely that European demographic trends will self-correct, especially if appropriate incentives are offered. But, as this chapter and Chapter 14 have demonstrated, predicting long-term migration trends in a world region as complex as Europe is fraught with difficulty.

Notes

1. In the British case, however, the disparity indicator is much lower at the outset (indicating more even immigrant employment distribution) and the sectors of original concentration have a much higher weighting of services. See the evidence in SOPEMI (1995, 41).
2. Asian Muslims were probably not flattered to learn that they were following a Jewish model of social progress. The real similarities between Irish and Caribbean migrants were never properly analysed beyond somewhat hypothetical analogies. Irish and Caribbean family structures are very different, for example. See also a letter by M. Coulter to the *Times Higher Education Supplement*, 30 August 1996, on the subject of the mobility of Irish and Jewish immigrants.
3. While there are data to demonstrate the low levels of self-employment and business activity among Caribbeans in the UK, less is known about the Irish because they are omitted from such comparisons. However, there are certainly many Irish-owned building firms which have grown out of the traditional Irish involvement with the construction industry, not to mention Irish-run pubs in centres of Irish settlement! It would also be a mistake to regard the Afro-Caribbean community as lacking business potential. A recent survey reveals this group's dynamism, as indicated by many recently established businesses run by highly motivated and well-educated individuals, nearly all of the second generation (Ram and Deakins, 1996).
4. Extracts from Cardinal Hume's speech taken from *The Guardian*, 7 September 1996.
5. Quoted in Öberg and Boubnova (1993, 253) who do not, however, give more details or the precise source of these calculations.

References

Black, R (1994) Refugees and asylum-seekers in Western Europe: new challenges, in R Black and V Robinson (eds) *Geography and Refugees: patterns and processes of change*, Belhaven, London, 87–103.

Blotevogel, H H and King, R (1996) European economic restructuring: demographic responses and feedbacks, *European Urban and Regional Studies*, **3**, 133–59.

Brochmann, G (1993) Control in immigration policies: a closed Europe in the making, in R King (ed) *The New Geography of European Migrations*, Belhaven, London, 100–15.

Caritas di Roma (1995) *Immigrazione Dossier Statistico*, Anterem, Rome.

Cashmore, E and Troyna, B (1983) *Introduction to Race Relations*, Routledge and Kegan Paul, London.

Castles, S (1993) Migrations and minorities in Europe: eleven hypotheses for the 1990s, in J Wrench and J Solomos (eds) *Racism and Migration in Western Europe*, Berg, Oxford, 17–34.

Castles, S and Miller, M J (1993) *The Age of Migration: international population movements in the modern world*, Macmillan, London.

Collinson, S (1996) Visa requirements, carrier sanctions, "safe third country" and "readmission": the development of an asylum "buffer zone" in Europe, *Transactions of the Institute of British Geographers*, **21**, 76–90.

Cross, M (1993) Migration, employment and social change in the new Europe, in R King (ed) *The New Geography of European Migrations*, Belhaven, London, 116–34.

Dell'Agnese, E (1996) Profughi politici e rifugiati "economici" in Italia: il doppio esodo albanese nel 1991, in M L Gentileschi and R King (eds) *Questioni di Popolazione in Europa*, Pàtron, Bologna, 69–81.

Drew, D and Gray, J (1991) The black–white gap in examination results: a statistical critique of a decade's research, *New Community*, **17**, 159–72.

Fakiolas, R and King, R (1996) Emigration, return, immigration: a review and evaluation of Greece's postwar experience of international migration, *International Journal of Population Geography*, **2**, 171–90.

Fassman, H and Münz, R (1994) Patterns and trends of international migration in Western Europe, in H Fassmann and R Münz (eds) *European Emigration in the Late Twentieth Century*, Edward Elgar, Aldershot, 3–33.

Findlay, A M (1995) The future of skill exchanges within the European Union, in R Hall and P E White (eds) *Europe's Population towards the Next Century*, UCL Press, London, 130–41.

Findlay, A M and Garrick, L (1990) Scottish emigration in the 1980s: a migration channels approach towards the study of skilled international migration, *Transactions of the Institute of British Geographers*, **15**, 177–92.

Frey, M and Mammey, U (1996) *Impact of Migration in the Receiving Countries: Germany*, International Organization for Migration, Geneva.

Hovy, B (1993) Asylum migration in Europe: patterns, determinants and the role of East–West movements, in R King (ed) *The New Geography of European Migrations*, Belhaven, London, 207–27.

Jones, P N (1994) Destination Germany: the spatial distribution and impacts of the "third wave" of post-war immigrants, in W T S Gould and A M Findlay (eds) *Population Migration and the Changing World Order*, Wiley, Chichester, 27–46.

Jones, P N (1996) Immigrants, Germans and national identity in the New Germany: some policy issues, *International Journal of Population Geography*, **2**, 119–31.

Kemper, F-J (1993) New trends in mass migration in Germany, in R King (ed) *Mass Migrations in Europe: the legacy and the future*, Belhaven, London, 257–74.

King, R (1993) Recent immigration into Italy: character, causes and consequences, *GeoJournal*, **30**, 283–92.

King, R and Rybaczuk, K (1993) Southern Europe and the international division of labour: from emigration to immigration, in R King (ed) *The New Geography of European Migrations*, Belhaven, London, 175–206.

Koser, K (1996) Recent asylum migration in Europe: patterns and processes of change, *New Community*, **22**, 151–8.

Kupiszewski, M (1996) Extra-Union migration: the East–West perspective, in P Rees, J Stillwell, A Convey and M Kupiszewski (eds) *Population Migration in the European Union*, Wiley, Chichester, 13–37.

Laziridis, G (1996) Immigration to Greece: a critical evaluation of Greek policy, *New Community*, **22**, 335–48.

Montagné-Villette, S (1994) Mobility and illegal labour in the EC, in M Blacksell and A M Williams (eds) *The European Challenge: geography and development in the European Community*, Oxford University Press, Oxford, 242–54.

Montanari, A and Cortese, A (1993) Third World immigrants in Italy, in R King (ed) *Mass Migrations in Europe: the legacy and the future*, Belhaven, London, 212–33.

Öberg, S and Boubnova, H (1993) Ethnicity, nationality and migration potentials in Eastern Europe, in R King (ed) *Mass Migrations in Europe: the legacy and the future*, Belhaven, London, 234–56.

Papademetriou, D G (1994) At a crossroads: Europe and migration, in K A Hamilton (ed) *Migration and the New Europe*, Center for Strategic and International Studies, Washington, DC, 12–36.

Peach, C (1996) *The Ethnic Minority Populations of Britain* Vol. 2, *Ethnicity in the 1991 Census*, HMSO, London.

Penninx, R, Schoorl, J and van Praag, C (1994) *The Impact of International Migration on Receiving Countries: the case of the Netherlands*, Netherlands Interdisciplinary Demographic Institute Report No. 37, The Hague.

Ram, M and Deakins, D (1996) African-Caribbeans in business, *New Community*, **22**, 67–84.

Salt, J (1984) High-level manpower movement in North-West Europe and the role of careers, *International Migration Review*, **17**, 633–51.

Salt, J (1992a) Current and future international migration trends affecting Europe, in *People on the Move: new migration flows in Europe*, Council of Europe Press, Strasbourg, 41–81.

Salt, J (1992b) Migration processes amongst the highly skilled in Europe, *International Migration Review*, **26**, 484–505.

Salt, J (1993) External international migration, in D Noin and R Woods (eds) *The Changing Population of Europe*, Blackwell, Oxford, 185–97.

Shuttleworth, I (1993) Irish graduate emigration: the mobility of qualified manpower in the context of peripherality, in R King (ed) *Mass Migrations in Europe: the legacy and the future*, Belhaven, London, 310–26.

SOPEMI (1995) *Trends in International Migration, Annual Report 1994*, OECD, Paris.

Tarrius, A (1992) Circulation des élites professionelles et intégration européenne, *Revue Européenne des Migrations Internationales*, **8**, 27–56.

Thomas-Hope, E (1994) *Impact of Migration in the Receiving Countries: the United Kingdom*, International Organisation for Migration, Geneva.

UNHCR (1995) *The State of the World's Refugees*, Oxford University Press, Oxford.

Waldinger, R, Aldrich, H and Ward, R (eds) (1990) *Ethnic Entrepreneurs*, Sage, Berkeley, CA.

Ward, R and Jenkins, R (eds) (1984) *Ethnic Communities in Business*, Cambridge University Press, London.

White, P and Sporton, D (1995) East–West movement: old barriers, new barriers? in R Hall and P White (eds) *Europe's Population towards the Next Century*, UCL Press, London, 142–60.

16
Urban life and social stress

Paul White
Department of Geography, University of Sheffield, UK

Introduction

A reading of recent media reports can very quickly lead to the conclusion that Europe's cities are in a state of decay and turmoil. There is a constant stream of newspaper and television reporting of drugs-related shootings, inter-racial tension, street prostitution, urban rioting, arson and vandalism. The cities affected are spread throughout the continent – Liverpool, Newcastle, London, the suburbs of Paris and Lyon, Amsterdam, Naples and Palermo in southern Italy, Prague and Budapest in central Europe, and Moscow and St Petersburg in Russia. To many commentators, particularly from the political right, it seems that European urban civilisation is at a crossroads, with the problems of the city (seen as emotional and social as much as economic) driving European populations into counter-urbanisation movements and the repopulation of rural spaces. Yet there is another side to this coin: it should not be overlooked that at the same time many European cities are witnessing processes of gentrification and *embourgeoisement* which are bringing the wealthy back to the city centres (Carpenter and Lees, 1995), and urban regeneration programmes are actively seeking to revive the economic fortunes of many cities and city regions throughout the continent (Figure 16.1). As throughout the whole

history of Europe, it is in the cities that the major forces of economic, political, cultural and social evolution are played through, and the results are manifest in a number of contrasted and divergent trends. Nor should it be assumed that the late twentieth century is particularly distinctive in the acuteness of the perceived urban issues – the same acuteness has been seen at many periods in earlier history, for example towards the end of the nineteenth century. Nevertheless, it could be argued that in the new Europe the particular circumstances attendant upon processes of economic restructuring, globalisation, ideological shifts, the crisis of welfare systems, and the opening of new market economies have created a particularly profound combination of pressures on urban life.

This chapter takes the details of economic changes dealt with in Part II of this volume and considers the reflection that these have within urban populations and societies, concentrating attention particularly on the more vulnerable and marginal groups of urban residents. It therefore touches upon several of the major debates and disputed concepts of urban social geography today, such as the emergence of an "underclass", the processes of "social exclusion", and the "polarisation" or "professionalisation" of urban social structures. The chapter also, however,

Figure 16.1   *Decayed and refurbished housing, Prenzlauer Berg, Berlin. (Photos: D A Pinder)*

argues that urban stress is not explicable solely in economic terms, but also relates to certain demographic changes taking place at a wider scale, and reflects current debates about social welfare provision.

The conceptualisation adopted here follows the *Oxford English Dictionary* in defining stress as the state that results from adverse circumstances which disturb the normal psychological or physiological functioning of an individual. The "stressors" in these adverse circumstances can be of many different kinds, a number of which overlap: lack of income (with both physical and psychological consequences), lack of employment, lack of adequate housing, lack of self-esteem (maybe brought about through other factors), various types of ill health, actual harassment, fear of violence, and lack of confidence in the future. A closely related concept is that of "insecurity", which can equally concern employment, housing or personal safety. All the stressors listed are attributes that can apply to individuals. But

through the spatial concentration of those suffering stress it is also possible to think of neighbourhoods and other spatial units that can be characterised as suffering stress. Stress can also be seen to apply to broader units such as social groups. Certain of the stressors outlined above commonly apply to considerable numbers of people drawn from identifiable sections of society – young unemployed males with low skill levels would be one such category, as would the physically disabled elderly. In some cases these social groups carry a strong locational attachment, but in others those involved are widely scattered. Throughout Europe populations of gypsy origin, for example, generally suffer from poor standards of living, harassment by local and national authorities, and prejudice from wider society (Humeau, 1994; Fonseca, 1995).

The measurement of stress at the individual level may be beyond geographers, but an approach through the identification of key stressors (as in the list given above) may yield acceptable indicators such as those based on housing variables, unemployment data, income levels and consumption patterns; these and other indicators form the basis of a number of well-known indices attempting to measure deprivation.[1] Two distinct problems arise, however, in trying to extend such indicators to produce comparative empirical data at the international scale. The first is that many stressed or marginal groups are identifiable only with difficulty (if at all) in official data sources. The most extreme case would obviously be clandestine migrants for whom no data exist, but data on urban alcoholics, the homeless or those suffering racial harassment are almost equally elusive. The second problem is that stress and marginality are relative concepts for which the boundaries vary from place to place. Thus poverty in different European countries may mean different things in absolute terms, but may be similar in the levels of stress produced for the individuals involved. For these reasons the argument offered in this chapter concerns more the current discourses surrounding urban stress, vulnerability and marginality in Europe, rather than presenting extensive (but possibly misleading) empirical detail.

Causes of Urban Stress in Contemporary Europe

The processes leading to stress for individuals, social groups and neighbourhoods in contemporary Europe can be identified under four headings – concerned with economic change, with socio-demographic change, with changing circumstances in European welfare regimes, and with specific spatial processes of segregation and separation. In considering these processes it must also be emphasised that the European context for their evolution is a particular one, and the transference of concepts from elsewhere is not necessarily helpful. To take two brief examples, ideas of the emergence of an "underclass" have been strongly developed in the United States (Wilson, 1987), but the concept cannot be straightforwardly adopted in Europe without some modification, since the existence there of Welfare State systems mediates certain of the influences at work. Similarly, as a number of authors have recently powerfully reiterated

(Peach, 1996; Vieillard-Baron, 1994), European cities do not have any districts that even approach the characteristics of the classic North American "ghettos".

Economic restructuring

The translation of the processes of economic change (Part II of this volume) into urban stress comes about through the selectivity of their effects on different individuals and social groups. Within western Europe restructuring is still involving reductions in manufacturing activities (see Chapter 5), but with a counterbalancing growth of producer and consumer services, although the former are more concentrated in the larger cities that participate more strongly in the global economy. The employment opportunities for low-skilled populations traditionally involved in manufacturing industry have been severely reduced, as production has shifted to more peripheral locations, both within individual states and also at the global scale. At the other end of the skill hierarchy, jobs in the high-level service sector have been increasing (see Chapter 7).

Among the important effects of these changes over the last two decades has been growing income polarisation, with a bigger gap between the income levels at the top end of the scale and those at the bottom. This phenomenon has been observed throughout western Europe in cities of very different kinds, for example in Bilbao (Martinez and Vicario, 1995, 350) as well as in London (Logan *et al.*, 1992). However, we should also note that the trend is not universal: in Stockholm, for example, there was evidence through the 1980s of relative stability within what were anyway relatively narrow income differentials – a point of some importance for the later discussion of the significance of welfare states (Borgegård and Murdie, 1994).

A thesis developed by Saskia Sassen in the United States has described a trend of "polarisation" involving the growth of (i) high-skill, high-pay jobs and (ii) unskilled, often part-time, temporary employment (frequently occupied by ethnic minority workers) in activities servicing the high-income sectors. Between these extremes there is said to be a reduction of the numbers of jobs available for the semi-skilled in the intervening areas of the employment hierarchy (Sassen, 1991). However, it has been argued that Sassen has incorrectly mapped American experience on to the European case, and that what is actually happening in European cities is not a joint process of proletarianisation accompanying high-skill employment growth, but a process of professionalisation in which the low skilled are being left behind. Hamnett (1994a, b) has sought to demonstrate that this is, in fact, the phenomenon applying both in London and in the Randstad in the Netherlands.

It is clear that economic restructuring in western Europe has created both income stress and the stress of unemployment for significant sectors of the urban population. It is also the case that such stress is selectively concentrated in segments of the labour force with low skill levels, who have nevertheless been accustomed to a continuity of employment through the manufacturing-based boom years of economic growth that pertained during the earlier post-war period. Retraining and other programmes to reintroduce the longer-term unemployed to the active labour force have met with limited success (Clark, 1995).

Issues concerned with economic change are rather different in the cities of eastern Europe. Comparative data on unemployment are poor, and time series are virtually non-existent (Gaspard, 1993). Nevertheless, the fragmentary evidence that does exist suggests that the effects of change are being felt in different ways. To take Budapest as an example, in 1993 the unemployment rate was only half that of Hungary as a whole, and the skill level of the unemployed in the capital was also higher than in the rest of the country (Dovenyi, 1994). Thus it has not been an urban industrial class that has been worst hit by change. In Hungary, as throughout much of eastern Europe, rural unemployment rates were much higher in the early 1990s (Fassmann, 1992; see also Chapters 17 and 19). In economies where gender equality in employment was much greater than in the West, it has also been women who have been particularly badly affected by rising unemployment – this is most especially true in the former Soviet Union, where female employment rates stood at the very high level of 76 per cent in 1989[2] (Kahn, 1993).

Socio-demographic change

It is well known that some of the most profound stress-related episodes in an individual's biography concern demographic events such as birth, death, marriage, divorce and migration. Changes in the rates of any of these can obviously alter indicators of satisfaction with life. In addition, changes in demographic structures can increase the susceptibility of a population to stress: for example, increased longevity may raise the proportion of a population suffering physical disability, or restricted in daily activities by long-term illness.

Throughout Europe the 1990s have witnessed profound demographic developments, affecting not just individual cities but whole nations and societies. From among the range of demographic indicators, it is useful here to highlight briefly three particular factors – divorce, rising numbers of single-parent families, and the growing proportions of the elderly. The emphasis here will again be placed more on the significance of these issues, rather than on empirical detail since the problems of definitions and data availability, particularly at the urban scale, militate against detailed comparisons.

Across the whole of Europe, divorce levels are generally increasing, with no distinction between western and eastern Europe. In 1995 the highest crude divorce rates at a national level were in Estonia, Belarus and the Russian Federation (all at over 4 divorces per 1000 population), with rates in a variety of other countries (the United Kingdom, the Netherlands, Belgium, Switzerland, Austria, Denmark, Norway, Sweden, Finland, the Czech Republic, Hungary, Moldova, Lithuania and Ukraine) being 50 per cent or more above the Europe-wide median national level of 1.9 per 1000 (Council of Europe, 1996). In Scandinavia high divorce rates, coupled with low marriage rates and an increase in extra-marital births, possibly indicate the establishment of a new set of life styles (Hall, 1995).

Information on single-parent families also suggests a relatively rapid rate of increase, largely relating to the trends outlined above. The household income stress induced by the circumstances of such families is generally exacerbated in a situation where two incomes per household are common and where additional costs for child care have to be found from within a single income.

The vast majority of single-parent households are headed by women, but it would be wrong to imply that all such households are economically vulnerable, or that some women have not specifically chosen this path. Certainly lone-parent families have often been identified as a strong indicator of poverty (Robertson, 1984) associated with other phenomena such as marginalisation within the housing stock, but it must also be borne in mind that in various cities women's movements have built a nexus of self-determination, self-help, political struggle and self-confidence around women who only a generation ago would have been completely ignored or vilified – examples reported include women in Athens and Berlin (Marouli, 1995; Mädje and Neusüss, 1994).

Cities have always had particularly strong representations of single-person households, and this phenomenon is growing rapidly. In the early 1990s 46 per cent of households in reunited Berlin, 45 per cent in Stockholm county, and 50 per cent in inner Paris consisted of only one person (Hall *et al.*, 1995). Apart from the demographic influences already mentioned, a further clear factor is the ageing of the population. This is, of course, a general phenomenon, but it is also one that tends to create residual groups of the impoverished elderly in certain city districts, with the exacerbation of problems of service provision that have become common to cities in both western Europe and in the old state-planned countries where the supply of facilities was sometimes better. (For examples from both West and East Germany see Köster, 1994, on the city of Aachen, and Gaube, 1991, on the suburb of Köpenick in East Berlin.)

Changes in European welfare states

In many ways, the influences already described under the headings of economic change and socio-demographic change ought to be strongly mitigated by the operation of the welfare states that have been such an important feature of European life in the post-war world. That these same welfare arrangements are themselves now often perceived to be in crisis is a strange paradox, since various systems of state support seemed to be at their strongest at a time of economic boom, but have proved susceptible to dismantling and dilution during precisely the period when they have been most needed. Clearly reservations can be expressed about the operation of the systems adopted by different countries.

The most penetrating analysis of welfare arrangements is that put forward by Esping-Andersen (1990). In this analysis welfare states in the capitalist world can be divided into three models (perhaps better seen in historical perspective as tendencies, since any particular welfare regime often combines elements from two or more of them). These models are labelled "liberal" (in reality "neo-liberal" might be better), corporatist and social democratic, and it could now be argued that each type has run into problems concerning its range of provision and its access criteria.

The neo-liberal welfare system puts greatest stress on the market, and in its more recent variants (such as in the UK under Mrs Thatcher) expects the individual to provide for their future welfare needs through "investment" in that market. State intervention is relatively limited and is generally means-tested. Corporatist welfare states, of which many aspects of the federal German scene can be taken as good examples, operate in such a way as to preserve sectional interests, with welfare rights dependent on membership of a particular group. What is then available in terms of welfare support is not constant or universal, but depends on previous (or continuing) membership of a specific trade union, company payroll or other organisation. Social democratic welfare states, such as have been particularly associated with Scandinavia, are characterised by universalism and the aim of bringing provision for the worst-off up towards standards for the better-off, with a narrowing of gaps, the elimination of dualism, and the provision of social goods at the widest level.

Social goods can be conceptualised as items where provision and consumption are regarded as being for the benefit of society as a whole, thus possibly including education, health care, pensions and unemployment benefits, public transport and sound housing conditions. Clearly different national welfare systems are structured around different beliefs concerning the desirable border between private and social goods, with these borders generally decided nationally since provision is costly and requires regulation at a high level. Esping-Andersen (1990, 35–54) terms the movement of provision into a welfare system "de-commodification", and shows that in an international analysis of the western European position in 1980 de-commodification within welfare systems had progressed furthest in the Netherlands, Austria and the Scandinavian countries: at the other end of the scale lay Ireland, Italy and the UK. Clearly events of the 1980s, particularly in the UK, have altered some of these findings. Privatisation policies operating in many European countries have resulted in the "commodification" of previously social goods and their movement into the private domain. Even where that has not happened, there have often been changes in the nature of provision that have altered the type of service provided as well as its possible efficacy – an example would be the closing of Italy's mental asylums under Law 180 of 1978, and the related instigation of community care policies for people with learning difficulties in the UK (Jones, 1996).

In a commentary on Esping-Andersen's ideas, Musterd (1994) has pointed out that they concentrate on social security, pensions and health insurance. Of equal interest to many is involvement in housing provision – a further core element in welfare ideologies. Again in western Europe, there are great diversities in the importance of the social housing stock – varying in the early 1990s from 36 per cent in the Netherlands and over 20 per cent in Germany, the UK, Austria and Sweden, to under 5 per cent of all housing in Greece, Spain, Luxembourg and Portugal.[3]

Esping-Andersen's analysis only applies to the capitalist world, but it can be partly extended (in terms of outcomes if not in terms of ideologies) to the new market economies of eastern Europe. Certainly here welfare arrangements are currently undergoing a profound alteration, with new systems not yet fully articulated (Crosnier, 1993). In the past, despite a theoretically egalitarian view on welfare provision that would accord with the liberal democratic model in a capitalist society, access and delivery systems contained strong corporatist elements. For example, many social goods were provided to their employees by the factories for which they worked – goods including

housing, crèche facilities, holiday camps, and special factory-run shops (Lefèvre, 1993). Housing was, of course, a wider issue catered for also by a number of other state-organised interests.

The widespread crisis of welfare provision has a number of roots. In many ways these relate to the two factors discussed earlier – economic restructuring and socio-demographic changes. Both of these continuing processes have heightened the demands made on welfare support – through increased unemployment and the need for labour retraining, income support, pensions and other welfare provision for the elderly. And these needs have grown faster at a time of generally low economic growth rates, during which post-war consensuses about the objectives of welfare states have started to disintegrate, particularly under the politics of the New Right with their championing of neo-liberal against corporatist or social democratic ideologies.

In the face of economic restructuring and socio-demographic change, however, it is arguable that all types of welfare regimes may fail to perform perfectly. Neo-liberal regimes provide only a safety net for the most disadvantaged, with means-testing operating to ration access. The generality of the poor, the sick or the badly housed are likely to be neglected, with limited intervention only being offered to the most extreme cases. Corporatist regimes inevitably tend to fail those in society who do not belong to the corporatist structures. Thus, for example, the young unemployed who have never worked may lack access to any form of unemployment benefit (as is the case in France). In eastern Europe the closure of many factories and the reductions of the labour forces of others have brought severe problems to those dependent on the social goods that have previously been provided through them. Meanwhile social democratic regimes tend to be high-cost structures, and here the crisis is one of funding in a situation of slow growth in governmental tax bases.

Particular emphasis must be placed here on the role of housing, and the retreat from social housing that has been occurring in various parts of the continent. In the UK there is a well-developed argument (Forrest and Murie, 1986) that council house sales are resulting in the marginalisation of those remaining in the sector, who increasingly are composed of the long-term unemployed, the poor elderly, single-parent female-headed households, and those who have entered the sector through a need for emergency accommodation, such as those rehoused after having suffered racial harassment. On the other hand in Sweden, where social housing has been intended for a wide range of the population and where privatisation is unimportant, there is much less evidence of marginalisation, although it does exist to a modest extent, most particularly in estates with a high proportion of foreign tenants (Borgegård and Murdie, 1995).

In eastern Europe the move towards the privatisation of previously state-owned housing has had a faltering start, with the aims and goals of programmes not yet fully articulated (Boyce,

Figure 16.2 *Privatisation and improvement of socialist housing, Leinefelde, former East Germany. An original entrance (bottom left) and its remodelled counterpart (bottom right). The end wall of the entirely refurbished building has been adorned with a portrait of Beethoven. (Photos: D A Pinder)*

1993). Progress has been greater in central Europe than in Russia, but everywhere the outcomes are somewhat uneasy, with increases in rent levels being almost universal (Figure 16.2). Property purchase by former tenants has not infrequently resulted in increased stress for many purchasers faced with unstable household incomes (Bodnár, 1996). In central Budapest international capital has moved into the real estate market, creating competition for housing from other potential land uses in what are currently slum areas: central city poverty has been accentuated and a form of planning blight has ensued (Lichtenberger, 1993, 1995). In East Berlin, where rent levels have once again risen (Schulz, 1993a), the major housing project areas of the socialist city have been brought under the control of what are effectively local housing associations, but with the requirement for a 5 per cent per annum rate of privatisation up to the year 2001.

These developments in European welfare regimes are highly complex, and take different forms in different countries, just as the actual development of such regimes was nationally differentiated. Throughout Europe, however, there are tendencies now for a retreat from welfare concerns by government, with the boundaries between social goods and private goods being redefined. Such changes, in part pragmatic (affecting welfare delivery) and in part ideological (involving the legitimation of welfare itself), are everywhere tending to exacerbate stress in the more vulnerable sections of society.

Stress and segregation

It was argued earlier that although stress was a quality affecting individuals, neighbourhoods and city districts could also be characterised as stressed when they sheltered a high proportion of such residents. There has been much discussion of the question of levels of segregation of the marginalised in European cities, considering the extent to which growing economic inequalities are reflected in greater spatial separation of different social groups, and in the increasing concentration of the vulnerable into what then become identified as "marginalised spaces" (Vant, 1986; Winchester and White, 1988). If segregation

of the vulnerable is occurring in this way it must relate either to differential processes of residential mobility, or to a process of downward social mobility *in situ*.

Residential mobility within the city can involve the removal of non-vulnerable people from a neighbourhood, or can result in the movement of the vulnerable into a district (White and Winchester, 1991). Longitudinal studies of intra-urban residential processes are remarkably rare in European cities, for despite the apparently useful data contained in the continuous population registers kept in many countries, information on accompanying personal social indicators is almost invariably lacking. What would appear to be the most common scenario is, however, for differential migration to bring a vulnerable population to a district of low-cost housing, perhaps created by slum conditions, by planning blight or by a city's housing allocation policy, which may concentrate the vulnerable in a specific social housing estate. There may then follow a longer-term process of increasing marginality, during which those most able to leave do so while a downward spiral sets in for those who remain. Effectively this is the familiar cycle of deprivation, concentrated in one place, which may operate on an inter-generational level.

Three examples might be used to highlight these processes. In Brussels, Mistiaen *et al.* (1995) have described the processes of marginalisation in two inner-city areas through the migration of Turkish and Moroccan workers into rented slum property close to their places of industrial employment, followed by the marginalisation of their offspring through unemployment. This produced a disaffected generation alienated from the Belgian systems of education and training, and inclined to indulge in petty criminality. With housing renovation elsewhere within the inner city, the districts in question have also undergone a further accentuation of the poor, forced to move there after rent increases elsewhere. Here there is clear evidence of an evolutionary cycle of increased deprivation and stress occurring through time, involving increasing segregation as a factor.

A different process of the spatial concentration of deprivation occurs in the Lisbon area where *bidonvilles* house poor families (often with a head who is out of work), single-parent families (almost

Figure 16.3 *A partment block on a socialist family estate, Leinefelde, former East Germany. The building is identical to the refurbished block in Figure 16.2. (Photo: D A Pinder)*

invariably headed by women), drug-dependants, and recent immigrants from Africa. The 1991 Portuguese census indicated that there were 14 000 units of *bidonville* housing around Lisbon, with particular concentrations in the north and east of the city, around the airport (Barata Salgueiro, 1995). In this case the segregation of a marginal population does not result from downward economic mobility of an existing population, but from the very process of in-migration and settlement of the district.

These examples are drawn from the free-market economies of western Europe, where residential segregation has a long history in circumstances of resource competition. In Eastern Europe such segregation has traditionally been less marked under the allocation structures of state socialism, with the separation of groups being more demographic in nature, for example with families allocated to "family estates" (Figure 16.3; Schulz, 1993b). However, there is now evidence of the emergence of areas of poverty or of minority group concentrations just as elsewhere. Budapest, for example, now has blackspots of accentuated poverty in its inner-city and industrial areas (Lichtenberger, 1995; Dovenyi, 1994), as well as a developing pattern of segregation involving gypsy families, particularly in certain slums in Pest (Ladanyi, 1993). Social polarisation between different districts is clearly increasing (Paal, 1995). The Hungarian geographer Enyedi (1994), in a wide discussion of post-socialist cities, has suggested that their internal spatial structures are likely to lose their socialist legacy over the years to come and will move to western European norms of segregation and spatial patterning, but that the process will take some time.

Stress and Social Exclusion

"Social exclusion" is a phrase that has passed into common use in recent years, but without much precision in its definition (White, P, in press).

Clearly, however, the concept is closely related to ideas of urban stress. Figure 16.4 illustrates the relationship between the four sets of stress-inducing factors already identified and various aspects of social exclusion. Four particular facets of exclusion are identified here, tied in different ways to the causes of urban stress and to wider influences. Although most attention is usually paid to unemployment and poverty as causes of a type of exclusion that basically revolves around the inability to indulge in "normal" consumption patterns, it is clear that other types of exclusion also exist. These are generally associated with processes operating in the political rather than the economic sphere. Changing welfare regimes obviously play a part, but other influences are wider and more "ideological" in origin. They reflect changing political discourses throughout contemporary Europe in the aftermath of the events leading to the conversion of the state socialist countries into market-based societies, as well as the increasing pace of liberal reform in most of western Europe. This liberal reform is partly driven by ideology, but is also a response to the tight public spending criteria for European Monetary Union and to increasing fears for Europe's competitive position

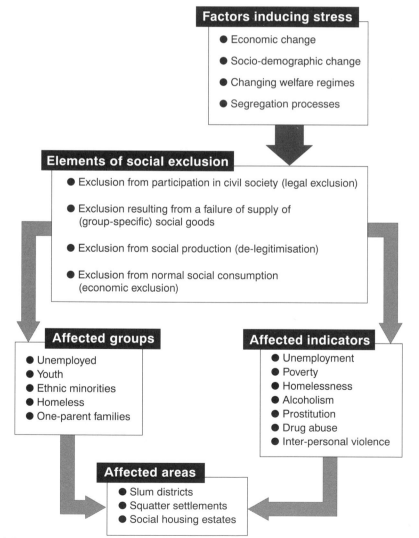

Figure 16.4 *Stress and social exclusion in contemporary European cities*

in the world economy. As Figure 16.4 also makes clear, and as was identified at the start of this chapter, stress and exclusion are disproportionately felt by certain groups of the urban population, showing up in a number of important social indicators. These are also then associated with certain types of urban location.

The first element of social exclusion identified in Figure 16.4 concerns exclusion from participation in civil society through legal restraint or regulation. Examples arise particularly through the failure to accord the full rights and duties of citizenship. Specific cases would include children born to foreign immigrants in Germany, who remain legally regarded as foreigners; the common practice of granting a form of "exceptional leave to remain" to rejected asylum-seekers in a number of countries; or the moves being made by the Baltic states to deny citizenship to Russian minorities who have long-standing residence in those countries. Throughout Europe the growing numbers of clandestine migrants obviously form an extreme group suffering this form of exclusion (see Chapter 15).

A second element of social exclusion can be conceptualised as occurring in situations where there is a failure to supply social goods (generally in the nature of services) to a group with particular needs and demands. Examples include the failure to adapt environments for the disabled; to provide official information in languages that can be read by residents who do not speak the official language; or to provide systems of emergency accommodation for the homeless. Although some of these issues may be ones that could be dealt with by private enterprises (such as wheelchair access to shops), many aspects of these forms of social exclusion result from the absence of state policies, sometimes relating to the crisis of European welfare regimes already discussed.

The third element of social exclusion is more ideological, and relates to the delegitimisation of the existence of certain groups in the discourse of politics and power. This is effectively a form of exclusion from social production – exclusion from being seen as a contributory section of society. Some forms of such exclusion are certainly legal or regulatory, as discussed above; but others act through hegemonic power structures or social control mechanisms, and result in certain groups

being labelled as undesirable, unacceptable or in need of control. The groups susceptible to exclusion in this way vary over time and through space. Some, such as the gypsies, have been generally so labelled throughout Europe; others have moved into and out of this category – examples might include unemployed youth (particularly where there is ethnic distinctiveness), gay and lesbian communities, and particular ethnic minorities who are officially described as "non-existent" (as happened to the Turks in Bulgaria in the 1980s).

The fourth and final element of social exclusion is the one that is most closely related to economic change as a cause of stress. This is exclusion from participation in the general local norms of social consumption through economic hardship. Exclusion in this form is effectively exclusion from many everyday aspects of the individualist consumer society that is rapidly coming to dominate the organisation of consumption throughout the whole of Europe, east as well as west.

All these forms of social exclusion clearly act to deny to certain individuals and groups what are seen by others as the normal perquisites, routines and experiences of everyday life. It is also clear that concepts of exclusion and of stress are not absolutes, but are dependent on the particular conjunctures of material, political, cultural and social circumstances operating in individual cities or other places at specific periods. Exclusion is likely to be contested and will therefore be unstable and evolutionary in nature, with the boundaries of the excluded and those suffering stress shifting in relation to particular issues and wider responses. It is, however, possible to identify a number of broad contemporary similarities among those disproportionately suffering stress and exclusion throughout the European urban realm.

Manifestations of Stress in Contemporary Urban Europe

Several studies and collections have recently addressed the question of whether there is now an emerging urban underclass in European cities (Musterd, 1994; van Kempen, 1994; Mingione, 1993). As discussed earlier in this chapter, the application of the term "underclass" in the European context must be different from its American origins. Nevertheless, as we have also seen, the welfare state basis for that difference is being eroded. As Musterd (1994, 190–1) sums up the present situation, there is certainly a current fear held by many commentators about the creation of underclass situations in European cities, with unemployment as the crucial (although not the only) dimension. Policy reactions could well produce paradoxical results – tackling unemployment while at the same time increasing marginality for those who fail to get jobs, and for the lowest-paid:

> "Nowadays, general reactions against the unemployment problems seem to be further economic restructuring, liberalization of the labour market and a wide revision of the welfare state in a more liberal direction. But, while there is a general belief that unemployment will be reduced because of that change, there is also the expectation that there will be an increase of social and socio-spatial segregation" (Musterd, 1994, 190–1).

High unemployment levels in many cities of Europe certainly constitute a major manifestation of urban stress and insecurity in the contemporary world, and are perhaps associated with a longer-term feeling of hopelessness than at any time since the Depression years of the 1930s. It is clear, not just to academic commentators and politicians but to the jobless themselves, that current unemployment is not simply cyclical but relates to major changes in the whole character of European economies. The unemployed cannot expect a return to the employment sectors they or their parents once occupied: future prospects are much less predictable.

However, there are further dimensions to unemployment that may increase levels of stress. In particular, the employment situation of many ethnic minority populations in European cities today is particularly poor, relating both to structural changes in their former employment sectors and to mechanisms (such as poor training and education, residential locations and discrimination by employers) that compound their specific disadvantage. In almost every city of western Europe, unemployment levels among ethnic minorities or foreigner populations are higher than the general level. Moreover, this is accentuated by the generally low activity rates of women, which increase the effective rate of non-employment (and therefore also the poverty level of any families concerned). This is not, however, a significant issue in eastern European cities, where immigrant populations are still relatively small.

Youth unemployment is a particular element of social stress throughout urban Europe, east and west, and unemployed young people have generally been seen throughout the continent as a "problem", especially when they are of working class and/or ethnic minority origin. It is here that we reach what is today one of the most excluded social categories throughout Europe, affected by a number of the processes and mechanisms described earlier in this chapter. In many corporatist welfare states the young unemployed have little or no access to independent welfare benefits, while elsewhere (as in the UK) increasing liberal ideologies in government have led to the reduction of certain welfare rights (e.g. housing benefits) for such claimants. Economic restructuring falls heavily on the young, who find the jobs that their parents' generation once entered have now gone, while in many societies they are seen as a dangerous and potentially violent "out-group", challenging the moral basis of society.

This element of vilification arises from the fact that in many European cities it is youth groups, particularly drawn from disadvantaged backgrounds, who are involved in particular episodes of contestation against the social controls and hegemonic structures that form the third, and ideological, element of social exclusion discussed above. Clearly there are possible feedback systems in operation here, linking youth contest to further exclusion and so on. Examples of youth challenges to "moral order" might include the "hot-rodding" of stolen vehicles; attacks on property and the police that have occurred sporadically in various suburban estates in the UK in the last few years (such as Meadowwell in North Shields, or Blackbird Leys in Oxford); the new "tradition"

Figure 16.5 *Contested urban space. Renovation in part of the former East Berlin is bringing high-income groups into a previously low-cost (and low-quality) district. The slogans sprayed on the refurbished buildings declare "If you don't fight, it's a slow death" and "stop touri[st] yuppies". (Photos: D A Pinder)*

of confrontations between young people and authority figures such as the police or fire services in many French cities (Joly, 1995); or the particular role of poorly educated and unemployed young people in violent activities associated with neo-Nazi groups in German cities, both in the former GDR and the Federal Republic. In all of these activities the manifestations of contestation can also reproduce stress and insecurity for the perpetrators as well as for others (particularly those living in the same neighbourhoods) in a self-fuelling process (Figure 16.5).

Others who have been involved in open contest over their marginal state in contemporary cities are the homeless who are involved in housing occupations or squatting (Figure 16.4). This is a phenomenon that was of considerable importance in the politically radical decade of the 1960s in western Europe, but which has re-emerged on to the contemporary urban scene in a number of cities, both in the west and the east. For example, a number of districts in the centre of East Berlin today have significant numbers of squats, where semi-derelict and abandoned flats have been occupied, often apparently by young people who have "come over" from the west of the city in order to do so.

One of the most visible "contests" of power launched by the homeless (and the unemployed) in many European cities today occurs in begging in streets and public spaces such as metro stations. These activities are supplemented by en-campments of the homeless, as have existed for many years at "Cardboard City" on London's South Bank, or more temporarily in the camp of homeless African families in the early 1990s in the Place de la Réunion in central Paris. Begging, street-sleeping and squatting are all challenges to modern societies, confronting them with the failures of neo-liberal political practices to ensure the "inclusion" of many individuals in everyday consumption, and the failure of welfare regimes to intervene.

There is, however, an element of concentration of such activities in certain cities, occurring particularly through the "opportunities" often provided by larger urban centres with their greater diversity of charitable and voluntary welfare organisations, and with their possibly greater offerings of temporary informal employment.

Such a concentration of groups suffering specific forms of stress can also occur through local policies which attract individuals to a city. Two examples from the realms of hard drug user communities can be used to illustrate this point. For several years Zurich's "Needle Park" behind the main railway station attracted many drug users from around Europe and beyond who were drawn by the liberal drug control regime adopted by the Zurich municipality until a change of policy in 1994. Similarly, Amsterdam has become a major focus for hard drugs as a result of locally liberal policies which have resulted in a district of the inner city (close to the red-light area) becoming a major location for many activities involving drug users (Koster, 1987).

Elsewhere certain standard indicators of urban stress are more evenly spread. For example, alcoholism is of general occurrence, although with a particularly strong incidence in Russian cities (White, S. 1995). Prostitution is another ubiquitous element, with reports of increasing activity in eastern European cities as a result of growing "sex tourism" from the West, and with growing numbers of girls of gypsy origin becoming involved, in an accentuation of long-standing social exclusionary tendencies affecting gypsy populations.

From a number of the examples discussed here it is clear that it is not just individuals who manifest aspects of stress, exclusion and insecurity, but that there are also, as argued earlier in this chapter, very important elements of spatial concentration at work, whereby individual districts can be characterised as stressed, deprived or dis-advantaged neighbourhoods. This recognition leads us to the geographically significant observation that stress levels for many people may be increased simply because of the district in which they live, and not just through who they are. The concentration into individual city districts of people classifiable as suffering individually or collectively from a variety of stressors may increase the "problems" they suffer, and reduce the possibility of mobility out of this situation. Many European cities today have such "residualised" areas. In Portugal and Spain they are often the squatter settlements increasingly populated by immigrants (Barata Salguiero, 1995), but older slum districts such as the Bario Xino in Barcelona still fulfil their traditional role for a population whose means of support is ever more lagging behind the local norm. In Budapest it is the Jozsefvaros area that is emerging as the residualised district (Dovenyi, 1994). In Brussels, it is the Schaerbeck and Cureghem *communes* towards the inner city (Mistiaen *et al.*, 1995).

In many cities of western Europe, however, although deprived inner-city districts of urban stress certainly exist (such as Spitalfields in London, or the Goutte d'Or in Paris), the neighbourhoods under the greatest threat of residualisation today are those social housing estates which are experiencing the most rapid increases in tenant families and individuals suffering from long-term unemployment, poverty, family breakdown, physical or mental disability, or social exclusion resulting from ethnicity. Through housing privatisation in certain cases, or the exodus of those who can afford to move, or the allocation of emergency cases to "difficult-to-let" housing, such concentrations are growing in many cities. The problems for the residents of these neighbourhoods often include stigmatisation through the labelling of the district in the media as a "problem area", with an accompanying "addressism" whereby job applicants, for example, are immediately rejected because of the reputation of their home locality (Waquant, 1993). Ironically, urban programmes that seek to ameliorate conditions (for example through retraining packages, or the provision of leisure services for the young) may help to reinforce the "problems" by drawing greater attention to them. It appears to be only in strongly social democratic welfare states such as the Netherlands or Sweden that issues of residualisation in social housing areas have largely been kept at bay, although even here we should note that these trends could be argued to be occurring in the Bijlmermeer estate in Amsterdam.[4]

With the exceptions of certain neglected inner-city districts (such as Jozsefvaros in Budapest, already referred to, or Friedrichshain in East Berlin), in eastern European cities there has to date been less spatial sorting by social categories, but in the next decade such sorting may well emerge, with the possibilities of residualised estates emerging in the same way – Marzahn and Hellersdorf in East Berlin are obvious possibilities.

Conclusions

Over recent centuries European economic history has been predominantly urban history. European economic evolution today is being transformed and, although certain cities are gaining new wealth and new activities from these changes, it is far from the whole urban population that benefits. Elsewhere urban societies are seeing their economic basis severely weakened, with no compensating replacement sectors arriving in sufficient force to ensure stability. To these economic changes is added, however, a series of further processes operating at a social, demographic and political level. Details of the population composition of European cities are changing (for example through population ageing, or through the growth of ethnic minority populations), while social norms are also in evolution (for example through increased rates of family breakdown).

It has been the argument of this chapter, however, that what are currently generally seen as increasing levels of stress and insecurity in European cities result in considerable part from a series of political forces. The economic, social and demographic changes described here have all created a challenge requiring a political response. That response has too often been inadequate or inappropriate. European welfare states, one of the glories of the post-war period, have been shown to be insecurely based and tending to underperformance just when they are needed most. In eastern Europe welfare regimes were broken by the events of 1989–92 and new forms have not yet emerged, creating a hiatus of uncertainty in the meantime, with many aspects of earlier provision effectively evaporating. Changing political ideologies, particularly in terms of a "New Right" political discourse, have strengthened the processes of stigmatisation and marginalisation affecting substantial groups in society, and by extension have encouraged increased spatial segregation. The details of the multiple processes involved certainly vary from country to country and from city to city, such that the outcomes also show some local variability, but the overall picture is everywhere composed from similar elements. One of the greatest challenges now facing the new Europe, at all levels of policy from the local to the international, is to seek to improve the everyday circumstances of those substantial sections of urban populations who fear for a tomorrow of unemployment, homelessness, poverty, unsupported old age, illness, violence or intolerance.

Notes

1. Such as the "Townsend Index" (Townsend, 1987).
2. Since then, however, female employment rates have fallen substantially.
3. Data from the Observatoire Européen du Logement Social.
4. The Bijlmermeer estate, south-east of Amsterdam, was the city's last major suburban expansion project. Unlike earlier post-war housing projects, which generally proved highly popular, this monolithic scheme was largely rejected by the Amsterdammers for whom it was designed. The city's solution was to house there disproportionate concentrations of disadvantaged groups.

References

Barata Salgueiro, T (1995) La pauvreté urbaine dans la région de Lisbonne, *Espace, Populations, Sociétés*, **1995/3**, 341–8.

Bodnár, J (1996) "He that hath to him shall be given": housing privatization in Budapest after state socialism, *International Journal of Urban and Regional Research*, **20**, 616–36.

Borgegård, L-E and Murdie, R (1994) Social polarization and the crisis of the welfare state: the case of Stockholm, *Built Environment*, **20**, 254–68.

Borgegård, L-E and Murdie, R (1995) Social polarization in Swedish metropolitan areas: the case of the public housing sector, 1980–1990. Paper presented at the International Conference on Population Geography, Dundee, September.

Boyce, N (1993) Russia on the way to a housing market: a case study of St Petersburg, *Environment and Planning A*, **25**, 975–86.

Carpenter, J and Lees, L (1995) Gentrification in New York, London and Paris: an international comparison, *International Journal of Urban and Regional Research*, **19**, 286–303.

Clark, M (1995) Unemployment, government training schemes and the perpetuation of marginality: evidence from the United Kingdom, *Espace, Populations, Sociétés*, **1995/3**, 381–90.

Council of Europe (1996) *Recent Demographic Developments in Europe, 1996*, Council of Europe Publishing, Strasbourg.

Crosnier, M A (1993) Russie: la protection sociale entre deux systèmes, *Courrier des Pays de l'Est*, **383**, 27–32.

Dovenyi, Z (1994) Adalekok a Budapesti munkanelkuliseg kerdesehez, *Foldrajzi Ertesito*, **43**, 257–64.

Enyedi, G (1994) Der Wandel postsozialistischer Städte, *Mitteilungen, Österreichischen Geographischen Gesellschaft*, **136**, 53–70.

Esping-Andersen, G (1990) *The Three Worlds of Welfare Capitalism*, Polity, Cambridge.

Fassmann, H (1992) Phänomene der Transformation. Ökonomische Restrukturierung und Arbeitslosigkeit in Ost-Mitteleuropa, *Petermanns Geographische Mitteilungen*, **136**, 49–59.

Fonseca, I (1995) *Bury Me Standing: the gypsies and their journey*, Chatto and Windus, London.

Forrest, R and Murie, A (1986) Marginalization and subsidized individualism: the sale of council houses in the restructuring of the British welfare state, *International Journal of Urban and Regional Research*, **10**, 46–66.

Gaspard, M (1993) Revenus et niveaux de vie en Europe centrale et orientale et en ex-URSS, *Courrier des Pays de l'Est*, **383**, 4–14.

Gaube, A (1991) Wohnbedingungen älterer Bürger in der ehemaligen DDR. Ein Zwischenbericht zu Untersuchungen in Berlin-Köpenick, *Informationen zur Raumentwicklung*, **1991/3**, 161–8.

Hall, R (1995) Households, families and fertility, in R Hall and P White (eds) *Europe's Population: towards the next century*, UCL Press, London, 34–50.

Hall, R, Ogden, P and Hill, C (1995) The pattern and structure of lone-person households in Great Britain and France. Paper presented at the International Conference on Population Geography, Dundee, September.

Hamnett, C (1994a) Social polarisation in global cities: theory and evidence, *Urban Studies*, **31**, 401–24.

Hamnett, C (1994b) Socio-economic change in London: professionalization not polarization, *Built Environment*, **20**, 192–203.

Humeau, J-B (1994) Les Tsiganes en Europe: problématique géographique, *Espaces, Populations, Sociétés*, **1994/3**, 349–58.

Joly, J (1995) Géographie de la violence urbaine dans les banlieues françaises, *Espaces, Populations, Sociétés*, **1995/3**, 323–8.

Jones, J (1996) Community-based mental health care in Italy: are there lessons for Britain?, *Health and Place*, **2**, 125–8.

Kahn, M (1993) La condition féminine en ex-URSS, *Courrier des Pays de l'Est*, **381**, 3–19.

Köster, G (1994) Zur Dynamik der Wohnorte älterer Menschen in der Stadt: Ausmass und Konsequenzen für die Stadtplanung am Beispiel der Stadt Aachen, *Geographische Zeitschrift*, **82**, 91–102.

Koster, L (1987) *Wandelaars in de Nieuwmarktbuurt: een onderzoek naar de invloed van de harddrugsscene op het wonen in een oude binnenstadsbuurt*, Amsterdamse Sociaal-Geografische Studies, 6.

Ladanyi, J (1993) Patterns of residential segregation and the gypsy minority in Budapest, *International Journal of Urban and Regional Research*, **17**, 30–41.

Lefèvre, C (1993) Le rôle social des entreprises industrielles en Russie, *Courrier des Pays de l'Est*, **383**, 33–9.

Lichtenberger, E (1993) Immobilienmarkt – Arbeitsmarkt – Wohnungsmarkt. Vergleichende Metropolenforschung: Wien – Budapest – Prag, *Mitteilungen der Österreichischen Geographischen Gesellschaft*, **135**, 7–40.

Lichtenberger, E (1995) Die Entwicklung der Innenstadt von Budapest zwischen City- und Stadtbildung, *Erdkunde*, **49**, 138–51.

Logan, J, Taylor-Gooby, P and Reuter, M (1992) Poverty and income inequality, in S S Fainstein, I Gordon and M Harloe (eds) *Divided Cities: New York and London in the contemporary world*, Blackwell, Oxford, 129–50.

Mädje, E and Neusüss, C (1994) Lone mothers on welfare in West Berlin: disadvantaged citizens or women avoiding patriarchy?, *Environment and Planning A*, **26**, 1419–34.

Marouli, C (1995) Women resisting (in) the city: struggles, gender, class and space in Athens, *International Journal of Urban and Regional Research*, **19**, 534–48.

Martinez, P M and Vicario, L (1995) Déclin industriel et polarisation socio-spatiale: le cas de Bilbao, *Espace, Populations, Sociétés*, **1995/3**, 349–68.

Mingione, E (ed) (1993) The New Urban Poverty and the Urban Underclass. Special issue of *International Journal of Urban and Regional Research*, **17**, No 3.

Mistiaen, P, Meert, H and Kesteloot, C (1995) Polarisation socio-spatiale et stratégies de survie dans deux quartiers bruxellois, *Espace, Populations, Sociétés*, **1995/3**, 277–90.

Musterd, S (1994) A rising European underclass? Social polarization and spatial segregation in European cities, *Built Environment*, **20**, 185–91.

Paal, M M (1995) La décomposition urbaine à Budapest: l'héritage du communisme, *Bulletin, l'Association de Géographes Français*, **1995/3**, 284–93.

Peach, C (1996) Does Britain have ghettos?, *Transactions, Institute of British Geographers*, **21**, 216–35.

Robertson, I M L (1984) Single parent lifestyle and peripheral estate residence, *Town Planning Review*, **55**, 197–213.

Sassen, S (1991) *The Global City: New York, London, Tokyo*, Princeton University Press, Princeton, NJ.

Schulz, M (1993a) Transformation des Berliner Wohnungsmarkts, *Mitteilungen der Österreichischen Geographischen Gesellschaft*, **135**, 63–86.

Schulz, M (1993b) Wohnbedingungen und innerstädtische Differenzierung in Ost-Berlin, *Geographische Rundschau*, **45**, 588–93.

Townsend, P (1987) Deprivation, *Journal of Social Policy*, **16**, 125–46.

Van Kempen, R (1994) The dual city and the poor: social polarization, social segregation and life chances, *Urban Studies*, **31**, 995–1016.

Vant, A (ed) (1986) *Marginalité Sociale, Marginalité Spatiale*, Editions du CNRS, Paris.

Vieillard-Baron, H (1994) *Les Banlieues Françaises, ou le Ghetto Impossible*, Editions de l'Aube, Paris.

Wacquant, L J D (1993) Urban outcasts: stigma and division in the black American ghetto and the French urban periphery, *International Journal of Urban and Regional Research*, **17**, 366–83.

White, P (in press) Ideologies, social exclusion and spatial segregation in Paris, in S Musterd (ed) *Segregation and Social Exclusion in Western Metropolitan Areas*, Routledge, London.

White, P and Winchester, H P M (1991) The poor in the inner city: stability and change in two Parisian neighbourhoods, *Urban Geography*, **12**, 35–54.

White, S (1995) *Russia Goes Dry: alcohol, state and society*, Cambridge University Press, Cambridge.

Wilson, W J (1987) *The Truly Disadvantaged: the inner city, the underclass, and public policy*, University of Chicago Press, Chicago.

Winchester, H P M and White, P (1988) The location of marginalised groups in the inner city, *Environment and Planning D: Society and Space*, **6**, 37–54.

17

Socio-economic stress, spatial imbalance and policy responses in the new democracies

David Turnock

Department of Geography, University of Leicester, UK

Under Communism growth was driven from the centre and it was widely asserted that location decisions reflected the principle of equal opportunity (Hamilton, 1971). Backward regions were endowed with new industries which often emerged in clusters reminiscent of Western "growth pole" concepts, while various steps were taken to restrain growth in capital cities and strengthen the lower levels of the central place hierarchy. By the late 1970s, however, it was clear that serious deficiencies remained. Widespread inequality still existed between countries and regions (Fuchs and Demko, 1979). Many rural areas had received relatively little investment and remained dominated by a labour-intensive agricultural sector that was used to employ the residual workforce and therefore maintain full employment (Pine, 1993). Neglect was particularly evident in the border regions because of the closed frontiers, but there were also big differences between districts where village people worked predominantly in agriculture and those where commuters could bring in salaries and manufactured goods from the towns. Meanwhile in the cities, pollution became a common health hazard; sharp contrasts in living conditions were brought out (Dangschat, 1987) while in the closing years of Communism much attention was given to variations in housing provision (Szelenyi, 1983; Zaniewski, 1991). And in both rural and urban areas there was an inadequate supply of consumer goods. Shortages were built into the system and it was necessary to queue for almost everything that was desirable.

Despite the attempts to achieve equity, it was common for communities and individuals to suffer social stress, and frequently for this to be linked with spatial imbalance at a variety of scales. These tensions, it is true, were often tempered by the fact that local officials were not usually privileged enough to create any great distance between themselves and the population; this helped communities to be cohesive. Also, most families enjoyed a large measure of security in return for politically correct behaviour, despite immense pressures on a heavily overloaded and under-funded tertiary sector. Nonetheless, perceptions of deprivation ran deep. Consequently, when enforced isolation from the West was ended in 1989, a "Dallas complex" of popular expectation

Figure 17.1   *Consumerism! (Orşova, Romania)*

was unleashed as it was assumed that living standards would rise quickly to reach Western levels (Figure 17.1).

This expectation, however, remains largely unfulfilled. Movement towards market economies is proving painful for many individuals and families (Ronge, 1991). The operation of the market is creating additional problems of spatial imbalance. And – in an environment in which state intervention is constrained by ideology and financial limitations – strategies to deal with inequality and alleviate social stress are far from fully developed. Given the fluidity of the situation and the extent of the problems, it would be unrealistic for this chapter to attempt a final analysis of the situation which now prevails. Even so, considerable progress can be made by focusing on three themes: the nature of socio-economic stress in the new system, its spatial dimensions at the national and international scales, and progress with policy responses and debates.

The Nature of Stress in the New System

By Western standards almost everybody in eastern Europe is under socio-economic stress because of the collapse of GNP in the early 1990s (Figure 17.2). Massive reorganisation is in progress in response to the global situation of intense competition for markets and investment. Simply coping with rapid change in telecommunications, the unprecedented choices under Western consumerism and the price variations between subsidised and non-subsidised services, causes many to think back to the days when life was simpler and in some respects easier. In addition, social and medical problems involving AIDS, drugs and prostitution pose challenges; the welfare of the institutionalised section of the population previously hidden by media censorship from public scrutiny must now be addressed by hastily reconstituted civil societies; and crime has achieved a new dimension in such areas as theft,

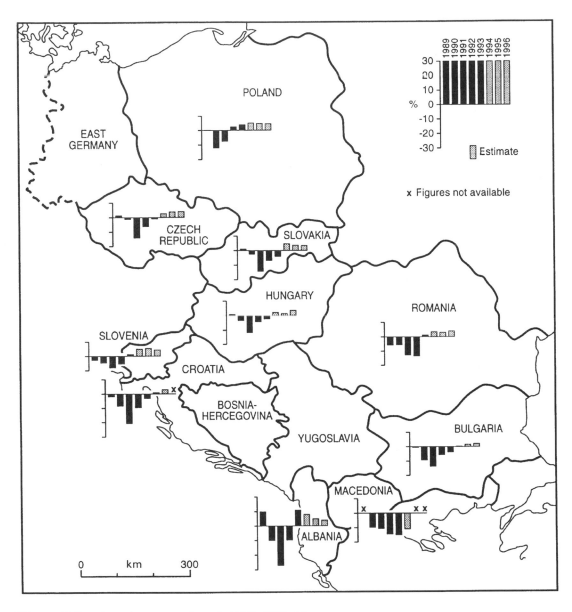

Figure 17.2 *Annual percentage change in GDP, 1989–96*

bribery and (in parts of former Yugoslavia) sanctions-busting. Drug-smuggling in the Balkans has increased alarmingly since 1989, and there is insufficient co-ordination between police forces to intercept any more than a small proportion. Moreover, the police are too poorly paid and equipped to check crime and avoid being involved in bribery.

In the workplace, adjustment by both management and workers to rising productivity through mechanisation, computerisation – and above all – an enterprise culture, is a formidable challenge to people who have been conditioned to seeing a job as a form of welfare with only a fuzzy relationship between effort and reward. People now have to work more efficiently, yet accept low wages in order to remain competitive with Asian "tiger" economies and also maintain the "wages precipice" on the German border. Similarly, entreprencurs cannot be taxed too

Table 17.1 *Annual percentage change in real wages, 1989–94*

	1989	1990	1991	1992	1993	1994
Albania	3.0	6.2	−42.3	18.6	1.1	1.1
Czech Republic	0.8	−5.5	−26.3	10.3	3.6	4.5
Hungary	0.8	−0.2	−3.7	1.7	−0.4	6.8
Poland	11.6	−27.4	0.2	−2.9	−1.1	2.9
Romania	2.1	5.6	−17.2	−13.0	−16.7	−6.7
Slovakia	1.4	−6.1	−25.2	0.7	−4.3	1.7

Source: EU Directorate-General for Employment, Industrial Relations and Social Affairs.

highly, otherwise the competition for investment with the tiger economies will be far too weak. As it is, the capital flowing into eastern Europe is a trickle compared with the money flooding into the Pacific Rim. In this way the global facts of life are being heaped upon a population that is scarcely prepared to receive them.

Inflation has eliminated small savings, while reduced government spending is evident in many ways, including reductions in free medical care and subsidised holidays. Older people lucky enough to have pensions have been severely affected by their falling value, while those who remain in employment have experienced a fall in the real value of their wages (Table 17.1). Workers in mining and heavy industry have suffered badly because these sectors were usually favoured under Communism with relatively high wages. Elsewhere in the economy, the oversupply of technicians is especially disconcerting for young engineers and their parents, who find that years of technical training to prepare for a privileged place in the Communist labour market have apparently been in vain.

One common outcome of all this has been widespread hardship. For example, more than a quarter of Hungary's population are now considered poor, according to studies of the "new" poverty (Vuics, 1992), while many families need "multiple incomes" in order to get by. Also, increased stress may well be reflected in falling birth rates. Thus, a drastic decline in the birth rate in the former East Germany reflects age-selective outmigration in search of employment, as well as the choice to be made between keeping a job and having a child (Fleischacker, 1995, 134).

Unemployment

Against this background, the geography of unemployment has become an important line of enquiry (Figure 17.3 and Table 17.2). Unemployment is in itself a traumatic experience for societies conditioned to associate the lack of a job with parasitism (Burda, 1993; Roesler, 1991), and the situation is even worse when, as is commonly the case, social security provision is very modest

Table 17.2 *Unemployment in central and eastern Europe, 1990–95*

	1990*	1991	1992	1993	1994	1995[†]
Bulgaria	1.6	11.9	14.0	15.5	na	na
Czech Republic	0.7	4.2	2.6	3.2	3.2	4.0
Hungary	1.5	7.8	14.0	13.7	na	na
Poland	6.1	11.5	15.9	15.0	na	na
Romania	na	3.0	8.3	9.5	10.9	14.5
Slovakia	1.5	6.6	11.4	14.4	14.5	15.0

na = not available.
[†] estimates.
* Poland 1989.
Sources: Blanchard (1994) and the Economist Intelligence Unit (1994 and 1995 data).

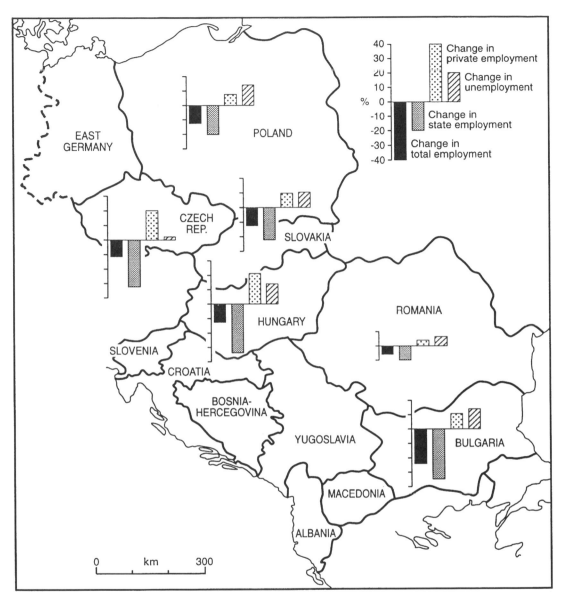

Figure 17.3 *Changes in aspects of employment and unemployment, 1990–92*

(Rupp, 1992). Much of the unemployment has arisen in industry controlled by state-owned enterprises (SOEs). Despite government attempts to limit the damage by providing subsidies, there has been a shake-out of labour, especially in heavy industry affected by the collapse of military procurement. Today's transition requires production to be related to market demand, world market prices and the profit motive, with greatly reduced government intervention. So it is

necessary to restructure and concentrate on profitable manufactures with substitution of high cost inputs.

Old industrial areas have suffered badly because their outdated plant is no longer competitive and there is little experience of diversification among enterprise managers. There are particular difficulties in towns with just one major industry, especially when this is heavy manufacturing (like the armaments industries of Slovakia) previously geared to Comecon markets. Many cities have also seen heavy lay-offs in the building industry when there has been insufficient funding to continue with large-scale central area redevelopments started before 1989. By contrast, light industry has suffered less severely, especially in the case of modern factories that have been able to negotiate joint ventures with Western firms. However, productivity levels are being driven up relentlessly. What may also be noted is that unemployment would be even higher but for acceptance of high levels of pollution. There are still many towns (like Copşa Mică in Romania) where emissions going way beyond the legal limit are tolerated in the interest of continued employment. This issue is considered further by Saiko in Chapter 20.

The impact of unemployment is increased by the limited protection for workers and the inadequate scale of retraining (Deacon, 1992). Germany's *Aufschwung Ost* (Upswing East) programme of retraining and job creation is very much the exception. Moreover, there is little prospect of improvement through union action, since these organisations are struggling for legitimacy and have lost much of the welfare role they enjoyed under Communism. Handicaps such as these offer few hopes of rapid solutions to the ingrained problems of poor health and short life expectancy that are so common throughout the region. However, there are some positive signs of change in the education system. Graduates from academic secondary schools have been doing better in the labour market recently, and academic courses have the advantage of being relatively cheap from the state's point of view. Appropriate education policies will also reduce isolation in countries where there is little knowledge of Western languages.

Ethnicity and gender

Care is necessary when considering the relationships between ethnicity and employment prospects. Ethnic tensions are easily exaggerated and Western perceptions tend to be clouded by the extreme conflict that has occurred in former Yugoslavia. None the less, given the inadequate legislation for worker protection, it is possible for dismissals to be disproportionately heavy among minority groups. The gypsies are frequently disadvantaged on the labour market, and more generally there is a need for confidence-building between ethnic groups. Consequently, it will be a big step forward if the Council of Europe framework convention on the protection of minorities is adopted in international treaties.

Gender issues are also relevant to the transition because, although the situation admittedly varies between countries, women have not yet achieved fundamental change towards equality, despite their involvement in political movements (Emandi, 1993). The transition may bring benefits for women in the longer term; indeed, hopelessness is hardly the predominant sentiment at the present time. But, for the moment, women face higher than average unemployment. In the former East Germany, for example, they are unemployed for longer periods than men and face greater difficulties getting jobs (Quack and Maier, 1994). Moreover, despite equal opportunity legislation now in force, there is concern over the erosion of child care facilities which complicates female employment where young mothers are concerned. Forced to choose between family and career, some women are opting for sterilisation in order to compete for jobs. More generally in the region women, as the homemakers, deal with most of the burdens of short-term scarcity, the difficulties engendered by the market mechanism and the price rises caused by the removal of subsidies. As mothers they have to cope with poor medical services, as in rural Albania where a single nurse may well be shared between two to three villages. And this is not to delve into the problems of overcrowding, malnutrition, alcoholism and domestic violence (Corrin, 1995).

Housing and transport

Movement in search of work is constrained by the very slow development of a Western-style property market. But housing is also a factor in

Figure 17.4 *Housing problems, Piatra Neamţ, Romania. Inner-city areas contain much run-down housing from the pre-Communist period, while new blocks in the suburbs are often poorly insulated and provide only small family apartments*

the wider poverty problem through the rise in rents and the eviction of many tenants from inner-city properties that are now being refurbished for a wealthier clientele. For the moment it seems that middle-class families (as well as the élite) are benefiting from privatisation of the housing market. In contrast poorer families, unable to find the resources to buy, are stranded in a spiral of rent increases aggravated by the withdrawal of subsidies. This raises the importance of housing benefit to limit the fall in real living standards (Pudney, 1995). Even when families have been able to exercise the right to buy, however, there is often a problem of heavy financial burdens for the repair of deteriorating inner-city housing (Hegedus and Tosics, 1994). Although economic difficulties make it necessary for the state to reduce its commitment, low-interest improvement loans (already available in the former East Germany) are needed if refurbishment by new owners on tight budgets is to succeed (Figure 17.4).

Meanwhile, in the rural areas especially, people have also been disadvantaged by the reduction of subsidies on public transport, leading to higher costs and lower levels of service. In some cases services have been withdrawn entirely and people no longer have the option of travelling daily to work in the town unless they can afford their own car. The purchase of second-hand vehicles from Austria and Germany has made car ownership much more feasible, but many of those without a vehicle have suddenly found themselves isolated. This in turn is all the more difficult to bear where the rural community has been transformed by forces such as migration, the politicisation of ethnic issues, or the restitution of land to previous owners (Verdery, 1994). Most of the Germans have left the commune of Brebu Nou in Romania's Caras-Severin county, leaving behind them a small elderly group without local transport and shops.

Agriculture

Apart from the growing difficulties of movement in rural areas, agriculture is relevant to the problems of stress because reform has taken place through various schemes of land redistribution. In many instances, large socialist farms (co-

operatives and to a lesser extent state farms) have been broken down, allowing land to be either allocated to its present occupiers or restituted to its former owners. A major effect has been a sharp reduction in employment and the closure of many linked enterprises in light industry and local services. This has created difficulties for food distribution and local infrastructure generally. In Poland, for example, there has been a break-up of the socialist food chain through division of the state monopoly trusts organised on a county basis (Stebelsky, 1995). Meanwhile in Nógrád (northern Hungary) privatised agriculture employs only a small proportion of the former agricultural workforce, at a time when many local industrial enterprises have closed and commuting to work in the towns is much reduced (Varga, 1996). Even when locally managed co-operatives have been retained, a drastic reduction in the demand for labour has usually resulted. And when co-operatives have been abandoned this has undermined an established marketing system, albeit one which involved bulk deliveries to government warehouses. Admittedly, change in this context should not be exaggerated: usually the state has retained at least a limited procurement role and some produce is still being offered at subsidised prices. But there is increasing private involvement, so prices for populations with generally restricted incomes are now much more variable.

Regional Outcomes and Responses

Although the geographical consequences of these interrelated problems are naturally complex, their impact on economic development patterns is now emerging. At the national level it is clear that the northern countries of the Czech Republic, Hungary, Poland and Slovakia (often referred to as the "Visegrád" group after the Hungarian town where close economic collaboration was first agreed) are emerging more quickly from the recession than the Balkan countries where the fall in GNP only bottomed out in the mid-1990s. At the same time, all countries have to wrestle with mounting regional differences. Many under-developed areas of the Communist period which were conspicuous because of their age and employ-

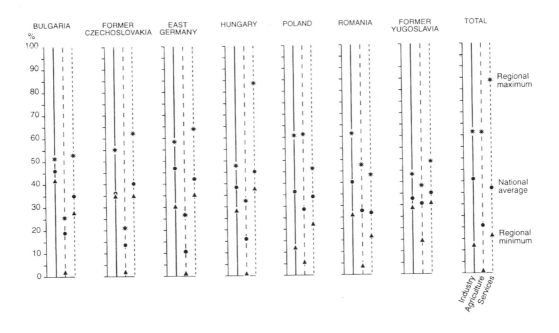

Figure 17.5 *Regional variations in employment structure* c. *1988*

ment structures (Bachtler, 1992b) are now even further disadvantaged by high unemployment

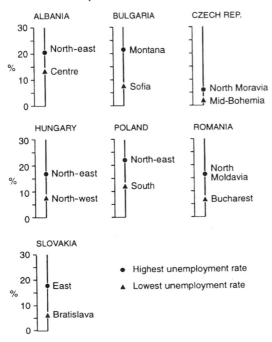

Figure 17.6 *Regional variations in unemployment, 1994*

(Csefalvay, 1994) (Figures 17.5 and 17.6). Hungary, for example, has a concentration of unemployment in its north-eastern regions. Industrial restructuring has naturally affected towns adversely, especially – though not invariably – in the more backward areas where industries tend to be less efficient. Thus high unemployment is characteristic of Poland's newer industrial regions, including Kielce, Lomza and Starachowice, where there was a heavy dependence on Soviet orders for products such as textiles and vehicles (Czyz, 1993). In such regions "overembedded" networks tend to remain locked into the rationality of the old regime, and change may occur largely through defensive measures as institutions attempt to insulate themselves from an increasingly threatening environment (Grabher, 1994). For example, now-separate divisions of some former large state enterprises may still rely partly on barter exchange between each other. Understandably, while new private firms are not absent from these areas, development is constrained by their restricted growth.

By contrast, economy-boosting joint ventures are over-represented in the capital cities and the Western regions of most countries, with the latter

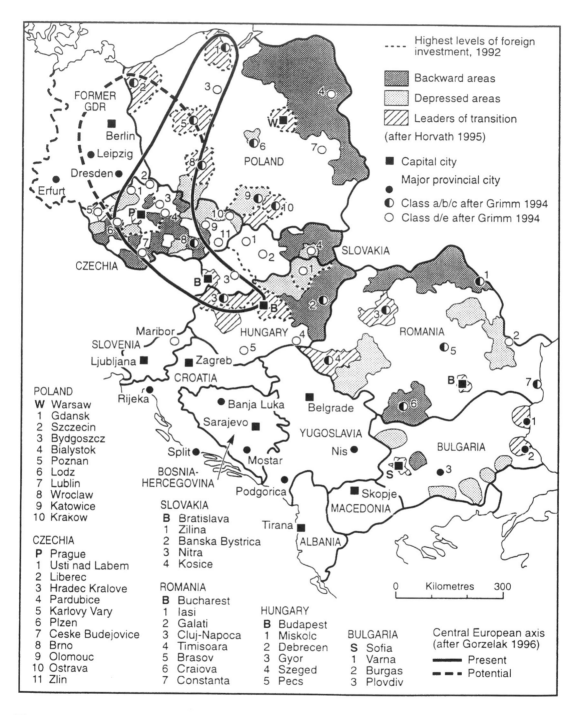

Figure 17.7 *Aspects of regional development*

benefiting from the relative proximity to western Europe. Hungary, for example, has a "fertile half moon" covering Budapest and a group of urban regions – Gyor, Kecskemet, Pecs and Szekesfehervar – in the centre and north-west of the country (Ivan, 1994). And the healthier performance of western regions generally has led Gorzelak (1996, 128) to refer to an advantaged "boomerang-shaped" area in the centre of Europe covering many of the major centres or cores of transformation (Figure 17.7). Even though there are dangers arising from heavy dependence on branch plants (Sadler, 1993), these stronger regions generally have the advantage of becoming "disembedded" from the old structures as they develop interregional linkages and relationships with external institutions. Thus serious imbalances are becoming increasingly evident both within individual countries and at the broader regional scale. There are severe inefficiencies in matching workers with jobs, not least because of constraints on mobility such as the poorly functioning housing markets (Blanchard, 1994, 7). And, understandably in view of the problems discussed earlier, regional variations are becoming a matter of great concern (Horvath, 1995). Indeed, Dovenyi (1994, 396) has gone so far as to warn of the danger that unemployment in the worst affected regions "may mean the last step in the disintegration of local societies".

Despite economic divergence, there are signs of progress. For example, some poorer regions are starting to benefit from growth occurring on the edge of large cities, especially Berlin, Budapest, Prague and Warsaw. More space is needed for recreation, for new industrial estates linked with motorways and for residential developments. Wealthy middle-class families are being encouraged to exchange their city apartments for up-market housing on the urban–rural fringe, and Gawryszewski (1992) raises the possibility of significant counter-urbanisation as professionals move to suburban zones with good conditions for high-tech industry. Meanwhile, in a number of genuinely rural regions, land reform has provided a form of welfare by enabling some of the people who have lost their jobs elsewhere in the economy to fall back on small-scale farming. Although there is little cash welfare for farmers (Kapitanski and Anastasova, 1994), tiny farms that can never be viable in the true sense do provide families with a means of feeding themselves and generating small surpluses that can be marketed (Figure 17.8). Moreover, there are prospects of further development based on this safety net, as

the experiences of many mountain dwellers in countries such as Poland and the former Yugoslavia demonstrate. For example, pluriactivity in the Polish Carpathians is well established, with agrotourism being particularly successful in a number of villages close to the Tatra and Babia Góra, (Pine, 1993). Large modern houses have been built on the strength of increased incomes and the demand for tourist accommodation, while summer visitors generate demand for locally produced food (Kurek, 1996).

While such examples may be encouraging, however, they are not generally representative. Consequently they have been paralleled by moves towards the introduction of regional policies reminiscent of those adopted by western European countries in the 1950s and 1960s. Thus regional aid is being made available for five years in all parts of the former East Germany through *Gemeinschaftsaufgabe*; and there is additional help for areas particularly affected by structural change. Similarly, the Hungarian government initiated a regional development fund in 1989 as part of a restructured regional policy (Horvath and Hrubi, 1992). Under this programme the Ministry for Environment and Regional Policy co-ordinates regional and urban development activities generally and supervises development programmes for underdeveloped and depressed areas such as Szabolcz–Szatmar–Bereg (Nefedova and Trejvis, 1994, 39). The Polish government too has been active in this sphere; in this case in establishing special economic zones to attract investment that could boost employment in problem regions. For example, located in southeast Poland between Sandomierz and Tarnów, Euro-Park Mielec offers 10-year tax holidays, with 50 per cent exemption to follow for another decade. The aim is to diversify the monostructural local economy, which is heavily bound up with an aircraft factory. Meanwhile in the Czech Republic, the current priorities are economically weak regions (mainly in Moravia); others vulnerable to structural change; border areas; and, especially in northern Bohemia, regions with unfavourable environmental conditions caused in part by industrialisation. Weak regions are benefiting from programmes to support small and medium-sized firms and a new Czech-Moravian Development Bank has been established for this purpose.

Figure 17.8 *Agriculture as a way of life. In much of eastern Europe all the "residual" family labour still goes into the intensive working of small farms. Horses are still widely used for traction since there is little capital available for investment, although ancillary income is derived from tourism in mountain regions*

As might be imagined, there are those who advocate substantial expansion of regional policies. Pavlinek (1992) has called for an effective regional social policy to deliver education and welfare. The latter would include job training and incentives such as capital grants, tax exemptions and relocation allowances. In similar vein, Nemes (1994, 368) has argued that "without revitalising and strengthening the role of regional policy, an eventual social and economic disruption of the northern and eastern regions of Hungary seems to be unavoidable". In reality, however, the emergence of strong regional policies is unlikely at the present time. This partly reflects the scarcity of financial resources to support them. It is a consequence too of the widespread belief that state intervention should be avoided. But it also reflects the view that the initial priority is clearly to develop strategies at the national level (Bachtler, 1992b, 135). Here again, a parallel with western Europe can be observed: regional policies there experienced their greatest development when national economies were expanding most successfully. With strong growth and favourable investment climates in central and eastern Europe, regional fortunes could easily change, as in the case of Mladá Boleslav in the Czech Republic. Here a one-sided industrial structure based on car manufacture has been revitalised by Volkswagen's investment. Yet, while it is one thing to advocate a strategy based on national growth, it is quite another to prescribe how this should be achieved. As a result a debate is now in progress between those advocating efficiency on the one hand and protection on the other. Thus Barta (1992) believes that competition policy should be used to strengthen national economies and major cities, while Bachtler (1992a) argues that policy should support potential growth areas that can lead the national restructuring process. Under this approach most attention would be given to diversified industrial regions with a relatively good technical and material base.

Although this debate is undoubtedly important it must also be noted that the improvement of regional economic prospects through a strategy based on spread effects, generated by national growth and supported by regional policy, is likely to require a long time horizon. Moreover, lessons to be learned from western European experience are again relevant. Few regions have had their development lags eliminated by "top down" planning, and recent recession has often led to the reversal of regional policy successes as external investors have closed plants. In response, many western European regions and cities have placed heavy emphasis on locality-based policies. This is an alternative approach that is increasingly feasible in central and eastern Europe as the powers and financial capacities of local governments increase. "An emancipational process of nationalities and regions can be expected" to follow the ethnic claims of groups such as the Moravians and Silesians, so that regions will develop more distinct economic and social profiles (Vaishar, 1992, 397). Toth (1993, 23) sees a logical evolution of democratic institutions towards greater decentralisation and regional autonomy, including tax-raising powers.

While this approach has considerable potential, however, it is evident that in each region consensus will be needed to forge links with businesses able to use resources and strengthen the economy by building on local traditions and cultural activities. Moreover it is also apparent that agriculture will not be able to provide the basis for development in the countryside. Agricultural employment is declining rapidly, and by the turn of the century is likely to provide only 5 per cent of employment. Hence the need for promotion of the secondary and tertiary sectors in rural areas (Klodzinski, 1992). Small businesses will need encouragement to support the large enterprises and develop the service sector, and in rural areas considerable growth could arise from clusters of small and medium-sized enterprises. In this way the "top down" process of breaking down the SOEs could be complemented by a "bottom up" programme to integrate the transformed state enterprises with the existing handicraftsmen and family-managed workshops (Swain, 1994). In important respects this would equate to the adoption of the "Bavarian model" of pluriactivity more widely. For example, in some regions quality products from a system of predominantly organic farming could be handled by an enlarged processing sector, while food processing, textile and craft industries could be complemented by various forms of rural tourism (Derounian, 1995). Indeed, agrotourism could well emerge as an important element in pluriactivity in areas such as Romania's Bran-Rucar corridor or Poland's north-eastern lake country.

Cross-border co-operation

Although there is debate as to the best way of dealing with the new regional problems, it at least seems certain that the immediate future will be characterised by cross-border co-operation programmes for regional development. Border areas constitute a special problem because the closed frontier of Communism created many backward areas. Here the dangers of instability may be increased by an ethnically mixed population (including Asians and refugees) trying to get into western Europe; by the failure of many people to identify with their social milieu; and by relatively low levels of religious adherence "which indicates lower social control" (Vaishar, 1993, 171). The first response to this specific challenge came after German reunification in the form of the 1990–91 border area programme (*Grenzraumprogramm*) for areas in both East and West Germany either side of the interzonal frontier and in Berlin. But since then the idea has been extended impressively.

For example, a tier of Euroregions now straddles Germany's borders with the Czech Republic and Poland. The programmes here include co-operation in culture, training and the environment, along with improved economic structures. While German firms are investing in projects that exploit the relatively cheap labour across the frontier, there is the prospect of technical progress through the plan for an industrial complex to develop both sides of the German–Polish frontier by linking the EKO steelworks of Eisenhüttenstadt with metal industries in Cybinka on the Polish side (Kratke, 1996). Elsewhere, the border areas of the Czech Republic have been boosted considerably by the financial incentives made available to Austrian and German businesses, while capital for economic restructuring has also been provided by the EU under a PHARE programme which includes projects in regions immediately adjacent to EU countries. Free trade zones have been established in Cheb and Ostrava, and centres of innovation ("economic and technology parks") in Cëske Valenice and Cheb. Like Germany's new *Länder*, north-west Bohemia has great potential in that it lies within eight hours' travel of over 80 million people. And for the rest of the Czech Republic, along with western Poland, western Slovenia and northern Croatia, the figure is more than 60 million.

Finally, the Carpathian Euroregion is a similarly interesting experiment bringing together the frontier districts of Hungary (Debrecen/ Miskolc), Poland (Krosno), Slovakia (Košice) and Ukraine (Mukačevo). Here the intention is to pool economic information and improve contact and trade through additional border crossings and better telecommunications. There is also a substantial environment programme through the East Carpathian Biosphere Nature Reserve established in 1993 to cover 164 000 ha in Poland, Slovakia and Ukraine. In one sense, the emergence of this Euroregion reflects the operation of "bottom up" processes. Local groups became active in 1990 and cross-border trade was recognised in treaties between the former Czechoslovakia, Hungary, Poland and Ukraine in 1992. The region was then created in 1993 on the

initiative of regional officials, with local contacts being supported by legal and political advice from central governments. The foreign ministers of Hungary, Poland and Ukraine signed a co-operation agreement in Debrecen in 1993, and since then Slovakia has become an associate. In addition, however, the operational aspect of the Carpathian region has an unusual international dimension in that it is to a great extent run by the Institute for EastWest Studies. This is an American–European–Japanese non-governmental organisation whose role is that of an honest broker helping to find "common language" across the region (Kaliberda, 1994).

The Way Forward

Eastern Europe is an area of stress yet, despite austerity during the early years of transition, economic growth is now picking up and people are generally confident about the prospects for a better future – especially if they can join an enlarged EU. Although only a minority feel better off now than they were under Communism, most are satisfied about the direction of change in terms of civil society in general and the economy in particular. Unemployment may still be high, yet there are opportunities in agriculture and service activities such as tourism and retailing. A particularly significant feature of the latter is that the collapse of state distribution systems has led not to their replacement by large capitalised trading and wholesale companies, but by a "bazaar economy" based on a host of very small operations. Opportunity costs for labour are low enough to draw many people into commerce using car-boots, kiosks or private houses, and there is also much trading on the streets away from the official markets (Figure 17.9) (Pedersen, 1993).

Despite these signs of progress, however, it will be a slow process for incomes to catch up with Western levels. Indeed, the European Bank for Reconstruction and Development suggests that, even in 2025, incomes will only run at half the

Figure 17.9 *Small-scale commerce based on local handicrafts. Activity of this type is commonplace both along the tourist highways and at country markets*

levels prevailing in western Europe. There is, moreover, a very strong probability that economic development will still be very uneven within the region, chiefly because restructuring is already forging ahead more rapidly in the north, where the Visegrád states hope they are on the fast track towards further enlargement of the EU. Elsewhere, and particularly in the Balkans – where economic change has been gravely hindered by war, sanctions, blockade and other less serious dislocations – the prospects are far less good.

Of course, as the discussion of spatial imbalance has already suggested, there are policy options for dealing with these issues. In essence the conventional wisdom – stressing open borders stimulating the growth of international trade and progressive entry to the EU – is challenged in some quarters by stronger nationalist policies that would reduce the influence of international organisations. Opting for one or other of these pathways would naturally have significant implications for economic planning. Open-door policies could result in the growth of foreign investment, including joint ventures, foreign-owned banks and the regional offices of multinational companies (leading, perhaps, to regional specialisation). However, the major pitfall associated with this strategy is that if – as seems certain – inward investment is concentrated on a limited number of countries, this could well force others to look inwards by giving greater protection to domestic industry and services. This, in turn, could produce two contrasted demographic scenarios: for the more advanced countries, low unemployment combined with rising welfare provision and low levels of international migration; and, for the remainder, the possibility of high unemployment, low welfare provision and higher levels of outmigration that could well place pressure on western Europe. Of course, the choices are not simple preferences between two sets of extremes, and the critical decisions involved are not being made by the east Europeans alone. On the contrary, some would argue that the room for manoeuvre within the region is extremely limited, and that precise outcomes will be shaped very largely by attitudes adopted in the EU and by the all-pervasive forces of globalisation. Having re-entered the capitalist economy, eastern Europe must learn to live by its rules.

References

Bachtler, J (1992a) Regional problems and policies in Central and Eastern Europe, *Regional Studies*, **26**, 665–71.

Bachtler, J (ed) (1992b) *Socio-economic Situation and Development of the Regions in the Neighbouring Countries of the Community in Central and Eastern Europe*, Commission of the European Communities Directorate-General for Regional Policies, Brussels/Luxembourg.

Barta, G (1992) The changing role of industry in regional development and regional development policy in Hungary, *Tijdschrift voor Economische en Sociale Geografie*, **58**, 372–9.

Blanchard, O (1994) Unemployment in Eastern Europe, *Finance and Development: A Quarterly Publication of the International Monetary Fund and the World Bank*, **31**(4), 6–9.

Burda, M (1993) Unemployment labour market and structural change in Eastern Europe, *Economic Policy*, **16**, 101–38.

Corrin, C (1995) Creating change or struggling to survive?: women's situation in Albania, *Journal of Area Studies*, **6**, 74–82.

Csefalvay, Z (1994) The regional differentiation of the Hungarian economy in transition, *GeoJournal*, **32**, 351–61.

Czyz, T (1993) The regional structure of unemployment in Poland, *Geographia Polonica*, **61**, 479–96.

Dangschat, J (1987) Sociopolitical disparities in a "socialist city": the case of Warsaw at the end of the 1970s, *International Journal of Urban and Regional Research*, **11**, 37–60.

Deacon, B (1992) *The new Eastern Europe: social policy past, present and future*, Sage, London.

Derounian, J G (1995) Rural regeneration in Romania, *Report for the Natural and Built Environment Professions*, **5**, 4–6.

Dovenyi, Z (1994) Transition and unemployment: the case of Hungary, *GeoJournal*, **32**, 393–8.

Emandi, H (1993) Development strategies and women in Albania, *East European Quarterly*, **27**, 79–96.

Fleischacker, J (1995) The impact of deindustrialization and unemployment on family formation in East Germany, *Geographia Polonica*, **64**, 117–35.

Fuchs, R and Demko, G (1979) Geographical inequalities under socialism, *Annals of the Association of American Geographers*, **69**, 301–18.

Gawryszewski, A (1992) Spatial population mobility in Poland 1952–1985, *Geographia Polonica*, **59**, 41–53.

Gorzelak, G (1996) *The Regional Dimension of Transformation in Central Europe*, Jessica Kingsley, London.

Grabher, G (1994) The disembedded regional economy: the transformation of East German industrial complexes into Western enclaves, in A Amin and N Thrift (eds) *Globalization Institutions and Regional Development in Europe*, Oxford University Press, Oxford, 177–95.

Grimm, F-D (1994) *Zentrensysteme als Trager der Raumentwicklung in Mittel- und Osteuropa*, Institut für Länderkunde, Leipzig.

Hamilton, F E I (1971) Decision making and industrial location in Eastern Europe, *Transactions of the Institute of British Geographers*, **52**, 77–84.

Hegedus, J and Tosics, I (1994) Privatisation and rehabilitation in the Budapest inner district, *Housing Studies*, **9**, 39–54.

Horvath, G (1995) Economic reforms in East-Central Europe, in S Hardy (ed) *An Enlarged Europe: regions in competition?*, Jessica Kingsley, London, 35–52.

Horvath, G and Hrubi, L (1992) *Restructuring and Regional Policy in Hungary*, Centre for Regional Studies, Hungarian Academy of Sciences, Pecs.

Ivan, L (1994) Spatial structure of the central system of the Budapest agglomeration, *GeoJournal*, **32**, 415–23.

Kaliberda, A (1994) The interregional association of transborder trade in the Carpathian Euroregion, in F Grief (ed) *Die Zukunft der landlichen Infrastruktur in Ostmitteleuropa*, Schriftenreihe der Bundesanstalt für Agrarwirtschaft 75, Vienna, 199–202.

Kapitanski, Y and Anastasova, M (1994) Problems of social insurance in the agricultural sector during the transition to a market economy, in F Grief (ed) *Die Zukunft der landlichen Infrastruktur in Ostmitteleuropa*, Schriftenreihe der Bundesanstalt für Agrarwirtschaft 75, Vienna, 33–8.

Klodzinski, M (1992) Processes of agricultural change in Eastern Europe, in R M Auty and R B Potter (eds) *Agricultural Change, Environment and Economy*, Mansell, London, 123–37.

Kratke, S (1996) *Where East Meets West: prospects of the German–Polish border region*, Europa-Universität Viadrina Faculty of Cultural Sciences, Frankfurt/Oder.

Kurek, W (1996) Agriculture versus tourism in rural areas of the Polish Carpathians. *GeoJournal*, **38**, 191–6.

Nefedova, T and Trejvis, A (1994) *First Socio-economic Effects of Transformation of Central and Eastern Europe*, Osterreichisches Ost- und Südosteuropa-Institut, Vienna.

Nemes, N (1994) Regional disparities in Hungary during the period of transition to a market economy, *GeoJournal*, **32**, 363–8.

Pavlinek, P (1992) Regional transformation in Czechoslovakia: towards a market economy, *Tijdschrift voor Economische en Sociale Geografie*, **83**, 361–71.

Pedersen, J S (1993) The Baltic region and the new Europe, in R Cappellin and P W J Batey (eds) *Regional Networks, Border Regions and European Integration*, Pion, London, 135–56.

Pine, F (1993) "The cows and pigs are his, the eggs are mine": women's domestic economy and entrepreneurial activity in rural Poland, in C M Hann (ed) *Socialism: ideals, ideologies and local practice*, Routledge, London, 227–42.

Pudney, S (1995) Income distribution and the reform of public housing in Hungary, *Economics of Transition*, **3**, 75–106.

Quack, S and Maier, F (1994) From state socialism to market economy: women's employment in Eastern Germany, *Environment and Planning A*, **26**, 1257–76.

Roesler, J (1991) Mass unemployment in eastern Germany, *Journal of European Social Policy*, **1**, 129–50.

Ronge, V (1991) Social change in Eastern Europe, *Journal of European Social Policy*, **1**, 49–56.

Rupp, K (1992) Democracy, market and social safety nets: implications for postcommunist Eastern Europe, *Journal of Public Policy*, **12**, 37–59.

Sadler, D (1993) The automobile industry and Eastern Europe: new production strategies or old solutions?, *Area*, **25**, 339–49.

Stebelsky, I (1995) *The Food System in the Post-Soviet Era*, Westview, Boulder, Colo.

Swain, N (1994) *Agricultural Development Policy in the Czech Republic: is one really necessary?*, University of Liverpool Centre for Central and East European Studies, Working Papers, Rural Transition Series, 34.

Szelenyi, I (1983) *Urban Inequalities Under State Socialism*, Oxford University Press, Oxford.

Toth, J (1993) Historical and today's socio-economic conditions of regionalism in Hungary, in A Duro (ed) *Spatial Research and the Socio-political Changes*, Centre for Regional Studies, Hungarian Academy of Sciences, Pecs, 15–28.

Vaishar, A (1992) Ethnic structure of the Czech Republic in the census of 1991 and its connections, *Geographica Slovenica*, **23**, 385–401.

Vaishar, A (1993) Ethnic, religious and social problems of frontier districts in the Czech Republic, *Geographica Slovenica*, **24**, 167–77.

Varga, S (1996) Changes in the agrarian sector of Hungary between 1989 and 1994 with special regard to the North Hungarian hilly regions, *GeoJournal*, **38**, 181–4.

Verdery, K (1994) The elasticity of land: problems of property restitution in Transylvania, *Slavic Review*, **53**, 1071–109.

Vuics, T (1992) The "new" poverty in the environment of Pecs, in W Zsilincsar (ed) *Zur ökonomischen und ökologischen Problematik der Stadte Ostmitteleuropas nach der politischen Wende*, Karl Franzens Universität Institut für Geographie, Graz, 53–66.

Zaniewski, K (1991) Housing inequalities under socialism: the case of Poland, *Geoforum*, **22**, 39–53.

18

The challenge of agricultural restructuring in the European Union

Brian Ilbery

Department of Geography, Coventry University, UK

Introduction

Farm income levels have long been of widespread concern in western Europe. While certain core agricultural areas are undoubtedly prosperous, low farm incomes have been a very real problem in many peripheral or marginal agricultural areas. One of the original objectives of the Common Agricultural Policy (CAP) in 1957 was to ensure a fair standard of living for the agricultural community, and in practice the policy has certainly played an important role in providing support for farm families. Recently, however, urgently needed reform of the CAP has meant a fairly radical rethink of that support in order to achieve a shift towards what has been termed a post-productivist farming system (Shucksmith, 1993). These changes have big implications for the economic and social well-being of many farming communities, especially those located in marginal agricultural areas.

Against a background of changing policy, this chapter aims to examine the challenge of agricultural restructuring in the EU; in particular it seeks to explore the ways in which farm families are attempting to maintain or increase income levels. Following a review of the characteristic features of the transition to a post-productivist agricultural system, the discussion charts agricultural policy reform in the EU since the mid-1980s, placing particular emphasis on the rationale and evolution of the set-aside policy. The spatially varied uptake of set-aside is then detailed, together with the ways in which farmers have used set-aside to strengthen their position by raising income and restructuring their businesses. The final section focuses on how farm families can adjust to the post-productivist transition, particularly through pluriactivity. This is seen as a potentially important means of supporting farm incomes and lessening farmers' dependence on an agricultural policy which is being made less socially oriented and more focused on economic and environmental issues.

The Post-productivist Transition

Agriculture in the EU has undergone two major phases of restructuring in the post-war period.

The first phase of agricultural *productivism* lasted until the mid-1980s and was characterised by a continuous modernisation and industrialisation of agriculture, with an emphasis on raising farm output through high levels of government support (Ilbery, 1990a). The second phase of *post-productivism* has developed since the mid-1980s and is characterised by the integration of agriculture within broader rural economic and environmental objectives, with an emphasis on reducing farm output.

Stimulated by overproduction and the environmental disbenefits of productivist agriculture, the transition to post-productivism does not, however, signal the end of productivist farm systems. Rather, two diverging systems are likely to coexist: first, an intensive, high input–high output system of farming which emphasises food *quantity*; and second, an extensive, low input–low output system of farming which emphasises sustainability and food *quality*.

Although the nature of post-productivist agriculture has yet to be defined by governments and society in developed market economies, a number of attributes can be identified for what has been referred to as the *post-productivist transition* (PPT) (Lowe *et al.*, 1993; Shucksmith, 1993; Ilbery and Bowler, 1998). These include:

- A reduction in food output
- Progressive withdrawal of state subsidies for agriculture
- The production of food within an increasingly competitive international market
- Growing environmental regulation of agriculture
- The creation of a more sustainable agricultural system

The PPT can be interpreted in terms of the progressive reversal of three trends which characterised the modernisation of agriculture during the productivist era. Following Bowler and Ilbery (1997), these bipolar opposites involve

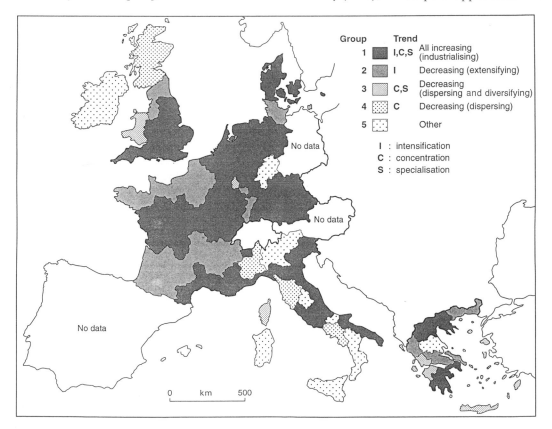

Figure 18.1   *Agricultural restructuring in the EC, 1979–87 (Bowler and Ilbery, 1997)*

the moves from *intensification* to *extensification*, from *specialisation* to *diversification*, and from *concentration* to *dispersion*. The first two have been actively encouraged by EU policy, but there has been little apparent attempt to disperse agriculture away from pockets of spatial concentration in core areas. Nevertheless, there are some early signs of a more extensive and diversified system of agriculture developing in some regions of the EU (Figure 18.1). Using data for 1979–87 (before set-aside and CAP reforms), a highly differentiated pattern of agricultural restructuring is apparent between regions, and it is almost certain that these trajectories will have been enhanced by policy reforms since 1988. The continuation of the "industrial" model of agricultural development (group 1) is dominant in much of England, central France, the Netherlands, Belgium and Denmark, and in certain regions in (the former) West Germany and Italy. However, extensification (group 2) is apparent in northern and southern regions of France and in northern England. Similarly, there is some evidence for diversification and dispersion (group 3) in Wales, Corsica, Luxembourg, Crete and the Greek islands, and for dispersion (group 4) in Scotland and three Italian regions – Piedmont, Tuscany and Campania.

The Post-productivist Transition, Policy Reform and Land Diversion

While both productivist and post-productivist phases of agriculture have been manipulated by state intervention, the PPT is being shaped by a rapidly changing international policy context. In particular, reforms of the CAP in 1992, the GATT[1] agreement on world agricultural trade in 1993, and the convergence between agricultural and environmental policy in the EU following the Earth Summit of 1992 (Agenda 21) have been instrumental in the move towards post-productivism.

Policy-makers in the EU realised in the mid-1980s that an agricultural system which does not produce for the market has few long-term prospects. Reform of the CAP thus became a priority and was based on three objectives (Ilbery, 1992a): first, to adjust supply to demand; second, to provide support (income) for farmers

experiencing difficulty during the adjustment period; and third, to increase concern for the protection of the environment.

A series of initial measures to control agricultural production was introduced in 1984. These included co-responsibility levies; guaranteed thresholds for cereals, sunflower seeds, processed fruit and raisins; and compulsory quotas in the milk sector (Robinson and Ilbery, 1993). Also introduced were such environmental measures as Environmentally Sensitive Areas (ESAs) and a farm woodland scheme, plus extra funding for diversification into tourism and crafts in less favoured areas (LFAs). However, a major effort to control the production of cereals came in 1988 with the introduction of set-aside, or land diversion (Regulation 1094/88). Land diversion involves compensating farmers for taking agricultural land out of production for a specified period of time. When it was introduced in 1988, estimates of the amount of land surplus to requirements in the EU ranged from 7 to 12 million ha (Conrad, 1987). Although compulsory for member states (with the exception of Portugal), set-aside was voluntary for individual farmers, who were to be compensated (by between 100 and 600 ECU per ha) for taking at least 20 per cent of their arable land out of production altogether for five years. The retired land could be left fallow (on either a permanent or a rotational basis), planted with trees or used for non-agricultural purposes (such as recreation).

By the late 1980s, however, it was becoming increasingly clear that production control measures were not solving the major problems of EU agriculture. Thus the European Commission recast the objectives of policy reform in agriculture, to include a more restrictive pricing policy involving a gradual scaling down of support prices for products in surplus; further application of the principle of producer co-responsibility, in which producers are made to bear a larger share of the costs of disposing of surplus production; and limits on intervention guarantees (stabilisers), coupled with a more stringent policy on quality in order to meet market requirements (Robinson and Ilbery, 1993).

A central aim since the late 1980s, therefore, has been to make producers more subject to market controls by reducing support prices and subsidies, with production above a specified limit resulting in a fall in average returns to the farmer. This aim has been translated into action through, first, the MacSharry proposals in 1991 and, second, the CAP reforms in 1992.

The MacSharry proposals

In 1991 the then agricultural Commissioner, Raymond MacSharry, presented a package of proposals to reform the CAP. The package consisted of a series of main points (Table 18.1) and advocated, for the first time, substantial cuts in support prices for cereals, with smaller cuts for milk, beef and butter. Controls on sheep farming were also advocated, together with extensions to the 1988 set-aside programme and early retirement for farmers. The proposals represented a concerted attack on the CAP's price guarantee system, linked with a framework of "income aid" to compensate farmers with small and medium-sized farms for their projected loss of income.

Not surprisingly, the proposals met opposition from farming bodies and some EU farm ministers, who felt that their own national interests might be damaged by these proposals. In particular, the UK criticised the suggestion of concentrating income aid on small and medium-sized farm businesses, and thus leaving the larger farms (many of which are concentrated in the UK) to compete in international markets with significantly reduced levels of price support. Nevertheless, the MacSharry proposals occupied an important position in the ongoing GATT negotiations and showed that the EU was willing to forward concrete proposals for restricting agricultural

Table 18.1 *The main MacSharry proposals*

1. Switching of support from prices to farm incomes
2. Breaking the links between price support and food production (decoupling)
3. Substantial cuts in price support, especially cereals (30%) but also beef and butter (15%) and milk (10%)
4. Compulsory set-aside of arable land
5. Income aid to smaller farms who set aside land
6. Provision for improved early retirement scheme for farmers at 55

support. Indeed, MacSharry engendered further discussions between farm ministers and quickened the pace towards final reform of the CAP.

Reform of the CAP

After 18 months of negotiations, agreement on restructuring the CAP was reached in May 1992. This attempted to break the link between farm incomes and the volume of food produced (decoupling) through a movement away from high support prices for food towards direct income aid for farmers. Such aid could be in the form of compensation for lower guaranteed prices and/or payments for "farming the countryside". The reform package sought to achieve:

1. A better balance of agricultural markets, through more effective control of production and keener efforts to stimulate demand.
2. More competitiveness in European agriculture, both internally and on the international market, through substantial price reductions.
3. More extensive methods of production, thus helping to conserve the environment and reduce surpluses.
4. A measure of support redistribution to benefit the more vulnerable enterprises.
5. Continued employment for an appropriate number of farmers.

Farmers were to be compensated for their loss of income from lower support prices and the measures were to be introduced progressively over a three-year period (from 1993). Especially in marginal areas, this delay was to allow them time to adjust to the new situation. The total reform package was quite complex, but the main measures are summarised in Table 18.2. Guaranteed prices for cereals were cut by 29 per cent over three years and, to compensate, *all* farmers became eligible for income aid in the form of area-based direct payments, irrespective of farm size. (Note the change from the MacSharry proposals.) However, these payments were made available only if farmers set aside a proportion of their arable land on a rotational basis over six years. (This proportion was 15 per cent in 1993/94, but varies in line with forecasts of market needs so that it was as low as 5 per cent in 1996/97.) Non-rotational set-aside is

Table 18.2 *Reforms proposed by EU farm ministers, May 1992*

Main points

1. 29% cut in cereal support over three years
2. Compensation for rotational set-aside (15% of arable area initially)
3. Set-aside to be compulsory for farmers wishing to qualify for regionally based income aid payable on each hectare of land left in arable production (i.e. on remaining 85% of original arable area)
4. Removal of co-responsibility levies
5. Farmers allowed to withdraw from original (voluntary) set-aside scheme
6. New non-rotational set-aside to be introduced
7. Additional aid for environmental protection, forestry and early retirement (accompanying measures)

also possible (18 per cent of arable area) and farmers can cultivate set-aside land for non-food crops (e.g. biofuels). So, farmers receive a lower guaranteed price for their cereals, plus regionally determined income aid (area payments) on the 85 per cent of arable land still in production and set-aside payments on the remaining 15 per cent. Effectively, set-aside is now compulsory if arable farmers wish to qualify for income aid, except for those producing less than 92 t. The co-responsibility levy was abolished in 1992/93. In the beef and sheep sector, meanwhile, a system of quotas was introduced to limit the number of livestock on which farmers can receive payments (Wynne, 1994); milk quotas were also retained. All of these changes are controlled through an integrated administration and control system (IACS), established under Regulation 3887/92; by completing annual returns, farmers have to report all details of crops, livestock and set-aside to this system.

Reform of the CAP also required member states to implement a package of "accompanying measures". These related to the afforestation of farm land, a new early retirement scheme and an ambitious agri-environmental action programme (Regulation 2078/92). The latter sought to limit agricultural production by encouraging farmers to adopt more extensive and less polluting farming practices. In today's world, it was argued, farmers needed to recognise their "public interest" role for

land management and protection of natural resources. Farmers participating voluntarily in this environmental protection programme for five years are financially compensated for loss of income if they abide by one or more of the following requirements:

- Substantial reduction in the use of fertilisers and/or the introduction or continuation of organic farming methods
- Change to more extensive forms of crop and livestock production
- Use of other farming practices beneficial to the environment and natural resource protection
- Upkeep of abandoned land
- Long-term set-aside of agricultural land for environmental reasons
- Land management for public access and leisure activities

For all accompanying measures, 50 per cent of the eligible expenditure is borne by the EU budget (75 per cent in Objective 1 regions). Each member state was asked to submit, and have approved by the end of 1993, an agri-environmental package. As an example, the UK's proposals included more ESAs, access to ESAs and set-aside land, new nitrate measures, an organic farming scheme, a moorland scheme, and a habitat improvement scheme through long-term set-aside (Table 18.3; Potter, 1993). These schemes are now operational, but still await detailed research.

Completion of the GATT negotiations in 1993 served to strengthen the CAP reforms, through agreements to reduce price support, export subsidies and border controls on agricultural commodities around the world (Arden-Clarke, 1992). In fact, the EU agreed to cut the volume and value of subsidised exports by 21 and 35 per cent respectively, and to limit the area of oilseeds to 5.13 million ha. Free access to the EU market is also to be allowed for imports of 3 per cent (and eventually 5 per cent) of the internal consumption of agricultural commodities produced within the EU. According to Naylor (1995, 283), the overall effect of the CAP reforms and GATT agreement is likely to be "a redistribution of aid to the less intensive and less well off areas, particularly within the livestock sector, and hence a contribution to the reduction in regional income disparities".

Table 18.3   *The UK's agri-environmental package, 1993*

Proposed scheme	Main objective
New ESAs	Extension of existing scheme, to increase ESA area to 1.17 million ha
Public access to ESAs	To enhance public enjoyment of the countryside
New nitrate measures	To protect groundwater catchments affected by high nitrate levels
Moorland scheme	To reduce the number of livestock grazing on moorland in areas outside ESAs
Set-aside management	To enhance the environmental value of lowland set-aside, including public access to set-aside land
Habitat improvement scheme	To encourage the long-term set-aside of land in areas suitable for conservation and wildlife
Organic farming	To provide aid for conversion of conventional systems to organic methods

Source: Based on various documents by the Ministry of Agriculture, Fisheries and Food.

However, the reform package does not modify the fundamental principles of the CAP, and problems therefore remain. For example, many agri-environmental schemes are restricted to a limited number of designated areas and are effectively "bolted on" to an economically driven policy (Robinson, 1991; Ilbery, 1992b). The CAP also remains full of contradictions: on the one hand, new technologies are being encouraged (e.g. genetic engineering) to develop higher yields yet, on the other hand, the EU is seeking to regulate and limit farmers' rights to produce food. While there may be a redistribution of aid to farmers and a decline in the total agricultural area as a result of CAP reforms, the spatial dispersion of production is not a likely outcome. Instead it is highly probable that the process which increasingly concentrates output in the most favourable areas will continue. This in turn will widen income disparities even further and create socio-economic problems for farm families in marginal agricultural areas.

Land diversion

Set-aside has become an important element of the PPT in EU agriculture, but its impact has been geographically uneven. Details on the uptake of the initial five-year scheme can be found elsewhere (Ilbery, 1990b, 1992a) and it is sufficient to note here that the initial response to set-aside in the EU was disappointing. After two years, less than

800 000 ha had been retired, equivalent to 1.3 per cent of the arable land and 2 per cent of the cereal area in the EU. By 1992, when the new scheme was announced, less than 2 million ha (2.6 and 5 per cent of arable land and the cereal area respectively) were set aside. Nationally, patterns of uptake were very uneven (Table 18.4), with Italy and the former West Germany accounting for over 60 per cent of the total. At the other extreme, there was minimal response from Denmark, Greece, Belgium, Luxembourg, Ireland and, to a lesser extent, France. (Portugal was exempt from the initial five-year scheme.)

Such varied rates of uptake can be explained in terms of two main factors: different levels of interest in, and commitment to, land diversion as a production control measure; and contrasting rates of compensation offered to farmers. While West Germany and the UK were strong advocates of land diversion, there was considerable opposition in southern states and such northern countries as France and Denmark. For example, because France was concerned that set-aside would damage its position as a major world exporter of agricultural products, a policy of extensification rather than set-aside was considered to be more appropriate as it would help to keep marginal agricultural areas in production. Similarly, Denmark advocated that each country should be allowed to introduce its own measures, as long as they reduced agricultural production by an agreed amount. As a consequence, Denmark was late in implementing set-aside.

Table 18.4   *National patterns of set-aside in the EU*

Country	1988–1992*		1993/94[+]	
	Area (ha)	% of EU total	Area (ha)	% of EU total
Belgium	880	0.05	19 000	0.41
Denmark	12 813	0.74	208 000	4.52
Germany	479 260	27.78	1 050 000	22.80
Greece	713	0.04	15 000	0.33
Spain	103 169	5.98	875 000	19.00
France	235 492	13.65	1 578 000	34.27
Italy	721 847	41.82	195 000	4.23
Ireland	3452	0.20	26 000	0.56
Luxembourg	91	0.01	2000	0.04
Netherlands	15 373	0.89	8000	0.17
Portugal	Exempt	–	61 000	1.32
United Kingdom	152 700	8.85	568 000	12.33
Total	1 725 790	100.00	4 605 000	100.00

* Voluntary set-aside.
[+] Compulsory set-aside.
Source: DG VI, European Commission.

Member states were allowed to fix rates of compensation between 100 and 600 ECU per ha, rising to 700 ECU in exceptional circumstances; they could also vary rates between different areas and according to particular criteria (e.g. land quality, less favoured areas, irrigated areas). The outcome was that some countries set flat rates of compensation (very high in the case of the Netherlands and low in both Ireland and Luxembourg), while other countries set variable rates (for example, high in the case of West Germany and quite low in the UK). Whatever the mechanism, however, in nearly all cases rates of compensation for set-aside were lower than farmers' potential earnings from growing cereals. This was especially so in such high-yielding cereal production areas as the Paris basin, the Po valley and East Anglia. In turn, this suggested that set-aside would be more attractive in marginal rather than core cereal-growing areas. Such a view has been confirmed in studies of the uptake of set-aside by Briggs and Kerrell (1992) and Ilbery (1992a) at the EU level, Jones (1991) and Jones *et al.* (1993) in West Germany, and Ilbery (1990b) in the UK. After two years of the scheme, Briggs and Kerrell (1992, 94) confirmed that it had not been sufficiently targeted on the key cereal growing areas in north and south-west France, the north

German plain, south and eastern England, northern Italy, northern Denmark and parts of Greece. Instead, set-aside was "concentrated in more marginal cereal-growing areas, where yields are lower and cereals are a smaller component of the agricultural system". Using multiple regression techniques, the same authors were also able to confirm that "adoption of set-aside is greatest in areas with a high proportion of land under cereals and relatively young farmers, but lower yields and population densities" (p. 98). This supports the generally held view that younger farmers are more innovative because they are aware of what is on offer (Ilbery and Bowler, 1993b). However, it also throws some doubt on the ability of voluntary schemes to initiate land-use change on farms which lack a history of change and innovation (Potter and Gasson, 1988).

The spatial pattern of set-aside uptake for the 1988–91 period is shown in Figure 18.2. Using the location quotient (LQ) statistic, where a value of over 1.0 highlights those areas setting aside more land than their area of arable land would suggest, regions of relatively high and low adoption can be seen. The main areas of concentration (LQ > 4) are in Sicily and Sardinia and around Potenza, Pisa and Siena on the Italian mainland. Italy and West Germany also dominate other areas of relative

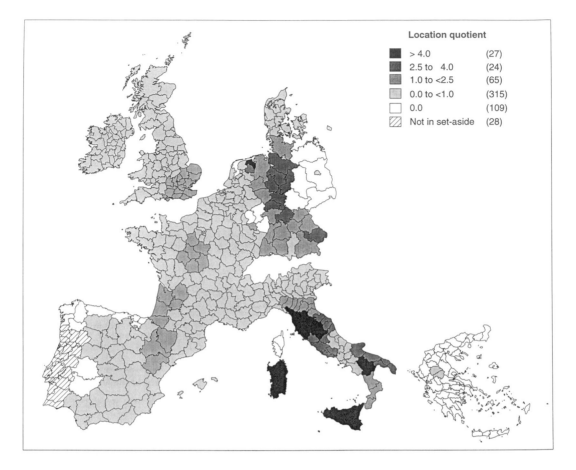

Figure 18.2 *Spatial patterns of set-aside uptake in the EU, 1988–91*

concentration (LQ 2.5–4). These include the heel of Italy, based on Bari and Taranto, the Rome and Ancona regions, and a large area in West Germany running from Lüneburg in the north to Unterfranken in the south. South-east England, the Paris basin, south-west France and north-east Spain join other parts of Italy and West Germany in having a less concentrated, but nevertheless significant, pattern of set-aside uptake (LQ 1–2.5). Figure 18.2 is also instructive in highlighting the relative lack of set-aside in such peripheral areas as Ireland, Scotland, northern Denmark, Spain and Greece. Farmers in just two regions of Greece – Thessalia and Karditsa – had joined the set-aside scheme by 1991.

Similar patterns of set-aside uptake were reported within England and West Germany. In England, set-aside was not concentrated in the "core" cereal-producing area of East Anglia and Humberside, but in those (marginal) areas with a weak competitive ability in cereals and a strong competitive ability in both mixed and part-time farming (Bowler and Ilbery, 1989). This meant a relative concentration of set-aside in the south-east and in close proximity to London in particular (Figure 18.3a), possibly reflecting market opportunities for other gainful activities (OGAs) and farm-based diversification (Ilbery, 1990b). Jones *et al*. (1993) confirmed the tendency for set-aside to focus on marginal cereal areas in a study of Rheinland-Pfalz in Germany. However, their survey also found that many farmers were using set-aside to restructure their farm businesses. Far removed from the original objective of introducing set-aside to control the output of cereals, farmers were using the financial payments from the scheme to secure generational continuity of the farm business; postpone new rounds of

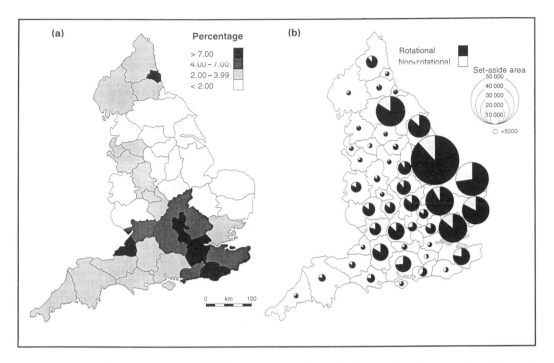

Figure 18.3 *The distribution of set-aside land in England: (a) 1991 (voluntary scheme) and (b) 1993 (compulsory scheme)*

capital investment in the farm; secure non-agricultural income; act as a pre-retirement strategy to run down the business; and make hired labour redundant.

Not surprisingly for a voluntary scheme, the amount of land set aside was relatively low and the overall impact was minimal because farmers were allowed to set aside their poorest arable land and intensify production on the remaining arable area. Consequently, production tended not to fall in proportion to the amount of land retired (slippage) and, despite a cost of 185 million ECU in 1988–89, cereal output in the EU hardly fell at all. In addition, set-aside had few environmental benefits because small and fragmented parcels of land were diverted out of production; far greater benefits would have occurred by targeting large tracts of land suitable for conservation.

In 1993, following reforms of the CAP, 4.6 million ha were set aside in the EU (Table 18.4). Just over one-third of this figure came from France, a major increase on its relatively low contribution under the voluntary scheme. The other major change involved Italy, which moved

from being the dominant "player" in 1988–92 to being almost insignificant under the compulsory scheme. As farmers are allowed to remain in the original voluntary set-aside scheme, this may help to account for the large discrepancy in the Italian figures between 1988–92 and 1993. Spain, the UK and Denmark have increased their relative proportion of set-aside land, while Germany joins Italy in recording a relative percentage decline.

By the 1994/95 agricultural year, 5.9 million ha of arable land had been set aside, an increase of 1.3 million ha (30 per cent). This reflected a rise in the premiums awarded and the availability of non-rotational and voluntary set-aside in addition to the rotational option. Including the old five-year scheme, the total area of set-aside had reached 7.2 million ha by 1995. One consequence of compulsory set-aside has been the better targeting of "core" cereal areas. However, this has been mainly on a rotational basis which yields few environmental and landscape benefits. In England, for example, the core cereal areas in East Anglia and Humberside are now setting aside more arable land (Figure 18.3b), but less than 20 per cent of the 553 175 ha involved in 1994 was non-rotational. Thus, set-aside continues to be criticised for its lack of environmental concern (Craighill and Goldsmith, 1994). This is why EU countries have been encouraged to consider long-term set-aside as part of their agri-environmental package. In the case of the UK, a voluntary 20-year Habitat Improvement Scheme has been introduced to present an opportunity for constructive use of set-aside land. But it is likely that less than 10 000 ha will be attracted into such a scheme and, until environmental conditions are attached to livestock headage and arable area payments (cross-compliance), set-aside is likely to remain a limited tool of environmental management.

Despite limited environmental benefits, the European Commission claims that the package of reform measures has been an undoubted success. They point to the following economic benefits:

1. An increase in the amount of arable land taken out of production.
2. A fall in cereal production since 1991, from 181 million t in that year to 161 million in 1994. Without compulsory set-aside, there is little doubt that cereal production would have continued to rise because of increasing yields per hectare. Effectively, therefore, the fall in production has been more than the recorded 20 million t.
3. A fall in stockpiles of grain, from 30 million tonnes in 1991 to less than 10 million in 1995. However, this caused an increase in cereal prices to levels well above those for intervention (support price). As a result rotational set-aside was reduced to 11 per cent and may be cut even further in future years.
4. A decline in beef intervention stocks, from 1.1 million t in 1991 to less than 100 000 t in 1994.
5. An increase in the use of EU cereals in animal feed because of their improved competitiveness following the decline in support prices.
6. A fall in the use of fertilisers and pesticides, as a result of less cereal production.
7. An increase in farm incomes, by over 10 per cent in some countries.

Today, therefore, more money from the CAP goes to farmers and less is used on storing surpluses and subsidising exports on the world markets. It would seem that EU farmers are becoming more competitive in the international arena, and there can be little doubt that the balance between supply and demand is much improved. Even so, the policy environment is now more fluid and there is increasing concern over the budgetary and environmental implications of the CAP. This in turn highlights the danger of farm families being over-dependent on CAP support. As a consequence, they have been encouraged to find alternative ways of maintaining or increasing their incomes. One popular option, especially for farmers not fortunate enough to be located in prosperous agricultural areas, has been to gain income from a range of non-agricultural activities, both on and off the farm.

Pluriactivity, the Post-productivist Transition and Farming Communities

There are a number of ways in which farm families can try to adjust to the PPT and thus ease financial pressures by maintaining or raising income levels. These have been termed *pathways of farm business development* (Bowler, 1992; Ilbery and Bowler, 1993a) and are summarised in Table 18.5. They fall neatly into three main strategies:

1. Maintaining a full-time, profitable food production element to the farm business (pathways 1 and 2).
2. Diversifying the income base by redirecting resources into non-farm enterprises and occupations (pathways 3 and 4).
3. Surviving as a marginalised farm business at a lower level of income, perhaps supported by investment income, pensions and other direct state payments (pathways 5 and 6).

The pathways are not mutually exclusive and so farm families may follow more than one pathway simultaneously. They may also make the transition from pathway 1 through to pathway 6, but once marginalised it is highly unlikely for a farm business to "move back" towards pathway 1. Because of their different histories, farming traditions and resource bases, it is likely that different localities will lend themselves to particular combinations of pathways. Although more research is needed on the spatial dimensions

Table 18.5 *Pathways of farm business development*

1. Extension of the industrial model of farm business development based on traditional products and services on the farm
2. Redeployment of farm resources (including human capital) into new agricultural products or services on the farm (agricultural diversification)
3. Redeployment of farm resources (including human capital) into new non-agricultural products or services on the farm (structural diversification)
4. Redeployment of human capital into an off-farm occupation (OGA)
5. Maintenance of traditional farm production and services with reduced capital inputs (extensification)
6. Hobby or part-time (semi-retired) farming

Sources: Bowler (1992); Ilbery and Bowler (1993a).

of agricultural restructuring and pathways of farm business development, a case study in the marginal agricultural region of the northern Pennines in England has shown that 80 per cent of farm households examined are following just one pathway (Bowler *et al.*, 1996). Not surprisingly for an EU less favoured area (LFA), only 12 per cent are following the "industrial" model of agriculture; in contrast, the traditional model of extensive farming dominates (pathway 5, 45 per cent), and is followed by other gainful activities off the farm (pathway 4, 33 per cent) and on-farm diversification (pathway 3, 29 per cent). It would seem, therefore, that in such difficult agricultural areas other pathways are considered only when traditional farming is unable to address the income needs of farm families. In other words, there is an apparent resistance by farm families to raising income from sources other than mainstream farming. This in turn suggests that there is considerable divergence between what policy-makers think should happen in theory and what is actually happening in practice.

It is possible to identify different types of farm household through different combinations of pathways (Marsden *et al.*, 1989; Ward and Lowe, 1994). *Accumulators* are more innovative and risk taking; they run large farm businesses and are able to redeploy capital and labour into on-farm diversification and agri-environmental initiatives. In contrast, *disengagers* often have small farms; they lack capital and so redeploy labour into OGAs off the farm. *Survivors* continue with traditional farming and often resist other pathways, although they may become "passive" adopters of agri-environmental schemes (Morris and Potter, 1995) and such agriculturally related OGAs as contracting.

Pluriactivity (pathways 3 and 4) has a long tradition in parts of the EU, but it has assumed unaccustomed relevance as post-productivist agricultural policies have developed since the mid-1980s. Defined as the generation, by farm household members, of income from either on- and/or off-farm sources to supplement earnings from primary agriculture, *pluriactivity* involves both on-farm *diversification* (Figure 18.4) and off-farm *other gainful activities*. The two elements of pluriactivity were, for a long time, examined in isolation, with OGAs incorrectly referred to as part-time farming, and farm diversification being typically divided into agricultural and structural activities. (The former included unconventional crop and livestock enterprises, farm woodland management, etc., while the latter added value through direct marketing and/or processing and also included farm-based tourism.) However, since the late 1980s research has been directed towards the wider and all-embracing concept of pluriactivity (MacKinnon *et al.*, 1991).

There can be little doubt that the incidence of pluriactivity in the EU has been increasing during the PPT. The proportion of farm household income arising from pluriactivity in France, for example, increased from 15 per cent in 1956 to 42 per cent in 1988, with regional variations between 25 and 52 per cent (Benjamin, 1994). Indeed, one major research project conducted by the Arkleton Trust in 24 regions of western Europe in the late 1980s suggested that 58 per cent of farm households are pluriactive (Fuller, 1990). By far the greatest proportion of pluriactivity was shown to be off-farm (over 50 per cent of all households compared with less than 10 per cent of households with on-farm diversification). However, this

Figure 18.4 *Tapping the tourist trade. A mountain farm in the Fimba valley, Silvretta Alps, Austria, offers summer walkers refreshments and farm produce. (Photo: D A Pinder)*

varied considerably between regions, from highs of 81 per cent in Freyung-Grafenau (Germany) and 72 per cent in West Bothnia (Sweden) to lows of 27 per cent in Picardy (France) and 33 per cent in Andalucia (Spain). Moreover, the breakdown of whether the operator, spouse or other family members have regular off-farm work also differs markedly (Table 18.6). For example, while both Freyung-Grafenau and Agueda (Portugal) have high rates of off-farm work, in the former this is dominated by the operator and, to a smaller extent, by other family members; whereas in Agueda there is a more even spread between operators, spouses and the remainder of the family. In none of the regions are there more spouses than operators involved in off-farm work, and in only five regions (in Italy, Spain, Ireland and Austria) do other family members outnumber operators.

Given these figures, it is not surprising that the Arkleton Trust project found that one-third of farm households obtained more than 50 per cent of their income from off-farm sources. This varied from a low of 10 per cent in Picardy to a high of 71 per cent in Freyung-Grafenau and generally reflected the distribution of dependence on non-farm work shown in Table 18.6. When the data were aggregated for the 24 regions, it was found that just 17 per cent of all farm households derive all of their income from agriculture; in contrast, 43 per cent derive less than 30 per cent of total household income from farming.

Thus it would seem from the Arkleton study that simple geographical patterns of pluriactivity do not exist in western Europe. As Fuller (1990, 368) concludes, "the degree of pluriactivity depends upon an interplay of farming, household and labour market characteristics, as well as cultural factors". Moreover, evidence from other studies similarly suggests that geographical patterns of pluriactivity in the EU reflect the interaction of a number of factors operating both externally and internally to the farm business. For example, a relationship has been shown to exist between regional socio-economic conditions (e.g.

Table 18.6 *Off-farm pluriactivity in European regions*

Region	% households with OFW*	% households with regular OFW:		
		Farmer	Spouse	Other family member
Freyung-Grafenau (FRG)	81	56	4	21
West Bothnia (Sweden)	72	57	11	4
Austria (West)	70	23	15	33
Austria (SE)	69	36	12	22
Agueda (Portugal)	68	29	22	17
Euskirchen (FRG)	65	41	4	20
Udine (Italy)	53	20	9	24
S. Lazio (Italy)	50	30	6	14
Asturias (Spain)	48	14	13	21
Languedoc (France)	48	36	8	4
Buckingham (UK)	44	25	14	5
Maas-Waal (Neth.)	44	27	7	10
Le Chablais (Switz.)	44	31	6	7
Ireland (East)	43	18	6	19
Devon (UK)	43	20	13	10
Calabria (Italy)	43	30	2	11
Grampion (UK)	40	20	12	8
Fthiotis (Greece)	40	26	4	10
Catalunya (Spain)	39	13	8	18
Korinthia (Greece)	36	22	3	11
Andalucia (Spain)	33	18	4	11
Ireland (West)	33	14	5	14
Savoy (France)	33	15	6	12
Picardy (France)	27	8	13	6

* Off-farm work.
Source: Fuller (1990).

local labour markets, unemployment, tourist activities) and rates of pluriactivity (Efstratoglou-Todoulou, 1990; MacKinnon *et al.*, 1991). Thus, pluriactivity is further developed in those regions where labour markets are well structured and diverse. Nevertheless, the evidence is not conclusive and a study of Scottish pluriactivity, for example, found that OGAs were more important in the least densely populated areas, reflecting social and cultural rather than economic factors (Edmond and Crabtree, 1994). The growing participation of women in the labour force for social rather than economic reasons is one such example of non-economic influences becoming important in the expansion of pluriactivity. Similarly, local cultural factors, and specific landscape designations such as National Parks, have been shown to be important in the distribution of pluriactivity in Wales (Bateman and Ray, 1994).

Because different types of pluriactivity are affected by different combinations of factors, spatial patterns of pluriactivity may be best explained in terms of personal preferences and "internal" household characteristics. This is the conclusion reached in a study of on-farm diversification in England and Wales, where "adopters" were shown to share certain characteristics which distinguished them from "non-adopters" (Ilbery and Bowler, 1993b). For example, they tend to have larger farm businesses, higher net incomes and a greater degree of indebtedness (features associated with accumulators). They are also younger than non-adopters, more educated and in receipt of more formal agricultural training. Stage in the family life-cycle is also a stimulus to farm diversification, with a greater proportion of adopters than non-adopters having successors wishing to continue the farm business. Similar associations have been found between pluriactivity and farm size (small farms favour OGAs and larger farms on-farm diversification), farm type and tenure, and also household composition (Ilbery *et al.*, 1996).

It is the interaction of many factors which shapes broad spatial patterns of pluriactivity and particular concentrations of OGAs and farm diversification. This is best demonstrated by taking two contrasting studies of pluriactivity, in France and Greece. Campagne *et al.* (1990) suggest that different types of region are developing particular forms of pluriactivity according to their own levels of agricultural modernisation. Three contrasting types of region in France were selected for detailed study: Picardy, an area of large farms and specialist arable production in northern France; Languedoc, a wine-growing region in southern France with a long history of combining farming with other work; and the Savoy valleys, a physically marginal area for agriculture in south-east France.

As suggested above, different processes are operating in these regions of varying levels of agricultural modernisation. The consequence has been the development of different types of pluriactivity. For example, the authors found that in Picardy household members are using agricultural resources to increase non-agricultural activities. Many wives work outside agriculture and there is an enterprise culture (accumulation) among the mainly family-based farms. Campagne *et al.* described this as a zone of *business pluriactivity*. However, in Languedoc income generated from mainly off-farm sources, especially by the spouse and children, is used to maintain and sometimes modernise the farm business. This is the *pluriactivity of maintaining farming*. Finally, in the Savoy valleys, farm households combine farming with a diverse range of on- and off-farm income-generating activities. Here, with the progressive abandonment of farming, there emerges *pluriactivity for survival*.

In Greece, Efstratoglou-Todoulou (1990) found pluriactivity to be a widespread phenomenon and not just associated with marginal areas. High rates were reported in regions where non-agricultural activities (e.g. manufacturing and tourism) are well developed, where agricultural structures are favourable, and where

natural resource endowments are poor. To examine regional patterns of pluriactivity in more detail, Efstratoglou-Todoulou hypothesised that the rate of pluriactivity of farm household members in a region is positively related to off-farm opportunities (so-called "pull" factors) and negatively related to favourable farming conditions ("push" factors) in that region. In other words, farm households become pluriactive because they are pushed by constraints on farming and pulled by off-farm opportunities.

Regression analysis confirmed the greater importance of the pull factor of off-farm opportunities over such push factors as farm opportunities and income. However, it was the interaction of push and pull factors that influenced regional patterns of pluriactivity. In particular, pull factors were stronger in areas with low farm incomes and low farm opportunities (i.e. less favoured areas); here pluriactivity had become a *necessity*. Where agricultural structures are favourable and farm opportunities and incomes are high, the impact of pull factors is reduced and the relative importance of push factors increases and exerts a significant inverse effect on pluriactivity. Farm households in such areas thus have alternative opportunities and so pluriactivity is the result of *choice*. Although some of the forces affecting regional patterns of pluriactivity were identified, Efstratoglou-Todoulou (1990) emphasised the need to incorporate "internal" characteristics of the farm household into the modelling exercise in order to gain a better understanding of the geography of pluriactivity in the EU.

It should be stressed that this section has focused on just two of the different pathways of farm business development that characterise the PPT. In reality, the development of one or two pathways should be evaluated in relation to the other available business development options; for example, OGAs could be combined with extensification, just as on-farm diversification could be developed alongside industrial farming. However, more research is needed on this topic, although the northern Pennine case study referred to earlier in the chapter did indicate that only 14 per cent of farm households combined two pathways and just 6 per cent had three or more pathways (Bowler *et al.*, 1996). Even in regions that are constrained by physical handicaps, there is a tendency for farm families to "survive" on traditional farming and to "resist" other pathways of farm business development. The future for such families and farming communities is thus in doubt, leaving policy-makers with the considerable problem of deciding how best to safeguard the social and economic make-up of marginal agricultural areas.

Conclusion

This chapter has provided a range of insights into agricultural restructuring in the EU since the mid-1980s and its spatially uneven impact on farm income levels. Four main points can be made by way of a conclusion, each with important implications for the welfare of rural communities and the geography of European agriculture. First, the pace of agricultural restructuring in the EU has increased significantly from 1984 onwards. In particular, there has been a movement towards post-productivism, characterised by extensification, environmental regulation and sustainable agricultural systems. State support for agriculture is being withdrawn at a time of increasing competition in the global agricultural market. Farmers are having to learn to adjust to this PPT by following different pathways of farm business development. As a consequence, the uneven development associated with productivist agriculture is being deepened during the PPT, as different regions become dominated by different pathway choices. This impacts directly on the prosperity and life prospects of individuals and families comprising many rural communities.

Second, the PPT is being manipulated by the state and in particular by reforms of the CAP and other international policies. Significantly, and for the first time, the CAP reforms of 1992 made substantial cuts in price support and began to decouple farm incomes from the amount of food produced. The reforms also introduced a series of accompanying measures relating especially to environmental objectives. Overall, the CAP reforms are already having different impacts in different areas in Europe, depending on the "commodity mix of production, farm and enterprise sizes (crop areas and livestock

numbers), the impact of set-aside measures, the relevance and likely uptake of 'accompanying measures', and the details of implementation of the regime at national and sub-national level" (Bryden, 1994, 388). As the reforms are concerned mainly with "northern" commodities, they are having most impact on the farming communities in these areas.

Third, pluriactivity has emerged as a characteristic feature of the PPT and is an important pathway of farm business development in many regions across the EU. The incidence of pluriactivity is increasing and the phenomenon is dominated by OGAs, especially on small farms. Spatially, pluriactivity is having a highly varied impact between different types of agricultural economy and region. This relates to such regional socio-economic conditions as local labour markets and unemployment rates and the way in which these interact with internal farm household characteristics, including stage in the family life-cycle, succession and levels of income and indebtedness. It is becoming clear that some farm families, especially in prosperous agricultural lowlands, are adopting pluriactivity as an accumulation strategy; but many others, especially in more remote and physically marginal agricultural regions, are using it as a survival mechanism.

Finally, it is now being realised that agriculture needs to be considered within a much broader rural policy framework (Bryden, 1994). Rural areas are experiencing other changes apart from agricultural restructuring, including counter-urbanisation, rural industrialisation, the growth of service sector employment and environmental enhancement. Such rural diversification is occurring as agriculture becomes more efficient and sheds yet more labour. As diversification takes place within individual farm households, agriculture needs to be viewed as just one element of an integrated rural development policy. Rural development is now high on the political agenda of the EU, and Saraceno (1994, 329, 330) warns that "rural development policies should not just be considered as a way to solve the shortcomings of agricultural policies". Rural development prospects vary for different types of rural region and, especially in remote mountainous areas and those with few alternatives and a heavy dependence on agriculture, the future is far from clear. In this context, Saraceno (1994) feels that "local" and "regional" are more useful concepts than "rural" and "urban". In consequence both she and Bryden (1994) call for more "bottom up" initiatives which cater for local needs. This, perhaps, is the most pressing conclusion to come from this analysis. There is a clear need to localise future development policies as policy-makers strive to meet the evolving challenge of safeguarding the socio-economic well-being of farm families on low incomes.

Acknowledgement

The author acknowledges the information for Figure 18.3 from Elaine Kerrell, Institute of Environmental and Policy Analysis, the University of Huddersfield.

Note

1. General Agreement on Tariffs and Trade. See also Chapter 4.

References

Arden-Clarke, C (1992) Agriculture and environment in the GATT: integration or collision? *Ecos*, **13**, 9–14.

Bateman, D and Ray, C (1994) Farm pluriactivity and rural policy: some evidence from Wales, *Journal of Rural Studies*, **10**, 1–13.

Benjamin, C (1994) The growing importance of diversification activities for French farm households, *Journal of Rural Studies*, **10**, 331–42.

Bowler, I R (1992) Sustainable agriculture as an alternative path of farm business development, in Bowler, I, Bryant, C and Nellis, M (eds) *Rural Systems in Transition: agriculture and environment*, CAB International, Wallingford, 237–53.

Bowler, I R, Clark, G, Crockett, A, Ilbery, B W and Shaw, A (1996) The development of alternative farm enterprises: a study of family labour farms in the north Pennines of England, *Journal of Rural Studies*, **12**, 285–95.

Bowler, I R and Ilbery, B W (1989) The spatial restructuring of agriculture in the English counties, 1976–85, *Tijdschrift voor Economische en Sociale Geografie*, **80**, 302–11.

Bowler, I R and Ilbery, B W (1997) The regional consequences for agriculture of changes to the Common Agricultural Policy, in Laurent, C and Bowler, I (eds) *CAP and the Regions: building a multidisciplinary framework for the analysis of the EU agricultural space*, INRA, Versailles, 105–15.

Briggs, D J and Kerrell, E (1992) Patterns and implications of policy-induced agricultural adjustments in the European Community, in Gilg, A (ed) *Restructuring the Countryside: environmental policy in practice*, Avebury, Aldershot, 85–102.

Bryden, J (1994) Prospects for rural areas in an enlarged Europe, *Journal of Rural Studies*, **10**, 387–94.

Campagne, P, Carrère, G and Valceschini, E (1990) Three agricultural regions of France: three types of pluriactivity, *Journal of Rural Studies*, **4**, 415–22.

Conrad, J (1987) Alternative land use options in the European Community, *Land Use Policy*, **4**, 229–42.

Craighill, A and Goldsmith, E (1994) A future for set-aside?, *Ecos*, **15**, 58–62.

Edmond, H and Crabtree, R (1994) Regional variations in Scottish pluriactivity: the socio-economic context for different types of non-farming activity, *Scottish Geographical Magazine*, **110**, 76–84.

Efstratoglou-Todoulou, S (1990) Pluriactivity in different socio-economic contexts: a test of the push-pull hypothesis in Greek farming, *Journal of Rural Studies*, **6**, 407–13.

Fuller, A M (1990) From part-time farming to pluriactivity: a decade of change in rural Europe, *Journal of Rural Studies*, **6**, 361–73.

Ilbery, B W (1990a) The challenge of land redundancy, in Pinder, D (ed) *Western Europe: challenge and change*, Belhaven, London, 211–25.

Ilbery, B W (1990b) Adoption of the arable set-aside scheme in England, *Geography*, **75**, 69–73.

Ilbery, B W (1992a) Agricultural policy and land diversion in the European Community, in Gilg, A (ed) *Progress in Rural Policy and Planning*, Vol. 2, Belhaven, 153–66.

Ilbery, B W (1992b) From Scott to ALURE – and back again?, *Land Use Policy*, **9**, 131–42.

Ilbery, B W and Bowler, I R (1993a) Land diversion and farm business diversification in EC agriculture, *Nederlandse Geografische Studies*, **172**, 15–27.

Ilbery, B W and Bowler, I R (1993b) The Farm Diversification Grant Scheme: adoption and non-adoption in England and Wales, *Environment and Planning C*, **11**, 161–70.

Ilbery, B W and Bowler, I R (1998) From agricultural productivisim to post-productivism, in Ilbery, B W (ed) *The Geography of Rural Change*, Longman, London, 57–84.

Ilbery, B W, Healey, M J, Higginbottom, J and Noon, D (1996) Agricultural adjustment and business diversification by farm households, *Geography*, **81**, 301–10.

Jones, A (1991) The impact of the EC's set-aside programme: the response of farm businesses in Rendsburg-Eckernforde, Germany, *Land Use Policy*, **8**, 108–24.

Jones, A, Fasterding, F and Plankl, R (1993) Farm household adjustments to the European Community's set-aside policy: evidence from Rheinland-Pfalz (Germany), *Journal of Rural Studies*, **9**, 65–80.

Lowe, P, Murdoch, J, Marsden, T, Munton, R and Flynn, A (1993) Regulating the new rural spaces: the uneven development of land, *Journal of Rural Studies*, **9**, 205–22.

MacKinnon, N, Bryden, J, Bell, C, Fuller, A and Spearman, M (1991) Pluriactivity, structural change and farm household vulnerability in western Europe, *Sociologia Ruralis*, **31**, 58–71.

Marsden, T, Munton, R, Whatmore, S and Little, J (1989) Strategies for coping in capitalist agriculture: an examination of responses of farm businesses in British agriculture, *Geoforum*, **20**, 1–14.

Morris, C and Potter, C (1995) Recruiting the new conservationists, *Journal of Rural Studies*, **11**, 51–63.

Naylor, E (1995) Agricultural policy reforms in France, *Geography*, **80**, 281–3.

Potter, C (1993) Pieces in a jigsaw: a critique of the new agri-environment measures, *Ecos*, **14**, 52–4.

Potter, C and Gasson, R (1988) Farmer participation in voluntary land diversion schemes: some predictions from a survey, *Journal of Rural Studies*, **4**, 365–75.

Robinson, G (1991) EC agricultural policy and the environment: land use implications in the UK, *Land Use Policy*, **8**, 301–11.

Robinson, G and Ilbery, B W (1993) Reforming the CAP: beyond MacSharry, in Gilg, A (ed) *Progress in Rural Policy and Planning*, Vol 3, Belhaven, 197–207.

Saraceno, E (1994) Recent trends in rural development and their conceptualisation, *Journal of Rural Studies*, **10**, 321–30.

Shucksmith, M (1993) Farm household behaviour and the transition to post-productivism, *Journal of Agricultural Economics*, **44**, 466–78.

Ward, N and Lowe, P (1994) Shifting values in agriculture: the farm family and pollution regulation, *Journal of Rural Studies*, **10**, 173–84.

Wynne, P (1994) Agri-environment schemes: recent events and forthcoming attractions, *Ecos*, **15**, 48–52.

19

Agricultural change and rural stress in the new democracies

Tim Unwin

Department of Geography, Royal Holloway, University of London, UK

Introduction

This chapter provides an overview of changes in rural society in the countries of eastern Europe since 1990, paying particular attention to the restructuring of agriculture. It begins by setting these developments within the broader context of changes in European rural society as a whole, focusing largely on the increasing integration of agriculture within the global economy. It then provides a summary of agriculture and rural society during the Soviet period, stressing in particular the great diversity of experiences in different places and at different periods, before analysing some key characteristics of the agrarian restructuring that has taken place during the 1990s. These are seen as having given rise to a range of problems, most notably difficulties associated with the implementation of land reform policies and increasing uncertainty for farmers now having to make decisions within a wider political and economic environment. The chapter concludes with brief case studies of the contrasting experiences of rural change in Poland, Hungary and Estonia.

Throughout this book, the term the "new democracies" has been generally used to refer to the countries that lie to the east of the EU. However, the single word "democracy" covers a wide spectrum of political experience. For Taylor (1994, 272) "Competition for government by multiple parties is at the heart of liberal democracy", but there are many other kinds of democracy (Sartori, 1987; Duncan, 1989), with Smith (1996), for example, seeing Estonia and Latvia as "ethnic democracies" reflecting primarily the interests of the majority ethnic group within them. The rallying cries of many people within eastern Europe during the late 1980s were nevertheless focused on the ideas of "democracy", and the "market economy". Lewis (1992, 2) thus notes that in the early stages of post-Communist change

> "Political democracy has been closely linked with the encouragement of market economics and the retreat of the state from the administration of economic processes; liberalism and the principles of free association have taken over from state organisation and the bureaucratic co-ordination of social life. The development of capitalist, market economies has been formally endorsed as a precondition for and concomitant of the development of political democracy."

Although the precise political and economic characteristics of the regimes which have

1985

Figure 19.1 *The states of eastern Europe, 1985 and 1995*

subsequently emerged remain relatively unstable and uncertain, most have followed a path which has led to the increased operation of market forces in the economy, and less direct government intervention in these processes. It is with the implications of these changes for people living in rural areas that this chapter is concerned.

Turnock (1989) has emphasised that it was the rise of Russia as a superpower based on Marxist ideology that converted the heart of Europe into a geopolitical watershed and gave special significance to the states to the east of this divide. In his words, "A substantial part of what used to be called 'Central Europe' has emerged as 'Eastern Europe', with coherence arising from government by Communist Parties conforming closely to the Soviet model" (Turnock, 1989, 1; Figure 19.1). The key common political factors uniting all of

1995

these countries, therefore, were their direct incorporation within the Soviet sphere of influence, and their rule by Communist Parties with greater or lesser control from Moscow. However, as Deutsch (1986, 2), writing in the mid-1980s, emphasised, "Despite Western stereotypes, the socialist part of Europe does not form an unchanging, monolithic bloc." Thus, five years prior to the collapse of the Soviet Union, some countries such as East Germany, Bulgaria and Hungary had achieved markedly more economic progress than others. In contrast, Romania, Poland and the USSR were in a period of deep economic crisis (Deutsch, 1986).

Two key principles underlay the economic heart of the political programmes imposed on these countries in the period following the Second World War: centralised planning and widespread industrialisation. Both were to have dramatic influences on the lives of people in rural areas. At a broad regional level, the establishment of the Council for Mutual Economic Assistance (CMEA) in 1949 was the main instrument through which the economies of the region were drawn into tight dependence on each other and in particular on the Soviet Union. Its central aims were to assist and co-ordinate the economic development of the six member states, the Soviet Union, Bulgaria, Czechoslovakia, Hungary, Poland and Romania. Albania joined later in 1949, the German Democratic Republic in 1950, and in 1965 Yugoslavia obtained associated status. Throughout the region, rapid industrialisation was fuelled by mass migration from the country-side to the towns, and the rural economies became increasingly unable to satisfy the growing urban demand for food. These changes, though, were taking place largely divorced from the broader social and economic transformations that were occurring in capitalist western Europe over the same period. Much of the stress being experienced in rural areas of the "new democracies" of eastern Europe in the 1990s has thus resulted from attempts to reintegrate their agrarian economies into a global system in which western European agriculture has been heavily subsidised. In order to understand the changes currently taking place in eastern Europe, it is therefore necessary briefly to highlight some of the key transformations that have taken place in western European rural life over the last 50 years.

European Rural Society

The words "rural" and "countryside" are in widespread use, and yet they remain elusively difficult to define. Cloke (1985, 4) has thus emphasised that "an all-embracing and long-term definition of rurality is ... very difficult to achieve", because it depends on the functions designated to the countryside, the rapid changes taking place in such areas, and the cross-cultural differences in meaning attributed to the term. Indeed, in much of western Europe urban society has so influenced traditionally defined rural areas that it is becoming increasingly difficult to separate out the two categories. There are nevertheless three main characteristics of the "rural" which continue to have widespread resonance (Unwin,

1996). First, it is a concept which applies essentially to places rather than to people. Thus it is still possible to refer to rural areas, although the people living in them may work in towns and maintain what most would see as an urban life style. Second, the rural is characterised by extensive land uses, such as agriculture, forestry and nature reserves. While there is a tendency for west European agricultural practices to become increasingly intensive, as for example with the 14 000 ha of intensive greenhouse cultivation in the Campo de Dalias to the west of Almería in south-east Spain (Porcel, 1994; Lorca, 1995), there still remain vast areas of extensive cereal cultivation across much of Europe, from the Alentejo in Portugal to the plains of Hungary in the east. Third, rural areas are imbued with deep cultural resonance, frequently associated with images of an idyllic past, more often than not linked closely to particular concepts of national identity (Hooson, 1994).

In western Europe, agriculture still remains an important form of economic activity in rural areas. However, the last 30 years have seen very considerable changes in the agrarian economy, through increasing intensification, concentration and specialisation (Bowler, 1986). As Ilbery (1990, 211) has argued,

> "in many areas agriculture has been transformed from little more than a peasant venture into a major business. Farms have become larger, fewer in number and more specialised. Farming has been modernised and, in some cases, industrialised as links with food processing and agricultural supply industries ... have been strengthened. Capital inputs into agriculture have increased substantially."

Although such a description could also be applied to much of east European agriculture during the period from 1960 to 1990, the changes that have taken place in western Europe have been much more dramatic in scale. Moreover, in western Europe, despite these changes there still remains a substantial sector of small, primarily subsistence oriented, and undercapitalised farms using family labour, particularly in the Mediterranean countries and Ireland.

Changes in agriculture and rural society in the countries of the EU have been driven largely by the

Common Agricultural Policy (CAP) (Hill, 1984; European Commission Directorate-General for Economic and Financial Affairs, 1994). This is widely seen as having over generously supported farmers with structural measures and price-support mechanisms during the 1960s and 1970s, leading not only to high prices for consumers, but also to substantial surpluses of products such as cereals, butter, beef and wine (Ilbery, 1990). The CAP is currently undergoing substantial reform, as the chapter by Ilbery in this volume describes (see also Marsh, 1991 and Folmer *et al.*, 1995), but its legacy will continue to have significant influences on rural life and landscapes well into the next century.

As well as the changes that have taken place in western European agriculture, the last decade has seen an increased recognition that rural areas are crucially important for other reasons, most notably their environmental role and their use for tourism and recreation. As a European Commission report at the end of the 1980s noted, "our rural areas are not only places where people live and work, for at the same time they have vital functions for society as a whole. As a buffer area and refuge for recreation, the countryside is vital to the general ecological equilibrium, and it is assuming an increasingly important role as the most popular location for relaxation and leisure" (Commission of the European Communities, 1988, 5). Agricultural restructuring has therefore been accompanied by substantial economic diversification in rural areas, and there has recently been a gradual reversal of the rural–urban migration so characteristic of the period between 1945 and 1970. The European Commission sees three key problems facing rural society into the next millennium: that of modern development, whereby areas of countryside are under increasing pressure from their neighbouring conurbations and heavy influxes of tourists cause yet further damage to the rural environment; that of rural decline, particularly in what are seen as "outlying Mediterranean parts of the Community", where there is a lack of economic diversification and development; and thirdly that of depopulation and land abandonment, leading to a collapse of the fragile environment, as is to be found in certain mountainous areas and islands (Commission of the European Communities, 1988, 6–7).

It is in the context of this background of a west European rural society, whose agricultural economy has traditionally been heavily protected and subsidised with reference to the world market, that the changes currently taking place in the rural areas of the new democracies need to be seen. While east European agriculture was itself subsidised under Communist rule, particularly through such things as cheap energy prices, many farmers are now caught in a double trap: not able to benefit from the subsidies enjoyed by their west European counterparts, they have to compete in the context of world market prices without the relative market protection that they enjoyed through their isolation under the previous regime. Most eastern European governments have therefore sought to protect their internal agricultural markets to some extent. However, as the Estonian example illustrates, this has by no means always been the case. Although so far Estonia is widely seen as having been among the most successful of the east European and former Soviet economies to adjust to the capitalist "free-market" economy, its farming sector has borne the brunt of the macro-economic policy instruments introduced by governments since 1991. As Maide (1995, 182–3) has commented,

> "State support to agriculture has been small . . . All the other post-socialist states besides Estonia have taken various measures to protect their agricultural and food markets (import duties, import licences etc.). Estonia has proceeded from the ideology of a fully free market and has not implemented any trade restrictions to protect the domestic market. This has created a situation where subsidised foodstuffs from foreign countries are flowing freely into the Estonian market but Estonian producers either cannot enter foreign markets or they face tremendous obstacles in their attempts."

Agriculture and Rural Society in the Soviet Period

Prior to the Second World War, and incorporation within the Soviet sphere of influence, eastern Europe was an important exporter of agricultural products. Turnock (1989, 223) thus notes that "over the period 1934–8 net exports were equivalent to the production from 3.74 million ha

Table 19.1 *Rural populations of selected European countries, 1960 and 1980*

	1960 % rural population	1980 % rural population	1980 figure as % of 1960 level
Eastern Europe			
Albania	69.4	63.2	91.1
Bulgaria	62.4	36.0	57.7
Czechoslovakia	53.1	37.1	69.9
German Democratic Republic	27.7	23.2	83.8
Hungary	60.0	46.6	77.7
Poland	52.1	43.4	83.3
Romania	65.9	52.1	79.1
USSR	51.2	35.2	68.8
Yugoslavia	72.1	67.7	93.9
Western Europe			
Belgium	34.0	27.6	81.2
Denmark	26.3	15.8	60.1
France	37.6	22.1	58.8
German Federal Republic	22.6	15.3	67.7
Greece	57.1	38.1	66.7
Italy	40.6	30.7	75.6
Netherlands	20.0	23.7	118.5
Norway	67.9	47.5	70.0
Portugal	77.5	69.4	89.5
Spain	43.4	25.7	59.2
Sweden	27.4	12.8	46.7
Switzerland	49.0	42.9	87.6
United Kingdom	14.3	9.2	64.3

Source: United Nations Fund for Population Activities (1980).

(6.4 per cent of the total area)". However, in the post-war period, while production broadly kept pace with the growth of population, it failed to satisfy rising demands and expectations (Deutsch, 1986). As a result, by 1962–66 the region had become a net importer of agricultural products, equivalent according to Turnock (1989) to the production from 3.97 million ha, or 5.9 per cent of the total land area. The agricultural structures and production methods introduced by the Communist governments of the region had therefore fallen markedly behind those of west European governments in delivering results.

At the same time, though, the overall share of the food and agricultural sector in the economy of eastern European countries has generally been much higher than in western Europe, as has been the percentage of employment in agriculture. Thus while agricultural employment in the European

Community fell from some 25.0 per cent of total employment in 1960 to only 6.7 per cent by 1979 (Hudson *et al.*, 1984), the share of agriculture in eastern Europe remained extremely high even into the late 1980s, ranging from 11.9 per cent in Czechoslovakia, the most industrialised country by this measure, to 35.0 per cent in Albania (Swinnen, 1994). For the majority of countries in eastern Europe, between one-fifth and one-quarter of the employed population were involved in agriculture. One key result of this has been that the percentages of the population living in rural areas have remained very much higher in eastern Europe than in the west. While there are undoubtedly problems in the use of varying definitions of rural and urban in different countries, Table 19.1 illustrates both that the percentages of people living in rural areas in 1960 were higher in the east than in the west, and also that they declined somewhat less rapidly over the next 20 years in the east. Thus for the eastern European countries shown in Table 19.1 the 1980 rural populations were on average 78.3 per cent of the 1960 levels, whereas for the western European countries shown the equivalent figure was 72.8 per cent. These averages nevertheless hide considerable variations, with the figures for eastern Europe being closer to those of Spain, Portugal and Greece, for example, than to those of the core European Community countries such as France and the Federal Republic of Germany.

At the heart of the rural changes introduced by the Communist regimes in the post-1945 period were centralised control over the economy, the imposition of widespread collectivisation of agricultural production, and the heavy subsidisation of food prices. However, the implementation of such policies varied greatly between countries and over time within individual countries. Figure 19.2 and Table 19.2 emphasise that the agrarian economy of eastern European countries was based upon a dual production structure. In general, a dominant collective and state farm sector existed alongside a small-scale private sector based on gardens and small plots of private land (Hedlund, 1989). However, in Poland and Yugoslavia collectivisation was never pushed as far as in other east European countries, and private farms continued to dominate their agrarian production systems throughout the period of Communist rule.

Originally, there were significant differences between collectives and state farms, but by the 1980s many of these distinctions had become blurred. Thus initially most workers on collectives held the title to their land, although non-land assets were held by the collective farm. The performance of a collective farm over a year determined the income received by the farmers, whose remuneration would be based on their relative inputs. On state farms, decision-making was much more centrally determined, the state owned all of the assets, and workers received fixed wages and social security benefits. These theoretical distinctions, however, had little meaning, with ownership titles in collective farms being effectively worthless. Swinnen (1994, 6) comments that "For all practical purposes collective farms were very much like state farms in most countries." An important difference

between state and collective farms, though, was that the former were generally very much larger. Thus by 1980 state farms in Czechoslovakia averaged some 10 500 ha, compared with only 2500 ha for collective farms, with the comparable figures for Hungary being 7590 and 3480 ha, and for Romania 5000 and 2260 ha (Turnock, 1989). Furthermore, there was a general tendency for the size of both collective and state farms to increase over time. The average sizes of collective farms in 1950 were thus only 310 ha in Czechoslovakia, 200 ha in Hungary and 280 ha in Romania (Turnock, 1989).

It is widely argued that the system of state and collective farms owed more to political and ideological imperatives than it did to rational economic arguments. Thus Turnock (1989, 227) has commented that

"Because of the emphasis placed on economies of scale, in contrast to the stimulation of initiative and innovation by dedicated workers, agriculture has been severely embarrassed by the political imperatives of Party control over the means of production. Also in so far as Marxist theory has been relevant to the decision to create collective/co-operative and state farms, then it has plainly been suspect through exaggerated expectations [that] productivity gains [would] follow simply from the abolition of private ownership."

Even in countries where collectivisation had progressed most extensively, private farming continued to play a very significant role in the production of fresh food, and particularly of fruit and vegetables. This was especially so during times of low production on state and collective farms, when private plots essentially provided much of the subsistence requirements of the population. In Hungary, for example, Juhasz (1991) has suggested that in 1987 three-quarters of all potatoes and vegetables were produced on small-scale private farms, with just under 60 per cent of all grape production and 56 per cent of pig breeding also taking place on such farms.

Overall, productivity levels were generally lower in eastern Europe than in the west, despite high levels of fertiliser applications and other energy inputs. But as Table 19.2 indicates, there were marked variations in such figures across eastern Europe, reflecting both the physical environment and also government policy. In

Figure 19.2 *Contrasting rural experiences: (a) an east German collective farm and (b) a farming landscape in northern Latvia*

Table 19.2 *Agrarian structure and production in eastern European countries in the 1980s*

	% Share of state farms in total output (1987)	% Share of collective farms in total output (1987)	% Share of private farms in total output (1987)	Arable land as a % of total area	Pasture as a % of total area	Forest as a % of total area	% Employment in agriculture and forestry (1980)	1981–85 cereal yield (quintals ha^{-1})	1981–85 average cereal production (million t)	Fertiliser application in 1984 (t per '000 ha)
Albania	21.1*	78.4*	0.5*	20.9	21.6	47.0	55.9	28.6	1.02	84.5
Bulgaria	90.0	0	10.0	39.5	16.3	34.6	18.1	41.4	8.55	171.2
Czechoslovakia	30.4	63.5	5.1	40.4	13.2	35.5	13.1	43.2	10.90	268.1
German Democratic Republic	7.7	82.5	9.7	46.4	11.4	27.2	10.6	41.4	10.37	182.4
Hungary	14.9	71.4	13.7	57.3	13.9	17.1	18.2	49.5	14.41	236.4
Poland	18.4	3.6	78.0	47.7	12.9	27.8	28.5	27.4	22.23	180.2
Romania	28.9	54.7	15.6	44.2	18.8	26.7	30.5	34.4	21.70	120.2
Yugoslavia	16.8	0.9	82.3	30.8	24.8	36.2	32.3	39.0	16.77	85.6

* Indicates figures for 1983.
Sources: Derived from FAO Yearbooks, Turnock (1989) and Swinnen (1994).

Czechoslovakia and Hungary, for example, fertiliser applications in the mid-1980s were very much higher than elsewhere, although this was not reflected in substantially higher yields. Table 19.2 also emphasises that the overall structure of land use varied significantly in the different countries of the region. In general terms, forest accounted for about one-third of the area, although this was much less in Hungary and much more in Albania. Likewise, pasture accounted for between 10 and 20 per cent of the total area of most countries, with arable generally covering between 40 and 50 per cent of the area.

The widespread use of inorganic fertilisers and pesticides, as well as the concentration of large numbers of livestock in intensive production units, has had considerable environmental implications throughout the region. Constantin (1996) has estimated, for example, that three-quarters of all Romania's agricultural soil has been damaged by pollutants, including pesticides, excessive chemical fertiliser use, heavy metals and petroleum, as well as by erosion, drought and increases in soil acidity. She goes on to note the following additional adverse environmental consequences of the previous agricultural regime: water pollution resulting from the discharge of pesticides into rivers; eutrophication caused by excessive use of chemical fertilisers; organic waste from livestock directly entering rivers and thus threatening the water supply of towns, particularly in the east of the country; and widespread problems caused by the need to dispose of substantial amounts of solid waste, including waste from the slaughter of livestock, harvest residues and orchard prunings. Such a catalogue of environmental damage resulting from poor agricultural management can be repeated across eastern Europe, and further examples are given in the next chapter of this book by Saiko.

Swinnen (1994) has emphasised another key component of the agricultural sector in eastern Europe prior to the reforms of the 1990s: not only were purchase prices for agricultural products relatively high, but there was also considerable price variation. In his terms,

"A peculiar feature of the former centrally planned system was that procurement organizations have traditionally paid different prices to different farms for the same product. Price differentiation entered through zonal pricing and through the bonus system. Several bonuses could raise received prices above base prices. The most important were quality differentials, bonuses for sales in excess of a moving average of past years and premia for farms in financial stress" (Swinnen, 1994, 8).

This provides some indication of the level and role of central planning in the agricultural sector.

Such state intervention nevertheless failed to provide food in sufficient quantity and diversity to satisfy the growing demands of the population. While during the 1980s the calorie and protein intakes of people living in eastern Europe were little different from those of their western neighbours, diets were generally much less diverse. Retail food prices for basic commodities were kept low by heavy subsidies, and these provided a serious drain on national budgets. Growing recognition of these difficulties caused governments to turn increasingly to new methods to improve food production. Thus, at a 1983 meeting of the CMEA in East Berlin, food diversification was ranked as a problem of at least as great importance as the growth in demand for raw materials and energy (Deutsch, 1986). However, the long tradition of emphasis on the urban-industrial complex as the driving force of economic development meant that it was extremely difficult to restructure the orientation of the economies of these countries. Indeed, commentators such as Deutsch (1986) have suggested that the inability of socialist planners to meet the new consumer demands which they had created was a key factor leading to the political instability that was eventually to result in the collapse of Soviet power in eastern Europe.

Restructuring and Agrarian Reform, 1989–96

Pressure for economic, social and political reform increased throughout eastern Europe and the former Soviet Union during the 1980s. However, the disintegration of the Soviet Union on 25 December 1991 precipitated a complete reorientation of the political and economic structures of the region (Bradshaw, 1993). It is still not clear what final direction these dramatic changes will take, but already it is evident that they have been marked by considerable diversity and divergence. In part this reflects the very diverse economic structures and environmental endowments of the relevant countries (see Table 19.2), but it is also a result of the particular political paths that their leaderships have followed. If the key characteristics of the former Communist regimes were their centralised planning, state ownership of the means of production, and their emphasis on the urban-industrial complex, the dominant motifs of restructuring and economic transformation have been decentralisation, privatisation and the introduction of a market economy. In the rural sector this has translated itself into the two distinct, but related, issues of land reform and agrarian restructuring.

Food price liberalisation

Throughout eastern Europe, the first measures of substantial rural economic reform were introduced by the Communist governments at the end of the 1980s. As indicated in the previous section, the driving motor for these changes was the mounting pressure to restructure the domestic food economies of the countries in the region. As Rowinski (1994, 211) has commented for Poland, the attempts at economic reform during the earlier 1980s

> "resulted in almost complete autarky of the Polish economy. The excess demand for basic food products was so strong that it lead [*sic*] to a controlled distribution of many of these products. Under these conditions, introducing any economic reforms of the food economy was impossible. Domestic food shortages induced a limitation on the role of market mechanisms."

Consequently the Communist government led by Mieczyslaw Rakowski introduced free purchase prices for agricultural products and free retail prices for many food products on 1 August 1989 (Rowinski, 1994; Centre for Co-operation with the Economies in Transition, 1995). Subsequently a range of other price liberalisation policies was implemented along with the removal of many subsidies, all of which have led to market prices increasingly coming to govern all levels of production and trading in the food economy.

Poland's example was rapidly followed by other countries, with Hungary and the Czech and Slovak Federal Republics introducing food price liberalisation policies in 1990, closely followed by Bulgaria in 1991 and Romania in 1992. Although such policies initially led to a dramatic increase in prices obtained by farmers for their products, this bonanza was extremely short-lived. In part this was because food price liberalisation policies were accompanied by the abolition of subsidies that had previously been directed towards the agricultural sector. However, in the longer term the dramatic rise in consumer prices has also served to reduce internal demand, and with weakly developed international trading links it has been difficult for farmers to develop new markets. Consequently most countries have reintroduced a range of measures designed to benefit farmers. As Swinnen (1994, 16) has noted,

> "It is remarkable ... how soon after the price liberalization and abolishment [*sic*] of subsidies government measures were reintroduced to protect farmers from negative reform impacts. During the second part of 1991 more and more interventionist and protectionist policies (re-)emerged as dramatic declines in agricultural incomes induced massive political pressure to intervene."

Land reform

Close on the heels of food price liberalisation policies, a series of land reform laws has been passed in all of the countries of the region. In order to understand the changes that have taken place, it is essential to distinguish between land reform (i.e. the actual redistribution of land) and agricultural reform (or the restructuring of the production units). Although closely related, the two have not always gone hand in hand, and this has given rise to considerable problems for rural communities. The history of previous land reforms suggests that they have rarely if ever been easy to achieve, and have almost always been associated with considerable short-term reductions in food production (Warriner, 1969; King, 1977). It is thus remarkable that there was such optimism in the late 1980s and early 1990s concerning both the desirability of this type of change, and its likelihood of achieving a rapid improvement in the standards of living of rural people.

Figure 19.3 *An Estonian private farm*

As Table 19.2 indicates, the balance between state farms, collective farms and private farms varied enormously in the region at the end of the 1980s (Figure 19.3). In Poland and Yugoslavia, for example, there were large numbers of small private farms, whereas at the other extreme Bulgaria was dominated by vast agro-industrial complexes. The land reform process itself has also varied greatly in terms of the methods used to implement it and in its intended results. Thus in Romania, Bulgaria and the former Czechoslovakia, local or municipal bodies have sought to administer the land-reform and farm-privatisation processes, whereas in Poland and Hungary control has been much more centralised at a national level (Swinnen, 1994). Estonia represents an extreme case, in that farm privatisation has been undertaken at a local level whereas land reform has been centralised at the national level (Unwin, 1994). In terms of the intended results, there is also marked variation. Thus in Bulgaria, Romania and Estonia there has been an attempt to return land to the original owners or their heirs, but in Hungary the principle has been to provide all previous owners with vouchers to purchase land or use for other purposes. To make matters worse, the long delays in implementing formal procedures resulting in the issuing of land titles, has meant that many people are taking things into their own hands, and unofficial privatisation has advanced rapidly, particularly in countries such as Romania, where the formal distribution of land titles has been delayed (Gavrilescu, 1994).

Land reform has been fraught with difficulty, not only because of problems involved in identifying former owners, but also because of the complexities involved in actually identifying the relevant parcels of land, and the sheer scale of the exercise that administrators unfamiliar with such procedures must undertake. As a result, land reform has been slower than many people anticipated. This has caused frustrations among those seeking to develop their own private enterprises, but it has also exacerbated the agrarian production crisis, because much land under disputed ownership has remained uncultivated. Moreover, this situation has further heightened tensions between, on the one hand, rural communities and, on the other, urban consumers intent on securing minimal price increases for their food supplies.

Agricultural reform

Just as the process of land reform has varied enormously throughout the region, so too has the process of farm reform. In Bulgaria it has had to concentrate primarily on the restructuring of the very large state farms, numbering only 283 in 1980, each at an average size of 16 870 ha (Turnock, 1989). At the other extreme, in the case of Poland, the necessity has been to enhance the previously dominant private sector while incorporating land formerly belonging mainly to the state sector (Table 19.2). In between, in the other countries of the region, the issue has primarily been concerned with determining the future of the thousands of medium-sized collective farms that dominated the agricultural production of countries such as Czechoslovakia, the German Democratic Republic, Hungary and Romania.

As yet, the complexities of agricultural reform and the turbulence of the transformation processes have meant that it is difficult to identify precisely what new farm structures are emerging. What is clear is that in the immediate aftermath of the introduction of reforms agricultural production levels have generally declined, with livestock numbers being particularly hard hit. In part this was exacerbated by drought in central Europe in 1992 (Centre for Co-operation with the Economies in Transition, 1995), but the continuing economic and political uncertainty facing many farmers is also acting as a considerable disincentive for development. Another apparent trend is for levels of production in private farms generally not to have declined as rapidly as those in the former collective sector.

Three main alternative organisational structures are emerging for former collective farms. First, some are simply being abandoned, with their livestock being slaughtered, and the former farmers either leaving formal employment or moving to urban centres in the search for jobs. This is particularly apparent in peripheral areas and on more marginal land. Second, other collective farms are being subdivided into separate units, with the assets being distributed among former members. Third, there are those collectives which have been restructured into a variety of joint stock companies. In numerous instances these are in effect little different from the former collective farms which they have replaced, and many are continuing to function at little more than subsistence level. Others, though, are adjusting to the economic environment, and are beginning to compete effectively in the new market economy. These are frequently those which benefited from skilful management under previous Communist regimes, and whose leaders have been able to manipulate the new conditions with equal success.

In the long run, providing that there is not a further dramatic political upheaval leading to a reversal of the trends so recently put into place, it is likely that a variety of farm types will emerge in the new eastern Europe. These will include both small and large private farms, joint stock companies, specialist state farms and a range of co-operative and collective enterprises. The precise farm structure of each country will then depend very much on its past economic and political history, as well as on the prevalent environmental conditions that influence the types of agricultural production that are most suitable. What is clear, though, is that this pattern will increasingly be decided by the economic and political relationships between these countries and the EU. As highlighted earlier in this chapter, the CAP has been highly significant in determining the rural landscape of western Europe in recent years, and it is likely to do so for the foreseeable future. What also seems inevitable is that many of the new small independent farms being created in eastern Europe will not be able to compete in the brave new world of the capitalist market economy, and that they will disappear just as have so many similar farms in parts of Portugal, Spain, Italy and Greece over the last decade.

The Practice of Rural Change: Agricultural Restructuring in Poland, Hungary and Estonia

In order to illustrate these themes in more detail, this chapter concludes with three contrasting case studies, each of which draws out elements of the above discussion in specific contexts. Poland has been selected because of the past importance of private farms within its agrarian structure, and its prominent role in leading to the break-up of the sphere of influence of the former Soviet Union. In contrast, Hungary has been chosen because it had a large collective farm sector, and since the introduction of the "new economic mechanism" in 1968 it had created a larger degree of market freedom than was typical of its neighbouring centrally planned economies. Finally, Estonia is used to exemplify the problems faced by rural communities in the small newly independent states of the former Soviet Union itself.

Poland: the uncertain future of private farms

The central elements of Poland's transition to a market-based economy include reforms to the tax system, privatisation and the establishment of market institutions. Most farm land in Poland in the post-1945 period was privately owned in highly fragmented small farms. Thus over half of the 2 million farms over 1 ha in size had less than 5 ha, and these accounted for some 23 per cent of total farm land (Centre for Co-operation with the Economies in Transition, 1995). Private farms dominated in the areas which before 1939 were in Polish territory, but in the northern and western regions which previously belonged to Germany, large state farms were introduced and these averaged some 2300 ha each in 1991. Under the Communist regime, the key instruments used by the state to try to achieve food self-sufficiency and food security were price-fixing measures for agricultural input, producer and food retail prices, alongside high consumer subsidies. In 1989, some 26 per cent of total employment was in agriculture, and in 1990 the sector contributed 15 per cent of GDP (Rowinski, 1994).

Since 1989, the main policy instruments used to implement the transition from a centrally planned economy have been concerned with the modernisation of the agricultural sector, while adjusting it to market mechanisms. However, as with many other states in the region, "The objective of creating a competitive environment for agriculture has been mainly implemented through general reforms of the economic system, rather than through policy reforms specifically directed to agriculture" (Centre for Co-operation with the Economies in Transition, 1995, 11). This has consequently given rise to considerable stress and anxiety in rural communities, who feel that the new governments have been primarily concerned with the interests of the urban, industrial and commercial sectors rather than with agriculture. There have, nevertheless, been two groups of policy instrument directed specifically towards agriculture: first, market price support mechanisms regulating domestic prices, import barriers and social measures contributing to farm incomes; and, second, structural policy measures and technical support to improve animal and crop yields.

These policies have as yet had little positive influence, but it must be emphasised that it is only five years since their introduction, and the complete restructuring of the agriculture sector is an enormous task. Agricultural production declined continuously between 1989 and 1992, with the 1992 figures being some 16 per cent below those of 1986 (Centre for Co-operation with the Economies in Transition, 1995). However, the most significant decrease occurred in 1992, and was largely the result of drought. More worryingly for farmers, the terms of trade have moved significantly against agriculture, with producer output prices rising less fast than input prices. The Centre for Co-operation with the Economies in Transition (1995) thus estimates that real farm incomes in 1993 were 43 per cent lower than in 1985. Rural families have therefore had to rely on alternative sources of income even more than they did under the old regime.

As yet, the privatisation of state farms has proceeded very slowly. By February 1994 only 2 per cent of the total area of land due to be privatised had been sold, despite preferential interest rates and favourable instalment plans. Just under one-third of land due to be privatised is currently being leased, mainly by enterprises created by former state farm employees. It seems that three main reasons underlie the slow rate of privatisation: uncertainty over the future of the agricultural sector, which makes it a less desirable option for investment than other sectors of the economy; the lack of available capital; and the location of much of the former state farm land in the north and west of the country, away from the traditional heartland of Polish private farming (Rowinski, 1994; Centre for Co-operation with the Economies in Transition, 1995).

The results of the decline in agricultural production within Poland have also been reflected in worsening agro-food trade figures. Agro-food imports have been growing more rapidly than exports with a deficit being recorded in 1993, when such products represented about 12 per cent of all Poland's trade. The disintegration of the CMEA has led to the need to establish new trade agreements with its member countries, and Poland has also been seeking to develop much closer trade links with the EU in the framework of its Association Agreement which came into force in March 1992.

In conclusion, Rowinski (1994) emphasises the dilemma facing the Polish agriculture sector. If it is to expand it requires considerable foreign investment, but such investment is unlikely to be forthcoming until the sector shows itself capable of appropriate levels of profit return. In the meanwhile, the introduction of protectionist policies in 1992, through the government's Opportunities for Rural Areas and Agriculture programme designed to assist rural communities, is leading to the weakening of Polish agriculture's competitive position in the international arena. This will in turn act as a further disincentive for the foreign investment that commentators such as Rowinski (1994) believe to be so essential for Poland's future.

Hungary: restructuring the collective sector

In contrast to Poland, Hungary's agricultural sector was dominated by collective farms (Table 19.2). However, these collectives were less rigid than those in many other CMEA countries, with individual farms retaining a relatively high degree of independence and private plots maintaining an important role in livestock and horticulture (Mészáros, 1994). The 1253 collective farms occupied about 70 per cent of the land, and on average in 1988 they farmed about 3600 ha and employed 400 people. The 133 state farms, in contrast, accounted for some 12 per cent of the agricultural land, averaging about 6000 ha and

940 employees each. As elsewhere in eastern Europe, both state and collective farms were involved in much more than just agriculture, with sales from non-farming activities usually exceeding those specifically from farming, even though less than 20 per cent of total fixed assets were devoted to non-farming activities (Centre for Co-operation with the Economies in Transition, 1994).

The relative success of Hungary's agricultural sector during the 1945–90 period has generally been attributed to the flexibility of its collective system, and its failure to implement the rigid centralised control experienced in many other countries. Moreover, a positive symbiosis existed between the private sector and the collective farms. It is thus estimated that the private sector contributed more than a third of agricultural output (Centre for Co-operation with the Economies in Transition, 1994), concentrating in particular on pigs, poultry, eggs, vegetables and wine, with much of the grain production and food processing being undertaken in the collective and state farms. Although some flexibility existed within Hungary's collective organisation, the agrarian sector was still subject to centrally determined production targets and price fixing as found within other CMEA countries.

The basis of Hungary's privatisation programme introduced since 1989 has been a compensation voucher scheme (Mészáros, 1994). The majority of claimants for compensation have based their cases on lost land, although other reasons such as imprisonment by the former regime are also counted. All recipients of vouchers can use them to bid for land or for other purposes, such as acquiring housing or shares in privatised state-owned industries. Former collective and state farm land that has been put into a compensation fund against possible claims is available for purchase through auctions, and the recipients must then agree to farm it for at least five years. While this system may seem relatively straightforward, the complexities involved in determining the validity of claims, and particularly the former ownership of land, have meant that progress has been slow. Thus, only one-third of land in compensation funds had been acquired at auction by July 1993 (Centre for Co-operation with the Economies in Transition, 1994). A key feature to note about this scheme is that it does not provide claimants with the land that they or their family once owned, but instead enables them to bid for land in any part of the country.

Delays in land reform have meant that progress towards the privatisation of state farms has also been slow. However, restructuring of the collective farms has been even more difficult, largely because of the complexity of their ownership structures, and the problems in identifying the precise landownership patterns of the collective farm members. Nevertheless, by the official deadline for transformation at the end of 1992, more than 90 per cent of former collectives had re-established themselves as co-operatives (Centre for Co-operation with the Economies in Transition, 1994). There has therefore been negligible conversion as yet to private farming, but this in part reflects the great speed with which the new policy was introduced, and the practical difficulties that were involved if former collective members actually wanted to withdraw their assets as was permitted by the law. It therefore seems likely that the initial co-operative structure that has been established will be subject to further change over the rest of this decade, particularly if it proves incapable of providing satisfactory levels of production.

The net effect of these reforms on production has been mixed. As in Poland, the 1992 harvest was hit by the drought conditions, although previously agricultural output apparently increased somewhat in nominal terms (Centre for Co-operation with the Economies in Transition, 1994). In 1991, for example, total grain production was around 15.6 million t, which was above earlier average figures. In part, this reflects Hungary's environmental endowment, which makes it particularly well suited to wheat and maize production. However, as in Poland, the terms of trade have moved against the agricultural sector, with farm input costs increasing more rapidly than output prices. This has once again led the government to adopt a range of farm support policies which conflict with the desire to create an open market-oriented agricultural sector. Looking towards the future, the government is intent on making agriculture competitive on the international market in order to gain export earnings, but to do so it will be necessary to ensure

that the new agrarian structures are able to sustain previous levels of production.

Estonia: agrarian change at the edge of Europe

The experiences of Estonian farmers following the republic's independence from the Soviet Union in 1991 are different yet again from those found in Poland and Hungary. Following the Soviet terror of 1940–41 and the deportations of many Estonian farmers in 1949 (Lieven, 1993), the introduction of collective and state farms dramatically altered the rural landscape. However, they failed to break the Estonian people's strong ties to their land, and the land reform legislation introduced in 1991 was thus based fundamentally on the principle that anyone who was a citizen of the Estonian Republic in 1940, or who is an heir of such a person, has the right to demand the return or substitution of land that was unlawfully alienated or, alternatively, compensation for it. Implementation of land reform, though, has been slow, in part quite simply because of the logistics of checking and processing claims. Moreover, many claimants are people who have for a long time lived in urban areas, particularly the capital Tallinn, and who have little interest in agriculture. Furthermore, the majority of new private landholdings are also extremely small, reflecting the structure of holdings that existed in the 1930s. By 1995, for example, the average size of newly registered holdings was only 12.3 ha.

In contrast to the centrally administered land reform programme, farm reform has been based at a local level, with the restructuring of the former collective and state farms being left largely to local negotiation. Almost all of Estonia's agricultural land was divided into either state or collective farms, there being approximately 150 of each in the mid-1980s. However, private plots, limited to 0.6 ha per household, played an important role throughout the Soviet period, accounting for between an estimated one-fifth and one-third of meat, vegetable and fruit production. It is not yet clear what has happened to many of the former collective farms, but estimates in 1995 suggested that perhaps one-third had collapsed altogether, one-third were functioning at more or less subsistence level, and a further third had been reorganised into joint-stock companies which were functioning as viable enterprises. The development of private farms has been much slower than was initially anticipated in the heady days of 1991, when it was thought that some 40 000–60 000 new private farms would be created by the end of the decade. In practice only 13 375 such farms had been created by April 1995, and many of these were finding the harsh realities of the market economy difficult to negotiate.

Farmers are faced with very severe difficulties. Estonia is a small country of only 1.5 million people. Its internal market is therefore small, and under Soviet rule its agrarian economy was fundamentally geared to providing dairy and meat products for the urban centres of neighbouring Russia. To this end energy and fodder prices were heavily subsidised. With dramatic rises in input prices since independence, and with the collapse of the Russian market following the introduction of punitive Russian import tariffs, farmers find it difficult to sell their produce at home or abroad. To make matters worse, the lack of import barriers in Estonia means that dumped foreign produce, particularly from EU countries, is undercutting local prices (Maide, 1995; Unwin, 1996).

Since independence the rural community has therefore been hit hard by government decisions to move as rapidly as possible towards a free-market economy. New initiatives have concentrated primarily on the introduction of macro-economic policy instruments designed to ensure financial stability and the privatisation of the means of production, but they have largely ignored the interests of rural society in general, and the agricultural sector in particular. The resultant discontent in rural areas has thus contributed to the victory of the Coalition Party and Rural Union in the March 1995 elections. However, despite agreement to move towards establishing a new Law on Rural Life in 1996, few direct benefits have so far been received from the government by farmers, who still have to operate in a highly uncertain environment.

The Future of Rural Life in "the New Democracies"

Democracy in capitalist societies serves those in power. The new élites of the former Communist states are primarily urban based, and concerned mainly with financial, commercial and industrial production. Such an urban-industrial emphasis was typical also of the Soviet period and, as Deutsch (1986) has argued, was one of the very reasons why this system collapsed. It is therefore not surprising that farming in eastern Europe is facing considerable difficulties in this period of economic, social and political transition. Although social inequalities undoubtedly existed under the previous Communist regimes, such inequalities will not be removed by so-called democracy and the free market. As Habermas (1994, 55) has so clearly argued,

> "The price of admission into a market economy has to be paid in the currency of social inequity, entirely new kinds of social divisions, and in higher long-term unemployment. A relatively higher level of base unemployment will persist in the new states, because one segment of the population is too old, and another too poorly trained, for a cognitively adequate and spiritually robust reaction to the considerable pressure for adaptation. As is always the case in accelerated social transformation, crises get shifted onto the life histories, onto the psyche and physical health of individuals."

If the lessons of western Europe are anything to go by, entry of the countries of eastern Europe into the global capitalist economy will – in the short term at least – result in considerable rural to urban migration. This will be the outcome both of the difficulties of finding employment in rural areas, and also of the psychological attractions for the young of the bright lights, fast food chains and discotheques of urban life (Figure 19.4). Faced with the rapidity of change seen in the urban commercial world of eastern Europe, it is scarcely surprising that few teenagers see their future lying in working as labourers on newly privatised farms in peripheral rural areas. Indeed, it is highly likely that the changes currently taking place in these areas are but the precursors of even greater transformations to be seen towards the end of this decade.

Two aspects of change seem particularly likely: a restructuring of the rural economies of eastern Europe to bring them closer to those of the EU; and the development of integrated rural development strategies that seek to provide a diversity of employment opportunities for people

Figure 19.4 *All roads lead to McDonald's in Torun, Poland*

living in rural areas. As Chapter 18 indicates, the changes implicit in the MacSharry reforms of the CAP and the 1994 GATT agreements will have far reaching implications for agriculture and the rural landscape in EU countries. Subsidy levels are being reduced, and farmers will increasingly have to face the much more competitive markets of the international arena. In this context, it is likely that many more of the small-scale farmers in peripheral parts of western Europe will continue to go out of business, and it is extremely hard to see how the tiny newly privatised farms in much of eastern Europe will be able to compete. Ironically, though, it may well be possible that in the longer term the exigencies of the market economy will make viable some very large production units, not that dissimilar from some of the state and collective farms found in eastern Europe in the 1970s and 1980s. Whether these are privately owned, co-operatives, or various forms of joint stock companies remains to be seen, but it is likely that a wide range of different farm structures will emerge, reflecting the diversity of their backgrounds and national identities.

It is also highly probable that levels of employment in agriculture in eastern Europe will continue to diminish. If alternative sources of work are not found in rural areas, then migration to the towns will increase at an even faster rate, and it is unlikely that the industrial and commercial sectors will be able to soak up this growing level of demand for jobs. It is increasingly being recognised elsewhere in the world that one strategy for coping with such rural change is to emphasise the need for integrated and sustainable approaches to rural development. This is true not only of the so-called "developing" countries, but also of the "developed" economies comprising the Organisation for Economic Co-operation and Development (OECD). For example, in a recent report the OECD (1995) has stressed the need for the introduction of new policy approaches to rural employment in order to provide an integrated approach to national development.

The "new democracies" of eastern Europe thus have an opportunity to develop innovative integrated approaches to rural development, combining not only agricultural interests, but also those of forestry, fishing, handicraft production, rural tourism, and nature reserves. It is only through such programmes that the stresses and strains of transition and restructuring can be minimised in rural areas. While the relative importance of agriculture will undoubtedly decline, rural livelihoods can be maintained and even enhanced through the application of policies that are both integrated and have an emphasis on sustainable development. Whether this will happen depends largely on the balance of power of different political interests within these countries themselves, but relationships with the EU are also relevant. In this latter context, accession agreements signed with the EU in recent years unfortunately give few grounds for optimism. While the urban commercial and industrial interests of the capitalist market economy continue to dominate the national and international political arenas, it seems inevitable that rural society in the countries of eastern Europe will continue to be disadvantaged.

Acknowledgements

Much of the research upon which this chapter has been based results from various grants from the British Academy, the Commission of the European Communities and the Estonian Academy of Sciences, which are hereby acknowledged with thanks. I am also particularly grateful to colleagues in Estonia, Poland and Germany for their relevant comments and advice, notably Wieslaw Maik, Jörg Janzen, Anton Laur and Reet Karukäpp.

References

Bowler, I (1986) Intensification, concentration and specialisation in agriculture: the case of the European Community, *Geography*, **71**, 14–24.

Bradshaw, M (1992) *The Economic Effects of Soviet Dissolution*, Royal Institute of International Affairs, London.

Centre for Co-operation with the Economies in Transition (1994) *Review of Agricultural Policies: Hungary*, Organisation for Economic Co-operation and Development, Paris.

Centre for Co-operation with the Economies in Transition (1995) *Review of Agricultural Policies: Poland*, Organisation for Economic Co-operation and Development, Paris.

Cloke, P (1985) Editorial: whither rural studies?, *Journal of Rural Studies*, **1**(1), 1–9.

Commission of the European Communities (1988) *The Future of Rural Society: Commission Communication to Parliament and the Council, Bulletin of the European Communities, Supplement 4/88*, Office for Official Publications of the European Communities, Luxembourg.

Constantin, D (1996) Environmentally sustainable regional development strategies in Romania – the challenges of transition, Paper read to the 35th Annual Meeting of the Western Regional Science Association, Napa, 25–29 February 1996.

Deutsch, R (1986) *The Food Revolution in the Soviet Union and Eastern Europe*, Westview Press, Boulder and London.

Duncan, G (ed) (1989) *Democracy and the Capitalist State*, Cambridge University Press, Cambridge.

European Commission Directorate-General for Economic and Financial Affairs (1994) *The Economics of the Common Agricultural Policy (CAP)*, Office for Official Publications of the European Communities, Luxembourg.

Folmer, C, Keyzer, M A, Merbis, M D, Stolwijk, H J J and Veenendaal, P J J (1995) *The Common Agricultural Policy beyond the MacSharry Reform*, Elsevier, Amsterdam.

Gavrilescu, D (1994) Agricultural reform in Romania: between market priority and the strategies for food security, in J F M Swinnen (ed) *Policy and Institutional Reform in Central European Agriculture*, Avebury, Aldershot, 169–210.

Habermas, J (1994) The past as future, in M Pensky (ed) *The Past as Future. Jürgen Habermas Interviewed by Michael Haller*, Polity Press, Cambridge, 55–72.

Hedlund, S (1989) *Private Agriculture in the Soviet Union*, Routledge, London.

Hill, B E (1984) *The Common Agricultural Policy: past, present and future*, Methuen, London.

Hooson, D (ed) (1994) *Geography and National Identity*, Blackwell, Oxford.

Hudson, R, Rhind, D and Mounsey, H (1984) *An Atlas of EEC Affairs*, Methuen, London.

Ilbery, B W (1990) The challenge of land redundancy, in D Pinder (ed) *Western Europe: challenge and change*, Belhaven, London, 211–25.

Juhasz, J (1991) Hungarian agriculture: present situation and future prospects, *European Review of Agricultural Economics*, **18**, 399–416.

King, R (1977) *Land Reform: a world survey*, G Bell and Sons, London.

Lewis, P G (ed) (1992) *Democracy and Civil Society in Eastern Europe*, St Martin's Press, New York.

Lieven, A (1993) *The Baltic Revolution: Estonia, Latvia, Lithuania and the path to independence*, Yale University Press, New Haven and London.

Lorca, A M G (1995) From traditional agriculture to technology, from emigration to immigration, in J Puigdefábregas and T Mendizábal (eds) *Desertification and Migrations*, Geoforma Ediciones, Logroño, 281–93.

Maide, H (1995) Transformation of agriculture, in O Lugus and G A Hachey Jr (eds), *Transforming the Estonian Economy*, Institute of Economics, Estonian Academy of Sciences, Tallinn, 169–86.

Marsh, J (1991) *The Changing Role of the Common Agricultural Policy: the future of farming in Europe*, Belhaven, London.

Mészáros, S (1994) The reform process in Hungarian agriculture: an overview, in J F M Swinnen (ed) *Policy and Institutional Reform in Central European Agriculture*, Avebury, Aldershot, 77–106.

Organisation for Economic Co-Operation and Development (1995) *Creating Employment for Rural Development: new policy approaches*, OECD, Paris.

Porcel, C H (1994) Evolucion de la estructura de la propiedad en El Ejido. 1933–1993, in J M M López and N Y Rossell (eds) *Sociedad y Espacio Geografico: Homenaje a la Professora Esther Jimeno López*, Universidad de Almería, Almería, 63–94.

Rowinksi, J (1994) Transformation of the food economy in Poland, in J F M Swinnen (ed) *Policy and Institutional Reform in Central European Agriculture*, Avebury, Aldershot, 211–36.

Sartori, G (1987) *The Theory of Democracy Revisited*, Chatham House Publishers, Chatham, N J.

Smith, G (1996) When nations challenge and nations rule: Estonia and Latvia as ethnic democracies, *Coexistence*, **33**, 25–41.

Swinnen, J F M (1994) Overview of policy and institutional reform in Central European agriculture, in J F M Swinnen (ed) *Policy and Institutional Reform in Central European Agriculture*, Avebury, Aldershot, 1–30.

Taylor, P J (1994) Party systems, in T Unwin (ed) *Atlas of World Development*, Wiley, Chichester, 272–3.

Turnock, D (1989) *Eastern Europe: an economic and political geography*, Routledge, London.

United Nations Fund for Population Activities (1980) *Population Facts at Hand*, United Nations Fund for Population Activities, New York.

Unwin, T (1994) Structural change in Estonian agriculture: from command economy to privatisation, *Geography*, **79**, 246–61.

Unwin, T (1996) Agricultural restructuring and integrated rural development in Estonia, *Journal of Rural Studies*, **13**, 93–112.

Warriner, D (1969) *Land Reform in Principle and Practice*, Clarendon Press, Oxford.

Part IV
Environmental Challenges

Economic development processes, such as those examined in Part II, can have far-reaching environmental consequences. Part IV explores a range of these impacts, starting with Tatyana Saiko's analysis of the legacy of post-war socialist industrialisation in central and eastern Europe. Environmental damage is shown to have been closely associated with attitudes which regarded resources as free and, at their most extreme, interpreted industrial pollution as evidence of progress. Since the fall of socialism, gains have been made through "transitional environmental improvement" – decreased pollution as a result of the collapse of economic activity. As Saiko demonstrates, however, there remains a need for urgent measures to improve the state of the environment, which is still critical in many parts of the former socialist bloc. Equally, there is a need to debate how this is to be achieved, since central and eastern Europe are dominated by underperforming economies in which meeting the costs of pollution control is not seen as a priority objective.

In the very different context of the EU, the issue of how to promote environmental protection and improvement is considered by Richard Williams and Holmfridur Bjarnadottir. Central to their discussion is the argument that, although a top-down approach has tended to be pursued in the past, effective environment policies cannot be pursued simply at the Union and governmental levels. Local action to implement environment policy, by integrating it into spatial planning and related measures, is also necessary to achieve widespread commitment and progress. Their argument is that pragmatic recognition of this is to be seen in an EU tactical shift in the 1990s, which has produced a marked swing towards networking, liaison with pressure groups and funding allocated competitively to environmental projects originating at the local level. What Williams and Bjarnadottir also demonstrate, however, is that in the environmental field – as in many others – behavioural factors can exert a strong influence on policy evolution. Thus the improved balance between top-down and bottom-up approaches has only been achieved since 1991, following the resignation of Ripa de Meana, a Commissioner for Environment strongly committed to the concept of progress through top-down legislation.

Two chapters then examine issues surrounding transport and the environment. For David Pinder and Julia Edwards the focus of concern is the potential conflict between EU policies in these fields. On the one hand, through its Single Market and trans-European infrastructure projects, the EU facilitates movement in the interests of economic development. On the other it has a strong commitment to limiting environmental pollution, which may clearly be out of step with the policy of promoting mobility, particularly for some transport modes. Against this background Pinder and Edwards examine the activities of one of the EU's foremost funding agencies, the European Investment Bank. This now operates in western, central and eastern Europe, allowing Europe-wide conclusions to be drawn concerning the Bank's ability to channel funding into environmentally sustainable transport projects.

Derek Hall's discussion, meanwhile, centres on transport problems and environmental pressures in urban Europe. His analysis is that urban transport policies are at a crossroads. Technological fixes designed to give the car more freedom are increasingly being rejected in favour of strategies to achieve sustainability ideals by exploiting new technologies; enhancing the appeal of public transport; and transferring the external costs of motoring in urban areas on to those responsible for them. But although this shift is now evident, Hall demonstrates that much remains to be done. Attitude, it is argued, is a deep-seated brake on progress and, in a deregulated and privatised climate, central and local governments frequently find it difficult to resist market-led forces. Moreover, while this is the case Europe-wide, in central and eastern Europe car-borne freedom is now a potent symbol of the break with the past, and has therefore become an additional powerful attitudinal constraint.

Finally, Brian Woodruffe turns the spotlight from urban to rural environments. Europe has a rich diversity of rural landscapes, and the immediate aim of the chapter is to elucidate the very complex range of approaches that have been adopted to restrain environmental damage in valued and pressured areas. Beyond this, however, the analysis identifies fundamental questions requiring extensive research and debate. Will the economies of western European states still enable them to afford protection as the number of protected areas continues to increase? How will central and eastern European states manage to meet the costs of effective conservation? Is it feasible to shift these costs more firmly on to visitors, who currently "consume" valued environments yet pay little in return? And, if the economic issues can be resolved, how is the use of Europe's kaleidoscopic rural heritage to be regulated and managed to ensure that its value is maintained and enhanced as the twenty-first century progresses?

20
Environmental challenges in the new democracies

Tatyana A Saiko

Department of Geographical Sciences, University of Plymouth, UK

Introduction

The 1992 UN Rio Conference highlighted growing concern about the global environmental disaster and the need for ecologically sound sustainable development. The latter was understood differently by various experts and has not yet been taken on board by the majority of countries, even in the developed world. However, given the collapse of the socialist system, it seemed that the emerging democracies of central and eastern Europe (CEE) occupied a relatively advantageous position in this respect. Unencumbered by Western countries' constantly diversifying consumerist attitudes, it was argued, these liberated states had the unrivalled opportunity to avoid the West's mistakes by integrating environmental policies into economic programmes.

After nearly a decade, it is evident that early hopes have been dashed. Initial optimism discounted the scale of major challenges – amounting to acute ecological crisis – inherited from previous regimes. In addition, the processes of economic and social transition proved to be more complex than most observers envisaged. Consequently this chapter is not primarily concerned with the evaluation of progress but, instead, with attempting to understand its disappointing pace. What are the environmental problems inherited from the past? How have they been exacerbated by transition? And what are the fundamental obstacles to improvement in the later 1990s?

The standpoint adopted to address these questions is that Europe – east and west – is a single environmental complex with a diverse range of interdependent links. This may be demonstrated with respect to transboundary pollution. CEE as a whole exerts a manifest influence on the state of the environment in western Europe through transboundary atmospheric pollution and water pollution of shared rivers and seas. Russia, for example, is responsible for one-fifth of the sulphur deposition in Finland and 11 per cent in Norway. At the same time, however, the generally accepted idea of a one-way environmental impact of CEE countries on western Europe is a myth, not least because of a purely geographical phenomenon: the predominantly westerly direction of winds in Europe. In reality, therefore, many airborne pollutants move within CEE and are also drawn in from the west. Continuing the Russian example, almost half of all sulphur deposition in the Russian Federation in 1992 came from transboundary

Table 20.1 *Trans-boundary pollution: sulphur dioxide deposition in and from European Russia in 1992*

Recipient country	Sulphur deposition				Deposition ratios	
	In Russia		From Russia		Difference between deposition in and from Russia	Ratio between deposition in Russia and deposition from Russia
	Amount ('000 t)	% total deposition in Russia	Amount ('000 t)	% total deposition in recipient country		
Russia	1302	52.0	1302	52.0	0	1
Ukraine	395	15.8	37	3.0	358	11
Germany	129	5.1	0	0	129	>100
Poland	128	5.1	5	0.4	123	26
Byelarus	87	3.5	14	4.3	73	6
Romania	69	2.8	0	0	69	>100
Czech Republic and Slovakia	62	2.5	0	0	62	>100
Estonia	46	1.8	2	5.0	44	23
Bulgaria	40	1.6	0	0	40	>100
Finland	39	1.6	28	20.3	11	14
United Kingdom	38	1.5	0	0	38	>100
Former Yugoslavia	28	1.1	0	0	28	>100
Caucasus countries	11	0.4	4	6.8	7	3
Lithuania	9	0.4	4	3.8	5	2
Sweden	8	0.3	6	5.0	2	1
Moldova	6	0.2	0	0	6	>100
Latvia	4	0.1	2	2.6	2	2
Turkey	4	0.1	4	1.2	0	1
Norway	0	0	10	11.1	−10	∞
Other sources	101	4.0	74	nd	27	−
Total	2506	100.0	1696	−	810	3
Of which trans-boundary:	1204	48	190	1.8	1014	6

Source: Adapted from Ministry of Ecology and National Resources of the RF (1995).

sources, and particularly from the Ukraine, Germany and Poland; and the total amount of sulphur deposited in Russia from sources in other countries was 6.3 times greater than the amount received by them from the Russian Federation (Table 20.1). Similarly, with respect to marine pollution, a Norwegian–Russian project has recently begun to examine formerly "closed" strategic research fields such as radioactive contamination of the marine environment. This initiative started in April 1992 within the framework of a Joint Commission on Environmental Protection, and a major result has been the revelation that 60 per cent of radioactivity accumulated in the Barents Sea during 1961–90 originated in the West and was "imported" by a branch of the Gulf Stream. The sources of this contamination were discharges from nuclear reprocessing plants at Sellafield in the UK and Cap de la Hague in France (*Nezavisimaya Gazeta*, 16 July 1996).

As yet, however, this interdependence between west and east and between countries within CEE is not sufficiently reflected in the literature. For CEE, most existing research focuses either on the former Soviet Union (FSU) (Feshbach and Friendly, 1992; Mnatsakanian, 1992; Peterson, 1993; Pryde, 1991; Stewart, 1992) or on the FSU's former "satellites" (Alcamo, 1992; Carter and Turnock, 1993, 1996; DeBardeleben and Hannigan, 1994; Fisher, 1992;

Manser, 1993; Vari and Tamaz, 1993). Meanwhile, relatively few studies cover eastern and central Europe as a whole (IUCN, 1990–93; Fodor, 1994; Nefedova, 1994). Thus an important task of this chapter is to help to bridge this gap. In doing so it recognises that the concepts of "central" and "eastern" Europe are currently undergoing change and are used with different meanings by various authors. Here the term "eastern Europe" is used to refer to the newly independent countries which previously formed the Soviet Union, including the European part of Russia, while "central Europe" is reserved for the former socialist bloc partners of the USSR. Bordered by the Ural mountains in the east, central and eastern Europe occupy a vast territory of 7.5 million sq. km, roughly two-thirds of which lie in central Europe. In comparison, the rest of Europe covers only 2.5 million sq. km.

The Environmental Inheritance of Socialism

By the 1970s a number of very successful integrated interdisciplinary studies were being carried out in Hungary to research the condition of the environment. As part of this initiative a nation-wide environmental monitoring system was established by the Academy of Sciences, in co-operation with the State Statistical Office and the National Office for Water Management (Carter and Turnock, 1993). This country, along with the Czech Republic, has remained in the forefront of advanced scientific investigations into environmental problems during the last decade. But although factual data existed in these countries, and also in the German Democratic Republic (GDR) and the USSR, it was politically embarrassing to admit the real extent of environmental problems, which "by socialist definition" could only be inherent to the capitalist system. Elsewhere, for example in some of the Balkan countries, the overall low level of economic development, coupled with the lack of the necessary environmental infra-structures and seriously inadequate allocations for research, led to a genuine absence of data which similarly disguised the severity of the situation. As a result, only since the advent of

glasnost (publicity) during the Gorbachev era in the mid- and late 1980s have circumstances improved sufficiently to produce the revelation of environmental disasters in many countries of the region. Moreover, although censorship of environmental information was lifted in Russia as early as 1986, much of the relevant data – for instance, relating to the Chernobyl catastrophe – were still not available to the public until the early 1990s (Yaroshinskaya, 1992).

Magnitude and scope of ecological problems

The magnitude and nature of the inherited environmental problems were extremely variable in each of the CEE countries, but there was good reason to describe the overall situation as a crisis. Of course, severe pollution was not something completely new to these countries; indeed, in some of them industrial development and associated environmental degradation originated in the nineteenth century. However, intensive indus-trialisation after the Second World War, enforced by the Stalinist regime and carried on for four decades of socialism, resulted in much more extensive ecological damage, with a multitude of adverse implications. This type of crisis has been described as a "creeping environmental phenom-enon" (Glantz, 1994) and is characterised by a long-term process of accumulation of ecological changes until they reach a critical threshold, which is often a point of no return for an ecosystem. In the CEE countries this threshold was most often associated with the rapid growth of environmental awareness towards the end of the Cold War period, when the real scope and magnitude of environmental problems became known to the public at large and environmentalism temporarily acquired the strength of a political opposition.

The actual magnitude of the ecological problems is still quite difficult to assess. As Fodor (1994, 35) has emphasised, the scale of environmental damage "can ... at the moment only be estimated ... our knowledge is very limited as far as the health damaging effects are concerned ...". This statement is particularly true for the past, when the first attempts at the overall assessment of environmental damage were made. Despite this uncertainty, the situation in many ways is worst in the FSU, which in the whole "socialist camp" had the longest record of accelerated industrialisation based on the command economy. Indeed, the spread and gravity of ecological problems throughout the FSU have encouraged some experts to describe it as "a united front of ecological degradation between Scandinavia and the Black Sea" (Stewart, 1992). Even so, in many respects it appears that in some central European countries environmental damage is even more serious and intense than in the FSU.

Probably the major irreversible problem area is the territory affected by the Chernobyl nuclear accident, which took place in April 1986. The present-day country which suffered most from the accident was Belarus, where 16 500 sq. km were contaminated with caesium-137, including over 2000 sq. km with concentrations of more than 40 curies per sq. km (Pryde, 1991). The total contaminated area exceeded 28 000 sq. km, and there has also been a lesser impact on other European countries (Medvedev, 1990). The impacts of this disaster, to which we will return later in this chapter, are enormous both for present and future generations, and it seems that we are only now approaching the point at which they can be examined in detail.

The second-worst affected region of ecological disaster was the so-called "black" or "sulphur triangle" of central Europe (Figure 20.1). This includes the Silesian district of Poland, northern Bohemia in the Czech Republic and the south-eastern part of the former GDR. This industrial heartland of the former socialist partners of the

Figure 20.1   *Heavy industrialisation and derelict land in the "black triangle": Kapowice, Poland*

USSR has probably paid the highest price in terms of air pollution because of its rapid industrialisation between the 1950s and the 1980s, although 80 per cent of the rivers are also contaminated (IUCN, 1991). During this period total industrial production in Poland increased by 12–13 times, while in the former GDR and Czechoslovakia the rise was at least eightfold (Nefedova and Treivish, 1994). In 1988 Czechoslovakia produced 74 per cent of the total volume of east European sulphur dioxide emissions (Carter and Turnock, 1993), and the severity of air pollution problems in the black triangle as a whole appears substantially greater than in the Donetsk Basin (the "worst" polluted industrial region of the Ukraine) or in the industrial centres of the Ural mountains in Russia.

Several factors have been responsible for the gravity of the environmental situation in this region. As has been indicated, nineteenth-century industrial development in the former Czechoslovakia and the GDR was further accelerated by intensive industrialisation during the Soviet period. The Stalinist model of economic development, adopted under pressure from the FSU, included assigning the greatest priority to heavy and energy industries and was based on very high consumption of raw materials. This type of economy created a development pattern found in all countries of the former socialist bloc, namely the concentration of industrial and mining enterprises – and therefore of pollution – in a single geographical region.

To add to the problem, industries and power stations generally burned brown coal and low-quality lignite with a high sulphur content. Heavy reliance on these low-grade fuels was the consequence of the lack of oil and other energy

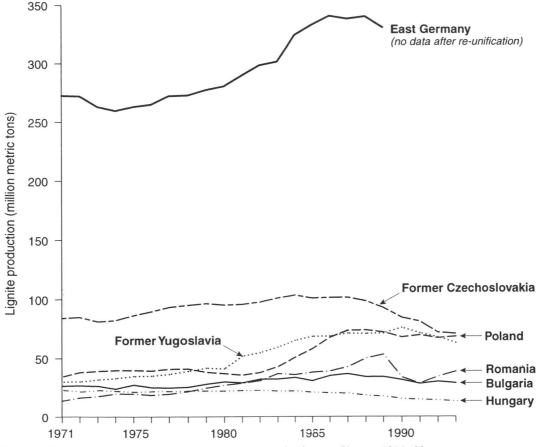

Figure 20.2 *Production of brown coal and lignite in central and eastern Europe, 1971–90*

sources, which resulted in the substantial expansion of lignite production and consumption during the socialist period (see Chapter 4). For example, lignite output in the former Czechoslovakia peaked at 102.9 million t in 1984 (Figure 20.2) and in 1991 brown coal and lignite accounted for over 80 per cent of the country's total coal production (EIU Country Profile, 1996–97). One consequence was that Czechoslovakia produced more pollutants per head of population than any other European state (IUCN, 1990). Meanwhile in the GDR, brown coal and lignite production was three times greater than in Czechoslovakia (OECD, 1991), and energy installations produced 94 per cent of sulphur dioxide, 73 per cent of dust and 81 per cent of nitrogen oxides (Manser, 1993). Against this background, Alcamo (1992) has estimated that a 70 per cent reduction in sulphur dioxide in the region as a whole will cost US$8.6bn. It is also clear that a significant clean-up of the degraded areas will take a long time. The open-cast mining districts, for example, have been devastated by the industry, and little attention has been given to remedial measures long considered standard practice in the lignite mining areas of western Germany.

Beyond this, the whole drainage basin of Europe's longest river – the Volga – which historically was the industrial heartland of Russia, was struck by a multitude of problems. These reached such a level that the massive degradation of ecosystems became almost irreversible. Chiefly in response to increased water demand, between the Second World War and the late 1980s the annual discharge of the Volga and its tributaries decreased by 20–30 per cent, and the upper reaches of thousands of small rivers and streams retreated by dozens of kilometres from their original springs. Because of heavy industrial development in the Volga basin, over 10 million t of pollutants were emitted into the atmosphere each year. Even more seriously, many tributaries of the Volga became heavily polluted with industrial, agricultural, domestic and, sometimes, radioactive wastes. In 1992 the volume of polluted wastes discharged into the river system accounted for 39 per cent of all such pollution in the Russian Federation. According to some estimates (Goskompriroda SSSR, 1990) by the late 1980s only 20 per cent of the basin's ecosystems remained

in a "normal" state, while conditions in the remaining 80 per cent were equally divided between those that were either "critical" or "catastrophic". This situation is, of course, extremely serious because the Volga basin occupies 62 per cent of European Russia; moreover, the river system exerts a tremendous influence on the overall "health" of the environment in this part of the Russian Federation and in the Caspian Sea region, which is currently shared by five independent countries. In addition, water pollution is a major problem in other countries as well. For instance, in the former GDR half of all available water sources are unusable for drinking and another 38 per cent are usable only after heavy treatment operations (Jones, 1995).

Although this discussion has highlighted major problem regions, this does not mean that other areas have remained unscathed. On the contrary, many other regions in both central and eastern Europe have suffered a whole range of environmental problems with varying degrees of severity. To quote Alcamo once more: "The damage is as diverse as the landscape" (Alcamo, 1992, 1). One telling statistic in this context is that, in 1991, 13 regions in Russia, including 9 within her European territory, were officially designated as "ecological disaster areas" (Ministry of Ecology and Natural Resources of the RF, 1992). In Poland 27 areas, occupying 11 per cent of the country and with 35 per cent of the total population, have been recorded as ecologically damaged (IUCN, 1990). In the former Yugoslavia it has become apparent that one-third of the forests have been destroyed, due mainly to air pollution, and that heavy loads of polluted wastes have been discharged annually into the River Danube from 150 industrial enterprises. There is much degradation in agricultural areas as well. For example, in Hungary 60 per cent of all groundwater has been affected by nutrient pollution, due to a rapid increase in the use of mineral fertilisers from 50 kg of active agents per hectare in 1962 to above 300 kg in 1983 (IUCN, 1991, 1992).

In addition, as is now widely appreciated, an important outcome of this extensive and intensive environmental damage has been its detrimental impact on people's health, which has led some authors to talk of "ecocide" (Feshbach and Friendly, 1992). One of the indices of this impact is the rate of infant mortality, which in 1991 reached 26.9 per 1000 new-born babies in Romania, 19.8 in Moldova, 17.8 in Russia, 16.7 in Bulgaria, 15.6 in Latvia, 15.2 in Poland and 14.8 in Hungary. These figures may be compared to 7.9 in the UK and 7.1 in Netherlands (*Russian Statistical Yearbook*, 1995). Another reliable index of well-being – life expectancy – is similarly much less favourable in most of CEE than in the developed countries of western Europe. For example, in the former Czechoslovakia it is five to seven years lower (Alcamo, 1992; see also p. 15).

These health problems, and more mainstream environmental threats, are at least partly related to the transboundary air pollution discussed earlier. As has already been indicated, however, the dramatic environmental crisis has other very deep-rooted causes stemming from the essence of the socialist system. Given the earlier discussion, and the fact that many causal factors have been widely examined in the literature (e.g. Fullenbach, 1981; Manser, 1993; Vari and Tamaz, 1993), they need not be examined at length here. What must be emphasised, however, is that they go beyond state attitudes which cultivated "pollution economies" with antecedents dating back to nineteenth-century or inter-war industrialisation. In particular, it is important to recognise the role of political, legal and social forces in the creation of the current environmental crisis.

One of the most important political factors was the general attitude taken by the state towards the environment and natural resources. As Hungarian geographers have noted, "human dominance over nature was regarded as the strength of socialism" (Juhasz *et al.*, 1993, 227). This political concept had a profound impact on the prevailing attitudes of both decision-makers and ordinary people for several decades after its initial introduction in the USSR during the Stalinist era. The most dramatic consequence of this was the dominant tendency to regard nature only as a source of free resources, which ultimately resulted in the devastation of multiple resource bases by inefficient and wasteful practices. Availability of natural resources, rather than demand, was the major limiting factor for the planned administrative command economies of the socialist countries. Most technologies continued to be very resource- and energy-consuming. Unsurprisingly, this type of economy allotted very low priorities to environmental issues. Highly prioritised industrial development was essential for the construction of Communism, and it was assumed that the totally controlled system could easily overcome any possible negative side-effects. "Moral persuasion" was used as a mechanism for the enforcement of environmental protection measures and, as Fullenbach noted, a frequent argument presented by the socialist system was that "pollution is a structural problem in capitalist societies, [and] therefore in principle insoluble, while the environmental problem in a socialist system is simply a question of motivation, and thus easily capable of solution via political decisions" (Fullenbach, 1981, 106). These dogmas were apparently supported by a multitude of environmental laws, acts, regulations and resolutions, but CEE states demonstrated an overall inability to enforce the legislation effectively. Similarly, there was a marked lack of economic instruments designed to foster environmental protection. Problems grew inexorably as a result, while blanket ideological controls effectively prevented the "seepage" of any politically unfavourable information until the 1980s. This censorship, in its turn, contributed significantly to a general lack of public awareness of actual environmental impacts, which made matters even worse.

Despite the ideological controls, awareness of the severity of environmental problems improved significantly towards the end of the socialist era. *Glasnost* contributed greatly to this but, in any case, widespread major damage cannot be passed off as normal or acceptable indefinitely. When the socialist period ended, therefore, it was natural that there were widespread hopes for environmental improvement associated with the transformation of society and the help that was expected from the West. The relatively clean environment in western European countries supported this assumption, and in many quarters the idea took root that the transition to the market economy would be a panacea for the environmental disasters now seen to be associated with the previous regime. As Manser noted, in 1990 "... it was still believed that the introduction of the free market would make a major contribution to environmental restructuring" (Manser, 1993, 148). Economic restructuring in the form of the decentralisation of power, deindustrialisation, privatisation and liberalisation of the economy would – it was widely argued – create the mechanisms needed for the rehabilitation of the environment and the prevention of any further destruction. As has been indicated, progress in this context has so far fallen well short of expectation, but what has been achieved and why has the pace of change been so disappointing?

Environmental Action and Change in the Transition Period

The main environmental challenge faced by the emerging democracies at the beginning of the transition period was the continuing ecological crisis. "As Central and East European societies move into a new era of their histories, they drag along with them the environmental costs of their recent past" (Alcamo, 1992, 1). The main asset, also inherited from the former regime, was the ecological diversity and richness of many virtually "untouched" or almost pristine landscapes in the region. It is estimated that these cover about 30 per cent of central Europe (Klarer *et al.*, 1994) and about 16 per cent of the Russian Federation (Danilov-Danilyan and Kotlyakov, 1993). These areas need even more careful protection from the encroachment of industrial development. Ideally, therefore, the situation requires a long-term sustainable economic development strategy, designed both to ameliorate past environmental damage and prevent further deterioration. Arguably, this strategy should incorporate a set of environmental objectives related to:

(a) Urgent action to minimise further adverse health effects in the ecological disaster areas.
(b) Improvement of the environmental situation in the region as a whole.
(c) The provision of nation-wide monitoring networks.
(d) The protection of pristine nature areas.
(e) The development of effective economic mechanisms to avoid further damage to the environment. This is probably the most important.

Unfortunately the initial collapse of the economies, subsequent economic problems suffered by all countries of the region, and the low priority given to environmental issues during this early transition period, have combined to become serious impediments to the evolution of such an integrated strategy. This has naturally made it difficult to achieve significant progress towards many of the above goals.

Achievements and failures of the perestroika period

As we have seen, successes in this period included institutional changes and the abolition of censorship of environmental information. But the main achievement of environmentalism in the *perestroika* (restructuring) period, started by the Soviet leader Mikhail Gorbachev in 1986, was improved environmental awareness and a new level of public participation in the political process (Matthews and Saiko, 1994). As a survey conducted early in 1990 in the former Czechoslovakia has revealed, for 29 per cent of the population environmental issues seemed very important (Wolchik, 1991). Although this was still less than the proportion giving priority to the economic reform (40 per cent), it was none the less a major advance. Before the fall of the Berlin Wall attitudes to environmental degradation were especially heated, particularly in the Baltic republics of the USSR, the former Czechoslovakia and Poland, where environmental movements took the form of political opposition and actively participated in the dismantling of the former regimes. Dozens of polluting enterprises in the USSR were temporarily or completely closed during the "Gorbachev era", which ended in December 1991, and many more environmentally damaging projects were abandoned. However, although this initiated progress towards the reduction of environmental impacts, it was still not matched by constructive efforts to enforce legislation and to apply an effective economic system of incentives for strict environmental control. Instead, due to the economic collapse of the previous administrative command economy system in most countries of the region, there was a general failure of environmental policies to bring any serious ecological progress.

Change and challenge in the transition period

Since 1989, as a result of economic collapse and the decline in industrial production during the transition period, *transitional environmental improvement* has been recorded in many parts of the region. Sakwa has noted that "the collapse of the Soviet economy … had a beneficial environmental impact, as plants closed and industrial activity declined …" (Sakwa, 1993, 263). One positive change is the overall reduction in sulphur dioxide emissions in many parts of CEE; in the Russian Federation, for example, the actual decline in these emissions between 1980 and 1993 was estimated at 51.7 per cent (Ministry of Ecology and Natural Resources of the RF, 1995) (Figure 20.3). Although this was in part due to the influence of the 1979 Convention on Long-range Transboundary Air Pollution, it is known that much of the reduction was a consequence of the new economic environment.

Similarly, recent data indicate that there has been a decrease in these emissions even in the black triangle (Swedish Environmental Research Institute, 1996). This phenomenon can be attributed to a cutback in lignite production in the countries of central Europe, again associated with general industrial decline during the transition period. Thus brown coal and lignite production in the Czech Republic fell by 22.3 per cent between 1991 and 1994. Compared with the peak value recorded in 1984, production has declined by almost one-third (OECD, 1991; EIU Country Profile, 1996–97).

Despite these encouraging trends, however, the justification for optimism is limited. For example, while the overall decline in economic production in the Russian Federation in 1993–94 amounted to 21 per cent, the total volume of air pollution decreased by only 12.7 per cent and water pollution by 9 per cent (Ministry of Ecology and Natural Resources of the RF, 1995). From this it appears that environmental gains are not directly proportional to economic losses. Also, it is very likely that recent reductions in pollution will be shown to have given only temporary relief. Many countries of the region, particularly in central Europe, are already showing various signs of economic revival, unmatched by highly desirable improvements in environmental control. And in the Russian Federation there is already evidence that one-quarter of the surviving enterprises have actually increased their polluting discharges (*Nezavisimaya Gazeta*, 2 February 1995). This may well mean that they have tended to economise on necessary environmental measures during the economic

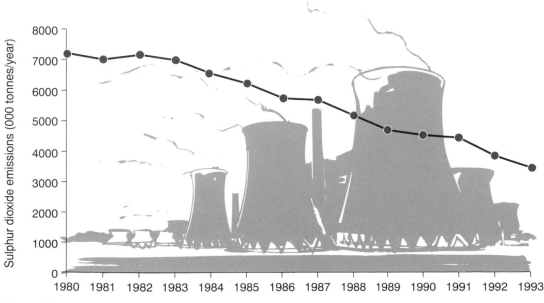

Figure 20.3 *Reduction in the Russian Federation's sulphur dioxide emissions, 1980–93*

recession. Indicators such as these point clearly to the conclusion that "deindustrialisation [is] hardly a long-term solution to the crisis" (Sakwa, 1993, 263).

There are also good reasons for believing that the task of environmental protection is becoming progressively harder, and may well continue to be so. Implementation of the adopted Western model of economic development has been accompanied by change in the system of values in society, and by the growth of consumerism with its subsequent additional impact on the environment. In all countries the number of private cars has increased significantly, aggravating the previous problems of traffic pollution, which were already quite severe in most of the capital cities. For example, the number of cars in the Russian Federation almost doubled from 1985 to 1994 (*Russian Statistical Yearbook*, 1995). What is also relevant here is that many of the additional vehicles are second-hand imports from western Europe, and are therefore considerably more polluting than new vehicles.

At the same time, the production decline in traditional industrial sectors has led to decreased consumption of some waste products, which were previously recycled. In the Ukraine in 1993 used tyre demand was 82 per cent lower than in 1990, while for solid domestic waste and phosphogypsum the equivalent declines were 86 and 95 per cent respectively (*Russia and Eurasia Facts and Figures Annual*, 1996). This clearly raises important disposal issues in countries where regulation is seriously deficient. It is further aggravated by the fact that in the last few years there have been many reported cases of exports of toxic ecological wastes from developed countries to CEE. This problem has acquired a particular significance in the Russian Federation, which on 1 July 1996 adopted a special Governmental Resolution on the State Regulation of Transboundary Transfers of Dangerous Wastes.

An additional significant fact is that improved environmental information has shown that some disasters were more serious than initially believed, and has also exposed previously unknown catastrophes. For instance, recent assessments have greatly increased the previous estimates given by Soviet and Western experts soon after the Chernobyl disaster. It is now estimated that at least 170 million Ci of radioactivity, and not 50 million

as was first announced, were released into the environment during the accident (Medvedev, 1990, 1994). Environmental surveys in the FSU carried out over the last few years have also significantly increased the initial estimates of the total contaminated area and have included many new regions in the list of affected territories. Detailed health studies have recorded hundreds of cases of thyroid cancer in children associated with the Chernobyl catastrophe. Elsewhere, in the last few years it has been revealed that at least two regions of the Urals are heavily contaminated with radioactivity, as well as some areas in the Kara Sea. Other examples of environmental degradation include the former military bases of the USSR in central Europe (Fodor and Walker, 1994).

There have also been new challenges stemming from the dissolution of the USSR, and resulting changes in the geopolitical situation. These are primarily attributable to the complex problems of internationally shared water bodies, such as the River Danube, the Baltic and the Black and Caspian seas (Galambos, 1993; Preis, 1996; Ozturk *et al.*, 1996; Saiko, 1996). "The disintegration of the USSR jeopardised Soviet environmental and conservation legislation as each republic sought maximum advantage for itself, leading, for example, to sea fishing of sturgeon in the Caspian, banned in 1962 by the Soviet Ministry of Fisheries" (*Moscow News*, 4 February 1993, cited by Sakwa, 1993, 263). International tensions, and sometimes even conflicts, related to shared natural resources and the state of the environment in the above regions have already taken place.

Political instability in a number of "hot spots" of the region has similarly added to the scope of environmental problems. Grave ecological consequences of the wars in Chechnya and the former Yugoslavia, coupled with conflicts in Pridnestrovye and Caucasus, have taken their own toll on the environment, and have also diverted many of the resources needed for economic development and environmental enhancement. For example, in Chechnya the total cost of damage and necessary restoration investments has been estimated at over US$9bn (*Izvestiya*, 27 October 1995). Three cities of the Chechen Republic – its capital Grozny, Argun and Goudermes – have been largely destroyed during the course of the war, as have several major

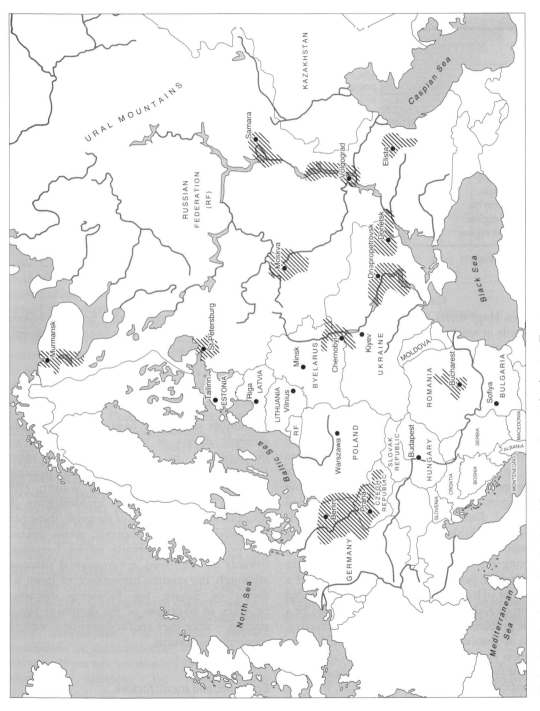

Figure 20.4 *Distribution of selected ecological disaster areas in central and eastern Europe*

investment in protection and improvement. Monitoring systems in a number of countries have been further undermined by the current economic difficulties, as was the case in 1995 when over 300 hydrometric posts along the River Volga were closed because of the lack of funds (Zonn, 1996). Economic difficulties have been responsible for a growing lack of properly staffed and equipped environmental infrastructures at the local level, while bribery of poorly paid officials has become a common practice. This has allowed existing polluting enterprises to avoid paying the prescribed fees, and new ones to ignore the requirement to undertake environmental impact assessments.

A further economic factor is that, although restructuring has hit established industries, many of the past causes of environmental degradation have continued to operate during the transition period. State monopolism remaining in many economic areas appears to be one of the persisting obstacles for effective change in the environmental sphere. In fact most of the old enterprises have survived, as Preis (1996, 15) has highlighted in the context of continuing Baltic Sea pollution problems: "... in Russia, Estonia, Latvia, Lithuania and Poland many industrial plants are technologically outdated and need to be rebuilt to meet the present environmental demands". New investments are rarely diverted to expensive programmes intended to renovate their obsolete technologies. Thus energy- and resource-intensive technologies are still widely used. Beyond this the continuing lack of environmental control measures reflects an important conflict between the environment and employment. In most countries the need to close polluting enterprises with outdated equipment has often been counter-balanced by the threat of increased unemployment. Faced with this dilemma, decision-makers at the highest levels have frequently been reluctant to take hard decisions which might generate social discontent. As Sakwa has noted "the tension between environmental security and economic well-being is an acute one in developed countries and all the more painful in countries close to economic catastrophe" (Sakwa, 1993, 263).

Not all industries, of course, are old. New ones are springing up, and the industrial sector's share of GDP in the former socialist countries continues

to be relatively high. In 1993 it amounted to 35.9 per cent in Russia, 32.7 per cent in Poland and 27.6 per cent in Hungary, compared with 23 per cent in the UK and 21.9 per cent in the USA (*Russian Statistical Yearbook*, 1995). But, all too frequently, new industrial investment brings new dangers. For example, many of the new élite entrepreneurs rely heavily on exports of raw materials as a means of earning quick profits. Typically, this is done with little concern for the environment. Linked with this, additional threats are related to a recent trend to locate new enterprises in areas previously untouched by human activities, thus undermining – in some cases literally – the few remaining assets of the former socialist countries (Klarer *et al.*, 1994). Generally speaking, in most countries recent commercial activities have been largely unregulated from the viewpoint of their environmental impacts, and transition to the free market may contribute to further environmental degradation. The role and mechanism of market incentives for environmental control, which are still being debated in developed countries, appear to be a complete mystery for decision-makers in the emerging democracies. Moreover, the basic contradiction between the goals of economic development and environmental improvement seems to be increasing during the current transition period, when the former administrative controls fail to operate and new market mechanisms are almost non-existent. This is particularly true for countries such as Russia or the Ukraine, where different forms of "hybrid" or even "mutant" capitalism have evolved, and where the development of a true market economy is complicated by corruption and other features inherited from the past.

Generally speaking, long-term sustainable approaches are a rare exception rather than normal attitudes in economic development. This strongly suggests that too many hopes have been pinned on privatisation as a vehicle for environmental protection (Manser, 1993). As Fodor (1994) has demonstrated, privatisation does not automatically lead to a decrease in pollution and is mainly effective in specific areas, such as waste management. Socio-economic restructuring via privatisation can even create the "new sources of danger" (Fodor, 1994, 40). For example, an influx of numerous small businesses with outdated technologies from the West, coupled with less strict environmental regulations in CEE countries, have aggravated the existing pollution problem. The emerging market economies are chiefly concerned with profit and – in a politico-social environment which is opposed to market regulation and the imposition of "unnecessary" costs – liberalisation cannot reasonably be expected to be a panacea for environmental problems.

From a social perspective, the most significant point is that the acute economic and social problems that have emerged in the transformation period in all spheres of life have pushed environmental issues down to a significantly lower level of priority. This has been the case even in the countries which had them very high on their agendas prior to the end of socialist period. Other concerns have taken the place of environmental ones in the face of the dramatic socio-economic change. This was underlined, for instance, by a recent opinion poll among Russian voters in the 1996 presidential elections. Forty-eight per cent were primarily worried by the high cost of living, 24 per cent by the threat of unemployment and 23 per cent by crime. In a second survey, in which respondents could list more than one concern, 18 per cent said that they were worried by the decline in state authority, 14 per cent complained of the collapse of morals in society and 14 per cent identified the war in Chechnya as their major anxiety. In stark contrast less than 3 per cent of the respondents were concerned with environmental problems (*Segodnya*, 26 June 1996).

Reflecting this trend, the level of activity of the "green" movement has also declined significantly throughout CEE over the last few years. Many of the former green leaders have abandoned their initial goals after becoming well established in the new parliaments or governments, while others have lost much of their former influence in the face of the ever-increasing pressures from industrial lobbies. At present the majority of environmental groups in the region have no serious impact on decision-makers, and there is an overall lack of public activism at the local level. Despite some regional successes, overcoming the lack of environmental concern remains a major problem in most countries.

Political and other reasons

Despite the obvious political transformation processes in individual countries, with a few exceptions former Communist Party bosses continue to dominate the top-level official posts and there has been little change in their attitudes towards natural resources and the environment. As a result no coherent integrated environmental policy has been developed in any country and, though some improvements have been made in most countries, in general a piecemeal approach has prevailed both in the realms of economic transition and environmental policy. This has produced a lack of effective legal and economic instruments to enforce stricter environmental regulation on old and new enterprises alike. This problem, it is true, must not be overemphasised. For example, in Russian watercourses the permitted levels of some pollutants, e.g. nitrates, copper and cadmium, are lower than those allowed by the World Health Organisation (WHO). But for others, including molybdenum, arsenic, lead, zinc, mercury, nickel and benzene, the permitted concentrations are higher. Indeed, for DDT the officially acceptable level is 50 times higher than the WHO guideline value (Bridges and Bridges, 1996).

While many of the political problems are internal, others reflect the international political dimension, particularly with respect to aid. According to a survey conducted by the Regional Center for Central and Eastern Europe, " … a considerable amount of foreign environmental aid has flowed into the region in recent years ..." (Klarer *et al.*, 1994, 86). Structurally, much of the environmental aid to the CEE countries has taken the form of international and bilateral projects. Various positive developments have resulted from this assistance, including support for the training of government and NGO officials; the production of environmental assessments, surveys and feasibility studies; the establishment of monitoring systems; and technology transfers and advice.

None the less, in many respects aid to date has provoked extensive criticism. For example, Manser (1993) has shown that very often the European Community has been unwilling to agree to projects in economic sectors in which the western and eastern interests are competitive. Outstanding examples have related to agriculture, steel and textiles. Thus "in several of the principal sectors, where Central and Eastern Europe had a comparative advantage . . ., the EC was reluctant to allow any significant access" (Manser, 1993, 153). Bilateral programmes, meanwhile, have often been limited to assisting countries which clearly have a direct environmental impact on the donor states because of their proximity. Thus Sweden channelled more than US$19m. to the Baltic states in 1994 in the form of environmental aid, above all to reduce air pollution by replacing boilers burning heavy fuel oil with advanced equipment based on biomass. Although some of this aid was also directed to another nearby state, Poland, none went to the other countries of the region.

Similarly, a recent examination of the effectiveness of the Nordic environmental aid to the countries of eastern Europe has identified negative as well as positive effects. One of the main criticisms relates to the neglect of local expertise in the recipient countries, even though it has become clear that the participation of local experts in these projects may be crucial to their success. As the authors note,

> "It is obvious that environmental aid to Eastern Europe is seen by Western countries as a way to generate jobs and thus support their own economies. One way of doing this is by funding the pre-feasibility studies carried out by domestic consultants, or implementing tied-aid schemes in which the recipient nation has to use the aid money to buy the donor's goods. BITS in Sweden, for instance, is required by law to fund only Swedish firms and consultants" (Lofstedt and Sjostedt, 1995, 368).

Other criticisms highlight the low economic efficiency of many aid projects and their lack of cost-effectiveness evaluation. This, it is argued, reflects the fact that "many countries, such as Sweden and Denmark, do not have clear environmental strategies for their East European environmental-aid programmes" (Lofstedt and Sjostedt, 1995, 369). In addition, inter-agency rivalry between the different donor organisations adds to the scope of problems. What is particularly striking about this substantial range of concerns is its similarity to the objections frequently raised in

connection with Western aid to developing countries.

Finally, it should be emphasised that progress is hampered by a continuing dearth of reliable and comparable environmental data for the whole region, even though the "revolutions" were in 1989–90. This is not to say that no information is available; but as Alcamo (1992, 28) has pointed out, "While there is a flood of information on the environment in Eastern Europe, the reliability of many of these data is in doubt. Moreover, there is still no agreement in Europe on which pollutants are [the] best overall indicators of environmental quality . . . ." In this context, it is true, improvements are becoming evident. Since 1990 substantial annual reports on the state of the environment have been published in the USSR and, subsequently, in Russia by the Ministry of Ecology and Natural Resources (1991–95). However, as was mentioned earlier, such progress tends to be restricted to the more developed countries of the region; elsewhere – and particularly in Romania and Albania – very few advances have been made in this respect. This problem, of course, reflects both the economic constraints and attitudinal influences discussed above. Moreover, even when progress is made there is no guarantee that it will be permanent. Recently, for example, Russia's Ministry of Ecology and Natural Resources has been transformed into the Russian State Committee on Environmental Protection, thus losing some of its power and functions.

Conclusion

This study has highlighted slow progress towards environmental enhancement in the countries of CEE. This chiefly reflects the influence of numerous constraints to improvement, constraints whose origins lie partly in the past and partly in the current transition period. There is a vital link between the ecological legacies of the former socialist system and the future well-being of central, eastern and – indeed – western Europe. Meanwhile, new environmental challenges are closely related to the processes of political, economic and social transformation which are under way in the countries in transition. The idealised model of a "clean" environment "inherent" to the free market economy has failed to produce the expected results. Moreover, problems of environmental degradation, in their turn, have contributed to the aggravation of economic decline and to the acceleration of social and even ethnic tensions. Although what may be called "transitional environmental improvement" has in some respects drawn a temporary veil over the crisis situation, this should by no means distract us from the need for urgent measures to improve the state of the environment, which is still critical in many parts of CEE. This is the reality, even though it is difficult to assess the precise magnitude of ecological crises in specific localities, and even more problematic to make a reliable and comprehensive ecological evaluation of the entire region.

To a great extent, the current absence of highly active environmental improvement programmes is readily understandable. Economic problems demand greater attention from governments, and environmental issues have therefore lost much of their "pre-revolutionary" urgency in the eyes of politicians and peoples. What is also becoming evident, however, is that environmental problems, in their turn, could make the successful implementation of economic reforms more difficult. And there is an increasing realisation that the challenges of environmental rehabilitation cannot be divorced from the prevailing economic, social and political issues. Instead, significant progress is likely to depend on the adoption of holistic strategies of sustainable development which take these issues fully into account. This, of course, will require CEE governments to show more political will towards environmental protection than they have since the start of the transition period, while a preparedness to channel growing economic gains into policy implementation will also be crucial.

What is also arguable, however, is that it would be a mistake to expect progress to come solely from developments within CEE. On the contrary, external forces may well have an important contribution to make towards the adoption of more effective policies. One aspect of this is that the prospect of the eventual integration of CEE countries into European and global structures, such as the EU and OECD, should provide an important stimulus. For example, with respect to the EU, the goal of accession should act as a significant inducement for individual states to harmonise their environmental legislation – and also its implementation – with the EU's requirements. Hungary has already made progress in this direction. Similarly Poland, which was awarded OECD membership in July 1996 largely on the strength of its economic restructuring, will now have to promote international standards of environmental protection within its borders (*The Economist*, 13 July 1996).

In addition, progressive external forces are likely to include the availability of aid. Although to date – as we have seen – environmental aid programmes have had many drawbacks, in some cases significant strengths can also be identified. One instance of this is provided by what are known as "joint implementation programmes", involving strong participation of both the donor and recipient countries. This approach has emerged as one of the key policies for managing financial and labour-resource transfers in order to meet international targets for environmental improvement. Because of its success, it is currently being considered as an implementation vehicle for four major international environmental agreements related to climate change, sulphur pollution, biodiversity and ozone depletion. There are also encouraging signs that progress may be achieved through the "debt-for-nature" swaps concept. This seeks to gain benefits from the problem of heavy external indebtedness experienced by many CEE countries. With this type of scheme, Western creditor governments buy back debt in exchange for a commitment from debtor states to enhance environmental protection (Manser, 1993). Thus the rationale of the Polish Environmental Fund, started in 1991, is to use debt-for-nature swaps to achieve environmental protection plus a 10 per cent reduction of the official national debt, a decline equivalent to US$3.1bn (Levy, 1993; Lofstedt and Sjostedt, 1995).

Finally, the argument that better progress will be made through the effective combination of internal reforms and external forces suggests that new perceptions and attitudes are required outside CEE. In particular, the time has come for Western countries to stop thinking in terms of CEE's "environmental guilt", especially as the West is itself a source of international pollution. Effective co-operation measures to protect our "common" environment will be enhanced substantially if there is the widest possible acceptance that "equal partnership" approaches have much to offer as we seek to maximise success in achieving the urgently needed environmental gains.

References

Alcamo, J (ed) (1992) *Coping with Crisis in Eastern Europe's Environment*, Parthenon Publishing Group, Carnforth.

Bridges, O and Bridges, J (1996) *Losing Hope: the environment and health in Russia*, Avebury, Aldershot.

Carter, F W and Turnock, D (eds) (1993) *Environmental Problems in Eastern Europe*, Routledge, London.

Carter, F W and Turnock, D (1996) *Environmental Problems in Eastern Europe*, 2nd edn, Routledge, London.

Davilov-Danilyan, V I and Kotlyakov, V M (eds) (1993) *Russia in Environmental Crisis*, Federal Ecological Fund, Moscow (in Russian).

DeBardeleben, J and Hannigan, J (eds) (1994) *Environmental Security and Quality after Communism in Eastern Europe and the Soviet Successor States*, Westview Press, Boulder, Colo.

EIU Country Profile 1996–9 (1996) *Czech Republic*, The Economist Intelligence Unit, London.

EIU Country Reports (1996) *Albania, Belarus, Bulgaria, Czech Republic, Estonia, Hungary, Latvia, Lithuania, Moldova, Poland, Romania, Slovakia, Slovenia, Ukraine, First Quarter 1996*, The Economist Intelligence Unit, London.

Europa Publications (1994) *Eastern Europe and the Commonwealth of Independent States: regional surveys of the world*, Europa Publications Limited, London.

Feshbach, M and Friendly, A (1992) *Ecocide in the USSR*, Auzum, London.

Fisher, D (1992) *Paradise Deferred: environmental policymaking in Central and Eastern Europe*, Royal Institute of International Affairs, London.

Fodor, I (1994) Characteristics of environmental problems in Eastern-Central Europe, in I Fodor and G P Walker (eds) *Environmental Policy and Practice in Eastern and Western Europe*, Centre for Regional Studies, Pecs, 33–41.

Fodor, I and Walker, G P (eds) (1994) *Environmental Policy and Practice in Eastern and Western Europe*, Centre for Regional Studies, Pecs.

Fullenbach, J (1981) *European Environmental Policy: East and West*, Butterworths, London.

Galambos, J (1993) An international environmental conflict on the Danube, in A Vari and P Tamas (eds) *Environment and Democratic Transition*, Kluwer, Dordrecht, 176–226.

Glantz, M H (1994) Creeping environmental phenomena in the Aral Sea basin, *NATO Advanced Research Workshop on Critical Scientific Issues of the Aral Sea Basin: State of Knowledge and Future Research Needs*, 2–4 May 1994, Tashkent.

Goskompriroda SSSR (1990) Special Report on the Catastrophic Situation in the Volga Region, Moscow (unpublished, in Russian).

IUCN (1990) *Environmental Status Reports: 1988–1989*, Volume One: *Czechoslovakia, Hungary, Poland*, International Union for Conservation of Nature and Natural Resources, Geneva.

IUCN (1991) *Environmental Status Reports: 1990*, Volume Two: *Albania, Bulgaria, Romania, Yugoslavia*, International Union for Conservation of Nature and Natural Resources, Geneva.

IUCN (1992) *Interaction between Agriculture and Environment in Hungary*, International Union for Conservation of Nature and Natural Resources, Geneva.

IUCN (1993) *Environmental Status Reports: 1993*, Volume Five: *Estonia, Latvia, Lithuania*, International Union for Conservation of Nature and Natural Resources, Geneva.

Jones, A (1995) *The New Germany. A human geography*, Wiley, Chichester.

Juhasz, J, Vari, A and Tolgyyesi, J (1993) Environmental conflict and political change: public perception on low-level radioactive waste management in Hungary, in A Vari and P Tamas (eds) *Environment and Democratic Transition: policy and politics in Eastern Europe*, Kluwer, Dordrecht, 227–48.

Klarer, J, Sitnicki, S and Zlinszky, J (1994) Strategic environmental issues in Central and Eastern Europe, in I Fodor and G P Walker (eds) *Environmental Policy and Practice in Eastern and Western Europe*, Centre for Regional Studies, Pecs, 73–97.

Levy, M A (1993) East–West environmental politics after 1989: the case of air pollution, in R O Keohane, J S Nye and S Hoffman (eds) *After the Cold War: international institutions and state strategies in Europe, 1989–1991*, Harvard University Press, Cambridge, Mass, 310–41.

Lofstedt, R E and Sjostedt, J (1995) Environmental aid to Eastern Europe: problems and possible solutions, *Ambio*, **24**(6), 366–70.

Manser, R (1993) *Squandered Dividend*, Earthscan Publications Limited, London.

Matthews, J A and Saiko, T A (1994) Environmental policies and public participation during transition periods: a comparison between Britain and Russia, in I Fodor and G P Walker (eds) *Environmental Policy and Practice in Eastern and Western Europe*, Centre for Regional Studies, Pecs, 223–34.

Medvedev, Z A (1990) *The Legacy of Chernobyl*, Basil Blackwell, Padstow.

Medvedev, Z A (1994) The Chernobyl legacy, *The Moscow Times*, 6 May 1994, 5.

Ministry of Ecology and Natural Resources of the RF (1992) *Report on the State of the Environment in the Russian Federation in 1991*, MENRRF/CIP, Moscow (in Russian).

Ministry of Ecology and Natural Resources of the RF (1995) *Report on the State of the Environment in the Russian Federation in 1994*, MENRRF/CIP, Moscow (in Russian).

Mnatsakanian, R A (1992) *Environmental Legacy of the Former Soviet Republics*, Centre for Human Ecology, University of Edinburgh.

Nefedova, T (1994) Industrial development and the environment in Central and Eastern Europe, *European Urban and Regional Studies*, **1**(2), 168–71.

Nefedova, T and Treivish, A (1994) *Regions of Russia and Other European Countries with Economies in Transition*, Institute of Geography of the Russian Academy of Sciences, Moscow (in Russian).

OECD (Organisation for Economic Cooperation and Development) (1991) *Energy Statistics and Balances of Non-OECD Countries*, OECD, Paris.

Ozturk, M, Ozdemir, F and Yucel, E (1996) An overview of the environmental issues in the Black Sea Region, paper presented at the NATA Advanced Research Workshop on *Scientific, Environmental and Political Issues in the Circum-Caspian Region*, 13–16 May 1996, Moscow.

Peterson, D J (1993) *Troubled Lands: the legacy of Soviet environmental destruction*, Westview Press, Oxford.

Preis, S (1996) Environmental problems of the Baltic Sea Region, paper presented at the NATO Advanced Research Workshop on *Scientific, Environmental and Political Issues in the Circum-Caspian Region*, 13–16 May 1996, Moscow.

Pryde, P R (1991) *Environmental Management in the Soviet Union*, Cambridge University Press, Cambridge.

Russian and Eurasia Facts and Figures Annual (1996), 21, Academic International Press, Gulf Breeze.

Russian Statistical Yearbook (1995) Goskomstat, Moscow.

Saiko, T A (1996) Environmental problems of the Caspian Sea Region and the conflict of national priorities, paper presented at the NATO Advanced Research Workshop on *Scientific, Environmental and Political Issues in the Circum-Caspian Region*, 13–16 May 1996, Moscow.

Sakwa, R (1993) *Russian Politics and Society*, Routledge, London.

Stewart, J M (ed) (1992) *The Soviet Environment: policies and politics*, Cambridge University Press, Cambridge.

Swedish Environmental Research Institute (1996), Press release.

Vari, A and Tamas, P (eds) (1993) *Environment and Democratic Transition: policy and politics in Eastern Europe*, Kluwer, Dordrecht.

Wolchik, S (1991) *Czechoslovakia in Transition*, Pinter Publishers, London.

Yaroshinskaya, A (1992) *Chernobyl: top secret*, Drugiye Berega, Moscow (in Russian).

Zonn, I S (1996) Personal communication.

Zonn, I S and Zonn, S V (in press) On the geoecological impacts of the military actions in the Chechen Republic, *Izvestiya Rossiiskoi Academii Nauk, Seriya Geographicheskaia*, 1 (in Russian).

21

Environmental protection and pollution control in the EU

Problems and progress in the 1990s

Richard H Williams and Holmfridur Bjarnadottir

Department of Town and Country Planning, University of Newcastle upon Tyne, UK and Skipulags Stofnun, Iceland

This chapter aims primarily to explore the scope and evolution of environmental policy-making in the EU. As a result of the periodic expansion of the original European Community, it is therefore concerned with the large majority of western and southern Europe. Indeed, within this broad region, only Norway, Iceland, Switzerland and Liechtenstein are excluded. None of these can be said to be a source of major environmental degradation, and only Switzerland falls outside the European Economic Area, to which some of the EU legislation also applies.

While the geographical arena for the analysis is relatively straightforward, however, the subject itself is highly complex. This partly reflects the sheer numbers of member states now involved, with the added dimension of their relations with the European Commission in Brussels. But it is also a consequence of a wide range of other factors which have become potential or actual impediments to attempts to formulate and implement environmental protection measures. To clarify recent developments in this vital yet highly complex field, the chapter looks first at the broad strategic framework devised for environmental policy-making, and in particular

at the legal basis for intervention. Attention then focuses on the policy framework itself, turns to the expanding armoury of tactical measures available to translate policy into practice, and finally examines the not inconsiderable range of challenges still waiting to be addressed.

Given the scope of the subject relative to the space available for discussion, detailed consideration of the state of the environment itself is impractical. However, this is well covered by Stanners and Bourdeau (1995) in their recent audit of Europe's environment. The initiative to undertake this was taken at the first pan-European Conference of Environment Ministers, held in Dobris Castle near Prague in June 1991: hence the title by which the study is commonly known, the Dobris Assessment. Similarly, for a comprehensive guide to the whole range of environmental policies and programmes, the institutions and officials responsible, and the non-EU bodies and pressure groups active in this sector, the guide published by the EU Committee of the American Chamber of Commerce in Belgium (AmCham, 1995) is very useful. Haigh (1995), meanwhile, offers a detailed account of each item of legislation and its significance for the UK.

The Strategic Framework: Treaties, Powers and the International Perspective

The authors of the EU's founding treaty, the Treaty of Rome of 1957, saw no need to refer to the environment (Wurzel, 1993). Article 2, which stated the task of the then European Economic Community, called for promotion of "continuous and balanced expansion". By 1972, public and political opinion was more aware of the environmental costs and pollution implications of economic growth, and a number of environmental measures had already been adopted. The Paris summit of 1972 therefore took the decision to establish an environmental policy sector. The question of whether the treaty needed to be amended was also discussed, but at that time the view taken was that it was sufficiently flexible to provide the necessary powers without amendment (Haigh, 1996).

Despite this decision, during the 1980s there was growing acceptance that the Treaty of Rome in fact provided insufficient powers for the action required. This was eventually rectified by the passage of the Single European Act of 1987, which paved the way for the Single European Market (SEM) and provided an explicit legal basis for EU environmental legislation. Even so, by this time over 100 environmental measures had been enacted (Wurzel, 1993).

Although it started slowly, environment policy had become a rapidly growing and influential policy sector by the early 1990s, with a high political profile. The need for collective environmental standards throughout the EU received greatly increased emphasis with the adoption of the programme to create the SEM by the end of 1992. It was recognised by this time that varying standards of pollution control among member states could result in unfair economic advantage which would constitute distortions of the SEM through the creation of pollution havens (Williams, 1986) or differing levels of liability for pollution costs. Therefore, in order to ensure its successful implementation and operation, harmonised environmental standards throughout the EU were seen to be necessary.

More recently, the Treaty of European Union, agreed at the Maastricht Summit in December 1991 and in force since 1993, has enhanced still further the scope for intervention in the environmental field. The Maastricht Treaty is clear about the place that environmental considerations must have in all EU policy instruments and EU legislation. Title XVI, the Environment Title, sets general objectives to which EU policy on the environment must contribute:

- "preserving, protecting and improving the quality of the environment;
- protecting human health;
- prudent and rational utilization of natural resources;
- promoting measures at [the] international level to deal with regional or worldwide environmental problems".

It goes on in the second paragraph to state that, *inter alia*,

> "Community policy on the environment shall aim at a high level of protection . . . shall be based on the precautionary principle and on the principles that preventive action should be taken, that environmental damage should as a priority be rectified at source and that the polluter should pay. Environmental protection requirements *must* be integrated into the definition and implementation of other Community policies" (Article 130r, EC Council 1992, 58; author's emphasis).

All member states can therefore be said to have accepted, when they ratified the Treaty, the obligation to give high priority to the environment, to seek high environmental standards and to accept the incorporation of these in all other EU policies. Some commentators go so far as to assert that this obligation overrides the exercise of all the other competences given to the EU. However, as a matter of practical reality this interpretation does not always prevail, as the European Environmental Bureau has acknowledged (EEB, 1994; Williams, 1996).

The Treaty on European Union reinforces the decision-making procedures for environmental legislation first established by the 1987 Single European Act. It does so by introducing three major changes to environmental policy-making at the EU level. These are the introduction of qualified majority voting (QMV); a stronger role for the European Parliament; and the creation of the Cohesion Fund.

QMV is intended to make the adoption of new environmental measures easier, but this is limited by the retention of unanimity (i.e. national vetoes) in some environmental sectors of significance in relation to pollution control. The European Parliament's stronger role, with powers of co-decision and of initiation of environmental legislation, is noteworthy because the Parliament has taken a firm stance in promoting environmental policies and has earned a reputation for being the most environmentally concerned of all the EU institutions (Barnes, 1995). The Cohesion Fund is focused on infrastructure investment and environmental improvement. It makes available for the first time substantial financial resources to help the four least prosperous member states implement environmental legislation (AmCham, 1995; Williams, 1996).

It may also be argued that the 1995 enlargement, with the accession of Austria, Finland and Sweden, has important implications for the development of EU environment policy. Finland and Sweden have the highest environmental standards of the 15 in a number of respects, and have clearly stated that they do not intend to allow environmental protection standards already set in their national legislation to be eroded as a result of adopting common EU standards. They can therefore be expected increasingly to perform the role of environmental pusher-states, pressing for the adoption of the highest standards.

Beyond this, progress on the environmental front is likely to be assisted by the European Environment Agency, established in Copenhagen in 1994. This is an EU institution, although it is also open to non-members. It is expected that it will not only work with national governments, but also with the numerous international organisations with environmental concerns, including the OECD, the International Energy Agency and the United Nations Environmental Programme. Currently, its main role is to provide technical and scientific support to the EU and its member states in the area of environmental protection and implementation of environmental policy. It was envisaged in 1990 that it would take an enforcement role in EU environment policy, but this has not yet been accepted in practice. The agency has, however, been involved in reporting on the state of the environment across the whole

of Europe, through the Dobris Assessment noted earlier (Stanners and Bordeau, 1995). This is the most comprehensive report and audit currently available.

At the inter-governmental level, the momentum for environmental protection has developed appreciably since the late 1980s. What must also be noted is that movement in this direction is by no means always smooth, as attitudes to the sustainability concept well illustrate. One of the single most influential events in the environmental discussion was an OECD conference in Oslo in 1987. This introduced and defined the concept of "sustainable development" in the context of the developed world, and highlighted the need for international action to tackle problems such as climate change, ozone depletion and diminution of biodiversity (Brundtland, 1987). In line with this new perspective, at the 1991 Inter-Governmental Conference (IGC) on political union, member states accepted the argument that Article 2 of the Rome Treaty should be amended to replace "continuous expansion" with "sustainable development". In contrast, the separate IGC on monetary union wanted to amend the same article so that it called for "sustainable non-inflationary growth" (Haigh, 1996). Although Haigh suggests that the intention was to incorporate the Brundtland concept of sustainable development (Brundtland, 1987), the final version contains elements of both formulations: "balanced development of economic activities . . . sustainable and non-inflationary growth respecting the environment" (Council of the European Union, 1992, 11). The end result is thus a rather equivocal commitment to sustainability, highlighting the continuing tension between economic growth and environmental protection. Understandably, at the time of writing the environment lobby has continued to press for adoption of the term "sustainable development" (EEB, 1995).

The Policy Framework: Action Programmes on the Environment

Since environment became a recognised policy sector in 1973, the Commission has adopted the practice of setting out a multiannual environment programme in the form of successive Action Programmes on the Environment. There have now been five of them (Figure 21.1). Although these programmes, containing reviews and statements of policy development intended for the period covered, are non-binding, many proposals have been adopted as law. A few measures, such as the Environmental Assessment Directive of 1985 (Williams, 1986; Wood, 1988; Glasson *et al.*, 1994) have been explicitly cross-sectoral, but the bulk of this legislation has been concerned with one of the following sectors of the environment: water, waste, air, chemicals, wildlife and countryside and noise.

Haigh (1989) listed over 200 items of European environmental legislation, while more recent work has shown that the rate of adoption increased from around 20 per annum to over 30 per annum by the late 1980s, reaching a peak of nearly 40 in 1993 (Williams, 1990, 202; Haigh, 1995). Against this background it is necessary to examine the current Action Programme in some detail.

The Fifth Action Programme

The Fifth Action Programme, covering the period 1992–2000 and entitled *Towards Sustainability*, is

the most comprehensive to date (Commission of the EC, 1992). It addresses issues of both global and local relevance, having sections on problems such as climate change and ozone layer depletion; acidification and air pollution; depletion and pollution of water resources; deterioration of the urban environment; noise; deterioration of coastal zones; and waste. The wide range of issues addressed in the programme points to a move away from focusing exclusively on environmental problems within the EU's boundaries, and also recognises the EU's wider political role in promoting sustainable practices at a global scale.

The programme is published in three volumes. Volume I is the formal *Proposal for a Resolution of the EC on a Community Programme of Policy and Action in Relation to the Environment and Sustainable Development*. This was adopted by the Environment Council in December 1992, with revisions to the text to incorporate the Council's views concerning key issues and priorities for Commission attention. Volume II, to which the overall title *Towards Sustainability* is specifically attached, is the main text of the programme. This sets out the policies, proposals for EU action and responsibilities for implementation. Volume III, entitled *The State of the Environment in the European Community*, provides a review of the problems

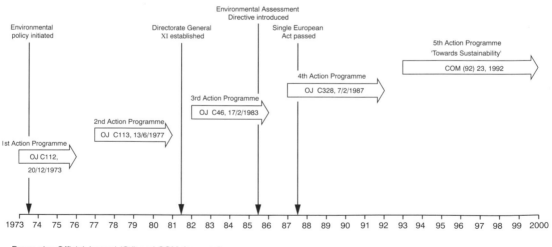

Boxes give Official Journal (OJ) and COM document reference for details of individual programmes.

Figure 21.1 *Action Programmes on the Environment*

being faced, and also presents an analysis of, and justification for, the policy proposals.

In addition, five key sectors are identified for intervention: agriculture, energy, industry, transport and tourism. For these, the argument advanced is that integrated approaches to sustainable development must be adopted in order to protect the future environment. Interestingly, it also develops the theme that industry should be seen as part of the solution to environmental problems, rather than being viewed simplistically as a source of degradation.

Given the Action Programme's wide-ranging perspectives, exhaustive analysis of its intentions is not possible. None the less, proposals for progress in various priority areas can be explored. With respect to pollution control, air quality is identified as a continuing concern, especially in urban areas, and in spite of several existing Directives. Proposals to deal with air quality and acidification by setting specific targets for the reduction of nitrogen oxide and sulphur dioxide emissions include revisions to the existing Directive on municipal waste incineration and a new Directive on the incineration of hazardous waste.

Water is the sector with the longest list of existing EU legislation, but problems still grow. Consequently, prevention of groundwater pollution by the further control of sources, and also by extensive monitoring, is proposed. Soil quality, which has been relatively neglected compared with water pollution, is now identified as a sector to be addressed. And, in relation to the improvement of both water and soil pollution, the problem of inadequate waste disposal techniques is identified as a target for corrective measures. Problems of industrial waste disposal are rapidly becoming prominent in those parts of the EU, such as some Objective 1 and Cohesion Fund areas, which are undergoing rapid industrialisation. It is anticipated that substantially improved land-use planning and environmental assessment, as well as better monitoring and technical controls, will be required.

The more general issue of quality of life is one where spatial planning is identified as playing a key role. Urban areas, although they provide the base for most economic activities and accommodate 80 per cent of the EU's population, are seen as deteriorating due to the abandonment of disused industrial land and a lack of investment in renewal. Noise in urban areas is also an issue to be addressed, not only by noise abatement programmes and limits on acceptable noise exposure levels, but also by spatial planning of infrastructure development, industrial areas, land use around airports and other noise sources.

Rural areas, meanwhile, are considered to present problems arising from changes in farming methods, the need to take some land out of agricultural production and find alternative land uses, desertification and, especially around the Mediterranean, coastal development. In this context, it is suggested that land-use planning can provide the basis for optimal management of growth, protection of the cultural and natural heritage, protection of open spaces, traffic management and promotion of public transport.

Transport is clearly recognised never to be environmentally neutral. Consequently, spatial planning and the integration of environmental assessment into the land-use authorisation process are seen as critical to the reconciliation of the conflict that can clearly be expected between, on the one hand, the EU's cohesion strategy and ambitions for trans-European networks and, on the other hand, its aspiration for "high environmental standards". And, apart from spatial planning's potential to reduce the environmental impact of transport and infrastructure networks, it is argued that improved planning has the capacity to reduce transport needs and car dependence, particularly through integration of public transport and the utilisation of more extensive rail and water transport.

Tourism, meanwhile, is seen as critical because in this sector the interconnection of economic and environmental factors could not be closer (Figure 21.2). Given its importance to the economy, its dependence on a clean environment to attract customers, and the pollution often left behind after the tourists have gone home, intervention in this sector is considered essential. Tourism along the Mediterranean littoral has given rise to widespread problems of waste management and water supply, while the scale of urbanisation needed to maximise the throughput of visitors has in some places exceeded the capacity of the local infrastructure and natural visitor attractions

405

Figure 21.2 *Tourism pressures on Dartmoor, UK. Visiting holidaymakers queue to enter an already overcrowded car park. (Photos: D A Pinder)*

to absorb the numbers. Indeed, in some cases such development has proved unsustainable as visitor numbers have fallen in the face of these problems. Similarly, Austria is especially concerned about the sensitive environment of mountain areas, especially in the context of holiday home development in the Alps, where tourist pressures can prove unsustainable and cause lasting environmental damage. Finland has comparable concerns in relation to holiday home developments along its many shorelines, for which special planning procedures exist.

Spatial policies, proposed as at least a partial solution, include strict land-use planning and traffic management, the application of more rigorous environmental standards, protection of sensitive areas and the creation of buffer zones, plus diversification of the economic base. What is evident from consideration of member states' planning systems is that most of these activities are primarily the responsibility of the lower tiers of the planning system. Local and regional authorities are therefore recognised as playing a key role through controls on development, management of tourist demand, the development of pilot projects and the exchange and promotion of good practice.

The Tactical Framework: Implementation Approaches in the 1990s

While the Fifth Action Programme may have strong ambitions, much will depend on the tactics adopted for implementation (Commission of the EU, 1994a). Until the early 1990s, these tactics were relatively straightforward, but there have since been significant changes in both their style and form. Further evolution is likely as the decade progresses.

In the 1980s, DG XI earned for itself the reputation of being a "legislative factory" because of its rather top-down legislation-based style of implementing its Action Programmes. As has been indicated, its productivity in this respect was very high, particularly under the leadership of the energetic and ambitious Ripa de Meana, the Environment Commissioner from 1989 until his resignation in 1991.

Since he departed, pressures have grown to modify this approach. DG XI now recognises the importance of being seen to respond to the needs and interests of local citizens, to apply the subsidiarity principle, and to achieve greater integration between the environment sector and other sectors of EU policy-making. To a great extent these responses have come in the form of networking and acceptance of pressure group lobbying, and in the development of funding initiatives. These are considered below.

Networking and lobbying

The swing towards networking, liaising with pressure groups and accommodation of their demands, can be demonstrated in the context of urban policy.

It has been recognised for some time that one of the problems affecting the public perception of the EU is the dominant role that the Common Agriculture Policy plays in the budget and legislation. This contrasts with the fact that approximately 80 per cent of the EU population live in urban communities. Consequently, there have been a number of attempts to develop an urban policy, several of which have been linked to Community initiatives established under the ERDF Regulation and administered by DG XVI.

During its period of prominence in 1989–91 under Ripa de Meana, the Environment Directorate sought to take the initiative in respect of urban policy by publishing a Green Paper, the so-called Green Book on the urban environment (Commission of the EC, 1990). This was an ambitious attempt to develop new spatial planning principles for urban areas, couched in a rather philosophical discussion of the concept of the European city. Proposals were developed for action on urban planning, transport and conservation, and on policies to reduce the impact of urban activities on the environment by measures such as emission controls and water and energy management.

Some people expected that the Green Paper would be followed by proposals for legislation in the normal way, and the Commissioner was also hoping that he would acquire responsibility for urban affairs within the Commission, with associated financial instruments for funded interventions. When it became clear that this was not to be, other ways forward were sought. At this point, DG XI officials recognised that they did not have strong links with local and regional authorities, or access to urban and regional planning expertise (Ward and Williams, 1996). They therefore set about remedying this by developing dialogue with these sectors by means of networks.

Typically, networks consist of a group of municipalities who undertake to share experience; explore opportunities to transfer technical advice, ideas and expertise; and pool their resources to act as a lobby on government, including the Commission. Examples include the Car-Free Cities Club and the expert group on sustainable cities. The latter has led to the Sustainable Cities and Towns Campaign and the adoption of a Charter of European Sustainable Cities and Towns (Williams, 1996). Several groups, including the examples noted above, have received start-up funding by the Commission. In contrast to the situation often found with national government departments, what is also very noteworthy and significant is that the Commission positively welcomes a situation in which networks that it funds come to act as a lobby directed at itself.

In the light of the earlier discussion, this attitude on the part of the Commission is readily understandable. In the first place, such networks are able to represent local opinion in several member states, since it is usually a condition of funding that they have a broadly based membership drawn from several countries. Secondly, lobbying is a means whereby the Environment Directorate, which is a relatively weak DG, can strengthen its hand in proposing legislation by being able to point to pressure for certain proposals coming from localities in different parts of the EU.

Networking is therefore a prime example of how DG XI has placed greater emphasis on working with local and regional authorities and non-government bodies, rather than on its more traditional top-down legislative style, targeted at national governments. Related to this shift, it has recently been estimated that, for 40 per cent of all

proposed environmental measures, implementation will be the responsibility of local government (Commission of the EC, 1992; Hams and Morphet, 1994).

Funding programmes

In contrast to the high profile given to legislation, dedicated funding did not play a major role in EU environment policy until the 1990s. However, this situation has now changed significantly: there is now acceptance, first, of the idea that the allocation of financial resources directly to environmental protection is within the EU's competence and a legitimate use of its resources and, second, of the need for greater synergy between the different sectors of EU policy. From modest beginnings in 1989, substantial funding is now available to eligible locations (Williams, 1996).

A Community initiative named ENVIREG operated from 1989 to 1993 in the least favoured regions and coastal areas. This provided funds for the reduction of pollution and management of waste, as well as for the promotion of land-use planning and development of pollution control expertise. ENVIREG was replaced by a financial instrument known as LIFE, which has a bigger budget and wider scope. The main objectives of LIFE are to promote sustainable development and environmental quality, and to protect habitats and the natural environment. The first of these objectives is allocated 40 per cent of the budget and includes the development of new technologies and the integration of environmental factors into land-use planning decisions. The second is allocated 45 per cent, with the remainder being available for education, training and improvement of administrative support for environmental services (Haigh, 1995).

The biggest funding programme is the Cohesion Fund, which was agreed at the Maastricht Summit in 1991 and came into operation in 1993. This is designed to help the poorest member states (i.e. those with per capita GDPs of less than 90 per cent of the EU average), so that Greece, Ireland, Portugal and Spain are eligible for assistance in the first funding period up to 1999. The purpose is to assist these countries overcome problems of peripherality and competitiveness, so that existing economic disparities are reduced or at least do not worsen, in preparation for the single currency.

To this end, transport and energy infrastructures have to date absorbed the majority of funding in each beneficiary country except Greece. However, investment in environmental protection, which is the other activity for which substantial funding is available, is gaining momentum. The rationale for including this sector within the Cohesion Fund is that economic growth in the periphery should not be allowed to take place through the development of pollution havens which would have the effect of distorting the SEM. As this environmental investment grows, it will be instructive to analyse the types of project funded. So far, many of the allocations have been for "end-of-pipe" technologies to cleanse emissions, rather than for preventative measures to achieve sustainable development (Haigh, 1995).

Continuing Challenges

Although considerable progress has been made with the problems of implementing environmental protection measures, this is a highly complex field and much remains to be achieved. Moreover, although the EU is a supranational jurisdiction, the many obstacles which can cause progress to be very slow must be recognised. These include conflicting national environmental priorities, procedures and perceptions of national interests, compounded by linguistic differences and technical problems of harmonisation and co-ordination. While recognising the scale of recent progress, it is appropriate to examine the impact of such issues, starting with the retarding influence of national attitudes as exemplified by the challenge presented by contaminated land (Figure 21.3).

Contaminated land, and fear of liability associated with it, is an issue of major concern to developers, investors in development and policymakers concerned with the regeneration of urban brownfield sites. Contamination tends to occur most in the older industrialised areas in Belgium, Germany, France, Spain and the UK (RETI, 1992; Meyer *et al.*, 1995; Stanners and Bordeau, 1995).

The worst problems in the EU are found in the former German Democratic Republic (GDR), for example in the Bitterfeld area, the site of one of the largest chemical engineering complexes in Europe, characterised by out-of-date technology and minimal maintenance and pollution control.

For the EU, an important issue arising from contamination is the extent to which public sector bodies accept risk of liability from past pollution by industrial processes and enterprises no longer in existence. In the former GDR and other parts of Germany such as the Ruhrgebiet, private developers are protected from much or all of the risk by the various public–private partnerships created to promote local economic development. But elsewhere the levels of protection are normally lower, and it is therefore argued that the risk of liability for any contamination may be deterring developers from sites, even if contamination is only suspected and not proven. Moreover, this deterrent effect is likely to be heightened whenever the developer is from another member state and may therefore be unsure of the legal position and extent of risk. Contaminated land is consequently a problem capable of distorting the operation of markets in land, property development, investment and insurance, and it is on this basis that it becomes a single market issue (Meyer *et al.*, 1995; Williams, 1995).

The Commission made its first move to solve the problem in 1989, when it put forward a proposal for a *Draft Directive on Civil Liability for Damage Caused by Waste* (Commission of the EC, 1989). As with environmental assessment and a number of other environmental proposals, this was to some extent based on experience of federal legislation in the USA. After consultations, an amended version which raised the possibility of a "European fund for compensation for damage and impairment to environment caused by waste" was presented to the Council of Ministers in 1991.

Since then, however, progress towards adopting this proposed Directive, and another on landfill waste, has been stalled by opposition from Greece, Ireland, Portugal and the UK. As a result, the Commission has had to step back from its specific proposals, and instead issue a *Green Paper on Remedying Environmental Damage* (Commission of the EU, 1993), based on the premise that different systems of civil liability could lead to

Figure 21.3   *Contaminated land clearance on the New Millennium Experience site, Greenwich, UK. (Photo: the New Millennium Company.) In the late nineteenth and early twentieth centuries the site was an important energy port, where coal shipped in from north-east England was converted into gas for London consumers. In common with most gasworks sites it became heavily contaminated with volatile hydrocarbons, necessitating extensive clean-up operations before reuse was possible. After the worst contaminated land was removed to licensed landfill sites (see photo), the site was treated by sinking 300 vapour extraction wells to draw air through the soil and stimulate biological degradation. Vapour extraction allowed 106 t of contaminants to be extracted in 20 weeks. (Information source: Institute of Petroleum)*

distortions of competition. Although the Commission retains the intention of proposing a Directive, it has not been able to finalise its proposals and is seeking further debate, despite considerable study (EIS, 1996).

On the positive side, the European Parliament has called for a draft Directive, and it is possible that revised proposals would be more likely to find a majority under QMV since the 1995 enlargement. What must also be noted, however, is that long-term developments are likely to be influenced by eventual EU expansion to include former Communist states. A further whole swathe of countries from Estonia to Bulgaria has indicated interest in membership, those in the forefront being the Visegrad Four, namely the Czech Republic, Hungary, Poland and Slovakia. Within these, and especially in Polish Silesia and northern Bohemia in the Czech Republic, there are some of the worst polluted environments and cases of contaminated land to be found anywhere in the world (Meyer *et al.*, 1995; see also Chapter 20).

While delays over contaminated land legislation have been primarily political, slow progress also reflects the impact of a second issue that always has the potential to complicate EU policy-making, namely the problem of ensuring consistency of meaning between specialist terminology in different languages. In this example, both the Commission's 1993 Green Paper and a report compiled by RETI (1992) have argued that contaminated land is an issue on which common European definitions are needed, as at present considerable potential exists for confusion. Thus, for example, words must be found in all 11 official languages to communicate the difference between derelict land and contaminated land, as understood in the UK; or the German distinction between *Altlasten* and *Brachflächen* areas (both implying land abandonment, but with the former particularly associated with industry and greater contamination). Without this progress, terminologies cannot be interpreted consistently throughout the EU by planning practitioners and lawyers.

Third, it is evident that considerable scope remains for progress to be made by co-ordinating different policy sectors in order to achieve improved environmental protection. It is now recognised that sectoral integration has long been a weak link in EU policy structures. In response, a

stronger treaty basis for a role in spatial planning was sought at the 1996–97 IGC. To support this proposal, a number of studies were undertaken of the spatial structure of the EU as a whole, and proposals leading to a spatial policy framework were formulated. Chief among these were the EUROPE 2000 and EUROPE 2000+ studies (Commission of the EC, 1991; Commission of the EU, 1994b); the work on behalf of DG XVI to produce a *Compendium of Spatial Planning Systems and Policies* (Shaw *et al.*, 1995); and the Committee on Spatial Development's preparation of the *European Spatial Development Perspective* (Shaw *et al.*, 1996; Williams, 1996).

The principal assumptions underpinning this intense activity are that national land-use planning and authorisation procedures may have the effect of non-tariff barriers and therefore impede operation of the SEM; that an overall spatial policy framework will provide an effective basis for enforcing greater coherence of EU spatial policy instruments; and that spatial planning – especially when harmonised throughout the EU – is one of the most widespread means whereby potential problems can be identified and ameliorated before polluting development occurs.

At the time of writing it is unclear what the IGC will ultimately achieve. However, from the viewpoint of this chapter, the key possibilities are an extension of QMV in the environment sector, the addition of an Urban Title to the treaties, and the creation of an effective competence in respect of spatial planning. While the latter two may not seem central to environmentalists' concerns, in reality they would both contribute to a strengthening of this sector and to its more effective integration with other policy sectors. Not least, this reflects growing recognition of the importance of integrating environmental requirements into projects and proposals financed by the EU.

Conclusion

Understanding of the need for effective implementation of Europe-wide policies in this, as in any other sector, requires good insights not only into specific environmental policies and programmes, but also into the logic behind their inclusion in the European integration project as a whole. The emphasis on common standards in environment policy plays an important role in achieving objectives relating to the single market, sustainability, cohesion and quality of life. This widespread relevance ensured that environment was an issue in the 1994 enlargement negotiations which produced the present EU of 15 member states, and one consequence of this expansion may ultimately prove to be a changed balance of power, favouring higher standards, in the Council of Ministers. What can certainly be anticipated is that environment policy will become very prominent in any future enlargement negotiations with the former Communist countries.

What has also been shown, however, is that environment policy is not just an issue at the EU and governmental levels. As a reflection of this there is growing emphasis on local action to implement EU environment policy, by integrating it at this lower level into spatial planning and other measures. This will inevitably have an increasing impact on local and regional authorities in all countries. To a great extent this impact is likely to be achieved by inducing authorities to integrate environment policy with EU economic development initiatives and funding programmes. The interests of the environment will be served by linking protection measures with funding criteria and developing greater policy coherence through horizontal measures such as EU spatial policy. New EU policy initiatives in fields such as urban policy and tourism can similarly be expected to stress implementation and environmental protection at the local scale. Finally, however, we must note that this reorientation is not simply a development that is being imposed from above. An important recent change has been increased recognition of grass-roots feelings; indeed some observers would now argue that the weight of public and political opinion, expressed directly and through networking and lobbying, will be a key factor in the future evolution and impact of EU environment policy.

References

AmCham (1995) *EU Environment Guide*, The EU Committee of the American Chamber of Commerce in Belgium, Brussels.

Barnes, P (1995) *Environmental Policy Discussion Paper 14*, Jean Monnet Group of Experts Centre for European Union Studies, University of Hull.

Brundtland, G H (1987) *Our Common Future*, World Commission on Environment and Development (the Brundtland Commission), Oxford University Press, Oxford.

Commission of the EC (1989) *Proposal for a Council Directive on Civil Liability for Damage Caused by Waste*, Brussels, Commission of the European Communities, COM (89) 282 final.

Commission of the EC (1990) *Green Paper on the Urban Environment*, Brussels, Commission of the European Communities, COM (90) 218 final.

Commission of the EC (1991) *Europe 2000: outlook for the development of the Community's territory*, DG XVI, Commission of the European Communities, Brussels.

Commission of the EC (1992) *Fifth Action Programme on the Environment: towards sustainability*, Brussels, Commission of the European Communities, COM (92) 23 final.

Commission of the EU (1993) *Green Paper on Remedying Environmental Damage*, Brussels, Commission of the European Union, COM (93) 47 final.

Commission of the EU (1994a) *Interim Review of Implementation of the European Community Programme of Policy and Action in Relation to the Environment and Sustainable Development "Towards Sustainability"*, Brussels, Commission of the European Union, COM (94) 453 final.

Commission of the EU (1994b) *Europe 2000+: cooperation for European territorial development*, DG XVI, Commission of the European Communities, Brussels.

Council of the European Union (1992) *Treaty on European Union*, Office of Official Publications of the European Community, Luxembourg.

EEB (1994) *EEB Twentieth Anniversary*, European Environment Bureau, Brussels.

EEB (1995) *Greening the Treaty: a manifesto for the Intergovernmental Conference (IGC) from UK members of the European Environmental Bureau (EEB)*, European Environmental Bureau, London.

EIS (1996) *European Information Service 167*, Local Government International Bureau, London, 29.

Glasson, J, Therivel, R and Chadwick, A (1994) *Introduction to Environmental Impact Assessment*, UCL Press, London.

Haigh, N (1989) *EEC Environmental Policy and Britain*, Longman, Harlow.

Haigh, N (1995) *Manual of Environment Policy: the EC and Britain*, Institute for European Environment Policy, Cartermill Publishing, London.

Haigh, N (1996) "Sustainable development" in the EU Treaties, *International Environmental Affairs*, March.

Hams, T and Morphet, J (1994) Agenda 21 and Towards Sustainability: the EU approach to Rio, *European Information Service 147*, Local Government International Bureau, London, 3–6.

Meyer, P B, Williams, R H and Yount, K R (1995) *Contaminated Land Reclamation, Redevelopment and Reuse in the United States and the European Union*, Edward Elgar, Cheltenham and Brookfield, Vermont.

RETI (1992) *Study of Derelict Land in the ECSC*, Vol A, *Summary and Recommendations*, RETI, Brussels.

Shaw, D, Nadin, V and Westlake, T (1995) The Compendium of European Spatial Planning Systems, *European Planning Studies*, **3**, 390–5.

Shaw, D, Nadin, V and Westlake, T (1996) Towards a supra-national spatial development perspective: experience in Europe, *Journal of Planning Education and Research*, **15**, 135–42.

Stanners, D and Bourdeau, P (1995) *Europe's Environment: the Dobris Assessment*, European Environment Agency, Office of Official Publications of the European Community, Luxembourg.

Ward, S and Williams, R H (1996) From Hierarchy to Networks? Sub-central government and EU urban environment policy, unpublished research paper, Centre for Rural Economy, University of Newcastle upon Tyne.

Williams, R H (1986) The EC environment policy, land use planning and pollution control, *Policy and Politics*, **14**, 93–106.

Williams, R H (1990) Supranational environmental policy and pollution control, in D Pinder (ed) *Western Europe: challenge and change*, Belhaven, London, 195–207.

Williams, R H (1995) Contaminated land – a problem for Europe?, *BrachflächenRecycling*, **1/95**, 19–25.

Williams, R H (1996) *European Union Spatial Policy and Planning*, Paul Chapman Publishing, London.

Wood, C (1988) The genesis and implementation of Environmental Impact Assessment in Europe, in M Clark and J Herington (eds) *The Role of Environmental Impact Assessment in the Planning Process*, Mansell, London, 88–102.

Wurzel, R (1993) Environmental policy, in J Lodge (ed) *The European Community and the Challenge of the Future*, Pinter Publishers, London, 178–99.

22

Transport, economic development and the environment

Squaring the policy circle?

David Pinder and Julia Edwards
University of Plymouth and University of Wales College, Newport, UK

As Vickerman and Hall note in Chapters 12 and 23, transport policy presents the European Commission, and EU institutions more generally, with a fundamental dilemma. On the one hand, transport is intimately connected with economic growth. This is a powerful consideration in an era in which the EU is beset by serious structural unemployment problems; strenuous efforts are being made to foster cohesion by extending the benefits of the single market more effectively to lagging parts of the EU (Figure 22.1); and increasing emphasis is being placed on supporting central and eastern European countries by integrating their fledgling market economies with those of western Europe. The importance attached to such concerns is amply demonstrated by a stream of transport-related reports published by the Commission in the late 1980s and early 1990s (European Commission, 1986a, b, 1988, 1989a, b, 1990, 1992a, b, 1994a, b). It is also underlined by the European Commission's recent push to ensure that momentum is maintained towards completion of trans-European networks (TENs) within the EU, and also to extend them beyond

the former Iron Curtain. These TENs can be viewed conceptually as strategic road, rail, air and energy infrastructures, and in the early 1990s continuing failure to complete them provoked the Commission to identify key gaps to be addressed as a priority (Figure 22.2).

On the other hand, however, there is the Commission's commitment to environmental protection. As Williams (1990, 202) has demonstrated, this grew rapidly after the mid-1970s, leading to the creation of an Environment Directorate (DG XI) in 1981 and to an impressive increase in Directives and Regulations intended to improve environmental protection. Although the approaches adopted by DG XI have evolved over the years, this environmental concern remains very real (Blacksell, 1994; see also Williams and Bjarnadottir in Chapter 21). But it is potentially diametrically opposed to a policy which aims to promote economic growth through the creation of more complete and more elaborate transport systems and networks. In most instances such a policy actively induces movement, thereby generating highly undesirable environmental

Figure 22.1 *Cork airport, Ireland. The development of air links with other parts of the EU is often considered a prerequisite for cohesion in such peripheral regions. (Photo: Finbarr O'Connell Photography and AerRianta)*

effects at a variety of scales (Bonsall, 1996; Coombe, 1996; Mackie, 1996). Locally, for example, the serious consequences may include greater noise pollution, the visual impact of new infrastructures, or increased levels of exhaust hydrocarbons and particulates. More broadly there is the issue of the relationship between, firstly, the exhaust emissions from a whole range of transport modes and, secondly, the accumulation of greenhouse gases.

While this is the central policy contradiction, the severity of the tension between improved communication and environmental protection varies with the type of investment in question. In terms of "traditional" transport modes, rail projects are likely to have less serious energy implications than major road schemes, and energy consumption per passenger kilometre is still higher for air travel (Table 22.1). Equally importantly, although any transport project will have its adverse aspects – energy consumption, exhaust emissions, noise, etc. – for some the gross impact is likely to be reduced to a net effect because of an ability to divert passengers or freight away from more damaging transport modes. Thus rail has the potential to impact on car travel at many scales, and can also aspire to compete with airlines inter-regionally and internationally. Similarly, as many European cities are now demonstrating, urban public transport systems offering speed, attractive fares and reasonable comfort can be effective alternatives to car-based mobility.

As a result, any attempt to evaluate the EU's involvement in the development of the transport

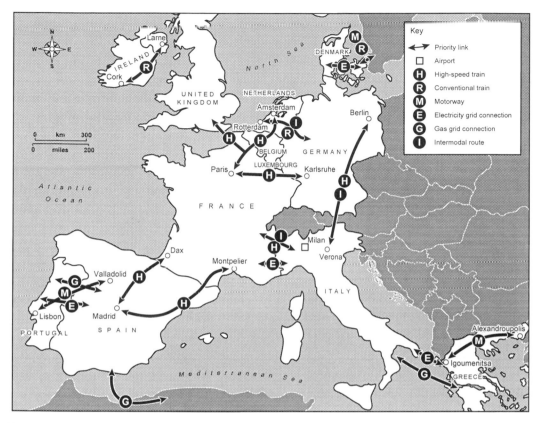

Figure 22.2   *EU Commission TEN priority projects sent to EIB for evaluation in 1994*

Table 22.1   *Energy efficiency in passenger transport modes*

	Persons carried	Energy used per passenger km (MJ)	Energy used per passenger km (fully laden) (MJ)
Petrol car			
under 1.4 litre	1.5	1.73	0.65
over 2.0 litre	1.5	3.08	1.15
Diesel car			
under 1.4 litre	1.5	1.50	0.56
over 2.0 litre	1.5	2.44	0.91
Train			
InterCity 225*	289[†]	0.65	0.38
InterCity 125[‡]	294[†]	0.59	0.35
Electric suburban	180[†]	0.48	0.26
Bus			
Double-decker	25[§]	0.52	0.17
Express coach	30[¶]	0.38	0.25
Aircraft			
Boeing 737	100[†]	2.42	1.45

*125 mph electric. [†]60% full. [‡]125 mph diesel. [§]33% full. [¶]65% full.
Source: Adapted from Farrington (1992, 64.1).

and communication sector must take into account the types of movement that are being promoted. Given that there are strong economic and political motivations to encourage the sector within the EU, this chapter addresses a number of central concerns. To what extent is there evidence of support for the less damaging transport and communication modes? Are there signs that these modes are being increasingly favoured? And, of rapidly growing importance in the 1990s, what are the implications of EU involvement in the modernisation of transport systems and communications in central and eastern Europe? In sum, how far can it be argued that support for infrastructure investment is linked with progress towards squaring the circle of tension between transport, economic development and the interests of the environment?

These questions are given added significance by the argument that the assumed link between infrastructure investment and economic growth is questionable. In Chapter 12 Vickerman warns that the assumption may lead to overinvestment and therefore inefficient use of resources as attempts are made to improve transport provision in lagging parts of Europe. Similarly Hurst (1994), in an exhaustive literature review of more than 70 papers, has concluded that "the statistical basis of many studies that show supra-normal returns for public infrastructure [is] weak". Other observations were that "there is some evidence to suggest that 'excessive' public investment hinders growth" . . . "causality from public investment to output is not proven" . . . and "it is not clear how new infrastructure will benefit a new location". Clearly, if the presumed economic spin-offs are in fact in doubt, it becomes even more important to examine the environmental implications of the sector's development.

Various data sources could be used to pursue this theme. Since the mid-1970s, for example, European Regional Development Fund grants have been an important source of finance for transport infrastructures. More recently, Cohesion Fund initiatives have been closely linked to transport developments and environmental protection. However, there are considerable problems with the evaluation of these funding streams. Cohesion Fund expenditure is too recent for trends through time to be established with

certainty. Neither fund extends to central and eastern Europe, and Cohesion grants are confined to Greece, Spain, Portugal and Ireland. Perhaps surprisingly, there is no EU-wide register of funded projects suitable for use in database construction. And, when projects are examined individually, there can be great difficulty in establishing how much has been allocated to transport, let alone to individual transport or communication modes. This is because quite different types of project are frequently clustered together to create packages qualifying for EU assistance.

As an alternative, therefore, this chapter is based on the analysis of funding provided by the European Investment Bank (EIB) since the mid-1980s. As will shortly become apparent, the Luxembourg-based Bank is a very large and active EU institution. Transport and communications have been among its long-term concerns, and a broad definition of the sector has ensured that there has been large-scale investment in telecommunications and energy infrastructures. This broad outlook is very similar to that currently held by the European Commission. Moreover, in the large majority of cases EIB lending in this field is tied to very specific schemes, so that there is little ambiguity about the nature of the projects funded. Over the years large sums have been invested throughout the EU, and since 1990 the Commission and EU member states have encouraged it to extend its activities beyond the former Iron Curtain. Consequently, while it cannot be argued that the EIB necessarily provides a perfect cross-section of all EU support for transport and communications infrastructures, it does at least offer a good starting point for studies of the nature and environmental implications of the EU's intervention in the sector.

Much of the chapter concentrates on three themes. First, a clearer picture is established of the types of project funded by the EIB within the EU. Attention then turns to the scale of investments in these various branches of the sector since the mid-1980s. Here the concerns are to identify biases towards, or away from, the less environmentally damaging modes, and to identify significant trends between the mid-1980s and today. Finally, the dominant characteristics of the EIB's recently initiated transport investments in central and eastern Europe are identified and assessed. Before turning to these themes, however, a review of the Bank's origins, *raison d'être* and operating procedures is appropriate.

The EIB: Origins and Approaches

The European Investment Bank was founded by the six European Economic Community member states in 1958, primarily as a regional development agency. Experience with the European Coal and Steel Community in the mid-1950s had demonstrated that market integration and increased competition could cause severe regional economic problems, and Italy in particular feared that the development of the EEC's Common Market might accentuate the disadvantages of peripherality.

Operationally the EIB was established to borrow investment finance in the world's capital markets, and to do so as cheaply as possible. Obtaining low-cost finance depended to a great extent on the fact that it was owned by the EEC countries, which could guarantee repayment. This eliminated risk, reduced the interest rates which the EIB was required to pay on its borrowings, and therefore allowed it to on-lend the money cheaply in Community countries where weak economic conditions meant that interest rates were high. Without resorting to direct subsidies to the private sector, therefore, a growing stream of investment finance could be channelled into lagging areas. This, it was assumed, would accelerate the development process and lead to the reduction of regional economic disparities.

Although it was empowered to finance industrial loans, a major target of the EIB's regional development work was infrastructural investment. This chiefly reflected the belief that infrastructural spending improved the operational environment for all businesses, allowing the existing regional economy to develop more effectively, and reducing obstacles to the attraction of mobile external investment by companies from other regions or countries. This led directly to large-scale funding for transport and communications projects, an emphasis that has been maintained to the present day.[1] Between

1991 and 1996, for example, loans for surface and air transport amounted to almost 23 billion ECU, and accounted for almost a third of all EIB activity in the EU. In addition telecommunications, and the main energy transmission systems, absorbed nearly 15 billion ECU.

Three further points relating to the EIB's operations must be underlined. First, it is not empowered to impose blueprint plans on would-be borrowers. Instead it was created as an agency whose function was to respond to projects proposed at the grass-roots level. The prevailing market-oriented view was that – compared with centrally conceived plans – national, regional or local perceptions of investment needs were far more likely to match reality. As the EIB endeavours to reconcile its investments with EU policy goals, therefore, it must do so within a framework dictated largely by customer demand.

Second, in much of the EU at least, it is now apparent that the need for EIB funding is far less than in its early years. High interest rates are less problematic and capital markets and banking systems have matured, so that there are often good alternative sources of finance (Honohan, 1995). Consequently the argument that EIB loans are necessary to ensure the implementation of new projects is considerably weaker. One consequence of this is that, given the official expectation that the EIB will pursue EU objectives, EIB support is perhaps best seen as a sign of approval, a signal that a project has been evaluated and found to conform with those objectives.

Third, linked with this, all schemes for which EIB funding is requested have for some years been subject to an environmental evaluation. At face value this could be taken as an assurance that the projects supported are fully in line with EU environmental protection objectives. Certainly the EIB itself argues that:

> "The process of financing only those projects which are efficient in resource allocation is probably the biggest contribution that the EIB can make to economic development which is 'sustainable . . . respecting the environment' (Treaty of European Union, Article 2)" (EIB, 1996, 7).

Closer examination, however, suggests that caution is necessary. For example:

"The main aim of the Bank in the environment field is to support projects that [contribute to] one or a number of the following objectives: improvements in drinking water supplies and waste water treatment; the introduction of environmentally sound techniques to process solid, in some cases toxic, waste; a reduction of atmospheric pollution, especially from power stations and industrial plant; the promotion of environmentally sound industrial processes or products; and the protection of the environment and the improvement of the quality of life in urban areas" (EIB, 1996, 5).

Although these targets are in some cases related to transport, the sector is clearly not placed centre stage. Beyond this, the EIB's statement on project evaluation reveals that a main aim is to ensure that, if implemented, a scheme will comply with "the relevant prevailing laws and regulations" in the country concerned. It is not considered appropriate to aim for environmental standards well within the regulations, although the latter may in some instances be lax; and in some cases it is envisaged that – especially outside the EU – projects which fail to comply with local standards could be countenanced. Finally – and very importantly from the transport viewpoint – judgements are not made in terms of the environmental outcomes of alternative solutions. Thus, for example, a proposed road project would be unlikely to be refused funding because its environmental costs exceeded those of rail.

On the one hand, therefore, it is evident that every transport-related project is subject to some form of environmental scrutiny. Yet, on the other, the approaches cannot be said to contribute to the minimisation of the sector's environmental impacts by promoting the best transport mode for a specific purpose. This is a major distinction to be borne in mind as we turn to consider in more detail the relationships between environmental issues and the EIB's transport and communications investment portfolio.

EIB Transport and Communications Support in the EU: an Overview

As we have noted, all transport and communications infrastructures involve environmental costs. However, these vary from one mode to another, and some are able to produce gains

through substitution effects. Against this background it is arguable that – at least through the EIB – the EU is promoting four relatively benign forms of transport.

Rail system investment

As has been emphasised, during the 1990s the European Commission has placed great stress on the development of trans-European networks (TENs). This reflects a concern to encourage integration within the single market, and also to support the Commission's growth initiative which aims to foster conditions suitable for future projects, such as monetary union (European Commission, 1994c).

One strand of this policy push has been to emphasise the importance of merging Europe's gradually developing high-speed rail systems into a recognisably international network (Blum *et al.*, 1992; Charlton, 1994; European Commission, 1986b, 1989b; Ross, 1994). High-speed rail is not, of course, entirely benign environmentally. For example, if new lines are necessary there is an inevitable impact on local ecosystems, and high-speed trains can also create significant noise pollution. None the less, environmental benefits related to exhaust emission control are to be gained by diverting passenger traffic from the roads and from the air, and it is in this context that EIB involvement is most significant. Its stake in the promotion of high-speed train travel began with its support for the French TGV system, and more recently it has diversified to invest in the Belgian, German and Spanish systems, as well as in international links between them. In addition, although the UK is still far from developing high-speed rail, the EIB has invested heavily in the Channel Tunnel, a key piece of infrastructure in terms of long-term network development (Gibb, 1994).

Less obviously, yet still importantly, EIB rail investment has included support for projects to encourage the modal shift of long-distance freight traffic from road to rail (European Commission, 1992a). Once again, this offers environmental gains with respect to vehicle emissions, with additional spin-off effects including noise reduction. Above all, the EIB's support has taken

Figure 22.3 *Intermodality in the global vehicle trade. Ocean-going car carrier and berths for specialised car transporter trains. (Photo: Associated British Ports, Southampton)*

the form of investment in intermodal freight depots. So far as rail network development is concerned, the purpose of these is to ensure maximum efficiency in the transfer of freight loads from the lorry or ship to the train, and vice versa (Figure 22.3). The swifter this transfer process is, the greater will be the chance of diverting road traffic to rail. Long-distance axes linking the major economic centres within the EU are obvious candidates for such developments (Charlier and Ridolfi, 1994), as the concentration of EIB investment in northern Italy in the late 1980s and early 1990s emphasises (Figure 22.4).

Quite apart from fostering long-distance rail passenger and freight traffic through TEN development, the EIB's investments also contribute to improvements in the standard national and regional rail networks. The projects funded in recent years have been extremely diverse: schemes involving track replacement, upgrading

from single to double track, the modernisation of signalling systems and the purchase of new rolling stock have all been supported. Thus examples of loans in the mid-1990s were those for the modernisation of rolling stock and infrastructure around Spain's nine largest cities; the upgrading of Stuttgart's suburban railway system; the improvement of rail networks in Campania and Abruzzi, Italy; and modernisation of the West Yorkshire rail network. Whatever a specific project entails, however, the general objectives remain constant. Investment aims to improve the appeal of rail transport at the local, regional and inter-regional scales, primarily by improving capacity, speed, passenger comfort and safety. Economically the expected outcome is an enhanced climate for business development, but environmentally these programmes are intended to underpin the diversion of individuals and freight from road to rail.

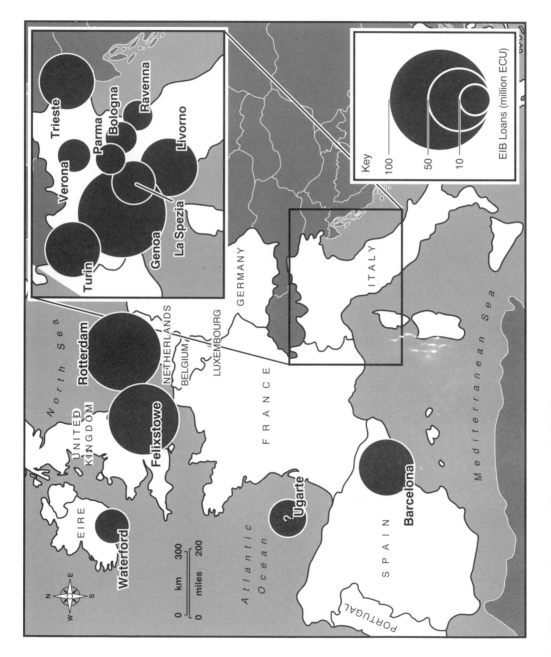

Figure 22.4 *EIB investment in intermodality projects, 1986–92*

Energy TENs

Energy TENs were defined by the early 1990s (European Commission, 1994b) and EIB support for these networks also contributes to environmental gains. Natural gas first began to impact on western European energy markets in the 1960s (Chapter 4). Thereafter it rapidly became necessary to transport this new fuel in large volumes from a small number of source regions – essentially the Netherlands, Norway, the Soviet Union and Algeria – to western Europe's widespread and burgeoning markets. This was achieved by heavy investment in a natural gas pipeline network, which from an early stage attracted large-scale EIB funding. This network now extends throughout the large majority of western Europe.

Initially, it is true, the motivation for network development was chiefly to improve western Europe's energy security. Especially after the 1973–74 oil crisis, it was recognised that the Community was over-dependent on oil imported from politically unstable source regions in the Middle East and North Africa. Increasingly, however, the environmental benefits of the natural gas TEN have become apparent. In part these benefits are related to construction: pipelines affect corridors only a few metres wide and, once the pipeline is laid, the land can be restored effectively. Visual intrusion and disruption of flora and fauna are therefore minimised. In addition, however, natural gas brings gains because it is the cleanest mass-consumption fuel and is generally used to substitute for fuels which are substantially more polluting (Estrada *et al.*, 1995). For example, whereas pollutant-rich fuel oil once ousted coal as the main energy source for industry and electricity generation, since the 1970s there has been an impressive switch in favour of gas. Between 1980 and 1996 the consumption of fuel oil in western Europe fell by 42 per cent while natural gas consumption almost doubled. Similarly in the domestic market, consumption of coal and heating oil has declined – although less spectacularly than in the industrial sector – while domestic natural gas usage has grown by almost 50 per cent.

This is not to argue, of course, that natural gas use entails no environmental costs; while its contribution to particulate and sulphur-based pollution is extremely low, its carbon dioxide output – and thus its contribution to the greenhouse effect – is substantial. Even so natural gas is much better than coal or oil in this respect,[2] and its substitution effects have therefore produced significant environmental gains. Achieving these gains has been entirely dependent on the development of a single transport mode – the natural gas network – in which the EIB has been a major investor. Moreover, continued EIB support for this TEN remains a feature of the 1990s. Recently, for example, substantial loans have been made available to increase the capacity of trans-Mediterranean pipelines, and also to extend gas availability into newer parts of the EU, where the substitution effect will continue. Thus the main natural gas grid is currently being extended to Spain and Portugal with EIB support, while a pipeline link from Italy to Greece is also considered a priority (Figure 22.1).

Although improved connectivity between national electricity generation and transmission systems is normally justified on efficiency grounds, it also offers the prospect of environmental gains. Detailed data on the pattern of international energy exchanges rarely appear. None the less, 1989 figures reveal that in western Europe numerous international links between national grids have been established, allowing sales to be made in neighbouring countries on a significant scale (Figure 22.5). France, Belgium, Spain, Norway and Sweden form a net exporting bloc, while Germany, Italy, Greece, Finland and the UK are net importers. So far as individual countries are concerned, these flows may be far from trivial. Indeed, France exported 12.3 per cent of her electricity production in 1989, while Italy imported 14 per cent of her requirements. Without this ability to even out imbalances between demand and supply through international exchanges, generating capacities in the deficit countries would have to have been increased. In most instances this would have resulted in more power stations burning fossil fuels; and, even if HEP had been an alternative, there would have been an environmental price to pay with respect to the ecological and landscape impacts of new dams.[3]

Historically EIB investment has contributed to the development of various international grid connections, and recent loans to projects of this type have included funding for links between the

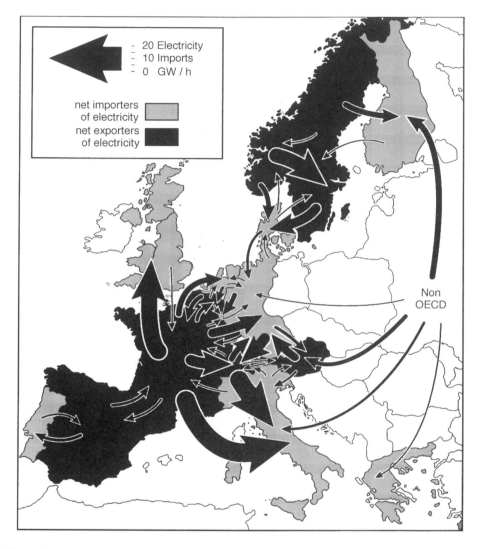

Figure 22.5   *International electricity exchanges, 1989*

German and Swedish, and Spanish and Portuguese, transmission systems. In addition there have been moves to ensure that the EIB plays a role in eliminating remaining serious gaps in the system, at least in western Europe. EU Commission priorities in the mid-1990s emphasised the need for improved connectivity within Denmark and also between the national grids of Spain and Portugal, France and Italy, and Italy and Greece (Figure 22.1). EIB expertise has already been involved in the assessment of these priorities, and further EIB funding will certainly follow over the next ten years.

Urban transport

Recognition of the EIB's growing involvement in the improvement of urban transport, and especially of urban public transport, is also necessary.[4] Most of these investments are clearly intended to encourage reduced dependence on the private car, thus ameliorating the effects of fumes, particulates and noise at the local scale, as well as the more global effects of greenhouse gas emissions. To some extent this funding has been directed at somewhat unusual alternative transport modes. In Naples, for example, two projects have involved support for funicular rail systems. One aims to keep tourism-related road traffic out of the historic core, while the other links a major residential area and the city centre, with obvious potential to divert shoppers and employees from inner-urban roads.

As might be anticipated, however, the leading investment targets are more mainstream. For example, among the cities and conurbations that have developed fast tram or light rail systems with partial funding from the EIB are Sheffield, the West Midland conurbation, Stuttgart, Toulouse, Rouen and Strasbourg. Especially in southern Europe, investments in the construction, extension and improvement of underground networks have figured prominently in the EIB's urban improvement activities. The Madrid, Valencia, Lisbon and Athens metro systems have all recently secured EIB development loans. And there has also been support for a wide range of other urban transport projects, such as the replacement of tram and urban bus fleets in Rostock (former East Germany), and construction of a public transport interchange system in Lisbon.

The downside

Despite the encouraging indicators noted above, other aspects of the EIB's investment portfolio are less reassuring. In part the problem is that of low funding levels for desirable transport systems, and above all for intermodality schemes. In the 1990s less than 1 per cent of the EIB's transport and communications investments have contributed to supporting the intermodality concept. This, it is true, owes much to the fact that EIB activity is demand led; operators of intermodal freight depots have in many cases turned to commercial funding sources instead of the EIB. Yet the fact remains that the EIB is scarcely represented in this important arena.

There are also issues associated with telecommunications. Throughout its history the EIB has been a staunch supporter of tele-communications investment, essentially because of the growing contribution effective communications networks have made to economic development. Particularly in peripheral problem regions, inadequate telephone systems have been

seen as a serious handicap to business and, therefore, to economic and social progress.

In recent years it has been argued that improved telecommunications bring environmental benefits, chiefly because of their propensity to promote activities such as teleworking, teleconferencing and home shopping (Capello and Gillespie, 1993). But, as Burt and Dawson argue in Chapter 9, and Vickerman emphasises in Chapter 12, at present reality does not match this assumption. In an era in which certain types of shopping have become significant leisure activities, electronic retailing has gained little ground in western Europe. Teleworking is limited, and is often used to change the timing of journeys, rather than to avoid them altogether. The linkage of telecommunications and computer systems has done much to enable the internationalisation of retail corporations, encouraging large-scale long-distance movement of commodities across western Europe, chiefly by road. And this link between information technologies, effective communications and the growth of international traffic is also fundamental to large sections of the manufacturing sector as they exploit the single market. All this would suggest that, while theoretically telecommunications may have great potential to bring environmental benefits by curtailing movement, their actual exploitation has frequently had the reverse effect.

Apart from this, evidence that EU support is provided for environmentally questionable transport modes and systems is particularly associated with investment in road and air transport infrastructures.

Road investments

Between 1980 and 1996 western European consumption of gasolines – chiefly petrol for cars – rose by almost 25 per cent. Over the same period diesel fuel consumption by road vehicles virtually doubled. Despite growing concern about the environmental effects of such trends, many EIB loans have continued to support road projects. In this context it is true that – in sharp contrast to the 1960s and 1970s, when motorways dominated EIB road funding – recent schemes have been much more diverse. Many are regional or local in nature, and are designed to eliminate bottlenecks. Frequently the investment is in road improvements, rather than the construction of new roads. Consequently it is normally possible to argue that such schemes are environmentally beneficial because, for example, they reduce congestion and the attendant high emission levels of crawling traffic.

However, investment in the motorway TEN – with its emphasis on the long-distance movement of people and goods by road – is by no means entirely a thing of the past. Motorway developments within Greece, between Portugal and Spain, and between Denmark and Sweden have all been funded in the 1990s and are likely to receive further EIB investment in the near future. France, too, has recently borrowed heavily for motorway construction. Morover, as Vickerman stresses in Chapter 12, while local and regional road improvements may produce some environmental gains through reduced congestion, as with inter-regional networks they induce further road traffic and, therefore, emissions.[5] This offsets gains made by, for example, increased use of catalytic converters (Eurostat, 1995, 106). A particular concern is nitrogen oxide (NO_x) output which, like carbon dioxide, is an important greenhouse gas. Although the data are as yet incomplete, it is probable that in 1992 the current 15 EU member states produced over 10 million t of NO_x, over 40 per cent of which was attributable to road transport.

Air transport investments

The EIB's transport investment portfolio also includes numerous air transport projects, often designed to encourage economic development and associated cohesion by more effective integration of the EU's core and periphery. To this end the purchase of new aircraft has been supported by EIB loans, and there have been investments in the expansion and upgrading of airports and terminal facilities in both the congested heart of the EU and its lagging areas. In the late 1980s and early 1990s Alitalia (the Italian national airline) contracted numerous EIB loans, almost all of them to purchase aircraft to improve

services within Italy or between Italy and the remainder of the EU. Safety, too, has been an important target, with loans being provided for improved air traffic control and new radar systems, partly in peripheral regions but also to serve the congested air lanes of the core. Thus Eurocontrol at Haren, Belgium, has received substantial funding.

Yet whatever the precise nature of the investment, and despite the importance of the integration goal, the price paid has been increased exhaust emissions (which, per passenger, are high relative to other transport modes) plus growing disturbance for local communities as a result of more frequent aircraft movements. As the European Commission has itself argued, part of the problem with air transport is that, by international agreement, aviation fuels are tax free. As a result there is insufficient pressure on engine manufacturers to produce fuel-efficient engines, which in turn encourages substantial exhaust emissions to be delivered into the upper atmosphere.

EIB Lending: Breakdown and Trends

Mediated by the EIB, therefore, EU support is provided for a wide range of transport and communications projects. Some are likely to mitigate environmental impacts while others may well exacerbate them. Against this background two questions arise. What is the balance between funding for these alternative outcomes? And to what extent is there evidence that funding is shifting to restrain damage to the environment?

As recently as the late 1980s it was striking that several of the transport media closely associated with environmentalism were absorbing low levels of EIB finance. As we have already noted, investment in freight intermodality was negligible, while loans for urban transport systems totalled only 727 million ECU (Table 22.2). Railways performed rather better, as did gas and electricity transmission and supply systems, yet each of these was outstripped by support for air transport projects. Moreover, the types of infrastructural investment most likely to promote the environmental problems associated with road transport – i.e. telecommunications and road

Table 22.2   *EIB investment in transport and communications systems in the EU, 1986–95*

	1986–90 (m. ECU)	1991–95 (m. ECU)	Change (%)
Roads/motorways	4070	9663	+182
Rail systems	1788	5034	+137
Air transport*	2659	2301	−13
Urban transport systems	727	3937	+441
Intermodal freight terminals	187	173	−7
Telecommunication networks and exchanges[†]	4295	7741	+80
Energy transmission and supply systems			
Natural gas	1920	4063	+111
Electricity	1573	2966	+89

* Includes loans for airport infrastructures, aircraft and air safety.
[†] Excludes satellites, cellular networks, etc.
Source: EIB *Annual Reports*, 1991 and 1996.

network development at all scales – were the leading investment categories.

In the 1990s, however, there have been clear signs of a shift in favour of the European Commission's environmental goals. Although the time periods detailed in Table 22.2 were identical, and although total transport funding grew impressively, air transport secured less investment in the early 1990s than in the late 1980s. In sharp contrast, loans for urban transport schemes rose by more than 400 per cent, to nearly 4 billion ECU; and those for rail systems similarly increased by almost 200 per cent, in this case to more than 5 billion ECU. Consequently EIB support for both these branches of the sector has recently exceeded that for air transport by a large margin.

Yet while these trends clearly suggest that there is good news with respect to convergence between environmental policy and practice, there is also another side to the coin. One aspect of this is the failure of intermodal freight projects to secure a high profile. A second is the expansion of road scheme funding by 137 per cent – despite the arguments for alternative transport modes. Over the 1991–95 period, indeed, road networks secured more EIB funding than any other transport mode, and almost twice as much as rail systems, even though funding for the latter had grown impressively. Such countervailing evidence prompts a further important question: why has movement towards greater sustainability not been more rapid, despite some encouraging trends?

Mixed results partly reflect the political realities

created by EU expansion in the 1980s and by the EU's economic growth and competition policies. Because Greece, Spain and Portugal all have low per capita GDP and poorly developed transport infrastructures, EIB investment has flowed impressively into projects intended to redress these deficiencies. Although they only joined the EC in 1986, Spain and Portugal accounted for a third of all EIB TEN investments in the first half of the 1990s. As in the 1960s, when Italy was the dominant EIB client, in practice this has often meant heavy investment in road projects. Consequently, while funding for rail system upgrading has not been eclipsed, there has been a strong push to improve all types of highway within individual countries and to extend the motorway TEN. In an integrationist era, any argument that road network upgrading should be held back because of the environmental implications of induced traffic would have been politically untenable. Road construction sites can be potent symbols of EU cohesion policy in practice.

Beyond this there are less obvious yet still significant contributory factors: the EIB's terms of reference and its organisational practices. Earlier it was noted that the EIB – like Structural Fund institutions aiming at regional development – is not an organisation charged with top-down blueprint planning. For 40 years, therefore, it has operated as a demand-led agency, required by its terms of reference to function in a responsive mode, rather than propose projects conforming with Commission priorities of the day. Only in the

1990s, following a Commission request for greater EIB involvement in the completion of TENs, has it been able to adopt a rather more proactive approach.[6] More rapid investment to promote the less damaging transport modes has therefore been inhibited by the ground rules of the past.

Uneven progress towards sustainability goals also reflects the EIB's internal organisational system. A key point is that, although annual investment is now almost 20 billion ECU, the EIB has less than 1000 employees. Moreover, while this total has almost doubled since 1980, the number of member states has risen from 9 to 15 and – at constant prices – turnover has more than quadrupled. To cope with relatively restricted human resources, and large-scale investment, the EIB has developed an organisational strategy based on strong relationships with relatively few customers who typically borrow for a series of projects over a lengthy period. Between 1986 and 1992, for example, 11 clients absorbed 85 per cent of EIB funding in Italy, the equivalent figures for Spain being 5 clients and 56 per cent, and for Ireland 4 clients and 70 per cent (Pinder *et al.*, 1995, 173). Historically most of these borrowers have been nationalised companies and government ministries or agencies responsible for transport infrastructure investments. Their strong relationships with the EIB have provided it with very effective conduits to channel funding from EIB headquarters in Luxembourg to member states and regions. Structurally, however, this convenient and efficient system is by no means ideally suited to a rapid shift of investment towards the more environmentally acceptable transport projects. Change can be retarded by established customers maintaining a strong influence on the EIB's investment profile.

In addition to influencing the types of investment supported, the EIB's operating procedures and terms of reference have a strong spatial dimension. The vast majority of the EIB's funding has always been channelled into EC (and now EU) member states, but for many years modest sums have also been made available to other countries. African, Caribbean and Pacific (ACP) states have qualified under the Lomé Convention; there is a scheme for lending to non-EU Mediterranean states; and small sums also go to some Asian and Latin American countries, mainly for energy projects. Since the fall of Communism, however, what is potentially a major new market for EIB involvement has been officially recognised: central and eastern Europe. At this point, therefore, it is appropriate to turn the spotlight eastwards, to explore transport funding trends in a region where strong economic imperatives undoubtedly have the potential to clash sharply with environmental objectives (Hall, 1993a, b; Lijewski, 1996; Pucher, 1995).

The EIB in Central and Eastern Europe

EIB loans to central and eastern Europe began in the early 1990s, the argument being that it was in the EU's interests to support the democracy movement, encourage political and social stability, and assist countries to strengthen their economies with eventual EU membership in mind. Funding provision for these countries was strongly supported by the EU Commission and member states, and was part of a package of measures initiated by the West. These included the EU's PHARE programme, which provides grant aid,[7] and the European Bank for Reconstruction and Development (EBRD).[8] As yet, total EIB lending in the region has been modest, partly because viable projects were at first limited, but also because ceilings were imposed on lending levels. However, these ceilings have been raised as demand has developed, so that by 1996 more than 4 billion ECU had been invested in these countries.

Loans have been concluded in all central and eastern European states (Table 22.3). Borrowing levels have naturally varied according to the scale of individual countries, but the maturity of their economies and public sectors has also been a powerful influence. As a result the Visegrad Four – the Czech Republic, Hungary, Poland and Slovakia – have established themselves as the main client states, absorbing 75 per cent of all EIB funding in the region. Table 22.3 also demonstrates that, sectorally, transport and communications have rapidly become the chief sources of funded projects: on average they have accounted for 60 per cent of all EIB investment, while individual national figures have typically varied between 50 and 85 per cent.

Table 22.3   *National distribution of EIB investment in central and eastern Europe, 1989–95*

	Total investment (m. ECU)	Transport* and telecommunications[†] (% of national total)	TENs (% of transport total)
Albania	34	85	100
Bulgaria	286	74	38
Czech Republic	737	52	49
Estonia	68	75	69
Hungary	832	65	23
Latvia	20	0	0
Lithuania	59	92	0
Poland	1306	62	57
Romania	455	75	50
Slovakia	253	47	8
Slovenia	120	100	100
Total	4170	60	36

* Includes loans for airport infrastructures, aircraft and air safety.
[†] Excludes satellites, cellular networks, etc.
Source: EIB *Annual Reports*, 1991 and 1996.

What is equally evident is that, within this sector, projects related to TENs have secured a significant share of available finance (Table 22.3). Although allocations have varied greatly between countries, by the mid-1990s TEN-related investments had absorbed more than a third of EIB transport loans. This closely reflected the EU Commission's concern to extend western European networks in order to underpin the eventual economic integration of East and West. Clearly, therefore, transport and communications are being treated as a priority sector of fundamental importance for long-term economic development. But to what extent does the evidence suggest that the pursuit of economic goals is being effectively co-ordinated with the promotion of transport sustainability?

To a degree the indications are positive. In particular it is notable that, while air transport has attracted a number of loans in Bulgaria, Hungary, Lithuania, Poland and Slovakia, these have accounted for less than 10 per cent of all investment. However, what may be questioned in this connection is whether investment rates will remain low as pressure develops for the creation of air transport networks which link central and eastern Europe more effectively with the western European and, indeed, global economic systems.

It seems inevitable that the region's air traffic will grow impressively, fuelling and feeding on economic development; it also appears unlikely that environmental arguments will hold in check the investments necessary to support this growth; and political expectations mean that partial funding for such projects will in all probability continue to come from the EIB.

With respect to other transport modes, there are already signs that the interests of economic development are overshadowing environmental considerations. A notable omission from Table 22.4, for example, is EIB investments in intermodality, although there is great potential to promote long-distance freight movement by rail to and from western Europe, as well as within the region. Equally obviously, in sharp contrast to recent trends in the EU, urban transport is not generating demand for investment. Because of their political history, central and eastern European cities have a tradition of low car ownership and extensive public transport systems (Pucher, 1995). Yet today the demand among large sections of the population is for private transport, a potent symbol of convergence on western Europe's life styles. This powerful trend is one factor holding back public transport refurbishment projects and, until there is much stronger

Table 22.4 *Modal distribution of EIB investment in transport and telecommunications systems in central and eastern Europe, 1989–95*

	m. ECU	%
Roads/motorways (TENs)	917	36.4
Other roads/motorways	70	2.8
Rail systems (TENS)	225	8.9
Other rail systems	36	1.4
Air transport (TENS)*	20	0.8
Other air transport	183	7.3
Urban transport systems	0	0.0
Intermodal freight terminals	0	0.0
Port developments (TENs)	55	2.2
Other port developments	14	0.6
Telecommunication networks and exchanges	760	30.1
Energy transmission and supply systems		
Natural gas	140	5.6
Electricity	0	0.0
Oil pipelines	100	3.9
Total	2520	100

* Includes loans for airport infrastructures, aircraft and air safety.
Source: European Investment Bank, EIB Financing in Central and Eastern Europe, press release, 4.11.96.

local political will to adopt a different course, the EIB's scope for promoting sustainable urban transport will remain limited.

Finally it is important to compare investments in road and rail projects. In one sense funding for these modes has been similar, in that both have chiefly attracted EIB support for TEN development, primarily to promote integration. To quote just three examples, in the Czech Republic finance has been provided to contribute to upgrading of the Berlin–Prague–Vienna railway; in Poland loans have supported rehabilitation of the Wroclaw–Opole motorway and an extension to Gliwice; and the EIB's largest loan in Romania has been for modernisation of the trunk road system.

In other respects, however, the contrasts between these modes could scarcely be greater. Even at this early stage it is clear that road transport improvements are establishing a commanding lead over rail investments. Altogether, rail projects have accounted for only a tenth of all EIB funding for the transport and telecommunications sector,

whereas road systems have secured virtually 40 per cent (Table 22.4).

This is not to argue, of course, that all road improvements are inappropriate. Economic imperatives are far too pressing for this to be the case. But it does strongly suggest that, as in urban areas, the forces acting in favour of the more environmentally damaging transport systems are strong. Particularly when intermodality is poorly developed, the speed, flexibility and cost of road transport are highly attractive. Moreover, as with the private car, in the new market-oriented climate the dominantly road-based western European industrial economy has become a highly influential role model for the central and eastern European countries. Against this background the number of road improvement projects is likely to remain high, and as yet there are no signs that the dominantly demand-led EIB has the means to steer its investment in favour of more environmentally acceptable rail transport schemes.

What must be added is that, as in western Europe, there is every prospect that telecommunications projects will boost the dominance of road transport. As Michalak has emphasised in Chapter 8, far-reaching telecommunications improvements are essential to economic development throughout central and eastern Europe, and to date they have accounted for almost a third of EIB loans in the region (Table 22.4). Yet it appears that an inevitable consequence of this will be to encourage sharp increases in long-distance freight movements. Most of these will be captured by the road haulage industry as road modernisation moves ahead of rail network improvements.

Conclusion

This review of recent investment trends has highlighted some progress but also continuing tensions. What is abundantly clear is that the EIB has little difficulty in making available large-scale investment for the transport and communications sector. This has long been the case in the EU and, although investment in central and eastern Europe is naturally much more limited, there too the upward trend is well established. Within these western and eastern investment streams the most positive signs from the environment's viewpoint are those identified in the EU. Good examples are provided by greatly increased loans for rail network development and urban transport systems in the 1990s.

Despite such indicators, however, conflicts between the interests of economic development and the environment remain prominent. The EIB's road network funding in EU member states has also grown substantially in recent years, to the extent that in the 1990s it has absorbed more than any other mode of transport or communication. In central and eastern Europe support for road transport is in the ascendant, while urban public transport developments and the modernisation of rail networks are far less buoyant. And, in both West and East, telecommunications developments which are essential for growth are likely to fuel trade and the seemingly inexorable rise of road traffic.

To some extent these trends reflect political realities. Thus the accession of Spain and Portugal in 1986 added to the EC many areas of poor road infrastructure, and also highlighted road integration problems at the international level. Inevitably an expectation arose that these difficulties would be tackled by available European investment, including that from the EIB. But the pole position enjoyed by road projects in both western and eastern Europe also reflects the realities of the economy, the strong preferences of individuals and the EIB's operational procedures. The economy is very firmly road based; individuals, in their private lives and in their business transport decisions, greatly value the flexibility and convenience of road transport; and the peoples of central and eastern Europe aspire to emulate western life styles and economic development processes. In these circumstances it is unavoidable that road transport projects will be very numerous, making it difficult for the EIB to engineer a dramatic shift in an alternative direction, designed as it is to respond to demand rather than plan strategically. By the same token, it is difficult to discriminate against air transport projects. As a result, if we regard EIB investment as a stamp of EU approval, we must accept that for the foreseeable future it will be given to many schemes whose presumed economic advantages are linked with distinct environmental drawbacks. In particular, the exhaust gases, particulates and

noise produced by road vehicles and aircraft are likely to be pervading problems.

What must be reiterated here is that these conclusions are based solely on an analysis of EIB activity, and it is possible that other forms of funding are producing different outcomes. For example, many small sustainable transport projects might be much more feasible with ERDF grants rather than EIB loans. None the less, the general picture does not look encouraging. This in turn suggests that it is necessary for the EU to deploy other instruments in its attempts to square the circle of transport, economic development and environmental protection. Of particular importance is the fact that the European Commission is also able to impact directly on transport-related pollution through Regulations and Directives, for example concerning emissions and noise levels. The potential gains from such measures are readily apparent on the roads: the switch to unleaded fuel; catalytic converters on new cars; tighter exhaust emission standards; and the reduction of sulphur and particulates in diesel fuel are all examples of what can be achieved. Moreover, a proposal by the EU in June 1997 that taxes should be imposed on aircraft fuel indicates recognition that this regulatory approach need not be confined to road transport.[9]

Yet if the imperfect progress made by EIB-type direct investment is to be reinforced in this way, the outcome will be heavily dependent on the commitment of individual EU governments to implement standards effectively. This is not guaranteed, not least because in some countries there are still strong vested interests who regard the costs of environmental protection as an unjustifiable burden on business. If this is a lingering problem in the West, however, it is likely to be an even greater factor in the East, where economic growth freed from restrictions is the central imperative. Against this background, although some progress is being made, there seems little prospect of the EU securing a rapid Europe-wide shift towards greater transport sustainability.

Notes

1. The commitment to transport infrastructures has so far been maintained despite the cautionary note sounded by

Hurst (1994), whose work in fact appeared in one of the EIB's own publications.

2. The carbon dioxide emission coefficient for natural gas is 56 t per terajoule (TJ); for liquid fuels it is approximately 75 t/TJ and for coal it is 94 t/TJ.

3. In most instances HEP was not an option because potential sites were generally exploited.

4. A quite different approach to the improvement of urban infrastructures is support for urban district heating systems designed to promote environmental protection through energy conservation and emission reductions. However, these are essentially highly localised developments that have received very limited funding and have therefore been excluded from the discussion.

5. The most notorious European example of induced growth is the traffic generated by the completion of London's orbital motorway, the M25.

6. A somewhat more proactive approach has become possible because the EIB has been made the lead agency for a new EU loan guarantee scheme, the European Investment Fund. A primary function of this is to encourage borrowing by public authorities and the private sector for TEN investment. Also, the EIB has evaluated for the Commission two lists of priority projects relating to transport and energy infrastructures (Figure 22.1). These lists were prepared by the Christophersen Group, established at the Brussels Council Meeting in December 1993. There is an expectation that the EIB will now contribute to meeting these priorities.

7. The PHARE programme is a European Union initiative providing grant aid to support economic transformation in eastern and central Europe. Launched in December 1989, PHARE aid was originally created for Poland and Hungary, but the geographical scope has been broadened so that well over 5 billion ECU have been made available in 11 central and eastern European countries.

8. The EBRD was established on 15 April 1991. The are 59 members in total, but 51% of the capital is held by EU member states, the Commission and the EIB; 10% by the USA; 8.3% by Japan; 4% by Russia; and 3.4% by Canada. The EBRD has both a financial and a political function since it must promote the market economy and democracy simultaneously in the countries of central and eastern Europe and the CIS. It is also a development bank which makes investments at very low rates of interest and makes loans to public and private enterprises. In connection with privatisation it is involved in acquisitions, mergers and the purchase of holdings for profit. The EBRD's statutes state that 60% of its operations must be in the private sector and 40% in the public sphere.

9. The EU proposed a world-wide air fuel tax following the New York Earth Summit, organised by the UN. The proposal was opposed by the United States but supported by the UN, not least because it envisaged that part of the proceeds would be channelled into environmental projects in developing areas.

References

Blacksell, M (1994) Environmental policies and resource management, in M Blacksell and A M Williams (eds) *The European Challenge: geography and development in the European Community*, Oxford University Press, Oxford, 323–42.

Blum, U, Gercek, H and Viegas, J (1992) High-speed railway and the European peripheries: opportunities and challenges, *Transportation Res-A*, **26**, 211–21.

Bonsall, P (1996) Can induced traffic be measured by surveys?, *Transportation*, **23**, 17–34.

Capello, R and Gillespie, A (1993) Transport, communications and spatial organisation: future trends and conceptual frameworks, in G Giannopoulos and A Gillespie (eds) *Transport and Communications Innovation in Europe*, Belhaven, London, 24–56.

Charlier, J J and Ridolfi, G (1994) Intermodal transportation in Europe: of modes, corridors and nodes, *Maritime Policy and Management*, **21**, 237–50.

Charlton, C (1994) The development of high-speed passenger rail services in Europe, in R Gibb (ed) *The Channel Tunnel: a geographical perspective*, Belhaven, London, 31–54.

Coombe, D (1996) Induced traffic – what do transportation models tell us?, *Transportation*, **23**, 83–101.

Estrada, J, Moe, A and Martinsen, K D (1995) *The Development of European Gas Markets: environmental, economic and political perspectives*, J Wiley & Sons, Chichester.

European Commission (1986a) *Communication from the Commission to the Council: Medium-term Transport Infrastructure Programme*, COM (86) 340 final, European Commission, Brussels.

European Commission (1986b) *Towards a European High-Speed Rail Network*, COM (86) 341 final, European Commission, Brussels.

European Commission (1988) *Triannual Report of the Commission on the Work of the Transport Infrastructure Committee (1984–1987)*, COM (88) 289 final, European Commission, Brussels.

European Commission (1989a) *Communication from the Commission to the Council Regarding a Transport Infrastructure Policy*, COM (89) 238 final, European Commission, Brussels.

European Commission (1989b) *Communication on a Community Railway Policy*, COM (89) 564 final, European Commission, Brussels.

European Commission (1990) *Towards Trans-European Networks for a Community Action Programme*, COM (90) 585 final, European Commission, Brussels.

European Commission (1992a) *Communication from the Commission Concerning the Creation of a Combined Transport Network and its Operating Conditions*, COM (92) 230 final, European Commission, Brussels.

European Commission (1992b) *Commission Communication: transport infrastructure*, COM (92) 231 final, European Commission, Brussels.

European Commission (1994a) *Proposal for a European Parliament and Council Decision on Community Guidelines for the*

Development of the Trans-European Network, COM (94) 685 final, European Commission, Brussels.

European Commission (1994b) *Commission Communication to the European Parliament and Council on Community Guidelines on Trans-European Energy Networks*, European Commission, Brussels.

European Commission (1994c) *Growth, Competitiveness and Employment*, Office for Official Publications, Luxembourg.

European Investment Bank (1996) *Environmental Policy Statement*, EIB, Luxembourg.

European Investment Bank (Annually) *Annual Report*, EIB, Luxembourg.

Eurostat (1995) *Europe in Figures*, Office for Official Publications of the European Communities, Luxembourg.

Farrington, J (1992) Transport, environment and energy, in B S Hoyle and R Knowles (eds) *Modern Transport Geography*, Belhaven, London, 51–66.

Gibb, R (1994) The Channel Tunnel project: origins and development, in R Gibb (ed) *The Channel Tunnel: a geographical perspective*, Belhaven, London, 1–30.

Hall, D R (1993a) Impacts of economic and political transition on the transport geography of Central and Eastern Europe, *Journal of Transport Geography*, 1(1), 20–35.

Hall, D R (ed) (1993b) *Transport and Economic Development in the new Central and Eastern Europe*, Belhaven, London.

Honohan, P (1995) The public policy role of the European Investment Bank within the EU, *Journal of Common Market Studies*, 33, 315–30.

Hurst, C (1994) Infrastructure and growth: a literature review, *EIB Papers*, 23, 57–76.

Lijewski, T (1996) The impact of political changes on transport in Central and Eastern Europe, *Transport Reviews*, 16(1), 37–53.

Mackie, P J (1996) Induced traffic and economic appraisal, *Transportation*, 23, 103–19.

Pinder, D A, Edwards, J B and Wise, M (1995) The European Investment Bank, transport investment and European Union objectives: an exploratory analysis, *Journal of Transport Geography*, 167–77.

Pucher, J (1995) The road to ruin? Impacts of economic shock therapy on urban transport in Poland, *Transport Policy*, 2(1), 5–13.

Ross, J F L (1994) High-speed rail: catalyst for European integration? *Journal of Common Market Studies*, 32, 191–214.

Scholl, L, Schipper, L and Kiang, N (1996) CO_2 emissions from passenger transport – a comparison of international trends from 1973 to 1992, *Energy Policy*, 24(1), 17–30.

Williams, R H (1990) Supranational environment policy, land use planning and pollution control, in D Pinder (ed) *Western Europe: challenge and change*, Belhaven, London, 195–207.

23
Urban transport, environmental pressures and policy options

Derek Hall

Leisure and Tourism Management Department, The Scottish Agricultural College, UK

Introduction

Transport represents a key element in Europe's changing geography, not just in terms of the movement of people, goods, information and ideas, but also in maintaining standards of living and in improving the quality of life. Yet transport is also a major consumer of non-renewable sources of energy and is responsible for much of the growth in atmospheric emissions. Not least in urban areas, the congestion and delay, negative health effects and accidents associated with transport have rendered it a major and largely unresolved issue – or series of issues – facing Europe's local, national and supranational decision-makers (Banister, 1996).

The nature and problems of urban transport articulate changing economic and societal priorities: questions of congestion and competition for access, environmental well-being and personal freedoms, private–public partnerships and funding sources, planning and control, notions of community, equity and sustainability. In the face of such issues, this chapter has two major aims. The first is to highlight the environmental impacts and external costs of urban transport within a European context, while the

second is to review the policy options available to raise the sustainability of urban transport development. Both entail an examination of the relationships between urban transport and land-use issues, a debate that has embraced a wider environmental dimension in recent years, not least in the UK. In addressing questions of sustainability, as exemplified in urban transport policy approaches across Europe, evaluation is necessary of the issues surrounding the modal split in urban transport use, particularly in relation to the roles of integration, co-ordination, deregulation and privatisation.

Following a brief examination of the evolution of European urban transport, the chapter addresses the nature of transport costs. In particular, debates concerning the external costs of car use in urban areas are examined, and the nature of these costs is exemplified. The policy options available for restraining, and providing sustainable alternatives to, car use in urban areas are evaluated, together with the environmental implications of these polices. Finally it is suggested that, if urban transport is to be sustainable, a mix of policy options will need to be adopted, with the balance varying from country to country. A central element, however, will be the need for more realistic attitudes to the external costs of motorised transport, a reoriented perspective that is an essential precondition for policies aimed at both reducing those costs through modal shift, and transferring them on to motorists themselves.

Urban Transport Evolution

The late-nineteenth-century development of suburban trains and electric trams (Figure 23.1) sustained a rapid outward growth of European

Figure 23.1 *Electric tram, Blackpool, UK. In contrast to the UK, tram systems have survived in many east and west European cities. (Photo: D R Hall)*

towns and cities and, for the first time, encouraged the separation of place of residence and work for large numbers of working people. Underground railways reinforced this process in the larger cities, while many urban railway systems developed a distinctive radial form as they were initially designed for travel to the principal sources of employment in city centres. Concentric routes were less common, although London, Paris, Berlin and a number of central and east European cities developed such links to permit direct movement circumnavigating the central area.

From the 1930s motor buses, and later widespread access to motor cars, encouraged suburbanisation and urban dispersal to occur on a much larger scale than hitherto. Tramways, and later trolleybus services, were enhanced and extended in many continental European cities. In post-war central and eastern Europe they often provided the backbone of heavily subsidised, if underfunded, urban public transport systems (Machon and Dingsdale, 1989). (West) Germany upgraded a number of its urban tram systems into light rail (LR) services, and put them underground through reconstructed urban centres to avoid conflict with road traffic, as in Cologne and Hannover. Suburban railway electrification, and the elaboration of underground systems, were particularly successful where land-use zoning powers were used to concentrate high-density suburban development around railway stations. The five suburban rail corridors developed from Copenhagen's 1947 Plan provide a notable example.

Bypasses began to be constructed during the interwar period, to divert through traffic away from small towns or from districts of larger urban centres. During the 1950s and 1960s construction of additional road capacity became the conventional wisdom as an effective solution to congestion problems, such that urban freeways, bypasses, ring roads and motorways were built in and around many urban settlements across (western) Europe. It soon became evident, however, that in many cases the capacity gained from additional road construction would be quickly filled with extra traffic generated by the new facility: "induced traffic". Subsequently, estimating induced traffic has become a major consideration when attempting to measure likely benefits from road improvements (Bonsall, 1996, Coombe, 1996, Mackie, 1996), and many would now argue that the induction effect is a good reason to curtail most new urban road building. The M25 motorway, opened in 1986 around Greater London, provides a prime example of underestimated induction, and the construction of additional carriageways now appears a very costly counter-productive exercise. More generally in much of western Europe, it was obvious by the 1970s that investing large amounts of capital in new highways dedicated to the rapid movement of motor traffic was not necessarily the most effective transport policy option.

At the same time, rebuilding community and identity of place, together with the "re-imaging" of urban areas (Law, 1993; Ashworth and Larkham, 1994) have become components of what may be viewed as the post-modernist fragmentation of contemporary Western urban experience. While developments in transport and communications, not least the widespread use of motor vehicles, have both permitted many individuals and organisations the luxury of spatial, social and economic flexibility and accessibility, these elements of modernisation and "progress" have also contributed to this fragmentation by compromising and devaluing many built and natural environments and by radically changing patterns of social and economic activity, such that freedom for some has been constraint and imposition for others.

During much of the twentieth century Europe has been characterised by ideological and physical division, the consequences of which could be recognised in differing urban transport policies and priorities. Following political and economic change in central and eastern Europe from 1989 onwards, characteristics and problems familiar in the West began to emerge as market-led policies began to be applied (Hall, 1993a, b; Lijewski, 1996). A rapid rise in car ownership and use, freight transport modal shift from rail to road, and problems of maintaining public transport services in times of economic restraint, have echoed west European trends, albeit within a telescoped time frame. However, the impacts on urban transport of deregulation, privatisation, inward investment, consumer choice, changing levels of personal mobility, domestic and international tourism and recreation in central and eastern Europe are yet poorly represented in the literature (Hall, 1995; Pucher, 1995).

Concerns over traffic accidents and health risks, social and spatial intrusion, and environmental damage from vehicle emissions have been reinforced by projected road traffic growth figures: many European countries anticipate a doubling of road traffic over the next 20–30 years. Yet trends in land use and transport have reinforced each other over several decades to produce a situation in which, for many who are locked into land-use patterns where they cannot do without their cars, high mobility is felt not to be a matter of choice but of necessity. The convenience, familiarity, privacy and perceived "security" of the motor car for its driver are cultural considerations which are heavily reinforced by government rhetoric which opines that road building reflects, and is essential for, national prosperity, and that the motor car symbolises the democratic ideals of freedom and consumer choice. But it is equally arguable that the roads-based mind-sets of decision-makers have acted to restrict choice for many people: in a UK survey, for example, 82 per cent of drivers agreed that it would be difficult to adjust their life styles to being without a car (Jones, 1992).

Such mind-sets, which have diluted any political will to intervene substantially in the life styles of the car-owning and car-using sectors of European society, have also acted to polarise the benefits and costs of transport. This is because a fundamental problem facing urban transport policy is the fact that car users do not pay for the environmental and social costs that they impose on others. While car users pay for the private costs of motoring – fuel, parking fees, road tolls, vehicle depreciation – society as a whole experiences and pays for the unintended external costs such as noise and pollution. The sum of both private and external costs represents the full cost of private motoring, yet car drivers only weigh up their private costs when making decisions about driving because they do not pay for the external costs involved. In economic terms this represents a market inefficiency, and in environmental terms it means that – unless politicians summon the courage to begin to charge drivers the full costs of their activities – urban environments, together

with human and economic health, will continue to deteriorate.

External Transport Costs

The external costs of transport are considerable (Figure 23.2 and Table 23.1), and raise major policy questions concerning the nature of urban land-use relationships, restrictions on personal freedoms, environmental impacts and economic efficiency. Around 92 per cent of all transport external costs in the European Union derive from road transport. Cars account for around 60 per cent and freight vehicles for 20 per cent. One relatively narrow estimate of the breakdown of the external costs of transport within the EU attributes 54 per cent to road accidents, 16 per cent to air pollution, 16 per cent to climate change and 14 per cent to noise nuisance (Rothengatter and Mauch, 1994). However, the full range of external costs is wider than this, and includes congestion; general disruption and intrusion; the resource depletion associated with the exploitation of natural materials used to construct and fuel motor vehicles; the resources used to build roads and other transport-related infrastructures; and the environmental costs of the disposal of vehicles, liquids (such as sump oil) and roads and buildings when their working lives are ended. It will be noted that many of these impact on urban environments, and it is hardly surprising that public concern about them has grown. For example, interviews undertaken for the UK Department of the Environment show that the

Table 23.1 *Estimates of the external costs of road transport (% of GDP, 1991)*

Belgium	5.4	Portugal	9.8
Denmark	3.2	Spain	4.9
Finland	3.3	Sweden	3.0
France	4.2	Switzerland	3.1
Germany	4.5	UK	3.7–4.7
Greece	5.6	Europe 17	
Ireland	4.2	(including	
Italy	3.8	Norway)	4.2
Netherlands	3.3		
Norway	4.9		

Sources: Pearce and Maddison (1994); Rothengatter (1994).

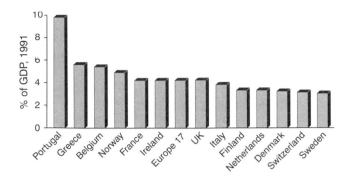

Note: UK figure is mid-point of estimated range 3.7 to 4.7%

Figure 23.2 *Estimates of total external costs of road transport, 1991*

proportion of respondents "very worried" about traffic exhaust fumes and urban smog has risen from a quarter in 1986 to a third in 1989 and to 40 per cent in 1993 (DoE, 1994).

If this is the general background, a range of recent studies has added more detail to the picture. Many questions revolve around the issue of congestion, which has both adverse economic effects and diminishes the quality of life for many urban residents and travellers (Whitelegg, 1992). Across the EU, the costs of transport congestion to industry have been estimated at more than 500bn ECU, and in the UK alone they have been put at £19bn per year, adding £6 per week to the average household budget (CBI, 1995).

Road transport accounts for one-fifth of world carbon dioxide output and, as carbon dioxide is recognised as the most important greenhouse gas (IPCC, 1990), transport is one of the sectors from which climate-related environmental impacts are increasing most rapidly (Scholl *et al.*, 1996). Urban congestion exacerbates air pollution problems: fuel consumption increases as speed decreases in congestion. A Danish study has shown that the emissions of carbon monoxide and volatile organic compounds (VOCs) from catalyst-equipped passenger cars in urban traffic are 100 per cent higher per kilometre at 20 kph than at 40 kph; similarly, nitrogen oxide emissions are 50 per cent higher during the slower peak times (Crawack, 1993).[1] Moreover, transport accounts for 55 per cent of total European emissions of nitrogen oxide, the major contributor to acid rain. Swedish researchers have attempted to establish a monetary valuation of the human health effects of

exhaust emissions in urban areas, but different methods of valuing the environmental effects of air pollution across Europe render comparative analyses at best tentative (ECOPLAN, 1992). Even so, extrapolating US findings, it has been suggested that vehicle exhausts may be responsible for 10 000 extra deaths annually in England and Wales alone (Brown, 1994).

Road accidents represent a dreadful human and economic waste: in the UK alone over 300 000 people were injured and 3665 killed in this way in 1995. Although there are significant variations in road accident fatalities (Figure 23.3), the greater proportion of serious accidents occur in urban areas. Roads in built-up zones may have accident rates up to three times greater than those elsewhere, although the relationship between accident rates and traffic volume is debated (DTp, 1987; Vitaliano and Held, 1991). What is also significant is that those who benefit least from the motor vehicle (the young, the old and the poor) seem disproportionately likely to die in road traffic accidents (Erskine, 1996). Pedestrians and cyclists are especially vulnerable. In the UK, 95 per cent of pedestrian accidents are recorded in urban areas, with half of these occurring in town centres. Children account for 39 per cent of all pedestrian casualties, and 90 per cent of accidents involving the under-fives happen within 400 m of home, often on minor roads in residential areas (Whitelegg, 1987).

Loss of net output to society is commonly argued to represent the major external cost of fatal accidents (Jones-Lee and Loomes, 1995), but estimation is made difficult by the fact that the notional

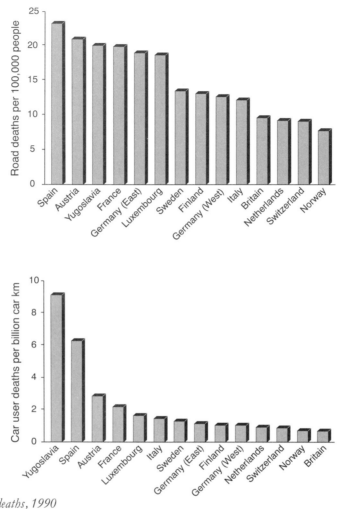

Figure 23.3   *Road deaths, 1990*

value of a statistical life (VOSL) varies considerably across Europe (from £13 000 in Portugal to £2.1m. in Sweden; Hansson and Markham, 1992). What is clear, however, is that such values are usually based on projected lost personal earnings and/or the ability of the liable party to pay. If anything, therefore, they are likely to be underestimates because they rarely consider the wider external costs to society: the expense of medical care and rehabilitation, plus the various economic, social and emotional penalties of supporting those permanently disabled by road accidents.

Apart from decreased quality of life, transport noise is also responsible for productivity losses caused by an inability to concentrate at work, or by disrupted sleep resulting in tiredness. Both the type and range of variables included, and the methodology employed to calculate the costs of such negative impacts, have varied considerably across western Europe, producing estimated costs of road traffic noise ranging from 0.02 to 2.27 per cent of GDP (Table 23.2). One calculation has suggested that the annual total cost of noise from transport in the UK alone was approximately £3bn, £2.43bn of which was attributable to the car and £0.55bn to heavy goods vehicles. Noise cost (in pence per passenger/kilometre) emerged as 0.097 for buses, 0.41 for cars, 1.18 for motorbikes and 1.96 for HGVs (Peirson and Vickerman, 1994).

Most forms of transport set up vibration which can not only progressively undermine older

Table 23.2 *Selected estimates of the costs of traffic noise*

Date	Country	Per cent GDP	Method/basis
1983	Europe	0.10–0.20	Comparison of studies
1983	France	0.30–2.27	Insulation costs for a 50 to 40 dB(A) norm
1986	France	0.04	Loss in property values
1989	General	0.10	Comparison of studies
1987	Netherlands	0.02	Government expenditure on abatement
		0.02	Loss in property value
1988	Netherlands	0.03–0.08	Extra prevention and remaining loss in property values
		0.03–0.08	Potential insulation
		0.12–0.24	Abatement at source
1983	Norway	0.22	Loss in property value
		0.17	Loss of sleep
		0.07	Existing protection
		0.12	Potential vehicle protection programme
1986	West Germany	0.02–0.05	Loss in property value
1987	West Germany	0.15	Productivity losses
		1.45	Loss in property values with 30 dB(A) norm
1991	West Germany	0.03	Roads: avoidance cost
		0.03	Rail: avoidance cost
		0.52	Roads: willingness to pay
		0.22	Rail: willingness to pay

Source: Verhoef (1994).

buildings and other structures, but also intrude into people's daily lives, diminishing their physical and mental well-being. Construction of new urban highways (and large-scale public transport schemes) can produce temporary or permanent community disruption, combining visual intrusion, polluted atmospheric conditions, noise and physical dislocation. Associated demolition of housing and commercial properties induces further social and economic disruption. The increasing proportion of urban land that car-related uses occupy reduces both environmental quality and the degree of mobility and access to other activities. The barrier effects of roads are well known, physically dividing communities, and cutting off potential pedestrian use of shops, schools and other services. This often necessitates the use of the car for safety and security reasons for adults and children who would otherwise prefer to walk, and whose health (barring traffic-derived pollution) would be enhanced by doing so. The land-take of roads, car parking areas – on-street or in purpose-built car parks – and other traffic-related infrastructures also reduces personal freedom, spreads accident and pollution risks,

and often causes massive visual intrusion. Not surprisingly, sites for new major road developments have sometimes become the symbols of, and battlegrounds for, the polarised values held within urban society in the late twentieth century, graphically expressing the need for more consensus over environmentally and socially sustainable agendas (Bryant, 1996).

Policy Options

Because individual country conditions will favour one particular approach rather than another, no single set of policy measures can adequately address the need to develop a sustainable urban transport programme. In fact, some seven complementary and closely related types of policy instrument are deployed to restrain car use in democratic European societies: restrictive policies, economic incentives/disincentives, integrated land-use planning, priority for public transport, support for benign modes, policies to influence attitudinal change, and the application of technological innovation.

Restrictive policies

Engineering traffic management measures have at best postponed congestion problems, and at worst have exacerbated or simply shifted them. The reorganisation of traffic flows through one-way and gyratory systems, by speeding up traffic, can have the effect of isolating groups of buildings and sections of communities, and of increasing noise, air pollution, accidents, barrier effects for pedestrians and other intrusion problems. The knock-on effects in terms of easing or constraining access, raising or lowering land values and thus influencing land uses, may be profound. To be effective, therefore, rather than simply alleviating congestion, restrictive policies need to embrace wider objectives likely to receive public support. Examples include restricting cars in central Athens and in Italian cities such as Florence for explicit environmental reasons, and lowering speed limits in urban residential areas for safety, environmental and energy considerations, rather than for increasing road capacity (Jones, 1991).

The development of traffic-free zones often meets initial opposition from retailers who perceive that a lack of motorised access to their premises will result in a loss of sales. Recognition of the legitimate interests and concerns of groups affected – adversely or beneficially – by any restrictions on car use in urban areas is important, and good communication and sources of information concerning changes are vital. Even so, support for restraint schemes has often increased after their introduction, once drivers and retailers have become used to them and recognise the benefits derived (Hass-Klau, 1993).

Speed restrictions on roads need to be considered in terms of saving fuel and reducing the number and severity of accidents. The concept of "traffic calming", conceived in response to problems of vehicle noise, vibration, atmospheric pollution and, above all, accident risks, especially to the young, involves the attempt to create an environment within urban residential areas in which cars are impeded but not excluded. In such environments priority is accorded to the pedestrian, thereby improving road safety; reclaiming space for pedestrian and non-traffic activities; improving pedestrian mobility and reducing traffic barriers to that mobility; promoting greater security, in particular among residents, pedestrians and cyclists; and creating an improved residential environment (Pharaoh and Russell, 1989; Hine, 1994).

Carefully planned street-width channelling, parking restrictions and speed-control devices (such as ramps) can help to alter the balance in favour of pedestrian mobility and safety (Tolley, 1990). Evidence from Denmark and elsewhere suggests that actual and perceived barriers to pedestrian mobility can be substantially reduced following the introduction of traffic-calming schemes, particularly on main roads. However, such schemes are not without their critics. This is partly because often they have been implemented where it is easiest to do so (on minor, less busy roads) rather than where they are most needed (Hass-Klau *et al.*, 1992). But a second contributory factor is that they can actually encourage car use by increasing the number of locally available parking spaces (TEST, 1989). In addition, urban bus operators tend to object to the siting of ramps on their routes, because of the negative impact on timetables and problems of vehicle wear and tear, particularly on the new generation of low-floor designs. (Here we are confronted with a welfare policy conflict.)

Economic incentives/disincentives

That the full external costs of each car journey are not borne by the motorist suggests a need for the application of economic incentives and disincentives to correct market inconsistencies and to encourage the use of less environmentally damaging urban transport modes. Two overarching objectives in employing taxation and/or economic disincentive measures are to increase the relative costs of car travel to represent its true external cost to society, and to encourage changes in land-use policy. The advocacy and implementation of various forms of ecological tax and fiscal impositions represent policy measures which are only slowly gaining ground in Europe (Whitelegg, 1993), although a carbon-related tax was introduced in Sweden in 1990 and was revised upwards in 1994 (Sterner, 1994). Such approaches include a uniform tax on carbon emissions, fuel prices related to each fuel's environmental damage, and purchase or ownership taxes differentiated to reflect vehicle emission characteristics (Maddison *et al.*, 1996).

Open access to the urban road network could be rationed through area licensing systems or by employing electronic distance charging. Differential rates could be charged according to the time of day and congestion conditions using roadside monitors. Noise costs could be incorporated into congestion pricing. Charges for road damage could be related to the distance a vehicle travels, its weight and the number of axles.[2] Charges for the external costs of road accidents could be based on distance travelled and differentiated with respect to different classes of road users. The use of a statistical value for a life which is commensurate with actual empirical evidence would be able to redirect road transport investments towards projects intended to reduce accidents. In Europe, however, although high fuel taxes are more widely accepted than in the USA, experiments to reduce congestion by charging car commuters have repeatedly been postponed.

One notable exception has been the introduction of toll cordons in Norway's three largest cities. In a country noted for its rural bias in regional and transport policy, tolls were introduced in Oslo, Bergen and Trondheim between 1986 and 1991 as a means of raising money for road building. They have reduced the volume of car traffic crossing during their periods of operation, but appear to have exerted only a minor impact on modal choice. However, it has been argued that, as people become conditioned to them, toll systems become easier to deploy both to restrain car traffic in general and to stimulate congestion pricing (Larsen, 1995).

Road pricing is to be introduced in Stockholm in 1998, with the levy earmarked for construction of further sections of the city's ring road. The aim is to reduce by 25 per cent the number of cars entering the city centre. When this has been achieved, a programme of environmental improvements will be undertaken, including noise reduction measures. In the UK, road pricing is being considered, with experiments taking place in Cambridge. Most of these schemes and plans need to be underpinned by at least four important and complementary elements: the application of new appropriate technology; a significant shift in personal behaviour and political attitudes in relation to the motor car, an attractive public transport system which also recognises the role of benign modes; and the ability of urban authorities to integrate land-use planning with that for transport.

An ideal set of policy instruments would be able to differentiate charges between vehicles with respect to emission profiles, noise characteristics, congestion factors, location, time, weather conditions, driving behaviour, traffic conditions and other variables. Development of information technology in the traffic sector has rendered much of this technically possible. Road pricing tests held in Germany, for example, have been undertaken based on a combination of the digital mobile phone system GSM and the satellite global positioning system (GPS). At any given moment, such systems allow a vehicle to know precisely where it is located, and hence what charge per kilometre it currently should face. It would not be too difficult to supplement such a system with variations in the weather, the speed of the car and other variables.

Integrated land-use planning

In recent years, a "new urbanism" has emerged which recognises the necessity to reconnect transport, land use and environmental concern. It represents a recognition that land-use planning is significant in the context of climatic change and that one of the strongest connections in this relationship is through the transport system. In particular, it aims to reduce the amount of urban travel by minimising the need for it. This can be sought particularly in the development of higher-density, mixed-use areas around high-quality transport systems, to provide a focused urban structure that can help to reduce car dependence. This shift in thinking, legitimising land-use planning as an instrument of environmental policy, was given a (west) European lead in the EU's *Strategy for Sustainable Mobility* (CEC, 1992). Applications of this approach in Europe have taken place in Copenhagen, Freiburg and Zurich (Newman and Kenworthy, 1996). In the UK, government planning policy guidance (PPG13: DoE/DTp, 1994) has been intended to promote these aims. Notably, PPG13 indicated a policy reversal by encouraging the avoidance of development locations which reinforce car dependency, such as out-of-town sites for shopping centres and business parks: in 1980 only 5 per cent of UK retail sales were made in out-of-town locations, but by 1992 this proportion had risen to 37 per cent (RCEP, 1994). PPG13, and similar policies elsewhere, urge local planning authorities to take account of the travel, energy and environmental implications of all their policies and location decisions. Yet their successful implementation will require wider policy aims, reregulation of public transport and better strategic and regional planning (Pharaoh, 1996), including a clearer understanding of the means to constrain (or contain) discretionary travel.

A further challenge for integrated land-use planning is that the scope to influence travel patterns directly through redevelopment processes is relatively limited, because only around 1 per cent of urban land is available for replanning in any given year. Further, the historical evolution of much urban structure often inhibits the ability to introduce dedicated public transport routes, cycleways or pedestrianised areas. Nevertheless, over a period of perhaps 25 years, land-use planning measures, combined with other policies, might be able to reduce atmospheric emissions by around 15 per cent (ECOTEC, 1993). But planning is unlikely to achieve a reduction in travel unless economic mechanisms are employed in a complementary way, alternatives to the private car are available and attractive, and a political commitment to sustainable transport policy is established. In the absence of these other policy elements, integrated land-use planning will not in itself be effective in reducing traffic growth (Owens, 1995).

Priority for public transport

Policy towards public transport in (western) Europe has encompassed a mix of economic efficiency, social equity and environmental responsibility. The relative weights of these three considerations have varied between countries, and indeed have also differed in time and space within individual countries according to the political complexion of central and local governments. In Scandinavia and the UK, structural change in public transport provision has shifted the balance away from social equity and towards economic efficiency; and the same could be said of post-Communist central and eastern Europe (Pucher, 1995). Here, public transport has been in retreat in a number of central and east European cities, as a rapid rise in post-Communist car ownership levels, loss or reduction of public transport subsidies, privatisation and fare inflation have been piled on top of several decades of underinvestment. In Kiev, for example, where the trolleybus is the principal form of surface transport, five cross-city routes were closed between 1992 and 1995, while other service frequencies were reduced. Shortages of spare parts for buses and trams have accompanied poor track conditions throughout many city tram systems, rendering journeys slow, unreliable and increasingly unattractive to a newly mobile society where modal choice is gradually increasing.

In all but a few countries the environmental argument for public transport provision tended to play a rather muted role until commitments to attain "Agenda 21" environmental objectives, stimulated by the Rio "Earth Summit", helped to focus governmental thinking. To entice motorists and their passengers back to public transport across Europe, in the absence of draconian proscriptive legislation, targeted inducements are necessary. These can include service enhancements and/or fare reductions, user-friendly vehicles, the adoption of new technologies to improve convenience and accessibility, the promotion of multimodality by improving facilities at interchanges, co-ordination between timetables and the provision of high-quality information to public transport users[3] (Montès, 1995; Priemus, 1995). Above all, however, political commitment to support public transport improvement and to pursue goals of integrated land use and transport planning is required.

The role of public transport as a planning tool is pivotal in assisting the development of an integrated and rational transport system as part of a sustainable urban environment. Yet deregulation and privatisation tend to reduce this potential because disparities between the uncertainties of market-driven, deregulated transport provision, and the broader needs of urban transport management are difficult to reconcile (Knowles and Hall, 1992; Tyson, 1995; DTp, 1996). In Denmark, deregulation and a degree of privatisation have been carried out in stages since 1989 in the Greater Copenhagen region, but within the framework of a metropolitan public authority responsible for inviting tenders, planning and co-ordinating all bus services, and for marketing public transport. In Greece, following successive changes in the political complexion of the national government, bus services in Athens have been renationalised (Matsoukis, 1996).

Successful transport planning depends to a large extent upon integration of the various modes of transport and the co-ordination of their operations. The forerunner of London Transport was established in the 1930s, while Greater Stockholm was one of the first mainland west European cities to establish a fully integrated public transport system when, in 1964, bus, metro and tramway services in some 55 county municipalities were brought together under a unified organisational framework. In Germany, a number of regional public transport co-ordinating authorities (*Verkehrsverbunden* or *VV*) act to integrate multimode public transport across urban and suburban areas and conurbations. In Augsburg, for example, the *AVV* was established in 1985 to co-ordinate 6 rail lines and 97 regional bus routes operated by 19 companies. Full integration of these was completed in 1992, and current plans are to create 2500 park-and-ride spaces and 780 cycle racks at 20 rail stations. Frequency on bus and tram routes has been improved, and reserved rights of way for both modes are being extended. Full integration between city and regional services took place in 1995. Probably the best known *VV*, that for the Rhine–Ruhr conurbation, incorporates 19 municipal transport undertakings which provide over 700 routes, supplemented by both park-and-ride and bike-and-ride facilities (Bushell, 1995).

The rebuilding or remodelling of commercial centres to accommodate covered malls or precincts can provide the opportunity to site transport terminals in more convenient locations for shoppers and employees. Major reconstruction of rail stations can assist multimode integration, and

park-and-ride schemes, introduced extensively in Luxembourg but also adopted much more widely in Europe, can reduce the number of cars entering central areas, particularly at weekend peak shopping periods. Commuters may be catered for in a similar manner with the provision of large-capacity car (and bicycle) parks adjacent to suburban rail stations.

Many transport planning proposals have been directed specifically towards increasing the speed and schedule reliability of bus and/or tram/light rail (LR) services. Indeed, most large European cities have adopted priority plans for these modes in an attempt to boost the attractions of public transport. Although time savings secured by bus-only lanes can be lost when vehicles enter inner-city areas where priority lanes are absent, buses may be accorded priority turns at intersections, and certain streets may be reserved for buses and/or trams only, particularly in pedestrianised shopping areas. Traffic-light priority systems operate for buses in Stockholm's city centre, for example, while Essen operates a tram priority scheme. Reserved tracks have long been a characteristic of many tram/LR systems, while in Milan reserved lanes are provided for trolleybuses with priority mechanisms at junctions.

In an attempt to assist public transport to keep to timetables, installation of automatic vehicle monitoring has been undertaken in a number of European cities, with Budapest being notable in applying it to both articulated buses and trams. Underground, the installation of automatic train control (ATC) equipment permits the reduction of headway between trains, thereby increasing capacity by permitting a greater frequency. In Moscow, for example, where 47 per cent of all public transport journeys are made by metro, this development has permitted frequencies of less than one-and-a-half minutes on some lines.

To enhance the attractiveness of bus services in suburban residential areas, small-capacity mini-buses may operate on a "hail and ride" system, whereby they can be stopped in the same way as a taxi, picking up and dropping passengers at their own chosen location along a fixed route. Minibuses are particularly useful in being able to negotiate the complex street patterns of housing estates more easily than larger buses. These vehicles can only cope with a limited demand, however, and their layout does not necessarily assist passengers with objects such as baby buggies or large amounts of shopping (Hall, 1993c).

In extending market penetration while pursuing altruistic welfare policies, bus and rail undertakings have slowly recognised the needs of certain types of disabled traveller through modifications such as wheelchair access ramps and lifts at terminals and stations. Buses with low-level access are now being mass-produced and put into service across Europe (Morris, 1996), often alongside longer-standing specialised (e.g. "dial-a-ride") provision. Thus, in Berlin, lift or ramp-equipped single-deck bus operation now extends to about 40 regular routes, while a separate "Telebus" network of low-floor, wheelchair-accessible midibuses is operated by a special agency (Bushell, 1995). Experimental studies for the design of taxis suitable for elderly and disabled passengers have also been undertaken.

In addition to providing an alternative to the car, investment in rail-based rapid-transit schemes has been used to encourage suburban develop-ment, and to help regenerate the declining economies of city centres, inner cities and derelict docklands (Figure 23.4; see also Williams, 1985; Knowles, 1996). About 40 metro systems are operational in Europe, with at least a further 14 proposed or under construction (Table 23.3). In the 1980s and 1990s investment interest switched from metro and suburban heavy rail to light rail (LR) schemes, notably in France, Ireland, Italy, Spain and the UK[4] (Lesley, 1993). Electrified LR systems offer many of the advantages of metros and suburban rail, but at much lower costs and with greater flexibility. They are now operational in over 70 European cities (Table 23.4) and are being constructed or proposed in several others. An increasing number, as in Sheffield and Zurich, can cross the city centres on wholly or partially segregated streets where use can be made of otherwise pedestrianised thoroughfares, as in the recently opened system in Strasbourg. This arrangement permits a level of access to central shopping and business districts not available to the car.

Figure 23.4 *Docklands Light Railway and station, London. (Photo: D R Hall)*

Table 23.3 *European underground railway (metro) systems*

	No.	Cities
Existing		
Austria	1	Vienna
Belgium	1	Brussels
Belarus	1	Minsk
Czech Republic	1	Prague
Finland	1	Helsinki
Greece	1	Athens
Hungary	1	Budapest
Norway	1	Oslo
Poland	1	Warsaw
Portugal	1	Lisbon
Romania	1	Bucharest
Sweden	1	Stockholm
Ukraine	1	Kiev
Netherlands	2	Amsterdam; Rotterdam
Spain	2	Barcelona; Madrid
United Kingdom	2	Glasgow; London
Italy	3	Milan; Naples; Rome
France	5	Lille; Lyon; Marseille; Paris; Toulouse
Germany	6	Berlin; Cologne; Frankfurt am Main; Hamburg; Munich; Nuremberg
Russia	6	Gorky; Kharkov; Kuibyshev; Moscow; Nijni Novgorod; St Petersburg
Proposed or under construction		
Bulgaria	1	Sofia
Denmark	1	Copenhagen
Latvia	1	Riga
Poland	1	Łódz
Slovakia	1	Bratislava
Spain	1	Bilbao
France	2	Bordeaux; Rennes
Italy	2	Florence; Palermo
Ukraine	3	Dnepropetrovsk; Odessa; Rostov

Source: Bushell, (1995).

Table 23.4 *European light rail systems*

	No.	Cities
Existing		
Austria	1	Vienna
Bosnia-Hercegovina	1	Sarajevo
Finland	1	Helsinki
Hungary	1	Budapest
Ireland	1	Dublin
Norway	1	Oslo
Slovakia	1	Bratislava
Spain	1	Valencia
Turkey	1	Istanbul
Ukraine	1	Krivoy Rog
Poland	2	Częstochowa; Warsaw
Russia	2	Naberezhnye-Chelny; Volgograd
Sweden	2	Gothenburg; Stockholm
Belgium	3	Antwerp; Brussels; Charleroi
Italy	3	Genoa; Rome; Turin
Netherlands	4	Amsterdam; Rotterdam; The Hague
UK	5	Blackpool; London Docklands Manchester; Newcastle; Sheffield
Romania	6	Braşov; Cluj; Constanţa; Craiova; Ploieşti; Reşiţa
France	8	Grenoble; Lille; Marseille; Nantes; Paris; Rouen; St Etienne; Strasbourg
Germany	21	Bielefeld; Bochum-Herne; Bonn; Braunschweig; Bremen; Chemnitz; Cologne; Dortmund; Duisberg; Düsseldorf; Essen-Mulheim; Frankfurt am Main; Freiburg; Gelsenkirchen; Hannover; Karlsruhe; Krefeld; Mannheim-Ludwigshafen; Stuttgart; Wuppertal*; Wurzburg
Proposed		
Italy	2	Bologna; Florence
Spain	3	Malaga; Seville; Zaragoza
UK	7	Birmingham; Bristol; Cardiff; Croydon; Leeds; Liverpool; Sheffield

* Suspended monorail.
Source: Bushell (1995).

The environmental credentials of urban public transport are mixed: trams, LR and metros cause vibration and noise, recently reflected in the architect's approach to the design of Manchester's Bridgewater Hall (Figure 23.5). To insulate this new concert hall from vibration caused by the nearby LR system, the entire auditorium is built on a spring suspension system. These types of public transport development induce much disruption in their construction phases and, together with trolleybuses, are powered by electricity which may have been generated by the burning of fossil fuels. Diesel buses produce particulates, and have tended to be noisy and dirty, or at least perceived as such. However, new generations of quieter engines, experiments with "bio" fuel (in Rouen and Reading, for example), and projects to ameliorate diesel emissions have all been employed by transport authorities in an attempt to promote buses as "greener" forms of transport. For example, in response to high atmospheric pollution levels in Athens, all diesel buses have been fitted with particulate trap oxidisers to work alongside the largest fleet of

Figure 23.5 *The Bridgewater Hall, Manchester, the home of the Hallé Orchestra. A spring suspension system is incorporated in the structure to avoid vibration from the nearby light rail line. (Photo: Len Grant)*

trolleybuses in western Europe. Within the framework of recent Swedish legislation, however, municipal environmental regulations could force diesel-engined vehicles off the streets of Stockholm by the year 2005, with the consequence that various options for electric traction and gas-powered vehicles are being considered.

It is evident that many urban transport authorities across Europe are working hard to render their services more environmentally acceptable, and at the same time combat the perceived greater convenience of private motor travel. But while public transport is generally significantly more "green" than the use of cars and lorries, it is far inferior to the genuinely benign modes – cycling and walking.

Support for benign modes

Walking can account for up to 35 per cent of all journeys in Western cities, and in the Netherlands cycling and motorcycling are used by one-third of all commuters. Several arguments are put forward for promoting walking and cycling as fundamental elements in any sustainable urban transport policy (Cleary, 1992; McClintock, 1992; McClintock and Cleary, 1996):

1. Social equity: on average, more than 90 per cent of any European country's population is able to walk or ride a bicycle in comparison with only around 40 per cent having the optional use of a car.
2. Altruism: pedestrians and cyclists, unlike motorists, do not inhibit the choices or movements of other road users and pose a minimal threat to them.
3. Versatility: cycling and walking provide "transport" for almost any individual at any time for shorter trips, and are easily combined with other modes for longer journeys.
4. Efficiency: journeys of 5 km or less could easily be covered by most people on a bicycle within the current average journey time of 25 minutes. In the UK at least, over 60 per cent of all trips are within this distance, of which 60 per cent are by motorised means, indicating the potential for a significant modal shift, particularly as in many urban areas cycling can offer a faster journey time than other modes for up to 10 km.

5. Public expenditure: a small proportion of the current expenditure on roads would, if reallocated, provide a significant investment in infrastructure and maintenance for pedestrian and cycle networks.
6. Health: daily exercise plays a major preventative role in lowering the incidence of both heart and respiratory diseases, and in increasing longevity, yet only a small proportion of adults undertake sufficient exercise to maintain their fitness. Walking and cycling are ideal ways of keeping fit, are possible for most of the population, and would therefore reduce national medical costs.
7. Air pollution: walking and cycling are non-polluting means of travel.
8. Energy conservation: the only major energy source required by walkers and cyclists – food – is renewable.
9. Land-take and congestion: 10 bicycles can be accommodated in the space taken by one car, and walkers have no vehicles to use or leave unattended.
10. Intrusion: walking and cycling have a minimal impact in terms of noise, vibration and community disruption.

Attitudinal change

It would appear that for sustainable transport policies to be both acceptable and workable, they need to be aimed at changing attitudes at a number of levels. These policies – educational campaigns (Peake, 1994) – should aim both to emphasise the full effects of travel behaviour, thereby helping to promote acceptance and understanding of the need for change, and to change attitudes towards the use of non-car modes – public transport, cycling and walking – by highlighting their positive aspects.

Three constituencies in particular stand out for targeting, although the first poses a conundrum, as it comprises politicians and decision-makers themselves. The frequent apparent lack of political will to implement available sustainable transport policy options in a coherent way is particularly related to the fact that – while many environmental problems have long time horizons in terms of their effects and the outcomes of potential solutions to them – European political systems are based on obtaining positive, quantifiable policy returns within electoral cycles of four to seven years. Under these circumstances, the long-term policies of sustainability are likely to be given a low political priority. Further, far too many European governments, politicians and bureaucrats still see roads as the key to, and symbol of, prosperity. Politicians' self-imbibed propaganda and sense of self-importance are reinforced at a personal level by the cultural determinance of the need for a car to reflect self-perceived status. This syndrome is particularly heightened currently in central and eastern Europe, where possession of (certain marques of) western European cars is viewed as a clear and essential indication both of one's new elevated economic status and of the ideological break with the past. How then to educate eastern and western European politicians into an attitude change? As the attainment of sustainability is concerned with reappraising policy goals, there is the requirement for a fundamental scrutiny of the values upon which decisions are made. Is it not time for a quality audit of the sustainability of decision-makers' values?

Employers form a second appropriate target group. There would appear to be a wide range of measures which companies can be persuaded, or given encouragement, to undertake in the pursuit of sustainable transport options. Policies to reduce travel volumes during the journey-to-work periods by encouraging the staggering of employment start and finish times, although a palliative rather than a radical policy for change, can lead to a substantial and effective reduction in the congestion attributable to commuting. The widespread adoption of "flexi-time" in the service sector helped to flatten the commuter-travel peaks in many major cities during the 1980s, and the extension of opening hours in city centres during the week encourages more workers to shop later and delay their journey home.[5]

Through the expansion of telecommunications, personal computing facilities and information technology generally, it has been recent conventional wisdom that many jobs traditionally carried out in city-centre offices could be accomplished as effectively at home (Graham, 1991). In 1994 the European Commission gave high priority to the adoption of telework as part of the Bangemann Report's list of actions to improve European competitiveness, setting a target of 10 million teleworkers in Europe by the end of the century. In theory, significant increases in the numbers of employees who can work at home in this way could contribute to a reduction in peak-hour traffic and the demand for road space generally within urban areas. Certainly the Dutch Ministry of Transport appears to have devised successful teleworking structures, and the municipal authorities in Paris, Madrid and The Hague continue to examine the potential of teleworking to relieve traffic congestion. Conversely, however, such dispersal of work can generate more discretionary travel, diffused both spatially and temporally, while predictions of the growth of teleworking could be over-optimistic. Many early teleworkers gave up this mode of work because of feelings of isolation and poor relationships with management, including a perceived marginalisation for promotion purposes. Finding household space to set aside for a dedicated work room has also posed domestic problems.

More tangible and immediate ways in which companies can influence travel behaviour is through the adoption of integrated plans for their employees. In the UK, the CBI has already taken a lead in encouraging company good practice for staff travel schemes, and legislation has been in place in the Netherlands since 1995 which requires companies with more than 50 employees to produce a transport plan. These plans can include arrangements for tailor-made public transport (usually bus) services for commuters; incentives for car-sharing and the collective use of pool vehicles; increasing parking charges for private cars; the provision of cash or perk alternatives to the use of company cars; and encouragement for in-house bicycle users' groups, including investment in secure cycle storage areas, cycle tracks, cycleways and ample shower and changing facilities for cycling commuters (of both sexes).

Despite successive attitude surveys indicating that the general public across Europe recognises, and is concerned about, the pollution and congestion problems arising from car-led transport, car owners and users appear loath to forsake their vehicles. Educational policies therefore need to be targeted specifically at relating people's personal experiences directly to the wider environmental consequences of their travel behaviour. But, of course, they first need the sanction of politicians who, over much of Europe, have revealed only a limited inclination to tackle the problem – and their own constituents – head-on.

Application of technology innovation

The misapplication of technology can exacerbate transport problems by, for example, permitting an increase in existing road capacity and thus encouraging induced traffic. Also, the UK government's climate-change strategy (Secretary of State for the Environment, 1994) has acknowledged that if traffic grows in line with current predictions, technological improvements to reduce environmental impacts will not be able to keep pace with emission growth. Yet, despite such drawbacks, the appropriate application of technology clearly has the potential to make a number of contributions to the promotion of sustainable urban transport policies, albeit in conjunction with one or more of the options outlined above.

The major arenas in which progress may be made towards technological innovation to support sustainable urban transport policies can at present be identified as:

1. Assistance in the reduction of the adverse effects of motorised transport, through improved fuel efficiency, use of alternative fuels, anti-pollution technology applied to emissions, and the introduction of roadside or on-board monitoring equipment (such as advanced vehicle identification) to permit pricing of congestion, emissions and other forms of external cost. For example, an electronic smart card can now be implanted into car engine-management systems to monitor the quantity of polluting emissions. This could be complemented by the real-time monitoring of air pollution in main streets so that urban dwellers are informed about the quality of air that they breathe.

2. Provision of better traffic control and management techniques, including giving priority to public transport at junctions, the use of advanced transport telematics (ATT) for improved logistics, and improved signalling and control mechanisms to increase the frequency (and thus capacity) of rail-based urban transport.

3. Provision of technological alternatives to travel, such as videoconferencing and teleworking.

4. Enhancement of the convenience of non-car transport use. Possibilities in this context are the introduction of rechargeable smart cards ("electronic purses") for the payment of fares, car parking fees, and road and bridge tolls (as employed in Berlin, Dublin and Marseille); and the provision of advanced information systems for intending public transport passengers in order to reduce waiting times and uncertainty (Kanninen, 1996; Nijkamp and Pepping, 1996).

Conclusions

Urban transport policies in Europe are at a crossroads. There is a growing resistance to major new road construction in urban areas; existing road networks have in many instances reached near capacity; parking controls are approaching their limits as an effective means of traffic restraint (Jones, 1992); and the environmental consequences of giving free rein to the car are increasingly recognised as unacceptable by national and international organisations (OOPEC, 1996). In many European cities there has taken place a discernible shift. This has seen a move away from employing technological fixes to give the car more freedom, towards policies which exploit technologies in order to seek sustainability ideals. Attempts are now being made to enhance the appeal of public transport and to transfer more fundamentally and more accurately the external costs of motoring in urban areas on to those responsible for them, while at the same time trying to minimise those costs through realistic restraint measures.

None the less, much remains to be done. Urban transport policies now need to establish a sustainable balance between demand and supply. Constraints on private motor travel need to complement an equitable redistribution of the car's external costs. Improvements in public transport supply – in terms of quality and efficiency – should be devised within a more integrated framework relating land use to transport and transport to wider environmental considerations. Improved co-ordination of different transport modes – encouraging multi-modality and the use of environmentally friendly means of travel such as walking and cycling – should be an important goal. Above all, significant attitude changes are required. But how far is this realistic in a deregulated and privatised climate in which central (and local) government may choose to follow market-led forces? Governments have their "Agenda 21" targets to meet, but many also find themselves in tight financial and ideological circumstances. In former Communist central and eastern Europe such an attitude and policy shift may take even longer to bring about: car-borne freedom is seen as a potent symbol of the break with the past. In Europe as a whole, a much more co-ordinated approach to the public promotion of the disbenefits of car use is required, at supranational, national and local levels. Until motorists are aware of the consequences of their travel behaviour, and carry the external costs, sustainable transport will not be achieved. Yet, almost certainly, a twenty-first century urban Europe will not be able to sustain car-led policies.

Notes

1. Swedish studies have placed the figures even higher.
2. Sweden used to have such an odometer-based system for charging trucks, but this system was abandoned in 1993 as part of the country's adaptation to EU rules.
3. Experiments with advanced information systems are particularly well developed in France and the Netherlands.
4. In the UK's case this occurred partly as a response by local authorities to their loss of bus operating and regulating roles through privatisation and deregulation.
5. Extended shopping hours, however, may not always produce unmitigated gains. They may, for example, increase return movement back into the city on specific late night shopping days. There is also the question of shop workers' conditions of employment. Germany, for example, has until recently had rigid and restrictive shop hours, not least because of the labour unions' concern to protect workers' rights.

References

Ashworth, G and Larkham, P J (1994) *Building a New Heritage: tourism, culture and identity in the new Europe*, Routledge, London.

Banister, D (1996) Energy, quality-of-life and the environment – the role of transport, *Transport Reviews*, **16**(1), 23–35.

Bonsall, P (1996) Can induced traffic be measured by surveys?, *Transportation*, **23**(1), 17–34.

Brown, W (1994) Dying from too much dust, *New Scientist*, **141**(1916), 12–13.

Bryant, B (1996) *Twyford Down: roads, campaigning and environmental law*, E & F N Spon, London.

Bushell, C (ed) (1995) *Jane's Urban Transport Systems*, Jane's Information Group, Coulsden, Surrey, 14th edn.

CBI (Confederation of British Industry) (1995) *Moving Forward*, CBI, London.

CEC (Commission of the European Communities) (1992) *The Future Development of the Common Transport Policy: a global approach to the construction of a Community framework for sustainable mobility*, Commission of the European Communities, Brussels.

Cleary, J (1992) Benign modes: the ignored solution, in J Whitelegg (ed) *Traffic Congestion: is there a way out?*, Leading Edge, Hawes, 153–68.

Coombe, D (1996) Induced traffic – what do transportation models tell us?, *Transportation*, **23**(1), 83–101.

Crawack, S (1993) Traffic management and emissions, *The Science of the Total Environment*, **134**, 305–14.

DoE (Department of the Environment) (1994) *Digest of Environmental Protection and Water Statistics no. 16*, HMSO, London.

DoE/DTp (Department of the Environment and Department of Transport) (1994) *Planning Policy Guidance on Transport*, *PPG13*, HMSO, London.

DTp (Department of Transport) (1987) *Values for Journey Time Savings and Accident Prevention*, Department of Transport, London.

DTp (1996) *Transport: the way forward*, HMSO, London.

ECOPLAN (1992) *Damage Costs of Air Pollution: a survey of existing estimates*, ECOPLAN, Bern.

ECOTEC (1993) *Reducing Transport Emissions through Planning*, HMSO, London.

Erskine, A (1996) The burden of risk – who dies because of cars?, *Social Policy and Administration*, **30**(2), 143–57.

Graham, S (1991) Telecommunications and the local economy: some emerging policy issues, *Local Economy*, **6**, 116–36.

Hall, D R (1993a) Impacts of economic and political transition on the transport geography of Central and Eastern Europe, *Journal of Transport Geography*, **1**(1), 20–35.

Hall, D R (ed) (1993b) *Transport and Economic Development in the New Central and Eastern Europe*, Belhaven, London.

Hall, D R (1993c) United Kingdom bus deregulation and privatisation and the role of minibuses, in C Muica and D Turnock (eds) *Geography and Conservation*, Institute of Geography, Romanian Academy, Bucharest, 66–74.

Hall, D R (1995) Tourism change in Central and Eastern Europe, in A Montanari and A M Williams (eds) *European Tourism: regions, spaces and restructuring*, Wiley, Chichester, 221–44.

Hansson, L and Markham, J (1992) *Internalization of External Effects in Transportation*, UIC Strategic Planning Committee, Paris.

Hass-Klau, C (1993) Impact of pedestrianization and traffic calming on retailing. A review of the evidence from Germany and the UK, *Transport Policy*, **1**(1), 21–31.

Hass-Klau, C, Nold, I, Boecker, G and Crampton, G (1992) *Civilised Streets: a guide to traffic calming*, Environment and Transport Planning, London.

Hine, J (1994) Pedestrian behaviour and safety on radial routes – initial study findings, in J Smith (ed), *Transport and Welfare*, Transport Geography Study Group, Institute of British Geographers, Salford, 35–49.

IPCC (Intergovernmental Panel on Climate Change) (1990) *Climate change: the IPCC scientific assessment*, Cambridge University Press, Cambridge.

Jones, P (1991) *Devising New Options for Tackling Traffic Congestion in City Centres*, University of Oxford Transport Studies Unit, Oxford.

Jones, P (1992) What the pollsters say, in J Whitelegg (ed) *Traffic Congestion: is there a way out?*, Leading Edge, Hawes, 11–31.

Jones-Lee, M W and Loomes, G (1995) Scale and context effects in the valuation of transport safety, *Journal of Risk and Uncertainty*, **11**(3), 183–203.

Kanninen, B J (1996) Intelligent transportation systems: an economic and environmental policy assessment, *Transportation Research A: Policy and Practice*, **30**(1), 1–10.

Knowles, R D (1996) Transport impacts of Greater Manchester's Metrolink light rail system, *Journal of Transport Geography*, **4**(1), 1–14.

Knowles, R D and Hall, D R (1992) Transport policy and control, in B S Hoyle and R D Knowles (eds) *Modern Transport Geography*, Belhaven, London, 33–50.

Larsen, O I (1995) The toll cordons in Norway, *Journal of Transport Geography*, **3**(3), 187–97.

Law, C (1993) *Urban Tourism*, Mansell, London.

Lesley, L (1993) Value for money in urban transport public expenditure – the case of light rail, *Public Money and Management*, **13**(1), 27–33.

Lijewski, T (1996) The impact of political changes on transport in Central and Eastern Europe, *Transport Reviews*, **16**(1), 37–53.

Machon, P and Dingsdale, A (1989) Public transport in a socialist capital: Budapest, *Geography*, **74**(2), 159–62.

McClintock, H (1992) *The Bicycle and City Traffic: principles and practice*, Belhaven, London.

McClintock, H and Cleary, J (1996) Cycle facilities and cyclists' safety – experience from Greater Nottingham and lessons for future cycling provision, *Transport Policy*, **3**(1–2), 67–76.

Mackie, P J (1996) Induced traffic and economic appraisal, *Transportation*, **23**(1), 103–19.

Maddison, D, Pearce, D, Johansson, O, Calthrop, E, Litman, T and Verhoef, E (1996) *Blueprint 5: the true costs of road transport*, Earthscan, London.

Matsoukis, E C (1996) Privatization of bus services in Athens, Greece – an assessment of a 14-month experiment, *Transport Reviews*, **16**(1), 67–78.

Montès, C (1995) Transport and land-use planning: the case of British and French conurbations, *Journal of Transport Geography*, **3**(2), 127–41.

Morris, S C (1996) Lowering standards, in S J Brown (ed), *Buses Yearbook 1997*, Ian Allan, Shepperton, 3–14.

Newman, P W G and Kenworthy, J R (1996) The land use–transport connection: an overview, *Land Use Policy*, **13**(1), 1–22.

Nijkamp, P and Pepping, G (1996) The relevance and use of information and telecommunications networks as strategic tools in the transport sector – a Dutch case study, *Annals of Regional Science*, **30**(1), 111–33.

OOPEC (Office for Official Publications of the European Communities) (1996) *A Green Paper of the European Commission: fulfilling the potential of public passenger transport in Europe*, HMSO, London.

Owens, S (1995) Transport, land-use planning and climate change: what prospects for new policies in the UK?, *Journal of Transport Geography*, **3**(2), 143–5.

Peake, S (1994) *Transport in Transition*, Earthscan, London.

Pearce, D and Maddison, D (1994) *Blueprint 3: measuring sustainable development*, Earthscan, London.

Peirson, J and Vickerman, R (1994) *The Microeconomic Analysis of the External Costs of Road Accidents*, Centre for European, Regional and Transport Economics, University of Kent, Canterbury.

Pharaoh, T (1996) Reducing the need to travel – a new planning objective in the UK, *Land Use Policy*, **13**(1), 23–36.

Pharaoh, T and Russell, J (1989) *Traffic Calming: policy and evaluations in three European countries*, South Bank Polytechnic, London.

Priemus, H (1995) Reduction of car use: instruments of national and local policies – a Dutch perspective, *Environment and Planning B, Planning and Design*, **22**(6), 721–37.

Pucher, J (1995) The road to ruin? Impacts of economic shock therapy on urban transport in Poland, *Transport Policy*, **2**(1), 5–13.

RCEP (Royal Commission on Environmental Pollution) (1994) *Transport and the environment*, 18th Report, HMSO, London.

Rothengatter, W (1994) Do external benefits compensate for external costs of transport?, *Transportation Research A: Policy and Practice*, **28**(4), 321–8.

Rothengatter, W and Mauch, S (1994) *External Effects of Transport*, Union Internationale des Chemin de Fers, Paris.

Scholl, L, Schipper, L and Kiang, N (1996) CO_2 emissions from passenger transport – a comparison of international trends from 1973 to 1992, *Energy Policy*, **24**(1), 17–30.

Secretary of State for the Environment (1994) *Climate Change: the UK strategy*, HMSO, London.

Sterner, T (1994) Environmental tax reform: the Swedish experience, *European Environment*, **4**(6), 205.

TEST (1989) *User Friendly Cities*, Transport and Environment Studies, London.

Tolley, R (ed) (1990) *The Greening of Urban Transport – planning for walking and cycling in Western cities*, Belhaven, London.

Tyson, W J (1995) Bus deregulation – the planning dilemma, *Transport Reviews*, **15**(4), 307–13.

Verhoef, E T (1994) External effects and social costs of road transport, *Transportation Research A: Policy and Practice*, **28**(4), 273–92.

453

Vitaliano, D F and Held, J (1991) Road accident external effects: an empirical assessment, *Applied Economics*, **23**, 373–8.

Whitelegg, J (1987) The geography of road accidents, *Transactions of the Institute of British Geographers*, **12**(2), 161–76.

Whitelegg, J (ed) (1992) *Traffic Congestion: is there a way out?*, Leading Edge, Hawes.

Whitelegg, J (1993) *Transport for a Sustainable Future: the case for Europe*, Belhaven, London.

Williams, A F (ed) (1985) *Rapid Transit Systems in the UK: problems and prospects*, Transport Geography Study Group, Institute of British Geographers, Aberystwyth.

24

Conservation and the rural landscape

Brian J Woodruffe
Department of Geography, University of Southampton, UK

Europe has a rich diversity of rural landscapes. Such diversity reflects the contrasts in topographic and terrain qualities as well as the multifarious fashioning, restoration and management measures that have been implemented over centuries of settlement. Particularly significant have been the changes which the twentieth century has wrought and which have probably been more extensive and pervasive than in any comparable period. Such diversity, too, presents taxing challenges to politicians, planners, landscape architects and environmental organisations seeking to conserve the inherent character and qualities of Europe's rural chequerboard of scenery. Finding means to meet these challenges for conservation is made more difficult by the different political, fiscal and managerial structures that characterise the countries of Europe today. It is evident, too, that there are significant differences in all these respects between western and eastern Europe. These are particularly noticeable where financial support for conservation measures is concerned. Western European states have benefited from a long period of government funding, and while financial constraints are now very evident, there has been a move towards private funding and sponsorship. In eastern Europe economic difficulties restrict the amounts that can be given over to conservation, and some countries rely heavily on grants and funding from outside organisations, such as the World Wildlife Fund, the World Bank and the European Bank for Reconstruction and Development, particularly to support larger projects (Centre Naturopa, 1994). The costs of such projects tend to be high because conservation programmes may be coupled with efforts to ameliorate the severe environmental problems afflicting many regions in eastern Europe. In a rural context, landscape issues and problems occur on different scales and in varying intensities, and affect a great many land uses and users of land. The way these issues are resolved depends on political attitudes and the implementation of legislation. In western European countries much of the essential legislation has been in place for decades; most eastern European states recognised that, in the immediate post-socialist period, new legislation was urgent if they were to measure up to the standards in place in the wider European realm. It will be some time before the results of these new approaches can be judged fairly, but the signs are that environmental conservation is very much on the political agenda at all government levels (Feher, 1995). This chapter aims, firstly, to consider the main reasons why conservation measures are necessary; secondly, to discuss the types of designated area used across Europe; and thirdly, to make a comparative analysis of the principal approaches, methods and measures employed to protect and conserve the features and character of rural landscapes. In the process, both natural and cultural environments are examined.

In recent years emphasis on conservation has shifted from national and local measures to policies and strategies drawn up by alliances of countries (Jongman, 1995). This shift has resulted in an overlapping mosaic of agreements, protocols, plans and schemes that sometimes supersede, sometimes augment and sometimes duplicate national options for conservation. The present European rural landscape is influenced by a welter of legislation over the use of land and by controls on appropriate uses; yet the urgency for conservation does not seem to diminish. Responses on a continental plane, whatever form they may take, are, however, unlikely to provide long-term solutions:

> "Blanket legislation, however well-intentioned, is more likely to be counter-productive as local people soon find that it is inappropriate to their particular problem. It is better to work towards developing general principles of conservation and then leave it to local bodies to implement them in the context of their particular situation" (HRH The Prince Philip, 1995).

Much has been proposed at a European level since environmental problems, such as acid rain, were recognised as having a continental dimension. The Berne Convention on the conservation of European wildlife and natural habitats, the European Conservation Strategy, the Biological Diversity Convention, the EEC Habitats Directive, events such as European Nature Conservation Year 1995 and programmes such as the Natura 2000 network[1] all represent attempts to encourage national governments and local organisations to implement policies and actions for the good of the rural environment (Council of the European Communities, 1992; di Meana, 1992; Fernandez-Galiano, 1994; Haapanen, 1995; Steele, 1993). By bringing governments together to examine environmental problems and by disseminating information, the Council of Europe

has been very influential in maintaining the continental perspective on issues relating to nature and landscape conservation. This has been particularly important for the states of eastern Europe and it has brought their ecological and landscape problems very much to the attention of the wider membership of the Council (Tardy, 1991; Krauklis, 1992).

The Need for Landscape Conservation

Landscape conservation measures are seen as necessary for several reasons:

* Landscapes, ranging from both the spectacular to the ordinary, have become increasingly recognised as valued features of Europe's heritage
* Attractive landscapes, together with their embedded array of historic settlements, hold a significant place in the tourist economy of most European countries
* The remaining tracts of natural environment are seen as valuable in their own right and of importance for scientific research
* And, not least, Europe's natural and man-managed rural environments are perceived as being threatened by development and change from a multiplicity of directions

With some 40 separate states in Europe it is very evident that the attention and significance given to these reasons will vary among governments and non-governmental organisations, and that the responses in the form of practical conservation measures will be likewise diversified.

Perhaps more than any other reason, it is the threats and the problems that inappropriate land-use changes bring which drive the efforts towards conservation. No landscape type can be free from change, although some are more vulnerable than others. Wetlands, river corridors, unbuilt-up coastlines, mountain tracts and intensively used agricultural lands feature frequently in media reports and in official documentation about problematic situations. The threats arise largely through urbanisation, industrial and highway construction, pollution of various kinds, the erosion and degradation of land, extraction of mineral resources, and the increasing intensity of recreation activities and mass tourism. Problems are exacerbated through a lack of firm planning structures or through weak management frameworks coupled with ineffectual legislation. Prior to discussing conservation measures, it is appropriate to exemplify a range of widespread and localised problems, and to outline the complexities that surround a selection of threatened tracts in rural Europe.

Urbanisation

While outwardly the rural landscape of many countries appears healthy and vibrant at the present time, a glance backwards will reveal the extent of change that has occurred. Recent reports for Alpine countries have identified a prevalent urbanisation of the Alpine landscape, and have noted the ineffectiveness of planning systems to control construction and limit environmental damage. In Switzerland between 1960 and 1990 the number of households increased by 79 per cent, the population by some 26 per cent. In real terms the population grew by over a million but so too has the number of dwellings. Of these extra million dwellings, the majority (70 per cent) are single-family homes occupying substantial areas of land outside the main towns and cities (Bundesamt für Raumplanung, 1988). Between 1980 and 1990 the number of *Gemeinde* (rural parishes) defined as "urban" rose from 508 to 806, and one in every four Swiss *Gemeinde* now belongs to an urban agglomeration (Meier, 1994). These changes have resulted not from a lack of planning but from approved plans, which initially scheduled far too much land for residential building; this in turn has led to the current sprawl across rural land, especially in the Mittelland. However, the threat from urbanisation does not end at the fringes of the metropolitan region; urban-style architecture

Figure 24.1 *Urban-style construction has infiltrated attractive rural areas and diminished landscape quality – Aminona, Valais, Switzerland*

has continued to infiltrate many mountain landscapes, sometimes in isolated locations unrelated to existing settlements (Figure 24.1). Much of this type of construction has been for second- and holiday-homes whose numbers have doubled since the early 1970s and which pose substantial problems for peripheral rural communities. Moreover, some of this construction has further implications for natural habitats because it may be linked to the development of new recreation activities such as golf courses. In 1992 there were 160 golf courses in the Alps, some of which were having adverse effects on wetland sites and on forested zones (Centre Naturopa, 1993).

In the canton of Graubünden in south-eastern Switzerland, the major problems relate to the growth in tourism: since 1965 the number of overnight stays has increased from 4.6 to 6.4 million in summer, whereas in winter there has been a rise from 4.7 to 8.0 million (Amt für Raum-planung Graubünden, 1995). In 1990 Graubünden contained the highest proportion of leisure-orientated dwellings (41.9 per cent), closely followed by the mountain canton of Valais with 41.7 per cent (Schuler, 1994). The consequence of such growth has been a diminished landscape quality through settlement dispersion (*Zersiedlung*), the conversion of relatively small, compact villages into rambling sporting centres, and the diffusion of multiform tourist infrastructures across cultural landscapes which previously had remained intact for centuries. However, the above report for Graubünden does acknowledge that not every community has been affected to the same extent, and planning policies have been able to conserve valued features of village character and villagescape (*Ortsbild*) of this distinctive part of the Alps.

Liechtenstein too has been very aware of the deficiencies of its planning system and of the

Figure 24.2 *Continuing urbanisation of villages has stimulated calls for stricter conservation policies within development plans – Natters and Mutters, Tirol, Austria, in 1996*

actual and potential urbanisation of its small number of rural communities. In 1988 it was calculated that the area zoned for building purposes was sufficient for a population of 100 000, whereas the contemporary population numbered only some 28 000 (Regierung des Fürstentums Liechtenstein, 1988). Here, the average size of plot for a new building has increased and the regulatory process has not been tight enough to ensure rational construction adjacent to existing settlements. To counter this trend, the Liechtenstein Parliament has required its rural communities to safeguard at least 30 per cent of the land for agricultural use and to create ecological compensation zones (Centre Naturopa, 1992). Similar patterns of incipient urbanisation and repopulation can be seen all over rural Europe, particularly within the commuting orbit of larger towns and cities (Figure 24.2). National and regional development strategies based on "decentralized concentration" are likely to augment these trends and emphasise the need for sustainable, equitable development (Bassi, 1995).

Depopulation

By way of contrast, the point should also be made that depopulation is still a dominant process in many parts of rural Europe; this trend is especially widespread in the countries of eastern Europe but is still a very evident process in south-central France, across much of northern Spain and inland Portugal, along the southern rim of the Alpine chain, and throughout rural Italy. Smaller pockets occur in western Greece, the west coast of Ireland, and in central and northern Sweden (Robert and Marcori, 1995). In such areas, the abandonment of land and of long-established settlements is having marked effects on the cultural landscape. Many of these depopulating areas are also recognised as important natural zones in which the maintenance of landscape quality depends on use and management by a resident population. These trends can be seen clearly in the Abruzzo region of Italy's central Apennines where 44 per cent of communities affected by outmigration lie within the boundaries of protected areas (Romano, 1995).

Efforts to conserve the integrity of such regions

– often border or cross-frontier regions – tend to be centred on wide-ranging programmes of economic regeneration and environmental renewal, as for example in the Czech Republic. Here, the problems came about because the socialist philosophy was to centralise both the farming system and the settlement pattern. This led to extensive and damaging changes to the cultural landscape, and to the partial or complete abandonment of small villages. Villages in frontier zones suffered particularly badly, and it is not unusual today to find substantial proportions of derelict or neglected properties. The renewal programme in the Czech Republic is based on a fresh evaluation of rural life and its economic base, but the finance necessary to deal with such a widespread problem has not yet been forthcoming (Kutej, 1992). Given such stressful socio-economic circumstances, it is understandable why renewal programmes do not always place conservation of the cultural landscape as a prime objective.

Wetlands

The conversion of many wetland sites and habitats to other uses is recognised as a major challenge to conservation throughout Europe (O'Sullivan, 1995). Data show that almost every country has been affected and in some the scale of change has been very substantial: in Greece, for example, it has been estimated that 61 per cent of wetland areas (300 000 ha) have been drained and put to other uses in the last 70 years (Tamisier and Grillas, 1994). It is not surprising therefore that many highly conserved areas now centre on wetland or riverine habitats. Yet, despite being protected, some never seem to be free of threat or conflict. The Doñana National Park in southern Spain is one of the last unspoilt tracts of marshland in Europe, but it has been threatened by water extraction schemes for agriculture and the construction of a recreation complex in recent years (Centre Naturopa, 1990a). The Doñana is of international ecological importance because it is one of the largest sites for migrating birds on the continent. The problem stems from the fact that no protected area is isolated from the changes that may occur, often quite legally, outside the designated zones. The changes outside the Doñana National Park will bring about a marked fall in groundwater levels and directly impinge on the wildlife that depends on the wetland tracts. Extending the reserve area to curtail the proposed developments is not a feasible proposition, although this alternative approach has been used elsewhere. Similar problems exist in other deltaic regions, notably in the Camargue of southern France and along the Baltic Sea coast.

In the last 50 years over 33 000 ha of wetlands in the Camargue have been transformed largely because fresh water has been extracted for irrigation and much of the hydrologic system has come under human control. A loss in biodiversity has resulted at site and regional levels, despite the Camargue being regarded as one of the most protected tracts of landscape in France (Tamisier and Grillas, 1994).

Along the Baltic coast it is anticipated that the pace of development will accelerate as a result of new economic programmes within the former Eastern Bloc states. Many wetlands and coastal lagoons urgently need protection and effective management to retain their inherent natural qualities. Some, such as the Curonian lagoon lying on the border between Lithuania and Russia, are threatened by pollution: pulp mills on the Nemunas river pump organic matter, phosphates, chlorinated compounds and various heavy metals into this lagoon, which acts as a buffer zone for the Baltic's marine environment. Similarly, the Vistula lagoon on the Gulf of Gdansk in Poland is heavily polluted from the industries of the Russian city of Kaliningrad. Solutions to such problematic situations will not be straightforward, not least because international co-operation is crucial for these frontier environments (Palmred, 1996). Damage to, and reductions in, wetland space have been a conspicuous feature of change in the rural landscape of Europe in recent decades and few countries are free of the problems these changes pose for conservation and management.

Earth-science sites

Peatlands are a different type of wetland and have been subject to extraction processes for centuries.

Of the three main types – fens, raised and blanket bogs – raised bogs have been disappearing rapidly from the European scene because they are more accessible than blanket peat and more usable. Both types have been identified as landscape features worthy of conservation, not simply because of their vulnerability but also because they are recognised as features of natural heritage and some are of scientific significance. Ireland and Finland contain the most extensive areas of remaining peatland in Europe. In Ireland, apart from their obvious ecological values, the peat landscapes have strong cultural and social associations and have inspired poets, musicians and artists, but some are under threat from drainage schemes, afforestation and continuing extraction. Only 7 per cent of raised bogs remain relatively intact, and it has been argued that they should be conserved simply for their value as relict features for earth-science research and education (Daly, 1990).

Several European countries have already recognised the importance of earth-science sites and have commenced work on identifying and registering these features (Black and Gonggrijp, 1990). It is the Scandinavian countries that have led the way in respect of recording, designating and protecting such sites; Sweden, for example, acknowledged the importance of geomorphological sites in the Nature Conservation Act of 1952 and has completed a geomorphological inventory for much of northern Sweden. Among the features the Scandinavian governments consider worthy of protection for their international scientific value are the Nigardsbreen glacier in Norway, sections of chalk cliffs on the Danish island of Mons, and the glacio-fluvial landscapes of central Finland, of which only about 1.5 per cent is as yet protected. In Finland 159 esker sites, covering 96 000 ha, have already been listed for conservation; some of these are of international significance in the field of Quaternary geology (Kontturi, 1990). In common with sites of ecological significance, earth-science sites can be easily and irretrievably damaged through mineral exploitation, urban expansion and construction, and tourist activities. Any damage diminishes the rich diversity of Europe's landscape and heightens the need for conservation measures and controls on changes.

Protected Areas and Landscape Designations

The safeguarding of landscape qualities takes several forms which include legislation at state and provincial level, controls on land-use changes, planning policies, management agreements, financial incentives and designations of various kinds. Common to almost all European countries is the designation of landscapes, cultural features and natural areas, but designation itself is only a starting point for effective conservation. More important is the legal backing that underpins the process of designation and gives meaning to the areas which have been identified as worthy of recognition and protection. Important, too, is the way in which the legislation is effected on the ground. Firm legislation may be of little value unless there are responsible authorities to take decisions and carry out control measures. It is evident that current problems afflicting some designated areas in Europe stem from internal administrative conflicts or from an inability on the part of a management authority to take action over issues that may arise (Framarin, 1994). Several countries have designated reserves and sites, but do not have the financial resources or trained personnel to manage all areas effectively and as necessary. Consequently, the question arises whether it is better to have long suites of designated areas with weak management or a representative selection with careful conservation. For some governments it may be solely a matter of prestige to designate a number of protected areas and achieve some international recognition in the field of environmental conservation. There are, therefore, several factors that may determine the degree and extent of protection which is afforded to any designated area.

The exact number and types of protected area found in Europe at the present time are difficult to assess because each country has different approaches to designation and not all record their designated areas according to standard definitions. Moreover, designations may overlap and some areas may be covered by several types. In an attempt to find a degree of common ground among national designations, the IUCN Commission on National Parks and Protected Areas has drawn up a set of five categories under which it recognises the great majority of protected areas. These five categories are set out in Table 24.1. The Commission's definition of a protected area is:

> "An area of land and/or sea especially dedicated to the protection and maintenance of biological diversity, and of natural and associated cultural resources, and managed through legal or other effective means" (IUCN, 1994).

The categories attempt to subdivide protected areas and sites into discrete types on the basis of three criteria:

1. Size – normally only sites larger than 1000 ha are included.
2. Management objectives – management must be sufficient to implement nationally legislated objectives.
3. Management authority – this must be a competent authority recognised by central government.

Sites and areas which do not meet these criteria are excluded and do not feature in the lists of protected areas recognised by IUCN. Category I areas are the least disturbed type of reserve and are protected mainly for their value for scientific research or as tracts of wilderness. Areas in Category II are National Parks that are managed primarily for the ecosystems found within them or for recreation. Category III areas – Natural Monuments – tend to be the smallest in size and comprise specific natural features. Areas which are set aside for habitat or species protection, and in which there is some level of management intervention, are included within Category IV. Lastly, Category V covers landscapes protected for their scenic, ecological and cultural qualities and where recreation may be a significant objective.

The distribution of protected areas according to these five categories is given in Table 24.2 for each country in Europe. Every country is represented with the exceptions of Andorra, Malta, Monaco and San Marino; for these four no areas qualify for listing. Turkey and the Russian Federation have been omitted because it has not been possible to determine precisely which of their designated areas are located within Europe or within Asia. However, in total there are 199 recognised areas in the whole of the Russian Federation and 44 within Turkey. Table 24.2 shows that the best protected and most valued areas (Categories I and

Table 24.1 *Protected areas: IUCN management categories, 1993*

I Strict Nature Reserve or Wilderness Area
Ia: Area of land and/or sea possessing some outstanding or representative ecosystems, geological or physiological features and/or species, available primarily for scientific research and/or environmental monitoring
Ib: Large area of unmodified or slightly modified land, and/or sea, retaining its natural character and influence, without permanent or significant habitation, which is protected and managed so as to preserve its natural condition

II National Park
Natural area of land and/or sea, designated to:
(a) protect the ecological integrity of one or more ecosystems for present and future generations
(b) exclude exploitation or occupation inimical to the purposes of designation, and
(c) provide a foundation for spiritual, scientific, educational, recreational and visitor opportunities, all of which must be environmentally and culturally compatible

III Natural Monument
Area containing one or more specific natural or natural/cultural feature which is of outstanding or unique value because of its inherent rarity, representative or aesthetic qualities or cultural significance

IV Habitat/Species Management Area
Area of land and/or sea subject to active intervention for management purposes so as to ensure the maintenance of habitats and/or to meet the requirements of specific species

V Protected Landscape or Seascape
Area of land, with coast and sea as appropriate, where the interaction of people and nature over time has produced an area of distinct character with significant aesthetic, ecological and/or cultural value, and often with high biological diversity. Safeguarding the integrity of this traditional interaction is vital to the protection, maintenance and evolution of such an area

Source: IUCN (1994).

II) comprise only about 14 per cent of the total, whereas protected cultural landscapes (Category V) make up almost half. Some countries hold few or no top-ranking areas – Austria, Belgium, Germany, Portugal, Switzerland and the UK – while others contain a spread across the category range – Bulgaria, Denmark, France, Iceland, Romania and the Netherlands. These distributions do not reflect a lack of sound designation and conservation procedures, but may have more to do with the criteria applied by IUCN and with the geographical structure of the countries concerned. This last point is supported by the fact that it is the Scandinavian countries which have the greatest number of areas in Categories I and II. Over 50 per cent (116 out of 205) of the Category I areas lie within these four states, where substantial tracts of wild and natural terrain still remain and where demands for land-use change are largely confined to the city regions of Oslo, Stockholm, Gothenburg and Helsinki. Even in Denmark,

where population density is higher, more than 1.3 million ha have been designated for conservation, almost a third of the national area (Table 24.3). Also worthy of note is that there is a greater area of land in Categories I and II than in the other three combined; this fact reiterates the opportunities available for, and emphasises the importance attached to, high-quality landscape conservation in these high-latitude regions of Europe. The 7 million ha comprise 61.3 per cent of the European total in these two categories (11.5 million ha).

The number of areas shown in Table 24.2 masks the great variety of titles used in the designation process. The IUCN category headings are by no means standard names and there are some 70 different titles applied throughout Europe. National Parks are found in 32 countries and there are 234 of these in all. Most are listed as Category II areas, but there are many with a Category V status, especially those which contain significant cultural

Table 24.2 *Protected areas in European countries, 1993*

Category*:	I	II	III	IV	V	Total
Albania	0	6	0	5	0	11
Austria	0	1	0	47	122	170
Belarus	1	1	0	0	8	10
Belgium	0	0	0	1	2	3
Bosnia-Hercegovina	0	1	0	1	3	5
Bulgaria	26	3	2	13	2	46
Croatia	4	5	1	5	14	29
Czech Republic	4	2	0	4	24	34
Denmark	9	0	2	61	41	113
Estonia	6	1	0	28	4	39
Finland	15	22	0	45	0	82
France	5	5	0	41	32	83
Germany	0	1	0	88	415	504
Greece	0	8	2	6	8	24
Hungary	0	5	0	6	42	53
Iceland	1	3	5	5	8	22
Ireland	0	5	0	7	0	12
Italy	0	11	1	86	74	172
Latvia	4	0	1	23	17	45
Liechtenstein	0	0	0	0	1	1
Lithuania	4	5	0	37	30	76
Luxembourg	0	0	0	0	1	1
Macedonia	0	3	5	5	3	16
Moldova	2	0	0	0	0	2
The Netherlands	3	4	23	47	0	77
Norway	54	20	0	8	31	113
Poland	1	15	0	21	74	111
Portugal	0	1	1	10	10	22
Romania	12	11	0	11	5	39
Slovakia	1	5	1	15	18	40
Slovenia	0	1	0	0	9	10
Spain	0	6	0	85	87	178
Sweden	38	15	0	135	26	214
Switzerland	1	0	0	48	60	109
Ukraine	13	2	0	4	0	19
United Kingdom	0	0	0	45	100	145
Yugoslavia	1	7	1	1	11	21
Europe	205	175	45	944	1282	2651

* For category definitions, see Table 24.1.
Source: IUCN (1994).

landscapes. Only two attain Category I status – the Swiss National Park and the Ojcow Park in Poland, both of which are relatively small in size. A point worthy of note is the number of areas designated since the late 1980s, especially in the former socialist states. For example, of the 76 protected areas in Lithuania, 54 have been established since 1989. In the same period, Romania has created 17 new reserves (out of 39), and Slovakia 12 out of a total of 40. The Natura 2000 network, set up by the European Commission in 1992 as part of the Community Directive on Natural Habitats, obliges governments to review existing situations and to

Table 24.3   *Area of protected land in Scandinavian countries*

	Categories*		Total (ha)	% National area
	I and II (ha)	III–V (ha)		
Denmark	23 838	1 364 912	1 388 750	32.3
Finland	544 810	2 183 835	2 728 645	8.1
Norway	5 054 493	482 019	5 536 512	17.1
Sweden	1 444 129	1 544 916	2 989 045	6.6
Total	7 067 270	5 575 682	12 642 952	10.9

* For category definitions, see Table 24.1.
Source: IUCN (1994).

look towards designating more reserves and National Parks (NPs). A start has already been made and new ones have recently been established in Finland (2), Italy (7), Estonia (3) and Poland (6). One of the Polish parks, the Biebrza NP, encompasses the largest wetland area in central Europe (Harabin, 1992).

Nature reserves are to be found in 21 countries, the most being in Sweden where 160 areas are listed. However, other titles cover much the same kind of reserve, although some countries have made individual distinctions and specified the actual type of reserve. This can be seen in Latvia where there exist botanical, mire, zoological, scientific and complex nature reserves, and the aptly named Cranberry Resources Reserve of Olla and Pigele. Similarly in Lithuania, fine distinctions have been made for the reserves based on natural features and earth-science sites: geomorphological, hydrogeological, hydrographical, hydrological, ichthyological and ornithological reserves (Baskyte and Lapelé, 1992). For landscape conservation the most widely used term is the "Landscape Protection Area" which appears in Austria (99 areas), Germany (335), Norway (31), Portugal (1) and Switzerland (60); it is also employed in some eastern European countries such as Bulgaria, the Czech Republic, Slovakia and Hungary. While these various terms and titles may make for confusion when trying to compare the types and quality of landscape conservation designations, they do, on the other hand, reflect the different approaches to

conserving natural and cultural landscapes; such approaches characterise the diversity, rarity and intrinsic values to be discovered in European landscapes.

Conservation Planning in Protected Areas

European planning organisations at all levels have become much more aware that designation of valuable areas is, in itself, insufficient to ensure proper conservation. This recognition of a need for more intricate planning and management can be illustrated with reference to three aspects that have gained in importance in recent years. First, there has been an increase in detailed plans for protected areas, and in plans backed up by firm policies in order to counteract development proposals and to control usage, especially of recreation activity. A second significant change has been the marked increase in cross-frontier co-operation on both conservation and broader environmental matters. This trend looks set to widen with the opening up of border zones in the 1990s between the countries of eastern Europe. Third, the widespread application of landscape planning has ensured that the debate about the appropriateness of approaches to conservation continues. As visitor numbers climb, and as pressure for cosmopolitan developments spreads across rural Europe, the means by which areas are protected is a particularly salient issue.

Comprehensive planning

The approach to more comprehensive planning can be illustrated from Südtirol in northern Italy, a region which includes the spectacular landscapes of the Dolomites and the Stelvio NP. The main, internationally recognised, designated areas are shown in Figure 24.3 but the full extent of protected landscapes in the region is summarised in Table 24.4. Over 75 per cent of the region's landscape carries some form of protective policy, a significant proportion of which is embedded in local landscape plans. In due course this locality-focused approach will become even more dominant when the remaining 12 communities (*Gemeinde*) in the region have approved plans. National and Nature Parks cover about 22 per cent of the land area of Südtirol, and this proportion too will rise when the eighth Nature Park (the Sarntaler Alps) is established. The conservation of all these areas goes beyond designation, however. The recent regional plan states that the prime aim for nature and landscape protection is the conservation, or creation, of optimum living conditions for people, flora and fauna on the basis of a sustainable, environmentally friendly use of resources and space. Throughout the whole region, natural conditions and the landscape are to be protected and carefully managed so that habitats, animals, plants and the identity, diversity and aesthetic qualities can be safeguarded. Specific environmental objectives have been set for the maintenance of pollution-free natural water sources, conservation of soil quality, the improvement of air quality and the reduction of noise pollution. Landscapes, which have been defined as having particular value because of their beauty, uniqueness, rarity or significance for recreation, will be kept free from building construction. Furthermore, all new building work is to be subject to landscape regulations, and unavoidable impacts on the natural environment are to be cushioned through landscape managment measures (Autonome Provinz Bozen-Südtirol, 1995).

To meet these objectives it is seen as essential that there is more co-ordination between the relevant authorities when measures are implemented on the ground and that local administrations, the rural *Gemeinde*, are fully

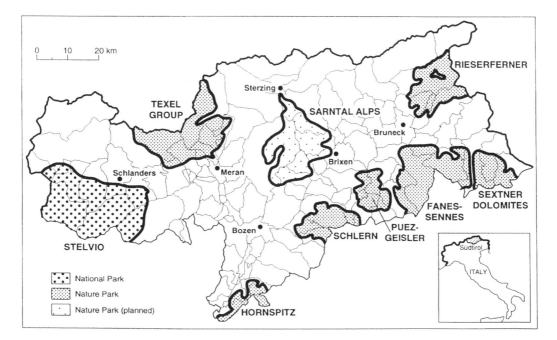

Figure 24.3 *Landscape protection areas in Südtirol, Italy*

Table 24.4   *Landscape conservation areas in Südtirol, Italy*

Protection category	Number	Area (ha)	% of total area
Areas in landscape plans (*Gemeinde* level)	81	353 606	47.8
Biotopes and protected landscape sites	117	1 997	0.3
Landscape protection zones	7	43 759	5.9
Nature parks	7	113 046	15.3
Natural monuments	565	–	–
National Park (Stelvio)	1	53 447	7.2
Total	–	565 855	76.5

Source: Autonome Provinz Bozen-Südtirol (1995).

involved in work that concerns landscape protection. One aspect common in conserved areas in Europe is the lack of up-to-date scientific information on the status of natural habitats and threatened plants and animals. In the Südtirol region this point is being covered by a strengthening of the administration, which will have monitoring of natural conditions as a principal function. As elsewhere in rural Europe, financial incentives for landscape conservation practices are to be extended to protect and maintain important biotope sites. Keeping the visiting public informed about the importance of nature and landscape conservation, and about the qualities of protected areas, is now well recognised as one means of helping management of people on vulnerable and pressured sites; accordingly, information centres are to be established in the Nature Parks and the ranger system is to be expanded.

Cross-frontier co-operation and planning

One aim of the European Strategy of Conservation, adopted in 1990, was to achieve more international co-operation across frontier zones so that valuable environments could be protected as a whole (Steele, 1993). This aim has been appreciated by the Südtirol administration and it is intended that the Rieserfernergruppe Nature Park (Figure 24.3) is to be enlarged to link up with the Hohe Tauern NP along the Austrian border, thereby creating a continuous protected tract either side of the main Alpine watershed. This demonstration of the potential for co-ordination is of no mean significance because there are 24 pairs of National or Nature Parks straddling national frontiers in Europe, and cross-border co-operation is vital to solve environmental problems (Thorsell, 1991). Examples of these include the Hautes Fagnes and the Nordeifel Nature Parks on the Belgium–Germany border; the Rago NP of Norway, which adjoins the Sarek NP and the Padjelanta NP in northern Sweden; and the Pyrénées Occidentales NP in France, which is coupled with the Ordesa NP in Spain. The only NP of the Südtirol, the Stelvio, borders the Swiss NP in the Engadine and a greater contrast in planning style and effectiveness would be difficult to find. The Swiss park is essentially a scientific reserve where access is restricted and where landscape change continues with very little management intervention. The Stelvio contains five ski-resorts and associated lifts and facilities severely affecting its wilderness qualities (Framarin, 1994). No amount of landscape planning is going to reverse this problematic situation and suggestions have been put forward to excise the inhabited lands and the skiing areas. Thereafter, landscape zoning may be a partial solution for more competent management. If effected, this reduction in area of a well-established and valued landscape will be a unique procedure in rural Europe.

It is in the predominantly land-locked states of central and eastern Europe that cross-frontier

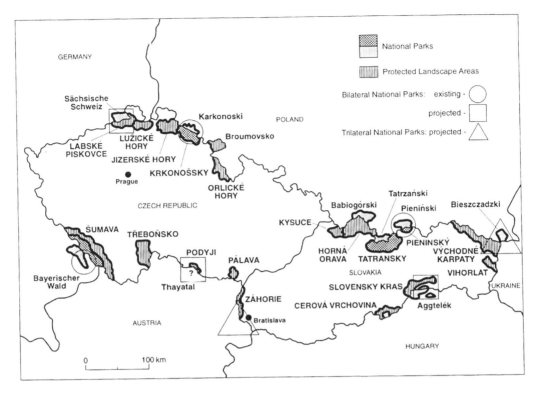

Figure 24.4 *Frontier parks and protected landscape areas in the Czech Republic and Slovakia*

planning has become significant for effective conservation of valued tracts of landscape. Most of the protected areas in the Czech and Slovak republics are located in border regions and over 800 km of their frontiers are covered by various categories of protection (Figure 24.4). In many instances the protected areas form only parts of natural landscape units, the other parts lying in adjacent states. Environmental conservation can be handicapped if planning and management measures are not co-ordinated across the frontier. Both the Czech Republic and Slovakia have placed great emphasis on co-operation with neighbouring states to ensure that protection is compatible either side. This has been particularly important for those zones which were forbidden territory during the "Iron Curtain" years and which became largely uninhabited; their landscape qualities and ecosystems were well preserved and many are acknowledged now as outstanding areas and of international distinction. Thus there is also a strong movement towards the establishment of bilateral or trilateral NPs. Several have been

proposed but some already exist, such as in the Bohemian–Bavarian Forest uplands along the German frontier. The Czech part, known as Sumava, was declared a Protected Landscape Area in 1963; in 1991 the best-preserved zone of 68 500 ha was upgraded to an NP with the status of IUCN Category II. In 1990 the whole area of Sumava was recognised as a Biosphere Reserve, thus making it completely compatible with the protective designations on the Bavarian side. This has enabled planning organisations to deal more efficiently with the problems of integrating management activities concerning fauna migration, threatened species, natural habitats and tourist development (Ministry of Environment, 1991).

Controlling development

Different ways of dealing with threats from development are in operation today, one of which is to create buffer zones around large conserved areas. This is a practice that has been in place in French NPs since their inception (Duffey, 1982). But it does not necessarily lead to effective conservation, because much depends on how the buffer zone is managed and on what kinds of development are permitted within it. In several French parks the buffer zones, or *pré-parcs*, have attracted far too much tourist construction and ski-centred infrastructure. For example, in the Vanoise NP, perhaps the most intensely developed, the core area has been kept free of new building, yet the number of visitors originating from the peripheral resorts has had a marked impact on the recreational use of land in the core. If buffer zones can deflect, rather than attract, most large-scale development, this concept would have much more credibility as a planning device. More successful is the system of graded zoning outwards from the core, which has been employed in the Gran Paradiso NP in Italy (Gambino and Jaccod, 1985).

Another variant of the core/fringe concept is to extend the core area so that the most fragile and valuable parts are better shielded from impacts along the fringes. This is a strategy that has been adopted in the Bieszczady NP in Poland. This park lies in the eastern Carpathians, contains ancient high-altitude forests and sub-alpine meadows, and is a site where bison were reintroduced in the 1960s. In 1988 a proposal for a winter sports centre sited within the park posed severe environmental threats and aroused fierce opposition from nature conservation interests. Not only was the project halted but, to counteract future development schemes, the park was substantially enlarged to more than 15 000 ha. Today it extends to the borders of Slovakia and the Ukraine, and there is the possibility of a tripartite NP being established (Centre Naturopa, 1990b).

Protection Measures for Nature Conservation

All European countries have defined areas and sites where wildlife and the natural habitat are protected. The status of this protection varies markedly according to how supportive the legal framework is and the ways in which this is put into practice on the ground. Since the mid-1980s there has been a move away from simply relying on protected areas as the means of nature conservation. Several countries – Belgium, Estonia, Denmark, the Czech Republic and Lithuania – are already aiming to secure networks of ecological sites linking small-scale tracts with much larger designated zones (Jongman, 1995). In 1990 the Netherlands established a network and this forms the focus of a national Nature Policy Plan (Horlings and Gersie, 1995). The network concept reflects the fact that wildlife does not respect designated areas, and also that even some large sites may not be sufficiently extensive to ensure interaction of species and individuals. The establishment of ecological networks thus gives nature conservation a more realistic spatial structure, and offers an approach which integrates more effectively with physical planning concepts (Jongman, 1995). Given these potential advantages, ideas are now being formulated for a European-wide system, the European Ecological Network or EECONET (Horlings and Gersie, 1995).

The introduction of network concepts demands a much more comprehensive approach to ecological assessment than has been the case in the past. It means that ecological mapping over large areas will be necessary to cover a wide range of habitats, including those within cultural environments. In some parts of Europe survey and mapping programmes are in place, the purpose being to identify those sites, zones and linear components in the rural landscape that are of importance, or have potential value, for nature conservation. One result of this research will be that the selection of areas for protection and conservation will be more representative of the whole range of habitats in a region, as Krahl and Marx (1996) explain in respect of Baden-Württemberg. New opportunities for nature conservation will arise, too, as landownership and land usage change: the former military land along the German borderland was quickly recognised as having conservation potential because of the contrasting habitat provided by the open land, as the view in the Harz mountains exemplifies (Figure 24.5).

The nature conservation programme for Schleswig-Holstein in Germany further exemplifies this comprehensive approach which, in some localities, is linked with proposals for less intensive

Figure 24.5 *Opportunities for new nature conservation areas have come about with the release of military lands – the former frontier zone in the Harz mountains, Germany*

farming methods (MELF Schleswig-Holstein, 1987). Here, selected parts have been intensively surveyed and landscape development plans (*Landschaftsentwicklungsplan*) have been produced for those areas which are either threatened by changes, or contain degraded landscapes or have important associations of natural or semi-natural features. Information collected in the field is assessed and sorted, and remapped to show how the various elements link together (Figure 24.6). Those components requiring managment action are identified, and an additional map is drawn up specifying where landscape measures are to be implemented (Rabius, 1990). A substantial programme of financial support backs up the whole process.

In the post-socialist period, reviews of conservation procedures for nature have taken place and new legislation has been introduced in several eastern European states, notably in the Czech and Slovak republics (Hromas, 1991),

Romania (Ceuca, 1994) and in the Baltic states (Baskyte and Lapelé, 1992). One difference with the former legislation in these eastern European countries is that recent laws tend to have more emphasis on the totality of the environment, and on protecting natural areas from all types of pollution, resource exploitation, and construction. Some states are now producing environmental plans; Latvia, for example, has drawn up a National Environmental Policy Plan, and this will be complemented shortly by an Environmental Action Plan (Centre Naturopa, 1996). Thus nature conservation, habitat protection and biodiversity will be treated in a broader context than perhaps is the case elsewhere. Spain, too, has adopted a new planning model which affords a stronger spatial component to the system of designating significant natural environmental resources (Schmidt, 1995). New regional resource plans are to set out strategies, zoning policies and effective measures; an

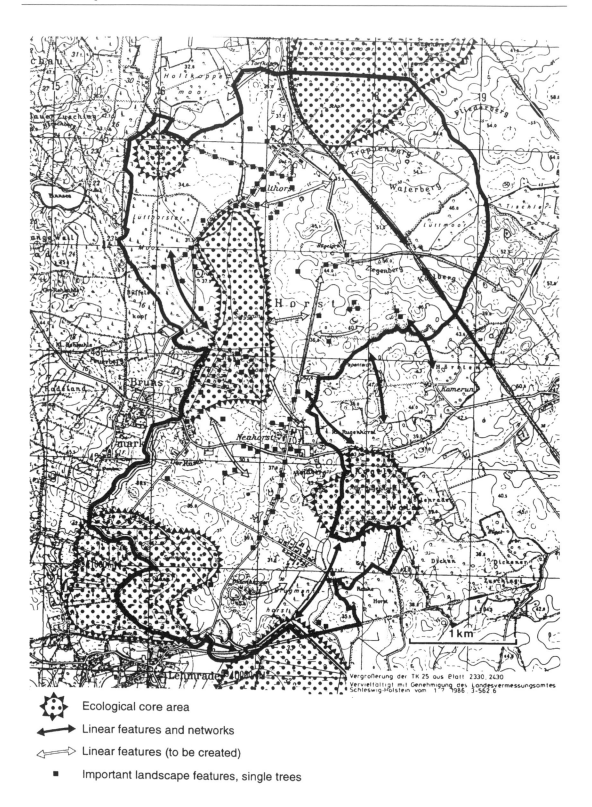

Ecological core area

Linear features and networks

Linear features (to be created)

Important landscape features, single trees

ecological development plan stipulates how these measures are to be integrated with other planning objectives and how new schemes will be funded. Land-use guidance plans for individual areas are to regulate land usage and conservation action.

These new ideas and approaches are a welcome sign that serious attention is being paid to wildlife and habitat conservation. What must be emphasised, however, is that not all new ventures may succeed, as is demonstrated with the Dutch concept of "quiet areas" (*Stiltegebieden*) (de Roo and Bartelds, 1996). This was an attempt to create in the Netherlands essentially undisturbed zones where wildlife could breed and in which man-made noise was kept to a minimum level. Perhaps surprisingly, recreational activity was also seen as an appropriate use of quiet areas and exemptions were made for certain sectors to allow for military flying. These examples, from the Netherlands and Spain, indicate both the difficulties of trying to develop new conservation concepts and the complexity of planning needed to ensure a place for nature in an already highly utilised rural space.

Conservation of the Cultural and Built Environment

Settlements and rural buildings feature prominently in conservation processes today. In the past conservation of the cultural environment was focused very much on the protection of historic features and areas through systems such as *Denkmalschutz* (Germany, Austria, Switzerland), the *sites classés* and *sites inscrits* (France), the *Monumentenlijst* (Netherlands) and the National Monuments listing (Ireland). More recently, conservation measures have become more problem-orientated, and for many European rural planning authorities there appear to be two critical problems to be tackled. First, there is a need to protect villages within urban-centred regions in order that their traditional character is neither diminished nor eroded by new residential and commercial construction. Second, in the less

accessible and economically fragile rural regions of Europe, where outmigration has been an inherent trend, many properties and villages have been abandoned or neglected and are in need of renovation and modernisation. It is not unusual to find such situations within highly valued and attractive landscapes. The challenge for conservation is to renew the building fabric and infrastructure, and find uses for the many traditional buildings that no longer have a role in the farming and rural economy.

The main answer to the first problem of protecting historic cores of villages and rural towns has been the zoning system. Zoning is a process in widespread use by planning departments in Europe. As with landscape designations, the kinds of zones employed vary substantially, often determined by the structures and uses found in rural localities. They do, nevertheless, tend to fall into two groups: one is concerned largely with development and the expansion of settlements, whereas the other is directed more towards protection and conservation objectives.

In Switzerland, for example, zoning of the cultural landscape can be very diversified, covering uses such as orchards, vineyards, open spaces, gardens, tree groups and green areas, as well as features such as attractive views, water-gathering areas, focal points and other historic qualities of settlement character (Bundesamt für Raumplanung, 1984). In practice, planning regulations may cover a series of building or development zonations, together with conservation zones for both agriculture and landscape. Some cantons stipulate that a separate plan (*Schutzzonenplan*) should be produced, showing the protection zones and containing a detailed inventory to accompany location maps. Legal regulations, relating to permitted uses and changes of use, back up the implementation of the zoning system. An example from the canton of Schwyz will suffice to show the procedure adopted for Tuggen, a village of 2340 inhabitants about 40 km south-east of Zurich (Spaargaren Partner AG, 1995). In addition to the demarcation of a development zone of the village centre (*Kernzone*), a townscape protection area (*Ortsbildschutzgebiet*) has been defined; this area covers parts of the central zone and an adjacent residential development zone, but also extends outwards to take in a section of the agricultural

Figure 24.6 *Map of ecological functions, from the* Landschaftsentwicklungsplan *for Horst, Schleswig-Holstein, Germany. (After Rabius, 1990)*

Table 24.5 *Specified features in the* Schutzzonenplan *for Tuggen, Switzerland*

	Number
Ortsbildschutzgebiet	2
Protected buildings (*Kanton* list)	29
Protected buildings (village list)	10
Nature conservation zones (incl. buffer areas)	8
Hedges and hedgerow trees	23
Dry-stone walls	2
Small woodland areas	11
Single trees	8
Geological objects (glacial erratics)	3
Stream and waterfall	1
Former stone quarries	2
River course and banks	1

Source: Spaargaren Partner AG (1995).

landscape. Within the *Ortsbildschutzgebiet* the aim is to protect the traditional character of the old village through controls on the scale, style and layout of new buildings. Protection measures also extend to smaller groups of old buildings away from the main village and to individual sites and features. In Tuggen the cultural features under protection are listed in Table 24.5; separate policy statements on the conservation of each of these are set out in the plan. This concept of zoning appears to be the most flexible approach for protecting the cultural qualities of rural settlements from damaging developments. The particular idea of a "conservation zone" has been taken up by planning authorities in several eastern European states; for example, in the Czech Republic, the historic centres of the Bohemian towns of Kadan and Zatec, both walled and with market squares enclosed by handsome arcaded buildings, are protected by special policy areas (*památková rezervace*). Demarcation of heritage zones alone will not ensure protection but they can reduce the impact of change, and also encourage the sensitive renovation and improvement measures that are currently under way in both these small towns.

As noted above, comprehensive renewal and enhancement of the built environment of rural towns and villages have become a principal objective of conservation policy in many European countries. West Germany was the first country to implement programmes on a substantial scale, largely to counteract depop-

ulation along its eastern frontier regions and in problem rural districts. Subsequently, the concepts and methods of these *Dorferneuerung* schemes have been applied to villages and smaller settlements throughout Germany, and particularly to the former GDR lands. The federal government has recognised that there is a pressing need for environmental renewal in the eastern *Länder* and currently has a model programme under way; some 600 towns and villages have been identified for renewal and improvement measures (BRBS, 1990a). Elsewhere in Germany hundreds of schemes have been completed, many are still at the planning stage, and there remain large numbers of villages that have not yet been accepted for a scheme. The map (Figure 24.7) for the Ahrweiler district in Rheinland-Pfalz exemplifies the extent of schemes in a small part of the northern Eifel region. The purposes of the *Dorferneuerung* process are to improve the quality of life for local residents, to encourage young people to remain in their home area and to help the rural economy. By using local firms to carry out some of the improvements, the schemes assist employment and also support the local economy. A wide range of measures can be included, most of which are concerned with enhancing the village environment and its cultural heritage, such as renovating historic and characterful properties, planting trees and shrubs, providing new open space for recreational activities, converting redundant buildings for community use and services, implementing traffic-calming measures along with new footpaths and cycleways, and creating ecological sites both within the village and outside (BRBS, 1990b).

Because of the very high financial costs to implement these schemes, the German federal authorities and some *Länder* governments have kept these programmes under constant review, and it is likely that the scale of schemes, particularly in the older (western) *Bundesländer*, may be less ambitious in the future (BRBS, 1990c). At the same time, the advantages of these renewal programmes for rural people, and for the cultural environment, have been recognised by planning authorities elsewhere in Europe and several countries have now initiated schemes along the German pattern: Austria, the Czech Republic, Slovenia, Poland, Hungary and Lorraine in north-eastern France (Pröll, 1992; Albrecht, 1995).

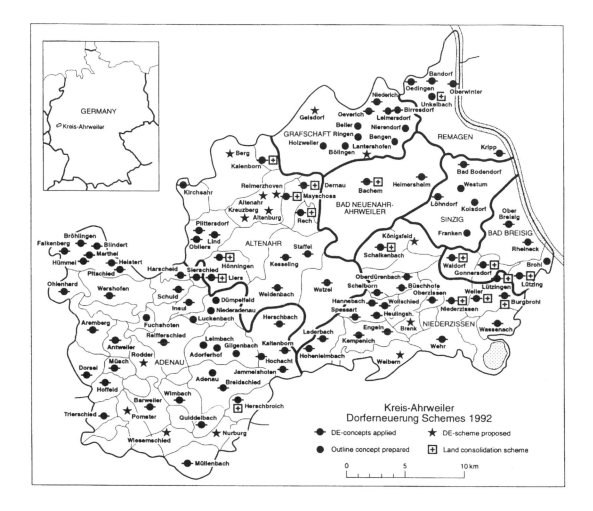

Figure 24.7 *Village improvement schemes in Ahrweiler district, Rheinland-Pfalz, Germany*

In the disadvantaged regions of the EU it is not unusual to find conservation measures integrated with small-scale rural development schemes under Community initiatives such as the LEADER[2] programme. One example of this integration is in Italy, where the restoration of ancient frescos on village houses is part of a scheme to promote rural tourism close to the nature park of Paveggio-Pale di San Martino in Trentino-Alto Adige (Donati, 1994). The same programme has supported village renovation projects in Oberfranken (Germany), Brittany (France), Alto Tamega (Portugal) and in Navarra (Spain) where the restoration of buildings of historic and artistic value along the pilgrimage route to Santiago del Compostella has been carried

out as part of a wider cultural development project (Verhelst, 1994). Other local means of conservation may be found through demonstrations of how historic buildings – often disused or underused farm buildings – can be converted to alternative uses while retaining their essential rural qualities and showing respect for their location (Landesamt für Denkmalpflege Schleswig-Holstein, 1989). Whatever the means of conserving the cultural landscape and the historic parts of the built environment, it is clear that more people and more settlements have been brought into the multi-pronged conservation strategies that have been applied to rural Europe in recent years.

Conclusion

This chapter has focused on a selection of issues concerned with the conservation of landscape, wildlife and the cultural environment. The intention has been to examine the main approaches that have been adopted to deal with some of the pressing issues within valued and protected areas. The situation in any one area is rarely straightforward and no one measure or course of action can suffice to resolve a problem, especially where fragile and sensitive environments are involved. Over time the sheer number of protected areas has grown very substantially and one does begin to question whether Europe will be sufficiently secure economically to be able to afford this scale of conservation. It is evident from the USA that protecting and managing, to a high standard, an increasing and large number of parks and reserves is a commitment which cannot be sustained continuously (Mitchell, 1994). Within the EU states, the European Commission supports conservation of protected areas through the part-financing of projects; in 1995 it committed 48.5m. ECU to some 59 projects (Commission of the EU, 1996). Such finance may help the less wealthy countries of the EU, but the major problems of funding fall within the non-EU countries of eastern and central Europe. It is here that international co-operation and financial support will have to be continued and increased if these states are to upgrade the quality of their environments. In the war-torn regions of, for example, Croatia, the difficulties of finding funding are already apparent, despite a firm commitment to augmenting the areas under protection (Centre Naturopa, 1995).

It is widely recognised that high-quality conservation demands a high price, irrespective of any reference to sustainability and irrespective of its significance to a tourist economy. A growing problem for many protected areas in Europe today is that the appreciative visitor pays very little, and often nothing, directly towards an area's conservation. The "windshield tourist" may contribute even less, probably creating costs because they arrive in excessive numbers and in vehicles that have to be accommodated.

Almost inexorably, perhaps paradoxically, the preservation ethic is growing among European peoples, and fuelling increasing demands for more protection procedures, not only in the most valued areas but also in familiar ones. Natural and cultural heritage are on many agendas from local societies to inter-governmental committees, and both are kept in the public eye through television programmes, holiday advertisements and popular magazines. Such exposure should help the conservation cause, as should the growing membership of environmental organisations. But, in the end, the use of Europe's rural heritage will have to be sensibly regulated and skilfully managed if its value is to be maintained, and hopefully enhanced, well into the next century (Messerli, 1993). Furthermore, to carry this kaleidoscopic heritage forward will need inspired co-operation on a much greater scale than at present, and in ways that will require the forging of innovative partnerships within the wider European community (von der Assen, 1993; Landenbergue, 1995). A European spatial development strategy has already been devised and a European nature conservation plan has been suggested (Robert and Marcori, 1995). Whatever direction is pursued, the foundations and frameworks for sound conservation of the rural landscape are already well established; the challenge is to progress to healthy, sustainable and adequately financed practices of conservation.

Notes

1. The "Natura 2000" network is an inventory of special protection areas, scheduled to be set up by June 1998. The idea of compiling the network was part of the European Commission's 1992 Directive on the Conservation of Natural Habitats and of Wild Fauna and Flora (Centre Naturopa, 1996). Member states are obliged to conserve representative areas to form a basic network for European nature conservation (Jongman, 1995).

2. LEADER stands for "Links between Actions for the Development of the Rural Economy". It is a Community initiative launched by the European Commission to encourage development in Objective 1 (development lag), Objective 5b (fragile rural areas) and Objective 6 (low population density) regions of the EU. The programme will run from 1994 to 1999, and is supported by 1500m. ECU from the three Structural Funds (LEADER European Observatory, 1996).

References

Albrecht, S (1995) Entwicklungsprobleme und Entwicklungsperspektiven im ländlichen Raum Lothringens, *Europa Regional*, **3**(1), 1–12.

Amt für Raumplanung Graubünden (1995) *Siedlungs- und Landschaftswandel in Graubünden*, Chur.

Autonome Provinz Bozen-Südtirol (1995) *Südtirol – Leitbild 2000. Landesentwicklungs- und Raumordnungsplan*, Südtiroler Landtag, Bozen.

Baskyte, R and Lapelé, M (1992) Lithuania – a world of lakes and rivers, *Naturopa Newsletter*, **92**(2), 3–4.

Bassi, T (1995) Framework and constraints for sustainable, equitable regional planning, *Naturopa*, **78**, 13–19.

Black, G P and Gonggrijp, G (1990) Space and time. A new approach, *Naturopa*, **65**, 10–13.

BRBS (Bundesminister für Raumordnung, Bauwesen und Städtebau) (1990a) *Stadt- und Dorferneuerung in der DDR*, Bonn-Bad Godesberg.

BRBS (1990b) *Städtebauliche Erneuerung von Dörfern und Ortsteilen – Ausgaben, Verfahren, Förderung*, Bonn-Bad Godesberg.

BRBS (1990c) *Bericht der Bundesregierung zur Erneuerung von Dörfern und Ortsteilen – (Dorferneuerungsbericht)*, Bonn-Bad Godesberg.

Bundesamt für Raumplanung (and Bundesamt für Forstwesen) (1984) *Landschaft und natürliche Lebensgrundlagen: Anregungen für die Ortsplanung*, Berne.

Bundesamt für Raumplanung (1988) *Lebensraum Schweiz wohin?*, Berne.

Centre Naturopa (1990a) Threats to the Coto Doñana, *Naturopa Newsletter*, **90**(6), 4.

Centre Naturopa (1990b) Extension of the Bieszczady National Park, *Naturopa Newsletter*, **90**(7–8), 3.

Centre Naturopa (1992) Liechtenstein: safeguarding farmland, *Naturopa Newsletter*, **92**(9), 3.

Centre Naturopa (1993) Over 150 golf courses in the Alps, *Naturopa Newsletter*, **93**(9), 1–2.

Centre Naturopa (1994) Ukraine, *Naturopa Newsletter* (special issue), 1–4.

Centre Naturopa (1995) Croatia, *Naturopa Newsletter* (special issue), 1–4.

Centre Naturopa (1996) Latvia: first National Environment Plan, *Naturopa Newsletter*, **96**(1), 3.

Ceuca, L (1994) Romania respects nature thinking of the future, *Naturopa Newsletter* (special issue), 1–4.

Commission of the EU (1996) Quality of the environment and natural resources, *General Report on the Activities of the European Union 1995*, Brussels, Commission of the European Union, 185–8.

Council of the European Communities (1992) Directive 92/43 on the conservation of natural habitats and of wild fauna and flora, *Official Journal of the European Communities*, L206/7–L206/15.

Daly, D (1990) Irish peatlands – valuable heritage, *Naturopa*, **65**, 20–1.

De Roo, G and Bartelds, H (1996) Quiet areas. A noble failure?!, *Town Planning Review*, **67**(1), 87–95.

Di Meana, C R (1992) Europe from 1993 onwards – a complete and coherent framework, *Naturopa*, **70**, 6 7.

Donati, P (1994) LEADER in action: restoration of ancient frescos and cultural promotion, *LEADER Magazine*, **7**, 12.

Duffey, E (1982) *National Parks and Reserves of Western Europe*, Macdonald, London.

Feher, F (1995) In central and eastern Europe, *Naturopa*, **79**, 8–9.

Fernandez-Galiano, E (1994) The Bern Convention: its next steps, *Naturopa Newsletter*, (special issue), 1–4.

Framarin, F (1994) The uncertain future of Stelvio National Park, the largest in the Alps, *Biological Conservation*, **67**, 85–7.

Gambino, R and Jaccod, P (1985) Le Parc National du Grand Paradis – une proposition de plan, *Revue de Géographie Alpine*, **73**, 217–46.

Haapanen, A (1995) The Bern Convention: its potential and objectives, *Naturopa*, **77**, 6–7.

Harabin, Z (1992) The natural world in Poland – a precious asset, *Naturopa Newsletter*, **92**(1), 1–3.

Horlings, I and Gersie, J (1995) Agriculture and nature in ecological networks in the Netherlands and Europe, *European Environment*, **5**, 7–12.

HRH The Prince Philip (1995) Editorial, *Naturopa*, **79**, 3.

Hromas, J (1991) Czechoslovakia and nature conservation, *Naturopa Newsletter*, **91**(1), 3–4.

IUCN (International Union for Conservation of Nature and Natural Resources) (1994) *United Nations List of National Parks and Protected Areas 1993*, Gland, Switzerland and Cambridge, UK.

Jongman, R H G (1995) Nature conservation planning in Europe: developing ecological networks, *Landscape and Urban Planning*, **32**, 169–83.

Kontturi, O (1990) Finnish eskers, *Naturopa*, **65**, 28–9.

Krahl, W and Marx, J (1996) Ansätze für grossflächigen Naturschutz in Baden-Württemberg, *Natur und Landschaft*, **71**(1), 15–18.

Krauklis, A (1992) Landscapes and nature conservation in Latvia, *Naturopa Newsletter*, **92**(2), 1–2.

Kutej, V (1992) Dorferneuerung in Tschechien, *Agrarische Rundschau – Dorferneuerung in Europa*, **3**, 30–2.

Landenbergue, D (1995) Partnerships with commercial companies in the Alps, *Naturopa*, **79**, 28–9.

Landesamt für Denkmalpflege Schleswig-Holstein (1989) *Kulturdenkmale auf dem Lande – Erhalten und Nutzen*, Baudenkmale in Gefahr 12, Kiel.

LEADER European Observatory (1996) LEADER profile, *LEADER Magazine*, **11**, 23–4.

Meier, H (1994) Daten der Volkszählung als Grundlage für die Raumplanung, *Raumplanung Informationshefte*, **94** (3–4), 3–5, Berne.

MELF (Minister für Ernährung, Landwirtschaft und Forsten) Schleswig-Holstein, 1987, *Extensivierungsförderung in Schleswig-Holstein*, Kiel.

Messerli, P (1993) Managing this vulnerable environment, *Naturopa*, **72**, 6–7.

Ministry of Environment (1991) *Frontier Parks in Czechoslovakia*, Prague.

Mitchell, J G (1994) Legacy at risk, *National Geographic*, **186**(4), 20–55.

O'Sullivan, J (1995) Wetlands of Europe, *Naturopa*, **77**, 19–20.

Palmred, J-E (1996) Eastern coastal diversity must be protected, *Enviro*, **20**, 4–5.

Pröll, E (1992) Beginn einer grossen Europäischen Burgerbewegung, *Dorferneuerung International*, **3**, 2–32.

Rabius, E-W (1990) Das Landesprogramm zum Schutz der Natur and zur Verbesserung der Struktur an der schleswig-holsteinisch-mecklenburgischen Landesgrenze – eine Zwischenbilanz, *Jahrbuch 1989*, Lauenburgische Akademie für Wissenschaft und Kultur, Mölln, 167–85.

Regierung des Fürstentums Liechtenstein (1988) *Veränderungen im liechtensteinischen Landschaftsraum*, Vaduz.

Robert, B and Marcori, C (1995) Towards a European Spatial Development Perspective (ESDP), *Naturopa*, **78**, 20–2.

Romano, B (1995) National Parks policy and mountain depopulation: a case study in the Abruzzo region of the central Apennines, Italy, *Mountain Research and Development*, **15**(2), 121–32.

Schmidt, G (1995) Naturschutzplanung in Spanien, *Naturschutz und Landschaftsplanung*, **27**(2), 69–75.

Schuler, M (1994) Tendenzen der Siedlungsentwicklung, *Raumplanung Informationshefte*, **94**(3–4), 15–18, Berne.

Spaargaren Partner AG (1995) *Gemeinde Tuggen: Verordnung über Natur-, Landschafts-, Ortsbild- und Denkmalschutz*, Rapperswil.

Steele, R C (1993) European Conservation Strategy, *Naturopa*, **71**, 8.

Tamisier, A and Grillas, P (1994) A review of habitat changes in the Camargue: an assessment of the effects of the loss of biological diversity on the wintering waterfowl community, *Biological Conservation*, **70**, 39–47.

Tardy, J (1991) Nature conservation in Hungary – living with changes, *Naturopa Newsletter*, **91**(1), 1–3.

Thorsell, J (1991) Twin parks, *World Magazine*, **47**, 38–46.

Verhelst, T (1994) Culture and rural development, *LEADER Magazine*, **8**, 10–16.

Von der Assen, F (1993) A green Europe without frontiers, *Naturopa*, **71**, 5–7.

Contributors

Holmfridur Bjarnadottir Environmental Planner, Environmental Assessment Division, Skipulags Stofnun, Iceland

Mark Blacksell Professor of Geography, Department of Geographical Sciences, University of Plymouth, Plymouth PL4 8AA

Steve Burt Senior Lecturer, Institute of Retail Studies, University of Stirling, Stirling FK9 4LA

P W Daniels Professor of Geography, School of Geography, University of Birmingham, Edgbaston, Birmingham B15 2TT

Andrew H Dawson Senior Lecturer in Geography, Department of Geography and Geology, University of St Andrews, St Andrews, Fife KY16 9ST

John Dawson Professor of Marketing, University of Edinburgh Management School, Edinburgh EH8 9XP

Michael Dunford Professor of Economic Geography, School of European Studies, University of Sussex, Falmer, Brighton BN1 9QN

Julia Edwards Lecturer in Geography, University of Wales College, Newport NP6 1YG

Richard Gibb Reader in Human Geography, Department of Geographical Sciences, University of Plymouth, Plymouth PL4 8AA

Derek Hall Head of the Leisure and Tourism Management Department, The Scottish Agricultural College, John Hannah Building, Auchincruive, Ayr KA6 5HW

Brian Ilbery Professor of Human Geography, Department of Geography, University of Coventry, Priory St, Coventry CV1 5FB

Russell King Professor of Geography, School of European Studies, University of Sussex, Falmer, Brighton BN1 9QN

Wieslaw Michalak Associate Professor of Geography, School of Applied Geography, Ryerson Polytechnic University, 350 Victoria St, Toronto, Ontario, Canada M5B 2K3

Peter R Odell Emeritus Professor of International Energy Studies, Erasmus University Rotterdam, and Visiting Professor of Geography, Department of Geographical Sciences, University of Plymouth, Plymouth PL4 8AA

David Pinder Professor of Economic Geography, Department of Geographical Sciences, University of Plymouth, Plymouth PL4 8AA

Tatyana A Saiko Senior Lecturer in Geography, Department of Geographical Sciences, University of Plymouth, Plymouth PL4 8AA

Michael Samers Lecturer in Geography, Department of Geography, University of Liverpool, Liverpool L69 3BX

Gareth Shaw Reader in Geography and Co-director of the Tourism Research Group,

477

Department of Geography, University of Exeter, Exeter EX4 4RJ

Adrian Smith Lecturer in Geography, School of Social Sciences, University of Sussex, Falmer, Brighton, BN1 9QN

David Turnock Reader in Geography, Department of Geography, University of Leicester, Leicester LE1 7RH

Tim Unwin Reader in Geography, Department of Geography, Royal Holloway and Bedford New College, University of London, Egham, Surrey TW20 0EX

Roger Vickerman Professor of Regional and Transport Economics, and Director of the Centre for European, Regional and Transport Economics, Keynes College, University of Kent, Canterbury, Kent CT2 7NP

H D Watts Reader in Geography, Department of Geography, University of Sheffield, Sheffield S10 2TN

Paul White Professor of Geography, Department of Geography, University of Sheffield, Sheffield S10 2TN

Allan M Williams Professor of Geography and European Studies, and Co-director of the Tourism Research Group, Department of Geography, University of Exeter, EX4 4RJ

Richard H Williams Senior Lecturer in Town and Country Planning and Associate Director of the Centre for Research in European Urban Environments, University of Newcastle, Newcastle upon Tyne NE1 7RU

Robert Woods Professor of Geography and Director of the Graduate Programme in Population Studies, Department of Geography, Roxby Building, University of Liverpool, Liverpool L69 3BX

Brian J Woodruffe Lecturer in Geography, University of Southampton, Southampton SO17 1BJ

List of figures

List of tables

Index

Index compiled by Geoffrey Jones